Handbook of
Theories of Aging

Vern L. Bengtson, PhD, is AARP/University. He received his B.A. at North Park College, and his M.A. and Ph.D. from the University of Chicago. For over 25 years he has directed the Longitudinal Study of Four Generation Families at U.S.C., doing research on the sociology of the life course, socialization, ethnicity, and aging. He has published 10 books and over 190 papers in professional journals and books. He is Professor of Gerontology and Professor of Sociology at the University of Southern California, and is Past President of the Gerontological Society of America. He has been awarded a MERIT grant from the National Institute on Aging and has twice won the Reuben Hill Award for outstanding research and theory on the family. He is the recipient of the Distinguished Scholar Award of the American Sociological Association (Section on Aging); Robert W. Kleemeier Award for outstanding research in the field of gerontology by the Gerontological Society of America; and the Ernest W. Burgess Award for career contributions to family research from the National Council on Family Relations.

K. Warner Schaie, PhD, is the Evan Pugh Professor of Human Development and Psychology and Director of the Gerontology Center at the Pennsylvania State University. He has previously held professional appointments at the University of Nebraska, West Virginia University, and the University of Southern California. Dr. Schaie received his BA from the University of California–Berkeley and his MS and PhD degrees from the University of Washington, all in psychology. He is the author or editor of 26 books and over 200 journal articles and chapters related to the study of human aging. Dr. Schaie is the recipient of the Distinguished Scientific Contributions Award of the American Psychological Association and of the Robert W. Kleemeier Award for Distinguished Research Contributions from the Gerontological Society of America. He was awarded the honorary degree of Dr. phil. h.c. by the Friedrich-Schiller-University of Jena, Germany.

Handbook of
Theories of Aging

Vern L. Bengtson, PhD
K. Warner Schaie, PhD
Editors

 Springer Publishing Company

Copyright © 1999 by Springer Publishing Company, Inc.

Springer Publishing Company, Inc.
536 Broadway
New York, NY   10012-3955

Cover design by Janet Joachim
Acquisitions Editor: Helvi Gold
Production Editor: Jeanne Libby

00 01 02 03 / 5 4 3

Library of Congress Cataloging-in-Publication Data

Handbook of theories of aging / edited by Vern L. Bengtson and K.
   Warner Schaie.
       p.   cm.
   Includes bibliographical references and index.
   ISBN 0-8261-1234-X
   1. Aging—Research. 2. Gerontology—Research. I. Bengtson, Vern
L. II. Schaie, K. Warner (Klaus Warner), 1928–   .
HQ1061.H3366   1999
305.26'07'2—dc21   98-40529
                                                                           CIP

Printed in the United States of America

Contents

Afterword

Preface

How important are theories of aging? Does the time-consuming exercise of building theories–by which we mean the development of explanations to account for empirical relationships—have much relevance to the rapidly. expanding field of gerontology recently? Has theory become outmoded, perhaps archaic, in the science and practice of aging today?

The purpose of this *Handbook* is to advance the development and applications of theories of aging. Its intended audience is the next generation of researchers in gerontology: graduate students, postdoctoral fellows, and junior investigators—those who will be charting the course of knowledge development in aging during the first decades of the 21st Century.

These future leaders in gerontological research have been learning the tools of their trade in an intellectual and scientific context that seems, at the end of the 20th Century, increasingly dismissive of the importance of theory. Technological sophistication in statistical modeling—but not theoretically-based explanations—appear to be demanded by journal reviewers today. Applications of research findings to specific problems—but not basic research to advance theoretical development—-seem to be the priority of NIH study sections reviewing grants. At the same time, some critics are saying that we are at *The End of Science* (Norris, 1996), while postmodernists have suggested that the very enterprise of theoretical explanation is little more than intellectual nonsense.

We feel that there is a need to reestablish the importance of theory in discourse about problems of aging. We feel it is valuable to emphasize the primacy of explanation in the vastly expanding scientific literature reporting empirical findings about aging.

The scope of this *Handbook* is multidisciplinary, reflecting the many scientific and applied disciplines engaged in gerontological research and interventions today, encompassing the biology of aging, the psychology and sociology of aging, as well as social policy and practice concerning problems of aging. These fields and others reflect the panorama of studies of aging today, one of the most intellectually-exciting areas of research and scholarship that has developed during the last few decades of the 20th Century. The chapters of this volume were commissioned from scholars whose research in aging has achieved international recognition and who we believe have something new to say about the advancement of theory in our field.

The *Handbook of Theories of Aging* is organized in five sections, reflecting major theoretical developments in the multidisciplinary enterprise of gerontology since 1988:

1. *Bases of theory-building in aging*: The four chapters in this section examine the history of theories and explanations in aging; prospects and problems for multidisciplinary theories in gerontology; phenomenology and postmodern thought in gerontology; and the interplay between theory and empirical research designs in research on aging.

2. *Biological and biomedical concepts and theories of aging:* Chapters in this section focus on genetics, evolution, and theories of aging; biological perspectives on explanations for aging; neuropsychological theories of stress and aging; and theories of health and functional capacity.

3. *Psychological concepts and theories of aging:* The five chapters in this section provide an overview of psychological theories of aging; theories of competence and aging; theories of cognition; personality change and continuity with aging; and theories of health and functional capacity with age.

4. *Social science concepts and theories of aging:* The chapters in this section focus on anthropological and ethnographic models in studying aging; social constructivist investigations and their application to aging; life course perspectives; developments in social-structural models of aging, including the "aging and society" paradigm; and political economy theories of aging.

5. *Applications and potentials for theories of aging:* In this concluding section authors explore the public policy applications of theories of aging; a methatheoretical analysis of theories of aging: application of theories of aging in gerontological practice and education; the theoretical problems posed by "a good old age;" and an examination of the dynamics of development and aging.

These chapters together represent the current status of theoretical developments in aging. In the first years of the 21st Century we can expect an avalanche in research publications reporting data about problems and processes of aging. We hope that the authors of these publications–as well as the editors and reviewers of the journals to which they have been submitted— will also address the theoretical implications of their findings. This is because theory, the pursuit of explanations that go beyond specific empirical findings, is of crucial importance to the cumulative development of knowledge concerning aging.

Vern L. Bengtson
K. Warner Schaie
September 1998

Acknowledgments

We want first to acknowledge the loss of our friend and colleague Jan-Erik Ruth, who died tragically in 1997. Dr. Ruth worked with us to develop this *Handbook* and was co-author, with Gary Kenyon and Wilhelm Mader, of Chapter 3. A professor of psychology at the University of Helsinki in Finland, Jan-Erik received his Ph.D. at USC under Jim Birren and collaborated with Jim on several volumes. Jan-Erik was an international leader in psychogerontology and a warm and wonderful person. We shall miss him greatly.

Second, we express our appreciation to the staff at various academic institutions who helped the chapter authors and editors put this *Handbook* together. Too often academic volumes are published without sufficient recognition of the staff whose labors enabled their completion, and we want to give credit where credit is due.

In particular the editors want to recognize the management skills of Linda Hall, Administrative Services Manager at the Andrus Gerontology Center, University of Southern California. Over the four years of this project's gestation Linda has nudged authors to meet deadlines, negotiated with potential publishers and financial supporters, deciphered exotic software files forwarded by authors, and organized the "Theories of Aging" workshop for the Gerontological Society of America. She shares the honors for this publication with the staff of work-study students she has trained, especially Jeff Foster, who is now Student Services Advisor for the Department of Environmental Studies at USC. We want also to acknowledge the efforts of Ann Shuey, research technologist at the Pennsylvania State University, the person who keeps Warner Schaie's transcontinental activities organized.

We thank the Gerontological Society of America and Carol Schutz, its Executive Director, for sponsoring a one-day pre-conference workshop on "Theories of Aging" prior to the 1997 annual meeting in Cincinnati, where a number of these chapters were presented and discussed.

We are grateful for the support of The Retirement Research Foundation and Dr. Marilyn Hennessey, its Director, who provided funds for the "Theories of Aging" workshop and for expenses associated with production of this volume.

Finally we want to express our appreciation to Dr. Ursula Springer of Springer Publishing Company. Dr. Springer read personally each of the 25 chapters. The field of aging is fortunate to have an advocate such as her in the publishing world.

Vern L. Bengtson
K. Warner Schaie

Contributors

W. Andrew Achenbaum, Ph.D.
Professor of History and Research
 Scientist
Institute of Gerontology
University of Michigan
Ann Arbor, MI

Margret M. Baltes, Ph.D.
Professor of Psychological Gerontology
Freie Universität Berlin
Medical School Benjamin Franklin
Department of Gerontopsychiatry
Berlin, Germany

Paul B. Baltes, Ph.D.
Director and Professor of Psychology
Max Planck Institute for Human
 Development
Berlin, Germany

Vern L. Bengtson, Ph.D.
AARP/University Professor of
 Gerontology
Professor of Sociology
University of Southern California
Los Angeles, CA

James E. Birren, Ph.D.
Associate Director
Center for the Study of Aging
University of California at Los
 Angeles
Los Angeles, CA

Richard T. Campbell, Ph. D.
Professor of Sociology
University of Illinois at Chicago
Chicago, IL

Laura L. Carstensen, Ph.D.
Professor of Psychology
Stanford University
Palo Alto, CA

Peter G. Coleman, Ph.D.
Professor of Psychogerontology
Department of Geriatric Medicine,
University of Southampton,
Southampton General Hospital,
Southampton, U.K.

Vincent J. Cristofalo, Ph.D.
Audrey Meyer Mars Professor and
    Director
Allegheny University of the Health
    Sciences
Philadelphia, PA

Dale Dannefer, Ph.D.
Professor of Education and Sociology
Margaret Warner Graduate School
    of Education and Human
    Development
University of Rochester
Rochester, NY

Caleb E. Finch, PhD
ARCO and William F Kieschnick
    Professor in the Neurobiology of
    Aging
University of Southern California
Los Angeles, CA

Anne Foner, Ph.D.
Professor Emerita, Rutgers University
New Brunswick, NJ

Mary Kay Francis
Research Assistant
Allegheny University of the Health
    Sciences
Philadelphia, PA

Christine L. Fry, Ph.D.
Professor of Anthropology
Loyola University of Chicago
Chicago, IL

Margaret Gatz, Ph.D.
Professor of Psychology
University of Southern California
Los Angeles, CA

Jaber F. Gubrium, Ph.D.
Professor of Sociology
University of Florida
Gainesville, FL

Jon Hendricks, Ph.D.
Director, Honors College
Oregon State University
Corvallis, OR

A. Regula Herzog, Ph.D.
Senior Research Scientist and
    Adjunct Professor of Psychology
The University of Michigan
Ann Arbor, MI

James A. Holstein, Ph.D.
Professor of Sociology
Department of Social and Cultural
    Sciences
Marquette University
Milwaukee, WI

Dorothy Jerrome, Ph.D.
Senior Lecturer in Social
    Gerontology
Department of Geriatric Medicine
University of Southampton
Southampton General Hospital
Southampton, U.K.

Malcom L. Johnson, Ph.D.
Professor of Policy Studies
University of Bristol
Bristol, England

Gary M. Kenyon, Ph.D.
Director, Institute of Gerontology
St. Thomas University
Fredericton, New Brunswick
Canada

Gisela Labouvie-Vief, Ph.D.
Professor of Psychology
Wayne State University
Department of Psychology
Detroit, MI

Wilhelm Mader, Ph.D.
Professor of Philosophy
Universität Bremen
Bremen, Germany

Hazel R. Markus, Ph.D.
Davis-Brack Professor in the
    Behavioral Sciences
Professor of Psychology
Stanford University
Palo Alto, CA

Victor W. Marshall, Ph.D.
Director, Institute for Human
    Development, Life Course and
    Aging
Professor of Sociology
University of Toronto
Toronto, ON, Canada

Angela M. O'Rand, Ph.D.
Associate Professor
Department of Sociology
Duke University
Durham, NC

Michelle Papka, Ph.D.
Neuropsychologist and Senior
    Instructor
Department of Neurology, and
Alzheimer's Disease Research Center
University of Rochester
Rochester, NY

Jill Quadagno, Ph.D.
Mildred and Claude Pepper Eminent
    Scholar in Social Gerontology
Professor of Sociology
Pepper Institute on Aging and
    Public Policy
Florida State University
Tallahassee, FL

Jennifer Reid, M.A.
Research Assistant
Pepper Institute on Aging and
    Public Policy
Florida State University
Tallahassee, FL

Cara J. Rice
Research Assistant
Leonard Davis School of Gerontology
University of Southern California
Los Angeles, CA

John W. Riley, Jr., Ph.D.
Consulting Sociologist
Silver Springs, MD

Matilda White Riley, Sc.D.
Senior Social Scientist
National institute on Aging, NIH
Bethesda, MD

Jan-Eric Ruth, Ph.D. (deceased)
Professor of Psychology
Helsinki University
Helsinki, Finland

Timothy A. Salthouse, Ph.D.
Regents Professor of Psychology
School of Psychology
Georgia Institute of Technology
Atlanta, GA

K. Warner Schaie, Ph.D.
Evan Pugh Professor of Human
  Development and Psychology
  and Director, Gerontology
  Center
The Pennsylvania State University
University Park, PA

Johannes J.F. Schroots, Ph.D.
Director ERGO/European Research
  Institute on Health and Aging
Adjunct Professor of Human
  Gerontology
Faculty of Psychology
University of Amsterdam
Amsterdam, The Netherlands

Teresa Seeman, Ph.D.
Associate Professor of Gerontology
  & Preventive Medicine
Andrus Gerontology Center
University of Southern California
Los Angeles, CA

David H. Solomon, M.D.
Professor Emeritus of Medicine
Director Emeritus, UCLA Center
  on Aging
University of California, Los
  Angeles
Los Angeles, CA

Jacqui Smith
Research Psychologist
Max Planck Institute for Human
  Development
Berlin, Germany

Maria Tresini
Research Assistant
Allegheny University of the Health
  Sciences
Philadelphia, PA

Peter Uhlenberg, Ph.D.
Professor of Sociology
University of North Carolina
Chapel Hill, NC

Alan Walker, Litt.D, FRSA
Professor of Social Policy
Department of Sociological Studies
University of Sheffield
Sheffield, UK

Sherry L. Willis
Professor of Human Development
The Pennsylvania State University
University Park, PA

Diana S. Woodruff-Pak, Ph.D.
Departments of Psychology and
  Diagnostic Imaging
Temple University and
Temple University School of
  Medicine
Philadelphia, PA

F. Eugene Yates, Ph.D.
Crump Professor of Medical
  Engineering
School of Medicine
University of California, Los
  Angeles
Los Angeles, CA

Steven H. Zarit, Ph.D.
Professor of Human Development
The Pennsylvania State University
University Park, PA

SECTION I

Bases of Theory-Building in Aging

1

Are Theories of Aging Important? Models and Explanations in Gerontology at the Turn of the Century

Vern L. Bengtson
Cara J. Rice
Malcolm L. Johnson

A re theories of aging important? Or have theories become irrelevant—perhaps archaic—in the broad, increasingly differentiated fields of inquiry that constitute gerontology today? Many researchers in gerontology seem to have abandoned any attempt at building theory.

The development of this chapter owes much to the seminar on "Theories of Aging" during 1997 at the University of Southern California. Many thanks are due to the members of that class (Barbara Chalmers, Grace Chen, Jeannine Diemoff, Sasha Enyart, Mary Gardner, Dipa Gupta, Anne Marenco, Carolyn Mendez, Brent Taylor, and Matthew Ting) for stimulating discussion of the themes of this chapter. Thanks also to Victor Marshall, Joe Hendricks, Maria Schmeeckle, Brent Taylor, and Danielle Zucker for helpful comments on earlier drafts, and to Linda Hall, whose encouragement and editorial competence guided the chapter into completion despite many challenges. Finally, we want to acknowledge our indebtedness to the National Institute on Aging's Social and Behavioral Sciences division, and in particular the leadership of Deputy Director Ron Abeles and Associate Director Jared Jobe. Their concern for theoretical development in aging and the social sciences has provided support for many investigators and students. Preparation of this chapter was supported by funds from research grant #R37 AG07977 and training grant #T32–AG00037.

Should we be concerned about this? What are the consequences of discounting theory for future knowledge development in gerontology?

These questions are particularly relevant at the beginning of the 21st century because of some fundamental challenges to science and the development of knowledge that have arisen recently. For example, John Horgan's (1996) *The End of Science: Facing the Limits of Knowledge in the Twilight of the Scientific Age* argues that the best and most exciting scientific discoveries are behind us, in part because of our inability or unwillingness to synthesize existing knowledge. Thomas Kuhn's (1962) *The Structure of Scientific Revolutions,* perhaps the most frequently cited book ever written about how science does (or does not) proceed, suggested that much of "normal science" has been reduced to what he called "mopping up": filling in the empirical details, solving relatively trivial puzzles, looking for practical applications of existing knowledge. Applied to aging, Kuhn's critique may be relevant to the observation that gerontology has been "rich in data but poor in theory" (Birren & Bengtson, 1988: p. ix); this has left researchers and practitioners with "many empirical generalizations but underdeveloped explanations by which to build upon in subsequent research" (Bengtson, Burgess, & Parrott, 1997, p. S72).

Another kind of challenge to theory—and to the scientific method itself—has resulted from the rise of critical analyses of knowledge over the past half century. The "critical theory" perspective, most often associated with the Frankfurt School of epistemology represented by Habermas (1970), questions positivism and the search for scientific natural laws as a principal source of knowledge. The understanding of *meanings* (which Habermas termed "hermetic/historical knowledge") and the analysis of *domination and constraint* in social forces (termed "critical" knowledge) are equally important as "objective knowledge" in understanding phenomena. These themes are central to what has become known as the "postmodern" movement in intellectual discourse (Lyotard, 1984; Rorty, 1991). Postmodernists have questioned the relevance of theory—indeed, the possibility of any useful theory—because of the inherent relativity of observed phenomena and the inescapable subjectivity of those who attempt to study it (Brown, 1986). Applied to gerontology, this critique focuses on the remarkable diversity in phenomena of aging, and the hazards of scientific reductionism in attempting to account for them. There is also the perspective that gerontology, the study of aging, should be regarded as an art, or perhaps a practice—but certainly not as a science, because of the inherently subjective nature of our inquiry concerning aging, dying, and death: none of which can be reduced to merely scientific or theoretical issues (see Katz, 1996).

These epistemological critiques about the development of knowledge and the role of theory are important to examine, particularly for gerontological researchers at the start of the 21st century. In this chapter we will address four questions: (1) What *is* theory—and how is it important in the development of knowledge about aging? (2) What is the state of theory in gerontology today? (3) Why has explicit theory development become devalued in gerontology during the past few decades? (4) How and why should 21st century researchers and practitioners in gerontology pay more attention to theory development?

WHAT IS THEORY? AND WHY IS IT IMPORTANT?

We feel the term *theory* is too often used ambiguously today. Its definitions run the range from *a guess or conjecture* to *a coherent group of general propositions used as principles of explanations for a class of phenomena* (Webster, 1998, p. 1471). We can excuse the lay public or the popular press for its imprecise usage of the term. However, within the scholarly community of gerontology it is important to recognize what theory is; how it is different from other epistemological terms (such as empirical generalizations, empirical models, simulations, or paradigms) that are sometimes used synonymously with it; and how theory can be useful in developing knowledge about aging.

The Focus of Theory

We define theory as *the construction of explicit explanations in accounting for empirical findings.* The key process—and this should be emphasized again and again—is *explanation.* There may be other ways to describe this, such as "telling a story" about empirical findings, or "developing a narrative accounting" about observations (see the chapters by Kenyon, Gubrium and Holstein, and Marshall in this volume). Nevertheless, the principal focus of theory is to provide a set of lenses through which we can view and make sense of what we observe in research. And the principal use of theory is *to build knowledge and understanding,* in a systematic and cumulative way, so that our empirical efforts will lead to integration with what is already known as well as a guide to what is yet to be learned (Bengtson, Parrott, & Burgess, 1996).

Facts, Models, and Paradigms

Theory should not be confused with other terms that reflect the process of knowledge development. First are what we define as *empirical generalizations: statements describing regularities observed over and over again in the course of systematic observation* (see Turner, 1988). Research involves observations, findings, "facts" that are generated through investigative methods intended to identify or reduce sources of "bias" in investigation. For example, the "scientific method" stresses reliability and validity of measurement as a means to reduce potential bias in observation by those collecting data.

Models represent another process in knowledge development, particularly in science: these are *descriptions or prototypes of how empirical generalizations may be related to each other*. Models describe the natural world and attempt to depict relations among variables that describe it. The development of "models" and "model-fitting" is a relatively recent contribution of 20th century statistical and engineering applications of basic science. Some of the chapters in this volume use the term "model" as a means to integrate empirical generalizations about age differences or processes of aging. Some scientific disciplines (for example, economics, demography, epidemiology, molecular biology) focus on models as a means of summarizing complex observations and describing their empirical interrelationships. But models are not theories; models do not engage the intellectual process of explanation. And what establishes the cumulative development of knowledge in science is explanation: the *why* behind the *what* that is observed.

A third term is *paradigm*. Kuhn (1962) introduced this in his analysis of the intellectual history of natural science, and because of his figurative and sometimes contradictory usage, it may be more useful as a metaphor than a definition. We characterize *paradigm* as *a movement in science brought about by a dramatic shift in efforts, reflecting the cumulation of empirical generalizations, models, and theories*. This in turn leads to a new epistemology of methods, research questions, interpretations, and explanations—what Kuhn (1962) has described as a "scientific revolution." The acceptance of a new paradigm can probably be recognized only from a broader historical perspective, often many years after its emergence as a mode of scientific inquiry. We note that there are alternative usages of the term "paradigm" within the field of gerontology. Some biologists use the term to describe what other biologists mean by "models;" Riley, Foner, and Riley (in this volume) use it to characterize a revolution in efforts within the sociology of age and aging during the past three decades.

These epistemological distinctions are not merely stylistic: they get to the heart of what theory is, and what the ultimate goal of inquiry should be. In the remainder of this chapter we will argue that gerontology has lost this focus on explanation—theory—in the latter decades of the 20th century; and that if gerontology is to prosper as a science or as a body of knowledge in the 21st century, it must rekindle its concern for theory development.

Why is theory important?

In the history of knowledge, from Aristotelian epistemology through modern sciences' applications in artificial intelligence, theory—the attempt to develop explanations—has proven to be extremely useful. In addition to the depth of understanding that theoretically based research provides, the breadth of pragmatic justifications for theory can be seen in four ways:

Integration of knowledge: A good theory summarizes the many discrete findings from empirical studies and incorporates them into a brief statement that describes linkages among the crucial observations, variables, or theoretical constructs.

Explanation of knowledge: A useful theory provides not only description of the ways empirically observed phenomena are related (this is what "models" reflect) but also *how* and especially *why* they are related, in a logically sound account incorporating antecedents and consequences of empirical results.

Predictions about what is not yet known or observed: Research based on theory can lead to subsequent discoveries based on principles proposed by earlier theory. Examples from the history of science include Darwin's theory of natural selection in biology; Mendeleev's theory leading to the periodic table of elements in chemistry; and Einstein's theory of relativity in physics.

Interventions to improve human conditions: Theory is valuable when we attempt to apply and advance existing knowledge in order to solve problems or alleviate undesirable conditions. The practical utility of scientific theory is evident in the advancement of instant communications from the telegraph to the world-wide Internet, and the near eradication of communicable diseases during the past century. Another kind of intervention is social: governments intervene through public policy, attempting to ameliorate problems of poverty in old age, delaying institutionalization of older persons through home assistance provisions like Meals-on-Wheels, and providing enriched educational opportunities to disadvantaged children through "Head Start" programs. These are indeed interventions; they are often experiments. How effective they are is open to further evaluation—and it must be noted that very little funding is available to provide evaluation research for public policy interventions. What is clear is that these social interventions often do not reflect well-digested theory—prompting the question: "If you don't understand the problem, how can you fix it?"

Alternative perspectives on theory have emerged from interpretive critiques of science (Featherstone, 1989; Giddens, 1996; Lynott & Lynott, 1996). In contrast to the procedures of positivistic science, interpretive and critical models of theorizing focus on process and understanding. Rather than emphasizing prediction and control, interpretive researchers collect data and make observations with the goal of identifying *themes of meaning* that emerge from the process of research (Glaser & Strauss, 1967). Critical theorists seek to question the underlying assumptions of scientific "knowledge"; to expose what they feel are political perspectives on that knowledge; and to give credence to the meanings and experiences of the underrepresented, less powerful groups in society. In social gerontology, for example, recent applications of chaos theory to problems of aging (Hendricks, 1997) have shifted the focus away from central tendencies and linear patterns toward an appreciation of diversity and complex, nonlinear progressions (see Hendricks and Achenbaum in this volume).

THE STATE OF THEORY IN GERONTOLOGY TODAY

Many researchers and practitioners in gerontology appear relatively unconcerned about theories of aging. In the biology of aging, for example, many researchers seem focused on empirical models of aging at the cellular or molecular levels, leaving integrative theories of aging to other investigators (for exceptions see Cristofalo et al., Chapter 6 in this volume and Finch, 1990, 1997). In the psychology of aging, the pursuit of experimental models of age differences has not been accompanied by similar efforts at integration of findings with theory (Birren & Birren, 1990; Salthouse, 1991). In the sociology of aging there has also been an increase in empirical analyses but a decrease in efforts at theoretical explanation concerning such critical phenomena as the consequences of population aging, the changing status of aging individuals in society, the social processes of aging in complex and changing societies, and the interdependency of age groups in the generational compact (Johnson 1995; Bengtson, Burgess, & Parrott, 1997).

The Problem of Theory Development in Gerontology

There may be some who feel that the problem of theory in gerontology today is that a few misguided gerontologists are still squandering their resources trying to construct theories of aging. Perhaps theory is the domain of armchair academics with too much time on their hands. Such an opinion is understandable given the many ways theory is miscast in gerontology and in the broader domain of science today. For example, theory is often held in opposition to "fact" and seen as no more than lofty speculation. Further, the desire for specific solutions to pressing problems facing elderly individuals can frame theory as a superfluous abstraction from practical concerns. The most radical critique comes from postmodernists, who claim there is no objective truth or reality to move toward, so theorizing amounts to grasping at thin air.

Within the relatively short history of gerontology as the scientific study of aging—which spans only a half century of sustained empirical research—

skepticism about the importance of theory has led some researchers to sub-stitute empirical models for theory and has led others to wash their hands of theory entirely. The effect of these reactions has been to substitute empirical monologues for theoretical dialogues about age and aging.

Thus, while we have developed many empirical generalizations *describing* aging, relatively few of these have been employed in the more fundamental tasks of *understanding and explaining* aging. We submit that this "disinher-itance of theory" in gerontological research recently has retarded the process of connecting findings to explanations, and thereby undermined the enrich-ment of knowledge about phenomena of aging.

For example, a recent study reviewed articles published between 1990 and 1994 in eight major journals relevant to the sociology of aging (Bengtson et al., 1997). By far the majority—72% of all publications reviewed—made no mention of *any* theoretical tradition in the literature as relevant to the em-pirical "findings" reported. The authors conclude that "the *ad hoc,* descrip-tive, model-based (rather than explanatory or theory-based) approach to research is ineffectual, over time" and that "if authors, journal reviewers, and editors ignore the need for explicit explanation in data analyses, it is not likely that we will achieve much cumulative knowledge development in so-cial gerontology" (Bengtson et al., 1997, p. S75).

An unfortunate consequence is that current gerontological research may be accumulating a vast collection of empirical generalizations without the parallel development of integrated knowledge. But the development of ex-planations—theories—is central to the variety of issues that gerontologists will be seeking to understand in the next few decades.

What Gerontologists Are Trying to Explain

Gerontologists—whether as scientists, practitioners, or policymakers—must deal with three general sets of problems as they attempt to analyze and understand phenomena of aging. The first set of issues concerns *the aged*: populations of those who can be categorized as elderly in terms of their length of life or expected lifespan, whether they be mice in the laboratory or humans as members of a society. The vast majority of gerontological studies in recent decades have concentrated on the functional problems of aged populations, seen in human terms as medical disability or barriers to inde-pendent living.

A second set of problems involve *aging as a developmental process* occur-ring over time. Here the focus is on how individuals of a species grow up and grow old—the processes of development, growth, and senescence over time—and the biological, psychological, and social aspects of that process, including its variable rates and consequences. Longitudinal research is nec-essary in order to address questions of processes of aging; unfortunately most studies of aging continue to be cross-sectional. But problems of the aged are inextricably related to issues of aging as a process, particularly in human populations.

Yet a third problem involves *the study of age* as a dimension of structure and behavior within species. This is of obvious interest to sociologists and other social scientists examining human populations, and the social organization they create and modify, in response to the age-related patterns of birth, socialization, accession to adult status, and retirement or death within the human group. The phenomena to be explained here concern how age is taken into account by social institutions; examples include the labor market, retirement, pension systems, and health care organizations. But it is also a concern of zoologists, primate anthropologists, and evolutionary biologists, who note the importance of age as an organizing principle in many species' behaviors—and their survival (Wachter & Finch, 1997).

These three concerns are quite different in focus and inquiry; yet they are inextricably interrelated in gerontological research and practice. The process of theorizing serves, in part, to disentangle these problems of aging and to address each as distinct but mutually dependent phenomena.

WHY HAS THEORY BECOME DEVALUED IN GERONTOLOGY?

Science, in common with all long-term human endeavors, is a social enterprise, and as such is reflective of the concerns, careers, and competitiveness of a collective group of practitioners. This is what Kuhn (1962) emphasized in his analysis of scientific discoveries in physics and chemistry. There are trends in what is considered as relevant inquiry, and there are trends going against this current.

Why has the concern for theory development become devalued in gerontology recently? We suggest that this trend, reflecting an impatience with theorizing in gerontology (and in scholarship more generally), stems from four other trends: (a) the failed quest for "grand theory;" (b) the drive for applications and solutions in gerontology; (c) postmodernist epistemological critiques; and (d) the resistance to cross-disciplinary and interdisciplinary investigations in gerontology. Ultimately, we argue that these challenges do not call for the devaluation or elimination of theories of aging; rather, they underline their utility for researchers and practitioners in the 21st century.

The Decline of "General Theory" in Scientific Inquiry

The profusion of scientific discoveries in the late 19th and early 20th centuries created an enthusiasm for theories of broad scope. There seemed no end to what science could explain and demystify. Scientific and technological advances rapidly transformed people's everyday lives. Applications of germ theory, for instance, led to the virtual elimination of childhood infectious diseases, so that for the first time in human history parents could take for granted that most of their children would survive infancy and grow up into adulthood. The automobile expanded the frontier "down the open road" in the early decades of the 20th century and astrophysicists extended it into outer space just 50 years later. If the social and cultural landscape could be so profoundly transformed by science, could not the scientific theory and method be applied to society itself?

Twentieth century social theorists began to abstract the fundamental ordering of the social world from empirical observations in the same way natural scientists abstracted laws of the physical world (Seidman & Wagner, 1992). As biological pathogens were identified and attacked by modern medicine, so modern social scientists envisioned their battle as exposing toxic societal ignorance and superstition to a healthy dose of the true social order. An overarching goal of this period was to provide a unified framework that would guide future research and analysis. Social theorists such as Parsons (1951) and Homans (1950) proposed that if we could articulate the laws and general principles of social action, then the specific problems of human society and their possible solutions would become more clear.

The current state of social theorizing is, by contrast, marked by doubt (Turner, 1992). Few scholars today would argue that we are converging on a teleological utopia of efficient society governed by science and free of conflict, or what Habermas (1972) called the "unfinished project of modernity." To the contrary, it can be argued that the attempt to filter complex social phenomena into universal principles can only lead to unwarranted reductionism and perhaps the perpetuation of inequalities. The history of Social Darwinism provides an example. When Darwin's *The Origin of Species by Means of Natural Selection* was published in 1859, it achieved recognition from most biological scientists within several decades. By the end of the 19th century, Darwin's "grand theory" of natural selection was modified and filtered into the formulation of Social Darwinism, which claimed that people and societies compete for survival and only the most "fit" survive. Before falling into disrepute in the 20th century, Social Darwinism was used to justify imperialism, colonialism, unbridled capitalism, and the superiority of the White race—all in the name of science.

Gerontology also has seen the rise and fall of "general theories" of aging (Achenbaum, 1995): for example Walter Cannon's (1942) theory of diminishing homeostatic capacity with aging, and the social science theories of disengagement, activity, and modernization. A case in point is disengagement theory (Cumming & Henry, 1961) which attempted to explain human aging as an inevitable process of individuals and social structures mutually and adaptively withdrawing from each other in anticipation of the person's inevitable death. This general theory of aging was elegant, multidisciplinary, parsimonious, and intuitively provocative. However, its ambitious magnitude was quickly challenged in widespread debate and ultimately denounced (Achenbaum & Bengtson, 1994).

Theories proposing universal mechanisms of social aging raise the issue of whether "old age" is a viable concept to apply equally to all people (Johnson, 1918). The many ways people will experience later life depend on how their life course trajectories are shaped by structural and personal factors (see O'Rand and Campbell; and Riley, Foner, and Riley in this volume). Increasingly, age-appropriate behaviors and roles are becoming more fluid. This complexity may be overlooked to the extent that theories focus on "the aged" as a unified category. Hence, theories that attempt to explain human aging as a general process are often oversimplified, and thus subsequently disregarded. At the same time, theories of aging can foster an appreciation of *aged heterogeneity* (Dannefer & Sell, 1988; Dannefer and Uhlenberg, this volume; Maddox & Clark, 1992) by addressing the ways in which diverse aging experiences converge in patterns and themes.

The Drive for Applications and Solutions in Gerontology

In contrast to grand theorists are the practical reformers who tend to ignore theory altogether as they pursue solutions to problems of aging. Maggie Kuhn, the fiery advocate for America's elderly and a founder of the Grey Panthers' movement, told an audience of the Gerontological Society of America that "We have enough research! We have enough theories! What we need are more programs to help senior citizens in need!" (M. Kuhn, 1983).

Unfortunately, the search for solutions without regard to theory can lead to several problems, including unchecked assumptions, a lack of evaluative criteria, and the inability to build upon previous efforts. Students and new professionals in gerontology are often motivated to identify the problems of aging and help devise appropriate ways of dealing with them. This assumes that aging is inherently problematic. Are gerontologists who define aging as senescence and decline actually helping older adults, or are they patronizing elders with "benign ageism" (Palmore, 1990)? Without theory, how can gerontologists decide which problems are caused by aging itself, which are age-related phenomena, and which are not due to age at all? Implicit theories and assumptions are left buried, where they can neither be evaluated for possible bias nor for further utility.

In an era when programs of intervention are held increasingly accountable for outcomes and results, what criteria are used to determine the utility of gerontological interventions? Without theoretical underpinnings, we cannot explain why some programs flourish and others flounder. The relationship between social support and well-being among older adults is a telling example of the crucial link between theory and application in gerontology. For years, the guiding assumption among practitioners was that more support to elders brought more psychological well-being. Explicit testing of this implicit theory reveals that there is "too much of a good thing," such that excessive amounts of intergenerational support can undermine autonomy and cause distress (Silverstein & Chen, 1996). Social breakdown theory provides one explanation of why this might be the case (Bengtson & Kuypers, 1986). It proposes a cycle of increasing dependency among vulnerable older people whose self-sufficiency erodes with high amounts of support. The curvilinear relationship between social support and well-being has significant bearing on family caregiving strategies and policy decisions.

Not only do theories allow us to predict the effects and evaluate the implementation of applied gerontology, but they also enhance our learning from the success and failure of these applications. By theorizing that social support may be harmful in excessive amounts, for example, we can shift time and resources toward identifying and facilitating other factors that may be beneficial. Interventions that are not integrated into broader efforts at cumulative theory-building risk not only coming short of their goals but undermining their very purpose.

If some theories of aging are more useful than others in generating meaningful explanations and effective interventions, we must develop systematic methods of evaluating theories. Achenbaum and Bengtson propose four criteria in evaluating the adequacy of theories in aging. These include (a) logical adequacy, a measure of clarity, internal consistency, parsimony, and explanatory content; (b) operational adequacy, or the ability of the theory to be empirically tested; (c) empirical adequacy, or the extent of credible and replicated evidence for the theory; and (d) pragmatic adequacy, the usefulness of theory in prediction and intervention as well as its feasibility and practical relevance (Achenbaum & Bengtson, 1994, p. 760). Theories of aging that meet criteria such as these will move gerontologists forward in generating answers and inciting further questions.

Postmodernism and the Uprooting of Theory

Postmodernists critique the theory-building process from its very foundations. Scientific theory—positivistic theory—is based on a hierarchical structure of observations and concepts. At its base are *constructs,* unobserved entities that stand for a repeated number of empirical observations that are linked in some sort of relationship. The term construct itself introduces the slippery differentiation (for postmodernists) between what is socially constructed and what is empirically "true." Is empirical reality itself a social construction, subject to the influence of moral, political, linguistic, and even observational biases? If so, what value does scientific theory have?

In gerontology, postmodernist scholars would hold that categories such as "old" do not equally represent their members, and that no person embodies such an abstraction (Katz, 1996). Beyond this seemingly semantic distinction, they call attention to the interests and values that are presupposed by such categories. On an epistemological level, postmodernists critique the privileging of "scientific" knowledge as purported truth. This challenge to positivistic theorizing stretches far beyond an interpretivist rejection of the inclination to overgeneralize from available data to an assault on the notion of data itself.

Postmodern critiques of scientific theory challenge not only what theoretical discourse includes but what it excludes, drawing attention to what is left out of the discussion. Postmodernists question the "metanarratives" that provide a context for theorizing. These "foundational discourses" are attacked for trying and failing to justify the legitimacy of Enlightenment traditions (Lyotard, 1984). The modernist idealization of reason as the key to enlightened society is rejected by postmodernist scholars, who tend to view science and social control, or knowledge and power, as inexorably linked (Foucault, 1972, 1973). Their "deconstructionist" critique of western philosophy cuts through the sterilized image of science. It calls for a dissolution of the binary oppositions or "black and white" dualities that hold science in contrast to politics, myth, and rhetoric (Derrida, 1978). These dualities are identified as leading to the intellectual positioning of science as truthful and nonscience as speculative "non-sense."

The pure relativism demanded by extreme versions of postmodernist critique suggests a kind of posttheoretical anarchy in which communication and thought itself are suspect. This position can be viewed as a hypothesis in its own right, whose soundness will be determined by the test of future scholarship. Before we prematurely accept the futility of theory, however, we must remember that the goal of science is to explain. Are all explanations equal? Bhaskar (1986) attributes the hasty rejection of theory to the common confusion in failing to distinguish between:

> . . . (a) the principle of epistemic relativity, *vis* that all beliefs are socially produced, so that knowledge is transient and neither truth-values nor criteria of rationality exist outside historical time and (b) the doctrine of judgmental relativism, which maintains that all beliefs are equally valid in the sense that there are no rational grounds for preferring one to another. (Bhaskar, 1986, p. 54)

Some contemporary scholars—including many gerontologists—would probably agree with the principle of epistemic relativism, rejecting scientific claims to absolute truth and reason. Theories are sociotemporally situated and produced by humans with particular interests and values. Judgmental relativism, on the other hand, is more difficult to accept because it is not easy to intuitively judge whether a given argument is good or bad. The social and motivational context of theories may not be grounds to negate them, but rather require critical awareness and reflective evaluation. There is little to be gained in shifting allegiance from abstract universality to an equally abstract postmodern rejection of the universal. Rationality need not collapse into universal truth claims, nor scientific inquiry into scientism. At the same time, there is much to be gained by recognizing the value of theory in generating more adequate and useful explanations.

Moreover, scientific theories have the capacity to effect practical changes in matters of great concern. Unprecedented population aging is one such matter that renders theory indispensable. Theoretical gerontology is relevant to both individual aging and the changing age structures of population, potentially helping both age "successfully."

The Resistance to Cross-Disciplinary and Interdisciplinary Investigations in Gerontology

If theory is pivotal to the continued growth of gerontology as a science, a practice, and an academic field of study, what will future theories of aging address? The study of individual and population aging and their societal consequences does not fall comfortably within one discipline. Levels of analysis and variables examined differ considerably between biologists, psychologists, sociologists, economists, and policy analysts. Each of these fields have contributed important insights to the study of aging, but it is no longer sufficient for researchers to analyze only the variables and empirical models specific to their respective disciplines. A comprehensive account rests on the ability of researchers to traverse disciplinary lines and develop a more common language of inquiry.

The advancement of pluralistic and contextualized social inquiry can be furthered by a commitment to cross-disciplinary and interdisciplinary investigations in aging (Rowe & Kahn, 1997). The scattered examples of this process signify the cross-fertilization of ideas and methods among scholars from widely divergent fields of study. They mark the possible emergence of a new era of inquiry in which researchers do not simply examine age differences and aging disorders from their various disciplinary empires but converge to explore the underlying mechanisms of aging and their multifaceted consequences. As of yet, however, such collaboration may be more rhetoric than reality. The enduring impact of gerontology depends on overcoming the resistance of some researchers to a broadened domain.

The knowledge that arises from "postmodernist" studies "...contests disciplinary boundaries, the separation of science, literature, and ideology, and the division between knowledge and power" (Seidman, 1994, p. 2). Such complexity does not imply the futility of theory; rather it suggests the demand for new approaches and truly interdisciplinary research. Theorists must conceive of ideas and knowledge as practical and purposive, examining the interests and goals reflected by their work.

If gerontology is currently assuming a unique multidisciplinary form at the start of the 21st century, the authors in this volume offer a contemporary snapshot of the metamorphosis (see particularly the chapters by Dannefer and Uhlenberg; Finch and Seeman; Fry; Hendricks and Achenbaum; and O'Rand and Campbell, in this volume). These suggest we are on the cusp of what promises to be a lively and creative dialogue about theories of aging in the coming decade. A commitment to the advancement of theory by the gerontological community will ensure that discussions continue to move forward.

WHY AND HOW SHOULD GERONTOLOGISTS FOCUS ON THEORY DEVELOPMENT IN THE NEXT DECADE?

We began this chapter by asking whether theory is important, relevant, or even possible within the broad and increasingly differentiated fields of inquiry that constitute gerontology at the end of the 20th century. We noted Kuhn's critique of "normal science" as an indictment of inadequate theoretical paradigms; the critical theory emphasis on the relativity of knowledge and the subjectivity of scientific research; and the postmodern dismissal of theory in the context of the relativity in discourse and claims to knowledge.

We then examined claims of these critiques as they relate to gerontology today. It appears that our field is rich in data but poor in theoretical integration. We argued that the focus of theory is on *explanation,* as distinguished from empirical generalizations, models of relationships or simulations. We noted that many researchers in gerontology today, along with many journal editors and reviewers, seem to have little concern for theory or its development. The disenchantment with "general theories" of aging, and the push for practical solutions to problems of the aged, have led to a devaluation of theory, particularly among gerontological practitioners and policy makers. We emphasized that applications of knowledge in gerontology—whether in medicine, practice, or policy—demand good theory, since it is on the basis of *explanations* about problems that interventions should be made; if not, they seem doomed to failure.

Without theory, the contributions of individual studies in aging are likely to have little impact. Even if we accept empirical generalizations at face value, these "facts" do not speak for themselves. They are but discrete building blocks in the development of knowledge. We suggest that researchers have a responsibility to act also as theorists, to interpret and explain their findings within a broader context of inquiry.

SUGGESTIONS FOR FUTURE RESEARCHERS IN GERONTOLOGY

We want to end this chapter with some suggestions for today's graduate students in gerontology—who will be the leading researchers and practitioners of aging during the first decades of the 21st Century—about how they can use theory to develop more cumulative knowledge involving processes of aging, or more successful interventions about involving problems of aging. We have noted that there are three basic areas of inquiry that gerontologists have been pursuing during the past half-century, and will be seeking to understand in future decades: concerns about *the aged* as members of increasingly aged populations in human societies; concerns about *basic processes and mechanisms of aging* in cells, organisms, and individuals within aging populations; and concerns about *age as a dimension* of social organization and public policy in industrialized societies. We have emphasized that cross-disciplinary and inter-disciplinary approaches to these three issues will be required in order to provide adequate understanding of these problems of aging, as well as the development of effective programs and interventions to alleviate them.

Thus, for the next generation of gerontologists, we offer five suggestions:

1. Remember that theory is crucial to the cumulative development of knowledge, whether in science or in any investigation. Don't attempt to publish results of your experiments, surveys, or observations without an explicit attempt to address the *why* behind the results.

2. Don't confuse empirical generalizations or models with theories. Theory involves explanation, and explanations develop knowledge.

3. Read the literature for previous attempts to "explain" the phenomena you are investigating. Science does not proceed in a vacuum, we stand on the shoulders of giants in terms of previous theory and attempts at explanation.

4. Scientific reductionism is not always the most important goal. Postmodernists challenge—rightly—the reductionist perspective by pointing to the understanding of diversity and complexity as equally important goals.

5. A single grand theory to explain aging—as has been proposed several times during the development of gerontology: in the past century—may be impossible; but we have many useful minitheories (what can be termed

"local knowledge") in the gerontological literature today. You will find these helpful as you frame your research questions, decide on appropriate methods to investigate them, and interpret the findings of your study.

CONCLUSION

Theory is important because it represents a sustained effort by a collective group of researchers to summarize what is already known, add to existing knowledge, and provide guidance for what is yet to be understood. Theory is the compass with which to navigate through vast seas of data. It is the means by which data are transformed into meaningful explanations, or stories, about the processes and consequences of aging.

REFERENCES

Achenbaum, W. A. (1995). *Crossing frontiers: Gerontology emerges as a science.* New York: Cambridge University Press.

Achenbaum, W. A., & Bengtson, V. L. (1994). Re-engaging the disengagement theory of aging: On the history and assessment of theory development in gerontology. *The Gerontologist, 34,* 756–763.

Bengtson, V. L, Burgess, E. O., & Parrott, T. M. (1997). Theory, explanation, and a third generation of theoretical development in social gerontology. *The Journal of Gerontology: Social Sciences, 52B(2),* S72–S88.

Bengtson, V. L., Parrott, T. M., & Burgess, E. O. (1996). Progress and pitfalls in gerontological theorizing. *The Gerontologist, 36(6),* 768–772.

Bengtson, V. L., & Kuypers, J. A. (1986). The family support cycle: Psycho-social issues in the aging family. In J.M.A. Munnichs, P. Mussen, & E. Olbrich (Eds.), *Life span and change in a gerontological perspective* (pp. 61–77). New York: Academic Press.

Bhaskar, R. (1986). *Scientific realism and human emancipation.* London: Verso.

Birren, J. E., & Bengtson, V. L. (Eds.) (1988). *Emergent theories of aging.* New York: Springer Publishing Co.

Birren, J. E., & Birren, B. A. (1990). Theory and measurement in the psychology of aging. In J. E. Birren & K. W. Schaie (Eds.), *Handbook of the psychology of aging* (3rd ed., pp. 3–20). San Diego: Academic Press.

Brown, H. (1986). *The wisdom of science.* New York: Random House.

Cannon, W. B. (1942). Ageing of homeostatic mechanisms. In E. Cowdry, (Ed.), *Problems of ageing* (2nd edition). Baltimore, MD: Williams & Wilkins.

Cumming, E., & Henry, W. E. (1961). *Growing old: The process of disengagement.* New York: Basic Books.

Dannefer, D., & Sell, R. (1988). Age structure, the life course and "aged heterogeneity": Prospects for research and theory. *Comprehensive Gerontology, 2,* 1–10.

Derrida, J. (1978). *Writing and difference.* Chicago: University of Chicago Press.

Featherstone, M. (1989). Toward a sociology of postmodern culture. In H. Hafner-kamp (Ed.), *Social structure and culture.* Berlin and New York: Walter de Gruyter.

Finch, C. (1990). *Longevity, senescence, and the genome.* Chicago: University of Chicago Press.

Finch, C. (1997). Comparative perspectives on plasticity in human aging and life spans. In K. W. Wachter & C. E. Finch (Eds.), *Between Zeus and the Salmon: The biodemography of longevity.* New York: National Academy Press.

Foucault, M. (1972). *The archaeology of knowledge.* Trans. A. M. Sheridan Smith. London: Tavistock.

Foucault, M. (1973). *The order of things: An archaeology of the human sciences.* Trans. A. Sheridan. New York: Vintage Books.

Giddens (1996). *An introduction to sociology.* New York: Norton.

Glaser, B. G., & Strauss, A. L. (1967). *The discovery of grounded theory: Strategies of qualitative research.* New York: Aldine.

Gubrium, J. F., & Wallace, J. B. (1990). Who theorizes age? *Ageing and Society, 10,* 131–149.

Habermas, J. (1970). Science and technology as ideology. *Towards a rational society.* Boston: Beacon Press.

Habermas, J. (1972). *Knowledge and human interests.* Trans. Jeremy Shapiro. London: Heinemann.

Hayflick, (1994). *How and why we age.* New York: Ballantine.

Hendricks, J. (1997). Bridging contested terrain: Chaos or prelude to a theory. *Canadian Journal on Aging, 16(3).*

Homans, G. (1950). *The human group.* New York: Harcourt, Brace and World.

Horgan, J. (1996). *The end of science: Facing the limits of science in the twilight of the scientific age.* New York: Broadway Books.

Johnson, M. L. (1996). Interdependency and the generational compact. *Ageing and Society, 15(2),* 243–265.

Katz, S. (1996). *Disciplining old age: The formation of gerontological knowledge.* Charlottesville, VA: University Press of Virginia.

Kuhn, M. (1983). Remarks to symposium at the Gerontological Society of America Annual Meeting, November 21.

Kuhn, T. (1962). *The structure of scientific revolutions.* New York: Norton.

Lynott, R. J., & Lynott, P. P. (1996). Tracing the course of theoretical development in the sociology of aging. *The Gerontologist, 35(6),* 749–760.

Lyotard, J-F. (1984). *The postmodern condition.* Minneapolis: University of Minnesota Press.

Maddox, G., & Clark, D. O. (1992). Trajectories of functional impairment in later life. *Journal of Health and Social Behavior, 33(2),* 114–125.

Marshall, V. W. (1995). Social models of aging. *Canadian Journal on Aging, 14(1),* 12–34.

Marshall, V. W. (1996). The state of theory in aging and the social sciences. In R. Binstock & L. George (Eds.), *Handbook of aging and the social sciences (4th edition).* New York: Academic Press.

Palmore, E. (1990). *Ageism: Negative and positive.* New York: Springer Publishing Co.

Parsons, T. (1951). *The social system.* New York: Free Press.

Rorty, R. (1991). *Objectivity, relativism, and truth.* Cambridge: Cambridge University Press.

Rowe, J., & Kahn, R. (1997). Successful aging. *The Gerontologist, 27(4),* 433–440.

Salthouse, T. A. (1991). *Theoretical perspectives on cognitive aging.* Hillsdale, NJ: Lawrence Erlbaum Associates.

Seidman, S. (Ed). (1994). *The postmodern turn: New perspectives on social theory.* Cambridge: Cambridge University Press.

Seidman, S., & Wagner, D. G. (Eds.). (1992). *Postmodernism and social theory.* Cambridge, MA: Blackwell.

Silverstein, M., & Chen, X. (1996). Too much of a good thing? Intergenerational social support and the psychological well-being of older parents. *Journal of Marriage and the Family, 58,* 970–982.

Turner, J. (1988). *The structure of sociological theory* (2nd edition). Homewood, IL: Dorsey Press.

Turner, J. H. (1992). The promise of positivism. In S. Seidman & D. G. Wagner (Eds.), *Postmodernism and social theory.* Cambridge, MA: Blackwell.

Wachter, K. W. &, Finch, C. E. (Eds.), (1997). *Between Zeus and the salmon: The biodemography of longevity.* Washington, DC: National Academy Press.

Webster (1998). *New world dictionary (29th edition).* New York: Random House.

2

Historical Development of Theories of Aging

Jon Hendricks
Andrew Achenbaum

THEORIES OF AGING AND CONTEXT OF IDEAS: MAKING CONNECTIONS

Regardless of specific focus, the puzzle-solving solutions scientists put forth are inevitably grounded in broader currents. Whether well defined or silent, theories have provided the perspectual eyeglasses that resolve how the so-called facts of aging are seen and how they are explained. We seek to highlight some of the issues and the controversies associated with theory-building in gerontology and to link them to social and professional considerations that shape the pathways to new knowledge. It is our assumption that to appreciate how change and innovation come about in theories of aging, scholars must be sensitive to the factors underpinning the study of aging. Our goal is to promote an understanding of the connections between scientific inquiry and tendencies extant in the land at any point in time that influence how a subject matter is conceived.

Historical Bases of Theories of Aging

The earliest historical records indicate that people in all times and at all places have tried to make sense of the way people age. Best-selling anthologies such as the *Oxford Book of Aging* (Cole & Winkler, 1994) use excerpts from the Koran, Confucius, and Langston Hughes, among others, to convey quintessentially human concerns about relationships and feelings over the course of life. Our generation is but the latest to look for lessons, in an effort to convert the mysteries of growing older into propositions that can be tested systematically. Just as surely as we have searched, so too will the next generation.

Gerontology's pioneers canvassed the historical treasure trove in order to put their own theories in perspective. The eminent psychologist G. Stanley Hall, for instance, devoted more than half of *Senescence* (1922) to premodern models of aging. In recent decades, various artists, historians, literary critics, philosophers, physicians, popular writers, and social scientists have surveyed the literature more systematically. Sanskrit and other ancient texts, archaeological evidence, the Bible, cave drawings, classical drama and poetry, medieval allegories, early modern medical reports, and alchemists' findings have been cast in precursory roles to draw parallels and contrasts between how humans past and present interpret "facts" of aging and explain variations in well-being and infirmity at various stages of life. (For overviews, see Achenbaum, 1985; Achenbaum, 1996; Cole, van Tassel & Kastenbaum, 1993; Gruman, 1966; Hendricks & Hendricks, 1978; Van Tassel, 1979).

Making sense of the historical record is an intricate task, one demanding a certain conceptual sophistication and contextual awareness. Analysts must constantly remind themselves that aging may be a universal phenomenon but its impact and meaning are mediated by economic, structural, and cultural factors. No text should be taken merely at face value. To make sense of the historic literature, its purpose and function, the conventions of genre and style, and the meaning of meaning during the period when a particular tract was created must be part of the analytic frame (Hendricks & Leedham, 1989). From the distillations that early gerontologists provided arise three generalizations about the foundations of gerontological theory-building before the 20th century:

1. *Most early models of aging reflected broader societal worldviews; few gerontologic prototheories were created through inductive reasoning.* To illustrate: the ancient Israelites accepted as truth the postulate that the human life span did not extend beyond 120 years (Gen. 6:3). That certain patriarchs lived far beyond that maximum was a sign of Providence that did not violate the divine order. Perhaps this is because diversity was taken for granted. Hebrew Scripture in their eyes abounds in the varieties of aging. Hence, according to Psalm 90, most who lived to age 70 or possibly 80 could expect to maintain their "strength," but thereafter "the hurrying years are labor and sorrow." The best predictor of longevity was obedience to God's commandments: the children of Israel were to honor their mothers and fathers "so that your days may be long and that it may go well with you in the land that

the Lord your God is giving you" (Deut. 5:16). Virtue was not always re-warded, however. Life could be hard for faithful elders: several books attest to the "reproach of widowhood" (Is. 54:4; Lam. 1:1, 5:3–4). The stages of human life never violated God's plans, but they were experienced in the life of a community subject to the vicissitudes of time and place.

2. *Because traditions matter, successive generations often reworked explana-tions of aging so that they made sense in new historical contexts.* For most Jews, ancient texts gave clear direction as to how the Ultimate Reality ex-pected them to comport themselves on their journeys through life. Neither infirmity nor poverty nor societal calamities such as exile and discrimina-tion were excuses for disobedience. The context is different but Cicero's *De Senectute* made much the same point: standards of behavior must not yield to insult or inequities of age. By the time the legend of *De Senectute* was translated into English in 1481, it was taken as proof positive that old age could be a time of virtue, a model of what life ought to be (Hendricks, 1993). Similarly, the lifestyles of the venerable Desert Fathers in fourth-century Egypt harkened back to ascetic customs practiced in the early Jesus movement. It is not coincidental that John Bunyan frequently cited biblical texts in *Pilgrim's Progress*. He described Christian's spiritual odyssey (1678) as different from that of his wife, Christiana (1684), but each on their sep-arate paths faced challenges comparable to those endured by Moses and Paul. Bunyan's allegory was the book most likely to be found in New En-gland households. Assuming that the settlers read the text, and there is ev-idence that they did, this fact corroborates historians' conclusions that Puritan divines transmitted biblical images of aging in crafting their model of Chris-tian charity (Haber, 1983). It is not too farfetched to suggest that layer upon layer of explanation about how women aged in past times might have reso-nated with the prevailing fears that culminated in the Salem witch trials. Even Soranus of Ephesus (c. 98–138 CE), did not refrain from certain mor-alizing about desirable lifestyles in one of the first volumes on diseases of women, *Gynaecia*. Reading it reveals that, through the eyes of men, the aging female body was full of abominations, thus reflecting tenets about sexuality in medieval Christianity.

3. *"Facts" may repeat themselves, but connections between aspects of aging and societal norms tend to be idiosyncratic and not widely shared.* Commen-tator after commentator throughout the centuries describes the physical marks of age in similar ways, almost as though identifying benchmarks along the way. They each note the thinning hair of the elderly, their stooping gait and failing senses. Sometimes, as was the case with Aristotle or Cicero, they also take note of wisdom and insight. In virtually all periods, commentators suggest that indignities in old age serve broader individual and relational purposes, though the precise formula varies by time and place. As with the

Greeks, the pattern is for wisdom to be more likely ascribed to elders than to youngsters. And yet, particularly in artifacts from ancient times and the early modern period, it is difficult to discern how pervasive competing theories of senescence truly were. Their correspondence to facts of individual aging is murky if for no other reason than it was an aging elite that was being depicted. More important, few authors made the connections between explanations of aging and their applications to real life societal circumstances. Then, as now, there was not always the will to do so.

There are exceptions, to be sure. Medieval iconography gives a rich sense of how contemporaries envisioned the relative status of various stages of life (Dove, 1986). Luigi Cornaro's practical *Discourses on the Temperate Life* (1558) was quickly translated into Latin, English, French, Dutch, and German; antebellum Americans adhered to his Renaissance prescriptions in caring for the aged (Cole, 1992). By and large, however, most explanations of aging were the product of either moralistic prescriptions or individual reflections; their influence on how people actually structured their lives was greatly circumscribed. For explanations of aging to insinuate themselves into contemporary culture or to attain the status of recognized theory, they need connections that make them testable on their own terms, and they must be congruent with developments in neighboring domains.

Building Theories Constructively

An emphasis on increasingly positivistic ways of knowing in Western Europe during the late Middle Ages and Renaissance set the stage for constructive theory-building in aging. "This shift made modern science, technology, business practice, and bureaucracy possible," observes Crosby (1997). The new pantometry combined observation with quantification, making it possible to discern and measure uniformities in a variety of domains. Yet the shift was gradual, hardly revolutionary. As far back as 1686, the philosopher Bernard de Fontenelle was lamenting that philosophy owed its popularity to a genuine curiosity and poor eyesight; once the *subvisibilia* could be seen, philosophy would yield to science except insofar as we want to know more than we can see (Hooke's microscope had been on the scene for two decades by that time). The availability of printed books, latitudes, and musical notations transformed many facets of life, including what counted as "knowledge," before they prompted fresh interpretations of aging.

Despite medical tracts dating from the ancient Egyptians or Soranus of Ephesus' two volumes, *Acute Disease* and *Chronic Disease,* in the first century CE, the 19th century endures as a watershed in gerontological thinking. Bold efforts to understand senescence in broad terms required two developments. On the one hand, theory-building in terra incognita awaited refinements in statistical techniques. Timely work was proffered by Adolphe

Quetelet, who declared that "man is born, grows up, and dies, according to certain laws that have never been properly investigated" (1842; see also Birren, 1986). Quetelet, through the application of what both he and Comte termed *social physics,* essayed to ascertain "the average man, amongst different nations, both physical and moral." His emphasis on the mean (while acknowledging diversity) remains central to those who formulate models of aging. The aftermath was that what was intended as a statistical average became an "ideal type" against which discrepancies are often contrasted.

On the other hand, advances in gerontological reasoning depended on both the invention of new techniques (such as the microscope and x rays) and the refinement of interventions (pharmaceutical, surgical, and psychiatric) with which to differentiate diseases and to treat disabilities over the life cycle. Thus, while early-19th-century investigators (such as Christian Wilhelm Hufeland and Sir Anthony Carlisle) had emphasized localized lesions that manifested themselves in late life, "pathological" models of aging did not gain salience in the United States until Jean-Martin Charcot's 1867 compendium, *Diseases of the Elders and Their Chronic Illnesses,* was translated into English in 1881. By then, U.S. biomedical researchers had the requisite etiological paradigms and techniques to test Charcot's taxonomy on patient complaints in their clinics and laboratories (Achenbaum, 1978). Timing in theory-building may not be everything, but it counts for a lot: Charcot's ideas were not so much original as they were congruous with new scientific methods and medical practices.

IS THERE THEORY IN AGING?

By the beginning of the 20th century a few U.S. scholars ventured beyond descriptive compilations of physical and pathological manifestations of growing older. Building on medical models, they began to construct holistic theories of aging that attempted to integrate the disparate yet seemingly complementary "scientific" techniques of biology and sociology. In part because of the work of the renowned French sociologist Auguste Comte, a contemporary and sometimes competitor with Quetelet, a quest for integrative frameworks was part of the scientific mind-set. Although Comte had formulated a hierarchy of the natural sciences, based on complexity and integration, that led from astronomy to physics, chemistry, and biology and ultimately to sociology, the principal inspiration in this instance can be found in the work of Elie Metchnikoff, a polymath who had distinguished himself in embryology, zoology, immunology, and pathology before grappling later in his life with the causes of old age.

The Nobel laureate's two major works on the subject, *The Nature of Man* (1903) and *The Prolongation of Life* (1908), vigorously defended his theory that microbes in the digestive tract caused "the morbid nature of old age." Unabashedly multidisciplinary in orientation, Metchnikoff conceived of later life as a time of continuing growth and development as well as of decline. Now, at the fin de siècle, the dynamic character of aging has been labeled as gerodynamics and is once again center stage as notions of predictable, continuous, and linear change are being scrutinized (Birren & Schroots, 1984; Hendricks, 1997). Metchnikoff was of the opinion that comparable variable patterns were evident among nonhuman young and even in senescent plants. His macrophage theory was intended to have practical applications for prolonging life; he vehemently insisted that yogurt would ward off illnesses that sap vital capacity, leading to decline and an "enfeebling of the noble elements." Metchnikoff was not without hubris, asserting that even those who did not benefit from his remedies would profit from his "optimistic" studies (Achenbaum & Albert, 1995).

Two eminent U.S. scientists followed Metchnikoff's lead in developing broadly based theories of aging. I. L. Nascher published *Geriatrics* in 1914. Although it resembles Charcot's compendium in format, Nascher's work is actually a precursory contribution that anticipates medical sociology. Its subtitle—*The Diseases of Old Age and Their Treatment, Including Physiological Old Age, Home and Institutional Care, and Medico-Legal Relations*—attests to the author's foci and cross-disciplinary breadth. *Geriatrics* displayed Nascher's ability to master disparate epidemiological data and analyze them in appropriate context. Not only does his volume introduce the term *geriatrics,* it establishes the agenda for comprehensive, integrative analyses of the conditions of later life. Nascher's training was in pharmacy and medicine, and he had honed his familiarity with social statistics in preparing an important urban epidemiological study, *The Wretches of Povertyville: A Sociological Study of the Bowery* (1909). In the course of these two works, America's first geriatrician set high standards for interpreting aging from a comprehensive perspective.

Similar in breadth and leverage was Hall's aforementioned *Senescence* (1922). G. Stanley Hall was a seminal figure in U.S. psychology who founded four journals and trained scores of graduate students. His two volume analysis of adolescence remains a classic and an archetype for field research. *Senescence* evolved out of Hall's interests in behaviorism, biology, and theology. And to the extent that he (at age 78) urged his peers to take advantage of "well-connected senectitude," Hall recast traditional paeans to old age into a compelling critique of contemporary societal arrangements. Like Metchnikoff and Nascher, both of whom are referenced in Hall's text, he melded basic research about aging with practical suggestions for the aged. As Birren and Birren (1990) note, it is too bad that psychologists in general have paid so little heed to Hall's counsel.

In the years following the turn of the century and prior to World War II, "holistic" approaches to the study of old age gained currency in the United States. The impetus for "grand theory" can be discerned in nearly all divisions of the scholarly endeavor, and a unifying thread running through them all was a desire to subsume knowledge from other disciplines into an overarching model. Philanthropic organizations such as the Josiah Macy, Jr., Foundation, which took "more interest in the architecture of ideas than in the architecture of buildings and laboratories," were effective in encouraging junior and senior researchers from a variety of disciplines to join forces in discerning the character and dynamics of senescence. Other foundations and many learned societies shared an interest in pooling resources to identify late-life "problems" and in proposing solutions to issues of both conceptual importance and practical relevance. Individual scholarship remained the norm, but theory-building on a grand scale, especially in boundary domains not claimed by any single profession or discipline, was likely to be an enthusiastic, collective undertaking.

Arguably, the most impressive achievement of this concatenated approach was *Problems of Ageing* (1939), assembled and edited by anatomist and cytologist Edmund Vincent Cowdry (see Achenbaum, 1995, p. 189). Having previously demonstrated to foundation officials the value of bringing together physicians and bench scientists to study arteriosclerosis, Cowdry secured additional funds from Macy to delineate all that was known about aging in order to provide a platform for further exploration. "The problems of growth, the upswing of the curve of vital processes, are being energetically attacked with adequate financial support," Cowdry argued. "Those of aging, the downswing of the curve resulting inevitably in death, are on the contrary, shamefully neglected." The appeal of the endeavor was underscored by others. Cowdry received support from the National Research Council's divisions of medical sciences, biology, agriculture, anthropology, and psychology. He then parlayed the resources available to him to recruit 25 scientists largely affiliated with the Union of American Biological Societies. Included among them were John Dewey, the nation's premier philosopher, and Lawrence K. Frank, one's of the Union's most savvy intellectual entrepreneurs, each of whom provided important contributions to *Problems of Ageing*.

In retrospect, Cowdry's volume stands as a benchmark by which subsequent efforts at gerontological theory-building can be assessed. *Problems of Ageing* did not so much settle issues as sharpen the focus of the debate. At the outset, Frank acknowledged the two poles that have continued to animate discussion throughout the remainder of the century. Then, as now, some experts asserted that old age resulted from "degenerative diseases," whereas others considered aging a natural process devoid of any particular pathology. Dewey, for one, emphasized the difficulty inherent in disentangling "scientific" data (rarely commensurate across disciplines) from "social" context. He was an early advocate for recognizing that regardless of underlying mechanisms, social context nuances their expression and can spell the difference between what Rowe and Kahn (1987) referred to half a century later as "normal" or "successful" aging.

Most contributors to *Problems of Ageing* stressed striking variations at the organic level, and a few made sweeping generalizations across species, but together they set the stage for a dramatic increase in attention to conceptual models in the next several decades. Seemingly, every contributor believed that appropriate application of the scientific method was the most expedient pathway to discovery. And they agreed that, whenever possible, cross-disciplinary collaboration was invaluable for tackling a multifaceted issue like aging. Had the counsel in *Problems on Aging* become the gold standard of gerontological theory-building, the quest for unified knowledge might have progressed further than it has.

In gerontology's earliest days many of its best-known proponents were committed to theory-building on a grand scale. As Lawrence Frank noted in the second (1942) edition of *Problems of Ageing,* "The problem is multidimensional and will require for its solution not only a multidisciplinary approach but also a synoptic correlation of diverse findings and viewpoints." Those remarks framed the agenda, and it was not long before Harvard physiologist and philosopher of science Walter Bradford Cannon incorporated some of the ideas he had gleaned from participants in the 1937 Macy-sponsored Woods Hole Conference on Aging in developing his perspectives on "the aging of homeostatic mechanisms" (pp. xvi–xvii). Taking such a point of view to heart, social scientists at the University of Chicago began to adapt Cannon's ideas in linking changes across biological, cultural, and psychological domains. At a time when scholars from a variety of disciplines were seeking the foundations of unified knowledge in many quarters, the search for the gerontological grail must have struck more than a few as an equally worthy quest.

THE DISCIPLINARY HERITAGE

Counterbalancing generous funding and inclusive affiliations conducive to multidisciplinary discourse were factors that narrowed the focus of individual researchers' inquiries as they broadened the field's vistas for pursuing knowledge. Most U.S. colleges were established to train young men for the ministry and to expose children of promise and wealth to the liberal arts; boards hired clergy and gentleman, more distinguished for character than intellect, to serve as professors. Priorities in higher education changed during the last quarter of the 19th century. To foster research and the creation of new knowledge, American universities organized their faculties into departments that generally corresponded to the ways that the arts and sciences were defined at that time (Veysey, 1965). Professional advancement thereafter required lengthy training, ending only upon receipt of professional certification or an academic degree beyond the B.A. and the publication of papers, reports, and books deemed acceptable by one's learned peers.

Other scholarly institutions beyond the academy reinforced the compartmentalization of information by privileging (intentionally or not) certain specialties over others. Hence, the Rockefeller Foundation invested heavily in medical research, political sciences, and sociology but declined requests for support in the Romance languages or cross-disciplinary activities in the biological sciences that its officers did not think would bear fruit. The federal government quite explicitly defined the parameters of its support for scientific inquiry. At first the National Academy of Science (established in 1863) and the National Research Council (founded in 1918) did little more than advocate activities in the private sector. During World War II, however, the Public Health Service took the steps that would make the fledgling National Institute of Health, created in 1939, into the world's most prestigious and richest cache of funds, especially for biomedical research.

Immediately after the war, the Veterans Administration forged a partnership with major U.S. medical schools whereby even more inclusive research initiatives were granted clinical license. Social science research also profited from new (though less generous) investments through the National Science Foundation (NSF) and its efforts to nurture centers of excellence. The NSF tended to allocate a higher priority to work in the natural sciences than in economics and history, and that pattern continues to be evident today. Even within areas of support, some initiatives, such as demographic research, were to prove more appealing than experiments in psychobiology.

This combination of intellectual and institutional trends affected theory-building in gerontology in postwar America in at least three ways:

1. Academic brokers such as E. V. Cowdry, John Dewey, and Lawrence Frank tried in the 1930s to nurture an "intensified collective consciousness" (Merton, 1972). Their enthusiasm for building theories based on multidisciplinarity were not pursued nearly so vigorously in the work of subsequent generations of researchers on aging. Seemingly, most gerontologists make their reputations by extending disciplinary-specific expertise to aging-related themes. Few master a second or third area of knowledge or find professional fulfillment in moving outside disciplinary paradigms, and few engage the work of scholars outside their own immediate realm in ways that are likely to extend understanding. Innovative theories, as a result, usually evolve from work done within fields, not from inquiries along the interstices of disciplinary frontiers that share common boundaries or are wildly dissimilar.

2. For millennia people have expressed interest in what it means to grow older, but aging per se has not been identified as a major "problem" or "issue" in most disciplines and professions during the 20th century. Big Science's interest in gerontology has been sporadic and transitory, and all too frequently sterile oppositions win out. Formulating a major theory about senescence might attract attention, but it is just as likely to be ignored by scientists intent on pursuing new wrinkles in traditional fields.

3. Not only is gerontology, like most hybrid endeavors, a marginal enterprise, but researchers on aging have as much difficulty as do outsiders in defining the contours of their interest. Methods and data vary across domains. Investigators use keywords differently (Achenbaum, Wieland, & Haber, 1996). "Schools" of thought are ephemeral; except for the University of Chicago's fabled Committee on Human Development, most places where established scholars reside generate a critical mass of like-minded students to be identified as "centers" for a particular style of research. In such an amorphous environment it would be hard to refine and extend the ideas of one generation of theory builders to the next.

As a result, the recent history of gerontological theory-building has largely been a succession of short-lived attempts to fashion middle-range theories focusing on one or another aspect of aging. These contributions usually have little salience beyond the academic disciplines in which they were created. Had Cowdry's *Problems of Ageing* become the *locus classicus* for those who followed, it might have been reasonable to expect theories of aging to step beyond "medical" models that sought to explain both the "normal" and "pathological" aspects of senescence and then to proffer practical applications based on paradigmatic assumptions. Yet physicians interested in the diseases of old age were more inclined to develop a medical subspecialty than to interact with psychologists and social workers. Hence, the American Geriatrics Society, founded in 1942, complements the mission of the Gerontological Society of America, but it subscribes to the canons and mores of the medical sciences, endorsing only secondarily the principles of cross-disciplinary research.

Similarly, one might have expected biologists to be major sources of theories on aging that extended metaphorically and otherwise across academic domains. In retrospect, one can invoke the names of a few true heirs to Metchnikoff, such as Charles Manning Child, Charles Sedgwick Minot, and Edmund B. Wilson. In postwar America one can point to W. Donner Denckla's theory of a brain-based hormonal clock on aging, Roy Walford's work on immunology, and George Williams's formulation of an evolutionary theory of aging (Rosenfeld, 1976). And many scholars have shaped current wear-and-tear theories of aging as well as radical gene models of how we age.

Indeed, the most important contributions thus far have been in the area of measurement, not theory-building. Leonard Hayflick's "correction" of Alexis Carrel's error, along with his demonstration that cells can divide only fifty times, contradicted the notion of immortality Carrel had advanced and thus re-formed the way we conceptualize senescence (Hayflick, 1994). Thanks to Nathan Shock's long tenure at the Gerontology Research Center in Baltimore, scores of researchers at the National Institute on Aging devoted their careers to collecting bits of data with precise calculations rather than pausing to theorize about the meanings of their findings.

Scholars in the social sciences, notably psychology and sociology, have been somewhat more intent on generating theories of aging. In the sociology of aging, three distinctive generations of conceptualization are apparent, each with subthemes. Each is also marked by methodological innovations that run parallel to the theories. The first generation of explicit theorizing arose during the 1960s, although there had been preliminary statements for more than a decade. In particular, the 1949 appearance of one of the early significant volumes by the Chicago School, *Personal Adjustment in Old Age* by Cavan, Burgess, Havinghurst, and Goldhamer, and the 1953 publication of *Older People,* by Havighurst and Albrecht, stand as precursors to what in retrospect are regarded as the first theoretical statements in social gerontology.

Not surprisingly, these early efforts were closely aligned with broader conceptual approaches characterizing social psychology, and each stressed various forms of activity and life satisfaction. Regardless of variant, each also relied on microlevel factors such as roles, norms, and reference groups for explaining adjustment in the face of taken-for-granted declines among the elderly. Functionialism and symbolic interaction are also theoretical precursors on which the more narrowly focused aspect theories of social gerontology built. Hence, disengagement, activity, subcultural, and continuity theories each stressed the individual as the appropriate unit of analysis in their quest to explain optimal and dysfunctional adjustment patterns. Each was put forth as a universally applicable model, not dependent on context or societal arrangements. Virtually without exception, the early efforts concentrated on individual adjustment, with social factors taken as unquestioned givens (Hendricks, 1992).

The second generation adopted a macrolevel structural approach and included age-stratification and modernization theories. Here the focus was on the ways in which changing structural conditions dictate the parameters of the aging process and the situation of the elderly as a collective category. Reacting to their first-generation counterparts, second-generation theorists went to considerable lengths to suggest that individual-level foci were reductionist and unnecessary as far as broad-brush interpretations were concerned. Deriving from a long-standing sociological contention that the whole is more than the mere sum of its parts, a position going back to Comte and especially to Marx and Durkheim, societal organization was conceived as establishing the terms by which people live. Hence, the way people age stems in part from societal organization, the political agenda, and individuals' location within social hierarchies. The proper unit of analysis was therefore a structural circumstance, not an individually derived attribute.

What followed was an attempt to be both more synthetic and more critical, to carve out an intermediate position; actors were viewed not as passive recipients of structural mandates but as active contributors to their own lifeworld. As a synthetic perspective formed out of the first two generations, the third generation incorporated the structuralists' concern with the distribution of resources, economic constraints, and the shape of the economy; but it also recognized that actors create meanings and that even structure is nuanced by the ways it is viewed by actors. Perhaps the most important transition was the recognition that aging is, by its very nature, an ecologically or (as we might say in the social sciences) experientially based process; it does not take place in isolation and is heavily influenced by surrounding conditions (Dannefer, 1996; Marshall, 1995). This latest round of theorizing is less concerned with parsimonious or even monolithic explanations as it seeks to bridge and to meld societal constraints, cultural meanings, individual meaning-giving, and the social forces that pattern the fabric of life (Dannefer, 1989; Marshall, 1986).

BREAKTHROUGHS AND EXPLANATIONS: ADVANCES IN GERONTOLOGY

Push and Pull of Success

Sociologists of science have long commented on the suzerainty that professional success exerts over subsequent practice. The gravitational pull of the successful application of any practice tends to extend beyond the realm of the original intent. As Pickering (1995) noted, there is not only an intertwining of machines, instruments, facts, theories, and practices within disciplines and areas of concentration but also across foci to neighboring disciplines. Success is a powerful attractor; it steers the careers of practioners and students trained in a given area while serving as a beacon for bordering disciplines where comparable questions may be under discussion. These cross-fertilizations pose quandaries as well as provide benefits. As much as in any instance, gerontology can be characterized by exactly this type of crossover and the dividends have often been palpable.

On the one hand, this should not be surprising because, to a certain extent, a comparability imposed by methodological canons for acquiring and verifying scientific knowledge will contribute to the definition of appropriate paradigms. As scientific methods have grown and been diffused across all manner of inquiry, explanatory models have grown out of methodological applications even as "knowledge communities" have been created by virtue of shared scientific conventions (Gergen, 1994). The mere practice of a particular way of knowing corroborates the "logic" of how knowledge is gained in the first place (Turner, 1994). One effect of the whole process has been a monopoly on legitimation as experts have claimed the Archimedean high ground to repel unruly challengers. The proliferation of professional affiliations, learned societies, and all the related associations to which scientists and scholars belong has ensured the certification of innovative models via peer review. That these can also be self-serving is a characteristic of all types of organizations.

Searching for Explanations

How does knowledge in gerontology come about? Even the recounting of early efforts that appears above does not answer that question. With each successive effort, the scientific milieu imposes a "bounded rationality"— providing guidelines for what researchers can or should do (Simon, 1991). Galton's collection of bodily and behavioral measurements at the 1881 London exposition is an excellent case in point. A *positivistic* approach would assert that once knowledge exists and once it is there for others to utilize, it forms a substrate for subsequent investigators and is therefore subject to the same laws of cause and effect as any other physical phenomenon. A *constructionist* approach maintains that knowledge and discovery are socially constructed, variable, and subject to differential interpretation. Under the terms of a constructionist perspective on how we know what we know, theory can never be finalized. Knowledge is always relative, and each new discovery will open new vistas of inquiry. A corollary of a constructionist approach to epistemology would assert that facts are inseparable from the scientist's "perceptual filters," be they conceptual, methodological, or political stipulations by which we organize what we perceive.

As Birren and Birren (1990) pointed out, once Quetelet, Galton, and others had set forth the rules of the scientific method for the human sciences, subsequent scholars were slow to challenge their modus operandi. Ironically, establishing the parameters for inquiry is also what theorizing is intended to do, for it also involves the imposition of an intentional scrim or filter through which the welter of phenomena can be organized into some type of meaningful taxonomy. It furnishes the boundaries for how we divide up the world and how we categorize what we perceive. Because each of the "scientific" disciplines that study aging shares a common intellectual tradition based on the scientific method, it is not surprising that their units of analysis and analytic techniques are variations on a theme. In their discussion of the evolution of developmental psychology, Birren and Birren (1990) made mention of Anderson's 1931 comment apropos psychology but applicable to all sciences: mustering facts and developing strategies and techniques of analysis mark the development of a mature science.

PROFESSIONAL RECOGNITION AND CREATIVITY

Just as theory shapes the creation of knowledge, so too does it affect those who create knowledge. The way we ply our profession, what we regard as data, and how we collect it and interpret it cannot help but reflect the application of those ways of thinking that we were exposed to as we were taught about aging in the first place. Which is not to say that progress does not occur or that innovative frameworks are not formulated, only to suggest it is more likely an incremental process than an unprecedented revolution in traditional modes of thinking. Conceptual frameworks that are widely acknowledged form persuasive and powerful lenses; they serve as reference points for what comes to count as knowledge and undergird its contingent nature.

Knowledge, like so much else in life, is communal; it adheres to recognizable principles and has recognizable consequences for those who share it. Unlike Kuhn's (1969) seemingly disembodied realm of scientific ideas, it is our contention that theory is written by real people with real careers. To whatever extent the succession of theoretical models demonstrates the history of dominant orientations, it simultaneously evidences the generational succession of researchers. Suffice it to say that newcomers launch their scholarly careers steeped in the practical reasoning and the genealogy and legitimacy of theoretical orientations. As practioners enter and leave, they formulate their agenda in terms of respected precedents. It is an ability to practice the lingua franca of the discipline that provides access to peer review, funding, publication, and all the other sentries one encounters in the practice of scholarship.

Free-floating models, those that appear to be created out of school, do not find a ready audience. The concepts that sustain, that create a recognized paradigm, also constrain. Polanyi (1966) spoke of the "tacit dimensions" of scholarly practice by which root metaphors establish credibility for the sorts of questions regarded as relevant and set the boundaries demarcating one group of practitioners from another. They also establish the protocols by which propositions are evaluated and constitute the vocabulary of appropriate application. It simply does not pay to be too obviously a heretic or to foster too great a breech with precedent. No better recent illustration can be found in the literature on aging than Hayflick and Morehead's early effort to publish their "correction" to a long-held misperception about the immortality of certain cell. First, they had to secure a favorable peer review if they were to publish their early identification of what came to be called the Phase III phenomena. Their manuscript was rejected by the prestigious *Journal of Experimental Medicine* on the grounds that it was "rash" in light of a universally recognized truth (Hayflick, 1994). But even then the scientific community remained rather skeptical for a full decade.

THE POWER OF PROFESSIONAL KNOWLEDGE

The lessons of Hayflick and Morehead are applicable for us all. Once in existence, data, techniques, and theory do not easily yield to contradictory evidence. And like all other perceptual schema, theoretical orientations, or at least their logic, tend to become like habits of the mind, something that researchers regard as natural, appropriate to the task at hand. As one of us has written elsewhere, it is not an overstatement to assert that theorizing circumscribes the world to which investigators attend. It is through the terms of our definition of what is important that we envelope as well as exclude portions of the world (Hendricks, 1992). Neyman (1977) was one of the first sociologists of science to suggest that in the world of ideas the pace of scholarly breakthroughs is influenced by the ebb and flow of demography, the aging of one cohort of scholars, the appearance of their followers, and succession in the scientific enterprise. Add to the mix the symbolic affiliations and allegiances to explanatory frameworks that scholars are likely to hold, and it is possible to see how the character of an entire generation of scholars coalesces (Neyman, 1977). The relevance of her remarks as far as our purposes are concerned is that gerontological novitiates are socialized to global theoretical positions that shape how they practice their science and that affect their own contributions and as well as their cohort identification. Science is, after all, a communal enterprise.

As each generation of theorizing gains acceptance within a subfield of gerontology, each provides a normative conceptual framework by which empirical data are interpreted. Be that as it may, no framework emerges on the scene fully formed; there is a developmental trajectory that is probably characteristic of the evolution of any way of knowing. First, there are formulative explorations, wherein *precursors* attempt to paint the broad parameters of a new way of looking at the world and what that might portend for the subject at hand. Early statements are not especially well formulated nor articulated with other dimensions of an issue, and they seldom contain full-blown theoretical statements. Next, *pioneers* apply the model to all manner of phenomena, provided they fall within the general rubric of the subfield; they seek and apply explicit labels for the theoretical statement. It is the pioneers who provide what amounts to the manifesto for the model and who issue articulated theoretical précis.

Entering a period of ascendancy, theoretical positions are taught in graduate school, underpin many empirical analyses, and are advanced as *exemplars* for how the world should be interpreted. Ultimately, an era of *reformulation* begins: modifications, qualifications, and critical reappraisals fuel many a professional career and focus much scientific effort. The original framework is sometimes refurbished by key contributors who came to the fore during the ascendancy period or by outsiders who are brought into the fold. In all instances, however, shortfalls and omissions are subjected to the bright light of professional scrutiny and serve to fuel many a career.

This last phase may also come to be regarded as the *precursory* launch for the next formulative theory. We contend that these same tendencies emerge in all types of conceptual model building, regardless of substantive focus in the social and behavioral sciences or in the life sciences. Part of the importance of this evolution of theoretical models is that once an author stakes a claim with one or another statement, he or she seldom shifts alliances by much. Rather, authors spend their careers demonstrating the application of this or that aspect of the theory itself. To the extent that an individual scholar-scientist is vested in a given way of explaining things, changes are unlikely. When looking across models, very seldom do investigators appear to advance more than a single model, save for those who fancy themselves theorists per se.

CONCLUSIONS

Theorizing is a reflexive activity shaping empirical investigations; it is a way to organize what we think we know about aging; it is critical activity. Theory is also fodder for careers and has served to orient successive generations of investigators and practioners. As a rule of thumb, most theory in gerontology falls into the category of what are sometimes termed "aspect theories" addressing some particular dimension of the puzzle that is aging. To date, relatively few efforts have successfully crossed disciplinary boundaries, and most theoretical statements have evolved from models that did not explicitly examine change (Birren, 1995). The absence of true multidisciplinary theory has less to do with the nature of aging than it does with professional concerns. Perhaps one of the reasons interdisciplinary work has found relatively little favor is that we live in a society that prides itself on specialization, well-honed divisions of labor, the merits of a "techno-fix" for everything that ails us (Hendricks, 1995). There is not much tolerance for the intellectual gadfly, and scientists in general seldom engage the work of other scholars that does not bolster the position they are advancing.

In commenting on the nature of theoretical models in biology, Cristofalo

(1996) commented that there may be a world of difference between aging in a petri dish and in an organism. If we interpret his point correctly, he is saying that there may be multiple cellular pathways to senescent phenotypes, some more relevant to the whole organism than others. His point is that even theories of cellular change vary according to whether they stress *stochastic* or *developmental-genetic* changes. Stepping beyond the particular focus of Cristofalo's point, he may be making as much of a call for multidisciplinary, nonlinear thinking and attention to aging mechanisms as would any of his brethren from the social sciences. In the psychology of aging, Birren and a number of colleagues have sounded the call for further multidisciplinarity and attention to what they termed *gerodynamics* (Birren, 1995; Birren & Schroots, 1984; Hendricks, 1997). Schroots, Birren, and Kenyon (1991) have gone so far as to suggest that the metaphors gerontologists employ may channel their interpretation of their "data" and the kinds of models they develop.

Once a scientific practice is established, it is a matter of considerable risk for a young scholar to depart from the tried and true. Habermas (1991) spoke of the hegemony of practice and implied in the process that part of its sway comes from the fact that their legitimacy is so taken to heart as to be virtually unchallenged. In gerontology, one unintended consequence has been an acceptance of the biomedicalization of all things having to do with growing old. One obvious repercussion has been the assignment of closely defined responsibilities that have insulated as they have attempted to bring solace. Perhaps it is a misconception to think of old age as a period requiring its own explanatory framework rather than a transitory phase of life having a great deal in common with any other rite of passage. By labeling a circumstance in a particular way, the meaning is managed even as attention is diverted from other plausible interpretations. Making old age a "special" period of life is not only self-serving but linked to political motivations (Estes, 1979; Quadagno, 1986).

Having made these claims, where do we go from here? The next state of theory-building, like those that preceded it, will be greatly influenced by major currents at the interstices of the biomedical and social sciences. We hope that theorists will appreciate the relevance of their work to coping with societal aging and as a factor in establishing the human condition. One benefit of postmodernist and feminist perspectives is the emphasis on the politics of difference and the relevance of difference in establishing identity.

REFERENCES

Achenbaum, W. A. (1978). *Old age in the new land: The American experience since 1790.* Baltimore: Johns Hopkins University Press.

Achenbaum, W. A. (1985). Societal perceptions of old age and aging. In R. H. Binstock & E. Shanas (Eds.), *Handbook of aging and the social sciences* 2nd ed. (pp. 129–148). New York: Van Nostrand Reinhold.

Achenbaum, W. A. (1995). *Crossing frontiers: Gerontology emerges as a science.* New York: Cambridge University Press.

Achenbaum, W. A. (1996). Historical perspectives on aging. In R. H. Binstock & L. George (Eds.), *Handbook of aging and the social sciences* 4th ed. (pp. 137–152). San Diego, CA: Academic Press.

Achenbaum, W. A. & Albert, D. M. (1995). *Profiles in gerontology: A biographical dictionary.* Westport, CT: Greenwood Press.

Achenbaum, W. A., Wieland, S., & Haber, C. (1996). *Keywords in gerontology.* New York: Springer Publishing Co.

Birren, J. E. (1986). The process of aging. In A. Pifer & L. Bronte (Eds.), *Our aging society* (pp. 263–281). New York: W. W. Norton.

Birren, J. E. (1995). Editorial: New models of aging: Comments on need and creative efforts. *Canadian Journal on Aging, 14,* 1–7.

Birren, J. E., & Birren, B. A. (1990). Theory and measurement in the psychology of aging. In J. E. Birren & K. W. Schaie (Eds.), *Handbook of the psychology of aging,* 3rd ed. (pp. 3–20). San Diego, CA: Academic Press.

Birren, J. E., & Schroots, J. J. F. (1984). Steps to an ontogenetic psychology. *Academic Psychology Bulletin, 6,* 117–190.

Cole, T. R. (1992). *The journey of life.* New York: Cambridge University Press.

Cole, T. R., van Tassel, D., & Kastenbaum, R. (Eds.). (1993). *Handbook of aging and the humanities.* New York: Springer Publishing Co.

Cole, T. R., & Winkler, M. (1994). *The Oxford book of aging.* New York: Oxford University Press.

Cristofalo, V. J. (1996). Ten years later: What have we learned about human aging from studies of cell cultures? *Gerontologist, 36,* 737–741.

Crosby, A. W. (1997). *The measure of reality.* New York: Cambridge University Press.

Dannefer, D. (1989) Human action and its place in theories of aging. *Journal of Aging Studies, 3(1), 1–20.*

Dannefer, D. (1996). The social organization of diversity, and the normative organization of age. *Gerontologist, 36,* 174–177.

Dove, M. (1986). *Perfect age of man's life.* Cambridge: Cambridge University Press.

Estes, C. (1979). *The aging enterprise.* San Francisco: Jossey-Bass.

Frank, L. F. (1942). Introduction. In E. V. Cowdry (Ed.), *Problems of ageing,* 2nd ed. Baltimore: Wilkins and Williams.

Gergen, K. (1994). *Toward transformation in social knowledge.* Thousand Oaks, CA: Sage.

Gruman, G. J. (1966) *The prolongation of life.* Philadelphia: American Philosophical Society.

Haber, C. (1983). *Beyond sixty-five.* New York: Cambridge University Press.

Habermas, J. (1991). *Knowledge and human interests.* Boston: Beacon Press.

Hall, G. S. (1922). *Senescence.* New York: D. Appleton's Sons.

Hayflick, L. (1994). *How and why we age.* New York: Ballantine.

Hendricks, J. (1992). Generations and the generation of theory in social gerontology. *International Journal of Aging and Human Development, 35,* 31–47.

Hendricks, J. (1995). The social construction of professional knowledge in aging. *Generations, 19,* (2), 51–53.

Hendricks, J. (1997). Bridging contested terrain: Chaos or prelude to a theory. *Canadian Journal on Aging, 16(2),* 197–217.

Hendricks, J. (1993). Cicero and social gerontology: Context and interpretation of a classic. *Journal of Aging Studies, 7,* 339–352.

Hendricks, J., & Hendricks, C. D. (1978). The age-old question of old age. *International Journal of Aging and Human Development, 8(2),* 139–154.

Hendricks, J., & Leedham, C. A. (1989). Making sense: Interpreting historical and cross-cultural literature on aging. In P. von Dorotka Bagnell & P. S. Soper (Eds.), *Perceptions of aging in literature: A cross-cultural study.* New York: Greenwood Press.

Kuhn, T. (1969). *The structure of scientific revolutions.* Chicago: University of Chicago Press.

Marshall, V. (1986). Societal toleration of aging: Sociological theory and social response to population. *Adaptability and Aging, 1,* 85–104.

Marshall, V. (1995). The state of theory in aging and the social sciences. In R. Binstock & L. K. George (Eds.), *Handbook of aging and the social sciences* (pp. 12–30). San Diego, CA: Academic Press.

Merton, R. (1972). Insiders and outsiders. *American Journal of Sociology, 78*(1), 9–47.

Neyman, E. (1977). Scientific career, scientific generation, scientific labor market. In S. Blume (Ed.), *Perspectives in the sociology of science* (pp. 71–94). New York: John Wiley and Sons.

Pickering, A. (1995). *The mangle of practice.* Chicago: University of Chicago Press.

Polanyi, M. (1966). *The tacit dimension.* Garden City, New York: Doubleday.

Quadagno, J. (1986). The transformation of old age security. In D. van Tassel & P. Sterns (Eds.), *Old age in a bureaucratic society.* Norwalk, CT: Greenwood Press.

Quetelet, L. A. J. (1842). *A treatise on man and the development of his faculties.* Gainesville, FL: Scholars Facsimiles and Reprints.

Rosenfeld, A. (1976). *Prolongevity.* New York: Avon.

Rowe, J. & Kahn, R. (1987). Human aging: Usual and successful. *Science, 237,* 143–149.

Schroots, J., Birren, J. E., & Kenyon, G. (1991). In H. A. Simon (Ed.), *Models of my life.* New York: Basic Books.

Simon, H. A. (Ed.) (1991). *Models of my life.* New York: Basic Books.

Turner, S. (1994). *The social theory of practices: Tradition, tacit knowledge, and presuppositions.* Chicago: University of Chicago Press.

Van Tassel, D. D. (1979). *Aging, death, and the completion of being.* Philadelphia: University of Pennsylvania Press.

Veysey, L. (1965). *The emergence of the American university.* Chicago: University of Chicago Press.

3

Elements of a Narrative Gerontology

Gary M. Kenyon
Jan-Eric Ruth
Wilhelm Mader

T he term *narrative gerontology* is intended as a root metaphor, or heuristic, for the field of aging. The term, which was first employed by Ruth (1994) and by Ruth and Kenyon (1996b), borrows from the call by authors such as Sarbin (1986) and Bruner (1990) for a narrative psychology. (For a review of the backgound and use of narrative in gerontology, see also Kenyon & Randall, 1997; Kohli, Freter, Langehennig, Roth, Simoneit, & Tregel, 1993; Mader, 1995; Ruth & Kenyon, 1996a.) As a root metaphor, narrative gerontology has the purpose of gathering together a particular set of insights about aging and about how we study this phenomenon. Most important among these insights is explication of the implications of the "life as story" metaphor for theory, research, and practice in the field of aging.

The narrative gerontology root metaphor possesses the following characteristics:

1. Narrative gerontology presupposes an existential-ontological image of human beings as storytellers and "storylisteners"; that is, human beings not

The authors would like to thank Bill Randall for useful comments on an earlier draft of this manuscript.

only *have* a lifestory, they *are* stories. This means that people think, perceive, and act on the basis of stories. Lifestories have cognitive, affective, and volitional dimensions.

2. Lives and lifestories are made up of facticity, which includes the outside aspects of the stories we are, such as the social and structural dimensions of stories described in the next characteristic of the metaphor, as well as the story that we tell ourselves (and therefore are) at any moment in time. In contrast to facticity, stories also consist of possibility, or the inner aspects of a story and a life that are changeable or subject to choice, new meaning, or "re-storying" (Kenyon & Randall, 1997). The term *re-storying* refers to the process by means of which people can enhance their sense of possibility by telling, reading, and retelling their lifestories. In this regard, a crucial aspect of understanding the narrative root metaphor and human aging from this perspective is the insight that, as Maddi (1988), explains, "Our sense of possibility is intertwined with what we perceive as given, and the dynamic balance between the two gives our lives its particular flavor" (p. 183).

3. There are four interrelated dimensions of lives as lifestories. First, there is a structural story, which includes such things as social policy and power relations in a society. Structural constraints, which are part of one's facticity, can effectively silence personal stories, voices, or the sense of possibility. Second, there is a sociocultural story, or the social meanings associated with aging and the lifecourse, including such things as relationships between employer and worker or between professional and client. This dimension also includes cultural, ethnic, and gender stories. Third, there is an interpersonal dimension to lifestories, which refers to relationships of intimacy"confidant or confidante, families, and love. Finally, there is the personal dimension of a lifestory itself. This dimension consists of the creation and discovery of meaning and coherence, the way in which the pieces make or do not make sense to a person.

4. In the final analysis, one's personal story is, to some extent, unique, idiosyncratic, and unknowable, both to oneself and to others. There is an element of opacity in lives and lifestories. The moment of meaning for a person contains a distinctly inner existential-spiritual quality; at the same time, that meaning is created/discovered in a fundamentally paradoxical social and interpersonal context. On the one hand, people can and do communicate, and we can learn a great deal about ourselves and each other; on the other hand, the claim here is that we will never have "the truth, the whole truth and nothing but the truth" about a life.

In what follows we will explore a number of implications that a narrative gerontology has for theories of aging and for understanding time, death, wisdom, and postmodern aging. We will also attempt to identify some important vantage points for research and theory development associated with this perspective. These vantage points are not all completely new; however, those that are not new are deserving of further study or reflection from a narrative gerontology perspective.

THEORIES OF AGING

Although narratives have been used in other disciplines and in gerontology as a method to access "subjective data," one would argue that this approach often represents a modern science perspective. That is, narratives are employed as a way to get at the more subjective aspects of a reality of aging that lies objectively behind the scenes and has its own rules. In contrast to this view and as explicated above, at the broadest level the contribution of narrative gerontology to the science of aging is the postmodern insight that all knowledge is metaphorical, historical, and contextual (Cole, Achenbaum, Jakobi, & Kastenbaum, 1993; Kenyon, Birren, & Schroots, 1991; Niethammer, 1985). In other words, it is storied. Among other things, this means that all theories of aging are narratives; that is what is meant by the term *hermeneutic circle*. There are certain ontological implications associated with the narrative root metaphor, and one of them is that the hermeneutic circle constitutes the bottom line. As Carr (1986) notes, "There is nothing below the narrative structure, at least nothing experienceable by us or comprehensible in experiential terms" (p. 66).

From this point of view, a theory of aging or a formal intervention strategy, by its very nature as a human activity, always contains a story with implicit and/or explicit meanings or ontological images of human nature, its development and its teleology. This postmodern argument is in distinct contrast to the modern science claims that the facts will "out" as long as one follows the scientific method and that there is both the possibility and necessity for objectivity in science. Rather, our argument here is that researchers and interveners bring their own stories (and values) to the professional situation, and those meanings and values are important components of what comes to count as valid knowledge of aging, as a good theory, as an appropriate intervention strategy, or as sound policy (see, for example, selected chapters in Birren & Bengtson, 1988, and in Birren, Kenyon, Ruth, Schroots, & Svensson, 1996).

To clarify this insight further, from the perspective of narrative gerontology there is no theoretical constraint on the employment of any particular method or approach to understanding the meaning (or meanings) of aging at the individual, group, and societal levels of discourse. In other words, quantitative or experimental methods and qualitative, hermeneutic, or biographical ones are in principle, depending on the phenomenon under inves-

Teleology — The study of design or purpose in natural phenomena

tigation, equally relevant or useful, as is any combination of the two (Reker, 1995). In addition to these approaches there is also an important contribution to narrative gerontology that originates in the insights of literary narratives, in that there is an intimate connection between "art and life" (see Cole, Van Tassel, & Kastenbaum, 1992).

The constraint that does arise and that points up the transition from the modern to the postmodern view is that many gerontologists (and other social scientists, particularly in North America) attach meaning to or live a particular story, namely, the scientific method story. Moreover, this story is not only lived by individual professionals, but it also extends to the social story in the training of graduate students and the priorities of funding agencies. In this way a scientific instrument or a methodological narrative can become an ontology. Although it is a feature of the postmodern world to have a variety of root metaphors, it can be argued that the modern emphasis on the scientific method has, in some cases, developed into an unreflected dogma-like story with its own "immune system," one that sometimes silences other voices—albeit often unwittingly in the sense that we all have our preferred metaphors and narratives, both professionally and personally.

Nevertheless, from a narrative perspective, a theory or method is, at least in part, socially constructed, and the process of theory construction involves "hidden references to the structural conditions that are imposed on us" (Alheit, 1995, p. 63). In this way, the method sometimes guides the research problem or the phenomenon to be investigated, rather than the problem suggesting the appropriate method to be adopted. One example is the study of wisdom, discussed later in this chapter. In Zen Buddhist terms this is a case of mistaking the finger pointing at the moon for the moon itself. Insofar as this is the case, we may not arrive at the whole story of aging, and we may actually do harm from an intervention perspective, as Gearing and Coleman (1996), for example, argue in extending some of the insights of Malcolm Johnson.

It is part of the agenda of a narrative gerontology to contribute to the process of what Hans Gadamer (1976), in discussing his notion of philosophical hermeneutics, calls recovering the meaning in something that we have come to take for granted. This approach has its counterparts in areas such as the sociology of knowledge, critical gerontology (Cole et al., 1993), and historical interpretations of cultural and scientific gerontology (Cole, 1992). It would also qualify as an instance of what Bengtson, Parrott, and Burgess (1996) discuss as critical theorizing. However, it should be noted that narrative gerontology also involves the consideration of a particular method as well as a form of practice. The activity of recovering meaning consists of making the "perceptual turn" to viewing a particular phenomenon "as a story," whether that phenomenon is a scientific theory or method or one's own life.

Ontology — branch of phil.

This initial turn, or re-storying moment, is not always an easy one because, as we mentioned earlier, stories sometimes have an immune system. This originates in the first characteristic of the narrative root metaphor, namely, that stories are constitutive of the way in which people express meaning in life (Birren et al., 1996). As theorists, researchers, and everyday persons, we begin with our own facticity, that is, with the story that we have told ourselves up to this point in time, along with the cultural, social, and personal resources we have available. This facticity, this "story that we are" (Randall, 1995), must be capable of being "read" as a story in order for our sense of possibility to become operative. Thus, adopting a new parenting style to deal with teenagers, grieving the loss of a loved one, and entertaining a new theoretical perspective on aging all require a re-storying (Kenyon & Randall, 1997) process involving more than just a new idea. In narrative terms, we need not only "have" a new story but "be" a new story as well. Actions, feelings, and ideas are all part of this human activity.

Vantage points for research and theory development:

1. Given the existential-ontological nature of narratives, it becomes important to investigate how theories are constructed in gerontology. For example, if there is no absolute reality, then we can ask whether knowledge of aging is, on the one hand, completely relative to a group and exclusively socially constructed or, on the other hand, an interpersonal and cultural co-authoring process based on a dialogue with many constituent epistemological variables.

2. A further research question concerns the elements of the story of theory construction in gerontology. The autobiographies of gerontological theorists could be analyzed to understand the contributions of different dimensions of their own lifestories to a better understanding of both aging and theories of aging.

3. We could inquire as to the nature of truth from a narrative gerontology perspective to distinguish appropriate from inappropriate theoretical stories to guide research and practice and thereby explicate the fundamental importance of the inside of aging to theorizing. A further related question is whether there is a moral imperative to knowledge of aging.

4. There may be some important education and training issues associated with theory construction in gerontology in terms of the range of conceptual frameworks to which students are exposed and which they are encouraged to explore. For example, perhaps students should be exposed to both humanities and scientific insights and to narrative and experimental methods. In gerontology it could be the case that the broader the exposure or the bigger the story, the better the theory, even though ultimately more specialized themes are adopted by gerontologists in their graduate work and professional life.

CLOCK TIME AND STORY TIME

The characteristics of the narrative gerontology metaphor suggest that human beings live more than one story of time. That is, human beings experience at least two different kinds of time. Following Achenbaum (1991), there is a physical, outer time and a psychological, inner time, or what Kenyon and Randall (1997) call clock time and story time. The experience of time is subject to the same tension as the rest of our being, namely, the tension between our inside story and the outer, larger story we live within. Throughout the lifespan we develop a relationship with outer time, or calendar time, and the way this form of time gets translated into social time and social clocks. As has been argued, human beings often judge themselves to be on-time or off-time with respect to such important activities as career development or starting a family (see Schroots & Birren, 1988). This experience of clock time can sometimes be crucial to a person who is, for example, looking at what sort of pension he or she has assembled compared to the threat of retirement or downsizing.

The crucial issue concerning time, from a narrative gerontology perspective, is analysis of the creative ways that people interact and can be helped to interact with this outer clock. Outer time, or clock time, must be dealt with, as it is part of our nature as interpersonal beings. However, the important point is that it is only part of the story of time. It is story time, which is subject to the dynamic between our facticity and our sense of possibility, that in the end may tell us more about the the nature of time.

This insight is expressed by Simone de Beauvoir (1973), who has noted that "our private inward experience does not tell us the number of our years, no fresh perception comes into being to show us the decline of years" (p. 420). In the same vein, Sharon Kaufman (1986), in her often cited study of older persons, found that people did not identify with aging as a significant part of their identity or inside story; rather, they felt that they were themselves, only older. These observations point us to the importance of examining the meaning of time and aging as it is experienced by human beings.

Time from the outside has a discrete past, present, and future. It is linear and unidirectional and is the commonly accepted measure of our finitude; that is, we are born, we grow, and we die. However, it is possible that this very definition of time, wherein people often feel that they are locked in by their past, is a construction. As Plank (1989) explains,

> We commonly accept this essentialistic view of the past as a thing or a series of events which happened once and for all in a specific way and which we, as historians, as witnesses in court, or merely as ordinary men who must live with what they have done, can grasp by a careful perusal of our memories or appropriate archives and documents. (p. 33)

The point here is that the deterministic assumptions contained in this view of time may themselves constitute only one story of time; they may be partly our own creation or even possibly a cohort phenomenon when we think of such things as predicted versus actual career and family life courses in a postmodern society.

It is interesting to note that consideration of these issues also calls into question the basic assumptions of a number of scientific theories in gerontology. We might ask, for example, whether continuity theory is about aging per se or whether in some cases it reflects a cohort, cultural, or period effect based on a widespread belief in a linear view of time that has created a "bondage to the past" (Plank, 1989). There are significant differences in an understanding of aging based on, on the one hand, outer or clock time and, on the other hand, inner or story time.

From a narrative point of view, although it is true that the stories of older persons involve a considerable past dimension, a past life, and include patterns of meaning created earlier on, this past is being reconstructed or re-storied creatively in serving the present. People ascribe present meaning to or express present metaphors of past events. In one sense the past exists only as it is remembered and created and re-created in the interaction with present and future experiences and with the meaning, interpretations, and metaphors ascribed to those experiences. Following Schroots and Birren (1988), "the psychological past and future are constructions, experienced as a series of presents" (p. 11). Human existence and action therefore consist, in agreement with Carr (1986), not in overcoming time, not in escaping it or arresting its flow, but in shaping and forming it. Human time is configured time in the sense that we tell ourselves a story of time.

Nevertheless, the time that is configured is not arbitrary. The future that is projected is not simply a picture of what might be, it is our very being. It is a future that we are already, that is based on this present and a particular past. This conclusion follows from the discussion that our personal meaning of time, as is the case with the rest of our being, is subject to the paradoxical dynamic between our facticity and our sense of possibility. That is, change is always possible in principle, but like stories, our lives come from somewhere, are something now, and are going somewhere.

Vantage points for research and theory development:

1. Existing life history data and further narrative studies could be analyzed with respect to the sequentiality of a lifestory. The purpose of such research would be (a) to understand the way in which different people order a lifestory, that is, the way they experience or live time; and (b) to analyze the influences that cause a specific person to live or find meaning in a specific version of story time and how that story may have changed over the lifespan.

2. It would be interesting to look at the way in which people of different ages and cohorts "story" and re-story time. For example, we can further investigate the claim that stories of time are cohort-based or gender-based. Related to the first vantage point, we need to know more about the inner logic that men and women, older and younger people, use to sequence time and to what extent that process is socially constructed or has other origins.

3. Research utilizing such approaches as guided autobiography could be undertaken as part of the foregoing and also as intervention research to facilitate a re-storying of time perspectives that may be problematic, by expanding one's sense of possibility in this area.

4. The phenomenon of "living in the moment" that is described by many spiritual traditions and by people who have had near-death experiences and is expressed in the stories of some older persons, would be useful in further analyzing the nature of story time and this aspect of the inside of aging. (For an indication of some of the existing work in this area, see Birren et al., 1996; Haight & Webster, 1995).

DEATH AND DYING

An existentialist dictum is that human nature is characterized by the search for love and meaning in the face of death. The subject of inner time-aging that we have just discussed suggests that, from the inside, time is not what it appears from the outside, that a narrative gerontology perspective expands its meaning. A similar point can be made about death. There are clinical and legal definitions of death, which are themselves sometimes complicated, but human beings really have access only to images, attitudes, or stories of death; there are no facts. Moreover, forms of death (Gass, 1997), both individual and cultural, influence the meaning of aging in a particular society, as well as behavior toward older persons and the behavior of older persons themselves (see also Cole, 1992). Thus, if we are to understand anything about our own death and dying and about important aspects of aging, narratives become indispensable. There are two main points to be made about death in the present context.

First, from a clock time point of view, we might expect that everyone who gets older would be expecting death and would want to review his or her life before that eventuality arrives. It has also been argued that the awareness of approaching death makes one lose a sense of the future (see Schroots & Birren, 1988). From a narrative gerontology perspective, neither of these claims is necessarily true, but both nevertheless require further investigation because they reflect the story of death by which many people live.

In this regard, a number of recent studies have shown that age is not a significant predictor of reminiscence frequency. As Webster (1994) points out in his review of these studies, if lifespan samples are employed, the expected triggers of advanced age and approaching death are not evident. Further, following Agren (1992), even the oldest old, although they must adjust to the limited number of years left, are still living time with a present, past, and future. Moreover, these dimensions are continuously interlocking and have meaning. Horner (1982), referring to her fellow nursing home resident, describes the situation in this way: "I don't think anyone old is afraid of death, though many, including Mrs. B., who will be 108 on Monday, may want life to go on" (p. 16). The first important point about death, then, is that it must be distinguished from the aging process. This point may be generally understood in the gerontological community, namely, that aging is not dying and not death. However, the implications of this distinction should be further explicated by analyzing older stories, as often the outer story of death is a guiding assumption in research and practice.

Second, in terms of its existential meaning, death is not something solid, like an object that we can face directly, nor do we automatically face it once we reach a particular age (Kenyon, 1990). In Heideggerian terms, death is a possibility, in that it is a concept with no specific meaning content. Yet it is also a very real certainty. As Pablo, who is sentenced to die in Sartre's (1969) play *The Wall,* puts it, "I can feel the wounds already; I've had pains in my head and in my neck for the past hour. Not real pains. Worse. That is what I'm going to feel tomorrow morning. And then what?" The other character, Tom, responds: "We aren't made to think that, Pablo. Believe me; I've already stayed up a whole night waiting for something. But this isn't the same; this will creep up behind us, Pablo, and we won't be able to prepare for it" (p. 8).

As with time, death is open to the dynamic of facticity and possibility. Our ontological situation as storied beings is such that the basis of our lives and our deaths is open-ended. We have choices that we make, whether we think we have them or not. Moreover, since we co-author our lives as interpersonal beings, we can help each other "to trade in and trade up our personal metaphors" of, in this case, death (Birren, 1987).

It is interesting to consider that, from this point of view, death as the annihilation of my being, which follows from a view of myself as a body only and as an egoistic being, is a choice. I can choose to think of myself and my death in this way. In fact, along with denial, this is the most common North American storyline of death. As Marcel (1952) notes, from this point of view, "death at first sight looks like a permanent invitation to despair" (p. 202). Moreover, it is possible for this despair to be virtually complete, in that I may see nothing else. The ultimate point of despair is manifested in suicide, as the extreme negation of oneself. An important aspect of suicide from a narrative point of view is that it represents the act of closing one's story in on oneself. This act creates special problems, different from other kinds of death, for those left behind, who must integrate this unknown story into their own lifestories.

Contemplation of human death can provide an excellent opportunity to experience existential meaninglessness, as we have just outlined. However, the very qualities of our being human, which provide this opportunity, also give rise to a very different story of death, one that is imbued with hope and existential meaning. The fact of death is a fundamental aspect of the human journey. Human life, as well as any consideration of the aging process, is not complete without the inclusion of death (Cole, 1992; Frankl, 1962). But because it is part of the opaqueness or indeterminacy of the journey that the nature of our death is unknown to us, at least experientially, it is possible to view death as part of the voyage. That is, we can consider death as another aspect of the path, as an open question (Kenyon, 1990). In this important sense, human life can be viewed as a journey that does not necessarily end as a fait accompli.

Death also becomes a powerful source of existential meaning (Reker & Chamberlain, 1988) insofar as we are able to live a more interpersonal story of ourselves. That is, from this point of view, death ends a life, but it does not necessarily end a lifestory or a relationship (Birren, 1988). The death of another may provide one of the most potent opportunities or catalysts for wonder, openness, or a search for meaning on the part of the survivor. Moreover, the loss of a fellow traveler does not remove the experience of what the person meant to the traveler who remains.

Vantage points for research and theory development:

1. Although a number of studies have been carried out, we have only stories of death. Much more must be done to help us understand the meaning of death from the inside through the narratives of older and younger persons, of men and women, and of different ethnic communities. We need to know more about the process by which a culture provides "forms" or metaphors of death and how they are storied by different persons and groups.

2. The fundamental relationship between aging and death must be analyzed further. For example, we might attempt to understand the distinction between the story of death as a "wall" (e.g., in a thoroughly secular society) or as a "door" and the effect such views have on a person's story and on the meaning that person assigns to his or her own aging.

3. Further analysis of the issue of continuity and discontinuity in one's story of death over time would make an interesting study.

4. As with the issue of time, guided autobiography might be a useful approach in assisting people to re-story their views of death and dying—their own death and dying and those of the people whom they survive.

WISDOM

Wisdom is a phenomenon with a long history and one that appears in many cultures around the world. However, for some decades it was relegated to a list of forbidden subjects by both philosophers and social scientists. One of the reasons for this is the kind of methodological story and related constraints described in the first section of this chapter: a case wherein the accepted methodological narrative takes precedence over the problem or theory narrative (Holliday & Chandler, 1986). However, a new interest in wisdom is emerging that includes its possibly intuitive association with age and experience.

Wisdom, as Birren (1988) has pointed out, is one of the potential end points for human development. As with many other phenomena of aging, wisdom is not a natural outcome of living longer, but it does require some level of experience. On the one hand, wisdom qualifies as a potentially positive outcome of aging that deserves serious attention. On the other hand, gerontologists are at the beginning stages of understanding the nature of wisdom and of how to identify wise people (Baltes & Smith, 1990; Sternberg, 1990).

One agenda here concerns the comparison of traditional interpretations of wisdom with current attempts to define and operationalize it. For example, important distinctions should be made between wisdom and other phenomena such as cleverness, specialized forms of intellectual functioning, and multiple intelligences (Gardener, 1993), some of which are measurable with experimental methods. In many wisdom traditions, the attribution of wisdom is reserved for those who may or may not be cognitively gifted but are capable in thought and action of doing the good, as the Greeks would say.

An understanding of wisdom may require a thorough evaluation of the meanings different people place on situations and a subtle assessment of interpersonal encounters, including the intentions different people bring to such encounters. That is, there may be an ethical dimension associated with wisdom. An important illustration of this is the example of a clever person who may appear wise and who may say and do the right things but for a very different reason than doing good. An extreme but illustrative example of this is the psychopathic personality.

Another feature of wisdom concerns whether it is one "thing" or many. Although we are interested in arriving at definitions and characteristics of wisdom as an aggregate phenomenon, a further question concerns the way in which people arrive at wisdom. That is, it may be possible that everyone possesses a unique wisdom story or ordinary wisdom that is intimately tied to a person's lifestory. These questions and others represent a context in which narrative gerontology can make a distinct contribution. That contribution originates first in the ontological nature of life as story. If we are stories, then, as Socrates pointed out, it might be that the "examined life" is worth living because "getting the story out," for those of us who wish to do so, may lead us closer to that wisdom story. A related point in this context is that there may be an ethical imperative on the part of interventionists to genuinely story-listen if the ultimate purpose is to facilitate the expression of another's wisdom story and not impose one's own story on others. That is, there is a particular set of constraints and expectations that is associated with various types of biographical encounters (Kenyon, 1996).

The consideration of wisdom leads us to intriguing questions such as whether there is a transition in aging that brings with it an increase in things like existential meaning, wisdom, and acceptance. Another question is whether there is a relationship between the suffering, loss, and disillusionment that the human traveler faces and a movement in life from having to being. It is this relationship to which Scott-Maxwell (1968) seems to refer in her autobiography, written when she was well into her 80s: "The hardness of life I deplore creates the qualities I admire" (p. 47).

Although more research and theorizing is necessary in this area, the list of preliminary observations supporting the insight that something like wisdom is both possible to experience and central to human development and aging continues to grow. Manheimer (1992), for example, captures this insight in a review of studies that "give dramatic form to retelling the story of late-life transformation in which disability, frailty, limitation, dependency, and despair undergo an inversion, becoming qualities such as capability, strength, possibility, autonomy, and wisdom" (p. 431).

Other narrative investigations have been carried out by Kaufman (1986), Coleman (1986), Ruth and Oberg (1996), and Gubrium (1993a), who have found that most of the older people they studied attained some degree of meaning and life acceptance. Such a view is echoed in the writings of Kubler-Ross and others who work with the terminally ill (see, e.g., Rinpoche, 1992). Still other sources relevant to this topic include interesting examples of radical re-storying. Important studies of this type are those carried out with victims of abuse, incest, and cancer, as well as with widows (for an expanded discussion of this topic, see Kenyon & Randall, 1997). The conclusions of these studies point to the ability of the human spirit, through a process of re-storying, to develop, create, and find meaning, a sense of possibility, and perhaps a form of wisdom in the midst of extreme circumstances.

Finally, researchers have begun to look specifically at the spiritual dimensions of aging as possible sources of wisdom and meaning (Cole, Van Tassel, & Kastenbaum, 1992; Kimble, McFadden, Ellor, & Seeber, 1995; Sherman & Webb, 1994).

These systematic findings, as well as other, more anecdotal and personal observations, invite philosophical speculation regarding our ontological roots and destiny. However, they also invite practical speculation that has a direct bearing on ourselves as meaning-seekers, personally and interpersonally. That is, if our lives truly are stories, then we are presented with a potentially positive and hopeful direction for the human journey. That optimism stems from the basic assumption that neither our lives nor our lifestories are ever locked in, that they are made up of facticity and possibility, that what is possible is not known in advance. Nevertheless, it should be noted that not everything is possible in any person at any particular time. Some people do not age well, and that is also a topic for narrative gerontology.

From a narrative gerontology perspective there is an aspect of openness and creativity built into the very fabric of human life. As Huxley (1944/ 1962) pointed out some 50 years ago, it is possible for just about any human characteristic to go with any other characteristic in a particular human being. Yet within the virtually infinite set of possible characteristics, we all have what Sartre (1956) calls a fundamental project, made up of our predispositions and basic attitudes; these form part of our facticity and could be called the raw material for our sense of possibility and for re-storying.

Vantage points for research and theory development:

1. A complex but important question is whether wisdom is one "thing" or many. Continuing to explicate different kinds and dimensions of wisdom could facilitate the identification of different types of wise people. It is possible that there are forms of wisdom in our culture that are hidden and that are reflected in yet unidentified storying styles or discourse patterns.

2. We need to inquire as to how a wise person becomes wise. It is possible that this process is a function of living one's own wisdom story. If so, then we can ask whether ordinary wisdom can be enhanced through biographical forms of intervention.

3. An interesting aspect of studying wisdom and age is the idea of the "unlived life"; that is, the acceptance of one's lifestory as it is and has been involves what it has not been, or the road not chosen. Existing and new narrative data could be analyzed from this point of view.

4. The manifestation or expression of wisdom could be investigated. The idea here is that wise people may behave in very different ways, from a silent gaze to political activism to social eccentricity.

NARRATIVES AND POSTMODERN AGING

As discussed in the first section of this chapter, lives and lifestories are not constructed in a personal vacuum. They are co-authored in an interpersonal, social, and structural context. It is therefore an aspect of narrative gerontology to explore this larger story we live within (Ruth & Kenyon, 1996a). That larger story may include, among other things, a class story, a gender story, a cohort-generation story, an ethnic and cultural story, a family story, a community story, a corporate or work story, and even, within ourselves, a basic emotionality story (Mader, 1996; for an expanded discussion of this issue, see Kenyon & Randall, 1997). All of the foregoing constitute part of our facticity.

A very significant issue in this context concerns the role of narratives in a postmodern world. Narratives themselves can be seen as, in part, a social construction that a person uses as a biography and as resources to create an identity and establish coherence and continuity. Biographical narratives, or lifestories, function as a temporal and continuous system of rules by which a person gives meaning to his or her life. The narrative is a means to avoid a fragmented, splintered life course in a postmodern world, in which traditional institutions and grand narratives such as family, work, and organized religion have diminished in their role of providing continuity and coherence.

If one accepts the characteristics of a future information society in which basic bodies of knowledge are not represented by persons in institutions (professors, teachers, parents) but by sociotechnical systems, then people of all ages will be forced to establish coherence and continuity in the face of vast, uncontrollable, and largely unevaluated bodies of knowledge. The impact of the information society on aging in the future, with its invention of such things as distance and multimedia education, makes for a wide range of research and speculation about the form and content of our future personal and societal narratives.

Insofar as this is the case, many of the issues of concern to the current cohorts of older persons will be of concern to us all. That is, in a modern society we have tended to see older people as a special group with respect to such things as attitudes, behavior, continuity of identity, and stability of social networks. We are concerned about such things as the role and meaning of being older in a society that has linear and age-based strata. From the point of view we have just outlined, issues that were special to older people become increasingly issues for an entire society in the face of a dramatic structural erosion resulting from an identification with global information streams.

The outcome of this situation is that narratives become crucial; they are the very structures of coherence, continuity, identity, and emotionality. A narrative gerontology, from this perspective, would be not only be part of the agenda of understanding older persons but would comprise an investigation into the principles of the socially constructed aspects of human beings in general, that is, an age-irrelevant society.

Vantage points for research and theory development:

1. An important first area of inquiry is whether and to what extent the postmodern changes just described are actually taking place. For example, we can ask whether the postmodern self is, in fact, "saturated" and has no center or whether meaning and new stories continue to be created.

2. A related question is whether and which master narratives have become meaningless and for whom. Paradoxically, perhaps as a result of radical change, work, family, and/or religion become more important life themes for some people. The interesting question then concerns the nature of an authentic life lived with conscious awareness of the relativity of values and the implication that my values should not be imposed on another. In other words, the postmodern world increases the tension between personal and social ethics. One could analyze lifestories with these themes in mind.

3. The stories of current cohorts of older persons provide a fruitful area for research. Perhaps their lessons of experience and possible wisdom can contribute important and practical insights into how to find hope and meaning in the face of change, loss, and disillusionment. Their stories may offer an antidote, as they have done in past eras, to the rapid advance of technical knowledge, with its impersonal character and its short half-life.

4. Following from the foregoing, a broader research issue is the process by which we create our personal stories and images of aging. We can ask under what conditions specific inner images or models become meaningful for us, not only in an intellectual sense but existentially. This issue is also important at the societal level of discourse: it concerns the role of images in a postmodern world that does not appear to organize one's inner life in such a way that a meaningful story of being older is carried forward from generation to generation.

CONCLUSION

The fundamental focus for a narrative gerontology is the lived experience or the life world of an aging person. The story of our aging takes place in a social and interpersonal context, yet this context is made meaningful by a unique person. The focus on this process of creating or finding meaning is particularly important in a postmodern world, where it is said that we are separated from master narratives with which we could previously identify. The narrative root metaphor, although not a theory of aging, offers an opportunity to inform theory by emphasizing the whole person. It offers the possibility and challenge to put the pieces back together, in conjunction with much research in aging that examines specific aspects of aging. Moreover, a major piece that requires attention is the inside of aging, aging as it is experienced and expressed by those living it. Narratives provide a structure or a lens by means of which the construction of new postmodern theoretical stories of aging can be facilitated.

We are only at the beginning of understanding the extent to which the story a person lives affects that person's quality of life and aging, biologically, psychologically, socially, and spiritually. We are only at the beginning of understanding the limits of facticity and the extent of possibility through re-storying. We are only at the beginning of understanding the power of story-telling and storylistening in co-authoring each other's lives and experiencing the best that human life and aging have to offer. Borrowing from Gubrium (1993b), the goal and challenge of narrative gerontology is a

critical empiricism; its aim, on the one hand, is to make visible the variety, contingency, and inventiveness in any and all efforts to present life and, on the other hand, to resist the temptation to put it all together into an analytically consistent and comprehensive framework privileging certain voices and silencing others. (p. 62)

REFERENCES

Achenbaum, W. A. (1991). Time is the messenger of the gods: A gerontologic metaphor. In G. Kenyon, J. Birren, & J. J. F. Schroots (Eds.), *Metaphors of aging in science and the humanities* (pp.83–101). New York: Springer Publishing Co.

Agren, M. (1992). *Life at 85: A study of life experiences and adjustment of the oldest old.* Gothenberg, Sweden: University of Gothenberg.

Alheit, P. (1995). Biographical learning: Theoretical outline, challenges, and contradictions of a new approach in adult education. In P. Alheit, A. Bron-Wojciechowska, E. Brugger, and P. Dominice (Eds.), *The biographical approach in European adult education.* (pp. 57–74). Vienna: Verband Weiner Volksbildung.

Baltes, P., & Smith, J. (1990). Toward a psychology of wisdom and its ontogenesis. In R. Sternberg (Ed.), *Wisdom: Its nature, origins, and development* (pp. 87–120). New York: Cambridge University Press.

Bengtson, V., Parrott, T., & Burgess, E. (1996). Progress and pitfalls in gerontological theorizing. *Gerontologist, 36,* 768–772.

Birren, J. (1987, May). The best of all stories. *Psychology Today,* pp. 74–75.

Birren, J. (1988). A contribution to the theory of the psychology of aging: As a counterpart of development. In J. Birren & V. Bengtson (Eds.), *Emergent theories of aging* (pp. 153–176). New York: Springer Publishing Co.

Birren, J., & Bengtson, V. (Eds.). (1988). *Emergent theories of aging.* New York: Springer Publishing Co.

Birren, J., Kenyon, G., Ruth, J. E., Schroots, J. J. F., & Svensson, T. (Eds.). (1996). *Aging and biography: Explorations in adult development.* New York: Springer Publishing Co.

Bruner, J. (1990). *Acts of meaning.* Cambridge, MA: Harvard University Press.

Carr, D. (1986). *Time, narrative, and history.* Bloomington: University of Indiana Press.

Cole, T. (1992). *The journey of life: A cultural history of aging in America.* New York: Cambridge University Press.

Cole, T., Achenbaum, A., Jakobi, P., & Kastenbaum, R. (Eds.). (1993). *Voices and visions of aging.* New York: Springer Publishing Co.

Cole, T., Van Tassel, D., & Kastenbaum, R. (Eds.). (1992). *Handbook of the humanities and aging.* New York: Springer Publishing Co.

Coleman, P. (1986). *Aging and reminiscence processes.* New York: Wiley.

De Beauvoir, S. (1973). *The coming of age.* New York: Warner.

Frankl, V. (1962). *Man's search for meaning.* New York: Simon & Schuster.

Gadamer, H. (1976). *Philosophical hermeneutics.* Berkeley: University of California Press.

Gardener, H. (1993). *Multiple intelligences: The theory in practice.* New York: Harper-Collins.

Gass, W. H. (1997). *Finding a form.* New York: Knopf.

Gearing, B., & Coleman, P. (1996). Biographical assessment in community care. In J. Birren, G. Kenyon, J. E. Ruth, J. J. F. Schroots, & T. Svensson (Eds.), *Aging and biography: Explorations in adult development* (pp. 265–282). New York: Springer Publishing Co.

Gubrium, J. (1993a). *Speaking of life: Horizons of meaning for nursing home residents.* Hawthorne, NY: Aldine de Gruyter.

Gubrium, J. (1993b). Voice and context in a new gerontology. In T. Cole, A. Achenbaum, P. Jakobi, & R. Kastenbaum (Eds.). *Voices and visions of aging,* (pp. 46–63). New York: Springer.

Haight, B., & Webster, J. (Eds.). (1995). *The art and science of reminiscing: Theory, research, methods, and applications.* Washington, DC: Taylor & Francis.

Holliday, S., & Chandler, M. (1986). *Wisdom: Explorations in adult competence.* Basel, Switzerland: Karger.

Horner, J. (1982). *That time of year: A chronicle of life in a nursing home.* Amherst, MA:University of Massachusetts Press.

Huxley, A. (1962). *The perennial philosophy.* Cleveland, Ohio: Meridian. (Original work published 1944)

Kaufman, S. (1986). *The ageless self.* New York: New American Library.

Kenyon, G. (1990). Dealing with human death: The floating perspective. *Omega, 22,* 59–69.

Kenyon, G. (1996). Ethical issues in aging and biography. *Ageing and Society, 16,* 659–675.

Kenyon, G., Birren, J., & Schroots, J. J. F. (Eds.). (1991). *Metaphors of aging in science and the humanities.* New York: Springer Publishing Co.

Kenyon, G., & Randall, W. (1997). *Restorying our lives: Personal growth through autobiographical reflection.* Westport, CT: Praeger.

Kimble, M., McFadden, S., Ellor, J., & Seeber, J. (Eds.). (1995). *Aging, spirituality, and religion: A handbook.* Minneapolis, MN: Fortress Press.

Kohli, M., Freter, H.J., Langehennig, M., Roth, S., Simoneit, G., & Tregel, St. (1993). *Engagement im Ruhestand-Rentner zwischen Erwerb, EHrenamt und hobby* [Engagement in retirement-pensioners between earnings, honoraria and hobbies]. Opladen, Germany: Leske & Budrich.

Maddi, S. (1988). On the problem of accepting facticity and pursuing possibility. In S. Messer, L. Sass, & R. Woolfolk (Eds.), *Hermeneutics and psychological theory* (pp. 182–209). New Brunswick, NJ: Rutgers University Press.

Mader, W. (1995). *Altwerden in einer alternden Gesellschaft* [Growing old in an aging society]. Opladen, Germany: Leske & Budrich.

Mader, W. (1996). Emotionality and continuity in biographical contexts. In J. Birren, G. Kenyon, J. E. Ruth, J. J. F. Schroots, & T. Svensson (Eds.), *Aging and biography: Explorations in adult development* (pp. 39–60). New York: Springer Publishing Co.

Manheimer, R. (1992). Wisdom and method: Philosophical contributions to gerontology. In T. Cole, D. van Tassel, & R. Kastenbaum (Eds.), *Handbook of the humanities and aging* (pp. 426–440). New York: Springer Publishing Co.

Marcel, G. (1952). *Metaphysical journal.* Chicago: Henry Regnery.

Niethammer, L. (Ed.). (1985). *Lebenserfahrung und kollektives Gedachtnis* [Life-experience and collective memory]. Frankfurt: Suhrkamp.

Plank, W. (1989). *Gulag 65: A humanist looks at aging.* New York: Peter Lang.

Randall, W. (1995). *The stories we are: An essay on self-creation.* Toronto: University of Toronto Press.

Reker, G. (1995). Quantitative and qualitative methods. In M. Kimble, S. McFadden, J. Ellor, & J. Seeber (Eds.), *Aging, spirituality, and religion: A handbook* (pp. 566–588). Minneapolis, MN: Fortress Press.

Reker, G., & Chamberlain, K. (Eds.). (1998). *Existential meaning: Conceptualization, research, and application.* Thousand Oaks, CA.: Sage.

Rinpoche, S. (1992). *The Tibetan book of living and dying.* London: Random House.

Ruth, J. E. (1994). Det aldrande berattarjaget: forsok till en narrativ gerontologi [Aging and personal storytelling: Attempts at a narrative gerontology]. *Gerontologia, 8,* 205–214.

Ruth, J. E., & Kenyon, G. (1996a). Biography in adult development and aging. In J. Birren, G. Kenyon, J. E. Ruth, J. J. F. Schroots, & T. Svensson (Eds.), *Aging and biography: Explorations in adult development* (pp. 1–20). New York: Springer Publishing Co.

Ruth, J. E., & Kenyon, G. (1996b). Introduction: Special issue on ageing, biography and practice. *Ageing and Society, 16,* 653–657.

Ruth, J. E., & Oberg, P. (1996). Ways of life: Old age in a life history perspective. In J. Birren, G. Kenyon, J. E. Ruth, J. J. F. Schroots, & T. Svensson (Eds.), *Aging and biography: Explorations in adult development* (pp. 167–186). New York: Springer Publishing Co.

Sarbin, T. (1986). The narrative as a root metaphor for psychology. In T. Sarbin (Ed.), *Narrative psychology: The storied nature of human conduct* (pp. 3–21). New York: Praeger.

Sartre, J. P. (1956). *Being and nothingness.* New York: Simon & Schuster.

Sartre, J. P. (1969). *The wall.* New York: New Directions.

Schroots, J. J. F., & Birren, J. (1988). The nature of time: Implications for research on aging. *Comprehensive Gerontology C, 2,* 1–29.

Scott-Maxwell, F. (1968). *The measure of my days.* New York: Penguin Books.

Sherman, E., & Webb, T. (1994). The self as process in late-life reminiscence: Spiritual attributes. *Ageing and Society, 14,* 255–267.

Sternberg, R. (Ed.). (1990). *Wisdom: Its nature, origins, and development.* New York: Cambridge University Press.

Webster, J. (1994). Predictors of reminiscence: A lifespan perspective. *Canadian Journal on Aging, 13(1),* 66–78.

4

On Reestablishing the Phenomenon and Specifying Ignorance: Theory Development and Research Design in Aging

Angela M. O'Rand
Richard T. Campbell

... But it is not yet known whether scientific disciplines differ in the practice of specifying ignorance—in the extent to which their practitioners state what it is about an established phenomenon that is not yet known and why it matters for generic knowledge that it become known. (Merton, 1987, p. 10)

Ten years ago, in the *Emergent Theories of Aging*, edited by Jim Birren and Vern Bengtson, we presented some reflections on the relationships among data, methods, and theory in aging research (Campbell & O'Rand, 1988). At that time we noted that social theories of aging were being recast in light of observations drawn from growing longitudinal databases and newly adopted dynamic analysis methods. These new methods, employing longitudinal data, revealed time-dependent contingencies in the construction of lives that linked early- and late-life transitions in ways unexplained by prior age-dependent theories. Life cycle and age norm theories were being challenged by "real time" constructions of the life course which yielded life transition sequences that were more heterogeneous and independent of age than prior theories predicted. Age norms were being superceded as the principal explanations for aging and human development by life course processes such as duration dependence, the timing of life events, and transition sequence. But little progress had been made at that time to link lives to structural and historical contexts. New methods were revealing much about the variable timing and sequencing of life transitions but less about how these sequences were oriented or reoriented by social structure or history.

In this chapter we address two general questions. First, what have we learned about the social phenomenon of the life course over the past decade? Second, what do we need to know to improve the theory of the life course? Our answers begin with a review of the changed conception of the life course that has emerged over ten years and has led to a reestablishment of the phenomenon of aging. Then we move to the argument that current theories in aging research largely fail to provide structural explanations for the re-established phenomenon of aging, although the most recent generation of aging theories includes some progress towards structural analysis (see Bengtson, Burgess, & Parrott, 1997). Contingency and comparison constitute the hard core of explanation in empirical science, but the widespread emphasis in aging research on short-run contingencies and proximate contexts falls short of explaining the phenomenon. We end with a call for theory development in the direction of better structural explanations. We need to know the structural-historical causes of changes in the life course using data that span comparable time periods and historical contexts and methods that accommodate robust cross-level analysis.

THREE CHANGES IN THE CONSTRUCTION OF THE SOCIAL PHENOMENON OF AGING

We began this chapter with a quotation from Robert K. Merton (1987), one of the premier American sociologists of this century and the founder of the field of the sociology of science, on the ongoing interaction among data, methods, and theory development in the sciences. His comments, following many others over the past five decades (e.g., Merton, 1948, 1959, 1971, 1981), suggest again how theoretical development is an ongoing response to both anticipated and unanticipated empirical generalizations, to strategic data, and to methodological innovations that often precede it. Two scientific practices of interest to Merton are labeled as "establishing the phenomenon" and "specifying ignorance." The first refers to a fundamental objective of any science to establish that a phenomenon actually exists, that it "is enough of a regularity to require and to allow explanation" (1987, p. 2). In this vein, Merton reviews episodes in the sciences when explanations have been provided without factual evidence that the phenomena of interest actually existed as defined, and then he reminds us that "mere fact-finding" is a necessary element of scientific efforts. The second, "specifying ignorance", refers to the successive process whereby specific new knowledge produces new specific ignorance or "a new awareness of what is yet not known or understood and a rationale for its being worth the knowing" (Merton, 1987, p. 8, citing Merton, 1981).

We find these Mertonian observations of scientific practice useful for an examination of theory development and research findings concerning aging. The phenomenon of aging in social theory has been reestablished over the past two decades on the bases of empirical observations, some of which may be attributed to "mere fact-finding," and the methodological innovations that have enabled these observations. These observations have revised our definition of the phenomenon. They have illuminated our ignorance. But they are not yet explained very well by our theories.

Accumulating empirical observations of the life course have changed the prevailing view of how it is organized. At least three major sets of findings have reestablished the phenomenon of aging:

1. Life course transitions are decreasingly tied to age: events in family, education, work, health and leisure domains occur across the life span at different (and many at increasingly later) ages than previously expected. Life transitions are less age-segregated and more age-integrated.

2. Life transitions are less disjunctive and more continuous: transitions are not necessarily abrupt nor irreversible events, but often gradual and reversible processes. Such transitions as family formation, education completion, career entry and exit, divorce and retirement are often more protracted and multidirectional than previously recognized.

3. Specific life pathways in education, family, work, health, and leisure are interdependent within and across lives. Trajectories within these domains develop simultaneously and reciprocally within and across individual lives.

From Age Segregation to Age Integration

The first generalization supports Matilda W. Riley's (1994) age-integrated conceptualization of the life course. A great deal of demographic, historical and sociological research on the life course shows that major life transitions are not as segregated by age as previous "life cycle" models suggested (O'Rand & Krecker, 1990). Marriage, childbearing, career entry and exit, and educational completion can and do occur variably across the life span. The variability is noticeable from adolescence, when diverse schedules of onset-of-sexual intercourse-education-work-and-family formation among the young anchor highly different and numerous age-related pathways into adulthood (see Rindfuss, Swicegood, & Rosenfeld, 1987). Recent census analyses, for example, reveal that in 1990 fully one third of American women between ages 25 and 34 were childless. Meanwhile, trends in adolescent pregnancy are declining across demographic groups while reproductive technologies such as in vitro fertilization have all but eliminated upper age boundaries in the reproductive process (Bianchi, 1995). Similarly, early and midlife patterns in delayed marriage, divorce, remarriage, childbearing, career entry and exit, and early retirement defy earlier normative and age-segregated conceptualizations that restricted these individual transitions to specific phases of the life span. Historical shifts in the timing of first marriage (nuptiality) among Whites in the United States are occurring and exemplify the empirical challenge to life cycle notions. After a century of decline in age at first marriage, reaching lows of 20 and 23 among women and men, respectively, in 1960, the trend has reversed. By 1990, White U.S. women and men were approximately 25 and 27 years of age, respectively, at first marriage (Haines, 1996).

One consequence is that adults are spending less of their lives as married. Bianchi (1995) observes changing gender role patterns using aggregate data across six 10–year cohorts of U.S. women: beginning with those born between 1906 and 1915 followed by four intervening cohorts (1916–1925, 1926–1935, 1936–1945, 1946–1955) and ending with those born between 1956 and 1965 (deemed the late baby boom). She reports that more than three fourths (77%) of the World War II (1936–1945) cohort in 1970 (then aged 25–34) were married and living with their husbands. By 1980 and 1990, the early and late baby boom (1946–1955 and 1956–65) women reaching the same age range, were less likely to be married: 64% and 60% of the early and late baby boom cohorts were married between the ages of 25 and 34. Observed patterns of delayed marriage and divorce are highly associated with these trends. Indeed, the growing heterogeneity of the timing and duration of marriage(s), childbearing, remarriage, and empty nest challenges any age-dependent theory of the family life cycle or the individual life course. Hiedemann and her colleagues (Hiedemann, Suhomlinova, & O'Rand, 1998) follow the mature women's sample of the National Longitudinal Survey, aged 30 to 44 in 1967, for 22 years. They report the increased risk of divorce among mature marriages (between 20 and 30 years' duration) in response to empty nest.

Labor force participation patterns are also less constrained by age. Women's lifetime labor force participation patterns have steadily increased over the century and have eroded gender norms that previously excluded women from market work. The fastest-growing subgroup of workers today includes mothers of young children (Bianchi, 1995). Meanwhile men's lifetime labor force participation patterns have steadily declined since the 1960s, primarily in response to early retirement incentives in particular employment sectors

(Quinn, Burkhauser, & Myers, 1990). More recently, trends towards postretirement returns to work by men and women alike are further evidence of the age independence of work (Doeringer, 1990).

Finally, forecasts of active life expectancy among recent cohorts of the elderly promise further challenges to an age-dependent process in the unfolding life course (Manton, Stallard, & Liu, 1993). Healthier lifestyles and improved delivery of medical care over the life span appear to be extending active lives into the seventh and eighth decades. Thus, empirical results have reconfigured the life course to be shaped by life transitions that are increasingly less dependent on age. However, so far our explanations for these trends are inadequate for the task at hand.

From Disjunctive to Continuous Transition Processes

The second generalization reveals that life transitions themselves are less disjunctive than earlier portrayed and more continuous and multidirectional. For example, the transition from school to work has become blurred and can no longer be restricted to early adulthood. Traditional life course models relegated all educational attainment to early adulthood; the number of years of schooling before work has been the conventional measure of educational attainment. Yet trends toward returns to formal education in midlife are growing, especially among women and less advantaged workers whose skill deficits in recent years have required a return to the classroom (e.g., Elman & O'Rand, in press). That these trends are generalizing to male workers caught in the global transformation of the work process are increasingly evident (Lewis, Hearn, & Zilbert, 1993; Office of Technology Assessment, 1986).

Family formation processes also are less clearly demarcated transitions. Trends toward cohabitation prior to marriage (or without marriage) render the unmarried-to-married transition less disjunctive and accompany delayed marriage and remarriage patterns that have blurred the boundaries of the marital state in the life course (Bumpass, 1990). Explanations for these patterns are matters of considerable dispute that range from broad cultural arguments regarding growing individualism in post-industrial societies (Ruggles, 1997) to middle-range hypotheses regarding declining male opportunity structures to support traditional marital and family institutions (Oppenheimer, 1997).

Finally, this generalization is clearly evident in retirement studies, where processes of gradual or partial retirement and the trend toward "bridge jobs" between major career and permanent withdrawal from work are blurring the boundary between work and nonwork at later ages (Doeringer, 1990; Quinn et al., 1990). Indeed, the increase in job mobility over the life span has rendered the retirement transition less distinguishable from job mobility transitions generally (Mutchler, Burr, Pienta, & Massagli, 1997).

From Separate to Mutually Contingent Pathways

The third empirical generalization reflects accumulating findings that trajectories observed within life domains such as family, work, or education are simultaneous and highly interdependent. Women's life courses have been especially illustrative of this phenomenon (Rossi, 1980). The family and work schedules of women, for example, are highly intertwined, making their separate analysis impossible, although their joint analysis makes rigorous demands on analytical precision only just beginning to be resolved (e.g., Lillard, 1993). Lives are lived along multiple temporal dimensions that are collinear (Upchurch, Lillard, & Panis, 1995; Waite & Lillard, 1991).

Complicating these observations further are the now obvious patterns by which multiple individuals' complex life courses influence each other. Elder (1994) refers to this as the principle of interdependent lives by which he describes how individuals' transitions are highly contingent on significant others' lives. Families are the most compelling proximate contexts of interdependent lives. Conger and Elder's (1994) study of Iowa youth in the recent midwestern farm crisis in the United States illustrates this point. Children's developmental patterns in the midst of this crisis are highly interdependent with parents' differential responses to these sociohistorical conditions.

The Longitudinal Study of Generations is another project revealing this principle within the family, defined even more broadly in temporal terms—across multiple generations (Bengtson, 1996). This project examines how intrafamily solidarity and conflict leads to common life trajectories across four generations over 2½ decades. Among these common trajectories are highly correlated patterns of occupational attainment between parents and children, with more attenuated associations across successively distal generations. Parents and children are more alike than grandparents and grandchildren in their occupational mobility patterns. The sociohistorical forces bearing on the interdependent lives of these families are now the concerns of this project.

Finally, the growing information on joint retirement among working couples exemplifies this phenomenon: modeling the retirement decision of spouses requires the joint consideration of their labor exits (Henretta, O'Rand, & Chan, 1993). Retirement is perhaps more a family than an individual transition when patterns of interdependency among married couples and between generations are reconfigured by transitions in the workplace which themselves are conditioned by family arrangements (O'Rand, Henretta, & Krecker, 1992). As such, there is growing evidence that retirement and other life transitions are more complicated than earlier constructions of them as single, age-dependent, and disjunctive events experienced by socially disconnected individuals.

The reestablishment of the social phenomenon of aging has consisted primarily of a reconceptualization of the dependent variable only. Indeed, the (arguable) case can be made that the major progress in aging research since 1965 has been in redefining aging but not explaining it very well. From the specification of the age-period-cohort problem (e.g., Ryder, 1965; Schaie, 1965) through the more recent explication of age-integrated, continuous and contingent life course processes (Elder, 1994; O'Rand & Krecker, 1990; Riley, 1994), real progress has occurred in establishing the dependent variable. Social aging is a time-driven process in which sequential contingencies make simple cause-and-effect relationships centered on chronological age difficult to sustain.

CONTINGENCY AND COMPARISON

These temporal processes have not been identified strictly through theory-driven research but more serendipitously in response to new methods or data opportunities. The application of new methods, such as event history analysis, provided a means of conceptualizing the life course in new and insightful ways—a process described in our earlier essay on the relationship between research design and theory development (Campbell & O'Rand, 1988). The data opportunities have been equally interesting. The mining of "strategic research materials" (another Mertonian concept), which were not originally collected in light of aging theory but which exhibit life course processes to practical advantage, is another feature of life course research (O'Rand, 1998). Significant exemplars are found in Glen Elder's work over 25 years, beginning with the Berkeley Guidance and Oakland Growth studies of two Depression-era samples, and more recently the Stanford-Terman sample (Elder, 1994; Elder & Clipp, 1988a, 1988b; Elder, Pavalko, & Hastings, 1991). These studies are based on "accidental data," that is, data that were either collected for another purpose or were collected at an arbitrary point in time. Even very large scale studies have this characteristic. For example, the National Longitudinal Surveys of Labor Market Experience, which have produced many aging-related publications, began as a longitudinal survey of the males aged 45–59 in 1966. A parallel study of women began in 1967, based on women aged 30–44 in that year. Why those years and those cohorts? There is no rational explanation; it just happened that the motivation, talent and money were available at that point to get the survey up and running. Another example is the Panel Study of Income Dynamics (PSID), which began as a study of poverty based on 5,000 households in 1966 and which has now emerged, with some sample supplementation, as a prime source of aging-related data.

Although methodological or data-based opportunities have redefined the endogenous phenomenon, they have not, however, aided in the specification of the social and historical processes that constrain and direct the life course. As noted above, until very recently most data sets employed in aging research were locked into a specific time and place and were rarely analyzed in conjunction with data from other contexts. Increasingly, though, one sees data collection of a more systematic nature. The full spectrum of available data could be the subject of another paper, but a few examples will make the point. First, we see systematic programs of repeated cross-sectional surveys, such as the General Social Survey begun in 1972 and continuing to the present. The March and October *Current Populations Surveys,* which contain a great deal of important data for students of aging, are now available on CD-ROM from 1968 to the present. Perhaps the most exciting development is the availability of easily accessible micro census data using a common format and codebook. Steven Ruggles and colleagues (Ruggles & Sobek, 1997) at the University of Minnesota have made every census available (with only a few exceptions) on an Internet-based files server.

In addition, more and more repeated longitudinal surveys of aging, based on representative national samples of the United States, are being produced. Of major interest are the two Longitudinal Studies of Aging, LSOA-I and II, sponsored by the National Center for Health Statistics; the first runs from 1984 to 1990, and the second is now in the field. In addition, the National Institute of Aging, in collaboration with the University of Michigan and various researchers from around the country, has launched an extremely ambitious program of longitudinal research known as Health and Retirement Study: Asset and Health Dynamics among the Oldest-Old, HRS/ AHEAD. The details of these surveys are too complex to relate here, but the basic plan is to carry out systematic longitudinal surveys of persons aged 50 and over, beginning with the cohorts of 1941–1951, with the "aging in" of new cohorts on a systematic basis (Juster & Suzman, 1995, Soldo, Hurd, Rodgers, & Wallace, 1997).

Short-Run Changes and Proximate Contingencies

The burgeoning database for the study of aging will have immense implications for the field. At the moment, the promise is more imagined than real. One problem already noted is that the specific data sets have no systematic relationship to social and cultural change. Hence, structural theory development is constrained by data. This results in a theoretical lag in the specification of exogenous factors. A related problem is that current social theories of aging focus nearly exclusively on short-run changes in the life course. In these theories, proximate environments and recent events are predicted to affect specific transitions in the life course. The findings are sometimes interpreted in light of assumptions about the probable or likely influences of more remote or broadly encompassing environments and more distal events.

But the near absence of structural or historical variables in most (nearly all) aging research relegates these considerations to concluding discussions and implications of the research.

In this vein, the argument has spread to move toward structural theories in epidemiological research, where the normative preference for individualistic over contextualized analyses has limited both the theoretical power of the field and its ultimate utility for broad-based social intervention (see Link and Phelan, 1995; Diez-Roux, 1998). This argument offers stringent criticism of the "individual risk factor" bias in this aging-related field and demonstrates the utility of turning to basic social conditions such as socioeconomic status. A key practice of epidemiology is to take strong observed correlations, such as the one between socioeconomic status and health, and attenuate it by the successive introduction of individual-level mediating or intervening factors. According to Link and Phelan, what is lost by this design is social explanation (or the specification of what they term "fundamental causes") and social intervention. Their critique is poignant testimony for how data limitations and analytical conventions can constrain theory development. Yet their essay is a self-exemplifying case of specifying ignorance: by examining the way that epidemiological research is conducted, they discover what is missing and specify what we need to know.

Aging theory that focuses on explaining only short-run changes in the absence of strong structural or contextual comparisons falls short of explaining the phenomenon. Modell's (1989) recent social history of the changing transition to adulthood among the young in the United States between 1920 and 1975 provides a strategic site for considering needs for improvement in theory. He reports a general trend toward the individualization of the life course, evident in the loosening of transition sequences in young adulthood. His historical account of these changes is grounded in period effects. Succeeding decades of the 20th century have brought more material and cultural resources, on average, to the young and thus introduced increasing individualization in the early life course. This historical argument suggests a multilevel theory of the growing structural diversity in life course processes. The transition to adulthood is represented by life course contingencies reflected in the onset of sexual behavior and educational, marital, fertility, and employment variables. These variables interact with gender and race, whose influences, in turn, have been modulated by historical factors to produce heterogeneity.

The examples from the United States provided above provoke another crucial issue, with direct relevance to the absence of fundamental comparisons in aging research. Much (but by no means all) research on the social aspects of aging has come from U.S. studies of various kinds. And in the United States a great deal has been written about how the Great Depression and World War II disrupted the lives of many in various ways. Glen Elder's pursuit of this issue by the sequential examination of multiple samples (panels) of individuals encountering these two events at different points in their lives has been among the few undaunted efforts toward the achievement of fundamental comparison. This research is fascinating, enlightening and illuminating—not least because it specifies our ignorance by pointing to what is left to be known. However, this literature has not and cannot provide definitive answers to the question of how depressions or wars affect the life course and why these effects follow. The reason is the absence of strong comparison. Our interpretation of the effects of one depression (the Great Depression in the United States) is confounded by the effects of one war (World War II as experienced by the United States), and vice versa. And although these two events are hardly trifling even when compared to the cataclysm of the Civil War, they are the only two such events in recent American history. Moreover, neither was the kind of all-encompassing, world-redefining event to serve as the source of definitive theoretical insight.

Although available data are less than definitive, it has been estimated that at the height of the Great Depression (1932–1933) about 25% of the American labor force was unemployed, and a substantial fraction of those who were working found themselves on short rations (Bordo, Goldin, & White, 1997; Chandler, 1970). For the majority of Americans, the Depression was a milestone not only because of its length but because it was the country's first experience with serious deprivation in more than a generation. Still, we would argue that although the Depression consisted of a serious downturn in the standard of living for many, it was not a life-threatening event except for a very few. Undoubtedly, it indelibly marked the psyches of those who lived through it, but it did not permanently change the social and cultural landscape. World War II was even less intrusive for the majority of the population; it signaled the return of good jobs and stable incomes even if it meant that luxuries were temporarily unavailable and plans had to be put on hold. Compared to the Civil War, its demographic effects in terms of casualties were relatively minor, particularly when one compares U.S. figures to Europe, China, and Japan.

To understand the effects of either the Great Depression or World War II, comparative examples are necessary. The ideal situation would be to have data on the effects of the Civil War, the Spanish-American War, World War I, the Korean War, and Vietnam in addition to World War II. Then statements such as "the effect of a war is to make draft-age cohorts do X" can be addressed. In the case of the Great Depression, comparative data on the effects of major business cycles and other depressions would produce the same sets of testable propositions. The obvious problem with existing U.S. data (censuses, panels, etc.) is that we lack replication of major historical events *within the range of the surveys or administrative data series available* (see Campbell, 1994). That is, from the standpoint of more quantitative studies of aging and the life course, the available database (with the exception of the census) begins in the early 1960s.

However, in aggregate data there is some opportunity for replication. For example, we have enough variation in fertility over time to gain some leverage for testing the Easterlin hypothesis (Pampel & Peters, 1995), although we lack a second Great Depression to which we could compare the effects of the first. The hypothesis argues that relative cohort size is a direct determinant of income potential and expected standard of living, with indirect effects on widely ranging micro-level behavioral outcomes such as fertility, marriage and divorce, and mental stress.

To date, the most effective analysis has occurred when researchers have sharp, clearly defined historical transitions to work with. That is one reason some studies of the effects of World War II and the Great Depression have been relatively fruitful in spite of the constraints in comparison. Both events have clear beginning and ending points, although it is still arguable exactly when the Great Depression ended (Bordo et al., 1997). In most circumstances, social change and the sequence of social events is more gradual. For example, the period following World War II, through the mid-1960s, was marked by high fertility rates, a strong economy, and with the exception of the Korean War, the absence of armed conflict using U.S. troops. But beginning in the late 1960s, many things began to change. By the early 1970s far grimmer times had arrived—marked by high inflation, an unpopular war, a decline in economic growth attributed to a growing competitive market, and a general decline in American optimism. As a result, discrete comparisons are not quite so easy. On the other hand, long swings in macro-level phenomena provide a good deal of theoretical leverage. Such swings are just now coming into view in light of more easily accessible data.

Some indication of the theoretical advantage to be gained from repeating economic and social cycles can be drawn from data reported by Levy (1987) on the extent to which the growth rate in real wages has changed over the past 40 years or so. Following Levy, Table 4.1 shows the extent to which persons born in various cohorts lived out their working lives in a period of real wage growth. The table shows the Depression and World War II but extends economic information to the present. Beginning in 1973 and continuing to at least the mid-1990s, there was no real gain in income beyond inflation for most workers. Only those workers who could expect to benefit from productivity gains drawing on human capital (education, training, and experience) over the course of their careers fared better than average. The table clearly reveals that each successive cohort since the turn of the century has spent a relatively lower proportion of its working career in periods of real wage growth. The important thing to understand about Table 4.1 is that change is gradual rather than abrupt. When real wages turn back, as some current evidence suggests is the case, we will gain needed theoretical lever-

TABLE 4.1   Years of Working Life and Percentage of Work Life Spent in
Periods of Real Wage Growth

Years Spent in Periods of Growth and Decline in Real Wages By Birth Cohort

Birth Cohort	Growth 1920–29	Decline 1930–39	WWII 1940–46	Growth 1947–73	Flat 1974–97	Year Retired	% Time Growth
1900	10	10	7	19		1965	79
1902	10	10	7	21		1967	79
1904	8	10	7	23		1969	79
1906	6	10	7	25		1971	79
1908	4	10	7	27		1973	79
1910	2	10	7	27	2	1975	75
1912		10	7	27	4	1977	70
1914		8	7	27	6	1979	70
1916		6	7	27	8	1981	70
1918		4	7	27	10	1983	70
1920		2	7	27	12	1985	70
1922			7	27	14	1987	70
1924			5	27	16	1989	67
1926			3	27	18	1991	63
1928			1	27	20	1993	58
1930				26	22	1995	54
1932				24	24	1997	50
1934				22	(24)	1999	—
1936				20	(24)	2001	—
1938				18	(24)	2003	—
1940				16	(24)	2005	—

Note: Table based on data reported in Levy (1987). Work life calculations are based on ages 18–65.

age (comparison), because it is only when transitions are repeated under differing historical circumstances that the assessment of effects is possible.

In short, at this stage of its development our understanding of the aging process is ignorant of the impact of broader exogenous processes and their complex effects on more easily measured endogenous life course transitions. Yet theoretical capital in aging research can be gained through more hierarchically structured examinations of the phenomenon based on longer historical and stronger structural comparisons.

International Comparisons

To press the argument one step further, think for a moment about the countries of the former Soviet Union, not just Russia but all of the countries that have emerged from the recent chaos. Suppose you were a male citizen of one of those countries, say Ukraine, born in 1900. At age 14 you found yourself wondering if World War I would go on long enough for you be conscripted. In 1917 you thought yourself lucky to have avoided becoming cannon fodder only to be swept up in the nightmare of the civil war and the eventual triumph of the Bolsheviks. Then came massive transformation of cultural, economic, and social systems; collectivization; and the total imposition of communism. The next decade brought the worst of the Stalinist nightmare, followed closely by the German invasion, the subsequent recapture of the area by the Soviets, and 10 more years of repressive Stalinism. Perhaps the period from 1960 to 1990 could be seen as relative calm, but it was followed in 1990 (a date to which you would have been very unlikely to live) by yet another massive upheaval—one that thankfully involved very little bloodshed but no small amount of economic hardship.

Here, given the availability of data, would be fertile ground for understanding the intersection of social structure and the life course. The comparison of data from U.S. and Soviet cohorts would be fruitful. Even if one doesn't focus on the Soviet Union or China, which also underwent successive large-scale social transformations in this century, think about the major industrial societies of Western Europe. Great Britain, France, and Germany twice suffered massive casualties in lengthy wars with a depression in between. Seen in that light, the United States and Canada offer slim pickings as empirical sources of theoretical insight. Granted, American historians would be surprised to have us tell them that not much has happened of a serious nature in the United States since the Civil War. But when it comes to identifying those events that redefine how human beings relate to one another and how they change their behavior in the face of massive social change, North Americans have been a privileged lot. Indeed, if one thinks about the life of a citizen in 20th-century Ukraine as akin to sailing through a hurricane in a rowboat, Americans have faced a thunderstorm from the comfort of a yacht.

International data exchange and formal cross-national partnerships in data collection and data linkage are bringing the opportunity for strong comparative studies within practical reach. Space does not permit an exhaustive inventory of international databases. Rather we will point to exemplary sources to illustrate the newly emerging possibilities for theory development stemming from new data and new methods.

An exemplary case of this trend in research design is the linkage of the German Socio-Economic Panel with the widely used U.S. Panel Study of Income Dynamics (GSOEP-PSID) over the period of 1980–1994 (available from the Center for Policy Research at Syracuse University). The GSOEP was drawn from 6,000 families in what was then West Germany and was later supplemented by 3,000 families from the former East Germany following unification. A matched file of equivalent socioeconomic data from both samples affords a more direct examination of differences between the United

States and Germany and between parts of Germany with distinctly different economic and political histories since World War II.

Although these data sets followed the typical pattern of not being developed originally to test specific theories of difference or change at the macroscopic level advocated in this essay, they hold much promise in this regard. Burkhauser and his colleagues (Burkhauser, Duncan, & Hauser, 1994) have already demonstrated the theoretical utility of comparative databases by showing the relative effects of different government redistributive policies on patterns of persistent poverty among the elderly in the United States and Germany. State policies in Germany protect more of the elderly population from povertyp however, both systems tend to disadvantage older women more than older men.

The Luxembourg Income Study (LIS) is a bank of comparable cross-national household income survey data linked over time (Gottschalk & Smeeding, 1997; Smeeding, O'Higgins, & Rainwater, 1990). Data from administrative records in government statistics bureaus and research centers are gathered by the LIS, converted to standardized values, and made available worldwide. The LIS expands beyond the GSOEP-PSID two-country comparison reported by Burkhauser et al. (1994) to multiple country cases. Comparison of seven countries (Australia, Canada, France, the Netherlands, Sweden, the United Kingdom, and the United States) reveals some of the consequences of American "exceptionalism"; whereas American older married couples are the best off economically, the worst off across eight countries are American single women (Smeeding, Torrey & Rainwater, 1993). And given the relationship between economic well-being and other social indicators of well-being in aging populations, the theoretical leverage gained by such comparisons is considerable.

Panel studies and administrative databases are available from a far larger number of countries than those archived in the two projects cited above. Similarly, U.S. governmental agencies, such as the Social Security Administration; the European Organization of Economic Cooperation and Development; the World Bank; and United Nations databases, such as the United National Development Programme (UNDP), are providing more and more comparable information to permit more comparison across social structures and historical periods. The UNDP produces the *Human Development Report*, which is providing increasingly rich, reliable, and comparable measures of social indicators as well as economic indicators for life course comparative research (UN Development Programme, 1995). Knowledge of cross-national variations in life expectancy, literacy, health services, school expenditure, women's citizenship and social rights, and other contextual indicators is in more limited supply but ultimately of greater sociological import. Problems persist in these data, particularly in their preparation for direct comparative study. Measurement, missing values, timing—these are a few expectable problems for research. But the trends in improved data are finally bringing life-course research to the threshold of genuine macro-micro analysis.

DATA AND METHODS FOR DETERMINING MACRO-MICRO LINKAGES

The analysis of macro-micro linkages requires at least three things: comparative historical or structural data of the kinds discussed above, historical sensitivity to asynchrony in the tempos of (lags in) change at different levels of analysis, and rigorous analytic methods. With regard to the latter, a great deal of progress in conceptualizing and modeling macro-micro relationships has taken place in the last decade.

Modeling Macro-Micro Relationships

Whereas 10 years ago dynamic methods imported from other fields were having an impact on recasting the phenomenon of aging, another class of statistical methods has emerged since that provides a means of linking macro and contextual variables to micro-level life course data. These multilevel methods—as in the case of event history methods before them—have again come from outside aging (they were independently developed by several groups of demographers and statisticians), with the major influence on gerontologists coming from demography.

As DiPrete and Forristal (1995) observe, the notion of contextual effects is by no means new. Multivariate studies have introduced contexts tied to individuals (e.g., urban vs. rural residence) as main effects. Similarly, interactions between contexts and individual attributes have been analyzed to ascertain the differential behavior of individual traits on life course outcomes across contexts (e.g., informal caregiving patterns across individuals living in rural vs. urban settings). However, this new generation of analytic methods permits the most rigorous approach to testing for contextual or structural effects while managing numerous technical problems associated with complications in error structure among non-independent observations. In other words, the method, like survival analysis, provides both conceptual clarification of time honored issues and statistical rigor in their solution.

Macro-level observations have been measured in main-or interaction-effects approaches in at least two ways: either as context-specific aggregate indices (means) of micro-level characteristics or as a global variables not expressed in terms of measured individual traits. Multilevel models go a long step further toward a direct test of contextual effects. The most frequent approach is a multiequation system in which, first, micro-level models are estimated within specified contexts and then the coefficients from these models become the dependent variables in the next phase, where contexts become the observations. Accordingly, the variations in micro-level coefficients are explained by the variation in contextual variables (see DiPrete & Forristal, 1994, for a thorough discussion). A key point is that data can be nested at several levels. For example, longitudinal data are nested within individuals, who in turn might share common environments such as a nursing home. Thus, multilevel models provide a new means of handling longitudinal data while at the same time dealing with sampling issues.

Multilevel models have been applied most frequently in the study of regional (village) effects on fertility behavior, school effects on academic and subsequent achievement, and national differences in job mobility patterns in the face of global market transformations. For aging research, given the availability of historical and cross-national data, these models offer much promise for theory building. Even the life course itself may be conceived of as a sequence of contexts across which individual variables may respond differently. Multilevel ideas generalize to a wide class of statistical models. For example, survival models, which have provided important conceptual tools for understanding and modeling the timing of life course transitions fit easily within the multilevel framework.

Appreciating Multilevel Asynchrony

Finally, given access to data that lend themselves to multilevel analysis, it is nevertheless important for life course research also to remain attentive to the asynchronies of social change across levels of study. Usually, historians are more appreciative of this problem than are other social and behavioral scientists. Social change occurs at different tempos across macro and micro levels. Schooler (1994) has recently reminded us of this problem. Micro-level processes occur at quicker tempos, whereas macro-level processes tend to change more slowly. Matilda White Riley's (1994) notion of structural lag captures this asynchrony quite succinctly. Even the most comprehensive data matched to robust analytical techniques for multilevel analysis do not eliminate the requirement of historically grounded and qualitatively informed interpretations of statistical models.

Matilda White Riley (1994) would also remind us that an overdeterministic theory of aging will misspecify the agentic demographic processes that have brought about structural change over this century. The transformation of gender roles over the past 100 years occurred steadily in women's life patterns, followed by institutional change. Women changed their lives in response to their changing historical circumstance; they changed frequently in the face of institutional inertia. Changing age-related roles and the social institutions that define and reinforce age roles are also being eroded by demographic pressure—but again, with some institutional resistance.

CONCLUSIONS

We are approaching a threshold in theory development permitting more macro-micro linkages. This is being occasioned by a Mertonian confluence of data, methods, and specified ignorance to develop theory and recast the phenomenon of aging. Reestablishing the phenomenon of aging requires that we address our specific ignorance about social and historical contexts of aging and account for observed variability in the life course with direct reference to the linkage among individual and contextual variables. There are systematic effects of historical events and structural cycles and trends on life patterns. Some of these effects are permanent; others are cyclical or short-lived. Without strong comparative data, these effects cannot be determined, and changes in the phenomenon of aging cannot be explained.

Our theories have not addressed these concerns very well for several reasons. Our data sets have traditionally not matched historical time. This has constrained theory toward focusing on short-run changes in the aging process. However, above and beyond data limitations, theories have moved more and more toward micro-level processes emphasizing proximal causes. As mentioned earlier, we are not alone in calling for an equally enthusiastic research agenda at the macro level. Both theory and social intervention require more attention to what Link and Phelan (1995) have aptly referred to as "basic social conditions" and "fundamental causes" of aging and life course processes that fall outside the boundaries of individual-level theorizing.

REFERENCES

Bengtson, V. L. (1996). Continuities and discontinuities in intergenerational relationships over time. In V. L. Bengtson (Ed.), *Adulthood and aging: Research on continuities and discontinuities* (pp. 271–324). New York: Springer Publishing Co.

Bengtson, V. L., Burgess, E. O., & Parrott, T. M. (1997). "Theory, explanation, and a third generation of theoretical development in social gerontology. *Journal of Gerontology: Social Sciences, 52B,* S72–S88.

Bianchi, S. M. (1995). Changing economic roles of women and men. In R. Farley (Ed.), *State of the Union: America in the 1990s. Vol. 1. Economic trends* (pp.107–154). New York: Russell Sage Foundation.

Bordo, M., Goldin, C., & White, E. (Eds.). (1997). *The defining moment: The Great Depression and the American economy in the twentieth century.* Chicago: University of Chicago Press.

Bumpass, L. L. (1990). What's happening to the family? Interactions between demographic and institutional changes. *Demography, 27,* 483–498.

Burkhauser, R. V., Duncan, G. J., & Hauser, R. (1994). Sharing prosperity across the age distribution: A comparison of the United States and Germany in the 1980s. *Gerontologist, 334,* 150–160.

Campbell, R. T. (1994). A data-based revolution in the social sciences. *ICPSR Bulletin, 14,* 1–4.

Campbell, R. T., & O'Rand, A. M. (1988). Settings and sequences: The heuristics of aging research. In J. E. Birren & V. L. Bengtson (Eds.), *Emergent theories of aging* (pp. 58–79). New York: Springer Publishing Co.

Chandler, L. (1970). *America's greatest depression, 1929–1941.* New York: Harper & Row.

Conger, R. D., & Elder, G. H., Jr. (1994). *Families in troubled times: Adapting to change in rural America.* Chicago: Aldine.

DiPrete, T. A., & Forristal, J. D. (1995). Multilevel models: Methods and substance. *Annual Review of Sociology, 20,* 331–357.

Diez-Roux, A. V. (1998). Bringing context back into epidemiology: Variables and fallacies in multilevel analysis. *American Journal of Public Health, 88,* 216–222.

Doeringer, P. B. (Ed.). (1990). *Bridges to retirement: Older workers in a changing labor market.* Ithaca, NY: Cornell University Press.

Duncan, G. J., & Smith, K. R. (1989). The rising affluence of the elderly: How far, how fair and how frail? *Annual Review of Sociology, 15,* 261–289.

Elder, G. H., Jr. (1994). The life course paradigm: Historical, comparative and developmental perspectives. In P. Moen, G. H. Elder, Jr., & K. Luscher (Eds.), *Linking lives and contexts: Perspectives in the ecology of human development.* Washington, DC: American Psychological Association.

Elder, G. H., Jr., & Clipp, E. C. (1988a). Combat experience and emotional health: Impairment and resilience in later life. *Journal of Personality, 57,* 311–341.

Elder, G. H., Jr., & Clipp, E. C. (1988b). Wartime losses and social bonding: Influences across 40 years in men's lives. *Psychiatry, 51,* 177–198.

Elder, G. H., Jr., Pavalko, E. K., & Hastings, T. J. (1991). Talent, history and the fulfillment of promise. *Psychiatry, 54,* 251–267.

Elman, C., & O'Rand, A. (in press). Midlife entry into vocational training: A mobility model. *Social Science Research.*

Goldstein, H. (1995). *Multilevel statistical models* (2nd Ed.). New York: Halsted Press.

Gottschalk, P., & Smeeding, T. M. (1997). Cross-national comparisons of earnings and income inequality. *Journal of Economic Literature, 35,* 633–687.

Haines, M. R. (1996). Long-term marriage patterns in the United States from colonial times to the present. *History of the Family, 1,* 15–39.

Heidemann, B., Suhomlinova, O., & O'Rand, A. M. (1998). Economic independence, economic status and empty nest in midlife marital disruption. *Journal of Marriage and the Family, 60,* 219–231.

Henretta, J. C., O'Rand, A. M., & Chan, C. G. (1993). Joint role investments and synchronization of retirement: A sequential approach to couples' retirement timing, *Social Forces, 71,* 981–1000.

Juster, T., & Suzman, R. (1995). An overview of the health and retirement survey. *Journal of Human Resources, 30* (Suppl.), S7–S56.

Levy, F. (1987). *Dollars and dreams. The changing American income distribution.* New York: Russell Sage Foundation.

Lewis, D. R., Hearn, J. C., & Zilbert, E. E. (1993). Efficiency and equity effects of vocationally focused post-secondary education. *Sociology of Education, 66* 188–205.

Lillard, L. A. (1993). Simultaneous equations for hazards. *Journal of Econometrics, 56,* 189–217.

Link, B. G., & Phelan, J. (1995). Social conditions as fundamental causes of disease. *Journal of Health and Social Behavior* (Special Issue), 80–94.

Manton, K. G., Stallard, E., & Liu, K. (1993). Forecasts of active life expectancy: Policy and fiscal implications. *The Journals of Gerontology, 48 (Special Issue),* 11–26.

Mason, W. M., Wong, G. Y. & Entwisle, B. (1983). Contextual analysis through the multilevel linear model. In S. Leinhardt (Ed.), *Sociological methodology 1983–84* (pp. 72–103). San Francisco: Jossey-Bass.

Merton, R. K. (1948). The bearing of empirical research upon the development of social theory. *American Sociological Review, 13,* 505–515.

Merton, R. K. (1959). Notes on problem-finding in sociology. In R. K. Merton, L. Broom & L. S. Cottrell, Jr.,(Eds.), *Sociology today* (pp. ix-xxxiv). New York: Basic Books.

Merton, R. K. (1971). The precarious foundations of detachment in sociology. In E. A. Tiryakian (Ed.), *The phenomenon of sociology* (pp. 188–199). New York: Appleton-Century-Crofts.

Merton, R. K. (1981). Remarks on theoretical pluralism. In P. M. Blau & R. K. Merton (Eds.), *Continuities in structural inquiry* (pp. i-vii). Beverly Hills CA: Sage.

Merton, R. K. (1987). Three fragments from a sociologist's notebooks: Establishing the phenomenon, specified ignorance, and strategic research materials. *Annual Review of Sociology, 13,* 1–28.

Modell, J. (1989). *Into one's own: From youth to adulthood in the United States 1920–1975.* Berkeley, University of California.

Mutchler, J. E., Burr, J. A., Pienta, A. M., & Massagli, M. P. (1997). Pathways to labor exit: Work transitions and work instability. *Journal of Gerontology—Social Sciences, 52B,* S4–S12.

Office of Technology Assessment. (1986). *Technology and structural unemployment: Reemploying displaced adults.* Washington DC: U.S. Government Printing Office.

Oppenheimer, V. K. (1997). Comment on 'The rise of divorce and separation in the United States, 1880–1990.' *Demography, 34,* 467–472.

O'Rand, A. M. (1998). Observations on the craft of life course research. In J. Z. Giele & G. H. Elder, Jr. (Eds.), *Life course research methods: Quantitative and qualitative* (pp. 52–74). Thousand Oaks, CA: Sage.

O'Rand, A. M., Henretta, J. C., & Krecker, M. L. (1992). Family pathways to retirement. In M. Szinovacz, D. I. Ekerdt, & B. H. Vinick (Eds.), *Family retirement* (pp. 81–98). Thousand Oaks, CA: Sage.

O'Rand, A. M., & Krecker, M. L. (1990). Concepts of the life cycle: Their history, meanings and uses in the social sciences. *Annual Review of Sociology, 16,* 241–262.

Pampel, F. C., & Peters, H. E. (1995). The Easterlin effect. *Annual Review of Sociology, 21,* 163–194.

Quinn, J. F., Burkhauser, R. V., & Myers, D. A. (1990). *Passing the torch: The influence of economic incentives on work and retirement.* New York: W. E. Upjohn Institute.

Riley, M. W. (1994). Aging and society: Past, present and future (1993 Kent Lecture). *Gerontologist, 34,* 436–446.

Rindfuss, R., Swicegood, C. G., & Rosenfeld, R. (1987). Disorder in the life course: How common and does it matter? *American Sociological Review, 52,* 785–801.

Rossi, A. S. (1980). Life span theories and women's lives. *Signs, 6,* 4–32.

Ruggles, S. (1997). The rise of divorce and separation in the United States, 1880–1990. *Demography, 34,* 455–466.

Ruggles, S., & Sobek, M. (1997). *Integrated public use microdata series: Version 2.0.* Minneapolis: University of Minnesota Historical Census Projects.

Ryder, N. B. (1965). The cohort as a concept in the study of social change. *American Sociological Review, 30,* 843–861.

Sampson, R. J., & Laub, J. H. (1993). *Crime in the making: Pathways and turning points through life.* Cambridge, MA: Harvard University Press.

Schaie, K. W. (1965). A general model for the study of developmental problems. *Psychological Bulletin, 30,* 843–861.

Schooler, C. (1994). A working conceptualization of social structure: Mertonian roots and psychological and sociocultural relationships. *Social Psychology Quarterly, 57,* 262–283.

Smeeding, T., O'Higgins, M., & Rainwater, L. (Eds). (1990). Poverty, inequality, and income distribution in comparative perspective. In *The Luxembourg income study.* Washington, DC: The Urban Institute; Brighton: Harvester-Wheatsheaf.

Smeeding, T. M., Torrey, B. B., & Rainwater, L. (1993). Going to extremes: An international perspective on the economic status of the U.S. aged. Working Paper No. 87. *Luxembourg Income Study.* Syracuse, NY: Syracuse University, Maxwell School of Citizenship and Public Policy.

Soldo, B. J., Hurd, M. D., Rodgers, W. R., & Wallace, R. B. (1997). Asset and health dynamics among the oldest old: An overview of the AHEAD study. *Journal of Gerontology: Social Sciences, 52B,* 1–36.

Uhlenberg, P., Cooney, T., & Boyd, R. (1990). Divorce for women after midlife. *Journal of Gerontology: Social Sciences, 45,* S3–S11.

United Nations Development Programme. (1995). *Human Development Report, 1995.* New York: Oxford University Press.

Upchurch, D. M., Lillard, L. A., & Panis, C. W. A. (1995, April). *Updating women's life courses: Theoretical and methodological considerations.* Paper presented to the Population Assocation of America, San Francisco.

Waite, L. J., & Lillard, L. A. (1991). Children and marital disruption. *American Journal of Sociology, 96,* 930–956.

SECTION II

Biological and Biomedical Concepts and Theories of Aging

5

Stress Theories of Aging

Caleb E. Finch
Teresa E. Seeman

Before describing our approaches to stress theories of aging, we wish to acknowledge our great esteem for Jim Birren, whose early work laid the foundations for our present approaches to the science of aging in general and to many of the specific topics that we study, as summarized in this overview. Of fundamental importance to the neurobiology of aging, Birren and Wall (1956) did the first cell-level analysis of electrical activity in nervous tissues of rats aged 8 to 26 months. In essence, age did not impair the ion channel–dependent membrane properties of peripheral myelinated nerve fibers, as measured by the conduction velocity and its temperature coefficient during calibrated electrical stimuli in sciatic nerve. Moreover, the numbers of sciatic nerve myelinated fibers did not change with age. These findings were the first clue that, merely because a cell was nondividing for extended times after development, it need not degenerate. These conclusions have been resoundingly supported by recent careful neuron counting in human and rodent brains that distinguishes relatively modest effects of aging from larger devastations of Alzheimer's disease and vascular dementia (Rasmussen, Schliemann, Sorensen, Zimmer, & West, 1996; West, 1993; Wickelgren, 1996). There is a growing belief that neurodegeneration is an epiphenomenon of aging, as we will describe later.

In 1959, Birren's great *Handbook of Aging and the Individual* was published. This landmark volume has long enjoyed its status as one of the great

This research was supported by grants to CEF from the NIA (AG13499, AG09793) and by grants to TES from the NIA (AG00586) and the John D. and Catherine T. MacArthur Foundation Networks on Successful Aging and on Socio-economic Status and Health.

books in the field, with outstanding articles that summarized the available data and theory, from the cellular level to the entire society. This volume and his other single-authored work, *Psychology of Aging* (1964), had great influence on the senior co-author (CEF) as he began his graduate work on aging in 1965–1969. Birren was prescient among his peers of that early era in understanding how the individual was, at all points in life, subject to the interplay between biological, psychological, sociological, and other environmental forces. It was this vision that attracted the senior author to the Andrus Gerontology Center at the beginning of his career in 1972.

Recent studies have shown that the influence of genetic variants on life span and on many outcomes of aging is smaller than unexplained variance, which is, by default, environmental (Finch & Tanzi, 1997). This conclusion was anticipated by Jim Birren (1959), for example: "As a man ages . . . he manifests his particular genetic disposition and the consequences of a unique set of cumulated experiences" (p. 36). Environmental influences on outcomes of aging are extensive, ranging from stress (our focus here), to lifestyle choices of food, physical exercise, alcohol, and tobacco. These same factors can also influence the developing fetus. Moreover, the domain of prenatal environment could extend to the grand-maternal uterus because the prefertilization ovum that each of us arose from was born as a cell when our mothers were fetuses themselves (Finch & Loehlin, 1998). Thus, in terms of our cell lineage, we were already typically more than 20 years old as a prezygotic cell before incorporating our paternal genes at fertilization (Figure 5.1). The "prezygotic domain" of human life history is completely unexplored for its influences on the individual.

With the rapidly growing older population, there is increasing interest in identifying factors that influence the different patterns of disease and disability observed within older age groups (Rowe & Kahn, 1987). Neuroendocrine regulation is a central facet of human physiological competence at any age, and differential patterns of neuroendocrine response to challenge have been hypothesized to contribute importantly to observed differences in trajectories of aging (McEwen & Stellar, 1983; Sapolsky, 1992; Seeman & Robbins, 1994). The idea that cumulative levels of "stress" may have deleterious effects on health and longevity can be traced to ideas of Bernard (1978) and Cannon (1929) regarding the importance of the "milieu interieur" and homeostasis to healthy functioning. In this half of the 20th century, Selye and others showed pathological consequences of excessive physiological activation (Krantz & Manuck, 1984; Sapolsky, 1992). The hypothesis that differences in neuroendocrine reactivity might influence patterns of aging is consistent with earlier research on the possible contributions of differential reactivity to risks for hypertension or cardiovascular disease. In regard to aging, the focus is not so much on a specific disease outcome but rather on

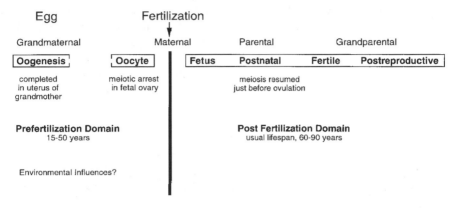

Pre- and Post Fertilization Domains of Life History: The Oocyte over Four Generations

FIGURE 5.1   The prezygotic environment, through which the unfertilized ovum (oocyte) may be subject to two distinct environments that have potential long-term and multigenerations effects on outcomes of aging. In humans, the grand-maternal environment is defined before birth of the mother, when the oocyte is generated as an individual cell in the developing ovary of the fetus. The differentiation of primary oocytes as distinct cells begins in the developing ovaries of fetuses that are about 2 months old, and it continues until about the time of birth. Oocytes in the maternal ovary could have been formed at any time in this phase, lasting 0–7 months. From Finch & Loehlin, 1998, with permission of the publisher.

the possibility that neuroendocrine reactivity might be related more generally to increased risks for disease and disability.

Stress mechanisms interact at many levels with processes of aging. We will describe age changes in the hypothalamic-pituitary-adrenal (HPA) axis, one of the body's two major regulatory systems for responding to external stressors and maintaining internal homeostatic integrity. The other key homeostatic system is the sympathetic nervous system (SNS). Specifically, we examine evidence of age-related increases in HPA dysregulation, sources of individual differences in HPA regulation, and finally, the consequences of dysregulation for health and functioning.

HPA AXIS AND AGING: DOES RESILIENCY TO STRESS CHANGE?

The possibility that changes in the regulation of the HPA axis may affect the aging process stems from the central role played by the HPA axis in the ongoing homeostatic regulatory processes of the body (McEwen & Stellar,

1983). As an individual interacts with the environment, the various stimuli encountered can serve as challenges, or "stressors," that elicit responses from the HPA axis as well as other internal homeostatic regulatory systems. There may be subtle but potentially important age changes in the dynamics of the HPA axis and other regulatory systems, resulting in impaired capacity to adapt to challenge, to maintain and/or regain homeostatic balance (Sapolsky, 1992).

A leading hypothesis posits an age-related decline in the resiliency of the HPA axis in response to challenge, with the greatest age-related changes seen in the resetting of the HPA axis poststimulation (Sapolsky, 1992). The result is a pattern of more prolonged elevation in glucocorticoids (GCs) and other hormones secreted by the HPA axis. The possible importance of such an age-related change in HPA resiliency, with prolonged elevation in GCs, stems from its potential for widespread effects on morbidity and mortality risks. HPA activation in response to challenge is designed to mobilize energy and cardiovascular functions that enhance survival during an emergency. Although essential for successful adaptation to short-term stress, more long-term, chronic exposure to increased HPA activity (with its elevations in GCs and associated increases in serum glucose and lipids, immunosuppression, and increased cardiovascular tone) has also been linked to increased risks for many age-related pathologies (e.g. cardiovascular disease, diabetes, hypertension, and cancer) (McEwen & Stellar, 1983; Sapolsky, 1992). Thus, age-related changes in HPA response to challenge, if they result in more prolonged exposure to elevated GCs, could increase risks for various types of pathology.

Studies of age-related differences in HPA function, primarily in rodents, have generally shown no age differences or slightly less response at older ages in terms of *initial* HPA stress responses (Seeman & Robbins, 1994; Sapolsky, 1992). However, most studies that examined both the initial response *and* the subsequent poststress "recovery period" reveal that older rats show more prolonged elevations in corticosterone. This decline in HPA resiliency—specifically, the prolongation of the poststress recovery phase—appears to result from decreased hypothalamic-pituitary sensitivity to negative feedback from GCs. Notably, cumulative exposure to GCs potentiates the loss of such hippocampal GC receptors.

An important target of stress is the hippocampal formation, which is a seat of declarative memory. In particular, astrocytes and neurons show extensive sensitivity to GCs with aging. This possibility was first reported by Phillip Landfield with Gary Lynch and others; they showed correlations between the numbers of fibrous (hypertrophied) astrocytes in the hippocampus of aging rats and the elevations of plasma corticosterone (Landfield, Rose, Sandles, Wohlstadter, & Lynch, 1977; Landfield, Waymire, & Lynch, 1978). Elevations of plasma corticosterone are generally observed in aging laboratory rats and include increases of free corticosterone (i.e., not bound to corticosterone binding protein) (Sabatino, Masoro, McMahan, & Kuhn, 1991). Much subsequent work by Landfield (1994), Sapolsky (1992), and McEwen (1992), among others, supports the concept that elevated GCs are associated with age-related neurodegeneration, particularly in the hippocampus.

Astrocyte activation during aging was initially characterized by metal stains that recognized the fibrous or reactive astrocyte phenotype (Landfield et al., 1977). Among the cytoplasmic constituents of fibrous astrocytes is the intermediate filament structural protein glial fibrillary acidic protein (GFAP), which is now established as a general marker for aging in mammalian brains. Progressively during aging, GFAP mRNA and protein increase in many brain regions of rodents and humans. The increases of GFAP mRNA per cell reach two– to three–fold by the life span but are detected by midlife, which is long before any indication of neuronal degeneration (Goss, Finch, & Morgan, 1990, 1991; Kohama, Goss, Finch, & McNeill, 1995; Nichols, Day, Laping, Johnson, & Finch, 1993; Morgan, Rozovsky, Goldsmith, Stone, & Finch, 1997).

Because GFAP is known to be posttranscriptionally regulated, a major question is whether the increase of GFAP expression is transcriptional. Initial efforts with a nuclear run-on assay showed a trend for increased transcription, which was not significant. However, the Finch laboratory showed that the increases of GFAP mRNA during aging are due to increased gene transcription, as found in a subpopulation of "hot astrocytes" (Morgan et al., 1997; Yoshida et al., 1996). The age-related increase of GFAP transcription is opposite to the more generally expected trend for decreased transcription, as reported for several genes expressed in the liver (Finch & Morgan, 1990).

Complex interactions of GCs with neurons may explain the paradox of GC association with hippocampal astrocytosis despite the evidence that diet restriction, which slows astrocytosis, also elevate GCs. In primary astrocyte cultures, GCs *induce* GFAP transcription (Rozovsky, Laping, O'Callaghan, & Finch, 1995), which would appear to compound the paradox. However, if co-cultured with neurons and astrocytes, then GCs *inhibit* GFAP transcription (Rozovsky et al., 1995), which is the *inhibitory* direction of response to GCs observed in vivo (Nichols et al., 1988; Nichols, Masters, & Finch, 1994; Nichols, Osterburg, Masters, Millar, & Finch, 1990).

Nonhuman primates show important parallels to the above rodent data regarding the association between age and more chronically elevated GC levels, increased HPA activity, and hippocampal degeneration but also show impaired immune and cognitive function (McEwen & Sapolsky, 1995; Sapolsky, 1992). Similarities have also been noted between pathologies observed in aging (e.g., diabetes, cardiovascular degeneration) and those seen in rats in response to excessive GC exposure (e.g., from exogenous GC administration or extreme social stress) (Sapolsky, 1992). Vervet monkeys that were exposed to chronic social stress showed extensive loss of neurons in the hippocampus (Uno, Tarara, Else, Suleman, & Sapolsky, 1989). An attempt to prove that GCs were the primary agents in this complex pathology, however, gave perplexing results. Implantation of cortisol pellets in the hippocampus of unstressed vervet monkeys caused neuron atrophy with perikaryal shrinkage in the GC-vulnerable CA2–CA3 regions (Sapolsky, Uno, Rebert, & Finch, 1990). Consistent with these mild effects, no gliosis or neuron death was obvious. Although this result appears to conflict with many studies showing cytotoxic effects of GCs on rodent neurons in vivo and in vitro, we suggest that local or systemic elevations of GCs may be necessary but not sufficient for neurotoxicity. Other factors found in socially stressed vervets that would not be produced by the stereotaxic cortisol could include systemic pathophysiological disturbances from impaired digestive and kidney functions and chronic autonomic arousal.

Data on humans show intriguing similarities to those on rodents and nonhuman primates. Studies of basal, nonstimulated HPA function have shown no age-related change or nonsignificant increases in corticotropin (ACTH) or serum cortisol at older ages (Seeman & Robbins, 1994). Data on patterns of HPA response to challenge also suggest little change with age in patterns of initial cortisol response to ACTH, dexamethasone, metyrapone, insulin-induced hypoglycemia, and corticotropin releasing hormone (CRH) challenge. The postchallenge recovery or resetting of the HPA axis, however, suggests that there may be age-related prolongations of the HPA axis response to ACTH, metyrapone, and CRH challenge.

Individual Differences in Patterns of HPA Regulation and Reactivity

Although much of the research on age-related changes in the HPA axis has focused on the axis itself—its "usual" characteristics, its patterns of response to challenge, and how these may change with age—observed interindividual differences in HPA responses to various stimuli suggest that individuals' psychological and/or social characteristics also play a significant role in modulating patterns of response to challenge (Seeman & McEwen, 1966). This is not surprising: the HPA axis does not operate in a vacuum but rather is responsive to external stimuli through the cognitions and interpretations we make about the stimuli. Notably, individual differences in reactivity appear to be fairly stable characteristics, suggesting that these differential patterns of neuroendocrine response are likely experienced repeatedly (perhaps throughout a lifetime) as the individual interacts with his or her environment. Over time, these different patterns of neuroendocrine response could lead to major individual variations in neuroendocrine aging as well as age-related risks for disease and disability (Sapolsky, 1992; Seeman & Robbins, 1994).

Gender and Reactivity

Gender differences in HPA reactivity might contribute to observed gender differences in morbidity and mortality. The HPA axis has widespread effects on nearly every bodily system. Evidence from rodent studies on sex differences in HPA basal activity is mixed, with some studies showing no effect of gender and others showing higher levels of activity in females (Seeman, Singer, & Charpentier, 1995). However, gender differences in patterns of response to challenge are more consistent with females exhibiting greater corticosterone response to challenges such as ether, ACTH, and restraint and greater ACTH response to challenge (e.g., ether or restraint). Females also show faster increase in ACTH and corticosterone in response to such stressors.

Data from humans indicate gender differences in HPA axis and sympathetic nervous system response to challenge, although the pattern of gender differences appears somewhat more complex than that seen in rodent models. Consistent with the rodent models, gender differences in reactivity become most apparent after puberty. There are several notable differences. First, under basal conditions, humans generally do not differ betweeen the sexes in cortisol levels at adult ages from 20 to 90 years old (Seeman, Singer, et al., 1995). However, one study of older men and women (aged 62–83) found significantly higher cortisol levels among the women (Greenspan, Rowe, Maitland, McAloon-Dyke, & Elahi, 1993). Second, with respect to patterns of response to challenge, whereas the rodent data indicate a consistent female excess (regardless of age), the human data suggest a possible age-related shift in observed gender differences. At younger ages, males more consistently exhibit greater sympathetic nervous system reactivity as indexed by blood pressure and catecholamines (Stoney, 1992). Data on possible gender differences in HPA axis reactivity at younger ages are more mixed, with some studies showing greater cortisol response among men while others report no significant gender differences (Seeman, Singer, et al., 1995).

Data on age-related alterations in patterns of diurnal plasma cortisol activity suggest, however, that women exhibit larger age-related increases in cortisol secretion. Specifically, postmenopausal women exhibit a shorter nocturnal nadir (i.e., period of lowest cortisol activity), higher morning acrophase (i.e., period of greatest cortisol activity) and higher overall mean 24-hour blood cortisol levels (van Cauter, Leproult, & Kupfer, 1995). Women may also experience a similarly greater age-related shift toward increased HPA axis response to challenge. Studies of older men and postmenopausal women show an intriguing pattern of greater HPA axis reactivity among women in response to corticotropin releasing hormone and to physostigmine, a centrally active cholinesterase inhibitor (Seeman, Singer, et al., 1995). There is a similar pattern of greater HPA reactivity in older women in response to a more naturalistic, "driving simulation" challenge (Seeman, Singer, et al., 1995). Moreover, postmenopausal women exhibit less feedback inhibition in response to cortisol infusion following metyrapone administration (i.e., showing a blunted ACTH decline) than do younger, premenopausal women and older men (Wilkinson, Peskind, & Raskind, 1996).

The possible role of reproductive hormones such as estrogen in this apparent age-related shift toward greater relative HPA axis reactivity among postmenopausal women is suggested by several lines of evidence. First, variations in estrogen levels have been linked to altered reactivity, periods of higher estrogen being associated with less reactivity (Marinari, Leshner, & Doyle, 1976; Stoney, 1992). Second, estrogen replacement therapy (ERT) has been related to reductions in blood pressure responses to challenge (Stoney, 1992). A study comparing pre-and postmenopausal women also found an association of ERT with a blunting of cortisol responses during cognitive and physical stress tests (Lindheim et al., 1992). These various findings suggest that the presence of estrogen may contribute to reduced cortisol reactivity through mechanisms that protect and promote negative feedback within the HPA axis. Indeed, one might speculate that the greater cumulative exposure to elevated GCs and the physiological sequelae of increased HPA reactivity postmenopause could contribute to the known increased risks among such postmenopausal women for congestive heart disease, diabetes, hypertension, and upper-abdominal obesity (McEwen & Stellar, 1983).

Psychosocial Factors and Reactivity

Growing evidence also indicates that psychological and social factors influence patterns of endocrine reactivity. Two classes of psychosocial factors, social integration and personal control beliefs, have frequently been singled out as important to health and aging (Henry, 1988; Rowe & Kahn, 1987). The centrality of these factors to patterns of aging is hypothesized to result from their association with basic, instinctually determined patterns of behavior. Social bonding and the desire for control are hypothesized to influence health and aging, in part via modulation of neuroendocrine response (Henry, 1988). Such modulation may result from the effects of social and psychological characteristics on cognitive-emotional interpretations of stimuli, which then influence neuroendocrine responses via neocortical and limbic centers (Seeman & McEwen, 1996).

Perceptions of personal control, for example, can attenuate neuroendocrine response to challenge (Houston, 1972). The Type A behavior pattern (which has been linked to perceived threats to personal control) is also associated with greater HPA axis and SNS activity (Krantz & Manuck, 1984; Williams, Suarez, Kuhn, Zimmerman, & Schanberg, 1991). Type A's increased reactivity may become more marked with age (Williams et al., 1991), a finding that is consistent with the hypothesis that the consequences of differential neuroendocrine reactivity become more apparent with time, as differences in the extent of "wear and tear" on the neuroendocrine regulatory mechanisms cumulate. Psychological characteristics reflecting self-esteem (Seeman, Berkman, et al., 1995), self-efficacy (Bandura, Taylor, Williams, Mefford, & Barchas, 1985) and positive self-concept (Kirschbaum, Wolf, May, Wippich, & Hellhammer, 1996) also predict reduced reactivity.

Social environment characteristics also have positive and negative effects on patterns of physiological response to challenge. Contact with others of the same species has been associated with reduced physiological arousal in response to stressors, and both dominant social status in a stable social environment and "social skills" have been associated with lower basal cortisols and less coronary atherosclerosis (Seeman & McEwen, 1996). By contrast, social stress (exemplified by subordinate status or dominant social status in an unstable social environment) has been associated with increased cortisol levels, increased HPA axis response to challenge, increased hippocampal damage, and greater coronary atherosclerosis. Among humans, the presence of a companion can decrease physiological stress responses, whereas interpersonal challenge has been shown to be a potent stimulus for increased SNS activity. Higher emotional support also predicts lower urinary cortisol and catecholamine levels in men. These associations of social support and personal control, with attenuations of endocrine response to challenge, suggest that individuals who enjoy greater support and/or greater sense of personal control may experience less cumulative exposure to the wear and tear of HPA and SNS activation, resulting in decreased risks of impaired neuroendocrine resiliency at older ages. If so, this may be one mechanism by which such psychosocial factors protect against risks for various forms of morbidity and mortality.

CONSEQUENCES OF ENDOCRINE DYSREGULATION

Significant health consequences of exposure to cortisol include increased risks for many cognitive and physical impairments that are commonly associated with older ages (e.g. atherosclerosis, hypertension, diabetes, hyperlipidemia, osteoporosis, reduced immune function, and cognitive deficits (McEwen & Sapolsky, 1995; Seeman & Robbins, 1994). Studies comparing patterns of HPA axis response to challenge in healthy versus patient populations also provide indirect evidence that declines in HPA axis resiliency may be associated with worse trajectories of aging. Patients with diabetes, hypertension, cancer, coronary artery disease, and depression exhibit more prolonged cortisol responses and greater escape from suppression by GCs or glucose. Cross-sectional, patient-nonpatient comparisons such as these do not, of course, indicate whether those with such diseases actually exhibited declines in HPA resiliency prior to the onset of the disease. Nonetheless, these data provide preliminary, though indirect confirmation of a possible association between HPA resiliency and the presence of such pathology.

Glucocorticoids (cortisol in humans, corticosterone in rodents) have significant effects on cognition (McEwen & Sapolsky, 1995). Both animal and human studies indicate that exposure to elevated levels of GCs can have detrimental effects on cognitive performance, particularly learning and memory. Dysregulation of the HPA axis, where there is increased exposure of the hippocampus to elevated GC levels, has been postulated to increase risk of decline in memory capacity. The central role of the hippocampus reflects its known role in aspects of learning and memory in rodents and humans and also the fact that it is a brain area extremely rich in adrenal steroid receptors; circulating adrenal steroids can easily cross the blood-brain barrier and reach the receptors.

Patient and healthy volunteer populations show negative associations between cortisol levels and memory (Seeman, McEwen, Albert, & Rowe, 1997). Administration of corticosteroids, as well as stress-induced elevations, reduced performance on tests of verbal memory (Kirschbaum et al., 1996). Moreover, a study of 19 healthy subjects, aged 60 to 87 years, showed links between longitudinal patterns of change in cortisol activity and memory performance at older ages (Lupien et al. 1994). Subjects were assessed annually on the basis of 24-hour "basal, non-stimulated" cortisol levels. Subjects who exhibited a pattern of increasing cortisol levels over the 4-year follow-up exhibited poorer memory performance at the end of the 4–year period, especially on a test of explicit/verbal memory.

Analyses of data from the MacArthur Successful Aging Study, a large community-based cohort of older men and women aged 70 to 79, revealed similar associations between increases in 12-hour urinary free cortisol excretion over a 2.5-year follow-up and declines in verbal memory (Seeman et al., 1997). The observed pattern showed a specific association between increases in cortisol and declines in delayed recall of a story. This observation is consistent with earlier reports from Lupien et al. (1994), who found that increasing plasma cortisol levels predicted declines in verbal memory but not visual reproduction, digit span, or divided attention. These patterns of association are also consistent with the hypothesis that higher levels of cortisol may be associated with increased risk of damage to the hippocampus, a brain region heavily involved in memory performance.

Notably, the association between cortisol and memory was strongest among the women in the MacArthur Successful Aging cohort ($r = -.33$, $p < .0001$, vs. $r = -.04$, for the men); women appeared to be somewhat more likely to exhibit increases in cortisol over time. These data appear to be consistent with those of Lupien et al. (1994). Although no formal tests for gender differences were performed in that study, the data indicate that women were more likely to exhibit the detrimental pattern of increasing cortisol: 50% of the women versus 36% of the men (Lupien et al., 1994). The predicted links are found between higher cortisol levels and smaller hippocampal volume in both normal controls and patients with Alzheimer's disease (McEwen & Sapolsky, 1995; Seeman & Robbins, 1994), and links between smaller hippocampal volume and poorer memory performance are found in healthy, cognitively normal older people.

PROMOTING SUCCESSFUL AGING: ARE PATTERNS OF ENDOCRINE REGULATION MODIFIABLE?

In light of this evidence indicating the potentially detrimental effects of greater endocrine reactivity on age-related risks for pathology, what can be done to counteract such risks? There are several lines of evidence suggesting that (a) aging per se is not uniformly associated with increased pathology and (b) patterns of endocrine reactivity that may contribute to increased risk of pathology are themselves modifiable. Besides the manipulation of glial aging by steroid hormones described above, glial aging is also retarded by diet restriction in rodents. In studies, rodents are given about 35% less than *ad libitum* food intake. As a result, diet-restricted rodents show slowed aging processes, with delayed onset of gross pathology and increased life spans. In parallel, the age-related increase in the activity of the astrocyte gene GFAP (see above) is slowed in the hippocampus of diet restricted rats (Morgan et al., 1997; Nichols, Finch, & Nelson, 1995). Because diet restriction causes an increase of plasma GCs (Sabatino et al., 1991), these finding pose a paradox to the earlier data that fibrous astrocytosis in the hippocampus of aging rats is associated with elevated corticosterone (Landfield et al., 1977; Landfield, Waymire, & Lynch, 1978). The resolution of this paradox may be found by understanding the transcriptional controls of GFAP.

Although age may indeed be associated with an increased prevalence of prolonged patterns of HPA response to challenge, aging per se is unlikely to be uniformly associated with such changes in HPA resiliency. Older age groups exhibit substantial heterogeneity in their relative burdens of morbidity and disability, indicating that increases in morbidity and disability are neither uniform nor inevitable consequences of aging (Rowe & Kahn, 1987). Such heterogeneity would suggest that aging may not be associated with uniform changes in HPA function either. Rather, aging can be hypothesized to be associated with heterogeneous patterns of change in HPA function with some individuals experiencing substantial change and others maintaining patterns of HPA function that are more like those of younger individuals. Thus, although age may be associated with an increased risk of diminished HPA resiliency, such declines would not be a uniform feature of the aging process.

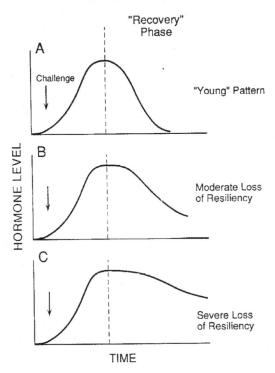

LEVELS OF RESILIENCY

FIGURE 5.2   Age-related change in patterns of response to challenge. Pattern A reflects an optimum of adequate response and efficient recovery. Patterns B and C illustrate progressively greater degrees of dysregulation, with growing failure to shut off
the response, even though the challenging stimulus was ended.

We hypothesize that the risk of decline in HPA resiliency with age is
related to lifelong, cumulative exposures to GCs. We also acknowledge that
other factors such as genetic endowment, initial number of hippocampal
GC receptors, and diet would be expected to influence this process as well.
Individuals with greater net GC exposure would be at increased risk for
decline, older age being the time when such declines in HPA resiliency become manifest. Some older individuals would thus develop a pattern of
prolonged HPA response, whereas others would maintain better HPA resiliency. Figure 5.2 illustrates some of the patterns of HPA resiliency that might
be observed in response to a challenge. Pattern A depicts good resiliency; it
would be most common at younger ages, where maximal resiliency is the
norm. Pattern B is associated with some minimal to moderate decline in
HPA resiliency (e.g., perhaps representing that seen at older ages among

those with less exposure to GCs). Pattern C represents that seen among older individuals experiencing substantial declines in HPA resiliency.

Data from the study of ACTH and cortisol response to a driving simulation test (Greenspan et al., 1993; Seeman, Berkman, et al., 1995) illustrate these differential patterns and their associations with both age and health. Data from the driving simulation test illustrate Patterns A and B, showing a possible effect of age rather than health status on HPA axis resiliency. In contrast to earlier studies using pharmacological challenges, we used a driving simulation as a more realistic type of challenge. The driving simulation, with its attendant requirements for responses to varied and sometimes dangerous situations, represented a challenge that all of our subjects actually deal with in their daily lives (i.e., driving a car). Preliminary data revealed that older "healthy" subjects (aged 70–79) had more prolonged cortisol responses, with levels remaining elevated above baseline after 2 hours (e.g., Pattern B). By contrast, younger individuals (aged 30–39) showed a rapid return to baseline before the end of the 2-hour follow-up period (e.g., Pattern A). The contrast between Patterns B and C can been seen in the study by Greenspan et al. (1993), which showed that older subjects with diabetes or high blood pressure had greater response to a CRF challenge than did older "healthy" subjects. These data suggest that there is heterogeneity within older age groups in terms of their patterns of HPA response to CRF and other challenges.

As a corollary to our hypothesis that those with greater cumulative exposure to GCs will be at highest risk for decline in HPA resiliency, we also hypothesize that they will exhibit increased prevalence of common, age-related diseases such as atherosclerosis, diabetes, and cancer. As indicated earlier, though short-term HPA activation in response to a challenging stimulus is clearly beneficial, more chronic exposure to elevated GCs and their physiological sequelae (e.g., increases in blood pressure, serum lipids, glucose, and immunosuppression) has been associated with increased risks for common age-related pathology such as atherosclerosis, diabetes, and cancer. The possible link between such age-related pathology and changes in HPA function is suggested by the patterns of more prolonged cortisol elevations in response to stimulation or greater escape from dexamethasone or glucose suppression seen among individuals with such conditions as compared to those without (see Seeman and Robbins, 1994 for review).

Evidence from observational studies also indicate that individual differences in diet and psychosocial characteristics (Seeman & McEwen, 1996) are associated with differences in HPA and SNS reactivity, and all of these are potentially modifiable characteristics. Future studies may reveal a hierarchy of response threshold to these counteracting regulators of gene activity in astrocytes. For example, co-culture of astrocytes with neurons inverts the transcriptional response of the GFAP gene to GCs. Therefore, we posit that there is some level of neuron dysfunction during aging that will stimulate activation of contiguous astrocytes more than any inhibitory effect of age-or disease-related GC elevations. This model would explain why GFAP elevations are found during aging in mice, which, unlike rats, have little or no increases of GCs during aging (see above). This model would also explain why diet restriction delays the increase of GFAP during aging, despite the elevations of GCs, if there is also maintenance of neuronal function by diet restriction, as appears to be the case (reviewed in Morgan et al., 1997).

The mechanisms by which diet restriction maintains neuron functions during aging could be numerous. A working hypothesis is that the lowered blood glucose of diet-restricted rats slows glycooxidative damage to extracellular macromolecules and therefore reduces the oxidative stress on neurons and glia. Hormone-metabolism interactions are fundamental to aging processes in many species of animals and plants (Finch & Rose, 1995), as well as in Alzheimer's disease and other neurodegenerative conditions of aging (Finch & Cohen, 1997).

Experimental data also suggest that interventions to promote regular exercise for older adults can result in more optimal endocrine regulation. For example, a 6-month program of moderate exercise was shown to result in more efficient insulin response and glucose regulation following a glucose-tolerance test challenge. Data such as these suggest that patterns of endocrine reactivity and regulation are potentially modifiable, suggesting that age-related changes toward less efficient regulation and its associated increased risks for various types of pathology need not be an inevitable consequence of the aging process.

Future research is needed to explore the extent to which endocrine regulation can be optimally maintained with aging. It is likely that no single intervention will be universally effective to maintain optimal responses to stress. It seems more likely that hormonal, nutritional, and drug treatments will be optimized for the individual in the context of daily activities. Moreover, we will come to appreciate more about the early developmental influences on outcomes of aging. Some influences may even precede fertilization, because the egg cell from which we grew was formed in our mother's ovary while she resided in our grand-maternal fetus. As we learn more about factors that protect against age-related declines in endocrine regulatory efficiency, it should be possible to achieve major enhancement of successful outcomes in aging for greater numbers of people.

REFERENCES

Bandura, A., Taylor, C. B., Williams, S. L., Mefford, I. N., & Barchas, J. D. (1985). Catecholamine secretion as a function of perceived coping self-efficacy. *Journal of Consulting and Clinical Psychology, 53,* 406–414.

Bernard, C. (1978). *Les phenomenes de la vie* (Vol 1). Paris: Librarie J-B Baillier et Fils.

Birren, J. E. (Ed.). (1959). *Handbook of aging and the individual.* Chicago: University of Chicago Press.

Birren, J. E. (1964). *The psychology of aging.* Englewood Cliffs, NJ: Prentice-Hall.

Birren, J. E., & Wall, P. D. (1956). Age changes in conduction velocity, refractory period, number of fibers, and blood vessels in sciatic nerve of rats. *Journal of Comparative Neurology, 104,* 1–16.

Cannon, W. (1929). The wisdom of the body. *Physiological Reviews, 9,* 399–431.

Finch, C. E., & Cohen, D. M. (1997). Aging, metabolism, and Alzheimer disease: Review and hypotheses. *Experimental Neurology, 143,* 82–102.

Finch, C. E., & Loehlin, J. (1998). Environmental influences that may precede fertilization: A first examination of the prezygotic hypothesis from maternal age influences on twins. *Behavior Genetics, 28,* 101–106.

Finch, C. E., & Morgan, D. G. (1990). RNA and protein metabolism in the aging brain. *Annual Review of Neuroscience, 13,* 75–87.

Finch, C. E., & Rose, M. R. (1995). Hormones and the physiological architecture of life history evolution. *Quarterly Review of Biology, 70,* 1–52.

Finch, C. E., & Tanzi, R. E. (1997). The genetics of aging. *Science, 278,* 407–411.

Goss, J. R., Finch, C. E., & Morgan, D. G. (1990). GFAP RNA prevalence is increased in aging and in wasting mice. *Experimental Neurology, 108,* 266–268.

Goss, J. R., Finch, C. E., & Morgan, D. G. (1991). Age-related changes in glial fibrillary acid protein mRNA in the mouse brain. *Neurobiology of Aging, 12,* 165–170.

Greenspan, S. L., Rowe, J. W., Maitland, L. A., McAloon-Dyke, M., & Elahi, D.(1993). The pituitary-adrenal glucocorticoid response is altered by gender and disease. *Journals of Gerontology: Clinical Medicine, 48,* M72–M77.

Henry, J. P. (1988). The archetypes of power and intimacy. In J. E. Birren & V. L. Bengtson (Eds.), *Emergent theories of aging* (pp. 269–298.). New York: Springer Publishing Co.

Houston, B. K. (1972). Control over stress, locus of control, and response to stress. *Journal of Personality and Social Psychology, 21,* 249–255.

Kirschbaum, C., Wolf, O. T., May, M., Wippich, W., & Hellhammer, D. H. (1996). Stress- and treatment-induced elevations of cortisol levels associated with impaired declarative memory in healthy adults. *Life Sciences, 58,* 1475–1483.

Kohama, S. G., Goss, J. R., Finch, C. E., & McNeill, T. H. (1995). Increases of glial fibrillary acidic protein in the aging female mouse brain. *Neurobiology of Aging, 16,* 59–67.

Krantz, D. S., & Manuck, S. B. (1984). Acute psychophysiologic reactivity and risk of cardiovascular disease: A review and methodologic critique. *Psychological Bulletin, 96,* 435–464.

Landfield, P. W. (1994). The role of glucocorticoids in brain aging and Alzheimer's disease: An integrative physiological hypothesis (Nathan Shock Memorial Lecture 1990). *Experimental Gerontology, 29,* 3–11.

Landfield, P. W., Rose, G., Sandles, L., Wohlstadter, T. C, & Lynch, G. (1977). Patterns of astroglial hypertrophy and neuronal degeneration in the hippocampus of aged, memory-deficient rats. *Journals of Gerontology, 32,* 3–12.

Landfield, P. W., Waymire, J. L., & Lynch, G. (1978). Hippocampal aging and adrenocorticoids: Quantitative correlations. *Science, 202,* 1098–1102.

Lindheim, S. R., Legro, R. S., Bernstein, L. , Stanczyk, F. Z., Vijod, M. A., Presser, S. C., & Lobo, R. A.. (1992). Behavioral stress responses in premenopausal and postmenopausal women and the effects of estrogen. *American Journal of Obstetrics and Gynecology, 167,* 1831–1836.

Lupien, S., Lecours, A. R., Lussier, I., Schwartz, G., Nair, N. P. V., & Meaney, M. J. (1994). Basal cortisol levels and cognitive deficits in human aging. *Journal of Neuroscience, 14,* 2893–2903.

Marinari, K. T., Leshner, A. I., & Doyle, M. P. (1976). Menstrual cycle status and adrenocortical reactivity to psychological stress. *Psychoneuroendocrinology, 1,* 213–218.

McEwen, B. S. (1992). Re-examination of the glucocorticoid hypothesis of stress and aging. *Progress in Brain Research, 93,* 365–383.

McEwen, B. S. , & Sapolsky, R. M. (1995). Stress and cognitive function. *Current Opinion in Neurobiology, 5,* 205–216.

McEwen, B. S., & Stellar, E. (1983). Stress and the individual: Mechanisms leading to disease. *Archives of Internal Medicine, 153,* 2093–2101.

Morgan, T. E., Rozovsky, I., Goldsmith, S. K., Stone, D. J., Yoshida, T., & Finch, C. E. (1997). Increased transcription of the astrocyte gene GFAP during middle-age is attenuated by food restriction: Implications for the role of oxidative stress. *Free Radical Biology and Medicine, 23,* 524–528.

Nichols, N. R., Day, J. R., Laping, N. J., Johnson, S. A., & Finch, C. E. (1993). GFAP mRNA increases with age in rat and human brain. *Neurobiology of Aging, 14,* 421–429.

Nichols, N. R., Lerner, S. P., Masters, J. N., May, P. C., Millar, S. L., & Finch, C. E. (1988). Rapid corticosterone-induced changes in gene expression in rat hippocampus display Type II glucocorticoid receptor specificity. *Molecular Endocrinology, 2,* 284–290.

Nichols, N. R., Masters, J. N., & Finch, C. E. (1994). Cloning of steroid-responsive mRNAs by differential hybridization. In R. de Kloet and W. Sutanto (Eds.), *Neurobiology of Steroids, Meth Neuroscience, Vol. 22,* (pp. 296–313). San Diego, CA: Academic Press.

Nichols, N. R., Osterburg, H. H., Masters, J. N., Millar, S. L., & Finch, C. E. (1990). Messenger RNA for glial fibrillary acidic protein is decreased in rat brain following acute and chronic corticosterone treatment. *Molecular Brain Research, 7,* 1–7.

Rasmussen, T., Schliemann, T., Sorensen, J. C., Zimmer, J. & West, M. J. (1996). Memory impaired aged rats: No loss of principal hippocampal and subicular neurons. *Neurobiology of Aging, 17,* 143–147.

Rowe, J. W., & Kahn, R. L. (1987). Human aging: Usual and successful. *Science, 237,* 143–149.

Rozovsky, I., Laping, N. J., O'Callaghan, J. P., & Finch, C. (1995) Transcriptional regulation of GFAP expression by corticosterone in vitro is influenced by the duration of time in culture and by neuron-astrocyte interactions. *Endocrinology, 136,* 2066–2073.

Sabatino, F,, Masoro, E. J., McMahan, C. A., & Kuhn, R. W. (1991). Assessment of the role of glucocorticoid system in aging processes and in the action of food restriction. *Journals of Gerontology: Biological Sciences, 46,* B171–179..

Sapolsky, R. M. (1992). *Stress, the aging brain, and the mechanisms of neuron death.* Cambridge, MA: MIT Press.

Sapolsky, R. M., Uno. H., Rebert, C. S., & Finch, C. E. (1990). Hippocampal damage associated with prolonged glucocorticoid exposure in primates. *Journal of Neuroscience, 10,* 2897–2902.

Seeman, T. E., Berkman, L. F., Gulanski, B. I., Robbins, R. J, Greenspan, S. L., Charpentier, P. A, & Rowe, J. W (1995). Self-esteem and neuroendocrine response to challenge: MacArthur Studies of Successful Aging. *Psychosomatic Research, 39,* 69–84.

Seeman, T. E., & McEwen, B. S. (1996). Impact of social environment characteristics and neuroendocrine regulation. *Psychosomatic Medicine, 58,* 459–471.

Seeman, T. E., McEwen, B. S., Albert, M. S., & Rowe, J. W. (1997). Urinary cortisol and decline in memory performance in older adults: MacArthur Studies of Successful Aging. *Journal of Clinical Endocrinology and Metabolism, 82,* 2458–2465.

Seeman, T. E., & Robbins, R. J. (1994). Aging and hypothalamic-pituitary-adrenal axis response to challenge in humans. *Endocrine Reviews, 15,* 233–260.

Seeman, T. E., Singer, B., & Charpentier, P. A. (1995). Gender differences in HPA response to challenge: MacArthur studies of successful aging. *Psychoneuroendocrinology, 20,* 711–725.

Stoney, C. M. (1992). The role of reproductive hormones in cardiovascular and neuroendocrine function during behavioral stress. In J. R. Turner, A. Sherwood, & K. C. Light (Eds.), *Individual differences in cardiovascular response to stress* (pp 147–163). New York: Plenum Press.

Uno, H., Tarara, R., Else, J., Suleman, M., & Sapolsky, R. M. (1989). Hippocampal damage associated with prolonged and fatal stress in primates. *Journal of Neuroscience, 9,* 1705–1711.

van Cauter, E., Leproult, R., & Kupfer, D. J. (1995). Effects of gender and age on the levels and circadian rhythmicity of plasma cortisol. *Journal of Clinical Endocrinology and Metabolism, 81,* 2468–2473.

West, M. J. (1993). Regionally specific loss of neurons in the aging human hippocampus. *Neurobiology of Aging, 14,* 287–293.

Wickelgren, I. (1996). Is hippocampal cell death a myth? *Science, 271,* 1229–1230.

Wilkinson, C. W., Peskind, E. R., & Raskind, M. A. (1996). Decreased hypothalamic-pituitary-adrenal axis sensitivity to cortisol feedback inhibition in human aging. *Neuroendocrinology, 65,* 679–690.

Williams, R. B., Jr., Suarez, E. C., Kuhn, C. M., Zimmerman, E. A., & Schanberg, S. M. (1991). Biobehavioral basis of coronary-prone behavior in middle-aged men: Part 1. Evidence for chronic SNS activation in Type A. *Psychosomatic Medicine, 53,* 517–527.

Yoshida, T., Goldsmith, S., Morgan, T. E., Stone, D., & Finch, C. E. (1996). Transcription supports age-related increases of GFAP gene expression in the male rat brain. *Neuroscience Letters, 215,* 107–110.

6

Biological Theories of Senescence

Vincent J. Cristofalo
Maria Tresini
Mary Kay Francis
Craig Volker

With the passage of time, organisms undergo progressive physiological deterioration that results in increased vulnerability to stress and an increased probability of death. This phenomenon is commonly referred to as aging, but as aging can refer to any time-related process, a more correct term is *senescence*. Most gerontologists would argue that there is no single cause, mechanism, or basis for senescence. Indeed, roughly 300 different theories have been proposed to explain the phenomenon (Medvedev, 1990). In this review we briefly discuss the salient points of several of the more commonly espoused theories of senescence and conclude with a discussion of cellular senescence, a major research interest in our laboratory.

EVOLUTION OF SENESCENCE AND LONGEVITY

One of the major theoretical advances in the past 10 years or so has been the consensus among most gerontologists that senescence is the result of the declining force of natural selection. Just as evolution has provided a unifying theme for biology, so the evolutionary biology of aging has provided a unifying theme for biological gerontology and has brought gerontology into the mainstream of biology. It has provided a realistic answer to the question, Why do we age? And it has given some clues to the biological mechanisms that orchestrate the phenomenon. This theoretical analysis has now allowed researchers to analyze empirical data on senescence within the tenets of this central theme. We believe this theoretical development has provided a major step forward in biological gerontology.

The deterioration that occurs with age is clearly not beneficial to the individual organism; yet the mechanism for biological evolution is mutation and natural selection. A key question is, Why should evolution have selected for a negative property?

In the wild, where most individuals succumb to predation, debilitating injury, disease, lack of nutrition, environmental factors, and so on, it seems unnecessary for an organism to invest substantial resources in repair and maintenance processes so as to prevent all physiological deterioration. Rather, it seems likely that an organism might instead invest its resources so that the rate of physiological deterioration does not interfere with the organism's ability to optimize reproduction during its anticipated life span.

Senescence and longevity are molded along with other traits as a species evolves to fill its niche. These characteristics are highly plastic, and animals live to widely different ages. For example, humans have a maximum life span of about 120 years, mice have a maximum life span of about 3 years, the European shrew has a maximum life span of only 3 months, and mayflies live only a day.

The physiological traits of an organism are manifest in that organism's DNA. The DNA encodes a variety of proteins that are made up of a string of amino acids. As organisms evolve, their DNA bases change. Some of these changes can result in changes to the sequence of amino acids in the string. As a result, differences between various organisms in DNA and amino acids in proteins give an indication of how closely related they are. For example, humans and chimpanzees are very closely related and have not evolved even a single amino acid difference in proteins such as hemoglobin and cytochrome *c* (Zwilling, 1992). Yet they have markedly evolved at least a twofold difference in life span. Even within the same species, specific populations have evolved different life spans. For example, an island population of Virginia opossums that is insulated from predators ages more slowly than an adjacent mainland population (Austad, 1997).

Evolutionary theory predicts that if an organism has a reduced chance of death from predation, that organism may evolve an increased life span. This is because, as threat of predation diminishes, traits that are beneficial for an organism to thrive and reproduce in old age have an increased selective pressure. In fact, animals protected from predation tend to have longer maximum life spans. Some animals with relatively long maximum life spans have shells (e.g., turtles, lobsters, and bivalves) or quills (e.g., porcupines) that protect them from predators. Similarly, animals that can fly away from predators, such as bats and birds, generally have longer maximum life spans than other animals of a similar size. Flight has other advantages and can be useful for migration and the search for food, but it also increases metabolic demand.

STOCHASTIC VERSUS PROGRAMMED THEORIES OF SENESCENCE

Most theories of senescence may be grouped into two general classes. Stochastic theories postulate that senescence is primarily the result of random damage, whereas programmed theories postulate that developmental/genetic processes direct senescence. Many theories incorporate aspects of both classes.

It is clear that species-specific developmental/genetic factors play a role in longevity. For example, the maximum life spans of different species vary widely (Comfort, 1979; Hakeem, Rodriguez-Sandoval, Jones, & Allman, 1996). Furthermore, although different species may share some common senescence mechanisms, the manifestations of senescence differ among species. Senescent mechanisms that operate over a large diversity of organisms have been termed "public" mechanisms, and those that are idiosyncratic of specific species have been termed "private" mechanisms (Martin, Austad, & Johnson, 1996). For example, the most common causes of death of elderly humans in industrial countries are vascular diseases (ischemic heart disease and cerebrovascular disease) and malignancies (Smith, 1993), whereas the primary causes of death in laboratory rodents are strain-dependent and include renal failure and malignancies not generally associated with death in humans (Adams & Cory, 1991; Yu, Masoro, Murata, Bertrand, & Lynd, 1982). Yet the observations that individual members of a species die of various causes over a range of ages, that identical twins do not die at identical times, and that environmental factors can shorten life span argue that stochastic events are important. In fact, the effects of random damage on an organism are intertwined with its ability to repair or protect itself from the damage, as well as its capacity to generate damaging agents itself.

ANTAGONISTIC PLEIOTROPY VERSUS LONGEVITY ASSURANCE MECHANISMS

Medawar (1952) and Williams (1957) argued that species might harbor deleterious genes whose time of onset has been delayed until the postreproductive period, when they would have little effect on subsequent generations.

They further suggested that there may, in fact, be a selective pressure to maintain some of these genes, for example, if the genes have beneficial effects early in life and enhance reproduction, an idea known as antagonistic pleiotropy. Sacher (1968) and Cutler (1979) have argued that the important question is not why we grow old, which one could think of as analogous to the decay of inanimate objects such as cars and buildings, but why we live as long as we do. Burnet (1974) proposed that certain genetically programmed mechanisms that may ensure the fidelity of an organism's physiology may do so only for a period consistent with reproductive success, after which the mechanisms lose function or are otherwise insufficient to prevent stochastic processes that result in dysregulation and death. Maybe it is not aging that is interesting but rather why the deteriorative cascade of physiological changes that we characterize as senescence does not become readily apparent until well into or beyond the reproductive period.

RATE OF LIVING THEORY

Pearl (1928) postulated that the metabolic potential (or total energy expenditure during life) is genetically determined, and thus longevity is dependent on the rate of metabolism (reviewed in Balin & Allen, 1986). Pearl's "rate of living" theory predicts that if the rate of metabolism of a particular organism is decreased, it will tend to have a lengthened life span, and vice versa. Cold-blooded animals, for example, tend to have reduced metabolism and live longer at lower temperatures. The metabolic rate of houseflies increases dramatically during flight, and houseflies that are confined to containers that permit walking but not flying live 2.5 times longer than controls (Balin & Allen, 1986). In addition, mammals induced to hibernate exhibit significant increases in longevity compared with controls (Lyman, O'Brian, Green, & Papafrangos, 1981; Sacher, 1977).

Exposure to low levels of ionizing radiation has been shown to increase the life span of insects (Allen & Sohal, 1982). As ionizing radiation can cause genetic damage, this observation at first seems counterintuitive. The most likely explanation is that the increase in life span resulted from a decreased metabolic rate. The flies exposed to radiation exhibited a lower metabolic rate and metabolic potential relative to the control flies. Furthermore, when both treated and control flies were confined in small vials to eliminate flight activity, the control flies exhibited the expected 2.5-fold increase, whereas these conditions exerted relatively small effects or no effect at all on the longevity of the irradiated groups of insects. It should be noted that the metabolic potentials of each group were unaltered by restriction of flight activity. These experiments would seem to preclude the existence of a radiation-stimulated, overcompensatory DNA repair mechanism, parasites killed by radiation exposure, or energy conservation due to inactivation or killing of gonads. The observations presented here support the hypothesis that in some organisms metabolic rate plays a role in the rate of senescent decline, yet they do not identify the mechanisms through which metabolism affects senescence or what genetic factors determine the metabolic potential of any given species.

CALORIC RESTRICTION

For several species, including rodents, fish, spiders, and water fleas, a decrease in caloric intake, without malnutrition, has been demonstrated to extend both mean and maximum life span. Furthermore, caloric restriction has been shown to increase the metabolic potential (estimated as the total caloric intake per body mass during life) of male Fischer 344 rats (46%) as well as female C3B10F$_1$ mice (25%). These results show that, at least in rodents, both life span and metabolic potential are not invariant and may be manipulated by diet. Experiments with primates (rhesus monkeys) are currently in progress. Although it is too early in the studies to determine the effects on life span, certain physiological effects of caloric restriction that occur in rodents have also been observed in rhesus monkeys, including lowering of body temperature and decreased blood glucose and insulin levels (Roth, Ingram, & Lane, 1995).

FREE-RADICAL THEORY

Harman (1956) proposed that free radicals generated during metabolism are a primary factor in senescence. Molecular species such as superoxide, hydrogen peroxide, hydroxyl radical, and other reactive oxygen metabolites can cause extensive damage, including lipid peroxidation, and modifications to DNA and protein. Steady-state levels of reactive oxygen metabolites depend on both pro-oxidant generation and antioxidant defenses. Antioxidant defenses include enzymes, such as superoxide dismutase, which removes superoxide, and catalase and glutathione peroxidase, which remove hydrogen peroxide, as well as low-molecular-weight antioxidants such as glutathione, ascorbate (vitamin C), tocopherols (including vitamin E), carotenoids (including vitamin A), ubiquinone (coenzyme Q), and urate. Exogenous administration of antioxidants does not appear to extend maximum life span, and in fact, such intake may suppress endogenous antioxidant defenses. Furthermore, the overall level of antioxidant defense enzymes does not seem to correlate with maximum life span. Still, the rates of generation of superoxide and hydrogen peroxide in mitochondria have been shown to increase with age in several different mammalian tissues, as well as in insects, and correlate inversely with maximum life span (reviewed in Sohal & Weindruch, 1996).

Mitochondrial oxidative phosphorylation, a process for usable energy production in the cell, diminishes in efficiency with age, a potential contributing factor in senescent decline (for a review, see Wallace et al., 1995). The cause for this decrease is not clear, but it may be damage to mitochondrial membranes and DNA (mtDNA), which are near the site of production of reactive oxygen species that are generated during the synthesis of adenosine triphosphate (ATP). Mitochondrial DNA is more susceptible to damage than nuclear DNA because it is not protected by histones, and the mechanisms of mtDNA repair are not as efficient as those for nuclear DNA. Oxidative damage to mtDNA, as measured by the presence of 8-hydroxy-2-deoxyguanosine, has been reported to be 10-fold higher than that found in nuclear DNA.

Furthermore, a large number of age-dependent mutations to mtDNA have been reported, although when quantified individually, such defects appear to occur in low amounts, generally less than 1% of the total mtDNA. As patients with mitochondrial diseases have been observed to harbor greater levels of defective mtDNA and still function well, such low levels seemed insufficient to cause senescent decline. Recently, however, mtDNA specimens from the hearts of eight individuals of various ages were examined, using a technique that allows for the detection of all possible mtDNA species over 500 base pairs that contain deletions. It was shown that the level of wild-type mtDNA decreased from more than 99% in the 3-year-old to only 11% of the total in the 97-year-old (Hayakawa et al., 1996).

As originally formulated, the free-radical theory regards senescence as resulting from stochastic damage inflicted by reactive oxygen metabolites. In the oxidative stress hypothesis (for a review, see Sohal & Weindruch, 1996), it is proposed that the damage-based free-radical theory may be too simplistic, as reactive oxygen metabolites also influence development and gene expression.

Substantial support for the free-radical theory/oxidative stress hypothesis comes from fruit flies (*Drosophila melanogaster*) that have been genetically manipulated to contain extra copies of genes that encode superoxide dismutase and catalase enzymes. These transgenic flies express 26% greater superoxide dismutase activity and 73% greater catalase activity than do control flies. In addition, the transgenic flies sustain a reduced rate of age-related oxidative damage, maintain enhanced physical vigor at later ages, and exhibit a 34% increase in maximum life span. The transgenic flies displayed not only increased life span but a comparable increase in metabolic potential as well (reviewed in Sohal & Weindruch, 1996).

SOMATIC MUTATION THEORY

The somatic mutation theory argues that genetic damage, originally suggested to arise from background radiation, causes senescence (Curtis, 1961). The most compelling experiments that address the somatic mutation theory are those of Clark and Rubin (1961). Exposure to ionizing radiation causes genetic damage and shortens life span. Clark and Rubin subjected haploid and diploid wasps (*Habrobracon*) to ionizing radiation and found that the haploid wasps were more sensitive to radiation treatment. Yet nonirradiated control populations of haploid and diploid wasps had the same life span, a result difficult to reconcile with the somatic mutation theory. It is interesting to note that these experiments do not address whether mutations to mtDNA play a role in senescence, as both haploid and diploid wasps would be expected to share comparable levels of mtDNA.

ERROR CATASTROPHE THEORY

The error catastrophe theory proposed by Orgel (1963, 1970) argued that senescence may result from a defect that arises in the machinery used for protein synthesis. Such a defect could lead to the production of a number of error-containing proteins, resulting in the dysregulation of numerous cellular processes. Whatever its intuitive appeal, a causal role for translation error catastrophe in senescence is not borne out by experimental evidence. The altered proteins that occur in senescence appear to result from posttranslational modification, such as oxidation and glycation, rather than errors at the primary amino acid level (for a review, see Rothstein, 1985). Furthermore, the accumulation of altered proteins appears to be due to decreased turnover in older cells.

HORMONAL THEORIES

Elevated levels of glucocorticoids (steroid hormones produced by the adrenal cortex) play a causal role in the rapid decline of both marsupial mice and Pacific salmon (Finch, 1990). This decline may not be an accelerated manifestation of typical vertebrate senescence but nonetheless indicates that hormones can affect deterioration and decline. Furthermore, the life span of a species appears to be tightly linked to its fecundity, and hormones are intimately involved in maturation and reproduction. In addition, various circulating endocrine hormones have a wide range of effects on many systems in the body, including growth, metabolism, temperature regulation, and inflammatory and stress responses. Thus, the neuroendocrine system is an obvious candidate for a system that might regulate an organism's rate of senescence. In fact, although very high levels of glucocorticoids may be detrimental to the survival of marsupial mice and Pacific salmon, there are indications that moderately elevated glucocorticoid levels may retard senescence in rats, mice, and humans (reviewed in Masoro, 1995).

Denckla (1975) reported a "decreasing oxygen consumption" pituitary hormone (DECO) that appeared to be responsible for the decreased efficacy of thyroid hormone observed with age. The pituitary secretes several hormones, and removal of the pituitary in a rat generally results in rapid death, unless there is a concomitant supplementation of specific beneficial hormones. Rats depleted of the putative DECO hormone through removal of their pituitaries (together with replacement of two adrenal steroids and thyroid hormone) displayed increased maximum aerobic capacity, increased aorta relaxation potential, improved T-cell-dependent functions, and an increase in the number of survivors at the maximum life span relative to normal rats. Shortly afterward, Denckla retired from research, and there are no subsequent reports in the literature to indicate that DECO has ever been isolated.

IMMUNOLOGICAL THEORIES

As with hormonal theories, the idea that the decline of the immune system may play a causal role in senescence (Finch & Rose, 1995; Walford, 1969) is attractive, as the immune system is integrally linked to the health and maintenance of the whole organism. Senescence results in reduced resistance to infectious disease and an increased incidence of autoimmune disease, indicative of deterioration of the immune system. The variety of age-related alterations in immune system components that have been reported include a decline in T-cell function with a shift in the T-cell population toward a reduced proportion of naive T cells and a greater proportion of memory T cells (reviewed in Miller, 1996). Walford (1969) and Finch and Rose (1995) have related immune system changes to the major histocompatibility complex. Mouse strains that have been constructed so that they differ genetically only at the major histocompatibility locus have different maximal life spans (Finch & Rose, 1995). Interestingly, this locus also regulates superoxide dismutase and mixed-function oxidase levels, relating the immunological theory to the free-radical theory of senescence.

SENESCENCE AT THE CELLULAR LEVEL

Cells have protective and repair mechanisms to ameliorate damage that occurs with age, but the mechanisms are insufficient, and damage accumulates. Cultures of bacteria can apparently grow and divide indefinitely provided they are supplied with sufficient nutrients. Cells with deleterious mutations die, but competent cells survive. A similar situation can be considered to occur in mitosis in eukaryotes. For example, bristlecone pines and the giant sequoias of California are purported to be several hundred years old, yet no individual living cells come close to the age of the plant. Similarly, many plants grown today have been serially propagated through cuttings from plants that died hundreds of years ago. In fact, all life presumably came from primordial cells that arose billions of years ago. Individual cells are renewed through division, followed by selection for the "fittest" cells.

In metazoans, the cells of the embryo differentiate into a germ cell lineage and a somatic cell lineage. The germ cell lineage is potentially immortal, in the sense that the complement of genes can be passed on indefinitely. In contrast, cells of somatic lineage are destined for further differentiation and ultimately for senescence and death (i.e., the soma is disposable and not required for species survival). Weismann (1882) proposed that senescence is the price somatic cells pay for their differentiation. He was also probably the first to suggest that the failure of somatic cells to replicate indefinitely limited the life span of the organism.

In contrast to Weismann's hypothesis, in vitro studies by Carrel and co-workers (summarized in Carrel & Ebling, 1921) suggested that individual cells, when separated from the organism, were potentially immortal in the same way that bacteria and most protozoa are considered immortal; that is, they could grow and divide indefinitely. This philosophy was generally accepted until the late 1950s and 1960s, when the work of Swim and Parker (1957), Hayflick and Moorhead (1961), and others established that cells derived from a wide variety of tissues from a wide variety of organisms were incapable of unlimited proliferation in culture. Hayflick and Moorhead (1961) interpreted these findings as a cellular expression of senescence.

There has been a long-standing debate as to whether in vitro studies using isolated populations of cells in culture, detached from the effect of neighboring cells in situ, accurately reflect the in vivo physiological processes of an individual cell in an organism. At present there is no evidence that the in vitro replicative life span of cells sets the life span of the organism. Still, many significant alterations that occur with in vitro senescence also occur with senescence in vivo. These changes include but are not limited to the overexpression of collagenase and stromelysin and a decrease in accumulation of a tissue inhibitor of metalloproteinases (TIMP-1). There are also differences; for example, the induction of EPC-1 mRNA in response to serum deprivation or density-dependent growth inhibition is diminished in late passage cells. Yet skin fibroblasts from old donors do not show reduced EPC-1 mRNA expression relative to that observed in cells from young donors. These and other alterations that occur with cellular senescence in vitro and in vivo are reviewed elsewhere (Cristofalo, Tresini, Volker, & Francis, 1998).

Furthermore, although the results of an early study (Stanley, Pye, & MacGregor, 1975) raise the possibility that it might not be true universally, cells from short-lived species have been reported to lose proliferative capability more rapidly than comparable cells from longer-lived species (Goldstein, 1990; Hayflick, 1977; Röhme, 1981). For example, fibroblasts from a Galapagos tortoise (maximum life span of more than 100 years) exhibit more than 100 population doublings, whereas those from a mouse (3-year maximum life span) achieve only 10–15 population doublings on average, before undergoing crisis and transformation. Thus, the maximum life span potential of a given species may be reflected in the proliferative ability of its derived fibroblasts in culture. Furthermore, these results suggest that the controlling elements for the chronological life span of the organism may partially overlap the control mechanisms during in vitro replicative senescence.

One might suppose that cells from larger animals would have enhanced replicative capacity because more cells are required to make a larger animal. Because there is a positive correlation between species size and maximum life span, it has been suggested that the number of population doublings characteristic of the fibroblast-like cells derived from any particular species may reflect the size of the animal rather than its life span. This seems unlikely, as a much smaller difference in the number of population doublings than that observed will account for the differences in size of the animals. As a typical example, suppose fibroblast-like cells derived from a 0.5-kg rat undergo approximately 15 population doublings. Each additional 10 population doublings gives a 2^{10}-fold (approx. 1000-fold) increase in mass. Thus, if body size were the only consideration, an additional 10 population doublings (25 total) would be enough to make cells for a 500-kg (1100-lb) human; yet fibroblast-like cells from humans generally undergo twice as many doublings as this, enough for a human with a mass greater than 17 billion kg (38 billion lb).

Martin, Sprague, and Epstein (1970) reported a decline in the replicative capacity of human skin fibroblasts with age of the donor (approx. 0.2 population doublings per year of donor age). In recent studies performed in our laboratory, however, we used skin fibroblast lines from 42 *healthy* individuals from the Baltimore Longitudinal Study on Aging and found no correlation between fibroblast proliferative life span and donor age. This suggests that perhaps some of the differences in replicative life span may be due to the health status of the donor.

The mechanisms that determine the limited replicative life span of cells in culture are not yet elucidated; however, as with intact organisms, there is evidence that favors both genetic and stochastic factors as contributors to the phenomenon of cellular senescence. Cells may be fused to form a single combined cell with two nuclei (heterokaryon) or a single cell with one combined nucleus (hybrid). When young (early population-doubling level) and senescent (late population-doubling level) cells are fused by either method, the senescent phenotype is dominant (for a review, see Smith & Pereira-Smith, 1996). In other experiments, individual chromosomes from young or senescent cells were fused to intact cells of the opposite population-doubling level. The results of these studies have implicated multiple chromosomes that are important in replicative senescence.

Another area of research has focused on why early passage cells respond to growth factors by proliferating and dividing whereas senescent cells do not (for a review, see Cristofalo et al., 1998). Surprisingly, much of the signal transduction machinery seems normal and functional in senescent cells. Recent evidence suggests that some steps in the cascade of protein phosphorylation as a consequence of growth factor stimulation may not function the same way in young and senescent cells.

Another interesting branch of studies on cells in culture deals with the phenomenon of telomere shortening. Telomeres are the ends of chromosomes. The way in which DNA is replicated requires the activity of an enzyme called telomerase to complete replication of the telomeres. In most normal cells, in vitro or in vivo, telomerase is not present; thus, with each replication of the DNA the ends are not completely replicated and the chromosomes become progressively shorter. This mechanism provides a theoretical basis for a "replication clock" that counts each replicative event until the telomere shortens to a length that does not allow any more replications.

The expression of several genes changes during cellular senescence. In addition, there are examples in which the orderly flow of events has been disrupted-for example, the uncoupling of translation from transcription and of transcription from cell cycle events. Apparently, there is widespread dysregulation in senescent cells. These observations suggest that mechanisms that maintain the integrity of early passage cells may fail as a result of stochastic processes.

In the use of cell culture as a model for human senescence, a fundamental question should be addressed: To what extent can we extrapolate from the phenomenon of replicative senescence in culture to the changes that occur in the body with age? Normal cells in culture express many of the characteristics they expressed in situ. An important question is, To what extent does the serial subcultivation of cells that were young when placed into culture, recapitulate the phenotype and mechanisms of senescence? One way to address this question is to make comparisons between cells aged in vitro and cells from different-age donors placed in culture and studied while young in culture for those differences observed in replicative senescence. For most of these studies, differences between fetal-derived cells and adult-derived cells were far greater than differences between cells derived from young and old adults. In addition, in most cases, regardless of donor age, cells that were still young in culture did not display the characteristic changes that occur when cells are aged in vitro.

The replicative senescence model in many ways shows characteristics similar to that of senescence of organisms. There are reproducible changes in structure and function; the process is deteriorative and leads to an increasing probability of cell death. In addition, many significant alterations that occur with in vitro senescence also occur with senescence in vivo. On the other hand, replicative senescence in culture shows no clear relationship to the processes that those same cells would undergo if they were to age in situ. Fibroblasts are in the category of reverting postmitotic cells; that is, they can replicate throughout life but do so only when called upon. Cellular senescence studies suggest that fibroblasts in situ (at least those derived from protected areas of skin) may be mitotically competent to last for several human life spans.

One possibility is that there are two pathways to senescence in cells like fibroblasts. Perhaps repeated replication leads to a senescence phenotype much faster than to the senescence that results from the passage of metabolic time in situ, during which only few mitoses occur. Alternatively, cells proliferatively aged in vitro may follow a different pathway but arrive at a final phenotype that is similar to cells aged in vivo. In either case, we can learn how these changes occur, what the regulatory mechanisms are, and how the changes can be delayed or accelerated, all under the controlled environmental conditions of culture and using cells derived from humans. Taken together, the findings suggest that there are multiple pathways to acquiring the senescent phenotype. For some cell types, the individual succumbs to death from other causes, involving other cells, long before those cell types have had time to senesce.

Cell cultures allow us to test the theories of senescence at the cellular level and in a controlled environment. What have cell culture studies taught us about senescence? First, we have learned a great deal of cell and molecular biology from studies of cellular senescence. We have learned about how cells recognize and interpret signals and how signals are amplified to trigger complicated events like DNA replication. We have even learned some things about why those functions fail. Perhaps we have also learned how to interpret the results of studies of senescence in models. In this respect, cell culture models are neither more nor less capricious than rodents, nematodes, *Drosophila,* and yeast and share with them the need for profound critical judgment in applying results of studies in these models to human senescence.

In conclusion, in this review we have briefly discussed several biological theories of senescence, some of which have empirical support and others do not. The realization that senescence may be explained by the declining force of natural selection has provided a major step forward in our understanding of the phenomenon. Models such as rodents, nematodes, *Drosophila*, yeast, and cell cultures have enabled us to test various theories of senescence. We can now control life span by a number a methods, including caloric restriction and manipulation of genes that affect oxidative stress and hormone levels. Future research to elucidate the biological causes, mechanisms, and basis of senescence will undoubtedly yield some exciting answers to the question: Why do we age?

REFERENCES

Adams, J. M., & Cory, S. (1991). Transgenic models of tumor development. *Science, 254*, 1161–1167.

Allen, R. G., & Sohal, R. S. (1982). Life-lengthening effects of γ-irradiation on the adult housefly, *Musca domestica*. *Mechanisms of Ageing and Development, 20*, 369–375.

Austad, S. N. (1997). Comparative aging and life histories in mammals. *Experimental Gerontology, 32*, 23–38.

Balin, A. K., & Allen, R. G. (1986). Mechanisms of biologic aging. *Dermatological Clinics, 4*, 347–358.

Burnet, M. (1974). *Intrinsic mutagenesis: A genetic approach for aging,* New York: John Wiley and Sons.

Carrel, A., & Ebling, A. H. (1921). Age and multiplication of fibroblasts. *Journal of Experimental Medicine, 34*, 599–623.

Clark, A. M., & Rubin, M. A. (1961). The modification by x-irradiation of the life span of haploid and diploid *Habrobracon*. *Radiation Research, 15*, 244–253.

Comfort, A. (1979). *The biology of senescence* (3rd ed.). New York: Elsevier.

Cristofalo, V. J., Tresini, M., Volker, C., & Francis, M. K. (1998). Use of the fibroblast model. In B. P. Yu (Ed.), *Methods in aging research.* Boca Raton, FL: CRC Press.

Curtis, H. J. (1961). Biological mechanisms underlying the aging process. *Science, 141*, 686–694.

Cutler, R. G. (1979). Evolution of human longevity: A critical overview. *Mechanisms of Ageing and Development, 9*, 337–354.

Denckla, W. D. (1975). A time to die. *Life Sciences, 16*, 31–44.

Finch, C. E. (1990). *Longevity, senescence, and the genome.* Chicago: University of Chicago Press.

Finch, C. E., & Rose, M. R. (1995). Hormones and the physiological architecture of life history evolution. *Quarterly Review in Biology, 70*, 1–52.

Goldstein, S. (1990). Replicative senescence: The human fibroblast comes of age. *Science, 249*, 1129–1133.

Hakeem, A., Rodriguez-Sandoval, G., Jones, M., & Allman, J. (1996). Brain and life span in primates. In J. E. Birren & K. W. Schaie (Eds.), *Handbook of the psychology of aging* (4th ed., pp. 78–95). San Diego, CA: Academic Press.

Harman, D. (1956). Aging: A theory based on free radical and radiation chemistry. *Journal of Gerontology, 11*, 298–300.

Hayakawa, M., Katsumata, K., Yoneda, M., Tanaka, M., Sugiyama, S., & Ozawa, T. (1996). Age-related extensive fragmentation of mitochondrial DNA into mini-circles. *Biochemical and Biophysical Research Communications, 226,* 369–377.

Hayflick, L. (1977). The cellular basis for biological aging. In C. E. Finch & L. Hayflick (Eds.), *Handbook of the biology of aging* (pp. 159–179). New York: Van Nostrand Reinhold.

Hayflick, L., & Moorhead, P. S. (1961). The serial cultivation of human diploid cell strains. *Experimental Cell Research, 25,* 585–621.

Lyman, C. P., O'Brian, R. C., Green, G. C., & Papafrangos, E. D. (1981). Hibernation and longevity in the Turkish hamster *Mesocritus brandti. Science, 212,* 668–670.

Martin, G. M., Austad, S. N., & Johnson, T. E. (1996). Genetic analysis of ageing: Role of oxidative damage and environmental stresses. *Nature Genetics, 13,* 25–33.

Martin, G. M., Sprague, C. A., & Epstein, C. J. (1970). Replicative lifespan of cultivated human cells: Effects of donor age, tissue, and genotype. *Laboratory Investigation, 23,* 86–92.

Masoro, E. J. (1995). Glucocorticoids and aging. *Aging, 7,* 407–413.

Medawar, P. B. (1952). *An unsolved problem of biology.* London: H. K. Lewis.

Medvedev, Z. A. (1990). An attempt at a rational classification of theories of aging. *Biological Reviews, 65,* 375–398.

Miller, R. A. (1996). The aging immune system: Primer and prospectus. *Science, 271,* 70–74.

Orgel, L. E. (1963). The maintenance of the accuracy of protein synthesis and its relevance to aging. *Proceedings of the National Academy of Sciences USA, 49,* 517–521.

Orgel, L. E. (1970). The maintenance of the accuracy of protein synthesis and its relevance to aging: A correction. *Proceedings of the National Academy of Sciences USA, 67,* 1476.

Pearl, R. (1928). *The rate of living theory.* New York: A. A. Knopf.

Röhme, D. (1981). Evidence for a relationship between longevity of mammalian species and life-spans of normal human fibroblasts *in vitro* and erythrocytes *in vivo. Proceedings of the National Academy of Sciences USA, 78,* 5009–5013.

Roth, G. S., Ingram, D. K., & Lane, M. A. (1995). Slowing ageing by caloric restriction. *Nature Medicine, 1,* 414–415.

Rothstein, M. (1985). The alteration of enzymes in aging. In R. C. Adelman & E. E. Dekker (Eds.), *Modern aging research: Modifications of proteins during aging* (Vol. 7, pp. 53–67). New York: Alan R. Liss.

Sacher, G. A. (1968). Molecular versus systemic theories on the genesis of aging. *Experimental Gerontology, 3,* 265–271.

Sacher, G. A. (1977). Life table modification and life prolongation. In C. E. Finch & L. Hayflick (Eds.), *Handbook of the biology of aging* (pp. 582–638). New York: Van Nostrand Reinhold.

Smith, D. W. E. (1993). *Human longevity.* Oxford, UK: Oxford University Press.

Smith, J. R., & Pereira-Smith, O. M. (1996). Replicative senescence: Implications for *in vivo* aging and tumor supression. *Science, 273,* 63–67.

Sohal, R. S., & Weindruch, R. (1996). Oxidative stress, caloric restriction, and aging. *Science, 273,* 59–63.

Stanley, J. F., Pye, D., & MacGregor, A. (1975). Comparison of doubling numbers attained by cultured animal cells with life span of species. *Nature, 255,* 158–159.

Swim, H. E., & Parker, R. F. (1957). Culture characteristics of human fibroblasts propagated serially. *American Journal of Hygiene, 66,* 235–243.

Walford, R. (1969). *The immunologic theory of aging.* Copenhagen: Munksgaard.

Wallace, D. C., Bohr, V. A., Cortopassi, G., Kadenbach, B., Linn, S., Linnane, A. W., Richter, C., & Shay, J. W. (1995). Group report: The role of bioenergetics and mitochondrial DNA mutations in aging and age-related diseases. In K. Esser & G. M. Martin (Eds.), *Molecular aspects of aging* (pp. 199–225). New York: John Wiley and Sons.

Weismann, A. (1882). *Über die Dauer des Lebens.* Jena, Germany: G. Fischer.

Williams, G. C. (1957). Pleiotropy, natural selection, and the evolution of senescence. *Evolution, 11,* 398–411.

Yu, B. P., Masoro, E. J., Murata, I., Bertrand, H. S., & Lynd, F. T. (1982). Life span study of Fischer 344 male rats fed *ad libitum* or restricted diets: Longevity, growth, lean body mass, and disease. *Journal of Gerontology, 37,* 130–141.

Zwilling, R. (1992). Aging—still a mystery. In R. Zwilling & C. Balduini (Eds.), *Biology of aging* (pp. 1–7). Berlin: Springer-Verlag.

7

Theories of Neuropsychology and Aging

Diana S. Woodruff-Pak
Michelle Papka

Neurological, physiological, and psychological changes accompany aging and affect both brain function and behavior. The field of the neuropsychology of aging involves scientific investigation, clinical assessment, and treatment of cognitive and behavioral changes that occur as a result of age-related changes in the brain. Neuropsychologists assess and aid in the treatment of individuals whose mental dysfunctions appear to be caused by damage or abnormalities in the brain. They also help to determine whether changes in behavior may be attributed to neurological dysfunction or to some other factor. In this regard, neuropsychologists attempt to differentiate normal from pathological aging. The basis for their assessment and treatment recommendations is neuroscientific research: inquiries about brain and behavior relationships in human and nonhuman animal species.

The term *neuropsychology* is relatively new, having purely 20th-century origins. William Osler, an internist at Johns Hopkins University Medical School, is credited with creating the term, although ironically, Osler attributed aging of the brain to changes in cerebrovascular (i.e., blood supply to the brain) rather than neural (i.e., cells of the brain) mechanisms (Birren & Woodruff, 1983). Donald O. Hebb, the celebrated Canadian neuroscientist and McGill University faculty member, used the term in 1949 when he published his influential book, *The Organization of Behavior: A Neuropsychological Theory.* Although neuropsychology was not defined in Hebb's book, the term apparently originated as an attempt to represent a scientific domain combining topics of interest in neurology and physiological psychology (Kolb & Whishaw, 1995). Further visibility was given to the term when the Harvard University neuroscientist Karl S. Lashley's works were collected and edited in 1960 under the title *The Neuropsychology of Lashley* (Beach, Hebb, Morgan, & Nissen, 1960).

The perspective represented in this chapter is derived from Donald Hebb's meaning of neuropsychology: the scientific study of brain function and behavioral relationships, using experimental evidence from human and non-human animal species as well as clinical evidence from humans with brain damage. Hebb's theories about brain function were conceptual, based on naturalistic observation. This tradition has been maintained, although contemporary theories also incorporate computer models and simulations of brain function.

There are a number of disciplines that are closely related to clinical neuropsychology, and they can best be conceptualized as a continuum between brain and mind. Disciplines focused on the brain include neurology and neuroscience, whereas disciplines focused on mind include behavioral neuroscience, cognitive psychology, and cognitive science. Loosely defined, brain can be thought of as the physical structures and processes of these structures, and the mind as the mental processes and manipulations that are based in the brain, enabling us to think and to respond in our environment. Computational modeling and artificial intelligence, as well as input from physics, mathematics, computer science, and engineering, are assimilated into neuropsychology and are used in applications such as brain imaging and modeling. Neuropsychology integrates data from these disciplines to facilitate assessment and understanding of brain and behavior relationships.

THEORIES AND MODELS IN A BOTTOM-UP DISCIPLINE

The very origin of the term *neuropsychology,* used first in book titles collecting the empirical work (primarily animal studies) of well-known neuroscientists, attests to the basis of the discipline in an inductive or "bottom-up" approach. Hebb and Lashley built their theoretical perspective from empirical observations rather than formulating theories first and then marshaling support for them. Indeed, in his search for mechanisms and neural substrates of learning, Lashley (1950) was frustrated, stating that his data on the localization of the memory trace led to the necessary conclusion that learning was just not possible.

The neuropsychology of aging is data-driven rather than theory-driven. As such, we might consider that this domain has more models (defined in this book as descriptions or prototypes of empirical relationships) than theories (herein defined as explanations to account for the empirical relationships). In an overview of this discipline, more theories have been evaluated and abandoned than maintained.

Some Early Neuropsychological Theories of Aging

Below, we describe and claim for the neuropsychology of aging any early theories that addressed brain and behavior relationships in aging. At the time they were created, these theories were not associated with the domain of neuropsychology because neuropsychology did not have a clear identity as a field until the late 20th century.

Underarousal

James E. Birren (1960) first articulated the theory of underarousal when he stated:

> There is the possibility that the well-established psychomotor slowing of advancing age is a consequence of reduced physiological activation. This agrees with what limited literature exists on age differences in activity and drive levels. Assuming a less energized or activated organism with age, in any unit of time there will be less interaction between the individual and his environment. This reduces the opportunity for all psychological processes to take place, e.g., perception, acquisition, manipulation of symbols, and storage. (pp. 326–327)

The major evidence for the underarousal hypothesis was provided by studies of brain electrical activity in the aged. In particular, studies assessing the relationships between behavior and brain wave activity, measured by the electroencephalogram (EEG), suggested that older adults were underaroused. For 50 years researchers have been aware of four major changes in the EEGs of older adults. These include (a) changes in the frequency and abundance of the alpha rhythm (8–13 cycles per second [cps]), the brain wave activity during periods of wakefulness; (b) changes in the incidence of beta activity (above 13 cps), associated with information processing; (c) diffuse slowing (especially noted in institutionalized elderly); and (d) slowing in particular areas of the brain (i.e., focal slowing), as well as abnormal activity in the temporal lobes. The most reliable age change in EEG activity is the slowing of the dominant frequency, the alpha rhythm. Because slower EEG frequencies are associated with lower states of arousal, EEG slowing in the aged may signify a lowered state of arousal in that population.

The mechanisms underlying EEG changes and their clinical significance remain unclear at present, at least in healthy, community-residing older adults. The association between measures of vascular function and EEG slowing in patient groups has raised the question of whether alpha slowing reflects cerebral metabolic changes. Reliable relationships between slowing of alpha frequency and cognitive impairment have been obtained in samples of elderly patients, which suggests that alpha frequency may be associated in some way with efficiency of information processing. However, attempts to find similar relationships between alpha frequency and cognition in healthy older adults have not been successful. Alpha frequency and cognition relationships may be an example of Birren's (1963) discontinuity theory, which states that behavior correlates with a physiological measure (in this case, alpha frequency) only when the physiological measure is in an abnormal range. Studies of event-related potentials (ERPs), which are measures of brain wave activity in response to specific stimuli, have also supported underarousal theory. These findings are too numerous and elaborate to detail in this chapter, but ERP evidence for underarousal was reviewed in Woodruff (1985).

Overarousal

One of the first gerontologists to articulate the theory of overarousal was Alan Welford (1965) who stated:

> Reduced activation would tend to lower both signal and noise, the former probably more than the latter, rendering the organism less sensitive and less responsive than it would otherwise be. At first sight the changes with age in neural structures make it seem obvious that older people would be likely to suffer from under-activation. Yet both clinical and everyday observations of middle-aged and older people often point rather to *over*-activation resulting in unduly heightened activity, tension and anxiety. (p. 14).

The data that have been used most frequently to support the overarousal hypothesis involve the measurement of lipid mobilization, a biochemical measure related to sympathetic nervous system function. Free fatty acid (FFA) level in the plasma component of blood is related to the level of autonomic nervous system arousal. To obtain this measure, an indwelling needle is placed in the subject's forearm, and sequential samples of blood are collected during simultaneous performance of an experimental task. Therefore, a major confound of the FFA measure is that regardless of the behavioral measure being assessed, there is a certain amount of stress involved in FFA data collection associated with the drawing of blood. Results of studies utilizing FFA measurements have indicated that during serial learning and stressful monitoring tasks emphasizing information overload, aged subjects had higher FFA levels, evidenced FFA increases comparable to young subjects while performing the tasks, and continued to show significantly higher levels of FFA for a minimum of 1 hour following the behavioral tests (Eisdorfer, Nowlin, & Wilkie, 1970).

Both over- and underarousal theories generated significant research interest in earlier decades, but they are seldom addressed by contemporary neuropsychologists. Neither theory was clearly refuted. However, these theories seem less useful in the interpretation of neuropsychological data in the late 20th century.

Right Hemisphere Aging

A neuropsychological theory that has received more direct disconfirmation is the postulation that there is selectively more rapid aging in the right cerebral hemisphere than in the left hemisphere. Visuospatial ability is associated with the parietal lobe, particularly the right parietal lobe. Deficits in visuospatial ability associated with normal aging are relatively large, and observations of selective impairment in older adults on right-hemisphere abilities led some investigators to formulate the theory that the right cerebral hemisphere is selectively impaired by processes of aging. Inasmuch as attention and vision are involved in visuospatial ability, the frontal and occipital lobes are also engaged. Demonstrations of the role of attention and frontal lobe involvement in visuospatial tasks have been used to challenge the postulation that the right hemisphere ages selectively. The initial suggestions that normal aging might affect the right and left cerebral hemispheres differently have not received empirical support (Libon et al., 1994).

Contemporary Theoretical Positions in Neuropsychology and Aging

In this bottom-up, empirically oriented discipline, it is unusual to label the current state of knowledge as theoretical. However, it is becoming increasingly evident as we approach the new millennium that in normal aging there are two major configurations of change in the brain that can be associated with cognitive aging. One change involves the prefrontal cortex, which is a critical substrate for a collection of abilities that neuropsychologists call executive function. A second age-related change in cognition involves the ability to form new declarative memories, a function that uses brain circuitry in the medial temporal lobes. Inasmuch as we are defining theories in this volume as explanations to account for empirical relationships, we will identify these two domains of demonstrated brain changes associated with cognitive aging as neuropsychological theories. The first "theory" of age-related change is identified as *prefrontal cortex executive function theory,* and the second is *medial temporal lobe declarative memory theory.*

Prefrontal Cortex Executive Function Theory

It cannot be overemphasized that frontal lobe functions are central to the understanding of the neuropsychology of aging. Executive function is one term that has been used to refer to the cognitive components controlled in the frontal lobes. Among these are planning, organizing, thinking divergently, inhibiting, and self-monitoring. Attention and working memory are terms used for metacognitive processes controlled in the frontal lobes and affecting aspects of most cognitive behavior. There is overlap in the cognitive functions assessed using the terms executive function, attention, and working memory, although the research encompassed under these three constructs has been carried out from somewhat different theoretical perspectives.

The term *executive function* is used primarily in neuropsychological assessment of frontal lobe function in normal adults or adults with brain lesions. Studies of working memory rely heavily on animal research in which direct assessment of neurophysiological function is made. Attention is a function studied in the domain of cognitive psychology, another discipline that has made significant contributions to the neuropsychology of aging. Executive function, working memory, and some aspects of attention have their neural substrate in portions of the frontal lobes of the cerebral cortex. The frontal lobes, perhaps more than any other region of the brain, are impaired by processes of aging (Woodruff-Pak, 1997).

The frontal lobes of the cerebral cortex subserve a number of diverse, higher-order functions and are at the top of a hierarchy of brain organization. Indeed, the frontal lobes, more than any other part of the brain, distinguish humans from other species. The concept of hierarchical organization in the nervous system was initiated by John Hughlings-Jackson (1835–1911), the founder of modern neurology. The ideas of Hughlings-Jackson were so modern that they may be receiving more serious attention in the present day than they did a century ago.

The frontal lobes of the human cerebral cortex are the last region to develop. The size of the frontal lobes increases dramatically from birth to the second year, and growth continues in childhood. The slow maturation rate of the frontal lobes has been associated with the relatively late development of some human abilities (Goldman-Rakic, 1987). One of the fundamental principles articulated by Hughlings-Jackson was that neural structures and associated abilities laid down earliest should be the most permanent and lasting, and the latest-developing structures and functions should be the most vulnerable to processes of aging. Neuropsychological, neuroanatomical, and radiological evidence that the frontal lobes are the part of the brain affected earliest and hardest by normal aging continues to mount (Albert & Kaplan, 1980; Coffey et al., 1992; Shimamura, 1990). Hence, capacities subserved by the frontal lobes show age-related impairment.

Age-related changes in emotion, arousal and sleep, response speed and timing, and some forms of memory are associated with neurobiological changes in the frontal lobes, along with age-related changes in executive function, working memory, and attention. The prefrontal cortex in conjunction with the hippocampus subserves working memory, which involves the temporary use of knowledge to guide behavior. Working memory deficits occur in nonhuman primates as well as in humans, and the deficit in animals parallels extremely well the working memory deficit observed in normal aging and exacerbated in Alzheimer's and Parkinson's diseases.

Frontal-Lobe Syndrome

The classic case of frontal-lobe syndrome was observed and treated by Harlow (1868) and more recently revived by Damasio, Grabowoski, Frank, Galaburda, and Damasio (1994). Although he was relatively young when he had his tragic accident, the patient, Phineas Gage, provided us with insights about aging as well as about frontal lobe lesions. A construction explosion hurled a tamping iron that was over an inch in diameter and 3½ feet long into the orbit of his eye and through the top of his skull. The blast was so powerful that the tamping iron passed completely through Gage's skull and brain, landing yards away on the ground. Miraculously, Gage never lost consciousness and survived this lobotomy-producing accident, but he was dramatically changed as a human being. Gage's physician, J. M. Harlow (1868) described him in what is a prototype of the frontal-lobe syndrome:

> He is fitful, irreverent, indulging at times in the grossest profanity (which was not previously his custom), manifesting but little deference to his fellows, impatient of restraint or advice when it conflicts with his desires, at times pertinaciously obstinate yet capricious and vacillating, devising many plans for future operation which no sooner are arranged than they are abandoned in turn for others appearing more feasible. His mind was radically changed so that his friends and acquaintances said he was no longer Gage. (p. 336)

Gage's disinhibition, or inability to inhibit inappropriate behaviors, such as using excessive profane language, is typical of the frontal-lobe syndrome and represents a change from premorbid behavior. A very mild form of disinhibition is seen in the garrulousness of old age. Older adults frequently tell and retell in extensive detail stories that their relatives have heard before. This pattern of verbal behavior is not inappropriate, but it may result as a consequence of very mild frontal-lobe syndrome in older adults (Shimamura, 1990).

More severe behavioral consequences of frontal lobe damage include lack of insight into one's problems and an inability to learn from mistakes. These characteristics are observed in patients with dementia, Korsakoff's syndrome, or Parkinson's disease or in individuals who suffered from tumors or strokes affecting the frontal lobe. Thus, the frontal-lobe syndrome is associated with a diminished sense of responsibility, impulsiveness, mild euphoria, and a tendency to make inappropriate and childish jokes. Another capacity that apparently resides in the frontal lobes that is impaired in this syndrome is the ability to initiate activities or to act spontaneously. Kolb and Whishaw (1995) characterized frontal lobe patients as appearing lethargic or lazy.

The Frontal Lobes and Cognitive Flexibility

The frontal lobes as the executive are involved in the planning and initiation of thought and action, cognitive flexibility, concept formation, and cue-directed behavior. A typical measure of cognitive flexibility assesses participants' ability follow one type of rule and then shift to another principle without explicit instructions to do so. The participant must infer than the rule has changed. The major challenge to the participant is determining which rule is in effect by way of continuous feedback from the examiner (i.e., "right," "wrong"). Such a task has been associated with dorsolateral frontal cortex function.

In a classic study testing cognitive flexibility, Brenda Milner (1963) assessed patients who had either dorsolateral frontal lobe lesions or lesions in other lobes of the brain. All patients had undergone neurosurgical lobectomies as a treatment for intractable epilepsy. Compared to patients with lesions in other brain locations, patients with dorsolateral frontal lesions had great difficulty in inferring that the rule had changed and switching to another principle. This type of error is called a perseveration, characterized by patients' inability to inhibit practice of the first learned rule and acquire a newly employed rule.

Parallel (less severe) deficits have been observed in normal older adults throughout almost five decades of investigation (Shimamura, 1990). Limiting comparisons to older adults of various ages, investigators have reported greater impairment in the oldest participants. Results of one study showed that healthy young-old adults (mean age, 67 years) performed significantly better than did old-old adults (mean age, 78 years) on a wide variety of tests of executive function that included assessment of cognitive flexibility (Wheilihan & Lesher, 1985). In a group of 75 older adults selected for optimal health, Haaland, Vranes, Goodwin, and Garry (1987) reported attainment of fewer categories and more errors in cognitive flexibility assessments in participants aged 80 to 87, compared to participants aged 64 to 69. Similarly, older participants (mean age, 81 years) made significantly more perseverative errors than did participants of a mean age of 68 years (Libon et al., 1994). In a sample of community-residing adults ranging in age from 20 to

75 years, it was reported that frontal lobe tests, as opposed to tests associated with parietal and temporal lobe function, were the best predictors of age (Mittenberg, Seidenberg, O'Leary, & DeGiulo, 1989). Age-related deficits were greatest on neuropsychological tests assessing components of frontal lobe function.

Prospective Memory. The term prospective memory has been used to identify three forms of executive function: planning, organizing, and self-monitoring (Shimamura, 1990), functions subserved by the frontal lobes. Functionally, the prospective memory system differs from the declarative memory system in that it manipulates and organizes memory, as opposed to acquiring and storing information. If there is a deficit in declarative memory, there may or may not be a deficit in prospective memory. For example, patients with medial temporal lobe lesions who are suffering from amnesia can perform prospective memory functions such as categorizing or organizing information. On the other hand, impairment in prospective memory can impair performance on declarative memory tasks because organizational and retrieval strategies may be underutilized.

Prospective memory includes the processes and strategies used to remember to perform future actions. Remembering to take pills at a certain time, to turn off the lights and lock the door before leaving the house, to make and keep appointments, and to remember birthdays, anniversaries, and other significant dates all require prospective memory. Keeping track of what information has been told to whom is another attribute of prospective memory that falls into the category of self-monitoring. Although almost everyone repeats the same story twice to a friend or a relative, the frequency of repeating the same story seems to increase with age.

In experimental tests, remembering to perform future actions is done more poorly by older adults (West, 1988). However, in real-life situations, older adults may compensate for this impairment by using external cues such as notes, reminders, and organized calendars. This may explain why, in one study, older subjects were actually more accurate than younger subjects in making telephone calls to an experimenter at scheduled times (Moscovitch, 1982).

Source Memory. Remembering the source of the information received, that is, remembering who told you something or where you read a piece of information, is yet another aspect of prospective memory. An aspect of source amnesia was assessed by Parkin and Walter (1992), using a technique they called the recognition and consciousness awareness paradigm. Participants in several age groups were shown stimuli and presented later with a larger group of stimuli, including foils, from which they were asked to specify which they had and had not seen previously. They also were asked to classify each recognized stimulus on a subjective basis: Had they specific recollection of the target's prior occurrence (e.g., an image of the target), or was recognition based simply on familiarity with the object? The effect of age on the distribution of subjective responses was dramatic. There were a substantially higher number of familiarity responses in older adults, and this measure was associated with a greater number of errors in tests of cognitive flexibility. Even in subgroups of older adults who performed the recognition task as well as younger adults, there were more familiarity responses than actual recollections. Older adults were less able to remember an image of the target that they had seen during the experiment.

Older adults also experience deficits in the organization of contextual and temporal information, as evidenced by their poor performance on a list discrimination test. On this task, participants are asked when a target was presented in relation to other targets. They must also specify which list the target was in and if the target was presented to their left or right. Comparing young and old participants on this task, Parkin, Walter, and Hunkin (1995) observed no age differences in recognition of the targets, but older adults were impaired in their memory for temporal context. The organization of incoming information in sequence has been localized to the frontal cortex (Milner, Petrides, & Smith, 1985). Using either male or female speakers, McIntyre and Craik (1987) presented fictitious facts such as "Bob Hope's father was a fireman." At a later time, participants were asked to recall the "fact" with prompts such as "What did Bob Hope's father do for a living?" Older adults were particularly impaired in source memory in that they forgot whether the fact was presented by the male or female voice (McIntyre & Craik, 1987).

In another study, memory for source was correlated with cognitive flexibility (Craik, Morris, Morris, & Loewen, 1990). Source recognition and source recall also were correlated with one another, but neither assessment was correlated with the declarative memory measure of fact recall. Taken together, these studies suggest that source memory relies on frontal lobe functioning. Accordingly, Craik et al. concluded that source amnesia was not reflective of a general memory impairment in the aged but rather that normal aging is associated with impairment in frontal lobe functioning, which in turn impairs memory for the source of information.

Medial Temporal Lobe Declarative Memory Theory

A decline in the efficiency of learning and memory processes is seen to some degree in all older adults. However, there is a subset of elderly adults who have severe memory impairment. These are the people most likely to be seen by a clinical neuropsychologist. Often these individuals are in the early states of Alzheimer's disease (AD).

Cognitive neuroscience studies of learning and memory in neurological patients with discrete brain lesions, in normal adults undergoing brain imaging with positron emission tomography (PET), and in animals in stimulating, recording, lesion, and pharmacological studies have converged to demonstrate that different types of learning and memory are performed by different brain systems. At present there is evidence for two major forms of memory systems, declarative and nondeclarative. These memory systems have been classified into forms that rely on medial temporal lobe brain circuitry (declarative) and forms that do not depend on the medial temporal lobe circuitry (nondeclarative) (Schacter, 1992; Squire, 1992). Brain substrates of separate memory systems are often physically remote from one another; they are composed of qualitatively different types of neurons, neurotransmitters, and projections; and they are likely affected differentially by processes of aging. Among brain memory systems, it is the medial temporal lobe circuitry for declarative memory that is most affected by processes of normal and neuropathological aging.

The subjective awareness of "trying to learn" is typically present in tasks that assess declarative learning and memory. In contrast, nondeclarative learning occurs primarily through the performance of a given task. Age-related changes in the medial temporal lobe region, including the hippocampus, are thought to be associated with deficits in declarative learning and memory. In a study by Golomb, de Leon, Kluger, George, Tarshish, and Ferris (1993) correlating brain scans (MRI and CT) with memory test performance, it was found that about one-third of 154 medically healthy and cognitively normal older adults, ranging in age from 55 to 88 years, had evidence of hippocampal atrophy. It was primarily the participants with hippocampal atrophy who performed more poorly on tests of immediate and delayed recall of prose paragraphs and paired associate words. Longitudinal investigation of this sample will determine whether the participants with hippocampal atrophy were actually in the early stages of AD. At present it is not clear that hippocampal degeneration is part of the normal aging processes. Golomb et al. (1993) may have been documenting neuropathological aging with their relatively unique and innovative imaging and behavior study. Frontal lobe impairment with aging may also contribute to poor performance on some declarative learning and memory tasks because frontal lobe function affects attention, motivation, regulation, and self-monitoring, which are components of declarative memory tasks.

THEORIES ABOUT NEURODEGENERATION

Approximately 10% of individuals over the age of 65 are affected by neurodegenerative disease, and by age 80 this risk increases to 15%. The most common cause of neurodegeneration in elderly adults is AD, which accounts for 50% to 60% of all age-related dementias. Lewy body disease, a more recently described disease entity, has taken the place of cerebrovascular dementia as the second most common cause of dementia in the elderly population. Graham, Bell, and Ironside (1995) reported that cerebrovascular dementia accounts for, at most, 15% of dementia cases; an even smaller percentage of older adults are affected by other, less common, neurodegenerative processes such as Parkinson's disease (PD), Pick's disease, and Creutzfeldt-Jakob disease. Each of these diseases is characterized by specific neuropathological changes, which, in turn, result in observable changes in cognitive and behavioral functioning.

One role of a clinical neuropsychologist interested in aging is to help determine whether cognitive changes experienced by an older adult are due to normal or pathological processes of aging. If pathological processes are suspected, differential diagnoses are postulated, and the one that is most consistent with the neuropsychological profile is suggested as the diagnosis. The basis for these decisions comes from neuroscientific research of brain-behavior relationships. The clinical diagnosis serves as somewhat of a "working hypothesis," from which various case management and treatment options may be considered. However, the definitive diagnosis can be determined only by the results of an autopsy. This procedure involves postmortem removal of the brain for extensive evaluation, utilizing various scientific techniques such as staining and microscopic observation.

Numerous theories have been proposed to account for neurodegeneration in aging, and interested readers are referred to the *Handbook of the Biology of Aging* series for detailed accounts (e.g., Schneider & Rowe, 1996). Below we discuss some of the theories that have received support in accounting for AD. Other neurodegenerative disorders associated with aging are discussed briefly. The reader is again reminded that the term *theory* used throughout this volume refers to explanations accounting for empirical relationships. Elsewhere, these "theories" may be thought of as working hypotheses or models.

Clinical Features of Alzheimer's Disease

The most prominent clinical feature of AD is a progressive dementia characterized by impairment of memory and other areas of cognitive functioning, including language, attention, executive functioning, and visuospatial skills. The onset of the dementia is insidious, and the specific deficits shown vary across affected individuals. The course of the disease is also variable, and stages are often classified as mild, moderate, or severe. Examples of typical scenarios described by AD patients and their families include episodes of getting lost, repetition of stories, and an inability to successfully perform usual functions (e.g., balancing the checkbook, cooking, taking care of household chores).

The cognitive impairment exhibited by these patients has been described as cortical, because functions subserved by the cortex seem to be affected. Disruption to cortical circuits corresponds with cognitive and behavioral dysfunctions, such as aphasia, apraxia, and agnosia. Respectively, these terms refer to impairments of language, coordination of goal-directed movements, and recognition of familiar stimuli. Interestingly, patients initially can remember information from their distant past although they may not be able to recall with whom they dined the night before. Presumably, this is because the consolidation of new memories is compromised by neuronal loss in the entorhinal cortex (and hippocampus), whereas stored memories may still be retrievable from unaffected areas of cortex.

Theories of Alzheimer's Disease

Neuropathological Mechanisms

The neuropathological hallmarks of AD are neurofibrillary plaques and tangles. The plaques, generally found in the cortex, are made up of neurodegenerative by-products and proteins called amyloid. Their location is extracellular. The tangles are intracellular fiber bundles found primarily in the cortex and hippocampus, although other areas such as brain stem nucleii may be affected. The relationship between plaques and tangles is not yet known, nor is the relationship between the presence of these neuropathological hallmarks, neuronal death, and subsequent manifestations in behavior and cognition. Some reseachers believe that the tangles, but not plaques, are responsible for neuronal death and behavioral change (e.g., Arriagada, Growdon, Hedley-Whyte, & Hyman, 1992), but this issue is still debated. Amyloid plaques have been observed in normal aging, although tangles are rarely found in normal, age-matched controls.

It is also not clear which type of protein or amyloid is responsible for the manifestations of the disease. The "BAPtists" believe a protein called β-amyloid is responsible for the disease; the "Tauists" assert that the tau protein plays a more critical role. Very recently, a third protein, called AMY protein, entered this theoretical debate (see Roush, 1997). Researchers at the University of Pennsylvania identified this protein serendipitously while testing different assays on AD brains. The role of this protein in the cognitive and behavioral indices of the disease has yet to be explored.

Genetic Predisposition

Why some people develop the neuropathological changes associated with AD and others do not is not known. Some theories focus on the role of external variables, such as environmental stimuli and chemical exposure, in the predisposition for AD; others focus on internal factors, such as genetics. Several genes have thus far been named for their involvement in AD. One that has received a large amount of attention and mounting support recently for its relationship to AD is apolipoprotein E (ApoE). Within the ApoE genotypes, individuals with at least one ε4 allele (i.e., heterozygous) are 2 to 4 times more likely to get AD, and people who have two ε4 alleles (i.e., homozygous) are 5 to 30 times more likely to get AD (see Rao, Cupples, & vanDuijn, 1996). Nevertheless, not all people carrying an ε4 allele develop AD.

Because inheritance of the ε4 allele does not reliably predict AD, other factors appear to modulate the expression of the disease. One of these variables may be gender. Rao et al. (1996) found that penetrance of the ε4 allele was greater for women because all women in that study who had even one ε4 allele developed AD. Only 62% of men with one ε4 allele developed AD. Until this and other potential modulating variables are better understood, the American College of Medical Genetics and American Society of Human Genetics Working Group on ApoE and Alzheimer's Disease has issued a warning against the use of genetic testing for the ε4 allele as a screening test for AD. The role of the ε4 allele in neuropsychological decline has not been documented, although results of one study indicate that the presence of the ε4 allele is not related to rate of cognitive decline (Growdon, Locascio, Corkin, Gomez-Isla, & Hyman, 1996). These researchers suggest that the effect of the ε4 allele may occur prior to the onset of AD or at the very early stages.

Biochemical Theories

The Cholinergic Theory. The cholinergic theory of AD associates memory impairment with a reduction in the neurotransmitter acetylcholine. This reduction is largely attributed to a loss of cholinergic neurons projecting from the basal forebrain to the neocortex, a discovery made by Whitehouse and colleagues in 1981. Subsequently, converging evidence from animal and human studies has shown that when levels of acetylcholine are increased, memory is facilitated. Likewise, when cholinergic activity is blocked, memory is impaired. A review of this research as well as a discussion of how the cholinergic hypothesis may account for neuropsychiatric manifestations of AD is offered by Cummings and Kaufer (1996).

This theory about the relationship between cholinergic deficiency and cognitive decline is the basis for the two pharmacological treatments for AD approved by the Food and Drug Administration in the United States. These drugs, tacrine and donepezil (E2020), are referred to as cholinesterase inhibitors because they increase acetylcholine concentration in the brain by inhibiting the enzymes that break down acetylcholine (i.e., primarily acetylcholinesterase). The efficacy of these drugs support the cholinergic theory, but the presently approved drug therapies represent just a beginning step in treatment of some of the cognitive symptoms of AD. Side effects, along with relatively weak cognition-enhancing properties of these drugs, indicate that additional drugs affecting the cholinergic and other neurotransmitter systems are needed to treat AD. Of course, these drugs do not cure AD; they merely treat some of the symptoms.

Cholinergic neurons are depleted in AD and continue to degenerate as the disease progresses. Drugs that have a neuroprotective effect, keeping the remaining neurons functional, are needed for the treatment of AD. In addition to the cholinergic system, other neurotransmitter systems, including serotonergic and dopaminergic systems, are grossly affected in AD. Pharmacological therapies aimed at the cholinergic system as well as at other neurotransmitter systems continue to be developed and tested. As neuroprotective drugs become available to treat AD, it becomes more essential to detect the disease early to preserve cognitive capacities and their underlying brain substrates.

The Estrogen Theory.   One type of pharmacological therapy that has received increased attention over recent years is estrogen replacement therapy for females with AD. The theory underlying this form of treatment stemmed from the observation of a higher prevalence of AD in women than in men. Evidence from animal and human studies have supported the potential role of estrogen in the manifestations of AD (see Simpkins, Singh, & Bishop, 1994). In general, these studies suggest that (1) estrogen may be linked to productivity of basal forebrain and hippocampal neurons (which are compromised in AD); (2) estrogen receptors in the brain seem to be located near nerve growth factor, which is known to be relevant to cognition and behavior; and (3) diminished levels of circulating estrogens in postmenopausal women might accelerate the onset of clinical symptoms of AD. Multicenter trials assessing the efficacy of estrogen as an intervention for AD and focusing on understanding the role of estrogen in cognitive and behavioral symptoms of AD are currently underway.

Threshold Theory and the Nun Study

According to the threshold theory of dementia, individuals with a lot of reserve (high cognitive function) may be less likely to show signs of dementia because their cognitive or neurological reserve capacity is less likely to fall below a certain threshold. Snowdon and colleagues set out to test this theory in a study of nuns who were members of the School Sisters of Notre Dame religious congregation (Snowdon et al., 1996). Their series of ongoing studies has come to be known as the Nun Study.

Each participating nun had written an autobiography at a mean age of 22 years, prior to taking her religious vows. Consistent with the threshold theory of dementia, Snowdon et al. hypothesized that sisters who evidenced high cognitive functioning in their writing samples 58 years prior would be less likely to have developed dementia. The earlier writing samples of 93 nuns were analyzed for idea density and grammatical complexity. In addition, the nuns, who were a mean age of 79.9 years at the time of the study, were administered a battery of neuropsychological tests. The threshold model of dementia was supported by the finding that low idea density exhibited on earlier writing samples was highly correlated with poor cognitive function measured by neuropsychological tests later in life. In addition, Snowdon et al. found that low idea density in early writing samples was predictive of large numbers of neurofibrillary tangles in the neocortex and hippocampus. In fact, low idea density appeared to be a better predictor of neuropathological markers than clinical evidence of decline, suggesting that the reserve hypothesis cannot fully account for the obtained results. Snowdon et al. have suggested that low idea density early in life may be an early expression of developing AD. Further validation for this theory is needed and may be obtained as the Nun Study continues.

Dementia Associated with Lewy Bodies

Other causes of dementia in the elderly population may be attributed to the presence of Lewy bodies in various parts of the brain. Lewy bodies are named after Friederich Lewy, who first identified them in the brain. They are the neuropathological hallmark of PD. Lewy bodies are eosinophilic structures located within the neuron. In PD, Lewy bodies are found in the brainstem nuclei (e.g., substantia nigra) and are associated with movement disorders such as rigidity, tremor, and bradykinesia (slow movement). In Lewy body disease, these neuropathological structures are found both in the brainstem nucleii and in the cortex; hence, this disease is sometimes called diffuse Lewy body disease, as Lewy bodies are present diffusely throughout the cortex.

Because special staining techniques are needed to recognize cortical Lewy bodies, this disease has gone underrecognized. Currently, neuropathologists are more aware of the possibility of cortical Lewy bodies and include the necessary staining procedures for revealing this pathology in autopsy protocols. As a result, Lewy body disease has quickly come to be recognized as the second most common cause of dementia in the elderly.

In addition to Lewy bodies, patients with Lewy body disease usually have the neuropathological features associated with AD (i.e., neurofibrillary plaques and tangles) as well. For this reason, these three neurodegenerative diseases, AD, PD, and Lewy body disease, may be thought of as a continuum of neuropathology, with PD the least severe, AD the most severe, and Lewy body disease falling somewhere in the middle. From a clinical standpoint, such a continuum also is applicable, as patients with Lewy body disease exhibit AD-like dementia as well as parkinsonism and other neuropsychiatric features, such as hallucinations and delusions (for a review of Lewy body disease, see Papka, Rubio, & Schiffer, in press). Because of this overlap in both clinical and neuropathological features, these three diseases are often difficult to distinguish in the living patient. In fact, it has been suggested that 36% of patients who meet clinical criteria for AD exhibit Lewy body pathology at autopsy. Furthermore, a large percentage of patients with PD, ranging from 20% to 50% in some studies, are said to be demented, and it is still not clear whether these patients may have Lewy body disease rather than idiopathic PD.

The recent recognition of Lewy body disease as a distinct nosological entity has led to the proposition of various neuropathological and clinical criteria for diagnosing this disease, as well as a range of associated terminology. Although promising, this research is still in preliminary stages. With increased dedication to the study of these patients, we can expect an improvement in our ability to accurately identify patients with Lewy body disease and to understand the relationships between the neuropathology and behavior associated with this disease. Such research is currently underway and will likely lead to additional theories about the neuropsychology of this form of neurodegenerative aging.

CONCLUSIONS

The rapid growth of the population of older adults in the 20th century has been accompanied by progress in theory-building about brain and cognition relationships in normal and pathological aging. Among the most promising theories about normal aging is prefrontal cortex executive function theory. Evidence from the domains of neuropsychology, neuroanatomy, and radiology continue to indicate that the frontal lobes and frontal-lobe-mediated executive function may be affected most in normal aging. Medial temporal lobe declarative memory theory suggests that normal aging may account for some changes in the ability to consciously acquire new information, but this impairment may have been overestimated in normal aging due to inclusion of significant numbers of participants with neuropathology such as AD. Lesions in the medial temporal lobes are a consequence of AD that occur early in the course of the disease, long before diagnosis. Recent evidence indicates that normal aging may not cause significant damage in the medial temporal lobes.

Genetically based theories such as the association of some ApoE alleles with increased incidence of AD may be useful in developing a risk profile for the disease. The theory addressing neurodegeneration that has been most useful in providing insights about cognition is the cholinergic theory, associating memory impairment and also AD with reduced levels of the neurotransmitter acetylcholine. In addition to explaining brain and cognitive consequences of reduced cholinergic levels, cholinergic theory resulted in the development and approval of the only existing drugs available to treat memory loss in AD.

The late 20th century is the most dynamic period for neuropsychology in its short history as a science. New technology invented and implemented only in the past decade is revolutionizing our ability to assess brain activity during cognition. This technology is just beginning to be applied to cognition and aging. In the face of these powerful new tools, it is hardly surprising that some theories and whole avenues of thought about aging and cognition have been abandoned. Perhaps it should be more surprising that some older theories continue to have utility. In this rapidly changing field, one inescapable conclusion is that new theories will emerge in rapid succession and older theories will likely be modified at a swift pace.

REFERENCES

Albert, M. S., & Kaplan, E. (1980). Organic implications of neuropsychological deficits in the elderly. In L. W. Poon, J. L. Fozard, L. S. Cermak, D. Arenberg, & L. W. Thompson (Eds.), *New directions in memory and aging: Proceedings of the George A. Talland memorial conference* (pp. 403–432). Hillsdale, NJ: Erlbaum.

Arriagada, P. V., Growdon, J. H., Hedley-Whyte, T., & Hyman, B. T. (1992). Neurofibrillary tangles but not senile plaques parallel duration and severity of Alzheimer's disease. *Neurology, 42,* 631–639.

Beach, F. A., Hebb, D. O., Morgan, C. T., & Nissen, H. W. (1960). *The neuropsychology of Lashley.* New York: McGraw-Hill.

Birren, J. E. (1960). Behavioral theories of aging. In N. W. Shock (Ed.), *Aging: Some social and biological aspects.* Washington, DC: American Association for the Advancement of Science.

Birren, J. E. (1963). Psychophysiological relations. In J. E. Birren, R. N. Butler, S. W. Greenhouse, L. Sokoloff, & M. R. Yarrow (Eds.), *Human aging: A biological and behavioral study.* Washington, DC: U.S. Government Printing Office.

Birren, J. E., & Woodruff, D. S. (1983). Aging: Past and future. In D. S. Woodruff & J. E. Birren (Eds.), *Aging: Scientific perspectives and social issues* (2nd ed., pp. 1–15). Monterey, CA: Brooks/Cole.

Coffey, C. E., Wilkinson, W. E., Parashos, I. A., Soady, S. A. R., Sullivan, R. J., Patterson, L. J., Figiel, G. S., Webb, M. C., Spritzer, C. E., & Djang, W. T. (1992). Quantitative cerebral anatomy of the aging human brain: A cross-sectional study using magnetic resonance imaging. *Neurology, 42,* 527–536.

Craik, F. I. M., Morris, L. W., Morris, R. G., & Loewen, E. R. (1990). Relations between source amnesia and frontal lobe functioning in older adults. *Psychology and Aging, 5,* 148–151.

Cummings, J. L., & Kaufer, D. (1996). Neuropsychiatric aspects of Alzheimer's disease: The cholinergic hypothesis revisited. *Neurology, 47,* 876–883.

Damasio, H., Grabowski, T., Frank, R., Galaburda, A. M., & Damasio, A. R. (1994). The return of Phineas Gage: Clues about the brain from the skull of a famous patient. *Science, 264,* 1102–1105.

Eisdorfer, C., Nowlin, J. B., & Wilkie, F. (1970). Improvement of learning in the aged by modification of autonomic nervous system activity. *Science, 170,* 1327–1329.

Goldman-Rakic, P. S. (1987). Development of cortical circuitry and cognitive function. *Child Development, 58,* 601–622.

Golomb, J., de Leon, M. J., Kluger, A., George, A. E., Tarshish, C., & Ferris, S. H. (1993). Hippocampal atrophy in normal aging. *Archives of Neurology, 50,* 967–973.

Graham, D., Bell, J., & Ironside, J. (1995). *Color atlas and text of neuropathology.* New York: Mosby-Wofe.

Growdon, J. H., Locascio, J. J., Corkin, S., Gomez-Isla, T., & Hyman, B. T. (1996). Apolipoprotein E genotype does not influence rates of cognitive decline in Alzheimer's disease. *Neurology, 47,* 444–448.

Haaland, K. Y., Vranes, L. F., Goodwin, J. S., & Garry, P. J. (1987). Wisconsin Card Sort Test performance in a healthy elderly population. *Journal of Gerontology, 33,* 345–346.

Harlow, J. M. (1868). Recovery from the passage of an iron bar through the head. *Publications of the Massachusetts Medical Society (Boston). 2,* 327–346.

Kolb, B., & Whishaw, I. Q. (1995). *Fundamentals of human neuropsychology* (4th ed.). New York: W. H. Freeman.

Lashley, K. S. (1950). In search of the engram. *Symposium for the Society of Experimental Biology, 4,* 454–482.

Libon, D. J., Glosser, G., Malamut, B. L., Kaplan, E., Goldberg, E., Swenson, R., & Sands, L. P. (1994). Age, executive functions, and visuospatial functioning in healthy older adults. *Neuropsychology, 8,* 38–43.

McIntyre, J. S., & Craik, F. I. M. (1987). Age differences in memory for item and source information. *Canadian Journal of Psychology, 42,* 175–192.

Milner, B. (1963). Effects of different brain lesions on card-sorting. *Archives of Neurology, 9,* 90–100.

Milner, B., Petrides, M., & Smith, M. L. (1985). Frontal lobes and the temporal organization of memory. *Human Neurobiology, 4,* 137–142.

Mittenberg, W., Seidenberg, M., O'Leary, D. S., & DiGiulio, D. V. (1989). Changes in cerebral functioning associated with normal aging. *Journal of Clinical and Experimental Neuropsychology, 11,* 918–932.

Moscovitch, M. (1982). A neuropsychological approach to perception and memory in normal and pathological aging. In F. I. M. Craik & S. Trehub (Eds.), *Aging and cognitive processes* (pp. 55–78). New York: Plenum Press.

Papka, M., Rubio, A., & Schiffer, R. (in press). A review of Lewy body disease, an emerging concept of cortical dementia. *Journal of Neuropsychiatry and Clinical Neurosciences.*

Parkin, A. J., & Walter, B. M. (1992). Recollective experience, normal aging, and frontal dysfunction. *Psychology and Aging, 7,* 290–298.

Parkin, A. J., Walter, B. M., & Hunkin, N. M. (1995). Relationships between normal aging, frontal lobe function, and memory for temporal and spatial information. *Neuropsychology, 9*, 304–312.

Rao, V. S., Cupples, A., & van Duijn, C. M. (1996). Evidence for major gene inheritance of Alzheimer's disease in families of patients with and without apoliprotein E epsilon 4. *American Journal of Human Genetics, 59*, 664–675.

Roush, W. (1997). New lesion found in diseased brains. *Science, 277*, 31–32.

Schacter, D. L. (1992). Understanding implicit memory: A cognitive neuroscience approach. *American Psychologist, 47*, 559–569.

Schneider, E. L., & Rowe, J. W. (1996). *Handbook of the biology of aging* (4th ed.). San Diego, CA: Academic Press.

Shimamura, A. P. (1990). Aging and memory disorders: A neuropsychological analysis. In M. L. Howe, M. J. Stones, & C. J. Brainerd (Eds.), *Cognitive and behavioral performance factors in atypical aging* (pp.37–65). New York: Springer-Verlag.

Simpkins, J. W., Singh, M., & Bishop, J. (1994). The potential role for estrogen replacement therapy in the treatment of the cognitive decline and neurodegeneration associated with Alzheimer's disease. *Neurobiology of Aging, 15*, 195–197.

Snowdon, D. A., Kemper, S. J., Mortimer, J. A., Greiner, L. H., Wekstein, D. R., & Markesbery, W. R. (1996). Linguistic ability in early life and cognitive function and Alzheimer's disease in late life. Findings from the Nun Study. *Journal of the American Medical Association, 275*, 528–532.

Squire, L. R. (1992). Memory and the hippocampus: A synthesis from findings with rats, monkeys, and humans. *Psychological Review, 99*, 195–231.

Welford, A. T. (1965). Performance, biological mechanisms and age: A theoretical sketch. In A. T. Welford & J. E. Birren (Eds.), *Behavior, aging and the nervous system*. Springfield, IL: Charles, C. Thomas.

West, R. (1988). Prospective memory and aging. In M. M. Gruneberg, P. E. Morris, & R. N. Sykes (Eds.), *Practical aspects of memory: Current research and issues* (Vol. 2, pp. 119–125). New York: John Wiley & Sons.

Wheilihan, W. M., & Lesher, E. L. (1985). Neuropsychological changes in frontal functions with aging. *Developmental Neuropsychology, 1*, 371–380.

Whitehouse, P. J., Price, D. L., Clark, A. W., Coyle, J. T., & DeLong, M. R. (1981). Alzheimer disease: Evidence for selective loss of cholinergic neurons in the nuclear basalis. *Annals of Neurology, 10*, 122–126.

Woodruff, D. S. (1985). Arousal, sleep, and aging. In J. E. Birren & K. W. Schaie (Eds.), *Handbook of the psychology of aging* (2nd ed., pp. 261–295). New York: Van Nostrand Reinhold.

Woodruff-Pak, D. S. (1997). *The neuropsychology of aging.* Oxford, U.K.: Blackwell.

8

The Role of Aging Processes in Aging-Dependent Diseases

David H. Solomon

A dramatic increase in longevity has characterized the 20th century and is continuing briskly at century's end. The social and economic impact of this "success story" will be influenced strongly by the relationship between aging and disease. The inescapable question is the one posed by Fries (1980): will morbidity, disability, and handicap be expanded or compressed? If aging-dependent diseases can be delayed in their onset by lifestyle change and medical interventions, compression of morbidity is possible. Furthermore, if efforts to slow the rate of aging are successful concomitantly in delaying the onset and slowing the progression of disease, morbidity may be compressed further, whereas the opposite will be true if aging is slowed and longevity is increased without a corresponding improvement in the pattern of chronic disease. Thus, the key to the future well-being of an aging global population rests to a large extent on how tightly linked the rate of aging is to aging-dependent diseases, especially those that are untreatable at any given time and are prone to cause long-term disability rather than early death. The example of Alzheimer's disease leaps to mind.

For this reason, gerontologists have a compelling interest in a careful examination of the aging–disease relationship. This analysis usually begins with definitions that attempt to distinguish between diseases and the fundamental process we call aging. However, it appears that this distinction is neither feasible nor useful. *Webster's Unabridged Dictionary* defines a disease as "an impairment of the normal state of the living animal or plant body or any of its components that interrupts or modifies the performance of the vital functions, being a response to environmental factors . . . , to specific infective agents . . . , to inherent defects of the organism . . . , or to combinations of these factors." Unfortunately, the manifestations of aging are diseases under this definition unless we constrain severely the meaning of the words "normal state."

A further problem is that we can recognize the presence of chronic diseases clinically only at an advanced stage in their development; thus, the underlying disease process is present but undiagnosable for variable, generally long, periods. How can we ever say that one or more diseases are not present and therefore that the individual is experiencing "normal" aging?

Meanwhile, aging has been defined in so many different ways, pretty much one per author writing on the subject, that one can only conclude that there is no agreed-upon definition of aging. Grimley Evans (1988) summarized the situation elegantly: "to draw a distinction between disease and normal ageing is to attempt to separate the undefined from the indefinable" (p. 3).

Acknowledging that a truly satisfactory definition of the aging process must await a fuller understanding of the details of that process than we have today, I will exercise author's license by choosing the comprehensive definition by Miller (1994): "Aging is a process that converts healthy adults into frail ones, with diminished reserve in most physiological systems and an exponentially increasing vulnerability to most diseases and death." In addition, Strehler (1982), later supplemented by Arking (1991), introduced specific criteria for an aging process as a "series of cumulative, universal, progressive, intrinsic and deleterious functional and structural changes" (p. 9). The criterion of irreversibility is often added. Unfortunately, none of these criteria truly separates disease from "normal aging." Diseases may be—in fact, often are—cumulative, progressive, and deleterious. Furthermore, many of the diseases of later life are essentially universal if we accept the earliest manifestations as defining the presence of the illness (see below). Acknowledging that normal aging is, by definition, intrinsic, it is also true that most diseases have at least some intrinsic pathogenesis, so this too fails as a distinguishing point. Finally, irreversibility is a characteristic that applies both to features of normal aging and to diseases. In both cases treatment can reverse at least part of the process. For example, the rate of accumulation of reactive oxygen species (ROS, free radicals) can be decreased by antioxidants, and the characteristic stiffening of muscles can be ameliorated by as simple an intervention as flexibility exercises.

Faced with such an array of logical inconsistencies, I propose a new concept with a set of definitions to match (see Figure 8.1). This begins with the term *fundamental aging processes* to describe the inevitable side effects of living, which would include ROS derived from respiration, glycation as a result of glucose metabolism, and telomere shortening as a consequences of

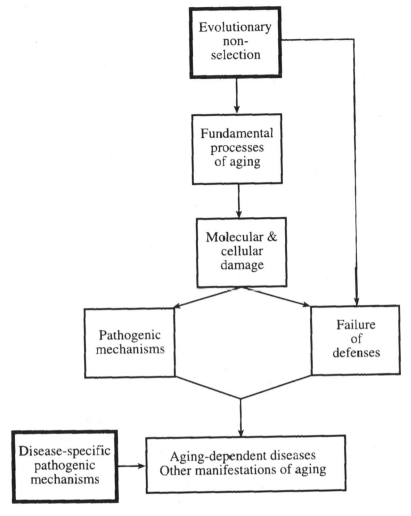

FIGURE 8.1 A model of the sequence of events made inevitable by the absence of genetic selection for genes that would maintain youthful physiological status indefinitely.

replication of cells, among others. These side effects are, by definition, universal. They lead, through three intermediate steps, to the "manifestations of aging," which are at a more clinical level and which vary in their specific characteristics across individuals and species. There is no qualitative distinction between aging-dependent diseases and other manifestations of aging, just as there is no valid distinction between these diseases and normal aging, but discarding the latter term at least frees us from the necessity to continue a pointless argument. So liberated, we can emphasize the distinction between fundamental aging processes and the manifestations of aging, an extremely useful distinction because it describes a direct predispositional relationship: fundamental aging processes sensitize the individual to clinically demonstrable consequences.

Parenthetically, even as innocuous a term as "other manifestations of aging" carries some ambiguity with it: these other manifestations are of two qualitatively different types. One is a change in structure or function that, if more severe, would be called a disease. For example, if creatinine clearance falls to 30% of the average youthful level by age 80, that is accepted as normal; whereas if it falls to, say, 15%, it is called chronic renal failure. The second type of other manifestation is a full-fledged characteristic of aging but one that is not usually referred to as a disease. Examples would be graying of hair and wrinkles in the skin.

Additionally, we define the terms used to describe diseases in relationship to aging. "Age-related diseases" has been widely used. However, as pointed out by Brody (1990), almost all diseases are age-related in the sense that they tend to achieve a peak incidence at a certain age. Some peak in childhood (e.g., acute lymphocytic leukemia), some in midlife (e.g., polycystic kidney disease, multiple sclerosis, and systemic lupus), and some fall into the area of interest of this chapter (i.e., those diseases whose incidence peaks at a late age). Brody proposed that age-related be reserved for diseases occurring at early and middle stages of life and falling to low incidence later and that those that peak in later life be called age-dependent. Later, he recognized that age-dependent is almost synonymous with age-related and accepted the suggestion that aging-dependent is a more accurate descriptor. I agree with that because aging-dependent signifies that the disease stems, at least in part, from fundamental aging processes. In using this term, I do not hold that aging is the *sole* etiology for aging-dependent diseases. The importance of aging processes is, in fact, as a potent predisposing factor for diseases and conditions whose etiology is actually multifactorial, as will be discussed below.

Finally, some diseases and conditions are age-related because they are, in fact, time-related; that is, they surface clinically at a certain age because time is required for the disease process to mature to that level, not because of the aging process. A classic example of a time-related condition is polycystic kidney disease, in which an inherited genetic abnormality leads to a disturbance in membrane permeability in the renal tubule, in turn leading to an abnormal accumulation of water. Many years are required for this misplaced water to build up to the point where the cysts become clinically evident. So the appearance of the disease has nothing to do with aging processes. I will exclude this type of disorder from the consideration of the aging–disease relationship that occupies the rest of this chapter.

EPIDEMIOLOGY OF AGING-DEPENDENT DISEASES

An essential component of any comprehensive definition of the aging process is that it predisposes to a rapidly rising age-specific incidence of aging-dependent diseases and of death. Mortality increases exponentially with age from a nadir in late childhood to approximately age 85, with a doubling time of approximately 8.5 years. Many of the aging-dependent diseases follow the same Gompertzian law of a linear relationship between the log of age-specific incidence and chronological age.

Mortality rate has decreased dramatically throughout the 20th century. In the first half-century this was largely accounted for by improvements in living environments, sanitation, other public health measures, and nutrition, with the result that the death rate at the age of onset of the exponential part of the curve declined sharply but the slope of the exponential rise remained relatively constant. During the second half-century a combination of healthier lifestyles and more effective preventive and therapeutic interventions has led to a further decline in the "age-zero" mortality, now accompanied by a decline in the exponential slope and a consequent slight increase in the doubling time.

Recently, as the population of extremely old people, nonagenarians and centenarians, has grown to researchable size, it has become increasingly evident that Gompertzian dynamics disappear after the age of 85 or 90. The rate of increase in mortality declines, reaching a point at which mortality rate is essentially constant with advancing age. These long-lived people, called "longevity outliers" by Smith (1993), seem to represent either healthful lifestyle choices, genetic selection of those with extraordinary resistance to the major fatal aging-dependent conditions, slowing of the rate at which aging processes occur in the oldest old, or all three.

Three-fourths of all deaths in the United States over the age of 65 are due to cardiovascular disease and cancer, and a small number of diseases account for most of the remaining mortality. Autopsies tend to emphasize terminal events rather than underlying causes, and clinical diagnoses and death certificate entries are more often wrong than right (MacGee, 1993). Few of these errors are corrected because only a small percentage of older people are autopsied. Thus, the exact order of frequency of diseases as causes of death is uncertain, but among the most frequent are ischemic heart disease, cancer, stroke, chronic obstructive pulmonary disease, pneumonia and influenza, diabetes, atherosclerosis, and accidents.

Of at least equal significance to the field of gerontology is the roster of aging-dependent diseases and conditions that lead to protracted disability more often than to death. In this instance, prevalences are the important statistic because they determine the burden of disability and need for care in the older population. The conditions, in order of prevalence, are osteoarthritis, hypertension, hearing impairment, cataract and other causes of visual impairment, ischemic heart disease, chronic obstructive pulmonary disease, diabetes, arteriosclerosis, orthopedic disorders (contributed to by osteoporosis), and cancer.

Armed with these two lists, we can select a sample of aging-dependent diseases for detailed analysis, limited by space considerations to ischemic heart disease, malignant neoplasms, diabetes, osteoarthritis, and in addition, Alzheimer's disease. The latter is not listed in mortality or morbidity statistics because of problems of diagnosis and reporting that have prevailed until recently, but it is of major importance in predicting disability, health care need, and loss of independence.

A BRIEF SUMMARY OF AGING PROCESSES

Before focusing on exemplary aging-dependent diseases, we must at least briefly summarize the components of the fundamental processes of aging, insofar as we can understand them today. I will confine this discussion to those components that are relatively noncontroversial and which are essential to theorizing about aging-dependent diseases. The reader is referred to a fuller analysis of aging processes in chapter 6.

To model the aging process it seems useful to describe a sequence of three steps leading all the way from evolutionary selection theory to a list of pathogenic mechanisms for disease or for other manifestations of aging (Figure 8.1). Rather suddenly, a consensus has developed that, at the most fundamental level, an accumulation of pathogenic processes is an *inevitable* accompaniment of aging. In simplest terms, this is because there is an almost complete absence of selection pressure for genes that would defend against aging processes and thereby prolong postreproductive, postparenting, and possibly postgrandparenting life. The lack of such genes guarantees a failure of maintenance systems in a complex organism whose evolution of specialized structures and functions has been driven by the need for fitness *during early life only*. Important variants of this theory, reviewed extensively in recent articles, are the disposable soma concept of Kirkwood (1985, 1996), the antagonistic pleiotropy concept of Williams (1962), and the metabolic-switch theory of Neel (1962), updated by Grimley Evans (1993).

Because older organisms are "twisting, twisting slowly in the evolutionary wind," to paraphrase John Ehrlichman's infamous Watergate metaphor, fundamental aging processes (Figure 8.1) accumulate while maintenance and repair mechanisms falter. Several key examples can be cited, although the list could probably be much longer. Reactive oxygen species (free radicals) are generated as an inescapable by-product of oxidative metabolism while, with age, enzymes equipped to detoxify these species decrease in activity (Horan

& Pendleton, 1995). Glycation of proteins leads to the accumulation of advanced glycosylation end products. It should be noted that these two pathogenic processes are synergistic because oxidation hastens glycation. Other posttranslational alterations in proteins may also be important (Gafni, 1997). Shortening of telomeres is still another example of a fundamental aging process.

The immediate results of these aging processes consist of damage to critical structures, molecules, and functions. The main targets of oxidation and glycation are DNA, protein, lipids, and lipid-layered membranes. Mutations accumulate in both nuclear and mitochondrial DNA, resulting in inaccurate synthesis of proteins and other macromolecules and probably accounting for inadequate energy production. Damage to proteins that are key elements in protection against the aging process establishes a vicious circle of accelerated aging. Examples of such critical proteins are enzymes (e.g., superoxide dismutase, catalase, glutathione reductase, DNA repair enzymes, detoxifying P450 cytochrome enzymes, and a variety of proteinases), receptors (e.g., beta-adrenergic, CD 28 in T cells), growth factors (e.g., fos), and structural proteins (e.g., collagen, elastin, and lens crystalline). The changes in structural proteins are particularly pervasive because these are long-lived and resistant to hydrolysis even when damaged. Collagen becomes extensively cross-linked as a result of oxidation and glycation, thereby losing flexibility and compliance. Elastin loses its elasticity as a result of fragmentation of its fibrils. Lens proteins undergo extensive changes in tertiary structure. Meanwhile, overall protein synthesis rate decreases with age for reasons not yet clear, cell division shows finite limits (possibly as a result of telomere shortening or defective action of cell-cycle enzyme systems), old cells develop a senescent phenotype, and apoptosis becomes faulty (Monti et al., 1992). Lipids undergo peroxidation, and lipid membranes become more viscous.

Such biochemical assaults lead, in turn, to pathogenic processes that express themselves both in the appearance of aging-dependent diseases and in other manifestations of aging. These pathogenic processes include atherogenesis, carcinogenesis, insulin resistance and diabetogenesis, microangiopathy, deficits in the immune system (both immunosenescence and autoimmunity), coalescence of pulmonary alveoli, altered chondrocyte physiology, and an excess of bone resorption over formation, as well as important declines in flexibility of skeletal muscle, compliance of heart muscle, elasticity of the skin and large arteries (leading to systolic hypertension), and compressibility of the lens (leading to the impairment of accommodation known as presbyopia, one of the earliest clinical manifestation of aging). Other pathophysiological mechanisms predisposing to manifestations of aging are accumulated structural damage to fixed, nonmaintained structures (e.g., teeth, lens, and intervertebral discs); replicative senescence in some mitotic cells (Campisi, 1997); accelerated apoptosis in some postmitotic cells (e.g., neurons, skeletal and cardiac myocytes); reduced wound healing and regenerative capacity; inefficient temperature-control mechanisms; and reduced capacity to maintain homeostasis after stress.

SELECTED AGING-DEPENDENT DISEASES

To illustrate the aging–disease relationship, I shall describe briefly the epidemiology and pathogenesis of the five model aging-dependent diseases previously cited.

Ischemic Heart Disease

Ischemic heart disease (IHD) is the most serious consequence of atherosclerosis, which, in turn, is the pathogenetic mechanism for essentially all cardiovascular disease in older people. It has a prevalence of 18% in persons age 65 and over (Verbrugge & Patrick, 1995). Age-specific incidence and mortality rise exponentially, with a doubling time of 8 years, closely paralleling the curve for overall age-specific mortality. Ischemic heart disease is a clear predictor of disability and of need for health care services. Age-specific mortality is 10 per 1,000 population at 65 to 69 years of age, rising to 76 per 1,000 for those over the age of 85 (Brody & Brock, 1986). Cardiovascular disease mortality has fallen sharply since 1968, although incidence has declined very little. Overall, mortality due to IHD has fallen by approximately 50%, and this has accounted for 55% of the recent decline in all-cause mortality.

Ischemic heart disease results from coronary atherosclerosis, whose pathogenesis is the result of an interaction between aging processes (e.g., oxidation by ROS and alterations in the collagen and elastin molecules) and disease-specific factors, both intrinsic and extrinsic. Genes for apolipoprotein(a), APO-E, LDL receptor, and homocysteine metabolism are involved and probably many more. Acquired conditions such as hypertension, obesity, hypercholesterolemia, and diabetes are important risk factors, as are smoking, a high-fat diet, and lack of exercise. These disease-specific factors would eventually cause atherosclerosis to reach a clinically evident stage, but this comes sooner because oxidation of LDL by ROS hastens the deposition of cholesterol in arterial walls, and the changes in collagen and elastin lead to accumulation of extracellular matrix, stiffening of the wall, and an increased tendency for thickening of the intima and media (Bilato & Crow, 1996).

Malignant Neoplasms (Cancer)

Although cancer occurs at all ages, all of the common cancers increase in frequency with age. For certain cancers, such as carcinoma of the prostate, the rise is exponential, but for many it is linear and quite gradual. Furthermore, cancer could technically be classified as age-related rather than aging-dependent because the incidence and mortality plateau after age 75 and decline after age 85. The commonest primary sites of cancer in people over 65 are lung, prostate, colon and rectum, and urinary bladder in men; breast, colon and rectum, lung, and pancreas in women.

Although cancers certainly take a toll as a result of symptomatology and mortality, their quantitative impact on disability is lessened by their high mortality and limited duration. Because incidence rises only gradually, compared to the exponential rise for other chronic diseases, and because cancer mortality rate falls with age, cancer causes only 12% of deaths from all causes for those over 85, compared to 20% at ages 75 to 84 and 25% at ages 65 to 74.

The pathogenesis of cancer is complex, and there has been controversy over whether the rise in incidence with age is due to aging processes or simply to the passage of time, allowing for accumulation of multiple damaging events such as somatic mutations in genes for growth factors, chromosomal breaks and translocations, internalization of immunogenic surface markers, alterations in cellular adhesive properties, and the like. In other words, according to this view, older persons develop cancer because they have a longer time to be exposed to carcinogenic influences. The alternative view, articulated well by Miller (1995), acknowledges the stepwise nature of carcinogenesis (initiation, promotion, and progression) but holds that the rate-limiting step(s) are controlled by the rate of aging processes. I favor the latter argument but must leave it to the reader to examine the evidence presented by Miller and other authors and, for the other side, by Newell, Spitz, and Sider (1989) among others.

Diabetes Mellitus

Type I, or insulin-dependent, diabetes is a classical example of an age-related disease. Its incidence peaks in youth, as is true of some other autoimmune diseases, and it rarely occurs de novo after the age of 50. On the other hand, Type II diabetes is an aging-dependent disease of entirely different pathogenesis. Its age-specific incidence and mortality rise exponentially with age, starting at about 40, with a doubling time of 6 to 8 years. The incidence then falls at very late ages. Diabetes causes disability in the later years of life, not because of hyperglycemia itself but as a result of the microangiopathic complications of diabetes, including retinopathy, peripheral nerve dysfunction, and diabetic nephropathy. In addition, diabetes predisposes to atherosclerosis, thereby increasing the frequency of IHD, cerebrovascular disease, and peripheral vascular disease with its accompanying threat of gangrene.

Type II diabetes is caused principally by disease-specific genetic predispositions and by lifestyle factors, especially overeating and underexercising. Although the incidence increases strikingly with age, so that age is the strongest risk factor for diabetes, the mechanism by which aging processes enter into the pathogenesis remains unclear. In fact, diabetes might conceivably be time-related rather than aging-dependent in the sense that older people have a longer time to be exposed to the consequences of disease-specific gene expression and adverse lifestyle factors (Heine, 1991), but it is more likely that the obligatory component in the pathogenesis is an effect of aging on the islet cells.

Osteoarthritis

Osteoarthritis is the most common disease of people over the age of 65 by a wide margin. The age-specific incidence rises exponentially with age, with a doubling time between 5 and 7 years. Prevalence in the United States is about 80% in the 75+ age group, when judged clinically, but is essentially 100% at autopsy. It is the greatest cause of disability in the later years because of its extraordinary prevalence and the fact that it lasts from onset to death from another cause. Arthritis is rarely fatal on its own. Progression of symptoms and x-ray abnormalities is very slow.

The pathogenesis of osteoarthritis is poorly understood. The role of genetic factors is unclear, but there certainly are extrinsic factors in some cases, perhaps 10% (e.g., trauma, meniscectomy, epiphyseal dysplasia, and joint instability). The remaining cases are unexplained, except for a presumed role for obesity (i.e., weight bearing). This leaves much room for a putative influence of aging, which might well be mediated by alterations in the structure and function of collagen as well as fundamental changes in the properties of chondrocytes.

Alzheimer's Disease

The most frightening consequence of our progressively increasing longevity is dementia due to Alzheimer's disease, vascular dementia, or other, rarer causes. The annual incidence of Alzheimer's disease is 1.4 per 1,000 in the seventh decade, 6.4 per 1,000 in the eighth decade, and 20.5 per 1,000 in those 80 years of age and older. This describes a Gompertzian exponential, with a doubling time of only 5 or 6 years from age 60 through 90. There is evidence of decreasing slope thereafter. The resultant prevalence figures are formidable: at least 6% of all people 65 and over and as many as 45% of those 85 and over. Disability is inevitable as the disease progresses and the severity of impairments grows. The disability burden accumulates sharply because the disease is long-lasting, averaging 12 years from diagnosis to death.

The pathogenesis of Alzheimer's diseases has been the subject of an explosion of recent research. Disease-specific factors include at least three genes that cause familial clusters, one allele (APO E4) that confers added risk of developing the disease, and certain unusual lifestyle issues such as chronic head trauma in pugilists. The exact role of aging processes is unknown, but it is clear that they must play a role if we are to explain the exponential increase in sporadic cases, which constitute the overwhelming majority. Oxidation by ROS and glycation appear to accelerate the deposition of amyloid in senile plaques, but there are probably many other mechanisms.

Comorbidity

Before completing this section, a few comments on the highly prevalent aging-dependent phenomenon of multiple coexisting diseases (comorbidity) are in order. Men in the United States report two or more chronic diseases or conditions with high frequency—35% in the 60–69 age bracket, 47% at 70–79, and 53% at 80 and above. For women the percentage frequencies are even higher—45, 61, and 70 for the same three age groups, respectively (Cauley, Dorman, & Ganguli, 1996). Comorbidity is a major factor in causing increased mortality and functional limitation. In one study, the concurrence of four aging-dependent conditions predicted future disability three times greater in prevalence than the average for any one of the conditions (Boult, Kane, Louis, Boult, & McCaffrey, 1994).

MODELS CONNECTING AGING PROCESSES TO AGING-DEPENDENT DISEASES

As discussed above, aging processes lead stepwise to pathogenic processes, intensified by a decline in the vigor of maintenance systems (Figure 8.1). This chain of events clearly predisposes an individual to one or more of the aging-dependent diseases and other manifestations of aging. The diseases are multifactorial, resulting from an interaction of aging processes with disease-specific factors, including (1) genes that increase the risk for developing the disease; (2) environment, which affects the individual as a result of inhalation, ingestion, or superficial exposure to toxins or radiations; (3) lifestyle choices, prominent among which are diet, exercise, smoking, alcohol, and prevention seeking through public health measures and medical advice; (4) psychosocial factors and access to education; (5) a host of continuously distributed physiological variables that, at the higher (or lower) end of the distribution, predispose to the development of what we call disease but that is actually just an extension, or shoulder, of the normal distribution (systolic blood pressure and isolated systolic hypertension represent an obvious example of this relationship); and (6) cumulative effects of the repeated application of physical forces, a factor particularly important in the pathogenesis of osteoarthritis.

In every instance the fundamental aging processes described above set the stage for the operation of disease-specific factors, doing so by a variety of mechanisms illustrated in the prior discussion of exemplary diseases. The variables affecting the pattern seen in an individual are the rate at which the aging processes progress and the intensity and diversity of disease-specific factors that determine which aging-dependent disease develops first, second, and so on (Horan & Pendleton, 1995).

Aging processes can predispose to the development of aging-dependent disease by mechanisms so diverse and so penetrant as to make it easily understandable that aging-dependent conditions account for the vast majority of illness in industrialized nations today (Holliday, 1995). Aging processes function as risk factors for disease, they accelerate the onset and rate of progression of disease, and they modify the manifestations of disease, generally making the disease worse.

To understand the dependency of diseases on aging, it is essential to emphasize that chronic diseases begin with subtle, currently undetectable abnormalities and progress slowly to produce functional changes, biochemical or cellular, and then histologically identifiable structural changes. Thus, the true duration of the disease is the sum of a preclinical (or predetectable) phase and a clinical phase. For each disease there is a biochemical threshold, a histological threshold, and finally, a clinical threshold (Figure 8.2). The clinical threshold varies, not only with the characteristics of the particular disease but very prominently with the ability of currently available methodology to detect the disease.

Many examples are available to illustrate these points. Fatty streaks, the primary event in the development of atherosclerosis, have been found in the aortas of children and young adults. The usual course is slow, steady progression, often with a steep, even exponential increase in severity at later ages. The full-fledged atherosclerotic plaque develops, leading eventually to symptoms and diagnosis. Note that diagnosis may occur earlier if the individual happens to have an exercise stress test or even earlier if an ultrasensitive high-speed CT scan detects tiny deposits of calcium in the coronary arteries.

Figure 8.2 illustrates the interaction of disease-specific factors, both intrinsic and extrinsic, with the effect of aging processes on the development and progression of aging-dependent diseases. Curve A diagrams schematically the severity of a disease process as a function of age, assuming only the operation of fundamental aging processes in an "average" individual, that is, one neither particularly predisposed to nor protected from the disease and one whose rate of aging processes is about average. Curve B suggests that a

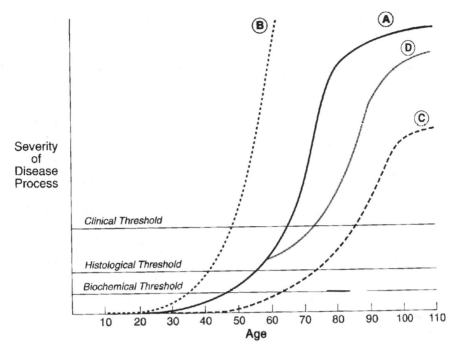

FIGURE 8.2 A diagrammatic representation of the probable course of a wide variety of aging-dependent diseases. See text for explanation of symbols.

person predisposed genetically and/or by lifestyle or other disease-specific factors would experience an earlier onset, earlier crossing of the three thresholds, and more rapid progression. Curve C diagrams the obverse situation in an individual blessed with protective forces, either disease-specific or in terms of rate of aging processes. Finally, Curve D depicts what would be expected if a person with an average rate of aging processes and disease-specific protections and predispositions suddenly changed some of the factors within the control of the individual, such as seeking and receiving preventive health care, changing lifestyle, or correcting a toxic environment.

THEORETICAL CONSIDERATIONS

Interpretation of the models in the previous section leads to several points of theoretical interest.

First, the basic theorem is that fundamental aging processes initiate a series of steps that increase the likelihood of developing one or more aging-dependent diseases. The evidence for this is very strong. The average old organism suffers from multiple diseases, each rising in incidence exponentially with age. It is unlikely that such comorbidity would result simply from greater time for disease-specific risk factors to operate. Actually, the effect of risk factors *decreases* with age because survivors without clinical evidence of the disease have been selected for resistance to the disease-specific risk factors. The weakness of serum cholesterol as a risk factor for coronary atherosclerosis after the age of 70 is an excellent illustration. Thus, longer exposure to risk factors would be unlikely to cause increasing age-specific incidences and certainly not the exponential rise characteristic of many aging-dependent diseases (Cauley et al., 1996). Further, the very multiplicity of aging-dependent diseases implies at least one common pathogenic mechanism, unless it is accounted for by one such disease leading to another. In fact, this very likely does occur, causing some clustering of diseases (e.g., hypertension, diabetes, central obesity, atherosclerosis, and hypercholesterolemia coexist more often than chance alone would dictate), but this mechanism could hardly link Alzheimer's disease, cancer, and osteoporosis, for example. So the breadth of pathology argues for a common aging-dependent pathogenesis.

Additional evidence comes from studies in animals. Caloric restriction in rodents mitigates and delays many stigmata of aging, increases longevity remarkably, and simultaneously reduces the incidence of a variety of strain-specific diseases (e.g., cancer, lymphoma, and chronic renal failure). The slowing of the rate of aging processes and of the incidence of disease seem to be quite parallel. In fact, in this classic model of increased longevity, it may well be the decrease in aging-dependent diseases that primarily explains the decrease in mortality, although Masoro (1988) presents some contrary evidence. In a different experimental approach, Covelli, Mouton, deMajo, Bouthillier, Bangrazi, Mevel, et al.(1989) and Miller, Bookstein, Van der Meulen, Engle, Kim, and Mullins (1997) have shown that mice bred for greater or lesser evidence of immunosenescence show corresponding differences in longevity; there were also correlations between markers of immunosenescence and sarcopenia. These experiments suggest that there is a basic aging process or set of processes that proceed at variable rates and lead to multiple correlated manifestations of aging. Covelli et al. (1989) presented preliminary evidence that the incidence of diseases (lymphoma and chronic nephritis) also correlated with the immunological marker of aging rate.

Finally, our knowledge about Werner's syndrome in humans provides strong support for the theorem that fundamental aging processes predispose to aging-dependent diseases. Its phenotype includes premature atherosclerosis, Type II diabetes, cataracts, osteoporosis, and cancers, along with replicative senescence in vitro. This disorder of recessive inheritance has recently been shown to be caused by a mutant gene that codes for a DNA helicase essential for normal cell division and DNA repair. This experiment of nature tells us that a genetic abnormality that accelerates the aging process is associated with an accelerated onset of aging-dependent diseases.

Second, aging-dependent diseases are essentially universal when considered as a group. Many of them may actually be universal even when considered alone. I believe that if the methods of detection were sensitive enough and age advanced enough, atherosclerosis, osteoporosis, osteoarthritis, and other diseases would be found to be just as universal as a decline in creatinine clearance or pulmonary forced expiratory flow rate, examples of widely accepted physiological changes of aging. The fundamental aging processes, taken together, predispose to all of the aging-dependent diseases, and the development of such diseases is a fundamental property of aging. It is possible that aging processes can cause aging-dependent diseases even when disease-specific factors are minimal, given a sufficiently long life.

Third, I believe that aging processes are rarely lethal on their own, at least until very advanced ages, if then. Mortality in the later years is largely explained by aging-dependent diseases, rather than by the aging processes that predispose to them or the changes with age that I have called other manifestations of aging and others have called normal aging. The empirical observation behind this position is that, although the fundamental aging processes are phenomena that pervade the entire organism, aging free of clinical disease is relatively benign. On the other hand, the incidence of aging-dependent diseases rises pretty much in parallel with the exponential rise in age-specific mortality. Thus, one can only conclude that aging processes do their damage by means of predisposing to diseases that, singly and in combination, lead to the impairments, disabilities, handicaps, and death that characterize the later years.

Recent studies of longevity outliers lead to one more theorem: the aging processes ultimately become less deleterious. This could be due to the survival of those with the greatest resistance to aging processes, to disease-specific factors, or to both; or it could be due to an actual slowdown in the rate at which aging processes, such as oxidation or glycation, take place. Like the other three theorems, this one should be testable by present and future research methods.

Beyond these theorems, I would like to make a suggestion regarding how we might think about the complex genesis of aging-dependent diseases. As expressed in Figure 8.1, these diseases result from interactions between the aging processes and a long list of disease-specific (or multiple-disease-specific) pathogenic factors, both intrinsic and extrinsic. Rather than quibbling about what is normal aging, I would suggest that we look on this as simply the most benign end of a spectrum of aging-related structural and functional changes and focus on describing quantitatively the contribution of aging processes, on the one hand, and the various disease-specific pathogenic factors, on the other hand, to the development of aging-dependent diseases and the other manifestations of aging. For example, the decline in creatinine clearance with age is largely dependent on aging processes, with other pathogenic factors playing a role in only a minority of individuals. At the other end of the scale, with a high ratio of disease-specific factors to aging processes, would be Type II diabetes. The fact of comorbidity would make estimations more complex, but the set-theory approach of Thompson (1996) would be useful in estimating the synergistic effects.

IMPLICATIONS

First, a major focus of research effort should be on the fundamental processes of aging, not because they are themselves highly malignant but because they predispose strongly to a broad array of aging-dependent diseases. The other major focus should be on the disease-specific pathogenic factors for the *nonfatal,* disability-causing diseases and conditions, particularly dementia, arthritis, osteoporosis, incontinence and impairment of hearing and vision. This dual strategy would go a long way toward assuring the compression of morbidity, which has been a consensus goal for the past 18 years (Fries, 1980). Fries predicted that a healthier lifestyle would accomplish the desired end, but many others have argued that this would be ineffective and even that expansion of morbidity would be inevitable. My hunch is that the dual research strategy described above would indeed lead to compression of morbidity; whereas incentives for healthier lifestyles, although beneficial, would probably be insufficient because they are unlikely to persuade the entire population, and even if they did, life span might well be prolonged as much as or more than the period of good health.

Second, the characteristic exponential curves describing the incidence (and progression rate) of aging-dependent diseases means that the first goal of research should be to *defer* the onset of clinical disease because this will halve the incidence and ultimately the amount of disability in society if deferral by one doubling time (5–8 years) can be achieved. It is likely that total prevention of aging-dependent diseases will not be accomplished for a very long time, so we should aim for "half a loaf." The focus on deferral should be directed primarily at the nonfatal or slowly fatal conditions cited above.

Third, the geriatrician should continue to follow what has become a basic tenet of geriatrics: assess whatever problems are detectable and treat whatever is treatable. A little improvement in each of several clinical problems often causes greater overall improvement than would be expected from their arithmetic sum. This axiom rests on the clear fact that aging-related diseases are usually multiple and on our growing knowledge of the effects of comorbidity. Synergy in deleterious effects mandates that the benefits of treatment will be synergistic as well.

Fourth, studies of extreme old age should be intensified because the slow-down in the rise in incidence rates of aging-dependent diseases and in the rates of progression of existing diseases may be an important clue to how to defer the onset of disease at earlier ages. I suspect that, from the earliest humans to the present, there has been compelling interest in the lifestyle of people who live exceptionally long lives. "Grandpa smoked like a chimney and drank like a fish, and he lived to be 102." Anecdotal information of this sort will continue to be presented, so it behooves us to study very seriously the genetics and the history of extrinsic factors that might affect the inci-dence of aging-dependent diseases and the longevity of very long survivors in comparison to people of average life span. Such studies would today be based on retrospective data, but as the major longitudinal study populations reach advanced ages, it should be possible to test hypotheses and theories by examining them prospectively.

REFERENCES

Arking, R. (1991). *Biology of aging*. Englewood Cliffs, NJ: Prentice Hall.

Bilato, C., & Crow, M. T. (1996). Atherosclerosis and the vascular biology of aging. *Aging Clinical and Experimental Research, 8*, 221–234.

Boult, C., Kane, R. L., Louis, T. A., Boult, L., & McCaffrey, D. (1994). Chronic con-ditions that lead to functional limitation in the elderly. *Journal of Gerontology: Medical Sciences, 49*, M28–M36.

Brody, J. A. (1990). Chronic diseases and disorders. In A. L. Goldstein (Ed.), *Biomed-ical advances in aging* (pp. 137–142). New York: Plenum Press.

Brody, J. A., & Brock, D. B. (1986). Epidemiological characteristics of the United States elderly population in the 20th century. *European Journal of Epidemiology, 2*, 15–25.

Campisi, J. (1997). Aging and cancer: The double-edged sword of replicative senes-cence. *Journal of the American Geriatric Society, 45*, 482–488.

Cauley, J. A., Dorman, J. S., & Ganguli, M. (1996). Genetic and aging epidemiology: The merging of two disciplines. *Neurology Clinics, 14*, 467–475.

Covelli, V., Mouton, D., DiMajo,V., Bouthillier,Y., Bangrazi, C., Mevel, J.-C., Rebessi, S., Doria, G., & Biozzi, G. (1989). Inheritance of immune responsiveness, life span, and disease incidence in interline crosses of mice selected for high and low multispecific antibody production. *Journal of Immunology, 142*, 1224–1234.

Fries, J. F. (1980). Aging, natural health and the compression of morbidity. *New England Journal of Medicine, 303*, 130–135.

Gafni, A. (1997). Structural modifications of proteins during aging. *Journal of the American Geriatric Society, 45*, 871–880.

Grimley Evans, J. (1988). Ageing and disease. In *Research and the Ageing Population* (pp. 38–57). Ciba Symposeium (#134). Chichester, U.K.: John Wiley and Sons.

Grimley Evans, J. (1993). Ciba Symposium (#134). Metabolic switches in ageing. *Age and Ageing, 22*, 79–81.

Heine, R. J. (1991). Non-insulin dependent diabetes mellitus: A phenomenon of aging? *International Journal of Epidemiology, 20* (Suppl. 1), S18–S24.

Holliday, R. (1995). *Understanding aging.* Cambridge, U.K.: Cambridge University Press.

Horan, M. A., & Pendleton, N. (1995). The relationship between aging and disease. *Reviews in Clinical Gerontology, 5,* 125–141.

Kirkwood, T. B. L. (1985). Comparative and evolutionary aspects of longevity. In C. E. Finch & E. L. Schneider (Eds.), *Handbook of the biology of aging* (2nd ed.). New York: Van Nostrand Reinhold.

Kirkwood, T. B. L. (1996). Human senescence. *Bio Essays, 18,* 1009 1016.

MacGee, W. (1993). Causes of death in a hospitalized geriatric population: an autopsy study of 300 patients. *Virchows Archiv. A. Pathological Anatomy 423,* 343–349.

Masoro, E. J. (1988). Food restriction in rodents: An evaluation of its role in the study of aging. *Journal of Gerontology: Biological Sciences, 43,* B59–64.

Miller, R. A. (1994). The biology of aging and longevity. In W. R. Hazzard, E. L. Bierman, J. P. Blass, W. H. Ettinger, Jr., & J. B. Halter (Eds.), *Principles of geriatric medicine and gerontology* (3rd ed., pp. 3–18). New York: McGraw-Hill.

Miller, R. A. (1995). Geroncology: The study of aging as the study of cancer. In K. Esser & G. M. Martin (Eds.), *Molecular aspects of aging* (pp. 265–277). New York: John Wiley and Sons.

Miller, R. A., Bookstein, F., Van der Meulen, J., Engle, S., Kim, J., & Mullins, L. (1997). Candidate biomarkers of aging: Age-sensitive indices of immune and muscle function covary in genetically heterogeneous mice. *Journal of Gerontology: Biological Sciences, 52A,* B39–B47.

Monti, D., Grassilli, E., Troiano, L., Cozzarizza, A., Salvioli, S., Barbieri, D., Agnesini, C., Bettuzzi, S., Ingletti, M. C., Corti, A., & Franceschi, C. (1992). Senescence, immortalization and apoptosis: An intriguing relationship. *Annals of the New York Academy of Science, 673,* 70–82.

Neel, J. V. (1962). Diabetes mellitus: A 'thrifty' genotype rendered detrimental by progress? *American Journal of Human Genetics, 14,* 353–362.

Newell, G. R., Spitz, M. R., & Sider, J. G. (1989). Cancer and age. *Seminars in Oncology, 16,* 3–9.

Smith, D. W. E. (1993). *Human longevity.* New York: Oxford University Press.

Strehler, B. (1982). *Time, cells, and aging.* New York: Academic Press.

Thompson, M. K. (1996). The need for a new biological model in geratology. *Age and Ageing, 25,* 168–171.

Verbrugge, L. M., & Patrick, D. L. (1995). Seven chronic conditions: Their impact on US adults' activity levels and use of medical services. *American Journal of Public Health, 85,* 173–182.

Williams, G. C. (1962). Pleitropy, natural selection and the evolution of senescence. *Evolution, 11,* 398–411.

SECTION III

Psychological Concepts and Theories of Aging

9

Multilevel and Systemic Analyses of Old Age: Theoretical and Empirical Evidence for a Fourth Age

Paul B. Baltes
Jacqui Smith

I s psychological aging best understood from an overall structural (systemic) level or in terms of specific processes and mechanisms? As the title of this chapter implies, our response to this question lies not in pursuing one or the other approach but in making efforts to join these different levels of theorizing and analysis. This line of approach owes much to the work of James Birren, whose lifetime oeuvre is characterized by a joint consideration of interdisciplinary as well as macro- and microperspectives on the nature of human aging (Birren, 1959; Birren & Bengtson, 1988; Birren & Schroots, 1996).

The task of joining levels of analysis within and across disciplines as well as between evolutionary and ontogenetic perspectives is not easy. To this end, life span developmental theorists have established a set of overarching propositions about ontogeny (e.g., P. B. Baltes, 1997; P. B. Baltes, Lindenberger, & Staudinger, 1997; Elder, 1997; Featherman, 1983). These propositions draw attention to the multiplicity of phenomena in late adulthood and the importance of utilizing different levels of theorizing and analysis strategies to examine age-related change. The propositions derived from an interdisciplinary integration of evolutionary and ontogenetic arguments provide a guiding framework for questions about the phenomena of aging as well as the design and interpretation of research. They are sufficiently general to be operationalized in the context of specific areas of functioning (e.g., intelligence, self-regulation) and across disciplines.

Research on very old age undertaken in the Berlin Aging Study (P. B. Baltes & Mayer, in press; Mayer & Baltes, 1996) represents one instantiation of the framework involving the disciplines of sociology, geriatric medicine, psychiatry, and psychology. In this spirit, findings from this study of a heterogeneous sample of 516 men and women between the ages of 70 and 100+ years will be used to illustrate aspects of the overall framework.

METATHEORETICAL OBSERVATIONS FROM LIFE SPAN THEORY: IMPLICATIONS FOR THEORIES OF PSYCHOLOGICAL AGING

One historical feature of lifespan theory is its joint consideration of evolutionary-historical and ontogenetic perspectives (Tetens, 1777). This chapter reviews various elements of the life span approach and describes empirical work that illustrates the application of the different levels of the metatheoretical framework. The family of overarching propositions that are the focus of this review are summarized in Table 9.1 (for additional propositions and details see P. B. Baltes, 1997; P. B. Baltes et al., 1997).

At the topmost level of the framework outlined in Table 9.1 are views about the general architecture of human ontogeny (P. B. Baltes, 1997). The fact that the evolutionary and cultural design of human development across the life span is essentially "incomplete" has strong implications for predictions about the nature of very old age and its modifiability. By incompleteness, a concept that is discussed in more detail below, we mean that the biological and cultural foundation of human development implies a life span script in which adaptive fitness must decline with increasing age, and the balance between gains and losses in developmental outcomes becomes increasingly less positive.

The second level includes general assertions about the dynamics underlying change. One set of arguments focuses attention on the multisided (e.g., different categories of behavior evince distinct age-change trajectories) and multifunctional (e.g., a given behavior can have distinct and varied functional consequences) nature of ontogenetic change in adaptive fitness. The other set on this level of analysis outlines the basic directional mechanisms and strategies of ontogenetic adaptation (e.g., selection, compensation, optimization). In line with propositions from the topmost level, it is suggested that old age is characterized by more losses than gains and that, during the second half of life, individuals need to invest more and more of their inter-

TABLE 9.1   Metatheoretical Perspectives on Human Aging Resulting from Joining Evolutionary and Ontogenetic Perspectives at Different Levels of Analysis

Level 1 *Biological and cultural evolutionary perspectives on life-span development*
   Proposition A: The co-evolutionary architecture of human ontogeny is biologically and culturally incomplete. Incompleteness increases with age. Why?
   (a) Evolutionary selection benefits decrease with age.
   (b) There is an age-related increase in the need or demand for culture.
   (c) There is an age-related decrease in the efficiency of culture.
   Proposition B: Current observations of phenomena in old age reflect this incomplete architecture and highlight the growing hiatus between what is desirable and what is biologically and culturally possible.

Level 2 *Life-span perspectives on age-related change: Aging is mMultidimensional, multidirectional, and dynamic*
   Proposition C: Age-related change should be viewed as being inherently multisided and multifunctional.
   (a) *Dynamics of gains and losses*: In human development, there is no gain without loss, no loss without gain. In old age the balance between gains and losses in outcomes becomes less positive if not negative.
   (b) *Deficits as catalysts*: Conditions of loss or limitations can provide a context for new forms of mastery and innovation.
   (c) *Potentials and limits*: Plasticity of human potential decreases with age.
   (d) *There is a life-span script in the allocation of resources to distinct goals: Growth, maintenance, and loss management.*
   Proposition D: Successful aging involves the collaborative interaction of three components: *selection, compensation, and optimization*. The need (demand) for the effective coordination of these components, especially the role of compensation, increases in late adulthood.
   Proposition E: Advanced old age is the most radical form of evolutionary and cultural incompleteness.

Level 3: *Aging at levels of behavior and mechanisms*
   (a) Example: Intelligence, personality, self
   (b) Example: Systemic-wholistic analyses
   Proposition F: The optimization of human development becomes increasingly more difficult as life is extended to its maximum biological life span. This is the basis for postulation of a fourth age.

nal and external resources in maintenance and management of loss rather than in growth or positive changes in adaptive fitness.

The third level deals with issues of differential aging within specific areas of functioning and from a systemic-holistic perspective. As to advanced old age, the findings converge in a way that suggests what could be called a fourth age. Specifically, the existence of a fourth age assumes that advanced old age is a state of functioning in which conditions prevail that are qualitatively distinct from earlier phases of life. Optimality of functioning, therefore, is more and more precluded. We argue that this is the direct consequence of what we label the radical incompleteness of the biological-cultural architecture of the life span.

Joining Biological and Cultural Evolutionary Perspectives

One of the lines of reasoning that resulted from and advanced the propositions summarized in Table 9.1 is outlined now in more detail. Consistent with recent interest in strengthening links between evolutionary and ontogenetic perspectives in the study of human behavior, one of us (P. B. Baltes, 1997; see also P. B. Baltes et al., 1997) outlined arguments about the general architecture of the life span dynamics between biology and culture. These proposals provide a metatheoretical guide for thinking about the dynamics and orchestration of biological and cultural forces that shape human ontogeny.

The architectural plan involves three elements and their life span functions (the three sections of Figure 9.1) that interact throughout ontogeny. A critical feature of Figure 9.1 is that the conjoint action of the three components of the architecture are required in order to understand phenomena of aging. No one element is proposed to be dominant or to take the leading role. Biological and genetic aspects, for example, are not viewed as more (or less) important than environmental and cultural forces in determining the phenomena observed in late adulthood. Each element has a specific directional pattern. The outcome at any age, however, reflects their reciprocal interplay and mutual conditioning.

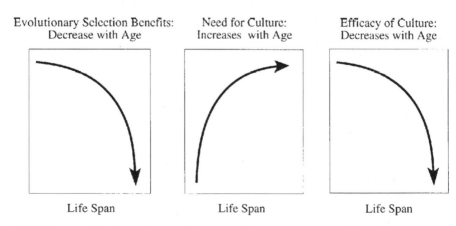

FIGURE 9.1   The incomplete architecture of human ontogeny: Schematic representation of three principles governing the dynamics between biology and culture across the ontogenetic life span (P. B. Baltes, 1997). Reprinted with permission.

1. Evolutionary selection benefits decrease with age. The first foundational life span principle (the leftmost panel of Figure 9.1) refers to the role of evolutionary-based genetic functions and their expression across the life span. It states that the benefits resulting from evolutionary selection decrease with age. Support for this principle comes from population geneticists, who argue in a similar vein (i.e., that there was an evolutionary neglect of old age). A related fact is associated with ontogenetic biological theories of aging that emphasize an age-associated loss in biological potential (Finch & Tanzi, 1997; Martin, Austad, & Johnson, 1996; Rose, 1991).

For the present purpose, the evolutionary argument is the more basic one. In humans, evolutionary selection pressure has operated primarily during the first half of life to ensure reproductive fitness (Partridge & Barton, 1993). Moreover, in earlier historical time few people lived to be old. As a consequence, compared to younger ages, it is likely that the "modern" human genome in older age groups contains a larger number of deleterious genes and dysfunctional genetic expressions. One concrete illustration of this age-based weakening of the benefits of evolutionary selection is the existence of late-life illnesses such as Alzheimer dementia (for other examples see Martin et al., 1996).

2. There is an age-related increase in the need (demand) for culture. The second life span principle depicted in the middle panel of Figure 9.1 suggests that for human development to extend itself farther and farther into the life span, there was an age-related increase in the need or demand for culture and its associated factors. Culture in this context refers to the entirety of psychological, social, material (environmental and technological), and symbolic (knowledge-based) resources that humans have generated and transmitted across generations (Cole, 1996; Durham, 1991; Shweder, 1991).

Two aspects underlie this second principle of the life span architecture. First, biological-genetic factors alone do not ensure the optimal expression of human development. Prerequisites for the fact that, over historical time, human ontogenesis has achieved higher and higher levels of functioning and longevity has been a conjoint evolutionary increase in the content and dissemination of culture. This idea of biological and cultural co-evolution (Durham, 1991) is illustrated in the changes in average life expectancy in industrialized countries during the 20th century. Life expectancy has increased from an average of about 45 years in 1900 to about 75 years in 1995. This increase is much more likely attributable to economic and technological innovations during this period than to changes in the genetic makeup of the population (Olshansky, 1995).

The second aspect underlying the age-related increase in demand for culture relates to the changing dynamic between biology and culture in the production of outcomes of adaptive fitness. As individuals approach old age, their biological potential declines (left part of Figure 9.1), so the demand for culture-based compensations (material, social, economic, psychological) to generate and maintain high levels of functioning increases. Examples of interactive trade-offs between biological characteristics and culture can be found in research on cognitive aging. With increasing age, individuals need more environmental support to perform at the same level of achievement, for instance in the memory domain (Craik & Jennings, 1992; Dixon & Bäckman, 1995; Kliegl, Smith, & Baltes, 1989; Lindenberger & Baltes, 1994; Salthouse, 1991).

3. There is an age-related decrease in the efficiency of culture. The rightmost panel of Figure 9.1 illustrates the third cornerstone of the overall life span architecture. With this foundational pillar, we argue that the relative efficiency (effectiveness) of psychological, social, material, and cultural interventions or inputs wanes during the life span, beginning at least in the middle years if not earlier (P. B. Baltes et al., 1997). This is not to deny that there continues to be plasticity in the second half of life. Indeed, the extent of plasticity within different domains of functioning and on an individual level may be larger than typically believed (P. B. Baltes et al., 1997; Schaie, 1996; Willis, 1990;). Rather, this third pillar draws attention to the proposal that the scope of plasticity of the human organism declines with age (see also Magnusson, 1996).

There are many examples from cognitive training studies to support this proposal of a negative life span script in cultural efficiency or efficacy (P. B. Baltes, 1997; Salthouse, 1991; Schaie, 1996). The older the adult, the more time, practice, and effort it takes to attain the performance levels and learning gains shown at younger ages. Moreover, when it comes to high, asymptotic levels of performance of memory functioning, for instance, older adults may never be able to reach the same levels of functioning that younger adults reach, even after extensive training (e.g., Kliegl et al., 1989; Lindenberger & Baltes, 1994).

4. Incomplete Architecture of Ontogeny. The implications for theories about old age and aging alluded to by the previous three propositions are summarized in Propositions A and B of Table 9.1, above. The architectural plan of human ontogeny is essentially incomplete in two respects (P. B. Baltes, 1997). Incompleteness results first from the fact that biological and cultural co-evolution (Durham, 1991) is not completed but continues. Second, incompleteness results from the fact that, relatively speaking, old age is young; therefore neither biological nor cultural evolution has had sufficient opportunity to evolve a full and optimizing scaffolding (architecture) for the later phases of life.

The evolutionary neglect of old age has been likened to an ill-designed building whose inherent vulnerabilities, as old age is reached, become more and more manifest and amplified by ontogenetic insults to the organism

(P. B. Baltes, 1997). The individual's capacity to compensate for these negative changes is more and more constrained. Furthermore, at the very time
that increased input from cultural factors (in the broadest sense) could alleviate some of the deficits produced by the negative biological trajectory and
perhaps even delay their onset, the potential and resources on the cultural
side are insufficient.

One fascinating area of research that has arisen because of this situation
of relative unpredictability is work examining functional status in advanced
old age and also the apparent decrease in mortality rates among the oldest
old (i.e., discrepant from those expected by the Gompertz model; e.g., Carey,
1997; Manton, Stallard, & Corder, 1997; Vaupel, 1997). What might be possible in terms of positive growth and maintenance of high levels of functioning into very old age if cultural (including technological) conditions were to
be further optimized and new resources introduced, including those that
would modulate genetic expressions? It may be possible, for example, to
identify cultural factors (including medical technological ones) already available to small subgroups of the population that could be made more widely
accessible and foster the general good of older persons in the population.
Despite its seeming pessimism about the future of advanced old age, it is
precisely the purpose of this proposition of incompleteness of the life span
architecture to facilitate such speculation and to challenge research impulses
in this direction.

The constellation of arguments, then, cannot be taken to suggest that
human aging is nothing but decline. This would be so if biological factors
were the only conditions shaping the course of aging. The fact that cultural
factors are operative, though at a reduced level of efficacy, entails the possibility of continued growth, selective as it may be. Moreover, the human
species and its associated cultural evolution has the power to outwit the
constraints imposed by biological-genetic conditions. "Declining the decline"
of aging is part of future-oriented gerontological work.

The Gain/Loss Dynamic

Beginning in late adulthood and certainly in old age, the overall balance
between gains and losses in adaptive fitness and associated ontogenetic outcomes becomes less positive. Nevertheless, it is important to place the interpretation of losses in old age in context and to ask whether or not some gain
is also present. Indeed, it is suggested that in ontogeny there can be no loss
without gain. A first illustration is research on wisdom (P. B. Baltes & Smith,
1990; Staudinger & Baltes, 1996). A second illustration of this idea is provided in Carstensen's (1993) socioemotional theory. Observed losses in old
age in the absolute size of the personal network of social contacts may be

balanced by a gain in the amount of time and energy invested in emotional contact with close partners and significant others. Similarly, dependency on others can generate new forms of personal control (M. M. Baltes, 1996).

The determination of what is a gain or a loss in old age is a topic of theoretical as well as empirical inquiry (see M. M. Baltes & Carstensen, 1996; Hobfoll, 1989; Schulz & Heckhausen, 1996). Suffice it here to mention that the nature of what is considered a gain or a loss itself can change with age; it involves objective as well as subjective criteria and is conditioned by theoretical predilection, standards of comparison, cultural and historical context, and criteria of functional fitness or adaptivity.

Deficits As Catalysts

Another script for viewing research on aging that involves a dynamic and future-oriented conception is the idea that a condition of loss, limitation, or deficit could also play a catalytic role for positive change. This view is derived from both evolutionary theory and ontogenetic theories of learning, where errors are considered to harbor potentially positive consequences. On the level of society and the individual, then, a deficit may serve as a catalyst for action by society, by the people themselves, or by significant others in their environment.

A better understanding of latent potential is critical for identifying those aspects of the current cultural and medical-technological context that are suboptimal or even detrimental to the well-being of older adults. It might enable the design of environments that harness more of the resources that remain in old age (P. B. Baltes & M. M. Baltes, 1990). The testing-the-limits approach (Kliegl et al., 1989) is one method that has been used to learn about developmental reserve capacity and to examine, under supportive and challenging conditions, the limits of performance potential. Similarly, the study of health behaviors (Vita, Terry, Hubert, & Fries, 1998) has opened new vistas on how society and individuals can extend the lifetime of functions.

Relative Allocation of Resources

A further conception (see Proposition D in Table 9.1) regarding the dynamics of development and aging relates to the extent to which resources are allocated to functions associated with growth (e.g., reaching higher levels of functioning), maintenance (e.g., sustaining or recovering normal levels of functioning in the face of a new contextual challenge or a loss in potential), and the regulation of loss when maintenance or recovery is no longer possible (P. B. Baltes, 1997; see also Marsiske, Lang, Baltes, & Baltes, 1995; Staudinger, Marsiske, & Baltes, 1995). In line with our view of the life span architecture outlined above, it is argued that there is a systematic shift in the relative allocation of resources to these three functions (growth, mainte-nance, regulation of loss) across the life span. As old age is approached, more and more resources are directed toward maintenance and the management of loss. Note in this context that the reallocation of resources toward main-tenance of functioning and regulation of loss is facilitated by the tendency of individuals to prefer avoidance of loss over enhancement of gains (Hobfoll, 1989; Taylor, 1991).

One telling example of the dynamics among the functions of growth, resilience, and regulation of loss is the life span study of the interplay be-tween autonomy and dependency in children and older adults (M. M. Baltes, 1996). Whereas the primary focus of the first half of life is the maximization of autonomy, in old age the productive and creative use of dependent behav-ior becomes critical. According to Margret Baltes, for older adults to main-tain autonomy in select domains of functioning, the effective exercise and use of dependent behavior is a compensatory must. By invoking dependency and support, resources are freed up for use in other domains "selected" for personal efficacy and growth. Moreover, dependent behaviors by themselves can produce positive outcomes as they often involve control over social contact.

Selective Optimization With Compensation

Life span theory has spawned one overall theory that is purported to represent how individuals orchestrate adaptive (successful) development. This theory of adaptive or successful development identifies three fundamental mechanisms or strategies: selection, optimization, and compensation (M. M. Baltes & Carstensen, 1996; P. B. Baltes, 1997; P. B. Baltes & Baltes, 1990; Carstensen, Hanson, & Freund, 1995; Dixon & Bäckman, 1995; Freund & Baltes, in press; Marsiske et al., 1995). The definition of selection, optimiza-tion, and compensation differs by theoretical framework and domains of functioning.

Within an action-theoretical framework (Brandtstädter, 1997; Freund & Baltes, in press), for instance, the following characterizations of the three components hold: Selection involves directionality, goals, or outcomes; opti-mization involves means to achieve directionality (desired outcomes); and compensation denotes a response to loss in means (resources) that is evolved in order to maintain success or desired levels of functioning (outcomes). Other theoretical frameworks place less emphasis on intention and rational-ity. Indeed, each concept (selection, optimization, and compensation) can be defined as active or passive, internal or external, and conscious or uncon-scious and can be applied to a large range of goals and means (Marsiske et al., 1995).

Central to the life span metatheory about ontogeny is the proposal that any process of development is expected to involve some orchestration of selection, optimization, and compensation. In late adulthood, because of the basic architecture of the life course, selection and especially compensation become increasingly important to maintain adequate levels of functioning and permit advances in select domains of functioning. Schulz and Heckhausen (1996) also address this topic in their model of successful aging and consider the role of adaptive combinations of primary and secondary control as instantiations of selection, optimization, and compensation.

ADVANCED OLD AGE: NEW FINDINGS

In this section we explore how the theoretical perspectives outlined might guide research design and analysis and, as well, provide an interpretative framework for findings from the recently evolving focus on advanced old age. To illustrate, we use findings from the Berlin Aging Study (BASE), a multidisciplinary study of a representative sample ($N = 516$) of men and women between the ages of 70 and 100+ years (P. B. Baltes & Mayer, in press; Mayer & Baltes, 1996).

Patterns of Aging and Age Differences in Intelligence

Figure 9.2 summarizes results from BASE for the age range 70 to 100+ years regarding two broad categories of intellectual abilities, the fluidlike mechanics and crystallized pragmatics of intelligence (Lindenberger & Baltes, 1997). In BASE, intellectual functioning was assessed by a computerized battery of 14 subtests. Previous research has shown that, up to age 80, performance on these two broad categories of abilities exhibit different patterns of maintenance and decline (e.g., Horn & Hofer, 1992; Schaie, 1996). The fluid mechanics thought to reflect the neurophysiological architecture or hardware of the human brain display instances of decline beginning in middle adulthood (30 to 40 years of age). In contrast, the crystallized pragmatics, understood as the culture-based software of the mind (P. B. Baltes, 1997), generally shows no decline in adulthood. Decline in these crystallized-pragmatic abilities begins later, on average around 60–70 years of age (Schaie, 1996).

The outcome pattern in old age is, however, more unidirectional and person-general. For advanced older ages, BASE findings presented in Figure 9.2 suggest general rather than dimension-specific age gradients. Across all cognitive dimensions, negative cross-sectional age differences between 70 and 103 years were substantial, representing a 1.8 *SD* difference in performance level and about 35% of the interindividual variance. Although the findings also suggest sizable heterogeneity on the individual level and some differences in the age gradients for categories of abilities, the evidence as a whole is consistent with the view that in advanced old age the biological incompleteness of the life course and its associated biological constraints come to the fore.

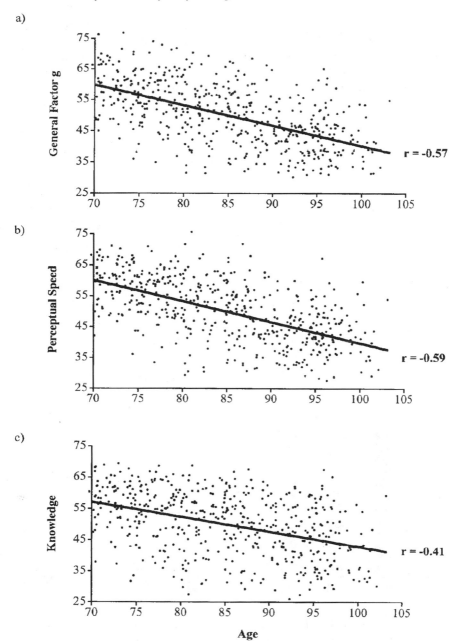

FIGURE 9.2   Berlin Aging Study: Age gradients in intellectual functioning (based on 14 tests). Measures of the fluid mechanics (e.g., perceptual speed) showed stronger negative age gradients compared with measures of the crystallized pragmatics (e.g., knowledge) (Lindenberger & Baltes, 1997). Reprinted with permission.

There is additional evidence: In a comprehensive set of analyses, Lindenberger and Baltes (1997) examined various relationships between intellectual functioning and other measures collected in BASE on sensory and functional capacity and life history. From these analyses, we highlight two findings that illustrate further the powerful role of biological constraints in old age and the parallel decrease in efficacy of cultural factors that was predicted by the life span architecture of ontogeny summarized above (Figure 9.1).

First, these analyses of intellectual functioning in old age revealed that all of the age-related individual-differences variance in intelligence within the BASE sample could be accounted for by differences in vision, hearing acuity, and sensorimotor balance. These relationships were not significantly reduced when subgroups (such as persons who were blind or deaf or who had a diagnosis of dementia) were excluded. In a comparative study with younger adults (15 to 54 years; P. B. Baltes & Lindenberger, 1997), the correlation between sensory functioning and intelligence was much lower. Lindenberger and Baltes (1997) suggest that this extraordinary nexus between sensory functioning and intelligence in old age demonstrates the importance of brain-related factors in the process of the aging of intelligence.

The second set of findings concerns analyses aimed at examining the relative role of biological factors in old age regarding intellectual functioning (Lindenberger & Baltes, 1997). As shown in Figure 9.3, biological factors or correlates

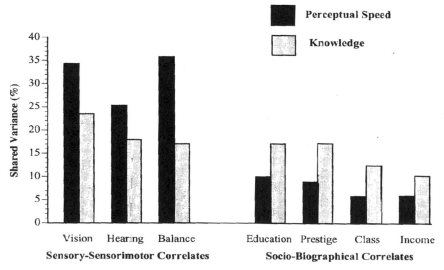

FIGURE 9.3   Berlin Aging Study: The divergent external validity of the two-component model of life-span intellectual development subsists into very old age. The figure displays differential correlational links of perceptual speed (a marker of the fluid mechanics of intelligence) and knowledge (a marker of the crystallized pragmatics of intelligence) to sociobiographical and biological variables (Lindenberger & Baltes, 1997). Reprinted with permission.

are more powerful predictors than sociocultural life history. This applies even to those categories of intellectual functioning, (i.e., the cognitive pragmatics) where culture-based knowledge and skills are critical ingredients.

The pattern of these two sets of findings, then, is consistent with the life span architecture outlined and the dual-process model of intelligence (i.e., fluid mechanics and crystallized pragmatics). When it comes to the hard-ware-like mechanics and the speedy and accurate functioning of basic mechanisms of information processing, old age takes its toll. In advanced old age, the compensatory role of culture and culture-based resources becomes less efficient (see also the lack of strong social-factor effects in health status of the oldest old in BASE; Mayer & Baltes, 1996). Biological-genetic factors gain in predictive power as advanced old age is reached.

Patterns of Aging and Age Differences in Personality

What about the self and personality in advanced old age? Thus far, personality and self-related functioning were considered more resilient to old age than intellectual functioning. Work on self and personality in old age has pointed less to age changes and developmental transformations than to understanding the mechanisms that afford the maintenance of personal integrity and well-being in the face of social loss and health constraints (e.g., P. B. Baltes & Baltes, 1990; Bengtson, Reedy, & Gordon, 1985; Brandtstädter & Greve, 1994). Indeed, some personality dispositions, especially neuroticism and extraversion, show much structural and mean-level stability (continuity) at least into the late 70s (McCrae & Costa, 1990). In a sense, personality and self-functioning have been seen as being age-friendly.

What about advanced old age, however? Figure 9.4 summarizes BASE findings regarding cross-sectional age gradients from 70 to 100 years in personality characteristics grouped in terms of social and psychological desirability (Smith & Baltes, 1996). Desirable characteristics were defined as those that researchers have found to influence positively the process of dealing with life problems: an interest in being with others (extraversion), openness to new ideas and experiences (openness), frequent experience of positive emotions (positive affect), and a feeling of being in control of one's life (internal control). Psychologically less desirable characteristics are those that are known to signal, either as antecedents or correlates, elements of dysfunctionality, such as neuroticism, negative affect, and the belief that one's life is controlled by others (external control).

At a general level, the BASE findings supported the view that aspects of personality seem to be less affected by age-related decline than is true for intellectual functioning. Age correlations were relatively small, and mean differences amounted to less than 0.5 *SD*. Closer examination, however, reveals that age differences on aspects of self and personality were all in a less

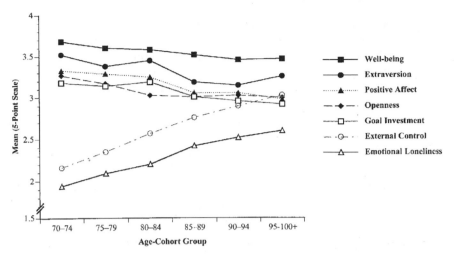

FIGURE 9.4   Berlin Aging Study: Age differences in personality characteristics (mean scores on a 5-point scale with 1 = low and 5 = high). (*a*) Small but mostly significant negative age differences in desirable characteristics. (*b*) Age increments in less desirable characteristics (Smith & Baltes, 1996). Reprinted with permission.

than desirable direction. Specifically, as to desirable characteristics and as shown in Figure 9.4, older participants in BASE reported less extraversion, openness, positive affect, and subjective life investment compared to participants aged 70 to 84 years. Conversely, as to less desirable attributes, older participants felt that their lives were more controlled by others (external control) and reported that they experienced more emotional loneliness. As a whole, these age gradients toward increased dysfunction could be interpreted as type of chronic stress reaction (Smith & Baltes, 1996; Staudinger et al., 1996). Such an interpretation would also be consistent with the architectural metatheory outlined above, including Propositions E and F (Table 9.1). In advanced old age, individuals may be pushed to the limits of their adaptive psychological capacity.

Aging as a Systemic Phenomenon

In line with the overarching life span metatheories, we believe that to achieve a comprehensive understanding of individual aging it is important to combine function-and mechanism-specific analyses with systemic-wholistic approaches that are aimed explicitly at the study of structural and functional interdependencies on the person level of analysis (see also P. B. Baltes & Smith, 1997; Birren & Bengtson, 1988; Birren & Schroots, 1996; Magnusson, 1996; Moen, Elder, & Lüscher, 1995). There is to date, however, little psychological work that addresses such questions about aging-associated differences in systemic-wholistic indicators or in structural interdependencies. This was one of the central aims of a series of articles published by BASE researchers (P. B. Baltes & Smith, 1997).

In our own contribution (Smith & Baltes, 1997) to this collection of articles on systemic-wholistic functioning in old age, we used cluster analysis as an unbiased method to identify individuals who were more or less similar to each other and to assign to all individuals, based on their cluster membership, a ranking in terms of an overall, systemic profile of desirability. These profiles, varying in desirability of functional status, were derived from scores on 12 measures of intellectual, social, and self-related functioning.

The cluster analysis illustrated that, even if individual variable comparisons did not demonstrate major age differences, combinations of such variables do, and the results were very much in line with the life span architecture and its age-associated increase in incompleteness. With increasing age and as described in the next section, more and more people belonged to the less desirable profiles.

THE MOST RADICAL FORM OF BIOLOGICAL AND CULTURAL INCOMPLETENESS: THE FOURTH AGE

The changing landscape of resources and potential for functioning inherent in the life span architecture presented in this chapter, as well as in the research findings summarized, carry implications for the nature of old age. Because of the increasing incompleteness of the architecture as old age is approached, the process of co-evolution of biological-genetic and cultural factors and generational transmission (Durham, 1991) that is basic to further progress in individual functioning is increasingly more difficult to achieve. One question in systemic-wholistic approaches that illustrates this constraint is whether the young old and the oldest old represent distinct subgroups on average, and whether we might be compelled to postulate the existence of something akin to a fourth age (P. B. Baltes, 1997). Such arguments can be linked to cultural-historical and medical-sociodemographic work (e.g., Laslett, 1991; Suzman, Willis, & Manton, 1992). In our view, understanding the nature of the fourth age, from about 80 years onward, constitutes the major new frontier for future research and theory in aging (see also Myers, Juster, & Suzman, 1997).

Regarding the third age, that is, the age span from about 60 to 80 years or so, culture and social forces in industrialized countries have been able to offset many of the weaknesses inherent in the biological life span architecture for the majority of individuals. What about advanced old age, however? The basic architecture of the life span presented in this chapter suggests that, although more people may expect to reach the fourth age, these added years may come with increased disability and diminished life quality. This proposition is indeed supported by Crimmins, Hayward, and Saito (1996) who suggested that the proportion of dysfunctional-inactive years of the remaining lifetime is 20% for 70–year-olds, whereas for 90–year-olds, close to 60% of their remaining years represent dysfunctional, inactive time. An opposing view would be expressed by Fries (1990) in his compression of morbidity model, which assumes a maximum biological life span. According to Fries, the closer, on average, that individuals approximate their maximum biological life span, the more it is possible to compress morbidity into the shorter time span before death. This model, then, would suggest that the fourth age, while existing, would be of increasingly shorter duration.

At present, gerontological research does not offer clear evidence on the question of the quality of functioning in advanced old age, and likely the picture is complex, with counteracting forces and processes. However, BASE, because of its wide age range and broad interdisciplinary assessment, offers a new window on the question of potential and quality of life in advanced old age. In total, 23 indicators stemming from geriatric, psychiatric, psychological, and sociological assessments were considered. When subjecting this information to a cluster analysis, groups resulted that differed in overall desirability of quality of functional status (P. B. Baltes, 1997; Mayer & Baltes, 1996; Smith & Baltes, 1997). Specifically, based on cluster analysis, the 516 participants in BASE were members of four subgroups, ordered in the quality of functional status from good to very poor (Figure 9.5).

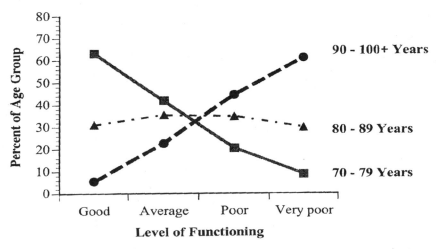

FIGURE 9.5   Berlin Aging Study: Distribution of research participants (by age) into four groups differing in functional status. Groups were formed by considering a total of 23 physical, mental, psychological, and social indicators (Mayer & Baltes, 1996; Smith & Baltes, 1996). Reprinted with permission.

The outcome is clear. The oldest old, perhaps because of increased closeness to death, are at a much higher risk for dysfunctionality than the young old. Risk of membership in the less desirable clusters (labeled poor and very poor) was three times larger for the oldest old than for the young old. Relative to 90–year-olds, for instance, 70–year-olds were five times more likely to be in the functionally best group (good). The reverse was true for the very poor group. Individuals over the age of 85 had a four times greater risk of membership in this extreme group of dysfunctionality than did persons aged 70–84 years. These are dramatic age differences in risk ratios. Although further analyses, including longitudinal, cohort-sequential and interventive ones, must be conducted to substantiate this pattern of results, the central outcome is unlikely to change.

This pattern of a major increase in risk and dysfunctionality in the fourth age is not noticeable only when physical variables are considered but also when the sole focus is on psychological measures such as intelligence, the self, personality, and social behavior (Smith & P. B. Baltes, 1997). Psychologically speaking, advanced old age appears to be a situation of great challenge and a period characterized by chronic stress or overdemand where adaptive fitness and resilience are concerned. In our view such findings suggest that advanced old age, the fourth age, represents a kind of testing-the-limits situation for resilience that is the direct consequence of the radical incompleteness of the biological-cultural architecture of the life span.

In his lifetime oeuvre, James Birren has forcefully and persuasively argued for a joint consideration of biological, sociocultural, and psychological forces in the study of human aging (e.g., Birren, 1959). In the present chapter we have added to these interdisciplinary and systemic arguments (see also Shock, 1977) a concern for the joint consideration of two temporal streams: evolution and ontogenesis.

Linking these several levels of analysis we described an overall biological-genetic and cultural-social architecture of the life span that suggests the exploration of a fourth age in which the basic incompleteness of this architecture is so radical that qualitative rather than quantitative as well as universal rather than specific aging losses become the rule. Because of the robustness of the incomplete architecture of the life course, it is likely that extending positive human development into higher and higher ages will be more and more difficult. To this end, collaboration of psychologists with other disciplines engaged in remedying the incomplete architecture of the life span, such as biology, medicine, the social sciences as well as practical anthropology, seems paramount.

REFERENCES

Baltes, M. M. (1996). *The many faces of dependency in old age.* New York: Cambridge University Press.

Baltes, M. M., & Carstensen, L. L. (1996). The process of successful ageing. *Ageing and Society, 16,* 397–422.

Baltes, P. B. (1997). On the incomplete architecture of human ontogenesis: Selection, optimization, and compensation as foundation of developmental theory. *American Psychologist, 52,* 366–381.

Baltes, P. B., & Baltes, M. M. (1990). Psychological perspectives on successful aging: The model of selective optimization with compensation. In P. B. Baltes & M. M. Baltes (Eds.), *Successful aging: Perspectives from the behavioral sciences* (pp. 1–34). New York: Cambridge University Press.

Baltes, P. B., & Lindenberger, U. (1997). Emergence of a powerful connection between sensory and cognitive functions across the adult life span: A new window to the study of cognitive aging? *Psychology and Aging, 12,* 12–21.

Baltes, P. B., Lindenberger, U., & Staudinger, U. M. (1997). Lifespan theory in developmental psychology. In R. M. Lerner (Ed.), *Handbook of child psychology: Vol. 1. Theoretical models of human development* (5th ed., pp. 1029–1143). New York: Wiley.

Baltes, P. B., & Mayer, K. U. (Eds.). (in press). *The Berlin Aging Study: Aging from 70 to 100.* New York: Cambridge University Press.

Baltes, P. B., & Smith, J. (1990). The psychology of wisdom and its ontogenesis. In R. J. Sternberg (Ed.), *Wisdom: Its nature, origins, and development* (pp. 87–120). New York: Cambridge University Press.

Baltes, P. B., & Smith, J. (1997). A systemic-wholistic view of psychological functioning in very old age: Introduction to a collection of articles from the Berlin Aging Study. *Psychology and Aging, 12,* 395–409.

Bengtson, V. L., Reedy, M. N., & Gordon, C. (1985). Aging and self-conceptions: Personality processes and social contexts. In J. E. Birren & K. W. Schaie (Eds.), *Handbook of the psychology of aging* (2nd ed., pp. 544–593). New York: Van Nostrand Reinhold.

Birren, J. E. (1959). Principles of research on aging. In J. E. Birren (Ed.), *Handbook of aging and the individual: Psychological and biological aspects* (pp. 3–42). Chicago: University of Chicago Press.

Birren, J. E., & Bengtson, V. L. (Eds.). (1988). *Emergent theories of aging.* New York: Springer Publishing Co.

Birren, J. E., & Schroots, J. J. F. (1996). History, concepts, and theory in the psychology of aging. In J. E. Birren & K. W. Schaie (Eds.), *Handbook of the psychology of aging* (4th ed., pp. 3–23). San Diego, CA: Academic Press.

Brandtstädter, J. (1997). Action theory in developmental psychology. In R. M. Lerner (Ed.), *Handbook of child psychology: Vol. 1. Theoretical models of human development* (5th ed., pp. 807–863). New York: Wiley.

Brandtstädter, J., & Greve, W. (1994). The aging self: Stabilizing and protective processes. *Developmental Review, 14,* 52–80.

Carey, J. R. (1997). What demographers can learn from fruit fly actuarial models and biology. *Demography, 34,* 17–30.

Carstensen, L. L. (1993). Motivation for social contact across the life-span: A theory of socioemotional selectivity. In J. Jacobs (Ed.), *Nebraska Symposium on Motivation* (Vol. 40, pp. 205–254). Lincoln: University of Nebraska Press.

Carstensen, L. L., Hanson, K. A., & Freund, A. (1995). Selection and compensation in adulthood. In R. Dixon & L. Bäckman (Eds.), *Compensating for psychological deficits and declines: Managing losses and promoting gains* (pp. 107–126). Mahwah, NJ: Erlbaum.

Cole, M. (1996). Interacting minds in a life-span perspective: A cultural/historical approach to culture and cognitive development. In P. B. Baltes & U. M. Staudinger (Eds.), *Interactive minds: Life-span perspectives on the social foundation of cognition* (pp. 59–87). New York: Cambridge University Press.

Craik, F. I. M., & Jennings, J. M. (1992). Human memory. In F. I. M. Craik & T. A. Salthouse (Eds.), *The handbook of aging and cognition* (pp. 51–110). Hillsdale, NJ: Erlbaum.

Crimmins, E. M., Hayward, M. D., & Saito, Y. (1996). Differentials in active life expectancy in the older population of the United States. *Journal of Gerontology: Social Sciences, 51B,* S111–S120.

Dixon, R. A., & Bäckman, L. (Eds.). (1995). *Compensating for psychological deficits and declines: Managing losses and promoting gains.* Mahwah, NJ: Erlbaum.

Durham, W. H. (1991). *Co-evolution: Genes, culture and human diversity.* Stanford, CA: Stanford University Press.

Elder, G. H. (1997). The life course and human development. In R. M. Lerner (Ed.), *Handbook of child psychology: Vol. 1. Theoretical models of human development* (5th ed., pp. 939–991). New York: Wiley.

Featherman, D. L. (1983). The life-span perspective in social science research. In P. B. Baltes & O. G. Brim Jr. (Eds.), *Life-span development and behavior* (Vol. 5, pp. 1–59). New York: Academic Press.

Finch, C. E., & Tanzi, R. E. (1997). Genetics of aging. *Science, 278,* 407–411.

Freund, A., & Baltes, P. B. (in press). The orchestration of selection, optimization, and compensation: An action-theoretical conceptualization of a theory of developmental regulation. In W. J. Perrig & A. Grob (Eds.), *Control of human behaviour, mental processes, and consciousness.* Mahwah, NJ: Erlbaum.

Hobfoll, S. E. (1989). Conservation of resources: A new attempt at conceptualizing stress. *American Psychologist, 44,* 513–524.

Horn, J. L., & Hofer, S. M. (1992). Major abilities and development in the adult period. In R. J. Sternberg & C. A. Berg (Eds.), *Intellectual development* (pp. 44–99). New York: Cambridge University Press.

Kliegl, R., Smith, J., & Baltes, P. B. (1989). Testing-the-limits and the study of age differences in cognitive plasticity of a mnemonic skill. *Developmental Psychology, 26,* 894–904.

Laslett, P. (1991). *A fresh map of life: The emergence of the third age.* Cambridge, MA: Harvard University Press.

Lindenberger, U., & Baltes, P. B. (1994). Aging and intelligence. In R. J. Sternberg (Ed.), *Encyclopedia of human intelligence* (Vol. 1, pp. 52–66). New York: Macmillan.

Lindenberger, U., & Baltes, P. B. (1997). Intellectual functioning in old and very old age: Cross-sectional results from the Berlin Aging Study. *Psychology and Aging, 12,* 410–432.

Magnusson, D. (Ed.). (1996). *The life-span development of individuals: Behavioural, neurobiological, and psychosocial perspectives.* Cambridge, U.K.: Cambridge University Press.

Manton, K. G., Stallard, E., & Corder, L. (1997). Changes in age dependence of mortality and disability: Cohort and other determinants. *Demography, 34,* 135–157.

Marsiske, M., Lang, F. R., Baltes, M. M., & Baltes, P. B. (1995). Selective optimization with compensation: Life-span perspectives on successful human development. In R. A. Dixon & L. Bäckman (Eds.), *Compensation for psychological defects and declines: Managing losses and promoting gains* (pp. 35–79). Hillsdale, NJ: Erlbaum.

Martin, G. M., Austad, S. N., & Johnson, T. E. (1996). Genetic analysis of ageing: Role of oxidative damage and environmental stresses. *Nature Genetics, 13,* 25–34.

Mayer, K. U., & Baltes, P. B. (Eds.). (1996). *Die Berliner Altersstudie* [The Berlin Aging Study]. Berlin: Akademie Verlag.

McCrae, R. R., Jr., & Costa, P. T., Jr. (1990). *Personality in adulthood.* New York: Guilford.

Moen P., Elder, G. H., Jr., & Lüscher, K. (1995). *Examining lives in context: Perspectives on the ecology of human development.* Washington, DC: American Psychological Association.

Myers, G. C., Juster, F. T., & Suzman, R. M. (1997). Introduction: Asset and health dynamics among the oldest old (AHEAD). [Special Issue]. *Journals of Gerontology, 52B,* v–viii.

Olshansky, S. J. (1995). Introduction: New developments in mortality. *Gerontologist, 35,* 583–587.

Partridge, L. & Barton, N. H. (1993). Optimality, mutation, and the evolution of ageing. *Nature, 362,* 305–311.

Rose, M. R. (1991). *The evolutionary biology of aging.* Oxford, U.K.: Oxford University Press.

Salthouse, T. A. (1991). *Theoretical perspectives on cognitive aging.* Hillsdale, NJ: Erlbaum.

Schaie, K. W. (1996). *Adult intellectual development: The Seattle Longitudinal Study.* New York: Cambridge University Press.

Schulz, R., & Heckhausen, J. (1996). A life-span model of successful aging. *American Psychologist, 51,* 702–714.

Shock, N. W. (1977). System integration. In C. E. Finch & L. Hayflick (Eds.), *Handbook of the biology of aging* (pp. 639–665). New York: Van Nostrand Reinhold.

Shweder, R. A. (1991). *Thinking through cultures.* Cambridge, MA: Harvard University Press.

Smith, J., & Baltes, P. B. (1996). Altern aus psychologischer Perspektive: Trends und Profile im hohen Alter [Psychological aging: Trends and profiles in very old age]. In K. U. Mayer & P. B. Baltes (Eds.), *Die Berliner Altersstudie* [The Berling Aging Study] (pp. 221–250). Berlin: Akademie Verlag.

Smith, J., & Baltes, P. B. (1997). Profiles of psychological functioning in the old and oldest old. *Psychology and Aging, 12,* 458–472.

Staudinger, U. M., & Baltes, P. B. (1996). Interactive minds: A facilitative setting for wisdom-related performance? *Journal of Personality and Social Psychology, 71,* 746–762.

Staudinger, U. M., Freund, A. M., Linden, M., & Maas, I. (1996). Selbst, Persönlichkeit und Lebensgestaltung: Psychologische Widerstandsfähigkeit und Vulnerabilität. In K. U. Mayer & P. B. Baltes (Eds.), *Die Berliner Altersstudie* [The Berlin Aging Study] (pp. 321–350). Berlin: Akademie Verlag.

Staudinger, U. M., Marsiske, M., & Baltes, P. B. (1995). Resilience and reserve capacity in later adulthood: Potentials and limits of development across the life span. In D. Cicchetti & D. Cohen (Eds.), *Developmental psychopathology: Vol. 2. Risk, disorder, and adaptation* (pp. 801–847). New York: Wiley.

Suzman, R. M., Willis, D. P., & Manton, K. G. (Eds.). (1992). *The oldest old.* New York: Oxford University Press.

Taylor, S. E. (1991). Asymmetrical effects of positive and negative events. The mobilization-minimization hypothesis. *Psychological Bulletin, 10,* 67–85.

Tetens, J. N. (1777). *Philosophische Versuche über die menschliche Natur und ihre Entwicklung.* Leipzig, Germany: Weidmanns Erben und Reich.

Vaupel, J. W. (1997). Trajectories of mortality at advanced ages. In K. Wachter & C. E. Finch (Eds.), *Between Zeus and the salmon: The biodemography of aging* (pp. 17–37). Washington, DC: National Academy of Sciences.

Vita, A. J., Terry, R. B., Hubert, H., & Fries, J. F. (1998). Aging, health risks, and cumulative disability. *The New England Journal of Medicine, 338,* 1035–1041.

Willis, S. L. (1990). Contributions of cognitive training research to understanding late-life potential. In M. Perlmutter (Ed.), *Late-life potential* (pp. 25–42). Washington, DC: Gerontological Society of America.

10

Theories of Everyday Competence and Aging

K. Warner Schaie
Sherry L. Willis

veryday competence in adulthood represents an important but complex domain of inquiry. The theoretical framework needed to organize and provide explanatory principles is equally complex. What is
required is an account that explains how an individual can function effectively on the tasks and in the situations posed by everyday experience (cf.
Willis & Schaie, 1986). To do so, the theoretical framework must incorporate
underlying processes, such as the mechanics and pragmatics of cognitive
functioning (cf. P. B. Baltes, 1987; Sternberg, 1977; Sternberg & Berg, 1987),
but it must also include the physical and social contexts that constrain the
individual's ability to function effectively.

Our position will be that a hierarchical model of competence must begin
with the underlying dimensions of the cognitive processes that are basic to
all meaningful behavior. Given the particular task attributes and constraints
in an everyday situation, different combinations and permutations of basic
cognitive skills will be required to successfully display competent behavior.
Alternative theoretical models that incorporate some or all of these features
will be elaborated. We then ask how developmental changes in the various
components constituting our theoretical framework will help us predict how

Preparation of this chapter was supported by grants R37 AG08055 and R01 AG11032 from the
National Institute on Aging.

everyday competence is likely to be maintained or to change with advancing age.

Historically, psychologists have addressed the study of competence by suggesting that an understanding of the wide array of dimensions of cognitive abilities would suffice to explain competence in everyday activities (Thurstone, 1938). Connolly and Bruner (1973) expanded the delineation of competence as a construct that implies action that may change the environment as well as adapt to the environment. They suggested that attributes of competence involved, first, the ability to select those features from the total environment that are required information for initiating a course of action; second, initiating a sequence of movements designed to achieve the planned objectives; and third, learning from successes and failures to form new plans.

From the above considerations it may be argued that competent behavior involves the application of cognitive mechanisms in specific situations, whose attributes may in turn interact with the developmental level of the individual. Because basic cognitive processes are typically operationalized so as to represent unitary trait characteristics, it is unlikely that any single process will suffice to explain individual differences in the exertion of everyday competence in any particular situation (Willis & Schaie, 1993). Hence, everyday competence could be characterized as the phenotypic expression of basic cognitive processes, which, given minimally required levels of motivational incentives, will permit adaptive behavior in a specific everyday situation or situations (Schaie, 1978).

In recent years a number of alternative approaches have been taken to define everyday competence. These can be represented as three different theories of everyday competence: componential theories that argue for different latent dimensions of competence, theories that take a strictly domain-specific approach, and those that are concerned primarily with the individual-environment fit. Because the definition of everyday competence has important societal implications, we next distinguish between psychological and legal definitions of everyday competence (cf. also Willis, 1996). We then address the question whether methods of measurement tend to drive theories of competence, and finally we present a view of competence within a life span perspective.

THEORETICAL APPROACHES TO EVERYDAY COMPETENCE

In this section we review three broad theoretical approaches to the study of everyday cognitive competence. The first perspective views everyday competence as a manifestation of latent constructs and as related to models of basic cognition. In the second approach everyday cognitive competence is conceptualized as involving domain-specific knowledge bases. In the third approach the focus is on the fit, or congruence, between the individual's cognitive competency and the environmental demands faced by the individual.

In all three approaches the focus is on problem solving with respect to everyday, real-world activities and demands. The concern is with the individual's ability to carry out the cognitively challenging activities of daily living. In this chapter we will be primarily concerned with the cognitive aspects of everyday competence. It is important, however, to acknowledge that the functional competence (Fillenbaum, 1987; Lawton & Brody, 1969) required to carry out everyday activities is multidimensional, involving physical and social as well as cognitive components. Medication compliance, for example, involves not only cognitive processes such as memory and reasoning but also the sensory ability to read the label, manual dexterity to open the bottle and measure the dosage, and social support.

Competence: Manifestation of Latent Constructs and Linkage to Basic Cognition

Within this approach we group such diverse perspectives as componential and hierarchical models of competence and theories of postformal stages of development (P. B. Baltes, Dittman-Kohli, & Dixon, 1984; Berg & Sternberg, 1985; Labouvie-Vief, 1992; see also Park, 1992). These diverse perspectives share some common themes.

First, each of these perspectives establishes a link between more basic forms of cognition and everyday competence. Within the componential and hierarchical approaches, the association of everyday problem solving with either psychometric intelligence or information processing approaches is considered. In the study of postformal thought, consideration is given to the evolution of relativistic or dialectical forms of thinking from formal operational thought.

Second, in this perspective competence is studied and assessed in terms of latent cognitive constructs. Observable everyday tasks/problems are seen as markers of these latent constructs. Competence is multidimensional in that there are multiple components or hierarchical levels, each represented at the latent construct level.

Third, everyday competence is not conceptualized in terms of specific substantive domains. Rather, competence in various everyday activities (e.g., managing finances, medication adherence) is seen as involving a parsimonious set of cognitive abilities or processes that cut across or apply to various substantive domains.

Fourth, the latent constructs perspective is concerned with age-related change and developmental trajectories in everyday competence. The developmental trajectories are determined in part by the particular model of basic cognition that serves as the underpinning of each perspective. For example, perspectives linked to basic cognitive processes such as speed of processing (or fluid) intelligence may be particularly concerned with decline trajectories. In contrast, postformal thought is concerned with more advanced or optimal levels of cognition.

Fifth, the role of the environment or context is of particular salience in determining the particular types of applied activities and problems in which everyday competence is manifested. Both the sociocultural context and the micro-environment determine the genotypic expression of everyday competence for a cohort or a given individual. For example, whereas ability to transport oneself beyond one's dwelling has been of concern through the ages, the ability to comprehend airline schedules and to operate computer-driven vehicles is only a recent expression of everyday competence with regard to mobility. The environment also plays an important role in the maintenance and facilitation of everyday competence in old age. Environmental stimulation and challenges occurring either naturally or through planned interventions have been shown to be associated with the maintenance and enhancement of everyday competence in the elderly.

Componential and Hierarchical Perspectives of Everyday Competence

One way in which various exemplars of this perspective differ is with regard to the model of more basic cognition with which they seek linkages. Sternberg and co-workers (Berg & Sternberg, 1985; Sternberg, 1985; Sternberg & Kolligian, 1990) have proposed a triarchic theory of adult intellectual development that involves metacomponents and experiential and contextual aspects. The metacomponential part of the theory is rooted in an information processing approach to cognition. This part of the theory is concerned with basic cognitive processes such as encoding, allocation of mental resources, and monitoring of thought processes. Of greater relevance to everyday competence are the experiential and contextual aspects of the theory. The theory posits that the metacomponential processes operate at diferent levels of experience with a task. The two levels of the theory that are of greater relevance for everyday competence have to do with whether the components are operative in a relatively novel fashion or are in the process of becoming automatized. According to Sternberg (1985), the most intelligent person (in this case having higher everyday competence) is one who can adjust to a change in problem situations and who can eventually automate the component processes of task solution. The third aspect of the theory is concerned with how the individual relates to the external world—the ability to apply the metacomponents at different levels of experience in adjusting to a change in the environment. Whether competence in a particular everyday activity declines or not would depend in part on the nature of environmental change and the ability of the individual to apply metacognitive processes to adapting to the change.

In a somewhat similar approach, Baltes and colleagues (P. B. Baltes et al., 1984) have proposed a two-dimensional componential model of cognition. In contrast to Sternberg, Baltes has conceptualized the mechanics of cognition (what Sternberg calls metacomponents) in terms of psychometric abilities, rather than information processing. Everyday competence is more closely associated with the second component of the theory—the pragmatics of intelligence. Although the mechanics of intelligence serve as underpinnings for the pragmatic component, the environmental context is critical to the particular form or manifestation in which pragmatic intelligence is shown. Baltes posits that although the mechanics of intelligence decline with age, there is enhancement in the pragmatic component through much of adulthood. The concept of wisdom has been linked and studied within the pragmatics of intelligence (Staudinger, 1996).

In our own work we have conceptualized a hierarchical relationship between basic cognition and everyday competence (Willis, 1987, 1996; Willis & Schaie, 1986, 1993). Basic cognition has been represented by domains of psychometric intelligence, such as the second-order constructs of fluid and crystallized intelligence and the primary mental abilities associated with each higher order construct. Like Berry and Irvine (1986), we propose that the cognitive abilities represented in traditional approaches to intelligence are considered universal across the life span and across cultures. When nurtured and directed by a favorable environment at a particular life stage, these processes and abilities develop into cognitive competencies that are manifested in daily life as cognitive performance.

Everyday competence, as represented in activities of daily living, are phenotypic expressions of intelligence that are context-or age-specific. The particular activities and behaviors that serve as phenotypic expressions of intelligence will vary with the age of the individual, that person's social roles, and the environmental context. Problem solving in everyday activities is complex and hence involves multiple basic cognitive abilities. For example, balancing one's checkbook involves verbal ability, inductive reasoning, and numerical skills. Our research has shown that significant variance in performance on everyday tasks can be accounted for by a combination of several basic abilities. The particular combination or constellation of basic abilities varies across different tasks of daily living. It is important to note that the basic abilities are seen as necessary but not sufficient antecedents for everyday competence (Willis, 1991; Willis & Schaie, 1993). Everyday competence also involves substantive knowledge associated with the particular everyday problem domain and the individual's attitudes and values with regard to the problem domain.

Postformal Forms of Reasoning

The postformal operational perspective has arisen as one that (a) is qualitatively different from prior forms or stages of reasoning, (b) develops in adulthood, and (c) is of particular interest in later adulthood. Of particular concern is the developmental timing of manifestation of this form of reasoning and the demonstration that it is different and often superior to prior forms of reasoning.

Labouvie-Vief (1992) and colleagues (Labouvie-Vief & Hakim-Larson, 1989) have proposed the development, in middle and later adulthood, of a more pragmatic, concrete, and subjective approach to reality. This mode of thinking reflects sensitivity to the interpersonal context and thus focuses on inner, personal experience. The study of cognitive aging until recently has focused almost exclusively on a youth-oriented mode that thinks of reality in a formalistic, abstract, and objectified manner. A vertical or hierarchical, rather than balanced or integrated, ordering of the two modes of thought were imposed. Pragmatic, emotive modes of thinking were devalued or subjugated. In adulthood there is the unique potential to integrate optimal use of both modes of thought. In related work, Blanchard-Fields (1986) has suggested that quantitative assessments of everyday competence or reasoning fail to tap the richness and complexity of older adults' thoughts and social attributional processes. Older adults use their postformal operational reasoning selectively, and such use is likely to occur in everyday problems that are emotionally salient and pertinent to their lives.

How Do These Perspectives Differ?

In spite of the commonalities earlier noted in this section, there are certain basic differences that may lead to competing research strategies and predictions. The Sternberg and Baltes positions are both parallel theories of competence; they suggest that there are different dimensions that conjointly affect everyday behavior but are weighted differentially for specific task demands and situations. The Willis-Schaie position is essentially a hierarchical model that argues for the aggregate importance of different combinations of basic cognitive processes as they apply to specific task demands and situational constraints. All these theories are continuity models: as adults age, certain processes may be weighted in a differential manner, but the latent constructs involved remain the same throughout the life span. By contrast, the postformal reasoning position represents developmental discontinuity by suggesting the importance of qualitative transformations, which may be unique to adulthood, as well as the increasing role of emotions as a major factor in everyday competence.

Competence as Domain-Specific Knowledge and Problem Solving

A second theoretical perspective conceptualizes competence as involving the development and organization of an increasingly complex and well-integrated body of knowledge that is domain-specific (Salthouse, 1990). Several themes associated with this approach can be identified. First, in contrast to the latent construct perspective, competence is considered to be domain-specific, that is, limited to a particular body of knowledge or substantive area. Second, the focus is not on identifying components or latent ability constructs but on describing the manner in which a problem is represented and the increasingly complex manner in which information is related and organized. Third, there is little focus on broad developmental trajectories. Rather, competence is seen as increasing as the amount of information grows and the organization of the knowledge becomes more integrated and complex. In later adulthood, everyday problem solving is seen as developing out of the older adult's familiarity and experience with problems within a specific life domain (Park, Morrell, Frieske, & Kincaid, 1992; Rybash, Hoyer, & Roodin, 1986).

Adults are seen as active problem solvers who construct a representation of both the problem and the process or strategies involved in solving the problem (Chi, 1985; H. Leventhal & Cameron, 1987). The adult's representation of the problem and of its solution involves factors that may vary with the type of problem being solved. A distinction is made between well-structured and ill-structured problems. In well-structured problems, research has focused on (a) declarative knowledge, the body of domain-specific knowledge possessed by the adult, and (b) procedural knowledge, the problem-solving strategies and skills that are relevant to the particular problem. In ill-structured problems, the problem is not well defined, allowing alternative solution strategies.

Research on ill-structured problems has often focused on adults' cognitions and beliefs about the problem and about solution or treatment alternatives (H. Leventhal & Cameron, 1987; Voss & Post, 1988). Some have argued that real-life problem solving is more closely associated with ill-structured problems (Sinnott, 1989; Sternberg & Wagner, 1986; also see Willis & Schaie, 1993, for an alternative view). Given their extensive lifetime experiences, the old might be expected to have larger stores of knowledge and to have hierarchically organized knowledge bases that are well integrated and that utilize lesser amounts but qualitatively higher order types of information.

Findings in support of the above hypotheses are mixed. Some studies report age-related reductions in the amount of information used and the extensiveness of the information search process undertaken by the old. Meyer, Russo, and Talbot (1995) examined decision making with respect to a health scenario about breast cancer. Older women had no greater prior domain-specific knowledge about breast cancer and remembered less information presented during the study. They sought less information before making a treatment decision. When given further information, older women typically did not change their initial treatment decision. In contrast, younger women were more likely to seek additional information while delaying a decision about treatment and more likely to compare and contrast various types and sources of information. In spite of these differences in use and recall of information, older women made the same decision regarding treatment as did middle-aged and young women. The older women reached the same decision based on less information earlier in the decision-making process.

Studies of managerial and of consumer decision making have found somewhat similar patterns of findings regarding age differences in problem solving (Schaninger & Schiglimpaglia, 1981; Streufert, Pogash, Piasecki, & Post, 1990). In a study of age differences in seeking medical care, the elderly were less likely to seek information from outside sources prior to contacting their physician and to contact their physicians earlier than did middle-aged individuals (E. A. Leventhal, Leventhal, Schaefer, & Easterling, 1993).

It should be noted that the domain-specific approach is essentially non-developmental. That is, competence is thought to arise out of automatization, prior experience, and the development of expertise. Hence, there are difficulties in accounting for age changes or age differences in competence that must be related to shifts in underlying physiological and psychological processes characteristic of normal aging.

Everyday Competence as the Person-Environment Fit

The third theoretical perspective to be reviewed is concerned with the degree of congruence between the abilities of the individual and the demands and resources available in the environment (Kahana, 1982; Lawton, 1982, 1987; Parmelee & Lawton, 1990). Competence does not reside solely in the individual nor in the environment. Competent behaviors occur when the capabilities of the individual match the environmental demands and resources. Hence, an older adult with some cognitive limitations may appear competent with respect to everyday activities when functioning in a supportive environment with many resources. In contrast, even the most capable individual appears less competent when functioning in a very demanding, resource-limited context. A loss of competence resulting from incongruence between the individual and the environment may reflect decreases in the abilities of the individual, changes in environmental demands or resources, or a combination of these.

The research on person-environment fit has examined the effects of different environments on older adults' ability to live independently, as well as on their morale and life satisfaction. Carp (1987) has suggested that the notion of fit should be considered at two levels. At the lower level are life-maintenance needs such as food, water, and adequate shelter. Fulfillment of these basic needs depends on the degree of fit between the person's ability to perform basic activities of daily living (ADLs; bathing toileting, feeding) and environmental resources. If the person is limited in these basic self-mainte-nance activities, then increased environmental support is needed to achieve a basic level of competence. Once these basic needs are met, the match between person and environment may then focus on the fit between the individuals' higher order needs and desires and the environmental resources.

Higher order needs may include the level of affiliation and social contact desired, need for privacy, and preferences for rural versus urban settings. With regard to affiliation, an appropriate match would involve a person with a strong desire for interpersonal contact living in a highly social environment. The impact of lack of congruence between the needs and desires of the individual and the environmental resources is illustrated in Carp's (1987) research on older persons moving to a new apartment facility. Older adults who, before moving, manifested the highest level of sociability were the ones most socially active after the move. Those who had been least socially active displayed even lower levels of socializing after the move. The inference is that those who were less comfortable in the closer environment of a housing project (greater incongruence between personal preferences and environmental conditions) withdrew and became more isolated. In contrast, those high on sociability took full advantage of increased contact with others and additional social activities.

The theoretical importance of the person-environment fit model lies in its ability to account for individual differences in competence in old age that can not be strictly attributed to the decay of the mechanics of cognition or the obsolescing of the information required by individuals to function adequately. It adds the important contextual dimension often ignored in person-centered developmental theorizing.

PSYCHOLOGICAL VERSUS LEGAL COMPETENCE

The previous section has reviewed three theoretical perspectives that characterize psychological approaches to the conceptualization and study of everyday competence. But psychological theories ought not to be mere sandbox exercises. Instead, they should abstract and systematize phenomena that are meaningful to real-world experience. In this section we briefly discuss how theories of psychological competence relate to the theoretical definition of competence as used in legal proceedings.

Legal competence is of significant practical importance because the legal determination of loss of everyday competence may result in legal judgments of guardianship or conservatorship. As we shall see, cognition is a critical aspect of legal judgments of competence. Interestingly, both legal and psychological considerations of competence have focused on two broad domains: competence with respect to the safety and well-being of the person and competence to manage one's property. In the social sciences, competence to care for oneself has been conceptualized and assessed in terms of the Activities of Daily Living ADLs (Katz, Ford, Moskowitz, Jackson, & Jaffee, 1963), including the ability to bathe, feed, toilet, and transport oneself. Management of one's affairs has been conceptualized to represent seven domains of ADLs defined as Instrumental Activities of Daily Living (IADLs; Lawton & Brody, 1969). These include the ability to use the telephone, shop for necessities, manage one's finances, prepare meals, manage one's medications, care for one's home, and transport oneself outside the home.

Legal determinations of inability to care for oneself often lead to appointment of a guardian, and incapacity to manage one's affairs may lead to appointment of a conservator. Grisso (1986) and others have argued that IADLs are of primary interest in legal guardianship cases. The elderly person may be able to engage in basic self-care activities and still have serious deficiencies in making decisions regarding independent living and management of property.

Definitions of legal competence are based on the need of the jurisprudence system to determine when a state legitimately may take action to limit an individual's rights to make decisions about his or her own person or property (Sabatino, 1996). Because the legal presumption is that adults are best able to decide what is in their best interest and ought to be left alone to pursue their own choices (Meisel, 1989), the burden of the judicial is system is on determining incompetence. Hence, legal definitions have focused largely on *incompetence* or *incapacity,* whereas psychological definitions are framed positively in terms of *competence.* Judgments regarding incapacity have recently become limited in scope to only certain domains of the person or property, such as financial management or health decision making. Global determinations of guardianship or conservatorship were more common in the past and reflected a concern with global incompetence.

In the legal system there is no national consensus on a standard for declaring an individual to be incapacitated (Anderer, 1990), just as there is little consensus in the social sciences on definitions of competence; statutes regarding competence vary widely from state to state. However, in both fields there is growing recognition of common themes or elements that are employed in conceptualizing and assessing competence (Altman, Parmelee, & Smyer, 1992: Grisso, 1986, 1994; Kapp, 1992; Sabatino, 1996; Willis, 1996). Of interest in this segment of the chapter are the similarities and differences between legal and psychological conceptions of competence.

Common Elements in Definition of Competence/Incompetence

At least four common themes or elements are frequently found in laws regarding guardianship and conservatorship and hence competence (Grisso, 1986, 1994; Sabatino, 1996).

1. *Assignment of status or disabling condition.* Until recently, a primary element in judgments of incompetence was the labeling or designation of a status for the individual. Courts and juries had the discretion to bestow the labels such as idiot, insane person, and lunatic on the individual, with the assumption that the label implied incompetence. Progressively state laws have refined the status approach in two respects. First, a more medicalized approach to defining a disabling condition has replaced the designation of a status. Second and more recently, some states no longer accept simply the identification of a disabling condition but require in addition a finding that the disabling condition has caused some dysfunctional behaviors (Parry, 1985).

2. *Cognitive functioning.* In some states the focus on a disabling condition (e.g., dementia) has been replaced with an emphasis on a more precise description of deficiencies in cognitive functioning. The critical aspect of cognitive functioning has been the individual's capacity to understand and to make and communicate responsible decisions; hence, legal definitions of competence are closely aligned with the forms of everyday problem solving of concern to psychologists. Cognitive functioning has been particularly salient in health care decision making and in advance directive statutes. Capacity with regard to health care decisions has been defined as the ability to understand the significant benefits, risks, and alternatives to proposed health care and to make and communicate a health care decision (Uniform Health-Care Decisions Act, 1993).

3. *Functional or behavioral impairment.* Recently, it has been argued that diagnosis of a disabling condition or poor performance on cognitive measures is insufficient for judging a person to be incompetent and for appointment of a guardian. The focus is on behavioral manifestations of incompetence rather than on less direct indicators such as diagnosis or mental tests. Thus, legal assessment of competence is following a trend similar to that in the social sciences—focusing on behavioral or performance indicators of problem solving and decision making rather than on measures of basic abilities and processes.

4. *Competence as congruence of person and environment.* Legal judgments are not concerned with assessment of absolute competence but rather with whether the individual is capable of functioning in a particular environment. The question is whether the person is capable of meeting his or her

essential needs for survival and is not endangering self or others in the current environment. Thus, competence in the legal sense does not reside solely in the individual but in whether the individual can survive and avoid risk of endangering self or others in a given context. Appointment of a guardian or conservator is seen as enhancing the environmental dimension when the individual's capabilities are not deemed sufficient in the present environment.

It may be noted that legal theorizing incorporates aspects of virtually all of the psychological theories of competence discussed earlier in this chapter. To the extent that these theories provide credible explanations, they also tend to affect and modify legal practice.

DO METHODS OF MEASUREMENT DRIVE THEORIES OF COMPETENCE?

As is true in other areas of gerontological theorizing, models built to systematize and explain empirical data are often driven by the methods of measurement used to collect such empirical data. At least three different approaches to the measurement of competence can be recognized. The first approach is open-ended, utilizing subject-generated responses and/or relying on the ability of rater-derived observations or judges' ratings of more global responses to determine the nature of competence as well as to judge the level of competence displayed by a particular individual. The second follows the psychometric tradition of building measurement models that dimensionalize the latent construct(s) of interest. Such models must of necessity involve objective assessment strategies that assume scientists can characterize response dimensions and specify appropriate (correct) subject response. A third approach is concerned with the person-environment fit, that is, the interaction between the actions of the individual (everyday competence) and the complexity or supportiveness of the context. The latter approach, of course, requires measurement of situations (environments) as well as performance of the individual.

Subjective Ratings

One way of measuring everyday competence is to consider whether a person "behaves" in a competent manner (Goodnow, 1984). Such an approach, of course, requires the use of judges to determine the attributes of everyday competence prevalent at various life stages (e.g., Berg & Sternberg, 1985). These attributes represent ways in which people combine or organize information about everyday events (Goodnow, 1986) or how psychologists perceive their own functioning (Mason & Rebok, 1984). Theories derived from taxonomies developed by judges or by various multidimensional scaling approaches tend to be essentially "nativistic." That is, they represent explications of the stereotypic conceptualization of the persons generating them. Hence, rating-derived theories may be quite specific to the age, social class, work setting, or other contextual dimensions of the raters and the target population (Scribner, 1984). One such prominent taxonomy that has widely influenced the field are the dimensions represented by the ADL and IADL checklists (Fillenbaum, 1985; Lawton & Brody, 1969). The IADL checklist in particular has been used widely to determine whether older individuals can function independently in the community as well to determine limitations on particular dimensions such as managing finances, using medications appropriately, using transportation, communicating via the telephone, being able to engage in household chores, and being able to shop and prepare food.

Subjective approaches to the definition of domain content play an important role in theory development and may be an essential first step in devising models that can be more formally operationalized with objective methods of assessment. Such methods provide the basis for data collections on which the viability of the theories can then be tested.

Objective Assessment

Objective measures for the assessment of everyday competence have been developed for quite some time. Early examples of such work are scales sampling everyday activities by Demming and Pressey (1957) and by Gardner and Monge (1977). Another set of items that has been used in aging research comes from the efforts of the Educational Testing Service (1977) to assemble an objective measure of competency in everyday tasks for high school graduates. This measure contains materials related to interpreting medicine bottle labels, bus schedules, road maps, Yellow Pages advertisements, warranties, newspaper editorials, and the like. Age changes on this global measure of everyday competence have been found to be comparable to those seen for fluid abilities (Schaie, 1996).

Willis and her colleagues (Marsiske & Willis, 1995; Willis & Marsiske, 1991; Willis & Schaie, 1993) have conducted an extensive program to operationalize objective assessment tools for each of the IADL domains, using printed materials that older persons must be able to deal with successfully in each of the seven categories. The plausibility of this measurement system was assessed by confirmatory factor analysis, as well as by replicating assessment with physical stimulus materials contained in older persons' homes (Diehl, Willis, & Schaie, 1995).

Just as subjective explorations may inadvertently bias the development of theoretical models and thus incorporate stereotypes that are largely time-, population-, and place-bound, so may objective measurement systems constrain the manner in which everyday competence is defined to the domain content of such measurement systems. Further restrictions are often introduced by the demand for ever more parsimonious assessment systems, which tend to lead to assessment procedures that, by their very nature, will be global. These procedures, in turn, may lead to the inappropriate inference that everyday competence is a unitary construct, even though we know intuitively and from empirical evidence that a multidimensional system of constructs must be involved to account for the complexitiy of human experience.

Person-Environment Fit

Given our definition of everyday competence as involving adaptive behavior within specific contexts, we now must consider the implications for theory of how to measure the context within which competence is displayed. A major approach to this issue has been the extensive literature on person-environment (P-E) fit (c.f., Lawton, 1982, 1989). In this approach it is sometimes argued that the action of persons within context can be treated only as P-E interactions; the effect of one on the other is seen as essentially reciprocal in nature. Nevertheless, the way in which the characteristics of the environment are described will obviously make a difference. For example, a number of efforts in this direction have appeared in the literature with respect to the characteristics of the physical environment (Regnier, 1997), of independent living arrangements (Carp & Christensen, 1986), and with respect to institutional environments (M. M. Baltes & Horgas, 1997; Moos & Lemke, 1985). Once again, whether the characteristics of such settings are measured as simple technical descriptors, as indicators of support, or along dimensions of dependency induction, such measurement will have theoretical implications for how the P-E interface is to be understood.

An alternative approach to contextual measurement is to take a quasi-ethnographic approach to discover the specific situations within which older adults are required to display competent behavior. This information can then be translated into a data language such as a Q-sort to discover the dimensions that are most likely to be perceived by older raters as characteristic of competency-demanding situations. In a study by Scheidt and Schaie (1978) situations were identified as ratable along the dimensions of social-nonsocial, common-uncommon, supportive-depriving, and active-passive. Age differences in perceived competence were found in the direction of greater competence for the elderly in situations involving social, common, and depriving elements (Willis & Schaie, 1986). It was also found that different basic cognitive skills were related to perceptions of effective functioning in situations with different attributes (Schaie, Gonda, & Quayhagen, 1983). A situational competence model here would be driven by the *perceived* attributes of the context rather than by its objective descriptors.

Measurement strategies are important in driving theory in gerontology because explanations must of necessity be based on how a domain of behavior is dimensionalized and whether objective or subjective experience is preferred for the source of one's data. Perhaps in the best of all possible worlds we would expect a dialectic process in which theory directs how we measure and in turn measurement impacts on theory.

EVERYDAY COMPETENCE WITHIN A LIFE SPAN PERSPECTIVE

We now come to the crux of the matter, namely, how should we advance theory development to better characterize the developmental course of everyday competence as we age? At least three aspects of such theory development must be considered. First of all, it must be stressed that the aging of everyday competence should be considered a dynamic process: competence of the individual as well as situational characteristics change both quantitatively and qualitatively over the adult life span. Second, adequate theoretical models must consider not only the level of functioning of the individual but also the matter of rate of change. Despite the remaining controversy over the importance of cohort differences in cognitive abilities and hence everyday competence, it seems likely that quantitative age differences in competence, prior to advanced old age, may to large extent be a function of obsolescence and cohort-related differences in opportunity structures. What is not clear, however, is whether there are also cohort-related differences in the *rate* of cognitive aging. The question of whether there has been a slowing of such change, particularly in advanced old age, remains open. Third, we need more theorizing about to what extent qualitative changes in the nature of individual response and in the characteristics of the eliciting situations contribute to apparently age-related differences in the display of everyday competence.

Clearly, whatever theory of everyday intelligence we care to espouse, we cannot escape the conclusion that decremental changes in the basic cognitive mechanisms will result in commensurate deterioration of performance of everyday tasks. To the extent that different psychological abilities decline at different rates, we will also expect to see differential change in everyday competence (Willis, Jay, Diehl, & Marsiske, 1992). In our research on the concurrent relationships between basic mental abilities and performance of cognitively demanding tasks in various domains of everyday competence, we have found that over half of the individual-differences variance in older adults' performance can be accounted for by mental abilities (Willis, 1997, Willis & Schaie, 1994).

A developmental theory of everyday competence would predict that adults will reach their asymptotic competence in midlife, when virtually all the basic cognitive processes are at peak levels. We would first expect difficulties in early old age for those activities that have relatively brief response windows—the inexorable increase in reaction time is most noticeable as tasks take on increasing complexity. We would next expect difficulties in those everyday tasks that involve strong components of processes identified as fluid or visualization abilities. Everyday competencies that involve primarily verbal (or other crystallized) processes are, by contrast likely to remain intact into advanced old age (cf. Schaie, 1996).

As we noted earlier, a comprehensive theory must also take into account the situational demands within which everyday competence must be exercised. These demands are likely to be life-stage-specific. Hence, lesser or greater amounts of underlying cognitive competence may be required. But we would also predict qualitative change in the situational context, depending on its complexity or supportiveness, that may permit the display of adequate everyday competencies even where cognitive resources have declined substantially. Moreover, motivational states (see chapter 14, this volume) and positive or negative shifts in the social support system (cf. Carstensen, Gross, & Fung, 1997) may markedly affect the expression of everyday competence.

We have previously described a stage theory of adult cognitive development that considers developmental changes in the demand context requiring adults' cognitive response (Schaie, 1977–78; Schaie & Willis, in press). The demand context defined by this theoretical model is also quite relevant for a theoretical framework of everyday competency. That is, the range of everyday competencies required of young adult or middle-aged individuals must necessarily differ markedly from those required of the old and very old. Just as a differentiation-dedifferentiation model fits the empirical data and makes sense for understanding the course of cognitive development (Reinert, 1970; Schaie, Maitland, Willis, & Intrieri, 1998; Werner, 1948), so we must consider a model for everyday competence whose ontogeny shifts from the simple demands of childhood, through the complexities of midlife, to a simplification of both situational context and extent of the individual life space in old age.

In the cognitive aging literature the process of development has been characterized by P. B. Baltes (1993) as selective optimization with compensation. We would propose that a similar process extends to everyday competence as well. Such a model would readily explain, for example, why 90–year-olds can make thoughtful dispositions of their personal property to selected friends and family members and at the same time are unable to take care of their financial affairs or engage in other IADLs that would be essential at an earlier life stage to successfully maintain independent living arrangements. We might conclude that everyday competence is of necessity constrained by the physical and cognitive capacity of the individual, the situational demands, and the environmental support that a given society deems appropriate at different life stages. We do not demand that children display competencies incompatible with their development stage. By the same token, competencies that we take for granted in midlife and early old age may well be inappropriate for the very old. Indeed, dependency and increased levels of societally approved support may obviate the display of many everyday competencies at both ends of life span.

Theory development in gerontology must provide explanations for both the continuities and the discontinuities of life span development. Perhaps theory development in the area of everyday competence can serve as a particularly useful example of how explanations may be found that showcase the remaining vitality of the aging individual as a contributing member of the species and at the same time explain the transformations in behavior and context that characterize the later stages of the life course.

REFERENCES

Altman, W. M., Parmelee, P. A., & Smyer, M. A. (1992). Autonomy, competence, and informed consent in long term care: Legal and psychological perspectives. *Villanova Law Review, 37*, 1671–1704.

Anderer, S. (1990). *Determining competency in guardianship proceedings.* Washington, DC: American Bar Association.

Baltes, M. M., & Horgas, A. L. (1997). Long-term care institutions and the maintenance of competence: A dialectic between compensation and overcompensation. In S. L. Willis, K. W. Schaie, & M. Hayward (Eds.), *Societal mechanisms for maintaining individual competence in old age* (pp.142–164). New York: Springer Publishing Co.

Baltes, P. B. (1987). Theoretical propositions of life-span developmental psychology: On the dynamics between growth and decline. *Developmental Psychology, 23*, 611–626.

Baltes, P. B. (1993). The aging mind: Potentials and limits. *Gerontologist, 33*. 580–594.

Baltes, P. B., Dittman-Kohli, F., & Dixon, R. (1984). New perspective on the development of intelligence in adulthood: Toward a dual-process conception and a model of selective optimization with compensation. In P. B. Baltes, & O. G. Brim, Jr. (Eds.), *Life-span development and behavior* (Vol., 6, pp. 33–76). New York: Academic Press.

Berg, C., & Sternberg, R. J. (1985). A triarchic theory of intellectual development during adulthood. *Developmental Review, 5*, 95–107.

Berry, J., & Irvine, S. (1986). Bricolage: Savages do it daily. In R. Sternberg & R. Wagner (Eds.), *Practical intelligence: Origins of competence in the everyday world* (pp. 271–306). New York: Cambridge University Press.

Blanchard-Fields, F. (1986). Reasoning in adolescence and adults on social dilemmas varying in emotional saliency: An adult developmental perspective. *Psychology and Aging, 1,* 325–333.

Carp, F. (1987). Environment and aging. In D. Stokols & I. Altman (Eds.), *Handbook of environmental psychology* (Vol 1, pp. 329–360). New York: Wiley

Carp, F. M., & Christensen, D. L. (1986). Technical environment assessment predictors of residential satisfaction: A study of elderly women living alone. *Research on Aging, 8,* 269–287.

Carstensen, L. L., Gross, J., & Fung, H. (1997). The social context of emotion. *Annual Review of Gerontology and Geriatrics, 17,* 325–352.

Chi, M. T. H. (1985). Interactive roles of knowledge and strategies in the development of organized sorting and recall. In S. Chipman, J. Segal, & R. Glaser (Eds.), *Thinking and learning skills: Current research and open questions* (Vol. 2, pp. 457–484). Hillsdale, NJ: Erlbaum.

Connolly, K. J., & Bruner. J. S. (1973). Competence: Its nature and nurture. In K. J. Connolly & J. S. Bruner (Eds.), *The growth of competence.* New York: Academic Press.

Demming, J. A., & Pressey, S. L. (1957). Tests indigenous to the adult and older years. *Journal of Counseling Psychology, 4,* 144–148.

Diehl, M., Willis, S. L., & Schaie, K. W. (1995). Older adults' everyday competence: Observational assessment and cognitive correlates. *Psychology and Aging, 10,* 478–491.

Educational Testing Service. (1977). *Basic skills assessment test: Reading.* Princeton, NJ: Educational Testing Service.

Fillenbaum, G. G. (1985). Screening the elderly: A brief instrumental activities of daily living measures. *Journal of the American Geriatrics Society, 33,* 698–706.

Fillenbaum, G. G. (1987). Multidimensional functional assessment. In G. L. Maddox (Ed.), *The encyclopedia of aging* (pp. 460–464). New York: Springer Publishing Co.

Gardner, E. F., & Monge, R. H. (1977). Adult age differences in cognitive abilities and educational background. *Experimental Aging Research, 3,* 337–383.

Goodnow, J. J. (1984). On being judged "intelligent." *International Journal of Psychology, 19,* 91–106.

Goodnow, J. J. (1986). Some lifelong everyday forms of intelligent behavior: Organizing and reorganizing. In R. J. Sternberg & R. K. Wagner (Eds.), *Practical intelligence: Origins of competence in the everyday world* (pp. 143–162). New York: Cambridge University Press.

Grisso, T. (1986). *Evaluating competencies: Forensic assessments and instruments.* New York: Plenum Press.

Grisso, T. (1994). Clinical assessment for legal competency of older adults. In M. Storandt & G. R. Vanden Bos (Eds.), *Neuropsychological assessment of dementia and depression in older adults: A clinician's guide* (pp. 119–139). Washington, DC: American Psychological Association.

Kahana, E. (1982). A congruence model of person-environment interaction. In M. P. Lawton, P. Windley, & T. Byerts (Eds.), *Aging and the environment: Theoretical approaches* (pp. 97–121). New York: Springer Publishing Co.

Kapp, M. B. (1992). *Geriatrics and the law: Patient rights and professional responsibilities* (2nd ed.). New York: Springer Publishing Co.

Katz, S., Ford, A., Moskowitz, R., Jackson, B., & Jaffee, M. (1963). Studies of illness in the aged: The Index of ADL, a standardized measure of biological and psychological functioning. *Journal of the American Medical Association, 185,* 94–99.

Labouvie-Vief, G. (1992). A neo-Piagetian perspective on adult cognitive development. In R. J. Sternberg & C. A. Berg (Eds.), *Intellectual development* (pp. 197–228). New York: Cambridge University Press.

Labouvie-Vief G., & Hakim-Larson, J. (1989). Developmental shifts in adult thought. In S. Hunter & M. Sundel (Eds.), *Midlife myths.* Newbury Park: Sage.

Lawton, M. P. (1982). Competence, environmental press, and adaptation of older people. In M. P. Lawton, P. Windley, & T. Byerts (Eds.), *Aging and the environment: Theoretical approaches* (pp. 33–59). New York: Springer Publishing Co.

Lawton, M. P. (1987). Contextual perspectives: Psychosocial influences. In L. W. Poon (Ed.), *Handbook for clinical memory assessment of older adults.* Washington, DC: American Psychological Association.

Lawton, M. P. (1989). Behavior-relevant ecological factors. In K. W. Schaie & C. Schooler (Eds), *Social structure and aging: Psychological processes* (pp. 57–78). Hillsdale, NJ: Erlbaum.

Lawton, M. P., & Brody, E. (1969). Assessment of older people: Self maintaining and instrumental activities of daily living. *Gerontologist, 9,* 179–185.

Leventhal, E. A., Leventhal, H., Schaefer, P. M., & Easterling, D. (1993). Conservation of energy, uncertainty reduction, and swift utilization of medical care among the elderly. *Journal of Gerontology: Psychological Sciences, 48,* 78–86.

Leventhal, H., & Cameron, L. (1987). Behavioral theories and the problem of compliance. *Patient Education and Counseling, 10,* 117–138.

Marsiske, M., & Willis, S. L. (1995). Dimensionality of everyday problem solving in older adults. *Psychology and Aging, 10,* 269–283.

Mason, C. F., & Rebok, G. W. (1984). Psychologists' self-perception of their intellectual functioning. *International Journal of Behavioral Development, 7,* 255–266.

Meisel, A. (1989). *The right to die.* New York: Wiley.

Meyer, B. J. F., Russo, C., & Talbot, A. (1995). Discourse comprehension and problem solving: Decisions about the treatment of breast cancer by women across the life-span. *Psychology and Aging, 10,* 84–103,

Moos, R. H., & Lemke, S. (1985). Specialized living environments for people. In J. E. Birren & K. W. Schaie (Eds.), *Handbook of the psychology of aging* (2nd ed., pp. 864–889). New York: Van Nostrand Reinhold

Park, D. C. (1992). Applied cognitive aging research. In F. I. M. Craik & T. A. Salthouse (Eds.), *Handbook of cognition and aging* (pp. 449–493). Hillsdale, NJ: Erlbaum.

Park, D. C., Morrell, R. W., Frieske, D., & Kincaid, D. (1992). Medication adherence behaviors in older adults: Effects of external cognitive supports. *Psychology and Aging, 7,* 252–256.

Parmelee, P. A., & Lawton, M. P. (1990). The design of special environments for the aged. In J. E. Birren & K. W. Schaie (Eds.), *Handbook of the psychology of aging* (3rd ed., pp. 465–489). San Diego, CA: Academic Press.

Parry, J. (1985). Incompetency, guardianship, and restoration. In S. J. Brakel, J. Parry, & B. A. Weiner (Eds.), *The mentally disabled and the law* (3rd ed., pp. 369–433). Chicago: American Bar Foundation.

Regnier, V. (1997). The physical environment and maintenance of competence. In S. L. Willis, K. W. Schaie, & M. Hayward (Eds.), *Societal mechanisms for maintaining competence in old age* (pp. 232–250). New York: Springer Publishing Co.

Reinert, G. (1970). Comparative factor analytic studies of intelligence through the human life-span. In L. R. Goulet & P. B. Baltes (Eds.), *Life-span developmental psychology: Research and theory* (pp. 468–485). New York: Academic Press.

Rybash, J. M., Hoyer, W. J., & Roodin, P. A. (1986). *Adult cognition and aging: Developmental changes in processing, knowing, and thinking.* New York: Pergamon.

Sabatino, C. P. (1996). Competency: Refining our legal fictions. In M. Smyer, K. W. Schaie, & M. Kapp (Eds.), *Older adults' decision-making and the law* (pp. 1–28). New York: Springer Publishing Co.

Salthouse, T. A. (1990). Cognitive competence and expertise in the aging. In J. E. Birren & K. W. Schaie (Eds.), *Handbook of the psychology of aging* (3rd. ed., pp. 311–319). San Diego, CA: Academic Press.

Schaie, K. W. (1977–78). Toward a stage theory of adult development. *International Journal of Aging and Human Development, 8,* 129–138.

Schaie, K. W. (1978). External validity in the assessment of intellectual development in adulthood. *Journal of Gerontology, 33,* 695–701.

Schaie, K. W. (1996). *Intellectual development in adulthood: The Seattle Longitudinal Study.* New York: Cambridge University Press.

Schaie, K. W., Gonda, J. N., & Quayhagen, M. (1983). Die Beziehung zwischen intellektueller Leistung und erlebter Alltagskompetenz bei Erwachsenen in verschiedenen Altersabschniten [Relationships of intellectual performance and everyday competence in adults of various ages]. In H. Löwe, U. Lehr, & J. E. Birren (Eds.), *Psychologische Probleme des Erwachsenenalters* [Psychological problems of adulthood] (pp. 43–67). Berlin: VEB Deutscher Verlag der Wissenschaften.

Schaie, K. W., Maitland, S. B., Willis, S. L., & Intrieri, R. L. (1998). Longitudinal invariance of adult psychometric ability factor structures across seven years. *Psychology and Aging, 13,* 8–20.

Schaie, K. W., & Willis, S. L. (In Press). A stage theory model of adult cognitive development revisited. In B. Rubinstein, M. Moss & M. Kleban (Eds.), *The many dimensions of aging: Essays in honor of M. Powell Lawton.* New York: Springer Publishing Co.

Schaninger, D. M., & Schiglimpaglia, D. (1981). The influence of cognitive personality traits and demographics on consumer information acquisition. *Journal of Consumer Research, 8,* 208–216.

Scheidt, R. J., & Schaie, K. W. (1978). A situational taxonomy for the elderly: Generating situational criteria. *Journal of Gerontology, 33,* 348–357.

Scribner, S. (1984). Studying working intelligence. In B. Rogoff & J. Lave (Eds.), *Everyday cognition: Its development and social context* (pp. 9–40). Cambridge, MA: Harvard University Press.

Sinnott, J. D. (1989). A model for solution of ill-structured problems: Implications for everyday and abstract problem solving. In J. D. Sinnott (Ed.), *Everyday problem solving: Theory and applications* (pp. 72–99). New York: Praeger.

Staudinger, U. M. (1996). Wisdom and the social-interactive foundation of the mind. In P. B. Baltes & U. M. Staudinger (Eds.), *Interactive minds* (pp. 276–315). New York: Cambridge University Press.

Sternberg, R. J. (1977). *Intelligence, information processing, and analogical reasoning: The componential analysis of human abilities.* Hillsdale, NJ: Erlbaum.

Sternberg, R. J. (1985). *Beyond IQ: A triarchic theory of human intelligence.* New York: Cambridge University Press.

Sternberg, R. J., & Berg, C. (1987). What are theories of adult intellectual development theories of? In C. Schooler & K. W. Schaie (Eds.), *Cognitive functioning and social structure over the life course* (pp. 3–23). New York: Ablex.

Sternberg, R. J., & Kolligian, J. (Eds.). (1990). *Competence considered.* New Haven, CT: Yale University Press.

Sternberg, R. J., & Wagner, R. (1986). *Practical Intelligence: Origins of competence in the everyday world.* New York: Cambridge University Press.

Streufert, S., Pogash, R., Piasecki, M., & Post, G. M. (1990). Age and management team performance. *Psychology and Aging, 5,* 551–559.

Thurstone, L. L. (1938). *The primary mental abilities.* Chicago: University of Chicago Press.

Voss, J. F., & Post, T. A. (1988). On the solving of ill-structured problems. In M. T. H. Chi, R. Glaser, & M. Farr (Eds.), *The nature of expertise* (pp. 261–285). Hillsdale, NJ: Erlbaum.

Werner, H. (1948). *Comparative psychology of mental development.* New York: International Universities Press.

Willis, S. L. (1987). Cognitive interventions in the elderly. *Annual Review of Gerontology and Geriatrics, 11,* 159–188.

Willis, S. L. (1991). Cognition and everyday competence. *Annual Review of Gerontology and Geriatrics, 11,* 80–109.

Willis, S. L. (1996). Assessing everyday competence in the cognitively challenged elderly. In M. Smyer, K. W. Schaie, & M. B. Kapp (Eds.), *Older adults' decision-making and the law* (pp. 87–127). New York: Springer Publishing Co.

Willis, S. L. (1997). Everyday cognitive competence in the elderly: Conceptual issues and empirical findings. *Gerontologist, 36,* 595–601.

Willis, S. L., Jay, G. M., Diehl, M., & Marsiske, M. (1992). Longitudinal change in prediction of everyday task competence in the elderly. *Research on Aging, 14,* 68–91.

Willis, S. L., & Marsiske, M. (1991). A life-span perspective on practical intelligence. In D. Tupper & R. Cicerone (Eds.), *The neuropsychology of everyday life* (pp. 183–198). Boston: Kluwer Academic Publishers.

Willis, S. L., & Schaie, K. W. (1986). Practical intelligence in later adulthood. In R. J. Sternberg & R. K. Wagner (Eds.), *Practical intelligence: Origins of competence in the everyday world* (pp. 236–268). New York: Cambridge University Press.

Willis, S. L., & Schaie, K. W. (1993). Everyday cognition: Taxonomic and methodological considerations. In J. M. Puckett & H. W. Reese (Eds.), *Mechanisms of everyday cognition* (pp. 33–54). Hillsdale, NJ: Erlbaum.

Willis, S. L., & Schaie, K. W. (1994). Assessing competence in the elderly. In C. E. Fisher & R. M. Lerner (Eds.), *Applied developmental psychology* (pp. 339–372). New York: Macmillan.

11

Theories of Cognition

Timothy A. Salthouse

I t is helpful to begin this chapter by documenting the phenomena in need of explanation by theories of aging and cognition. An effort of this type is desirable because one cannot hope to evaluate the success of alternative theories if there is no agreement with respect to what a successful theory of cognitive aging should attempt to explain.

I propose that the primary phenomenon requiring explanation by a theory of cognitive aging is the age-related decline in measures of process, or fluid cognition. This type of cognition refers to the efficiency or effectiveness of processing at the time of assessment and is typically evaluated with tasks of learning, memory, reasoning, and spatial abilities.

Figure 11.1 portrays representative data from cross-sectional samples involving experimental (free recall and paper folding) and psychometric (reasoning and associative learning) tests. The scores in each test were converted to standard deviation units to allow all variables to be expressed in the same metric. Although it is not represented in the figure, there is considerable variability at each age in every variable. It is important to note that many older adults perform at or above the average of young adults, and many young adults perform at or above the level of older adults. However, there are also pronounced age trends, and for many variables the magnitude of the difference in cognitive performance between the average at age 25 and the average at age 75 is about 1.5 standard deviation units. These phenomena clearly require an explanation because they are moderately large and have been well established in numerous studies.

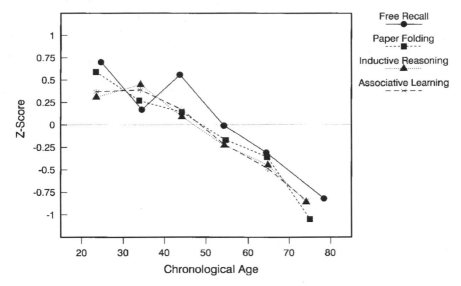

FIGURE 11.1 Performance in free recall, paper folding, inductive reasoning, and associative learning tests as a function of age decade. Free recall data from Salthouse (1993), paper-folding data from Salthouse (1994), and inductive reasoning and associative learning data from the normative sample for the Woodcock-Johnson Test of Cognitive Abilities. Reprinted with permission.

However, other aspects of cognition may not have to be explained by a theory of cognitive aging. For example, the relative stability of product, or crystallized, cognition is often assumed not to require a developmental explanation. This type of cognition refers to the accumulated products of processing carried out in the past and is typically evaluated with tests of acquired information and general knowledge.

Figure 11.2 portrays the cross-sectional age relations involving multiple-choice vocabulary and general knowledge tests from three recent studies conducted in my laboratory. Notice that in contrast to the fluid or process abilities, the trend in these variables is to remain stable or possibly to increase with advancing age.

The distinction between these two types of cognition is important because many researchers have assumed that it is not necessary to incorporate an explanation of why certain variables do not exhibit age-related differences into a theory of cognitive aging. The idea that the absence of a difference seldom requires an explanation may or may not be valid, but in any case there are apparently no theoretical accounts of the stability of crystallized or product cognition, and thus these aspects of cognition will not be discussed further in this chapter.

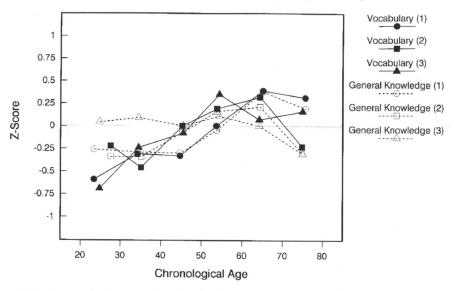

FIGURE 11.2   Performance in multiple-choice vocabulary and general knowledge tests as a function of age decade. All data from unpublished studies by Hambrick, Salthouse, and Meinz (1997).

THEORIES

How can these cross-sectional age-related differences in fluid or process cognition be explained? Before we turn to this issue, it should be noted that the phenomena are referred to as age-related because, although there is clearly a relation between measures of cognitive performance and age, one cannot necessarily infer that processes of aging are responsible for the observed differences. In fact, we will see that theories differ greatly with respect to the nature of the causal influences postulated to be responsible for the empirical relations between age and measures of cognitive performance.

Most theoretical perspectives in aging and cognition can be classified into one of two categories, depending on whether the primary hypothesized determinants are distal or proximal in nature. Prototypical theories within each category are briefly described in the following two sections.

Distal Explanations

In the present context, distal refers to factors that occurred at earlier periods in the individual's life but that contribute to the current level of performance. This type of explanation is particularly useful for specifying why the observed differences emerged, because there is wide agreement that the mere passage of time is not sufficient as a cause of behavior. It is therefore necessary to postulate factors that exert their influence over time and that are responsible for the age-related differences evident in the level of cognitive performance.

One type of explanation for distal factors focuses on a variety of sociocultural changes that might be presumed to affect cognitive performance. The distinguishing characteristic of this perspective is that it emphasizes changes occurring in the social and physical environment more than changes taking place within the individual. Some researchers use the term *cohort effects* to refer to the constellation of influences associated with physical, social, and cultural changes because people born in different periods (i.e., people comprising distinct birth cohorts) are likely to have experienced different physical and social environments as they were growing older. The strongest version of this environmental change perspective suggests that people experience little or no cognitive decline with increasing age but rather that they effectively become obsolete because people from more recent generations perform at successively higher levels on many cognitive tests than do those from earlier generations.

The most impressive evidence for an influence of some type of social, cultural, or physical change on cognitive performance derives from time-lag investigations. The relevant information in a time-lag study consists of comparisons of the cognitive performance of two or more samples of individuals of the same age but tested at different points in time. For example, Tuddenham (1948) compared the performance of soldiers in 1943 with the performance of soldiers in 1918–1919 on a test of general intelligence. He found that the average score in the 1943 sample was at the 83rd percentile of the distribution of scores from the 1918–1919 sample; therefore, Tuddenham's results are consistent with the view that cognitive performance is affected by changes occurring in the environment or culture in which one lives. Flynn (1987) and Schaie (1996) have also documented substantial time-lag effects in various measures of cognitive performance, including those reflecting process or fluid cognition.

Although the evidence for historical improvements in cognitive test performance now seems compelling, the implications of these results for the interpretation of age-related differences in cognition are not yet clear. For example, it is definitely not the case that all age-related cognitive differences are merely obsolescence effects because there have been numerous reports of substantial longitudinal (within-individual) age-related declines on a variety of cognitive measures (e.g., Hultsch, Hertzog, Small, McDonald-Miszczak, & Dixon, 1992; Schaie, 1996; Zelinski & Burnight, 1997). Furthermore, very little information is currently available about the factors responsible for the time-lag effects or about the age of maximum susceptibility to them, and consequently it is difficult to predict the impact that they might have on different types of age-related comparisons (see Salthouse, 1991, for further discussion of this issue). Many researchers seem to assume that environmental change influences are likely to have the greatest impact on cross-sectional comparisons, but that is not necessarily the case. As one illustration, if the change in the physical or social environment affects people of all ages equally, such as might be the case with exposure to toxins or pollutants in the air, water, and food supply, then the most serious distortions of developmental patterns might occur on longitudinal rather than on cross-sectional age relations. Admittedly, this is mere speculation at present, but if it should be the case, then the situation might be somewhat analogous to the effect of inflation on income; that is, large time-lag effects might occur that make longitudinal comparisons difficult to interpret, without seriously compromising the meaningfulness of cross-sectional comparisons obtained at any given point in time.

One example of a particular type of sociocultural change that might be presumed to affect cognitive functioning is that associated with educational patterns. There are well-documented increases across the decades of this century in the average amount of education completed by adults, and it is possible that these changes could affect the level of performance on at least some cognitive tasks. However, the available empirical evidence has not been very consistent with an educational change interpretation of age-related differences in cognition. For example, although negative age differences are sometimes attenuated when level of education is statistically controlled, additive rather than interactive effects of age and amount of education are usually found when relations of age to various measures of cognition are examined among people with the same levels of education. That is, people with more education tend to score higher on many cognitive tests than do those with less education, but in moderately large samples the patterns of age-related decline are typically quite similar across different amounts of education. Therefore, although amount of education is clearly related to cognitive performance, the existing evidence suggests that generational differences in the quantity of education completed are probably not responsible for more than a small proportion of the cross-sectional age-related differences evident in various measures of cognitive functioning. Because of difficulties associated with evaluating educational quality, no conclusions can be reached about the impact of possible generational differences in the quality of one's education.

Another possible distal determinant of age-related differences in cognitive performance is related to the amount and type of relevant experience the individual has acquired. The primary assumption of this experiential perspective is that the relations between age and measures of cognition vary as a function of the amount of recent experience. This view is sometimes known as the disuse perspective because age-related cognitive decline is postulated to occur largely because of lack of use, not because of maturationally determined deterioration.

Three types of evidence are relevant to the experiential or disuse perspective on age-related cognitive differences. One category of evidence consists of contrasts of the age relations across familiar and unfamiliar activities. The reasoning is as follows: If some activities are continuously performed across all periods of adulthood, then there would have been no disuse, and thus the disuse view would predict much smaller or nonexistent age relations for performance of familiar activities compared to unfamiliar activities. However, this expectation has not been supported because there are numerous reports of age-related differences favoring young adults in a wide variety of familiar cognitively demanding activities (e.g., comprehension of prescription medication information, memory for stories and movies, interpretation of bus schedules and government forms, etc.). (See Salthouse, 1991, for a review.)

A second category of evidence relevant to the disuse perspective consists of comparisons of age trends in people with different amounts of relevant experience. The disuse interpretation would predict smaller age-cognition relations for people who have used their abilities continuously than for people who seldom use their abilities because in the former case there would have been no period of disuse. Although this prediction seems quite plausible, moderate to large age-related differences have frequently been found in samples of adults with extensive amounts of experience in relevant activities. For example, similar age-related declines in measures of spatial ability have been found across groups of people with widely varying amounts of experience with spatial activities, including architects (e.g., Salthouse, Babcock, Skovronek, & Mitchell, 1990; Salthouse & Mitchell, 1990). Parallel age relations have been found for memory for music regardless of the individual's amount of musical experience (Meinz & Salthouse, 1998). There are some exceptions to these patterns (e.g., Morrow, Leirer, & Altieri, 1992), but they have been surprisingly difficult to find, and the factors responsible for the different patterns have not yet been identified.

A final type of evidence relevant to the experiential or disuse interpretation concerns the effects of manipulations of experience on the magnitude of age-cognition relations. If the source of the age-related differences in cognition is a lack of experience (or disuse) on the part of older adults, then one might expect those differences to disappear after everyone had received additional relevant experience. That is, the added experience could be assumed to remediate the disuse; and if disuse was the only factor contributing to the age-related differences in performance, then those differences should be eliminated when there was no longer any disuse. Once again, although the reasoning seems plausible, this result has almost never been obtained. In fact, in some cases the exact opposite has occurred: the magnitude of the age-related differences have actually increased rather than decreased after experimenter-provided experience (e.g., Kliegl, Smith, & Baltes,

1989). Almost every study has found that people of all ages benefit from training or practice, but there is little evidence that added experience results in a reduction of the age-related differences in measures of cognitive functioning. Specifically, when adults of different ages receive the same type and extent of training, there have been very few, if any, cases where older adults have been found to improve more than young adults.

Although the "use it or lose it" idea is popular among both the general public and researchers in the field of cognitive aging, it has surprisingly little supporting evidence. Therefore, although the disuse interpretation cannot be completely dismissed as a factor contributing to age-related differences in cognition, it should be acknowledged that this view currently does not have much empirical support.

The distal interpretations that have been discussed can be considered to be fairly optimistic because they suggest either that there is no age-related decline (obsolescence) or that the decline occurs only because of lack of the appropriate types of early or recent experience, which can presumably be remediated (disuse). Other types of distal interpretations of age-cognition relations have been proposed, but they have not yet been the focus of much systematic investigation.

Proximal Explanations

Proximal factors are those operating at the time of assessment that influence the current level of performance. Because theories at this level are focused on concurrent relationships, they may be more likely than distal-oriented theories to incorporate specific mechanisms linking the theoretical constructs to cognitive performance. However, because the emphasis is on characteristics of processing at the time of assessment, proximal theories seldom attempt to specify how or why the age-related differences in the critical mechanism or mechanisms originated.

A variety of proximal explanations of age-related differences in process or fluid cognition have been proposed. Moreover, because much of the contemporary cognitive research is of this type, there are many versions within each category.

One category of explanation for proximal factors postulates that the age-related differences originate because of some type of strategic deficiency manifested in qualitative differences in the manner in which the cognitive task is performed. Perhaps because of disuse or for other unspecified reasons, this interpretation proposes that there is a shift with advancing age in the efficiency or effectiveness of the strategies used to perform particular cognitive tasks.

There are at least two variants of strategy-based interpretations of age-related differences in cognition. The production deficiency version postulates that if the same strategies were used by adults of different ages, then everyone would have equivalent levels of performance. This interpretation assumes that there are little or no age-related differences in capability or capacity, but for some reason, as adults grow older, they tend to use suboptimal strategies to perform many cognitive tasks. The processing deficiency version of the strategic deficiency hypothesis asserts that there would still be age-related differences in cognitive performance even if everyone used the same strategy because the critical limitation is that the strategies cannot be performed at the same level of efficiency by people of different ages. In other words, this view maintains that the differences in strategy are secondary to differences in more fundamental abilities.

Most of the empirical research to date has been more consistent with the processing deficiency version than with the production version of the strategic deficiency hypothesis (see Salthouse, 1991, for a review). However, interpretations postulating adult age differences in metacognitive strategies and processes are still being investigated, and it is possible that at least some of the age-related differences in cognition might eventually be found to be attributable to these types of higher order strategic factors.

A second category of explanation attributes age-related differences in cognitive performance to quantitative differences in the efficiency and/or effectiveness of particular information processing stages or components. This specific-deficit hypothesis is based on the assumption that most cognitive tasks require a particular set of processing operations or components and that a useful investigative strategy is to try to determine which of them is (or are) primarily responsible for the observed age-related differences in performance.

As a somewhat dated example, a memory researcher could postulate that processes of encoding, storage, and retrieval are all required for successful performance. If one subscribes to this model of memory, then research could be designed to determine which of these components is most sensitive to age-related effects and is presumably responsible for much, if not all, of the age-related differences found in at least some memory tasks.

More recently there has been considerable interest in the view that both automatic and controlled attention processes are involved in many cognitive tasks, and there have been several attempts to derive measures of each type of process and then examine their relations to age. There are now quite a few reports that the age-related differences are greater in measures of controlled processing than in measures of automatic processing (e.g., Jennings & Jacoby, 1993).

The specific-deficit approach has had some success in the form of functional localization of age-related effects to particular aspects of processing within certain cognitive tasks. However, considerably more research is needed to investigate the construct validity of the measures of the targeted processes or components. In order to have confidence in the conclusions from this approach it is important to demonstrate that the target measures have at least moderate correlations with other measures of the same constructs and weak or nonexistent correlations with measures of other constructs. For example, if the critical construct is hypothesized to be encoding, it is important to demonstrate that there are similar patterns of age-related influences in measures of encoding derived from other cognitive tasks. Similarly, if aspects of controlled processing are presumed to be critical, then different measures of controlled processing should be expected to be related to one another and to exhibit the same pattern of age-related influences. Unfortunately, most of the existing research within this perspective has been restricted to measures derived from single tasks, and hence it is possible that many of the results are specific to those particular tasks.

A third major category of proximal explanation is based on the assumption that many of the age-related cognitive differences are related to an altered operation of one or more cognitive primitives. That is, age-related declines in the efficiency or effectiveness of elementary cognitive operations hypothesized to be involved in many different kinds of cognitive processes (and thus termed cognitive primitives) are presumed to be responsible for at least some of the age-related differences in fluid or process cognition. This type of explanation is similar to the specific-deficit interpretation, but it differs in that the key constructs are broader and are assumed to affect a wide variety of tasks. In fact, the constructs are sometimes referred to as processing resources, and they encompass concepts such as attention, working memory, and processing speed (see Salthouse, 1991, for a review).

Resource interpretations have been popular in part because age-related differences have been reported in a great many different cognitive variables (Salthouse, 1996). Interpretations based on task-specific strategies or components have therefore been argued to be inadequate because a very large number of specific deficits would have to be postulated to account for all of the age-related differences that have been reported. In contrast, if there were pronounced age-related effects on a small number of cognitive primitives that are involved in many cognitive tasks, then a more parsimonious interpretation of age-related cognitive differences might be possible. Although these arguments have been seductive, they sometimes run the risk of being circular because the age-related cognitive differences are attributed to a reduction in processing resources, but the reduction in processing resources is inferred on the basis of the same age-related differences in performance (Salthouse, 1991).

INVESTIGATIVE STRATEGIES

How can the different theoretical approaches to cognitive aging be investigated? A variety of analytical procedures are possible, but as with any type of research, it is important to select the methods that are most appropriate for the question of interest.

One investigative method involves some form of process analysis. This essentially consists of detailed analyses of the processes postulated to be involved in the performance of a particular task and then examination of the age relations on measures of each process. This approach is most consistent with the specific-deficit or strategic deficiency type of interpretation and is probably the dominant investigative method among psychologists trained in the cognitive psychology tradition.

An important advantage of process analysis is that it can be used to investigate the operation of hypothesized mechanisms; that is, once the relevant processes are specified, it should be possible to identify measures reflecting critical components of processing or particular types of strategies. However, a disadvantage of this approach is that the resulting information may be too task-specific, in the sense that the mechanisms may apply to only a limited set of cognitive tasks. It should be possible to overcome this limitation by relying on converging operations within a given task and following principles to investigate construct validity across tasks, but these procedures have not yet been widely employed.

Statistical control is another investigative strategy that has frequently been used in recent research on aging and cognition. For example, hierarchical regression and partial correlation procedures have been employed to investigate the mediational role of variables assumed to be involved in age-cognition relations. The rationale for this approach is that if measures of the hypothesized mediator can be obtained, then it should be possible to determine the extent to which the age-related effects in the target variable are reduced when the mediator is controlled. The greater the attenuation of the age-related variance in the target variable, the larger the inferred involvement of the mediator in those relations. To illustrate, if a researcher hypothesizes that particular early life experiences are critical for adult age-related differences in cognitive performance and if measures indexing those experiences can be obtained, the age-related declines in the measures of cognitive performance should be reduced after the effects of those experiences are statistically removed from the dependent variable of interest.

An advantage of the statistical control method is that it can be applied with many different types of theoretical interpretations as long as measures of the relevant constructs are available. However, it is not always possible to obtain sensitive measures of the relevant constructs from each individual, and thus there are practical limits to the usefulness of the method. Furthermore, because the method is based on correlational procedures, the standard caution about not inferring causation from correlation applies. Results from statistical control procedures are sometimes misinterpreted as identifying the cause of age-related differences, but instead they should merely be viewed as either consistent or inconsistent with particular causal assumptions.

A related strategy is based on structural equation models. The goal of this approach is to examine the interrelations among either manifest variables or latent constructs within path models. Structural models are particularly useful when investigating how several variables are simultaneously interrelated with one another. With certain combinations of variables, this analytical strategy can even be informative about the mechanisms involved in particular causal influences. Because of its close relations to the method of statistical control, the structural modeling approach shares many of the advantages and disadvantages of the statistical control approach.

There have recently been a number of attempts to link age-related cognitive differences to impairments in particular neuroanatomical processes or structures. These efforts have produced some fascinating results, but several important questions must be considered before their role in explaining cognitive aging phenomena can be fully evaluated. For example, one fundamental issue concerns the role of neuroanatomical localization in theories of cognitive aging. Specifically, what are the implications of a possible discovery that many age-related cognitive differences are associated with damage to a particular brain structure or region or to a certain neurotransmitter circuit? Is this type of localization equivalent to explanation? And how is it different from functional localization in which the source of the age-related differences is postulated to be localized within one or more components hypothesized to be responsible for a particular type of processing?

Neuropsychological research has the potential of being very useful in demonstrating similarities or differences among constructs that were not obvious on the basis of behavioral data. When successful, it is also informative about the physical substrate underlying the observed behavioral differences, and it presumably provides a more complete explanation than one expressed exclusively in terms of functional theoretical constructs such as processing stages or components. Nevertheless, the role of neuroanatomical localization in theories of cognitive aging is still unclear, as are the implications of this type of information for future efforts at prevention or intervention.

FUTURE DIRECTIONS

Which theoretical perspectives appear most promising in accounting for cognitive aging phenomena? And what analytical procedures can be used to investigate those perspectives? Even though some perspectives currently seem more plausible than others, it is probably still too early to reach strong conclusions about the types of theoretical explanations that will eventually be most successful. A useful approach at this time may be to attempt to identify broad constraints on theories before committing to very detailed interpretations. (See Salthouse, 1996, for an elaboration of this argument.)

It is clear that age-related effects are evident on many different process or fluid cognition variables. There is also evidence that the age-related effects on different variables are not independent (e.g., Salthouse, 1996; Verhaeghen & Salthouse, 1997). These findings must be taken into consideration in future theories, either with mechanisms that have broad applicability or with a wide range of more limited mechanisms.

Many questions still remain about the relative contributions of different types of determinants on individual variables. Analytical procedures are thus needed to evaluate the relative importance of shared and unique age-related influences, as well as theoretical perspectives that can account for both types of effects.

Finally, theorists should move toward a broader and more eclectic focus that acknowledges contributions of different types of developmental determinants. Even though the proportional contribution of each type will almost certainly vary as a function of a number of conditions, it is nevertheless important to seek a more integrated perspective, in which several factors demonstrated to be important contributors to the age differences are incorporated into the explanations. Theoretical models highly specific to a very limited set of tasks and isolated investigations of whether a particular factor has any contribution to the age-related differences in cognition are unlikely to lead to progress in explaining why there are age-related differences in so many different measures of cognitive functioning.

REFERENCES

Flynn, J. R. (1987). Massive IQ gains in 14 nations. What IQ tests really measure. *Psychological Bulletin, 101,* 171–191.

Hambrick, D. Z., Salthouse, T. A., & Meinz, E. J. (1997). *Predictors of crossword puzzle proficiency and moderators of age-cognition relations.* Manuscript in preparation.

Hultsch, D. F., Hertzog, C., Small, B. J., McDonald-Miszczak, L., & Dixon, R. A. (1992). Short-term longitudinal change in cognitive performance in later life. *Psychology and Aging, 7,* 571–584.

Jennings, J. M., & Jacoby, L. L. (1993). Automatic versus intentional uses of memory: Aging, attention, and control. *Psychology and Aging, 8,* 283–293.

Kliegl, R., Smith, J., & Baltes, P. B. (1989). Testing the limits and the study of adult age differences in cognitive plasticity of a mnemonic skill. *Developmental Psychology, 25,* 247–256.

Meinz, E. J., & Salthouse, T. A. (1998). The effects of age and experience on memory for visually presented music. *Journal of Gerontology: Psychological Sciences, 53B,* P60–69.

Morrow, D. G., Leirer, V. O., & Altieri, P. A. (1992). Aging, expertise, and narrative processing. *Psychology and Aging, 7,* 376–388.

Salthouse, T. A. (1991). *Theoretical perspectives on cognitive aging.* Hillsdale, NJ: Erlbaum.

Salthouse, T. A. (1993). Speed mediation of adult age differences in cognition. *Developmental Psychology, 29,* 722–738.

Salthouse, T. A. (1994). The nature of the influence of speed on adult age differences in cognition. *Developmental Psychology, 30,* 240–259.

Salthouse, T. A. (1996). Constraints on theories of cognitive aging. *Psychonomic Bulletin and Review, 3,* 287–299.

Salthouse, T. A., Babcock, R. L., Skovronek, E., Mitchell, D. R. D., & Palmon, R. (1990). Age and experience effects in spatial visualization. *Developmental Psychology, 26,* 128–136.

Salthouse, T. A., & Mitchell, D. R. D. (1990). Effects of age and naturally occurring experience on spatial visualization performance. *Developmental Psychology, 26,* 845–854.

Schaie, K. W. (1996). *Intellectual development in adulthood: The Seattle Longitudinal Study.* Cambridge, U.K.: Cambridge University Press.

Tuddenham, R. D. (1948). Soldier intelligence in World Wars I and II. *American Psychologist, 3,* 54–56.

Verhaeghen, P., & Salthouse, T. A. (1997). Meta-analyses of age-cognition relations in adulthood: Estimates of linear and non-linear age effects and structural models. *Psychological Bulletin, 122,* 231–249.

Zelinski, E. M., & Burnight, K. P. (1997). Sixteen-year longitudinal and time lag changes in memory and cognition in older adults. *Psychology and Aging, 12,* 503–513.

12

Social-Psychological Theories and Their Applications to Aging: From Individual to Collective

Margret M. Baltes
Laura L. Carstensen

S ocial gerontology includes and often blends both sociological and psychological theories, rendering the disciplinary source of particular theories and their underlying assumptions unclear (Achenbaum & Bengtson, 1994; Bengtson, Burgess, & Parrott, 1997; Birren & Bengtson, 1988; George, 1996; Hendricks, 1996; Marshall, 1995). Clarifying the particularities, however, is important to understand the uniqueness and commonalities in approach. With such an aim in mind, House (1977) and more recently George (1996) distinguish between sociological social psychology and psychological social psychology. They characterize one major difference between the two in terms of their focus on micro- versus macro-level influences on behavior. As House (1977) noted more than 20 years ago, sociologists tend to examine macro-level social structural variables and use survey methods to ascertain relationships among broad social structures and the location of individuals within those structures.

In contrast, psychologists are concerned primarily with the behavior of individuals as a function of micro-social variables (i.e., properties of other people present in a particular situation) and rely on experimental or quasi-experimental designs to assess their influences. To psychologists, the aim of social psychology is to understand social phenomena using person-centered paradigms in which structural and functional properties of the individual person is the core.

We want to argue in this chapter that the social phenomena to be studied should involve the collective as well. Such an emphasis on collective or social-interactive conceptualizations has been made explicit, for instance, in cognitive collaboration research (Dixon & Gould, 1996) and in research on shared understanding (Goodenow, 1996). For detailed examples and discussions, see the recently edited book *Interactive Minds* by P. B. Baltes and Staudinger (1996a).

We do not mean to suggest that the collective approach should replace the individual perspective in social psychology but rather that it might provide new theoretical insights and novel empirical research questions and thereby lead to progress in the field. Moreover, when speaking about the social, the collaborative, and the interactive-minds view, we do not assume that the collective is associated primarily with benefits. Indeed, the social is a major contributor to human evolution, including ontogeny (Cole, 1996). However, it is also true that some aspects of the social and collective have dysfunctional consequences. One telling example is work by Gottman (1997), who demonstrated that specific styles of parent-child interactions can have major long-term negative consequences. The same gain-loss dynamic thus applies as we move from individual selective optimization with compensation (SOC) to collective SOC.

A theoretical perspective that accepts the individual and collective as part of the phenomenon to be studied but rests firmly in the use of individual-paradigm theory might help to overcome serious criticisms leveled at the overemphasis on individualism and positivism in social psychology (e.g., Farr, 1996, but see also Brewster-Smith, 1997) or at its narrowness and artificiality (McGuire, 1973). It is an approach that is suited to study the social while maintaining a psychological orientation in theory and methodology.

In this chapter we concentrate on psychological social psychology. Instead of providing a comprehensive overview of theories in the field and their influence in gerontology, we provide a general comment on social psychological theories in gerontology and then focus on two specific ones, *the model of learned dependency* and *socioemotional selectivity theory*, to illustrate the person-oriented approach in social psychology. Both models have generated programs of research that have yielded new information about social aging. We then move to the metamodel of SOC and use it as an example of how an individual-level approach can be augmented by considering the social and collective. The result of this application of a collective social psychology perspective is the outline of what we label collective SOC.

CONTRIBUTIONS OF SOCIAL PSYCHOLOGY

Mainstream Social Psychology

Early work in mainstream social psychology focused on social ills and social problems, such as racism, mass hysteria, and the potentially pernicious effects of social influence. Despite much theoretical and methodological criticism, social psychology has promoted our understanding of social variables that influence a number of behavioral phenomena. Perhaps nowhere has this been more evident than in health psychology and behavioral medicine, where social variables have been linked to the etiology and course of diseases (e.g., Brezinka & Kittel, 1996; Holahan & Moos, 1991), attributions for the causes of illnesses and coping with diseases (e.g., Taylor, Repetti, & Seeman, 1997), and compliance with medical regimens (e.g., Bandura, Taylor, Williams, Mefford, & Barchas, 1985; Di Matteo, Reiter, & Gambone, 1994; Leventhal, Diefenbach, & Leventhal, 1992). In addition, it has been shown that social power, in the form of nonverbal cues and social behaviors of physicians, influence compliance with patients' medical recommendations (e.g., Di Matteo, Sherbourne, Hays, & Ordway, 1993). Social-psychological principles have also been applied in an effort to change behaviors and thus prevent disease (e.g., Hamburg, 1989; Hurrelmann, 1990).

Social psychology also has contributed to understanding the "burnout" syndrome (e.g., Cordes & Dougherty, 1993; Maslach, 1982), stressful life events (e.g., Hobfoll, 1991; Holahan & Moos, 1991; Lazarus & Folkman, 1984), and the influence of stressful work situations on individuals (e.g., Glass & Estes, 1997). A burgeoning area of research in social psychology addresses social support, again most frequently as it relates to health and mortality (e.g., Berkman, 1995; Holahan, Moos, Holahan, & Brennan, 1997). Similarly prominent is the work on social cognition, such as attributional styles (e.g., Taylor, 1989) and self-regulation (Higgins, 1997).

Other domains in which the force of social variables has been documented include law (e.g., the influence of social variables on jury deliberations [Boyll, 1991]), education (e.g., the relationship between teacher expectations and school performance [Saracho, 1991]), workplace effectiveness (e.g., Glass & Estes, 1997), and consumer behavior (e.g., Schroeder, 1996).

Thus, social psychology has helped to focus attention on the importance of environmental variables, person-situation interactions, social influences, social support, cognitive attributions, information processing, and decision making. Arguably, social psychology's major achievement has been the demonstration of the subtle but powerful influence of situational variables in both negative (Milgram, 1965; Zimbardo, 1970) and positive ways (Rosenhan, 1970) and the identification of the core mechanisms that mediate the respective effects.

Social Gerontology

The emphasis in mainstream social psychology on social ills and problems is shared by social gerontology. Indeed, for many years gerontological research was concerned nearly exclusively with problems of aging and old age and, in hindsight, clearly contributed to the problematization of old age from which gerontology is only now recovering.

Early work in social gerontology was very much concerned with negative aging stereotypes. The term *ageism* was coined to refer to age discrimination, which is considered conceptually analogous to racism and sexism (Butler, 1975). In this context the loss of and changes in roles and the apparent rolelessness of old people is highlighted. Parallels between social differentials of the young and old were compared to differences among ethnic groups, between men and women, and between rich and poor (i.e., Dannefer, 1987; Markides, Liang, & Jackson, 1990). At present, social-psychological research on the antecedents and consequences of caregiver burden is also of major interest (i.e., Zarit, Pearlin, & Schaie, 1993).

In addition to research focused on specific social problems, in more recent years there has been growing interest in social-psychological processes that influence life course change more normatively. Among these are control theories such as primary versus secondary control (Heckhausen & Schulz, 1995); coping theories, such as accommodative versus assimilative coping styles (Brandtstädter, 1984; Brandtstädter & Renner, 1990); theories about age-differences in attributional styles (Blanchard-Fields, 1996; Hess, 1994); and theories that blend psychological with sociological approaches to life course relationships, such as the convoy model (Kahn & Antonucci, 1980) and the support-efficacy model (Antonucci & Jackson, 1987).

Joint consideration of characteristics of the person and the environment has led to the conclusion that environments grow increasingly important as people age, serving to facilitate autonomy and well-being or, alternatively, placing barriers between individuals and their competent execution of daily life. Lawton's (1989) model of person-environment fit, which has been extremely influential in gerontology, suggests that a balance between environmental demands and personal skills is necessary for one to feel competent and be judged as competent by others.

In summary, social-psychological approaches to aging have been highly productive in past years, contributing a great deal to the understanding of numerous normal and pernicious age-related phenomena. In an effort to illuminate the traditional approach in social geropsychology and the types of empirical findings the approach can yield, we now detail two social-psychological theories of aging, the model of learned dependency and socioemotional selectivity theory. We offer these theories as prototypes of person-centered approaches to the study of social aging.

PERSON-ORIENTED APPROACHES IN SOCIAL PSYCHOLOGY AND SOCIAL GERONTOLOGY

The Model of Learned Dependency

In contrast to the frequently held belief that dependency is a necessary correlate of old age, the model of learned dependency postulates that dependency in old age reflects conditions of the proximal or micro-social system the elderly person inhabits. Based on a social learning theoretical framework, Baltes and colleagues define dependency as an overt behavior (viz., accepting or requesting help) that is learned (for extensive discussion, see M. M. Baltes, 1996). They employed "convergent operations"—experimental, sequential observational, and ecological intervention strategies—to uncover the social conditions and influences governing dependency in old age. They demonstrated reliably that many behavioral interactions between old people and their social environments are characterized by a stable pattern that reinforces dependency and ignores independence (for a summary, see M. M. Baltes, 1995, 1996). This dependence-support and independence-ignore script describes a social world in which dependent behaviors function to secure social contact. Learned dependency is thus a means or instrument to control specific aspects of the social environment (M. M. Baltes & Reisenzein, 1986; M. M. Baltes, Wahl & Reichert, 1991; Horgas, Wahl, & Baltes, 1996).

Dependency in old age is, therefore, not an automatic corollary of biological aging and decline, of illness and impairment, but in large part is a consequence of social conditions. On the basis of these findings we can draw several conclusions. For one, they challenge the widespread belief that dependency is a necessary corollary of disease and impairments. Second, they question the generalizability of the explanatory power of the model of learned helplessness proposed by Seligman (1975). The latter postulates that dependency is the outcome of noncontingencies rather than differential contingencies, and it characterizes dependency only as loss. Rather, our findings suggest that dependent and independent behaviors of old people experience systematically different social contingencies: reinforcement for dependency and neglect or even punishment for independence. Consequently, it is dependent behavior that serves to gain desired outcomes such as attention and social contact. In a socially deprived world such contingencies have special power, despite the fact that it is not the elderly individual herself who selects these contingencies but the social environment that determines them. Thus, dependency in old age represents both gain and loss.

Because the social environment prefers a specific interaction pattern over others, a social script—a *Drehbuch*—is created that judges dependency in old age as expected, adequate, and acceptable. This judgment, in turn, suggests that many old people are considered incompetent and prone to dependency (M. M. Baltes et al., 1991; Reichert, 1993; Wahl, 1991). The consequence is an environment that tends to overprotect older individuals while simultaneously neglecting existing strengths and reserves. Although reinforcement of dependence will have negative effects on the everyday competence of old people in the long run and thereby accelerate aging decline, it must be reiterated that, at the same time, the acceptance of the dependency-support script allows the elderly person to optimize or at least maintain social contact and to conserve energies for other pursuits that may have higher individual priority.

In sum, we have demonstrated that dependency can be the outcome of a learning process and that it is functional and adaptive when the aim is maintenance and optimization of social contact and avoidance of loneliness. Three qualifications should be emphasized: Dependency means passive control; reinforcement of dependency leads necessarily to nonuse of existing skills and thus to a possible acceleration of aging decline via disuse; and the compensation strategy, dependent behavior, is dictated by the environment; it is not self-selected. Dependent behaviors represent an adaptive reaction to forces or rules of the environment, and as such they secure social contact.

This function of dependency as a rather passive control instrument can be extended to many life domains. Bandura (1982) has coined the term *proxy control* to describe the delegation of control to others. Therewith the elderly person retains control over desired outcomes that cannot be reached any longer through his or her own power and avoids losing self-efficacy. An interesting question, therefore, is, Do elderly people actively select dependency to compensate for real or expected losses and thereby maintain and optimize goals that have higher priority? Such self-selected dependency (M. M. Baltes, 1996; M. M. Baltes & Carstensen, 1996; M. M. Baltes et al., 1991) would be an indicator of proxy control à la Bandura (1982).

Our argument for the existence of self-selected dependency is the following: Because of increasing losses with aging, the elderly person is confronted with the following alternatives: (a) to give up those goals and activities that are severely hindered by losses, (b) to compensate for losses by activating latent reserves, or (c) to become selectively dependent in the threatened domains or activities and thereby release energies and strengths for the pursuit of other activities that might be more important to the old person. In the face of increasing vulnerability the old person must thus be able to transform his or her agency into dependency where and when necessary in order to adapt and age successfully. This extension of the model of learned dependency leads to the hypothesis that the elderly person may use help from others in two situations: first, when aims or domains of high priority are endangered and reserves are lacking to rectify the situation; and second, when aims or domains of low priority but requiring much energy and time cannot be given up because they are necessary for survival. In sum, we have shown that dependency can have many etiologies and that it should not automatically be equated with incompetence. On the contrary, it might be necessary for successful aging.

Socioemotional Selectivity Theory

Socioemotional selectivity theory was initially formulated to explain the highly reliable, age-related decrease in social interaction evidenced in old age (Carstensen, 1991). At that time, two theoretical explanations for the age-related reduction in social contact, both grounded in sociology with a macro-level focus, were highly influential. Activity theory considered inactivity a societally induced problem rooted in social norms, such as mandatory retirement and an indigenous ageism in our sociopolitical structures (Havighurst & Albrecht, 1953). The alternative, disengagement theory, posited that the approaching death instigated a mutual, psychological withdrawal between the older person and society. Withdrawal is considered adaptive because it prepares the older individual for death and society for the loss of its member (Cumming & Henry, 1961).

According to socioemotional selectivity theory, however, the reduction in the breadth of older people's social networks and social participation reflects, in part, a motivated redistribution of resources by the elderly person, in which engagement in a selected range of social functions and a focus on close emotional relationships gives rise to meaningful emotional experience. In other words, reduction in social contact in old age reflects an active selection process in which emotionally close social relationships are maintained and more peripheral social relationships are discarded. Social networks that comprise a disproportionate number of emotionally close social partners, according to the theory, best serve older people's needs.

Socioemotional selectivity theory differs from previous ones in that it considers cognitive and motivational factors in changed social networks. According to the theory, people do not simply react to social contexts; they proactively manage their social worlds. As a life span theory it also adopts the assumption that adaptation is time- and space-bound and that one's life stage provides an important context to which one adapts.

The theory has been elaborated elswhere (see Carstensen, 1993; 1995; Carstensen, Gross, & Fung, 1997), so it will be only briefly summarized here. Socioemotional selectivity theory states that an essential set of social goals motivates social contact throughout life. According to the theory, specific social-psychological goals can be classified into two broad categories: (1) information (or knowledge) seeking and (2) emotional regulation (including emotional meaning). The theory claims that the activation of particular social goals is contingent on the social, psychological, and cognitive conditions the individual perceives. Perceived time plays a critical role in this context. When time is perceived as relatively unlimited, long-term goals are pursued, typically involving exploration of the world and the acquisition of novel information. In contrast, when time is perceived as limited, the constellation of goals is reorganized so that short-term goals, such as how one feels, assume greater importance than long-term goals, such as information acquisition.

Experimental research in which time perspective was manipulated supports the theoretical predictions. Under open-ended conditions older adults prefer familiar, emotionally meaningful social partners, whereas younger people do not; presumably that is because older people perceive time as limited. When time perspective is expanded, older people fail to show this bias. Under time-restricted conditions, younger people display the same bias that older people do. Similarly, closeness to the end of life, regardless of age, is associated with an increasing tendency to think about social partners in terms of their potential for emotional gratification, as opposed to their informational value (Carstensen & Fredrickson, in press; Fredrickson & Carstensen, 1990).

Theoretically, reductions in social network size reflect a diminished desire for contact with social partners who do not offer emotional rewards. If so, the number of emotionally close social partners should be highly stable across age, whereas the number of more peripheral social partners should be relatively low in old age. Both longitudinal (Carstensen, 1992) and cross-sectional (Lang & Carstensen, 1994; Lang, Staudinger, & Carstensen, 1998) findings support this hypothesis. In general, although there are differences in overall network size between younger and older subjects, these differences are not distributed evenly across social partners who are more or less emotionally close. Rather, reductions in more peripheral relationships account for most of the observed age differences. Perhaps even more important, there is also evidence for the adaptiveness of the reduction in network size. Older people who reduce contact with peripheral others while maintaining contact with emotionally meaningful social partners appear to profit in terms of psychological well-being (Lang & Carstensen, 1994; Lang et al., 1998).

In summary, old age represents the penultimate of social endings. Other conditions also influence construal of future time; and when they do, younger people evince behaviors and choices similar to those shown by older people. Thus, socioemotional selectivity theory holds relevance for understanding social preferences and social behavior across the life span. By molding social environments, constructing them in a way that maximizes the potential for positive affect and minimizes the potential for negative affect, older people increase the odds that they will regulate the emotional climate, which, at the end of life, may represent the supreme social goal.

TOWARD A COLLECTIVE SOCIAL PSYCHOLOGY

The models and findings presented thus far have provided examples of the ways in which social factors influence the expression of behaviors. The two models we described reflect traditional social-psychological approaches in that they adopt a person-centered approach to analyze the social antecedents and consequences of certain behaviors (i.e., dependency or social preferences). Both are theoretical conceptions that have generated research programs, which in turn have advanced new knowledge about aging processes (Bengtson et al., 1997).

We now turn to a perspective that treats individuals as elements of a social behavioral system, the social-interactive perspective. Group problem solving provides one example. Others include the behavioral dynamics of group conflicts and issues related to group solidarity and competition (e.g., Bengtson, 1996; Bengtson, Schaie, & Burton, 1996). Yet another collectivist view stems from contextualism (Lerner, 1997), suggesting that social systems and individuals who inhabit those systems exert reciprocal influences on each other.

A social-interactive perspective goes beyond the study of the effects of specific situations on specific individuals to consider the intertwining behavioral stream of two or more individuals. Such transactions can occur in proximal face-to-face interactions and can refer to internal (having an imaginary conversation with a significant other) as well as external (exchanging information directly) interactions. In any case, the focus always is on the transaction and collaboration between individuals. In the literature at large the social-interactive perspective has been studied under quite diverse labels, such as situated cognition, interactive minds, cooperation and collaboration, shared understanding, social construction, collaborative rules, or simply social context (for an overview, see P. B. Baltes & Staudinger, 1996a; Smith, in press; Staudinger 1996; Staudinger & Baltes, 1996).

Whereas the study of effects of social forces on individuals has a long history in psychology, the study of collectively based social actions and transactions has a more recent origin. Particularly in the study of aging, such a perspective holds several promises. Aside from its intrinsic theoretical interest, a social-interactive perspective adds to the understanding of how individuals age together as units. Such a collectivist view focuses the lens on groups of people such as married or partnership couples (e.g., Carstensen, Gottman, & Levenson, 1995), friendships (e.g., Blieszner, 1995), or kinship networks that coexist and co-function over time (Antonucci & Jackson, 1987). They can also involve long-term relationships between caregivers and care receivers, who exhibit interactional scripts such as the dependency-support or independence-ignore script (M. M. Baltes, 1996).

In the following, we apply this collective perspective, that is, an interactive-minds and collaborative behavior view—to a psychological theory of successful aging, the metamodel of selective optimization with compensation (Baltes & Baltes, 1990; Baltes & Carstensen, 1996; see also Baltes & Staudinger, 1996b).

FROM INDIVIDUAL TO COLLECTIVE SELECTIVE OPTIMIZATION WITH COMPENSATION

In the context of aging, the metamodel of selective optimization with compensation (SOC) has been developed to describe and explain the successful adaptation of individuals to aging losses by proposing the interplay among three processes: selection, compensation, and optimization (M. M. Baltes & Carstensen, 1995; P. B. Baltes, 1997; P. B. Baltes & Baltes, 1990; Marsiske, Lang, Baltes, & Baltes, 1995). The basic assumption of the SOC model is that the three processes form a system of behavioral action or outcome-oriented functioning. In their orchestration, they generate and regulate development and aging. Whereas selection processes address the choice of goals, life domains, and life tasks, both compensation and optimization are concerned with the means to maintain or enhance chosen goals.

Through selection, a given individual or group of individuals chooses from an array of possibilities or opportunities. Selection refers to a restriction of one's involvement to fewer domains of functioning as a consequence of new demands and tasks (elective selection) or as a consequence of or in anticipation of losses in personal and environmental resources (loss-based selection). Selection may mean avoidance of one domain altogether, or it can mean a restriction in tasks and goals within one domain or a number of domains. Although selection connotes a reduction in the number of high-efficacy domains, tasks, or goals, it does not only suggest continuation of previous goals, domains, or tasks albeit in smaller numbers. It can also involve new or transformed domains and goals of life. Selection can be proactive or reactive. It may be directed at environmental changes (i.e., relocation), active behavior changes (reducing the number of social partners), or passive adjustment (not climbing the stairs).

Compensation, the second component factor facilitating adaptation to loss in resources, becomes operative when specific behavioral capacities or skills are lost or reduced below the level required for adequate functioning. Compensation involves a response to a loss in goal-relevant means. The question here is, are there other means to reach the same goal, accomplish the same outcome in a specific domain? The need for compensation in old age stems mostly from person-or environment-associated changes in means-ends resources. Compensatory efforts can be automatic or planned and are not necessarily dependent on existing means. Compensation might require the acquisition of new skills, of new means not yet in the repertoire. Compensation thus differs from selection in that the target, the domain, the task, or the goal is maintained but other means are sought to compensate for a behavioral deficiency in order to maintain or optimize prior functioning.

Optimization, the third component factor, involves the probability, level, and scope of desirable outcomes or goal attainment (viz., the minimization of losses and maximization of gains). Therefore, the central themes of optimization are the generation and refinement of goal-relevant means (resources) associated with the generation and production of goal attainment (desired outcomes). Optimization and growth may relate to the perfection of existing goals and expectations (e.g., in the domain of generativity) but may also reflect new goals and expectations in line with developmental tasks of the third phase of life (such as acceptance of one's own mortality).

So far the model of SOC has been used in a person-centered framework. For instance, one example often used to illustrate the strategy of SOC was taken from an interview with the aged pianist Arthur Rubinstein, who indicated that he preserved high-level concert performance by playing fewer pieces (selection), practicing those more often (optimization), and using variations and contrasts in speed to generate the impression of faster play (compensation). This was one individual who orchestrated SOC for personal advancement.

Although we have not yet conducted research within a collective frame of reference, we can imagine how individual SOC manifestations can be expanded to include collective processes of selection, optimization, and compensation. Individuals age in social contexts. Needless to say, individuals striving for SOC at a personal level inevitably consider group processes that facilitate or hamper these strivings. We want to go a step further and look at ways in which couples, families, and other groups age together successfully. Some members of the social network, such as spouses, friends, and children, join in defining goals (selection), in providing improved means and opportunities (optimization), and in offering alternative means where one's own fail (compensation). As mentioned above, when defining the nature of interactive minds and collaborative social units, these processes can operate externally or internally, they can be active or passive, conscious or subconscious (see also P. B. Baltes & Staudinger, 1996b).

Let us look at two research examples that were not designed to test collective SOC but can serve to elaborate the concept of collective SOC. Roger Dixon and his collaborators (Dixon & Gould, 1996) have been working in recent years on a process refered to as collaborative memory. They have shown that story recall by a group, married couples, or even pairs of strangers leads to superior memory performance, compared to individuals' memory performance. Indeed, elderly couples show a much larger boost in memory performance over individual performance than do younger couples or older strangers. In the terminology of SOC, elderly spouses compensate for one another. As Dixon shows, they give each other memory cues by relating personal references to stories and discuss ways to improve their performance when reaching an impasse. They provide remarkable support for the adage "two heads are better than one."

A second empirical example is Birren's work on guided autobiography (Birren & Birren, 1996; Birren & Deutschman, 1991). Birren makes it very explicit that guided autobiography in contrast to individual autobiography combines individual and group experiences. The group interaction and leadership, because of its mutual encouragement and questioning, acts as a selective mechanism by "sensitizing people to the overlooked and unappreciated past" (Birren & Deutschman, 1991, p. 1). The group provides assistance in working through unpleasant memories (compensation). It also can help its members to optimize the effects of life review because group interactions often generate new perspectives on issues of their lives, thus enhancing meaning of life (optimization).

Collective SOC, therefore, results as a function of interactions between people. These interactions have, of course, a gain-loss dynamic (P. B. Baltes, 1997). For collective SOC to be positive in outcome there has to be a mutually facilitative, coordinated group structure to ensure collective successful aging. Similar to Bandura's (1997) notion of collective self-efficacy (see also Sampson, Raudenbush, & Earls, 1997), collective SOC has to be based on a shared understanding among members of the group regarding their respective goal structures and their respective strengths and weaknesses that defines the means or resources to reach goals and the ways to enrich opportunities or protect against constraints. If such conditions prevail, when and what to select and when and how to compensate and optimize can attain a higher level of functioning for all members. In such a collective endeavor, selective, compensatory, and optimizing strategies are not only tailored to a single individual's gains and losses but to a group's collective gains and losses. From an individual's perspective, collective SOC may differ from his or her personal SOC and may involve costs in that more personal resources have to be yielded for collective SOC.

Take a 70-year-old couple as a sample case. To collectively age successfully, they will have to select short- and long-term goals, take stock of the resources available to reach those goals, and consider potential obstacles and barriers (i.e., the losses they may encounter). The goals they decide on might be common goals (e.g., moving into a golf community). In contrast, they may also select goals that are one spouse's personal goals (e.g., accept a part-time job in a highly desirable area that has summer all year round). Taking on the new job might, however, be possible only if the other partner compensates by doing the driving to and from work. Both might be collectively optimizing their living environment and their leisure activities. As long as they collectively decide on the goals and collectively work toward reaching them, they both age successfully. If, however, personal and collective goals are too divergent, one partner might feel alienated and at increased risk for psychological and physical problems or even divorce. Thus, for collective SOC to work, there has to be a substantial overlap between collective goals and personal goals, collective SOC and personal SOC.

At a more macrolevel, collective SOC might entail the improvement of social systems and structures. Coordinated efforts to improve sanitation and hygiene and to employ major public health campaigns to ensure vaccination and healthier lifestyles are credited as the prominent reasons that individual life expectancy has almost doubled during this century. That is, through collective selection (investment of time and energy into physical exercise), compensation (reliance on medical assistance when sick), and optimization (use of improved knowledge and technologies, such as preventive vaccinations), more people are living longer than ever before in human history. These are social-interactional processes that could never be captured with traditional individual social-psychological paradigms. However, they have dramatically changed human aging and can be modeled with the collective SOC paradigm.

Thus, collective SOC can occur on a micro-level, as with a couple; on a meso-level, as with a family; or on a macro-level, as in the case of social institutions. At each level, collective SOC is conceptualized as an interactive process between people. How well the group fares in this process depends on the interactive dynamics of its members. To further the path of a social entity—the couple, the family, the community—toward successful aging, selective, compensatory, and optimizing actions have to be taken collectively.

Adopting such a collective social-psychological approach, which captures the dynamics of social phenomena, might enable Birren and Schroots's (1996) bold statement to come true: "It is conceivable that the introductory psychology books of the future will be organized around principles (or theories or models) of development and aging into which will be fitted the elements of perception, learning, memory, and personality" (p. 16; parentheses added by authors). Applied to the content of this chapter, the opening framework of such a book may include examples of successful development: how individuals select, optimize, and compensate in order to live good lives, individually and collectively. Subsequently, the textbook may turn to the specific components and mechanisms and conditions that allow this goal of a good life to come about.

REFERENCES

Achenbaum, W., & Bengston, V. L. (1994). Re-engaging the disengagement theory of aging: On the history and assessment of theory development in gerontology. *Gerontologist, 34,* 756–764.

Antonucci, T. C., & Jackson, J. S. (1987). Social support, interpersonal efficacy, and health: A life course perspective. In L. L. Carstensen & B. A. Edelstein (Eds.), *Handbook of clinical gerontology* (pp. 291–311). New York: Pergamon Press.

Baltes, M. M. (1995). Dependency in old age: Gains and losses. *Current Directions in Psychological Science, 4,* 14–19.

Baltes, M. M. (1996). *The many faces of dependency in old age.* New York: Cambridge University Press.

Baltes, M. M., & Carstensen, L. L. (1996). The process of successful ageing. *Ageing and Society, 16,* 397–422.

Baltes, M. M., & Reisenzein, R. (1986). The social world in long-term care institutions: Psychosocial control toward dependency? In M. M. Baltes & P. B. Baltes (Eds.), *The psychology of control and aging* (pp. 315–343). Hillsdale, NJ: Erlbaum.

Baltes, M. M., Wahl, H.-W., & Reichert, M. (1991). Successful aging in institutions? *Annual Review of Gerontology and Geriatrics, 11,* 311–337.

Baltes, P. B. (1997). On the incomplete architecture of human ontogeny: Selection, optimization, and compensation as foundation of developmental theory. *American Psychologist, 52,* 366–380.

Baltes, P. B., & Baltes, M. M. (Eds.) (1990). *Successful aging: Perspectives from the behavioral sciences.* New York: Cambridge University Press.

Baltes, P. B., & Staudinger, U. M.(Eds.). (1996a). *Interactive minds: Life-span perspectives on the social foundation of cognition.* New York: Cambridge University Press.

Baltes, P. B., & Staudinger, U. M. (1996b). Interactive minds in a life-span perspective: Prologue. In P. B. Baltes & U. M. Staudinger (Eds.), *Interactive minds: Life-span perspectives on the social foundation of cognition* (pp. 1–32). New York: Cambridge University Press.

Bandura, A. (1982). Self-efficacy mechanism in human agency. *American Psychologist, 37,* 122–147.

Bandura, A. (1997). *Self-efficacy: The exercise of control.* New York: Freeman.

Bandura, A., Taylor, C. B., Williams, S. L., Mefford, I. N., & Barchas, J. D. (1985). Catecholamine secretion as a function of perceived coping self-efficacy. *Journal of Consulting and Clinical Psychology, 53,* 406–414.

Bengtson, V. L. (1996). Continuities and discontinuities in intergenerational relationships over time. In V. L. Bengtson (Ed.), *Adulthood and aging* (pp. 271–303). New York: Springer Publishing Co.

Bengtson, V. L., Burgess, E. O., & Parrott, T. M. (1997). Theory, explanation, and a third generation of theoretical development in social gerontology. *Journals of Gerontology, 52,* 72–89.

Bengtson, V. L., Schaie, K. W., & Burton, L. (Eds.). (1996). *Intergenerational issues in aging.* New York: Plenum Press.

Berkman, L. F. (1995). The role of social relations in health promotion. *Psychosomatic Medicine, 57,* 245–254.

Birren, J. E., & Bengtson, V. L. (Eds.) (1988). *Emergent theories of aging.* New York: Springer Publishing Co.

Birren, J. E., & Birren, B. (1996). Autobiography: Exploring the self and encouraging development. In J. E. Birren, G. M. Kenyon, J.-E. Ruth, J. J. F. Schroots, & T. Svensson (Eds.), *Aging and biography* (pp. 283–299). New York: Springer Publishing Co.

Birren, J. E., & Deutschman, D. E. (1991). *Guiding autobiography groups for older adults.* Baltimore: Johns Hopkins University Press.

Birren, J. E., & Schroots, J. J. F. (1996). History, concepts and theory in the psychology of aging. In J. E. Birren & K. W. Schaie (Eds.), *Handbook of the psychology of aging* (4th ed., pp. 3–24). New York: Academic Press.

Blanchard-Fields, F. (1996). Social cognitive development in adulthood and aging. In F. Blanchard-Fields & T. M. Hess (Eds.), *Perspectives on cognitive change in adulthood and aging* (pp. 454–487). New York: McGraw-Hill.

Blieszner, R. (1995). Friendship processes and well-being in the later years of life: Implications for interventions. *Journal of Geriatric Psychiatry 28,* 165–182.

Boyll, J. R. (1991). Psychological, cognitive, personality and interpersonal factors in jury verdicts. *Law and Psychological Review, 15,* 163–184.

Brandtstädter, J. (1984). Personal and social control over development: Some implications of an action perspective in life-span developmental psychology. In P. B. Baltes & O. G. Brim (Eds.), *Life-span development and behavior* (Vol. 6, pp. 1–32). New York: Academic Press.

Brandtstädter, J., & Renner, G. (1990). Tenacious goal pursuit and flexible goal adjustment: Explication and age-related analysis of assimilative and accommodative strategies of coping. *Psychology and Aging, 5,* 58–67.

Brewster-Smith, M. (1997). Challenging Allport and Jones: A European perspective on the history of social psychology. *American Journal of Psychology.*

Brezinka, V., & Kittel, F. (1996). Psychosocial factors of coronary heart disease in women: A review. *Social Science and Medicine, 42,* 1351–1365.

Butler, R. N. (1975). *Why survive? Being old in America.* New York: Harper & Row.

Carstensen, L. L. (1991). Selectivity theory: Social activity in life-span context. *Annual Review of Gerontology and Geriatrics, 11,* 195–217.

Carstensen, L. L. (1992). Social and emotional patterns in adulthood: Support for socioemotional selectivity theory. *Psychology and Aging, 7,* 331–338.

Carstensen, L. L. (1993). Motivation for social contact across the life span: A theory of socioemotional selectivity. In J. E. Jacobs (Ed.), *Nebraska Symposium on Motivation 1992: Vol. 40. Developmental perspectives on motivation* (pp. 209–254). Lincoln: Nebraska University Press.

Carstensen, L. L. (1995). Evidence for a life-span theory of socioemotional selectivity. *Current Directions in Psychological Science, 4,* 151–156.

Carstensen, L. L., & Fredrickson, B. L. (in press). Socioemotional selectivity in health older people and younger people living with the human immunodeficiency virus (HIV): The centrality of emotions when the future is constrained. *Health Psychology.*

Carstensen, L. L., Gottman, J. M., & Levenson, R. W. (1995). Emotional behavior in long-term marriage. *Psychology and Aging, 10,* 140–149.

Carstensen, L. L., Gross, J., & Fung, H. (1997). The social context of emotion. *Annual Review of Gerontology and Geriatrics, 17,* 325–352.

Cole, M. (1996). Interacting minds in a life-span perspective: A cultural-historical approach to culture and cognitive development. In P. B. Baltes & U. M. Staudinger (Eds.), *Interactive minds: Life-span perspectives on the social foundation of cognition* (pp. 59–87). New York: Cambridge University Press.

Cordes, C. L., & Dougherty, T. W. (1993). A review and an integration of research on job burnout. *Academy of Management Review, 18,* 621–656.

Cumming, E., & Henry, W. E. (1961). *Growing old: The process of disengagement.* New York: Basic Books.

Dannefer, D. (1987). Aging as intracohort differentiation: Accentuation, the Matthew effect and the life course. *Sociological Forum, 2,* 211–236.

DiMatteo, M. R., Reiter, R. C., & Gambone, J. C. (1994). Enhancing medication adherence through communication and informed collaborative choice. *Health Communication* [Special issue], 6, 253–265.

DiMatteo, M. R., Sherbourne, C. D., Hays, R. D., & Ordway, L. (1993). Physicians characteristics influence patients adherence to medical treatment: Results from the Medical Outcomes Study. *Health Psychology, 12,* 93–102.

Dixon, R. A., & Gould, O. N. (1996). Adults telling and retelling stories collaboratively. In P. B. Baltes & U. M. Staudinger (Eds.), *Interactive minds: Life-span perspective on the social foundation of cognition* (pp. 221–241). New York: Cambridge University Press.

Farr, R. M. (1996). *The roots of modern social psychology 1872–1954.* Oxford, U.D.: Blackwell.

Fredrickson, B. L., & Carstensen, L. L. (1990). Choosing social partners: How old age and anticipated endings make us more selective. *Psychology and Aging, 5,* 335–347.

George, L. K. (1996). Missing links: The case for social psychology of the life course: Section 3. Cross-fertilization of the life course and other theoretical paradigms. *Gerontologist, 36,* 248–256.

Glass, J. L., & Estes, S. B. (1997). The family responsive workplace. *Annual Review of Sociology, 23,* 289–313.

Goodenow, J. (1996). Collaborative rules: How are people supposed to work with one another? In P. B. Baltes & U. M. Staudinger (Eds.), *Interactive minds: Life-span perspective on the social foundation of cognition* (pp. 163–197). New York: Cambridge University Press.

Gottman, J. M. (1997). *The heart of parenting.* New York: Simon & Schuster.

Hamburg, D. (1989). Preparing for life: The critical transition of adolescence: Preventive interventions in adolescence. *Crisis* [Special issue] *10,* 4–15.

Havighurst, R. J., & Albrecht, R. (1953). *Older people.* New York: Longmans

Heckhausen, J., & Schulz, R. (1995). A life-span theory of control. *Psychological Review, 102,* 284–304.

Hendricks, J. (1996). Where are the new frontiers in aging theory? The search for new solutions. *Gerontologist, 36,* 141–145.

Hess, T. M. (1994). Social cognition in adulthood: Aging related changes in knowledge and processing mechanisms. *Developmental Review, 14,* 373–412.

Higgins, E. T. (1997). Beyond pleasure and pain. *American Psychologist, 52,* 1280–1300.

Hobfoll, St. E. (1991). Traumatic stress: A theory based on rapid loss of resources. *Anxiety Research, 4,* 187–197.

Holahan, C. J., & Moos, R. H. (1991). Life-stressors, personal and social resources, and depression: A 4–year structural model. *Journal of Abnormal Psychology, 100,* 31–38.

Holahan, C. J., Moos, R. H., Holahan, C. K., & Brennan, P. L. (1997). Social context, coping strategies, and depressive symptoms: An expanded model with cardiac patients. *Journal of Personality and Social Psychology, 72,* 918–928.

Horgas, A. L., Wahl, H. W., & Baltes, M. M. (1996). Dependency in late life. In L. L. Carstensen, B. A. Edelstein, & L. Dornbrand (Eds.), *The practical handbook of clinical gerontology* (pp. 54–75). Newbury, CA: Sage.

House, J. S. (1977). The three faces of social psychology. *Sociometry, 40,* 161–177.

Hurrelmann, K. (1990). Health promotion for adolescents: Preventive and corrective strategies against problem behavior. *Journal of Adolescence, 13,* 231–250.

Kahn, R. L., & Antonucci, T. C. (1980). Convoys over the life course: Attachment, roles, and social support. In P. B. Baltes & J. O. G. Brim (Eds.), *Life-span development and behavior* (Vol. 3, pp. 253–286). New York: Academic Press.

Lang, F. R., & Carstensen, L. L. (1994). Close emotional relationships in late life: Further support for proactive aging in the social domain. *Psychology and Aging, 9,* 315–324.

Lang, F. R., Staudinger, U. M., & Carstensen, L. L. (1998). Socioemotional selectivity in late life: How personality does (and does not) make a difference. *Journals of Gerontology: Psychological Science, 53B,* P21–30.

Lawton, M. P. (1989). Environmental proactivity and affect in older people. In S. Spacapan & S. Oskamp (Eds.), *Social psychology of aging* (pp. 135–164). Newsbury Park, CA: Sage.

Lazarus, R. S., & Folkman, S. (1984). *Stress, appraisal and coping.* New York: Springer Publishing Co.

Lerner, R. M. (1997). Theories of human development: Contemporary perspectives. In R. M. Lerner (Ed.), *Handbook of child psychology,* 5th ed.: Vol. 1. *Theoretical models of human development* (pp. 1–24). New York: Wiley.

Leventhal, H., Diefenbach, M., & Leventhal, E. A. (1992). Illness cognition· Using common sense to understand treatment adherence and affect cognitions interactions. *Cognitive Therapy and Research,* [Special issue], *16,* 143–163.

Markides, K., Liang, J., & Jackson, J. S. (1990). Race, ethnicity, and aging: Conceptual and methodological issues. In R. H. Binstock & L. K. George (Eds.), *Handbook of aging and the social sciences* (3rd ed., pp. 112–129). San Diego, CA: Academic Press.

Marshall, V. W. (1995). The next half-century of aging research—and thoughts for the past. *Journal of Gerontology: Social Sciences, 50B,* S131–133.

Marsiske, M., Lang, F. R., Baltes, P. B., & Baltes, M. M. (1995). Selective optimization with compensation: Life-span perspectives. In R. A. Dixon & L. Bäckman (Eds.), *Psychological compensation: Managing losses and promoting gains* (pp. 35–79). Hillsdale, NJ: Erlbaum.

Maslach, C. (1982). *Burnout: The cost of caring.* Englewood Cliffs, NJ: Prentice-Hall.

McGuire, W. (1973). The yin and yang of progress in social psychology. *Journal of Personality and Social Psychology, 26,* 446–456.

Milgram, S. (1965). Some conditions of obedience and disobedience to authority. *Human Relations, 18,* 57–76.

Reichert, M. (1993). *Hilfeverhalten gegenüber alten Menschen: Eine experimentelle Überprüfung der Rolle von Erwartungen* [Helping older people: An experimental analysis of the role of expectations]. Essen, Germany: Blaue Eule.

Rosenhan, D. L. (1970). The natural socialization of altruistic autonomy. In J. Macauly & L. Berkowitz (Eds.), *Altruism and helping behavior* (pp. 251–268). New York: Academic Press.

Sampson, R. J., Raudenbush, S. W., & Earls, F. (1997). Neighborhoods and violent crime: A multilevel study of collective efficacy. *Science, 277,* 918–924.

Saracho, O. N. (1991). Teacher expectations of students performance: A review of the research. *Early Child Development and Care, 76,* 27–41.

Schroeder, J. E. (1996). An analysis of the consumer susceptibility to interpersonal influence scale. *Journal of Social Behavior and Personality, 11,* 585–599.

Seligman, M. E. P. (1975). *Helplessness: On depression, development, and death.* San Francisco: Freeman.

Smith, J. (in press). Perspectives on planning a life. In S. Friedman & M. K. Scholnick (Eds.), *Why, how and when do we plan? The developmental psychology of planning.* Hillsdale, NJ: Erlbaum.

Staudinger, U. M. (1996). Wisdom and the social-interactive foundation of the mind. In P. B. Baltes & U. M. Staudinger (Eds.), *Interactive minds: Life-span perspectives on the social foundation of cognition* (pp. 276–315). New York: Cambridge University Press.

Staudinger, U. M. & Baltes, P. B.(1996). Interactive minds: A facilitative setting for wisdom. *Journal of Personality and Social Psychology, 71,* 746–762.

Taylor, S. E. (1989). *Positive illusions.* New York: Basic Books.

Taylor, S. E., Repetti, R. L., & Seeman, T. (1997). Health psychology: What is an unhealthy environment and how does it get under the skin? *Annual Review of Psychology, 48,* 411–447.

Wahl, H.-W. (1991). Dependence in the elderly from an interactional point of view: Verbal and observational data. *Psychology and Aging, 6,* 238–246.

Zarit, S. H., Pearlin, L. I., & Schaie, K. W. (Eds.). (1993). *Caregiving systems: Informal and formal helpers.* Hillsdale, NJ: Erlbaum.

Zimbardo, P. G. (1970). The human choice: Individuation, reason, and order versus deindividuation, impulse, and chaos. In W. J. Arnold & D. Levine (Eds.), *Nebraska Symposium on Motivation, 1969* (Vol. 17, pp. 237–307). Lincoln: University of Nebraska Press.

13

The Self-Concept in Life Span and Aging Research

A. Regula Herzog
Hazel R. Markus

SIGNIFICANCE

How do people maintain active involvement and a sense of well-being across the life span? Why is it that despite the loss and decline apparently associated with aging, many older people experience themselves as feeling exceptionally good, often better than when they were younger? The life span literature is replete with concepts that provide some window on the dynamics of successful aging. Many studies emphasize that the key is to be found in fine-tuned, well-calibrated reactions to life events. Flexible goal adjustment (e.g., Brandtstädter & Renner, 1990), personalized strategies of control and management (Lachman, 1986; Heckhausen & Schultz, 1995), and the processes of selection, compensation, and optimization (Baltes & Baltes, 1990; Brim, 1992; Carstensen, 1993) all serve this purpose. Other research highlights planning and anticipation—setting goals, constructing possible futures, and developing new roles—as critical features of the adaptive aging process (Atchley, 1989; Breytspraak, 1984; Ryff, 1991).

The authors gratefully acknowledge the many intellectual contributions by their colleagues Melissa M. Franks and Diane Holmberg during their ongoing collaboration; the critical reading of this chapter by Robert Atchley, Melissa Franks, and Diane Holmberg; and the funding provided to their work by the National Institute on Aging (R01 AG08279).

In this chapter, building on the work of Brandtstädter and Greve (1994); Whitbourne (1986); Bengtson, Reedy, and Gordon (1985); and Markus and Herzog (1991), we suggest that the theoretical perspective of the self-system can bring a new organization and a more comprehensive understanding to these adaptive and proactive processes. The domains and dimensions that define the self provide the basis of selectivity, determining where time and energy will be invested, where efficacy and control (or the lack of it) will be experienced, what will be planned for, what will be compensated for, what will be discounted or ignored, and ultimately how individual lives accrue meaning and structure.

The self can be defined as a multifaceted, dynamic system of interpretive structures that regulates and mediates behavior. The multilevel self-system, comprising cognitive, affective, and somatic representations and routines—in the most general sense, an individual's characteristic ways of being a person in the world—is believed to be broadly consequential for individual experiences, activities, and well-being. Many current theoretical perspectives on the self can be described as a blend between cognitive approaches, which view the self-concept as an object of knowledge that can be analyzed for its content and functioning, and social constructionist approaches, which view the self as the subject of experience and thus as continually shaped by and also shaping the specific worlds within which it is engaged. Historically, despite many theoretical statements to the contrary, the tendency has been to reify the self and to regard it as a thing, as exemplified in thousands of studies on the self-concept, the self, or self-esteem. Currently, there is a move away from this perspective toward the view of the self as a set of processes or a system that is simultaneously a social construction and a social constructor or experience, actively selecting among various imperatives; claiming, elaborating, and personalizing some of them while ignoring, contesting, or rearranging others.

With a focus on the self-system we gain some insight into what is typically transparent—the coordinates of personal significance or one's individualized designs for meaning making. The self-system is more than just a reflection of one's previous actions or a representation of experience; it is also selective and creative and is continually involved in fashioning everyday experience. As Schaffer (1992) notes, experience is made, "it is not encountered, discovered or observed, except upon secondary reflection" (p. 23), and it is the self-system that is responsible for this construction. The experience of growing old; of becoming skilled or educated; of divorce, job change, or retirement; of children leaving home; of children returning home; of widowhood; of becoming bald, heavy, or unhealthy depends in large part on what self-relevant frameworks are invoked to lend structure to these events and to make them meaningful. Because of the self system's link to experienced behaviors and well-being, we suggest it as a useful focus for research on aging and adaptation.

Although self-systems incorporate individualized and idiosyncratic meanings, people construct and make sense of the world in terms of the categories and dimensions that are provided and valued by the social worlds in which they live. The self, then, can be considered a locus of sociocultural influence. It receives and integrates the diverse messages communicated by one's various social contexts about what matters in the world and how to be an appropriate or valued member within a given context (Oyserman & Markus, 1993), including how to mature and age and what to expect of the unfolding life span. These messages are then incorporated into a set of interpretive frameworks that give shape to what people are motivated to do, how they feel, and what they notice and think about, as well as their overt actions and ultimately how they live their lives.

Influenced by the social and cultural environment and in turn choosing and even creating its own current, future, and past environment, the self, we suggest, is intimately involved in the negotiation of the life span. Following Whitbourne (1986, 1987), we would argue that the self reveals the blueprint of a life anticipated and the adjustments made to a life lived. A focus on the self-system adds to the variable-centered approach that characterizes the psychology of aging a person-centered approach that has the potential to provide an integrative perspective on how individuals manage continuity and change in the many aspects of their lives as they mature and age.

In this chapter we will present the nature of the self-system, including its functions, content, and time dimensions. We will then discuss the social factors affecting the self system, focusing briefly on culture, gender, socioeconomic status, knowledge about the life span, and roles and resources. Finally, we will describe the links between the self-system and behavior and well-being. We will conclude by returning to the topic of adaptation to aging, briefly discussing how the theoretical perspective of the self can inform theorizing on this topic.

NATURE OF THE SELF

—Outgoing, a leader, I don't like to follow anyone. I love to lead. I love all sports and I love my children. My goal is to open up a home for children. Years ago I used to be a chaperone for the boxing team. 68–year-old man
—Independent, people-oriented, one who needs to keep busy. I rely a great deal on my faith in God. 52–year-old woman
—I'm a great-grandmother. Right now I'm in a situation that is not too happy. My son is ill with AIDS. I'm diabetic, phlebitis in my legs and I need medical

care for these conditions. I see myself as rather happy. I still have that much hope. 74–year-old woman
—out-going, problem-solving. I like a challenge and I like to help people solve their problems, family man, oldest man
—I see myself in a unique situation. I feel that as you age, description takes on a different meaning. Still looking for purpose in life. I'm a teacher and that's compensation for not having family and kids. I'm a good person, reasonably healthy, and active and creative. 49–year-old woman
(From research described in Markus, Holmberg, Herzog, & Franks, 1994).

These are quotes taken from a recent representative sample of Americans over 30. Overall the self-descriptions of these respondents reveal philosophies of life, descriptions of favorite actives, roles, traits, and preferences. Some are rich in detail, some sparse; some are built around clearly categorized attributes and roles, some are cast in terms of everyday actions and practices. Some frame the future; others highlight the past and the present. They are a diverse set of responses, yet all seem to provide viable answers to the question "Who am I?" And although clearly skeletal, they provide some insight into what matters to these people and into the nature of the frameworks or dimensions by which they understand and organize their lives. Taken together, these quotes reveal more than just different individual perspectives; they provide a rudimentary sense of how American adults in midlife and older age from a mostly middle-class background currently understand themselves.

Functions of the Self

In the words of Sullivan (1940), the self is what one takes oneself to be. It is not a special part of the person or the brain but the whole person considered from particular points of view (Neisser, 1991). The ideas and images that people have of themselves and the stories that they tell about themselves reflect what Bruner (1990) called "self-making." This term highlights the continual and dynamic process of organizing and providing form, meaning, and continuity to one's actions and reactions. Self-making requires fashioning together broad cultural mandates (e.g., remain active; be strong and independent), specific social expectations (e.g., a father's imperative to "make something of yourself," an adolescent daughter's advice to "chill"), one's own unique blend of hard-won insights and emotional understandings of one's abilities, temperaments, preferences, and behaviors. The result is a set of custom-crafted interpretive frameworks that create self-congruent structure and coherence in each individual's world and life. These frameworks form an account of the past, and they provide a blueprint for the future (Birren & Hedlund, 1985; McAdams, 1989).

Self-concepts, or self-narratives, are the socioculturally appropriate stories we learn to tell about ourselves. But they are not just the stories we tell to ourselves. They are not, as some have argued, simply justifications that people give to themselves and others when the need to explain themselves arises. Rather, understandings of the self that are enduring and recurrent are individualized, interpretive structures that organize both the micro and the macro levels of ongoing experience (Oyserman & Markus, 1993). These frameworks are not applied to behavior *after* it has occurred; they are an integral aspect of the experience itself, both affording and constraining experience. Self-concepts from this perspective are cultural, historical constructions but also constructors of experience. They achieve the power to structure personal experience, "to organize memory, to segment and purpose-build the very 'events' of a life. In the end, we become the categories and narratives by which we tell about ourselves" (Bruner, 1990, p. 15).

The evidence for the interpretive or integrative function of the self is of two types. The first comes from studies that document the information-processing consequences of interpretive structures, which are typically called self-schemas (Markus, 1977), salient identities (Ogilvie, 1987; Stryker, 1986), and core conceptions (Gergen, 1977). These structures reflect the domains of life that are illuminated and that stand out for people and represent the domains of expertise. They indicate what people will attend to, what they think about, what they care about, what they remember, and what they spend their time and energy on (Banaji & Prentice, 1994; Markus et al., 1994; Markus & Wurf, 1986). In the quotations given above, such domains include religion, health, leading or teaching others, problem solving, independence and sports. Such salient or schematic dimensions of the self are usually measured by self-ratings on a set of dimensions or attributes, by self-reports in open-ended measures, or by some combination of these methods. Attributes or domains that are rated as highly descriptive and as important to the self or dimensions that are frequently mentioned are likely to function as such organizing structures. In the sociological literature, identities are assessed through ratings of centrality of, commitments to, and meaning of various roles (Reitzes, Mutran, & Fernandez, 1994).

The second type of evidence for the interpretive and integrative function of the self comes from studies that show stability in how individuals describe themselves over time and tell their stories across the life span. Certain self-views can be shown to recur persistently as people tell the stories of their lives, and these narrative reconstructions of human lives show considerable thematic coherence (Costa & McCrae, 1988; McAdams, 1989; Mortimer & Lorence, 1981). Cantor and colleagues (Cantor, 1994; Cantor & Zirkel, 1990) study what people are trying to "do" in their lives and find that, even when engaged in activities that are quite diverse, they are often working on the same life task and using similar strategies. Cantor's work also suggests that stability alone is not the hallmark of a healthy self, that self-systems are flexible and learning, and that this is another feature of well-being and personal coherence.

In a study of the role of self-schemas in creating and maintaining a stable sense of self over time, Markus and her colleagues (Markus et al., 1994) found that respondents who held a self-schema in a particular domain showed a greater 1-month test-retest reliability in the domain-relevant self-rating than did respondents without a self-schema in the domain. Respondents who held a particular self-schema also perceived greater continuity between their current self-perception in the particular domain and how they saw themselves in the past and in the future. Further discussion of the functions of the self is provided in our earlier review (Markus & Herzog, 1991).

Content of the Self

Within the North American context, the self is understood to be rooted in a set of internal attributes such as abilities, talents, personality traits, preferences, roles, subjective feeling states, and attitudes. In one of the earlier statements of these ideas, James (1890) divided what he called the empirical self or "me" into three components: the material self, the social self, and the spiritual self. A major cultural task within Euro-American contexts broadly defined and one that is often mutually pursued by caretakers, friends, and teachers is the highlighting expressing, and affirming of attributes that identify the self. These attributes are assumed to be the basis of one's uniqueness and individuality.

American selves, although quite diverse, as the above examples indicate, show some clear commonalities in the form of the self. Markus, Herzog, and their colleagues (Markus et al., 1994), in their recent representative sample of 1,500 American adults, found that most respondents had no difficulty responding to a relatively unstructured request to "tell me about yourself." As is evident in the examples and supported by a quantitative analysis of the responses to this open-ended question, self-concepts were dominated by reports of attributes—physical attributes, personality attributes, and mention of family roles. Between 60% and 72% of the responses, depending on the age and educational background of the respondents, were attributes or roles (Herzog & Markus, 1993). The remaining responses focused on actions of the self, describing the self in terms of what the individuals were doing, rather than who they are; for example, "I've just gotten a divorce," "I work for a chip company," or "I do a lot of camping." A similar range of responses was reported by McCrae and Costa (1988) in response to the Twenty Statements Test.

Also, the viable self-concept, especially in the American context, seems to depend on being able to continuously and confidently express and affirm the positive features of the self (Taylor & Brown, 1988). The self-concepts of Americans contain about four to five times as many positive attributes as negative ones (Markus et al., 1994).

In a close-ended part of their survey, Markus and her colleagues asked respondents to rate themselves on 44 descriptors by using a 5-point scale; the descriptors were generated in pilot studies in which a diverse array of people were asked to describe themselves. Following a factor analysis of the responses to the 44 descriptors, it was evident that there are many independent areas of self-experience. The analysis yielded 11 factors that explained about half of the variance; almost half of the descriptors did not reach a loading of 0.5 or higher on any factor. The major factors might be labeled Mental Health (e.g., "depressed," "content"); Upstanding (e.g., "organized," "responsible"); Social (e.g., "caring," "friend"); Vocation (e.g., "involved in paid work," "hardworking"); Accommodating (e.g., "tolerant," "realistic"); Attractive (e.g., "physically attractive," "intelligent"); Inventive (e.g., "curious," "sense of humor"); Avocation (e.g., "involved in hobbies/leisure activities," "active"); Family Roles (e.g., "being a mother/father," "being a husband/wife"); Social Characteristics ("aware of race or ethnic background," "aware of being a man or woman"); and Autonomy (e.g., "dependent," "independent") (Franks, Herzog, Holmberg, & Markus, in press).

Although some analysts of self-reports suggest that the five factors of neuroticism, extroversion, openness to experience, agreeableness, and conscientiousness are sufficient to account for all self-characterizations (Costa & McCrae, 1988), the results reported here and by others (e.g., Rentsch & Heffner, 1994) suggest that the dimensions of self reflect a blending of personal attributes, sociodemographic characteristics, and social roles.

Among American adults of 30 and older a variety of specific descriptors were rated by almost everybody regardless of age, gender, or socioeconomic status as both very descriptive and very important to their views of self (Markus, et al., 1994). These included being a friend (91%), responsible (90%), aware of being a man/woman (88%), involved in family (85%), mature (82%), respected (78%), and sense of humor (78%). These widely endorsed self-descriptors probably reflect some current general norms or imperatives of how to be a "good" or "morally adequate" person and suggest a concern with community and relationship reflected in sevreal of the previously discussed dimensions.

Issues of agency, autonomy, and competence seem to be reflected among the descriptors that were endorsed somewhat more selectively. These included "independent" (74%), "intelligent" (72%), "active" (65%), "aware of your race or ethnic background" (64%), "healthy" (61%), "involved in a paid work" (57%), "spiritual or religious" (52%), "tolerant" (49%), and "conservative" (40%) and represent primarily the factors of vocation and avocation described before.

Taken together, these self-descriptions reveal that Americans in midlife and beyond think about themselves in varied and multifaceted ways. Many have positive, reasonably well articulated views of themselves that center on social attributes such as gender and race, having a family and friends, being competent and active, and being responsible.

Time Dimension of the Self

The self-system extends beyond a currently salient roles, social and personality attributes, to include possible as well as past selves (Cross & Markus, 1991; Markus & Herzog, 1991). As specific representations of desired and feared aspects of the self in the future, possible selves provide positive and negative visions and serve to simultaneously organize and energize one's actions. Possible selves illustrate how far one might go and how one might get there. Through possible and future selves, individuals cast themselves ahead and sketch out a road map of alternative and future trajectories. Through past selves, on the other hand, individuals organize and to some degree create a personal history. Past selves provide a basis of comparison, indicating how far one has come. Past selves may bolster the self, provide meaning to current and past life, and maintain well-being (Atchley, 1982). Past selves are not assumed to be veridical reflections of the past (Greenwald, 1980). Rather, past selves as well as possible selves are likely to be viewed through the lens of current selves. Through selectively choosing to adopt and elaborate past and possible selves that are consistent with or support it, the current self-system engineers a sense of continuity and change.

SOURCES OF THE SELF

Whereas people can be quite inventive and selective in how they think about themselves—indeed, this is one key to healthy adaptations and adjustment—they are also responsive to the requirements of their various sociocultural environments and typically create selves in ways that resonate with what is valued in those environments. The self-concept, then, is the personal locus of societal or sociostructural influences. It reflects and incorporates what others think of the person, how the person is treated, who are the relevant others, and what the person makes of all this. As the philosopher Charles Taylor (1991) contends, "My self-definition is understood as answer to the question `Who am I' and this question finds its original sense in the interchange of speakers. I define who I am by defining where I speak from in the family, in social space, and in the geography of social status and functions" (p. 35).

Cultural Differences

A variety of studies with Japanese respondents, for example, reveals that the question of "who are you" is not the reasonably natural question it seems in the American context, in which many people are at ease with both introspection and some degree of self-disclosure. The direct, certain, opinionated self-disclosures of the Americans in the examples at the beginning of the preceding section would often seem rude and inappropriate in a Japanese context. Japanese self-descriptions reflect an explicit concern with others and vary according to the nature of the social situation in which the "Who am I" question is being asked. In constructing a self, the relationships among individuals and the meanings created in interactions among people are emphasized over individual preferences and private or personal meanings (Bachnik, 1994).

Japanese respondents are less likely to use the type of personal attributes so common in American selves and are much more likely to describe the self in terms of habitual, everyday actions (e.g., I play tennis with sister, I try to avoid disturbing others). Moreover, when compared to American respondents, Japanese respondents are very likely, as indicated in the previous example, to incorporate another person into their own self-descriptions. The emphasis is not always on harmony or cooperation with others; in fact, sometimes the self-descriptions highlight conflict or tension, but there is a pervasive awareness that a person is an interdependent element in an encompassing social field and can be seen as the intersection of a number of relationships. As a consequence, self-descriptions reflect this self-defining relationality (Markus & Kitayama, 1991). Studies in other Asian cultural contexts (e.g., Korea and China) reveal a similar concern with relatedness to others and a tendency not to draw sharp boundaries between the self and close others and to characterize the self in terms of social roles (I am a daughter) and qualified social roles (I am Jane's friend) (Ip & Bond, 1995).

Studies that find cultural differences in the content of selves have led investigators to consider more specifically the broader cultural contexts within which people are living and to delineate the connections between the cultural criteria for selfhood and well-being. For example, North Americans show a strong tendency toward optimism—to overestimate the likelihood that desirable and fortunate events will happen to them and to underestimate the likelihood of undesirable events. And in fact such optimism has been clearly associated with good physical and mental health (Taylor & Brown, 1988). Recent studies with Japanese respondents, however, suggest that for them the healthy or appropriate attitude is a more fatalistic or pessimistic one—the belief that one cannot control everything and that a desirable outcome depends on a variety of factors other than the actions of oneself (Heine & Lehman, 1995).

These studies may be interesting in their own right, but for our purpose they highlight the ways in which the nature of the self is a product of the sociocultural context and how self-making is afforded and constrained by the imperative and demands of a person's various sociocultural environments. They suggest that, in future research, concepts such as effective coping and adjustment, well-being, successful aging, and even physical and mental health should be analyzed with reference to what is understood as "good" or "moral" or "healthy" in a given context.

The Self and Socioeconomic Status

A person's general socioeconomic context will also shape the self-system, and the little attention paid to socioeconomic status (SES) in current research on the self and identity is rather surprising. Socioeconomic status, with educational attainment as one of its main components, has several possible links to the self-system. First, the broader exposure to information and knowledge afforded by higher SES should result in a broader and more diverse self-system that includes a wider array of current and particularly possible selves. Supporting our hypothesis, we recently found a strong relationship between a multifaceted self and educational attainment which is a major indicator of SES among American adults (Franks et al., in press). The relationship holds for current self-schemas but extends also to the retrospective view of the past selves and particularly to the prospective view of the possible selves. Adults with higher education levels hold a broader and more textured view of themselves in the past, present, and future.

Lest one easily discard this finding as just a reflection of something like the higher cognitive complexity of the more highly educated, we did control on a short version of the WAIS-R Similarities measure as indicator of cognitive complexity and could not explain the observed relationship by such cognitive complexity. In the context of the well-established relationship between SES and health and well-being (for review, see Adler et al., 1994) we wish to suggest that the more elaborated selves among those of higher SES provide a possible mediating process (Herzog, Franks, Markus, & Holmberg, in press) that should be considered in the search for an explanation of the link of SES to health.

Second, aside from the increased breadth in knowledge, higher SES affords more opportunities and resources to pursue a wider array of goals and selves. Whether the focus is on the college student's occupational options, summer jobs, and trips abroad or on the retired professional's volunteer careers and leisure and social activities, higher SES affords a more varied and differentiated lifestyle (see also Franks et al., in press). Third, higher SES is likely to result in a different life span and its timing. For example, the educational phase lasts longer in the life of adults of higher SES, the uptake of marital and parenting roles occurs later, the occupational development peaks later, grandparenthood occurs later, and the retirement phase differs in terms of onset and the kinds of activities in which retirees engage. Thus, we would expect some self-schemas about life cycle changes to vary substantially by SES.

Finally, a possible impact of SES is on the specific self-schema of competence and control because of SES's link to better occupational attainment, higher income, and generally increased power in society. Confirming the impact of SES on this aspect of the self, several investigators have recently observed a relationship between education or SES and indicators of an agentic self and have proposed it as one particular mediating process of the effect of SES on health (Herzog et al., in press; House et al., 1994; Ross & Wu, 1995).

Gender

Although the meaning of gender and gender expectations is currently being renegotiated in many spheres, gender continues to have a powerful impact on self-making. Women's lives are still distinctly different from those of men; for example, women are typically responsible for raising children and maintaining relationships; they are often in low-power, subordinate, and gender-segregated positions within society; and they earn less money (Eagly, 1987; Ridgeway & Diekema, 1992).

In a recent theoretical integration of the gender difference literature, Cross and Madson (1997) suggest that because women participate in society in ways that highlight relationality (they fulfill roles that are defined by caring for and nurturing others), their selves will emphasize the fact of this connectedness. They suggest that, throughout the life span, women will view relationships as integral parts of their selves; their own thoughts and feeling will be understood in terms of the thoughts and feelings of close others, and the needs of others will shape moral decisions and social interaction. They contend that women are more likely than men to be characterized by an interdependent self-construal.

Maccoby and Jacklin reported in 1974 that social characteristics were a more important aspect of self-definition for women than for men, and this finding has been continually supported. Thoits (1992), for example, reported that women considered aspects of their identities associated with relationships as more important than did men. Using an innovative approach called an autographic method, Clancy and Dollinger (1993) asked men and women to compile pictures of themselves. Women included many more pictures of themselves with friends and families than did men, who included more pictures of themselves alone. In our own work with a representative sample of adults over 30 years of age we find that, although gender differences in self-description are not pronounced, women are indeed more likely than men to describe themselves in terms of social relations and gender; whereas men are more likely to describe themselves in terms of work and being independent and active (Markus et al., 1994). Markus and her colleagues found few gender differences in the possible selves; however, Ecuyer (1992), summarizing across a number of studies, noted that men and women are similar in the overall level of aspirations within the self-concept but that the content of their aspirations varied. In his studies women aspired to stay in good health and experienced greater possibilities of social activities and the financial means to help their children; men were more likely to mention changing careers, less tiresome work, and the possibility of retiring.

Life Span Knowledge

Expectations about possible and future selves are also informed by popular theories about the course of the average life cycle. Within the European-American context, Krueger and Heckhausen (1993) demonstrated that adults of all ages perceived increases during early adulthood and decreases during later adulthood across a broad range of personality characteristics. Similarly, Ross (1989) reported that students viewed life span trajectories as being either inverted-U-shaped or stable through older age. These and other related studies suggest a fair amount of consensus about life span patterns of various characteristics, which typically show expected decline or stability but almost never increase in the later part of the life span.

We are not aware of any published evidence that tests directly the hypothesis of the relationship between theories about the general life span and expectations for one's own future life, but some evidence suggests that even retrospective views of the self seem to be refashioned according to knowledge of the life span patterns (Ross, 1989). Also, in our own survey we observed a high rank order correlation between degree of life span stability attributed to certain descriptors and degree of stability expected for one's own life on the identical descriptors (Markus et al., 1994).

Recently, researchers have explored cultural variation in theories about the life cycle and have found considerable variability in how this period of life is understood and experienced (Lock, 1998; Shweder, 1998). For example, in Japan and India the period from 45 to 60 in a woman's life is framed very positively and understood as the time during which the woman has the most influence, power, and status within the extended family. Midlife is not marked as a separate period of life and is not associated with the empty nest syndrome or with the kind of crisis imagery that is common in the American middle class. Aging in general is associated with growth in maturity and wisdom and much less frequently cast in terms of loss and decline.

Explorations of variation in theories about the life span remind us that the psychological experience of decline or loss is not a reflection of a bare reality but, importantly, a construction. Loss may be experienced only if one assumes that the expected and preferred state is constancy or stability. Change can be experienced without being cast as loss, especially if variation and change are culturally valued.

Understandings and images of how to be a self and how to age do not vary just by cultural context but also historically. Gergen (1992) notes a period shift from the self-centeredness of the romantic self during the 19th century to the efficiency of the modern self during earlier parts of this century and finally to the multiple possibilities of the postmodern self of today. The current appreciation of the myriad of possibilities for selves is thought to be prompted by the explosion of opinions, values, personalities, and lifestyles communicated over the new media, although we believe that access to these selves, as well as the means to realize them, are very much conditioned by SES.

Roles and Resources

Roles that carry with them behavioral prescriptions that are shared by many members of a society or of a specific subgroup and thereby frame many individual experiences and expectations can affect the formulation of the self-concept through socialization and internalization processes (Morgan & Schwalbe, 1990). Because many roles are age-structured, they lend themselves to explaining the life span changes of the self-system. Similarly, some resources, such as health and wealth, are typically age-related and thus might be expected to leave their imprint on how an individual views him or herself across the life span. A paper by Logan, Ward, and Spitze (1992) illustrates these contentions. In a well-controlled study of a sample of middle-aged and older adults, these authors observed relationships between adult roles and health status and whether a specific self of young, middle-aged, or old was held: Healthier adults were more likely to view themselves as young, less likely to view themselves as old than as middle-aged. Adults who were not married were more likely to view themselves as old than as middle-aged; adults who had no children were more likely to view themselves as young than as middle-aged.

To summarize, although generalized views about the human life span are likely to affect what individuals expect, hope, and fear for their own lives, individual experiences framed by roles and resources will "individualize" these expectations.

The Self and the Life Span

Cross-sectional investigations of the content of the self reveal few age differences (Krueger & Heckhausen, 1993; Markus et al., 1994; McCrae & Costa,

1988). Whereas the current self-descriptions reflect a general lack of age differences, clear age differences emerge for possible and past selves. Adults at different stages of their life span take different foci in elaborating their future and their past, older persons holding more past selves than younger persons but fewer possible selves (Cross & Markus, 1991; Herzog, Franks, Markus, & Holmberg, 1996). These age differences are quite robust, replicated across a broad set of selves and with different methodologies. Similarly, Ryff (1991) reports a clear and statistically significant age-related decrease in the likelihood ratings of future selves in terms of the six domains of Ryff's measure of psychological well-being. What is most striking about the decrease reported by Ryff is the fact that it obtains even on measures that had been previously developed by Ryff to reflect areas of potential growth in older age. Ryff further reports an age-related tendency toward increased likelihood ratings of past selves that is consistent with our findings, although in her work the effect is clear only for men. Taken together, these findings suggest that, as people get older, they see their future consolidating around a few aspects of the self. This is consistent with Baltes and Baltes's (1990) principle of optimization (in older age efforts are concentrated on fewer goals or selves) as well as with the theorizing about the prevalence and importance of reminiscing in older age (Lewis, 1971).

A good deal has been written about the issue of stability or change in the content of the self. A large body of convincing evidence suggests longitudinal stability in adult personality characteristics—often measured by self-ratings (Bengtson, Reedy, & Gordon, 1985; Costa & McCrae, 1988)—a finding that is replicated in analyses of mean-level differences as well as of correlational stabilities. Yet such stability of the general current self-system may well be achieved by considerable change in its more specific aspects, such as in future and past selves, that allow maintenance of the current self by providing a point of comparison. Future and past selves, if different from current selves, may also reflect expectations about predictable life changes such as retirement. Following Carstensen and Freund (1994), we would argue that such perceived changes are not necessarily reactive and adaptive to challenges of aging but may reflect proactive changes in plans and goals for the maturing self. We speculate that such systematic life changes are more readily perceived for roles than for personality characteristics.

Ross (1989) has pointed out the inconsistency of some of these findings by demonstrating stability and change in the same individuals: individuals who show little change on independent longitudinal measures nevertheless retrospectively self-report change. Krueger and Heckhausen (1993) have raised issues with both measurements of change in an attempt to reconcile the inconsistency. We suggest that more attention should be paid in this research to how different time aspects of the self are being incorporated into the considerable continuity of the self-system and, more generally, how global stability and continuity in the general self may be achieved by modifications in the specific aspects of the self (see also Atchley, 1989).

Intersections Among Sources of the Self

Each person is characterized by a number of these sociocultural contexts, which make some claim on the person and are associated with separate ideas and practices about what matters in the world and how to be a "good" and "worthy" person in it. All significant social contexts have the potential to influence the kinds of accessible and acceptable selves—past, current, and possible. The self then becomes the locus of various and sometimes competing ideas and images and must evaluate contradictions and make choices between alternatives. Ultimately, the self is involved in negotiating a socially acceptable and personally comfortable set of descriptors and making them its own.

Most important for this discussion, the different social contexts are modified by the life span. In concluding this section we therefore provide a few examples of the intersection between the social contexts and age or life span. Cultural notions of "how to be a person" may vary by the stage of the life span. For the Western world, Erikson's (1959) well-known theory portrays the social dimensions of intimacy with a significant other and generativity toward the next generation as salient dimensions of identity in the middle years, whereas the competence dimension of industry is salient in late childhood and adolescence. In Japan, as in many East Asian societies, mature adulthood is a privileged status associated with influence, self-control, responsible judgment, and authority. In comparison with the United States, there is relatively little emphasis on older age as time of frailty, decline, or decay (Shweder, 1998).

Also, a socioeconomic differentiation in the processes of the self may intensify with increasing age, along with the growing heterogeneity in levels of economic resources (O'Rand, 1996; Smith, 1997). Gender differences in the content of the self have been described by Guttman (1987) as differing across the life span: differences between the genders in their affiliation and instrumentality are thought to become less pronounced with increasing age. Although this proposition has been widely accepted, in our opinion it has neither been completely articulated nor conclusively established (Fultz & Herzog, 1991). Finally, most roles are age-graded (Foner, 1996), possibly leading to changes that are conditioned by the life span.

THE SELF AND BEHAVIOR

Many theorists have recognized the link between the self-system and behaviors or activities, an important link for gerontological theorizing on maintaining activities into older age. Sociologists have conceptualized the self as commitment to the behavioral prescriptions associated with specific roles (Stryker, 1980). Similarly, some theorists of personality believe that the essence of an individual is best captured by understanding what he or she is "working on" or "striving for" (Cantor & Kihlstrom, 1987; Emmons, 1986). And some cognitive psychologists stress the ecological self or the self as a doer (Neisser, 1993). In other words, the self is as much about doing as about being, as much about process as about content. In behaviors, the self manifests, expresses, and maintains itself. The best way of laying claim to a particular self is to behave in accordance with it (Cross & Markus, 1990). It appears then that there is an ongoing process of mutual constitution between the self-concept and behavior—they create each other over time. Various actions are organized and integrated within the self, and the self then serves to construct or provide meaning and coherence to a person's experience.

Activities may also be chosen to promote a desirable possible self or to avoid an undesirable possible self. Shaped in part by expectations of normative changes such as retirement or ill health and in part by personal intentions such as new engagements and skills, people hold views about themselves in the future—about what might be possible, what desirable, and what feared. Such possible selves represent potent motivators to engage in relevant behaviors, and the existence of some discrepancy—a possible self that is better or worse than the current self—is thought to play an important role in related behavioral change.

Our comments are not meant to imply a simple one-to-one correspondence between specific self-schemas and specific behaviors. The correspondence is complicated by several recognitions. First, behaviors can be conceptualized at various levels. Single reactions, perceptions, and choices are combined into individual behaviors. Individual behaviors are usually part of more encompassing strategies, which, in turn, are developed in pursuit of larger tasks (Cantor, 1990) supporting current or possible selves. The correspondence to the self-system is probably more transparent for the larger tasks than for the single behaviors. Second, tasks and ultimately selves can be pursued with different strategies, and these with different behaviors. By the same token, the same overt behaviors may serve different purposes and overall tasks or selves. Third, although some activities may be routinized, part of a fine-tuned and well-rehearsed behavioral set, others may be less frequent peak experiences, explicitly sought because of their expression of the self (Csikszentmihalyi, 1993).

From a life span perspective, people refine their patterns of activities as they gain experience with behaviors, strategies, and tasks and harmonize them with their self-system to achieve continuity and satisfaction in their selves and their lifestyles (Atchley, 1993). In middle age, relative stability is achieved: some major tasks and lifestyles related to such life domains as occupation and marital and family roles have been chosen; others have been abolished. Strategies for their achievement have been established. The onset of older age often brings with it new challenges to this established equilibrium: the loss of social partners through retirement, illness, and death disrupts well-established patterns of social intercourse. The onset of illnesses reduces competencies in various activities.

Activity theory has drawn early attention to activities as an important factor in adaptation to aging because they allow expression of new selves (Lemon, Bengtson, & Peterson, 1972). More recently, at least three forms of behavioral adaptation to age-related challenges to established selves have been described in the literature. Atchley (1989) has presented continuity theory, which posits that, despite some disruptions of established patterns, many activities continue into older age, and therefore an overall sense of continuity of the self typically predominates. Baltes and Baltes (1990) have proposed the principle of compensation according to which activities are altered or replaced with other activities to accomplish the same tasks and express the same selves. Similarly, Brim (1988) has suggested a hierarchy of adaptive changes in response to experiences of failure or impairment of behaviors. According to Brim, an individual will first attempt to modify behaviors by taking more time and expending more effort; if this approach is unsuccessful, he or she will resort to different behaviors in support of the same goal. Only as a last resort will the individual change goals. In his provocative paper on the "busy ethic," Ekerdt (1986) has described a more general compensation mechanism: many different leisure activities can provide meaning to the retirement period because, as long as they are earnest and active, they create a semblance of work and thereby satisfy the strong work ethic in American society.

One specific dimension of the self, then, that may be threatened by aging is the competent, active, useful self, and activities may be sought that can continue or compensate for the productive roles of work and child rearing. We have called such activities productive and included in the category activities such as housework or upkeep of home and yard that "produce" a social or economic value (Herzog & House, 1991; Herzog, Kahn, Morgan, Jackson, & Antonucci, 1989). Findings from the longitudinal study of well-functioning older adults by the MacArthur Network on Successful Aging, which showed that change in productive activities was related to change in feelings of mastery and control (Glass, Seeman, Herzog, Kahn, & Berkman, 1995), confirms this hypothesis, as do findings from our own cross-sectional survey of older adults, which showed that the performance of productive activities was related to a competent self (Herzog et al., in press).

In older age, leisure activities may also become important in shaping, expressing, and maintaining the self-concept (Atchley, 1993; Mannell, 1993). Leisure activities include a broad range of activities; their defining criterion is that they are performed for their own sake. Through their experiential, developmental, and social qualities they may contribute to the social as well as the competent self-schemas. Our own research (Herzog et al., in press) confirms this hypothesis.

A current and possible self of good health grows ever more important as people get older, and the possible self of ill health becomes ever more realistic (Cross & Markus, 1991). A growing body of literature has begun to systematically implicate self-perceptions in the initiation and maintenance of health-promoting behaviors such as avoiding smoking and drinking or adopting healthy nutrition, regular exercise, weight control, and routine health examinations (Rodin, 1986). The popular health belief model, for example, posits that perceptions of one's own susceptibility to a particular disease—a possible self of being unhealthy—are critical in the decision to take health care actions. In gerontology, Hooker and Kaus (1992) have shown that persons who reported an important health-related possible self were more likely to engage in health-protective behaviors than those without such a self.

A recognition of the role of possible selves also seems to underlie public, corporate, and private attempts at retirement preparation. Formal and informal preparations for retirement promote the choice of activities that either prepare for a different possible self (e.g., financial and recreational planning for the leisure self) or ensure the continuity of a present self into the future (e.g., exploring opportunities for volunteer work in order to maintain a competent self).

THE SELF AND WELL-BEING

Because of its dynamic, adaptive nature, the well-functioning self is expected to bear a relationship to well-being. Well-being, of course, has been of particular interest in gerontology ever since disengagement and activity theories were first described and has presented a gerontological paradox when it became evident that older adults were no less satisfied than their younger counterparts. At least four different perspectives on the direct relationship between self and well-being have been offered. According to the first view, a diverse, multifaceted self may be adaptive in itself and thus lead to well-being, because it enables the individual to draw on different schemas in dealing with a complex environment. Gergen (1992) believes in the multifaceted self as a sign of our times, in which we continue to be exposed to a "social world of unbounded proportions" and learn about "myriad possibilities for being." He argues that this postmodern self has meant less self-centeredness and increased flexibility, which, we would postulate, can lead to enhanced well-being.

Supporting the belief in a relationship between the self and well-being, it has been known since the pioneering work by Linville (1987) that a complex multifaceted self is related to well-being. We recently replicated this finding (Herzog et al., 1996) by showing that the number of different self-schemas an individual reports is related to the level of well-being operationalized as depressive symptoms and self-esteem. Likewise, it has been known for quite some time that multiple role identities are important for sustaining general well-being in adulthood: the more roles individuals occupy, the better their mental health (e.g., Coleman & Antonucci, 1983; Thoits, 1983). Moreover, the benefit to well-being of multiple role involvements recently has been demonstrated in a study of older adults (Adelmann, 1994). In this study, those older adults who occupied a greater number of roles experienced less depression, higher life satisfaction and greater self-efficacy than did those who occupied fewer roles.

A second view may be described as portraying a more specialized role of the self in maintaining well-being. A large body of research demonstrates a positive relationship between a self-schema of competence—also called sense of control, self-efficacy, mastery, self-directedness—and health and well-being (for review of this literature, see, e.g., Ross & Wu, 1995; Rowe & Kahn, 1987). Likewise, a smaller body of research on identity and self-esteem suggests that those who hold the identity of competent workers and are committed to the worker role have higher self-esteem than those without such identity and commitment to it (Reitzes et al., 1994). Our own work (Herzog et al., in press) has confirmed the importance of a self-schema of competence for well-being among older Americans.

Another self-schema that has potential significance for well-being is the social schema—social acceptance and social engagement. An impressive body of research documents the effect of social connectedness on well-being and health (House, Landis, & Umberson, 1988). Yet other, more directly relevant research (Herzog et al., in press) casts doubt on the importance of the social self by demonstrating a weak and unreliable relationship to well-being. It may well be that the social self is necessary but not sufficient for well-being.

Whereas the first two conceptualizations may be termed main effect theories, a third view is more appropriately called an interaction or buffer model. According to the latter view, the nature of the self acts as a moderator of the impact of problems or stresses on well-being: A problem will have a stronger impact on an individual who holds a self-schema that is relevant to the area of the problem than on an individual who does not hold such a self-schema (Thoits, 1991). For example, retirement should reduce well-being for older workers who think of themselves as workers and care about their job but not for those who do not hold such a self-schema. On the other hand, we speculate that a problem will have a weaker effect on individuals who hold rich multifaceted self-schemas and who therefore have alternative self-schemas to draw on than on individuals who do not. For example, retirement should have less impact on older workers who also hold schemas as volunteers and grandparents. The buffering effect is implied by much of the writing on adaptation to aging, but it has not yet received much formal testing. A study by Brandtstadter and Rothermund (1994) best illustrates this approach. These authors showed that in a group of middle-aged and young-old adults the effect of loss of control depended on the importance attributed to control in the relevant domain.

A fourth approach links well-being to the processes by which self-perception is submitted to social, temporal, domain, or ideal comparisons in defending and promoting the self. To protect well-being, selective social comparisons with others who are worse off can be initiated by the self (Suls & Mullen, 1982). Temporal comparisons with a satisfying past or a promising future may serve the same purpose (Atchley, 1982). Domain comparisons by which negative self-perceptions in one domain are contrasted with positive self-perceptions in another domain represent another possible mechanism to enhance or maintain well-being. Finally, manipulating the discrepancy between ideal and current selves through modification of the ideal self can lead to well-being and has been proposed as one mechanism for the relative satisfaction of older Americans (Campbell, Converse, & Rodgers, 1976). Through these various processes of selective comparison the active self-system engages in emotion control and thereby builds well-being and self-esteem (Taylor, Wayment, & Carillo, 1995). More detailed discussion is provided in our previous review (Markus & Herzog, 1991).

CONCLUSION

We propose the self, or identity, as a useful theorctical perspective for studying personal adaptation to aging. We view the self-system as consisting of a number of knowledge structures that persons hold about themselves and a set of cognitive functions that actively integrate those knowledge structures across content areas and time frames. As such, the self-system is actively involved in structuring and interpreting experiences, motivating behaviors, managing emotions, and providing a sense of continuity; it is an integral part of all of them, shaping them and, in turn, being shaped by them. Because of its nature and its link to behavior and well-being the self-system provides us with a conceptualization of the adaptive and proactive processes that have been described by many life span developmentalists as critical in maintaining active involvement and well-being in older age and gives us a system's view on the interaction and integration among those processes. Although the self-system is fashioned by the individual as a unique set of images, characteristics, and themes relevant to the self, these themes are chosen from culturally and socially available and valued ones and thus reflect cultural and subcultural views of personhood.

Given the long life span and the mostly stable environments of persons in their second half of life, self-systems in older age are typically stable in content and well tuned in function. People of all ages seem to seek meaning in their experiences and try imposing directions on their future. Nevertheless, we suggest that change in the self-system is possible and manifests itself in several forms. First, overall stability in major self-perceptions may be achieved by considerable change in the details. For example, a sense of self as active or competent may be achieved by a number of specific activities. Thus, the committed and hardworking worker retains a sense of engagement after retirement through volunteer work or serious leisure activities (Ekerdt, 1986; Herzog et al., in press). Second, changes in the self-system may come about because of changes in the personal or social situation of the aging person. In the face of a serious disability or loss of a long-term spouse, an active and competent self possibly cannot be maintained, necessitating change in the self-system. Third, but not least, change may be self-initiated following an anticipated or actively pursued trajectory of change. For example, retirement will facilitate transition from a working to a traveling self.

Whether changing or not, we propose that the self-system provides us with a perspective on how the aging individual negotiates the life span and often comes out with a sense of continuity and indeed well-being, accomplishing, as it were, the last stage of ego integrity in Erikson's (1959) life stage theory.

REFERENCES

Adelmann, P. K. (1994). Multiple roles and physical health among older adults: Gender and ethnic comparisons. *Research on Aging, 16,* 142–166.

Adler, N. E., Boyce, W. T., Chesney, M. A., Cohen, S., Folkman, S., Kahn, R. L., & Syme, S. L. (1994). Socioeconomic status and health: The challenge of the gradient. *American Psychologist, 49,* 15–24.

Atchley, R. C. (1982). The aging self. *Psychotherapy: Theory, Research and Practice, 19,* 388–396.

Atchley, R. C. (1989). A continuity theory of normal aging. *Gerontologist, 29,* 183–190.

Atchley, R. C. (1993). Continuity theory and the evolution of activity in later adulthood. In J. R. Kelly (Ed.), *Activity and aging: Staying involved in later life* (pp. 5–16). Newbury Park, CA: Sage.

Bachnik, J. M. (1994). Introduction: Uchi/soto: Challenging our conceptualizations of self, social order, and language. In J. M. Bachnik & C. J. Quinn (Eds.), *Situated meaning.* Princeton, NJ: Princeton University Press.

Baltes, P. B., & Baltes, M. M. (1990). Psychological perspectives on successful aging:

A model of selective optimization with compensation. In P. B. Baltes & M. M. Baltes (Eds.), *Successful aging: Perspectives from the behavioral sciences* (pp. 1–34). New York: Cambridge University Press.

Banaji, M., & Prentice, D. (1994). The self in social contexts. *Annual Review of Psychology, 45*, 297–332.

Bengtson, V. L., Reedy, M. N., & Gordon, C. (1985). Aging and self-conceptions: Personality processes and social contexts. In J. E. Birren & K. W. Schaie (Ed.), *Handbook of the psychology of aging,* (2nd ed., pp. 544–593). New York: Van Nostrand Reinhold.

Birren, J. E., & Hedlund, B. (1985). Adult development through autobiography. In N. Eisenberg (Ed.), *Current perspectives in developmental psychology.* New York: Wiley.

Brandtstädter, J., & Greve, W. (1994). The aging self: Stabilizing and protective processes. *Developmental Review, 14,* 1–29.

Brandstädter, J., & Renner, G. (1990). Tenacious goal pursuit and flexible goal adjustment: Explication and age-related analyses of assimilative and accommodative strategies of coping. *Psychology and Aging, 5,* 58–67.

Brandtstädter, J., & Rothermund, K. (1994). Self-percepts of control in middle and later adulthood: Buffering losses by rescaling goals. *Psychology and Aging, 9,* 265–273.

Breytspraak, L. (1984). *The development of self in later life.* Boston: Little, Brown.

Brim, O. G. (1988, September). Losing and winning. *Psychology Today, 22*(9), 48–52.

Brim, G. (1992). *Ambition: How we manage success and failures throughout our lives.* New York: Basic Books.

Bruner, J. (1990). *Actual minds, possible worlds.* Cambridge, MA: Harvard University Press.

Campbell, A., Converse, P. E., & Rodgers, W. L. (1976). *The quality of American life: Perceptions, evaluations, and satisfactions.* New York: Russell Sage.

Cantor, N. (1990). From thought to behavior: 'Having' and 'doing' in the study of personality and cognition. *American Psychologist, 45,* 735–750.

Cantor, N. (1994). Life task problem solving: Situational affordances and personal needs. *Personality and Social Psychology Bulletin, 20,* 235–243.

Cantor, N., & Kihlstrom, J. (1987). *Personality and social intelligence.* Englewood Cliffs, NJ: Prentice-Hall.

Cantor, N., & Zirkel, S. (1990). Personality, cognition, and purposive behavior. In L. A. Pervin (Ed.), *Handbook of personality: Theory and research.* New York: Guilford.

Carstensen, L. L. (1993). Motivation for social contact across the life span: A theory of socioemotional selectivity. In J. E. Jacobs (Ed.), *Nebraska Symposium on Motivation* (pp. 209–254). Lincoln: University of Nebraska Press.

Carstensen, L. L., & Freund, A. M. (1994). Commentary: The resilience of the aging self. *Developmental Review, 14,* 81–92.

Clancy, S. M., & Dollinger, S. J. (1993). Photographic depictions of the self: Gender and age differences in social connectedness. *Sex Roles, 29,* 477–495.

Coleman, L. M., & Antonucci, T. C. (1983). Impact of work on women at midlife. *Developmental Psychology, 19,* 290–294.

Costa, P. T., Jr., & McCrae, R. R. (1988). Personality in adulthood: A six-year longitudinal study of self-reports and spouse ratings on the NEO Personality Inventory. *Journal of Personality and Social Psychology, 54,* 853–863.

Cross, S. E., & Markus, H. (1990). The willful self. *Personality and Social Psychology Bulletin, 16,* 726–742.

Cross, S., & Markus, H. (1991). Possible selves across the life span. *Human Development, 34,* 230–255.

Cross, S. P., & Madson, L. (1997). Models of the self: Self-construals and gender. *Psychological Bulletin, 122,* 5–37..

Csikszentmihalyi, M. (1993). *The evolving self.* New York: Harper Collins.

Eagly, A. (1987). *Sex differences in social behavior: A social role interpretation.* Hillsdale, NJ: Lawrence Erlbaum Associates.

Ecuyer, L. E. (1992). An experiential-developmental framework and methodology to study the transformation of the self-concept from infancy to old age. In T. M. Kipka & R. P. Lipka (Eds.), *The self definitional and methodological issues* (pp. 96–134). New York: State University of New York Press.

Ekerdt, D. J. (1986). The busy ethic: Moral continuity between work and retirement. *Gerontologist, 26,* 239–244.

Emmons, R. (1986). Personal strivings: An approach to personality and subjective well-being. *Journal of Personality and Social Psychology, 51,* 1058–1068.

Erikson, E. H. (1959). Identity and the life cycle. *Psychological Issues,* Monograph 1. New York: International Universities Press.

Foner, A. (1996). Age norms and the structure of consciousness: some final comments. *Gerontologist, 36,* 221–223.

Franks, M. M., Herzog, A. R., Holmberg, D., & Markus, H. R. (in press). Educational attainment and self-making in later life. In C. D. Ryff & V. Marshall (Eds.), *The self and society in aging processes.* New York: Springer Publishing Co.

Fultz, N. H., & Herzog, A. R. (1991). Gender differences in affiliation and instrumentality across adulthood. *Psychology and Aging, 6,* 579–586.

Gergen, K. J., (1977). The social construction of self-knowledge. In T. Mischel (Ed.), *The self: Psychological and philosophical issues* (pp. 139–169). Totowa, NJ: Rowman and Littlefield.

Gergen, K. J. (1992, November/December). The decline and fall of personality. *Psychology Today,* 59–63.

Glass, T. A., Seeman, T. E., Herzog, A. R., Kahn, R., & Berkman, L. F. (1995). Change in productive activity in late adulthood: MacArthur Studies of Successful Aging. *Journal of Gerontology: Social Sciences, 50B,* S65–S76.

Greenwald, A. G. (1980). The totalitarian ego: Fabrication and revision of personal history. *American Psychologist, 35,* 603–618.

Guttman, D. (1987). *Reclaimed powers: Toward a new psychology of men and women in later life.* New York: Basic Books.

Heckhausen, J., & Schultz, R. (1995). A life-span theory of control. *Psychological Review, 102,* 284–304.

Heine, S. J., & Lehman, D. R. (1995). Cultural variation in unrealistic optimism: Does the West feel more invulnerable than the East? *Journal of Personality Social Psychology, 68,* 595–607.

Herzog, A. R., Franks, M. M., Markus, H. R., & Holmberg, D. (1996, August). *Age differences in temporal orientation of the self: Current, past and possible selves.* Paper presented at the 14th biennial meeting of the International Society for the Study of Behavioral Development, Quebec City.

Herzog, A. R., Franks, M. M., Markus, H. R., & Holmberg, D. (1998). Activities and well-being in older age: Effects of self-concept and educational attainment. *Psychology and Aging, 13.*

Herzog, A. R., & House, J. S. (1991). Productive activities and aging well. *Generations, 15,* 49–54.

Herzog, A. R., Kahn, R. L., Morgan, J. N., Jackson, J. S., & Antonucci, T. C. (1989). Age differences in productive activities. *Journal of Gerontology: Social Sciences, 44,* S129–S138.

Herzog, A. R., & Markus, H. R. (1993, August). *The self in social context: Age, gender, and socioeconomic differences.* Poster presented at the Third Congress of the Swiss Society of Psychologists, Zurich.

Hooker, K., & Kaus, C. R. (1992). Possible selves and health behaviors in later life. *Journal of Aging and Health, 4,* 390–411.

House, J. S., Landis, K., & Umberson, D. (1988). Social relationships and health. *Science, 241,* 540–545.

House, J. S., Lepkowski, J. M., Kinney, A. M., Mero, R. P., Kessler, R. C., & Herzog, A. R. (1994). The social stratification of aging and health. *Journal of Health and Social Behavior, 35,* 213–234.

Ip, G. W. M., & Bond, M. H. (1995). Culture, values, and the spontaneous self-concept. *Asian Journal of Psychology, 1,* 29–35.

James, W. (1890). *Principles of psychology.* New York: Holt.

Krueger, J., & Heckhausen, J. (1993). Personality development across the adult life span: Subjective conceptions vs cross-sectional contrasts. *Journal of Gerontology: Psychological Sciences, 48,* P100–P108.

Lachman, M. E. (1986). Locus of control and aging research: A case for multidimensional and domain-specific assessment. In R. Abeles (Ed.), *Aging and quality of life* (Vol. 1, pp. 34–40). New York: Sage.

Lemon, B. W., Bengtson, V. L., & Peterson, J. A. (1972). An exploration of the activity theory of aging: Activity types and life satisfaction among in-movers to a retirement community. *Journal of Gerontology, 27,* 511–523.

Lewis, C. N. (1971). Reminiscing self-concept in old age. *Journal of Gerontology, 26,* 240–243.

Linville, P. W. (1987). Self-complexity as a cognitive buffer against stress-related illness and depression. *Journal of Personality and Social Psychology, 52,* 663–676.

Lock, M. (1998). Deconstructing the change: Female maturation in Japan and North America. In R. Shweder (Ed.), *Welcome to middle age! (And other cultural fictions).* Chicago: University of Chicago Press.

Logan, J. R., Ward, R., & Spitze, G. (1992). As old as you feel: Age identity in middle and later life. *Social Forces, 71,* 451–467.

Maccoby, E. E., & Jacklin, C. N. (1974). *The psychology of sex differences.* Palo Alto, CA: Stanford University Press.

Mannell, R. C. (1993). High-investment activity and life satisfaction among older adults: Committed, serious leisure, and flow activities. In J. R. Kelly (Ed.), *Activ-*

ity and aging: Staying involved in later life (pp. 125–145). Newbury Park, CA: Sage.

Markus, H. (1977). Self-schemas and processing information about the self. *Journal of Personality and Social Psychology, 35,* 63–78.

Markus, H. R., & Herzog, A. R. (1991). The role of the self-concept in aging. *Annual Review of Gerontology and Geriatrics, 11,* 110–143.

Markus, H. R., Holmberg, D., Herzog, A. R., & Franks, M. M. (1994, November). *Self-making in adulthood.* Symposium presented at the annual meeting of the Gerontological Society of America, Atlanta.

Markus, H. R., & Kitayama, S. (1991). Culture and the self: Implications for cognition, emotion, and motivation. *Psychological Review, 98,* 224–253.

Markus, H. R., & Wurf, E. (1986). The dynamic self-concept: A social psychological perspective. *Annual Review of Psychology, 38,* 299–337.

McAdams, D. P. (1989). The development of a narrative identity. In D. M. Buss & N. Cantor (Eds.), *Personality psychology: Recent trends and emerging directions* (pp. 160–174). New York: Springer-Verlag.

McCrae, R. R., & Costa, P. T. (1988). Age, personality, and the spontaneous self-concept. *Journal of Gerontology: Social Sciences, 43,* S177–S185.

Morgan, D. L., & Schwalbe, M. L. (1990). Mind and self in society: Linking social structure and social cognition. *Social Psychology Quarterly, 53,* 148–164.

Mortimer, J., & Lorence, J. (1981). Self-concept, stability and change from late adolescence to early adulthood. *Research in Community and Mental Health, 2,* 5–42.

Neisser, U. (1991). Two perceptually given aspects of the self and their development. *Developmental Review, 11,* 197–209.

Neisser, U. (1993). The self perceived. In U. Neisser (Ed.), *The perceived self* (pp. 3–21). Cambridge, U.K.: Cambridge University Press.

Ogilvie, D. D. (1987). Life satisfaction and identity structure in late middle-aged men and women. *Psychology and Aging, 2,* 217–224.

O'Rand, A. M. (1996). The precious and the precocious: Understanding cumulative disadvantage and cumulative advantage over the life course. *Gerontologist, 36,* 230–238.

Oyserman, D., & Markus, H. R. (1993). The sociocultural self. In J. Suls (Ed.), *Psychological perspectives on the self* (Vol. 4, pp. 187–220). Hillsdale, NJ: Erlbaum.

Reitzes, D. C., Mutran, E. J., & Fernandez, M. E. (1994). Middle-aged working men and women: Similar and different paths to self-esteem. *Research on Aging, 16,* 355–374.

Rentsch, J. R., & Heffner, T. S. (1994). Assessing self-concept: Analysis of Gordon's coding scheme using "Who am I?" responses. *Journal of Social Behavior and Personality, 9,* 283–300.

Ridgeway, C. L., & Diekema, D. (1992). Are gender differences status differences? In C. Ridgeway (Ed.), *Gender, interaction and inequality* (pp. 157–180). New York: Springer-Verlag.

Rodin, J. (1986). Aging and health: Effects of the sense of control. *Science, 233,* 1271–1276.

Ross, C. E., & Wu, C. (1995). The links between education and health. *American Sociological Review, 60,* 719–745.

Ross, M. (1989). Relation of implicit theories to the construction of personal histories. *Psychological Review, 96,* 341–357.

Rowe, J. W., & Kahn, R. L. (1987). Human aging: Usual and successful. *Science, 237,* 143–149.

Ryff, C. D. (1991). Possible selves in adulthood and old age: A tale of shifting horizons. *Psychology and Aging, 6,* 286–295.

Schaffer, R. (1992). *Retelling a life. Narration and dialogue in psychoanalysis.* Basic Books.

Shweder, R. (1998). Introduction. In R. Shweder (Ed.), *Welcome to middle age! (And other cultural fictions).* Chicago: University of Chicago Press.

Smith, J. P. (1997). *The changing economic circumstances of the elderly: Income, wealth, and social security* (Policy Brief No. 8). Syracuse, NY: Syracuse University, Center for Policy Research.

Stryker, S. (1980). Symbolic interactionism: A social structural version. Menlo Park, CA: Benjamin/Cummings.

Stryker, S. (1986). Identity theory: Developments and extensions. In K. Yardley & T. Honess (Eds.), *Self and identity* (pp. 89–104). New York: Wiley.

Sullivan, H. S. (1940). *Conceptions of modern psychiatry.* New York: Wiley.

Suls, J., & Mullen, B. (1982). From the cradle to the grave: Comparison and self-evaluation across the life-span. In J. Suls (Ed.), *Psychological perspectives on the self* (Vol. 1, pp. 97–128). Hillsdale, NJ: Erlbaum.

Taylor, S. E., & Brown, J. D. (1988). Illusion and well-being: A social psychological perspective on mental health. *Psychological Bulletin, 116,* 21–27.

Taylor, S. E., Wayment, H. A., & Carillo, M. A. (1995). Social comparison and self-regulation. In R. M. Sorrention & E. T. Higgins (Eds.), *Handbook of motivation and cognition* (pp. 3–270). New York: Guilford Press.

Thoits, P. A. (1983). Multiple identities and psychological well-being: A reformulation and test of the social isolation hypothesis. *American Sociological Review, 48,* 174–187.

Thoits, P. A. (1991). On merging identity theory and stress research. *Social Psychology Quarterly, 54,* 101–112.

Thoits, P. A. (1992). Identity structures and psychological well-being: Gender and marital status comparisons. *Social Psychology Quarterly, 55,* 236–256.

Whitbourne, S. K. (1986). *The me I know: A study of adult identity.* New York: Springer-Verlag.

Whitbourne, S. K. (1987). Personality development in adulthood and old age: Relationships among identity style, health, and well-being. *Annual Review of Gerontology and Geriatrics, 7,* 189–216.

14

Emotions in Adulthood

Gisela Labouvie-Vief

T here has been a recent upsurge in studying the role and functions of emotions development. After a long historical tradition in which emotions were construed as processes that were nonrational and subordinated under rational guidance, emotions have been redeemed as important independent systems that are not reducible to the cognitive system. Still, we humans cognize emotions, and cognition constitutes a natural part of our emotional lives. How the cooperation among cognition and emotion is to be construed has therefore been the focus of a plethora of writings.

Understanding the role of emotions in human adaptation and development also has enlivened the study of adulthood and later life. From their once secondary status, emotions have come to be implicated in all kinds of adaptive outcomes, and a growing body of theoretical and empirical inquiry has explored the role of emotions in adaptation. As part of this evolution, a number of different theoretical positions have emerged.

How individuals regulate their emotions at different stages of adulthood has been the subject of two rather different and sometimes oppositional theoretical and empirical perspectives. One set of writings on the topic has assumed that emotions should be viewed as fixed and innate biological programs; another, that culture and individual development provide a system of cognitive controls that significantly alter those programs.

According to the first model, emotions are relatively hard-wired systems selected by evolution for basic and universal adaptive requirements of our

Preparation of this chapter was supported by grant AG09203 from the National Institute on Aging.

species. These systems are prepotent over the cognitive system, and they show little variation as a function of experience, context, or development. Thus, the emotional state and subjective experience of emotion require minimal learning or, as Zajonc (1984) put it, "preferences need no inferences." According to the second class of theories, in contrast, emotions are filtered and transformed through the operation of cognitive mechanisms such as ego processes, schemata, and appraisal processes (e.g., Lazarus, 1991), and such cognitive mechanisms may bring new and more complex emotions (e.g., Labouvie-Vief & DeVoe, 1991). However, a third class of models proposes that even though such cognitive transformation is possible, biologically based emotion regulation processes on the one hand, and cognitively based ones on the other hand, can remain separate and unintegrated. Anticipated in the Freudian notion of defense mechanisms (e.g., A. Freud, 1965), this view is gaining increasing prominence in recent integrative theories about cognition-emotion linkages (e.g., Fischer & Ayoub, 1994; Weinberger, 1990). It proposes that although cognition and emotion systems can come to cooperate smoothly, they do so only in cases where cognitions remain cognizant of important prepotent emotion systems and integrate those systems into representations. However, it is also possible that cognition and emotion systems continue to function independently or, as in the case of defensive emotion regulation processes, in an antagonistic fashion.

In this chapter, I suggest that across these core approaches to the development of emotions, the various theories can be grouped into two metatheoretical prototypes. These prototypes conceive of the critical task of adult and later life adjustment in somewhat different terms. According to one prototype, development throughout adulthood is guided by the ideal of increasing openness and flexibility; according to a second, development in later life consists of an adjustment to the losses that come with increasing age. Both of these prototypes result from somewhat different views of the relation between emotion and cognition. I begin by outlining these core views in the context of biological theories of emotion and aging. In the sections to follow, I discuss the different metatheories of emotion and aging, while in the concluding section, I suggest several means of integrating the two.

BIOLOGICAL ASPECTS

From a biological perspective, emotions are often viewed as basic, built-in programs. These systems are relatively hard-wired by evolution such that basic adaptive needs for reproduction and survival are met. Such hard-wired emotional systems imply homeostatic mechanisms that set important priorities and defaults. They function as feedback-dampening or negative feedback systems, since they act to reduce or negate discrepancies from particular default values. This setting of defaults does not necessarily involve cognitive processes (see Izard & Ackerman, 1997). Indeed, the dictum that preferences need no inferences is supported by findings that important emotional systems are organized within subcortical systems that are shared by all mammals (Panksepp & Miller, 1996). To that extent, emotions are independent of higher-order cognitive systems. Nevertheless, these lower structures must be integrated with higher-order ones during the course of development.

The biological view of the emotions was stimulated by Darwin's (1965) work on emotional expression. In *The Expression of Emotion in Man and Animals,* originally published in 1872, Darwin suggested that emotions can be studied as specific behaviors, such as facial expressions and gross motor gestures, and he maintained that many of these movements are innate patterns that evolved for specific adaptive purposes in animals and human beings alike. More recently, this suggestion was incorporated in the proposal that there are distinct emotional systems, involving distinct patterns of expressive gestures and physiological responses (see Izard & Ackerman, 1997). These movement patterns are assumed to be organized by about seven basic emotional patterns: interest, joy, anger, sadness, fear, surprise, and disgust.

The notion of different and independent emotion systems also goes along with the observation (Panksepp & Miller, 1996) that there appear to be basic and separate emotion systems of circuits organized at subcortical levels. Several such subsystems have been proposed: ones relating to separation distress and sorrow (*Panic*), to playfulness and joy (*Play*), sexual desires and pleasures (*Lust*), nurturance and social bonding (*Acceptance*), the *Fear* and *Rage* systems, and perhaps several other emotion systems. Since these subsystems seem to be shared by all mammals, they appear to constitute a core emotional hardwiring of the brain.

The notion that there are basic emotional patterns fixed by biology has received considerable support not only from cross-species studies, but also from cross-cultural and life-span research. Cross-culturally, a body of research suggests that certain prototypical situations (e.g., spoiled food) arouse identical prototypical expressions (e.g., disgust) across a diversity of cultures. From a life-span perspective, it also appears that basic emotion patterns are fairly fixed across the life course. Basic patterns of emotional expression appear to be in place at birth or soon thereafter and do not change much thereafter (Izard & Ackerman, 1997). However, in line with the notion that aging brings decreases in the intensity of many motivation- and affect-related systems (see Lawton, 1996), there may be some decreases in intensity of expressive responses.

Such changes were demonstrated in a study by Levenson, Carstensen, Friesen, and Ekman (1991), who compared young and older subjects on physiological responsivity to a directed facial action task (moving muscles on the face to simulate an emotional expression) and a relived emotion task.

They found that for both tasks a similar pattern of responsivity occurred. However, the magnitude of these changes was much less for the older subjects than for the younger subjects. Thus, the autonomic reactivity of the older was less than that of the younger.

Such findings suggest that even though core emotional systems remain intact, their homeostatic functioning nevertheless may change as a function of age. For example, older individuals sometimes exhibit a restriction of affective arousal, whether as a result of a physiological blunting of emotional responses (Lawton, 1996), or because they find it difficult to deal with high levels of arousal and therefore have evolved complex strategies for the blunting of emotions. They may also exhibit a slowing of homeostatic regulation since patterns of activation appear to persist longer at older ages (see Lawton, 1996). However, the exact mechanisms for similar homeostatic changes are still rather poorly understood.

Findings such as those discussed above suggest that the tendency to view emotions as derived from cognitions—a tendency inherent in many past interpretations of emotions—needs to be tempered. Indeed, it now is often acknowledged that emotions can function independently of variations in experience and of higher-order cognitive processes. Nevertheless, it is true that in humans emotion-related cognitions can come to play a role as a function of development and experience. Specifically, this modification can happen in two prototypic ways (see Labouvie-Vief, in press).

The first of those ways functions through a stabilizing relationship. In such relationships cognitions essentially are put in the service of core emotional patterns. In that role, they function to maintain values that are set by prepotent emotional systems. Hence they operate as feedback processes that organize cognitions at higher levels.

In contrast to such relatively reactive emotion-cognition relations, however, there are also linkages that are more proactive and that work through expanding the range of emotional experience. This expansive and opening function relies on feed-forward processes rather than feedback dampening. In feed-forward processes individuals no longer dampen experiences that are too intense. Rather, they turn their attention to such experiences and begin to elaborate and amplify them. The original equilibrium is deliberately disturbed and explored in an effort to integrate the disturbing experience. Eventually, as a result of this process, individuals are able to reequilibrate at a new level. That is, by integrating into their cognitions an experience that was too disturbing originally, they can maintain a sense of emotional equilibrium even in the face of experiences and conflicts that previously could not be assimilated.

Ideally, feedback and feed-forward processes should work together in a cooperative fashion. In other words, there are important limits to the regulative power of cognition. If cognitions are integrated with important organismic-emotional programs, cognition may extend the power of those programs by monitoring processes such as intentions and flexible modulation. In such cases, the emotional programs and cognitive representations work together cooperatively. However, such cooperative functioning is not a given; cognition also may work to misrepresent, falsify, or distort core biological programs (Labouvie-Vief, in press). Thus in the ideal case, lower-order biological programs and higher-order cognitive programs need to engage in dialectical exchanges that augment and modulate, but do not thwart, emotional expression. Nevertheless, for better or worse, even though there are important biological constants in emotional physiology, experience, and expression, the how and why of emotion regulation is subject to considerable modulation by experience and development. How such modulation appears to happen in feed-forward and feedback processes will be discussed next.

EXPANDING EMOTION-COGNITION RELATIONS IN DEVELOPMENT AND AGING

From the perspective of cognitive development, increasing cognitive capacities are related to emotional repertories that become broader, more complex, and are able to carry representations that have the potential for more contrast and conflict. Such a cognitive-developmental perspective was first launched by Piaget (for review, see Labouvie-Vief & DeVoe, 1991). Piaget rejected a polarization between biology and experience, but suggested that the two modify each other in the process of development. Such modification happens as individuals in their development move away from preset equilibrium points by systematically exploring experience away from equilibrium (see Brent, 1978; Labouvie-Vief, in press). As a result of such feed-forward processes, the individual can form representations that permit more complex and varied forms of emotional experience.

Emotions in Early Development

Research has provided ample support for such a general developmental theory (for review, see Labouvie-Vief & DeVoe, 1991). First, many core emotions appear to be in place as a result of the hereditary organization of affect. However, these emotions become more and more linked to patterns of experience and, as individuals proceed to symbolic thinking, new emotional patterns emerge. Not only do children begin to experience emotion to symbolic stimuli (such as fear of an animal hiding under the bed), but new emotions can emerge that presuppose higher levels of self-differentiation. Examples are such emotions as shame or guilt—emotions that presuppose relations between the self's expression and experience on one hand, and the reaction of the social world, on the other. Izard (Izard & Ackerman, 1997) calls these emotions dependent, since they are affected by increasing cognitive maturity.

Such dependent or secondary emotions continue through later stages of development. In adolescence, when individuals operate in terms of abstractions, feelings can center on collective ideals and standards, dreams, life plans, and so forth. It is possible that even in adulthood and late life new emotions emerge: the fierce protectiveness of parents or the generative concerns of mature adults with mentoring the next generation all may be relatively novel emotions that first emerge in adulthood. Even in late life (or perhaps as a consequence of specific spiritual practices), new emotions may surface. For example, forgiveness, embracing compassion, serenity, and equanimity are emotions sometimes associated with optimal aging. However, so far there has been little research that has explored such life stage specific growth in the nature of emotions.

More important than new types of emotions, however, is the fact that in the course of development, already existing emotions can become more differentiated and interlinked with others. For example, as the individual becomes cognitively more sophisticated, emotions are understood as being modulated across time and space. This understanding permits the individual to maintain equilibrium in the face of temporary emotional disturbances. In addition, emotions also are related to other emotions than can occur simultaneously: for example, children begin to understand that they and others can be both nice and mean at the same time. Especially if the valence of emotions is different (as in mean and nice), the ability to coordinate emotions is strongly related to cognitive level in childhood and adulthood. Emotions can also be linked in means-end sequences, as when the expression of one emotion (e.g., pleasantness) becomes the means to achieve a higher-order emotional goal (e.g., acceptance). In the latter case, however, it is also possible that a focus on means-end relationships dampens the ability to express and experience opposite emotions—a mechanism that may contribute to emotional repression.

Emotions in Adult Development

In my own research over the years (see Labouvie-Vief, 1997), I explored what kind of developmental patterns of emotions characterize adulthood and later life periods. A major tenet of this work has been the proposition, first suggested by Jung (1933) and repeated in many emotion-related theories since, that the organization of emotions is strongly regulated by cultural and institutional scripts. If these scripts are transmitted in relatively fixed systems of power, a self emerges that is organized around the goals of acceptance and success within those scripts. At midlife, as individuals are at the peak of their cognitive capacities and as they move into more symmetrical power relations, these scripts need to be reexamined, and the construction of the self needs to be reevaluated. In turn, such reevaluations will free the individual's potential for openness and creativity.

Midlife reevaluations and reintegrations appear to be the result of a shift in a naive epistemology through which individuals re-construct the meanings of a number of everyday constructs from relatively external to more internal ones. One of those constructs relates to the nature of emotion. For young children, emotions are rather direct bodily experiences, but as children grow up, they come to see emotions more and more in terms of complex processes such as evaluating, deciding, delaying, controlling. By adolescence and young adulthood, individuals master a cultural language of emotions that emphasizes processes of valuation and control (not unlike the Freudian notion of the superego). Yet, there is little sense of a self that transcends these culturally valued controls.

In contrast, individuals throughout adulthood begin to redefine their emotions in relation to the cultural context that shaped their unique emotional repertoire. The search is for a self that transcends the cultural language of emotions, and that attempts to differentiate the self from that institutional/cultural language. In that process of searching for the real self, a new emotion language emerges. This language is both more complex and more spontaneous. On one hand, it acknowledges the reality of one's emotions as bodily symptoms and powerfully motivating subjective experiences; on the other, that language indicates that the individual can transform and regulate emotions in terms of broader, interindividual goals.

Because emotions ultimately are organized by core self-structures, more recent examinations have focused on how individuals represent their self and that of others—especially that of their parents (see Labouvie-Vief, 1997). In this research, younger or less mature individuals framed their self and that of others in terms of a conventional perspective: i.e., in terms of an organized, codified, and abstract set of role expectations. At a more advanced level, the institutional values become susceptible to doubt and criticism: for example, such values can be carried too far. Instead, a dynamic perspective evolves in which descriptions of one's self and that of others convey in vivid language the unique and evolving experience of individuals within the context of their particular life histories. Lives now are understood in the context of multiple frames—cultural, social, and psychological, for example. There is keen insight into the psychological dynamics that are at the root of human diversity, yet an understanding that such diversity appears to be regulated by a common human heritage. At the same time, awareness of emotional complexity is at its maximum, and individuals are able to view themselves and others in nonpolarized terms, as a collection of aspects that comprise the full range of negative and positive emotions.

Just as one's self becomes viewed more from the perspective of historical patterns and general emotional transformation, so do the selves of one's parents (Labouvie-Vief, Diehl, Chiodo, & Coyle, 1995). Younger individuals and those over the age of 60 primarily describe their parents in the interpersonal context of their roles as providers of emotional and financial support to the self, or, to a lesser extent, in the institutional context of their societal position. Few youthful individuals represent their parents as autonomous individuals in their own right. In contrast, around midlife there is a peak of responses that are appreciative of the unique individuality of parents: Participants describe their parents not just as carriers of parental and other social roles, but show an awareness of the conditions that shaped the parents and made them become the persons they are or were. These results are consistent with views (anticipated by the work of Jung, 1933) which suggest that a restructuring of representations of one's parents is part and parcel of the reorganizations in self often associated with middle adulthood.

Moves toward greater complexity at midlife have also been reported from Helson's longitudinal (see Helson, in press) study of Mills College women. Patterns of change differed for women who were engaged in different life paths or `social clocks.' Traditional women's life was dominated by adaptation to the roles of wife and mother which was frequently accompanied by a withdrawal from social life, the suppression of impulse and spontaneity, a more negative self-image, and decreased feelings of competence. Twenty percent of the women who adhered to this pattern relinquished this life structure and divorced between the age of 28 and 35. In contrast, women who had chosen a career path at age 28 were less respectful of norms and more rebellious toward what they experienced as constrictive pressures. Although these women did not score lower on femininity or on well-being, they were more independent and self-assertive than their traditional counterparts. Long-term follow-up of the women showed that those who continued to stay on the career path into middle adulthood showed greater confidence, initiative, forcefulness, and intellectual independence than women who did not continue on this path. Thus, Helson's data suggest that the move to greater complexity depends, in part, on the type of social-clock project individuals adopt.

In a quite similar vein, Stewart (1996) recently has proposed a contextual view according to which individuals face midlife challenges in different ways. Thus she argues that for most of the women studied, midlife may be a time of reexamination of their lives. If life patterns are found wanting, these women may experience regret and as a result engage in a midlife adjustment, correcting their patterns by such changes as moving from family to work orientation. This group of women subsequently shows a positive turn in their patterns of adjustment. However, not all women who are dissatisfied with their lives are able to readjust their pattern. For those women, the subsequent life course shows a picture of poor emotional health.

Cognition and Emotional Functioning in Late Life

How does the notion of continued cognitive-emotional development hold up in later life? Many authors have suggested that such movements may continue into late life, giving rise to advanced forms of knowledge in the form of wisdom (see Labouvie-Vief, 1997; Miller & Cook-Greuther, 1990). However, research does not hold up the notion that, as a group, older individuals are wiser. Indeed, it appears that wisdom, assessed by the cognitive-emotional integration measures in the above research, reaches a high point in middle adulthood rather than old age (see Blanchard-Fields, 1997; Labouvie-Vief, 1997). Indeed, even among middle-aged individuals, only a fairly small percentage appears to show evidence of a more complex form of emotional functioning; and those individuals who do generally are those who are more highly educated and socioeconomically advantaged (Labouvie-Vief, 1997).

That complex forms of reasoning should be strongly related to cultural experiences makes good theoretical sense, since culture plays a dominant role in enhancing or dampening the degree of individuation that is at the core of such reasoning (Labouvie-Vief, in press). For the same reason, it is quite possible that older individual's overall lower levels of emotional complexity is a result of cohort or generational changes; indeed, it is well known that less recent generations have experienced stricter socialization into emotional control and to that extent, one would expect their reasoning about self and emotions to be more conventional as well.

A second major reason older individuals may evidence lower levels of cognitive-emotional complexity is that there exist cognitive limits that restrict such complexity. In my own research (see Labouvie-Vief, 1997), cognitive-emotional complexity is consistently and strongly related to intellectual functioning. This finding suggests that complex forms of emotion regulation depend on general cognitive resources that are known to decline with age. Further, in our study of self and emotion representation, cognition-emotion relationships were especially strong in the older portion of the sample: those with lower levels of representation also used more controlling and defensive strategies of emotion regulation, and suffered from higher levels of depression. These findings suggest a third major reason why many individuals do not think about emotions in complex terms. These individuals' higher order cognitive-emotional integrations may be limited because due to their particular life histories, they have come to invest their cognitive capacities not in the expansion of emotional experience but rather in its restriction and fragmentation (see Labouvie-Vief, in press). Indeed, such an interpretation was foreshadowed by the work of Jung (1933), who emphasized the role of individual openness in later life.

Even though emotions of older individuals do not seem to display higher complexity, older individuals in general are effective at emotion regulation, giving an overall picture of well-controlled behavior. How such adaptive regulation can happen in the face of loss and declining resources has been the focus of a further class of theories of emotion and aging.

Loss and Emotional Resilience in Later Life

Rather than focusing on expanding ranges of emotions, another class of theories has addressed the issue that, despite the losses that aging brings, older individuals appear to be resilient and display a remarkably positive pattern of well-being. This suggests that even in the face of declining resources, there are unique, resilient ways of adaptation that optimize adaptation in later life.

Coping and Emotion Regulation

The observation that older individuals overall display a pattern of well-regulated behavior is compatible with a host of studies that have examined age-related differences in patterns of coping and affect regulation (for review, see Labouvie-Vief, 1997). This literature consistently indicates that older individuals are less likely to regulate their behavior through relatively impulsive strategies such as hostile acting out, projection, and turning against others. In contrast, they are more likely than younger individuals to use strategies such as reinterpreting situations, avoiding conflict, accepting negative events, and appealing to general norms and principles (see Blanchard-Fields, 1997; Labouvie-Vief, 1997). Thus, in general, older individuals are typically found to present a picture of well-being, good adjustment, and well-regulated behavior. Interestingly too, there is evidence that this pattern of age differences in part reflects the role of cultural change, since older individuals have been socialized into stricter rules of emotion regulation (Magai & Passman, 1997).

Age differences showing overall more well-regulated behavior in the older individual may tap a particular aspect of development. That aspect is different from the flexible control mechanisms discussed in the previous section. Instead, it indicates that some forms of development do not necessarily bring increasing expansion and flexibility of emotional experience, but that it also can be focused primarily on the mastery of and enmeshment in the social system and its rules and norms (see Labouvie-Vief, in press). Indeed, available data suggest that the good coping picture displayed by the elderly does not necessarily reflect a pattern of flexibility, but rather one of gating-out of negative experience. This notion is in line with two general proposals. First, many authors (see Lawton, 1996, for review) have noted that although older individuals are good at transforming negative affect, they also tend to do so at the expense of avoiding negative experience, even in vital interpersonal situations. Second, older individuals' regulation strategies rely primarily on greater norm orientation, at the same time as they experience decreases in flexibility (see also Helson, in press). Such findings suggest that as individuals experience changes in a variety of cognitive and emotional resources, they restrict their focus from an exploratory and open mode to one that is narrower and more self-protective. This observation also is in line with a recent proposition by Heckhausen and Schulz (1995). These authors suggest that with increasing age, individuals shift their mode of self-regulation away from one aimed at primary control through direct action, instead they focus on such secondary modes of control that disengage from action and instead adopt inner means of adjusting to a reality that is manipulated through cognitive means such as interpretation (Heckhausen & Schulz, 1995).

Assimilative and Accommodative Shifts

A somewhat similar perspective has been proposed by Brandstädter (e.g., Brandstädter & Greve, 1994). Brandstädter notes that impairments and losses are an inevitable fact of aging. We are faced with a decline of adaptive reserves of various kinds; we experience a shrinking of the temporal horizon and begin to experience ourselves as mortal; we increasingly experience bereavement and loss, failing health, and the restriction of more youthful roles, dreams, and ideals. From such evidence one might expect a picture of lowered self-esteem and identity problems in old age. Yet quite to the contrary, older individuals maintain a good sense of well-being. Indeed, rather than experiencing increasing rates of depression, older people even may be buffeted by high rates of depression.

Brandstädter proposes that this emotional resilience of the elderly can be accomplished by a shift from an assimilative to and accommodative mode of self-regulation. Assimilation, in that view, is aimed at strategies that attempt to realize or maintain desired self-aspects. For example, individuals may spend great efforts to enhance health or fitness, maintain physical or interpersonal attractiveness, maintain levels of competence. All of these strategies are assimilative activities.

Accommodation, in contrast, involves adjustments in normative self-representations that are aimed at buffering the experience of loss. For example, realizing that our resources are failing, we can adjust to such losses by rearranging our values, rescaling our goals, and adjusting aspirations so that they fit with given situations. In addition, we may engage in a variety of immunizing strategies—strategies that are aimed not so much at experiencing the full range of such losses, but that rely on such self-protective processes as palliative interpretations, putting negative experiences in a rosy light, and so forth.

Research by Brandstädter and his colleagues shows strong support for his theory over an age range from young to old adulthood. There are nearly linear declines in assimilation, with corresponding linear rises in accommodation. Yet, this switch in strategies is related to the recovery and maintenance of a positive view of self and personal development in later life. Thus, accommodative strategies should be distinguished from coarser processes of distortion of reality, such as denial and fragmentation. Further, the critical factor in such accommodative changes is not age per se, but rather a host of psychological, psychological, and social changes that usually accompany change over time, but that are conceptually different from age.

Social Networks and Emotions

One theory that also has addressed the older individual's resilient emotion regulation is Carstensen's social selectivity theory (Carstensen, Graff, Levenson, & Gottman, 1996). Rejecting views that consider the older person as bereft of resources and roles, Carstensen suggests that older individuals have become experts at investing their resources into optimizing the experience of positive aging. They do so by actively arranging their social environments so as to guarantee optimal well-being.

Carstensen's work is supported by studies that show that across the life span, individuals tend to gradually interact with fewer people; yet this restriction shows an adaptive pattern as they deliberately withdraw from social contact in peripheral relationships, while maintaining or increasing involvement in relationships with close friends and family. This selective narrowing functions to maximize gains and to minimize risks in social and emotional domains—and indeed, the restriction to a smaller but more intimate network, trading quantity for quality, is related to adaptive outcomes, consistent changes through the life span. Younger individuals tend to have larger and more peripheral social networks, while those of older individuals are restricted to the more central contacts. At the same time, older individuals are more satisfied than younger ones with their social networks, and less likely to want more friends.

Critical factors that bring about the adaptive restriction of social networks are awareness of one's mortality and limited time rather than age or cognitive complexity, per se. Specifically, the anticipation of endings rather than time per se appears to be the critical factor in effecting the social selection, since the effect is evident not only in aging individual but also in younger individuals facing death or imagined endings. Critical in this process is that as individuals age, they move from future-oriented goals to present-focused, emotion-related ones.

In sum, one important line of thinking focuses attention on the notion that older individuals have resilient strategies for coping with losses; indeed, that adaptive aging (in the sense of maintaining a sense of well-being) requires such optimization strategies. Individuals may become more self-protective and restrict their interactions to those that are not too disturbing. Still, a consideration that has not been highlighted in this group of interpretations is the general interpersonal and cultural consequence of this pattern of social restriction. What are the costs of this restriction for family and caregivers, and for culture at large?

DISCUSSION AND CONCLUSIONS

The two metatheoretical views outlined here entail two rather different visions of development. One of these visions is guided by the notion of openness to oneself and others alike. The goal here is to achieve maximum intersubjectivity by opening ourselves to all forms of human experience, whether positive or negative, whether in self or others. This goal is achieved through widening our emotional horizons to achieve fuller intersubjective partnership between individuals, and between individuals and institutions and cultures. The criterion for studying aging thus is placed in an intersubjective framework in which consideration is given not only to the well-being of the self, but also to that of others and culture at large. This view of development thus highlights the need for creativity and transformation rather than closure and stability at all points of adulthood, even into late life. In such a view, a unique role can accrue to elders, who due to their broad integration of reason and emotion can become mentors for younger generations, teaching them about the broad and central conditions of the human condition.

The second vision, in turn, is based on the view that individual adaptation is optimized by a process of closure and restriction to those goals that are most important for the individual. In this view, optimal aging is not so much defined by the more general location of the individual in culture, but rather by inner processes that maximize individual well-being. Yet evidence suggests that well-being is achieved at the expense of increasingly gating-out experiences and individuals that disturb one's equilibrium.

In the end, I suggest, these two views form the endpoints of what is a continuum, and future research will need to be aimed at describing aging as some form of balance individuals achieve on this continuum. From that perspective, individual aging can take on a number of outcomes. On one hand, restriction of resources will inevitably narrow individuals' focus; on the other hand, whether such a restriction is met with an increasing focus on the well-being of the self or a widening concern with that of culture remains a question that should invigorate future inquiries into the process of development in adulthood and later life.

REFERENCES

Blanchard-Fields, F. (1997). The role of emotion in social cognition across the adult life span. In *Annual Review of Gerontology and Geriatrics, 17.*

Brandstädter, J., & Greve, W. (1994). The aging self: Stabilizing and protective processes. *Developmental Review, 14,* 52–80.

Brent, S. B. (1978). *Psychological and social structures.* New York: Springer Publishing Co.

Carstensen, L., Graff, J., Levenson, R. W., & Gottman, J. M. (1996). Affect in intimate relationships: The developmental course of marriage. In C. Magai & S. H. Mc-Fadden (Eds.), *Handbook of emotion, adult development, and aging* (pp. 227–247). San Diego: Academic Press.

Carstensen, L. L., Gross, J. J., & Fung, H. H. (1997). The social context of emotional experience. In *Annual Review of Gerontology and Geriatrics, 17,* 325–352.

Darwin, C. (1965). *The expression of emotion in man and animals.* Chicago, IL: University of Chicago Press. (Original work published in 1872).

Fischer, K.W., & Ayoub, C. (1994). Affective splitting and dissociation in normal and maltreated children: Developmental pathways for self in relationships. In D. Cicchetti & S. L. Toth (Eds.), *Rochester symposium on developmental psychopathology: Vol. 5. Disorders and dysfunctions of the self* (pp. 147–222). Rochester, NY: Rochester University Press.

Freud, A. (1965). *Normality and pathology in childhood.* New York: International Universities Press.

Heckhausen, J., & Schulz, R. (1995). A life-span theory of control. *Psychological Review, 102,* 284–304.

Helson, R. (In press). Personality change in women and their adult development. *Polish Journal of Developmental Psychology.*

Izard, C. E., & Ackerman, B. P. (1997). Emotions and self-concepts across the life span. In *Annual Review of Gerontology and Geriatrics, 17.*

Jung, C.G. (1933). *Modern man in search of a soul* (Trans. W.S. Dell & C.F. Baynes). New York: Harcourt, Brace & World.

Labouvie-Vief, G. (1997). Cognitive-emotional integration in adulthood. In K. W. Schaie & M. P. Lawton (Eds.), *Annual review of gerontology and geriatrics, Vol. 17* (pp.). New York: Springer Publishing Co.

Labouvie-Vief, G. (In press). Self-organization and cognitive-emotional integration: The intersubjective link. In I. E. Josephs & S. Hoppe-Graf (Eds.), *Entwicklung als soziale Konstruktion* (Development as social construction). Lengerich, Germany: Pabst Verlag.

Labouvie-Vief, G., & DeVoe, M. (1991). Emotional regulation in adulthood and later life: A developmental view. In *Annual Review of Gerontology and Geriatrics, 11,* 172–194.

Labouvie-Vief, G., Diehl, M., Chiodo, L.M., & Coyle, N. (1995). Representations of self and parents over the life span. *Journal of Adult Development, 2,* 207–222.

Lazarus, R.S. (1991). *Emotion and adaptation.* New York: Oxford University Press.

Levenson, R. W., Carstensen, L. L., Friesen, W. V., & Ekman, P. ((1991). Emotion, physiology, and expression in old age. *Psychology and Aging, 6,* 28–35.

Lawton, M.P. (1996). Quality of life and affect in later life. In C. Magai & S. H.

McFadden (Eds.), *Handbook of emotion, adult development, and aging* (pp. 327–348). San Diego: Academic Press.

Magai, C., & Passman, V. (1997). The interpersonal basis of emotional behavior and emotion regulation in adulthood. In *Annual Review of Gerontology and Geriatrics, 17.*

Miller, M. E., & Cook-Greuther, S.R. (Eds.) (1990). *Transcendence and mature thought in adulthood: The further reaches of adult development.* Lanham, MD: Rowman & Littlefield.

Panksepp, J., & Miller, A. (1996). Emotions and the aging brain. In C. Magai & S. H. McFadden (Eds.), *Handbook of emotion, adult development, and aging* (pp. 3–26). San Diego: Academic Press.

Stewart, A.J. (1996, August). *Personality in middle age: Gender, history and mid-course corrections.* Murray Award Lecture presented at the American Psychological Association, Toronto, Canada.

Weinberger, D. A. (1990). The construct validity of the repressive coping style. In J. L. Singer (Ed.), *Repression and dissociation.* Chicago, IL: University of Chicago Press.

Zajonc, R. B. (1984). On the primacy of affect. In K. R. Scherer & P. Ekman (Eds.), *Approaches to emotion* (pp. 259–270). Hillsdale, NJ: Erlbaum.

SECTION IV

Social Science Concepts and Theories of Aging

15

Anthropological Theories of Age and Aging

Christine L. Fry

nthropological theories have their roots in an intellectual tradition
that is distinctive from the other social sciences. Nineteenth-century thinkers such as Edward B. Tylor and Lewis Henry Morgan
documented a natural universal history of humankind and the laws of evolution. We now see these theories as antique curiosities and points of departure. Largely through the research agendas of Franz Boas (Stocking, 1996),
who has been called the father of American anthropology, and the work of
Bronislaw Malinowski and Radcliffe-Brown in Great Britain, the foundations for contemporary anthropological thought were created (Goody, 1995;
Stocking, 1995). Anthropology, like other disciplines, has its share of schisms
and "isms," resulting in diverse perspectives.

Despite diversity in paradigms and a marked increase in specialization
during the last half of the 20th century, anthropological research and theory
generally embrace three tenets. First is a perspective that includes the entire
globe. This means attempting to apply anthropological theory to the entirety
of the human experience and explain variance. Second, anthropological theory is rooted in the comparative method. Ethnographic descriptions of specific cultures and contexts provide comparative data for theory-building and
evaluation on a global or regional basis (referred to as ethnology). Third,
anthropological theory is holistic. Because the comparative method requires
comparable data, anthropologists emphasize the context in which the data
are found. This usually means an entire context, which can include ecology,

social life, culture or meaning, and human variation and historical context as revealed by written records or archaeological reconstructions.

In this chapter we examine how the distinctive disciplinary perspective of anthropology has contributed to our theorizing about age and aging. First, we discuss anthropological theories of aging and old age. Second, because age is a temporal phenomenon, we review the nature of time and the distinctive ways in which humans use maturational differences. Third, we turn to the question of cultural variation in models of the life course. Fourth, we consider the strengths and promises of anthropological theories of age and aging. In conclusion, the possibilities of unified theories of age, aging, and the aged are appraised.

AGE IN ANTHROPOLOGICAL THEORIES

Once anthropologists began describing specific cultures, age became a part of anthropological theory. It was never very prominent, usually imbedded in discussions of kinship or the typical life cycle, with a focus of domestic groups. A major exception is the problem of age organization as a fairly esoteric problem in social anthropology, focused in the ethnography of Africa and of Native Americans on the Great Plains. In the few societies involved, males are formally ordered into classes by age. For social scientists interested in age and social organization, these cultures provided tantalizing models from simple societies, which could serve as heuristic contrasts for age in complex industrial societies. (See below, under "Age Class Systems" for discussion.)

Old age came late for anthropology. In fact it was the sociologist Leo Simmons who was the first to explore the accumulating ethnographic data organized into the Human Relations Area Files. In *The Role of the Aged in Primitive Society*, Simmons (1945) employed data from 71 nonindustrialized societies to statistically examine the status and treatment of the old from records of 19th-century ethnographers, missionaries, and colonists. His independent variables are ecological, economic, social, and political organization and religious beliefs. Although no singular hypothesis concerning better or worse treatment of older people in simpler societies emerged, Simmons's data documented the complexity and variability of the issues. Among the surprises were that some people lived a very long time (the superaged) in small-scale societies with little technology. Promoting their security was continued involvement in subsistence activities, personal services, and contributions to civil and religious life.

Nearly two decades later, Margaret Clark and Barbara Anderson (1967) used a culture and personality framework to examine mental illness and wellness in late life. In their volume *Culture and Aging* (1967), they assess the hypothesized relationship between cultural values and mental health. Adherence to American values involving independence and rugged individualism is maladaptive in late life. Changed value orientations, with different expectations, promote successful aging and mental health.

Perhaps the most explicit theory on aging was formulated by sociologist Donald Cowgill and anthropologist Lowell Holmes on aging and modernization. In *Aging and Modernization,* Cowgill and Holmes (1972) propose a quasi-evolutionary theory linking marginalization of older people to modernization (see also Cowgill, 1986). Explicit hypotheses involve independent variables of productive technology, health technology, urbanization, and education with the dependent variable, status of older people. Precisely because of its explicit hypothesis, this theory has received considerable debate and revision. In spite of difficulties with modernization and aging, this theory has done more than any other to remind us of the diversity of cultures in which humans live and grow old. It also reminds us of the cultural evolutionary changes that have occurred in the past 12,000 years. Modernization is too narrow a process to capture the broader picture of cultural evolution. Modernization refers to 20th-century economic and political changes and has shifted to a model of world systems. An evolutionary framework is desirable in conceptualizing the costs and benefits of increased scale, technology, intensification, and political centralization and their effects on peoples lives.

If the first four decades of anthropological theory and age are noted for the paucity of research, the last two decades are noteworthy for their abundance. An entire volume, *Age and Anthropological Theory* (Kertzer & Keith, 1984), invited anthropologists to theorize about age from evolutionary, social, and cultural perspectives. Anthropologists have investigated the contexts in which older adults are living, ranging from age-homogeneous retirement communities to inner cities and rural communities. Ethnographic research has explored special populations, including ethnic groups and older people with disabilities. Cross-cultural research continues, as seen in Project AGE (Keith et al., 1994). There have been many reviews of this research (see Albert & Cattel, 1994; Climo, 1992; Fry, 1996; Keith, 1990; Sokolovsky, 1997), and it cannot be covered in detail in this essay.

In generalizing from this third generation of anthropological work in aging, several themes are apparent. These are discussed below.

1. *Complexity.* As Leo Simmons (1945) discovered a half-century ago, aging is complicated. It is next to impossible to confirm a linkage between variables such as the social status of older people or even well-being of older people and an evolutionary transformation (simple to global or nonindustrial to industrial capitalism) or specific economic cores (foraging, domestication, peasantry or industry). The reason for this is that aging is experienced

in a *cultural* context. Because culture is adaptive, it presents multiple paths in decision making and reflection. In other words, there are multiple ways to get from here to there. If one thing does not work, humans will use their culture and knowledge to figure out a way that will work.

2. *Diversity.* There are many different ways of being human, and there are even more ways of being an older human. The diversity of aging experiences is one of the major discoveries in gerontological research. This diversity has been confirmed time and time again in cross-cultural and intracultural research on older people.

3. *Context specificity.* Living, aging, and growing old are experienced in specific contexts. What happens in one social context is not necessarily transferrable across cultures. For instance, in defining functionality, vision is likely to be a critical ability. For all primates, sight is a primary sense. Yet different contexts will place distinct demands on abilities. In contexts where management of daily life is predicated on literacy and recreation consists of reading, television, or driving a recreational vehicle, loss of sight is tragic. But where literacy is minimal and the environment familiar, reduction in vision may not be as catastrophic.

4. *Culture and understanding.* To understand age is to interpret phenomena of change over time and the rhythms of the normal life course. Interpretation of these changes involves culture. Everyone uses culture, and its multiple perspectives are to be expected. Culture is also at the foundation of evaluation. What is the best for people? For older people? When it comes to questions about social policy, we have learned to ask, Whose culture is it? For instance, if we had listened to the wisdom of Lewis Mumford (1956), who argued for the integration of older people, age-segregated retirement communities would never have been built. When anthropologists looked into life in these age-segregated settings, they found viable communities, not the projected geriatric ghettos.

Thus, in looking toward anthropological theories of aging, we must first look at time and how humans have culturally incorporated temporal phenomena in understanding age and aging.

THE CHALLENGE OF TIME

Time actually is not a challenge. Time just happens, as a property of the universe in which we live. Discontinuities and continuities in experience give the sensation of periodicity and duration of time. Because of the organization of the solar system, every living thing experiences the periodicity associated with the rotation of our small planet, Earth—night and day—

plus seasonality caused by the axis of the rotation and Earth's elliptical orbit around the sun. The challenge of time rests in how humans incorporate the experience culturally and thus interpret the phenomenon (Gell 1992).

Because culture is not completely arbitrary, we are in for no surprises. Virtually every culture organizes time by days, months, and years. Lunar months leave a few extra days that are worked into the calendar, similar to February 29 in a leap year. Calendrics, in fact, are very ancient for our species, dating to the Upper Paleolithic of Europe some 20,000 years ago, in the Magdalenian Period. The passage of time is noted ritually in fertility festivals and other rites, such as first fruits and harvesttime.

Although calendars calibrate time and schedule human events in time, they do not translate into age and aging. Indeed, age is that which happens in time from birth to the present or to death. To measure age calendrically, the calendar has to be transformed. Most cultural calendars reckon time in a relative fashion. Time is anchored in the present, which is forever changing. Events are seen as relative to each other—that is, earlier or later, before or after. People are seen as junior or senior, younger or older than one another. For age to be measured, three things have to happen to a calendar. First, the units of time must be rationalized into explicitly bounded segments. Second, and most important, time has to become absolute and fixed. The calendar has to be anchored at a specific point in time. Third, time so rationalized is seen as independent of any social order and thus politically neutral; that is, time and its prognostication are not dust in the hands of the priests but seen as an element in the universe.

Time as currently reckoned by the Christian calendar is based on the Gregorian calendar, which, in 1582, revised the Julian calendar. Our units are millennia, centuries, decades, years, months, days, hours, minutes, seconds. Time is anchored in the year 0 and the supposed birth of Christ (actually missing the event by 30 or so years). From 0 on the A.D. side, count forward to the present; on the B.C. side, count backward. Time is transcendent for societies, dating history; for individuals, it fixes their births on a day and a year. Without these conventions, age expressed chronologically would be a conceptual impossibility. Why were absolute time and chronological age invented? How has age been incorporated into specific models of the life course?

Chronological time is dominant for Euro-American culture and cultures incorporated into the 19th- and 20th-century industrial order. It is so central that an aging individual's confusion on questions dealing with present year, date, or hour can result in recommendations to institutionalize, as seen on Mini-Mental Status tests. In a broader time frame, long after an individual's biography has faded from memory the dates on the tombstone attest to that person's presence in time. It is not surprising that when observers from Europe and North America encountered peoples of smaller-scale cultures, they were blinded by their own temporal orientation. Smaller-scale cultures, using relative time, were misrepresented by ethnographers. Chronological age per se did not exist; but relative age, as expressed in kinship (generational differences) and in maturational stages, were translated into terms that could be understood by Euro-Americans. Age grades, often with chronological markers, were used to organize descriptions of domestic life. Even the chronological ages of informants are translated from relative time by creating local event calendars and birth orders.

If gerontology is as "chronocentric" as it seems to be, then we should critically reexamine our theories of age and social organization. Indeed, during the 1960s and 1970s, one of the major debates in social gerontology centered on chronological age, which became less useful than functional age (Austin & Loeb, 1982). The argument was that age based in functionality is more sensitive to an individual's abilities and needs. Yet when we turn to the conceptual building blocks of what theories we have, we find they are all cast in a chronometric framework. Here I am thinking of such concepts as age strata, cohorts, age grades, life stages, social clocks, on/off time, age norms, young old/old old, and even *the* life course. When we hedge our bets by pointing to variability and heterogeneity in searching for pattern, we are left with temporal order. Chronology may conceptually be appropriate for the contexts being modeled, but chronology is but one alternative. Hence time— its use and meaning—is best seen as a variable.

To begin a reexamination of age and culture for the 21st century, I see two necessary starting points. First, we need to examine maturational differences and how they are incorporated into a social order. Second, we must clarify variability as to how differences in maturity are modeled by human cultures in transforming maturation into ideas about age and aging.

SOCIETIES AND MATURATIONAL DIFFERENCES

Maturational differences are selected because we want to minimize our chronocentric view of age by looking at differences in the way maturity is used socially. The question I pose is, what possible advantages are offered to a social group by encoding and defining normative behavior for individuals who differ by maturity? We should answer this question on a pan-human basis, regardless of how time and its conceptualization creates variability.

To discover how maturational differences are used, we must look at humans in comparison with nonhumans for the most telling contrast. Social hierarchy is a common organizing principle for all social groups. For both nonhuman and the simplest of human societies, hierarchy is based on differential maturation. In chimpanzee societies, males organize themselves into a dominance hierarchy based on physical strength and abilities to manipulate and threaten others. Alpha males are those in their physical prime or allied with males who are in their prime and who will support their cause. The rewards are sex and privileges of power (de Waal, 1989; Heltne & Marquardt, 1989).

But here a marked contrast must be noted. *No human society invests power in young males.* The maturation and strength of young male individuals are superseded, culturally, by strong controls regarding generation and kinship. The young are, indeed, often excluded from full adulthood (namely, parenthood) until they are socially mature and ready to replace the senior generation in social leadership. In small-scale human societies, generational differences usually work to the advantages of seniority. From an evolutionary perspective, the reasons lie in the fact that humans are cultural, whereas chimpanzees are protocultural. Humans have the abilities, through language and culture, to encode experience and to share knowledge with each other. Senior members have more experience with diverse situations and potential novelty and therefore can provide solutions that enhance group survival.

In larger-scale societies, hierarchy and stratification are based more on material accumulation by senior generations, with resulting power differentials to the disadvantage of the young. Maturational differences are by no means neutral in the quest for wealth and influence, but these favor some, although not all, older adults. In short, in cultural evolution, *generational differences* have become an important axis of social life that is more important than the physical changes associated with maturation or the decrements associated with aging.

CULTURAL MODELS OF THE LIFE COURSE

If generations are a point of departure from nonhuman populations to the development of culture and human society, then generation should be a starting point for any anthropological theory of age. Each human culture can be seen as a "theory" about how things work or as a model for living. Through the transmission of knowledge, norms, and expectations, each culture provides guidelines for generational relations, for age, and for the life course. Although much has been written about the life course, theoretically our efforts have been tentative at best.

Anthropologists use the life course as a paradigm or heuristic device to organize our research. However, we haven't given the life course the benefit of theory to classify and clarify variation on a cross-cultural basis. Using generational and cultural comparisons as our starting point, I suggest that there are three major types of cultural models or theories of the life course: (1) generational systems, (2) age class systems, and (3) staged life courses.

GENERATIONAL SYSTEMS

Generations have been discussed and recommended as fruitful beginnings in thinking about the life course (see Bengtson & Cutler, 1976; Fortes, 1984; Kertzer, 1982). Generations are based on relative time: junior and senior. Generations have very little to do with chronological time. We are reminded of this when a cousin shows up who is old enough to be an uncle or when a stepmother is young enough to be a sister. Generational time places a person—or an "ego" in anthropological terminology—in a web of relationships by seniority. First there are seniors: parents and a class of people related to parents by generation. Second, there are juniors: children and other classes of people such as nieces and nephews. Third, there equals, who are ranked by birth order (siblings and cousins). The principles can be extended up through ascending generations and down through descending generations. Relative time and the work of kinship (reproduction) places each person in a fixed web of relationships. The language of generations is kinship. Every human society has generational principles that organize all or a part of social life. For small-scale, band, and tribal societies, generations and generational placement are primary mechanisms for organizing the life course.

Age Class Systems

Age class systems have long been an interesting problem in social anthropology and have offered inspiration for theorizing about the life course. S. N. Eisenstadt (1956) introduced the phenomenon to sociological thinking about age in *From Generation to Generation* with an explicit functional theory. Later Leonard Cain (1964), in a seminal article, saw parallels for age grading, age norms, and the life course in industrial societies. Even age stratification theory drew on ethnographic cases for illustration of simpler societies (Foner & Kertzer, 1978, Kertzer, 1978, 1989). As fascinating as age classes are for models of the life course, they are not helpful as models of the life course in complex societies (Spencer, 1990). Something very different appears to be at work in these societies.

One of the first challenges in understanding age classes is their variability (see Bernardi [1985] for a classification and alternative theories). In spite of variability, the defining feature of age classes is that males are ordered hierarchically by something that would appear to be age. The appearance of age is most likely the chronocentrisim of observers, who translate the relative age into chronological terms. Thus, the literature is full of the ages of initiates and ages of transition, which are not relevant to the actors. Males are grouped by generation and pass through life together as their class ascends generationally or as their class makes the transition into the next senior class. Each class is ranked, junior or senior. Women are rarely organized into age classes.

A number of theories have been proposed to explain this, ranging from mobilization of labor to population regulation. However, when we realize that generations are the foundation of age classes, it becomes clear that age class systems are a special case of generational systems. A minimal rule is that a son must belong to a different class from that of his father. In minimizing conflict between father and son, who may be competing for the same resources, age class systems have used generations to organize the political structure of the broader community. Age classes thus are kinship and generation projected onto the larger social fabric (Fortes, 1984).

Staged Life Courses

Even more has been said about the conceptual and theoretical development of the life course perspective (see Dannefer & Uhlenberg, chapter 17 in this volume, for a review). In addition to the often cited principles (Bengtson & Allen, 1993) underlying the idea of progressions and sequences of behaviors, the life course in complex societies is (1) based on a combination of generational and chronological age and (2) understood as staged or divisible into a variable number of age grades.

Chronological age as a marker of behavior had to be invented and needed a good reason to be created. We often look to the record keeping of churches and the emergence of vital statistics and demography in Europe as the origin of chronological age as a measuring point. The Romans were among the first to use age as a defining term, for conscription into their military forces. Chronological age is clearly associated with state-level societies. Age defined chronologically becomes the basis for universalistic (in contrast to particularistic) norms in regulating a large population. Age defines the responsibilities of citizenship. With capitalism and industry, age has further been used to define adulthood and labor force participation. Legal norms prevent children from working and force them into educational institutions. Legal norms define when one can enter into adult activities—voting, military service, marriage, driving, drinking, and so on. Legal norms also define if and when one is pensionable and expected to retire from the labor force.

Legal norms gauge the life course and calibrate a social clock of role entrances and exits. At minimum there is a stage of preparation, a stage of participation, and a stage of retirement. Preparatory stages are ones of enculturation and skill acquisition for an adult life of work and a career in the labor market. What begins at home, with nurturance by parents, is completed in formal educational institutions, with finely age-graded classes defined by chronological age. Children are launched into adulthood once they have completed their schooling and have attained the chronological age defined by the legal norms of adult privilege. Especially relevant are the norms concerning age of work and age of marriage as thresholds into the stage of adult participation. Retirement from participation in the labor force is similarly guided by chronological legal norms, most notably the age of eligibility for state social security programs or pensions. In the nation-states of the industrialized world the pensionable age has arbitrarily been set at 65, with some flexibility upward or downward and exceptions for specific occupations.

Legal norms defined by the state create an understanding of life as something that is staged. Beyond the basics of preparation, participation, and retirement we find considerable variability in how the life course is refined into smaller and more defined stages. For instance, Americans, Irish, and Hong Kong Chinese, when asked to divide adulthood (participation and retirement) into age groups, saw from 1 or 2 divisions up to 10, with an average of 5 (Keith et al. 1994; see also chapter 6 by Fry). In spite of the variability in number of divisions, they represent periods life that are graded by age. Passage through the stages is ordered by chronological expectations on work, marriage, family cycles, and especially the participation of children in schools.

Visions of a postmodern life course (Featherstone & Hepworth, 1991) and an age-irrelevant society (Neugarten, 1982) have been depicted as an ideal toward which gerontology should work. Family, work, and retirement could be significantly reconfigured and redistributed across the life course (Riley, Kahn, & Foner, 1994); yet the American age norms, first investigated by Neugarten (1982), display considerable stability from the 1960s to the 1990s (Settersten & Hagestad, 1996a; 1996b). The staged life course is an institution of regulation and rationalization of the labor force (Kohli, 1986, Mayer & Muller, 1986). Where adulthood is organized by labor force participation, life courses are staged. Where participation in labor markets is marginal to sporadic, generational principles organize life.

In our Project AGE, research communities in western Ireland and Africa did not see life as divisible into age-graded stages. Wage labor in these communities did not organize adult life. Even in marginalized minority groups, generational age, not chronological norms, are more important. Among African Americans an "age of wisdom" defines successful older women. Attaining wisdom is through parenting one's own children, grandchildren, and foster children (Peterson, 1997).

AGE, VARIABLES, AND THEORIES

Age and aging are clearly temporal phenomena at the core of gerontology and theories about becoming old. But on second thought, is age really a variable? The answer is yes and no. On the negative side, age is time, and time is not a variable. Time is a property of the universe. Time never caused anything. It is what happens in time that is of importance to theories of aging. Indeed, most research on aging in biology, psychology, and the social sciences has focused on what happens in time. Bodies are transformed and societies respond to individuals who are very young and those who have been here a long time. Age becomes a variable only insofar as it is culturally conceptualized and incorporated into social life. Age also becomes a variable when a society becomes aware of its own demographics and begins to worry. As suggested above, generational time and chronological time are two ways of conceptualizing age.

If aging is what happens in time, then theories have to be focused on specific issues for a hypothesis to be generated and evaluated. A central challenge for gerontology is that so much happens in time that it is difficult to establish a paradigm to order our theories and integrate our knowledge. Aging transcends disciplinary specializations. One alternative in organizing what we know about aging is to recognize a disciplinary division of labor and try to cross boundaries in maintaining a "big picture" view of aging. That is the approach taken by academic gerontology as reflected in this volume. Another option is an applied approach to practical difficulties in old age, using relevant but fragmentary theories from appropriate disciplines. Either way, we end up with the atheoretical gerontology described by Bengtson and his colleagues (Bengtson, Burgess, & Parrott, 1997; Bengtson, Parrott, & Burgess, 1996). Perhaps a unifying paradigm is not possible or even desirable for gerontology, simply because it is so complex and multidimensional.

One of the purposes of theory is to organize what we know. Anthropology offers some distinct advantages in its emphasis on holism, comparison, and global perspective. Although anthropology as a discipline embraces all aspects of humans, biological and cultural in all times and places, my suggestions are decidedly cultural. In over a century of anthropological thought, culture remains central to our understanding of human experiences. Culture can be seen as a theory about how things work. Each society, each social group, has worked out a collective folk theory about the world, people, and relationships. As people pass through time and their social world, they forever are learning their culture and organizing their lives and groups in the process. Age and aging are a part of those theories.

The holism, comparison, and globalism of anthropological theory enhance our efforts to construct theory about age and aging. Most positive is the recognition of diversity. It is in diversity that we find the variables comprising hypothesis and theories about cultural phenomena. A challenge to the construction of theories about aging is finding the classification of diversity that is theoretically productive but at the same time does not oversimplify and stereotype. Anthropologists have dealt with this issue either in terms of regional studies or by a theoretical organization of cultural types. How we approach diversity for theories of aging is something that must be theoretically driven.

For gerontology, anthropological theories offer an enticing promise. Aging is universal. All human beings experience temporal change from birth to death. In spite of the ubiquity of age and time, how these are experienced is subject to cultural interpretation. Each culture is localized knowledge anchored in specific circumstances and relationships. A significant challenge for a theory of aging is to disentangle what is universal from what is specific and locally defined. Anthropological theories have been developed for rather basic issues of human existence, such as kinship and economic organization. For investigating problems of aging, these efforts are maturing with much promise.

AGE, AGING, AGED

Age, aging, and *aged* are three words frequently used in gerontological discourse. Sometimes they are used interchangeably; sometimes they are used to argue for theoretical advances. Certainly, gerontology began with a focus on the old—the aged. Soon we recognized that the end of life had a beginning and a connection with what goes before—aging. Finally, we called for a theory of age. Age, aging, and aged are neither interchangeable nor mark theoretical advancement. As we work toward a more sophisticated body of knowledge in gerontology, we must recognize that age, aging, and the aged are indeed three windows into the phenomena we study.

Age

Theories about age are theories about cultural and social phenomena. How are time and age conceptualized? How is age used in the regulation of social life? How does age enter into the manipulation and negotiation of daily living? As we have argued above, the connections between time and the life course are variable on a cross-cultural and perhaps on an intracultural basis. Generations, age classes, and staged life courses based on chronological norms are at least three ways in which age is understood. Each conceptualization has its causes and consequences for the people who define their lives through the respective cultural models.

Aging

Theories about aging are theories about living. These theories are organized around a life span perspective and life courses. Because so much happens in living, the list of potential research topics and theories would appear to be vast. These include questions about aging and changes in health and functionality, changes in participation in the division of labor, changes in family roles, and changes in cultural values and safety nets—all subjects for anthropological theories of aging.

For example, kinship, like age, is a universal. Families are age-heterogeneous groupings in which and through which people live all or important parts of their lives. Like aging, families change through time as the cast of characters matures, passing through adulthood and age. Domestic groups pass through a cycle of formation (marriage), expansion (children), and contraction (marriage of children). Although universal, the relationships between parents and children as they pass together through life courses and domestic cycles are by no means identical across cultures.

In small-scale egalitarian societies, parents and children remain interdependent all of their lives. Families are groups of people who have learned to work together and support their membership. Kin and the work they do comprise the safety net. Parents can expect to and do command children in the interest of their kin unit. In contrast, families in large-scale capitalist societies are only a part of the safety net. Wage labor and market economies have reduced the role of families in production. Essential goods and services may be purchased in the marketplace. Relationships between parents and children are transformed from those based on economic interdependence to those of companionship, friendship, and intimacy. Children are nurtured as individuals, to be launched into a life course (Fry, 1995). A middle-class ideal is that children will continue to develop and grow independent of parental guidance. The failed "launch" and the resultant "domestic interdependence" are by no means desirable.

Aged

Theories about the aged are theories of old age. Without the focus on late life, gerontology as we know it would disappear. This focus on late life is the culmination of age and aging. It is the realization that lives, life chances, and the consequences of how age is understood are all culturally constructed. Here our theories are most important, because they have real consequences for people who are aged. Historically, with industrialization and urbanization, old age has been defined as a problematic state. Old age is seen not only as a medical and economic problem but also as a social problem, especially in terms of social support and caregiving. As defined, however, predicaments associated with the aged have potentials for improvement.

Our theories about the aged become relevant for social policy, legislation, and political action. In politics and policy there are winners and losers. Thus, any theory about old age must account for the diversity in the cultural contexts in which older adults who are classified as problematic are actually experiencing their old age. The reasons are straightforward: (1) Is what we see as problematic really a problem? (2) Are there any strengths in the context that can be improved or supported? (3) Are there any weaknesses that can be reduced? (4) Because old age is the culmination of aging, is there any way of preventing the future old from experiencing what is seen as problematic?

Over a half-century ago, Leo Simmons (1945), in the first systematic cross-cultural analysis of the problems of aging and the aged, documented a host of complex issues and no simplistic theories. Time is not complex; time is elementary. Age, aging, and the aged are a complicated part of the human experience because they are subject to cultural interpretations.

Culture is always perplexing. As a design for living, culture is central to the way humans comprehend, negotiate, and manipulate their natural and social worlds. Culture is not a property of the universe like space or time. Consequently, we should expect complexity and diversity. Although theoretical unification and parsimony are scientific goals, culture and what happens in time may not be amenable.

Any theory explaining the puzzles of age, aging, or the aged is likely to be multifaceted and eclectic. At the same time, if we are ever to arrive at scientific explanations of age, aging, and the aged, theory is *the* essential ingredient. Explicit theory is a tool that enables us to separate cultural inventions from more general explanations. Explicit hypotheses relating study variables in a specific way not only clarify our thinking about phenomena but lead to the appropriate methods for evaluation of the relationships. The cost of relying on implicit theory is to potentially perpetuate "home-grown" cultural models as scientific generalizations.

REFERENCES

Albert, S. M., & Cattell, M. G. (1994). *Old age in global perspective: Cross-cultural and cross-national views.* New York: G. K. Hall.

Austin, C., & Loeb, M. (1982). Why age is relevant in social policy and practice. In B. Neugarten (Ed.), *Age or need? Public policies for older people* (pp. 263–288). Beverly Hills, CA: Sage Publications.

Bengtson, V. L., & Allen, K. R. (1993). The life course perspective applied to families over time. In P. Boss, W. Doherty, R. LaRossa, W. Schumm, & S. Steinmetz (Eds.), *Sourcebook of family theories and methods: A contextual approach* (pp. 469–498). New York: Plenum Press.

Bengtson, V. L., Burgess, E. O., & Parrott, T. M. (1997). Theory, explanation, and a third generation of theoretical development in social gerontology. *Journals of Gerontology: Social Sciences, 52B*(2), S72–S88.

Bengtson, V. L., & Cutler, N. E. (1976). Generations and inter-generational relations: Perspectives on age groups and social change. In R. Binstock & E. Shanas (Eds.),

The handbook of aging and the social sciences (pp. 130–159). New York: Van Nostrand Reinhold.

Bengtson, V. L., Parrott, T. M., & Burgess, E. O. (1996). Progress and pitfalls in gerontological theorizing. *Gerontologist, 36*, 768–772.

Bernardi, B. (1985). *Age class systems: Social institutions and politics based on age.* Cambridge, U.K.: Cambridge University Press.

Cain, L. D., Jr. (1964). Life course and social structure. In R. L. Faris (Ed.), *Handbook of modern sociology* (pp. 272–309). Chicago: Rand McNally.

Clark, M. M., & Anderson, B. (1967). *Culture and aging: An anthropological study of older Americans.* Springfield, IL: Charles C. Thomas.

Climo, J. J. (1992). The role of anthropology in gerontology: Theory. *Journal of Aging Studies, 6*(1), 41–56.

Cowgill, D. O. (1986). *Aging around the world.* Belmont, CA: Wadwsorth.

Cowgill, D. O., & Holmes, L. D. (Eds.). (1972). *Aging and modernization.* New York: Appleton-Century-Crofts.

de Waal, F. (1989). *Chimpanzee politics: Power and sex among apes.* Baltimore: Johns Hopkins University Press.

Eisenstadt, S. N. (1956). *From generation to generation: Age groups and social structure.* New York: Free Press.

Featherstone, M., & Hepworth, M. (1991). The mask of ageing and the postmodern life course. In M. Featherstone, M. Hepworth, & B. S. Turner (Eds.), *The body: Social process and cultural theory* (pp. 371–389). Thousand Oaks, CA: Sage Publications.

Foner, A., & Kertzer, D. I. (1978). Transitions over the life course: Lessons from age-set societies. *American Journal of Sociology, 83*, 1081–1104.

Fortes, M. (1984). Age, generation and social structure. In D. I. Kertzer & J. Keith (Eds.), *Age and anthropological theory.* (pp. 99–122). Ithaca, NY: Cornell University Press.

Fry, C. L. (1996). Age, aging and culture. In R. H. Binstock & L. K. George (Eds.), *Handbook of aging and the social sciences* (4th ed., pp. 118–136). San Diego, CA: Academic Press.

Fry, C. L. (1995). Kinship and individuation: Cross-cultural perspectives on intergenerational relations. In V. L. Bengtson, K. W. Schaie & L. M. Burton (Eds.), *Adult intergenerational relations: Effects of societal change* (pp. 126–156). New York: Springer Publishing Co.

Gell, A. (1992). *The anthropology of time: Cultural constructions of temporal constructions of temporal maps and images.* Providence, RI: Berg Publishers.

Goody, J. (1995). *The expansive moment: Anthropology in Britain and Africa, 1918–1970.* Cambridge, U.K.: Cambridge University Press.

Heltne, P. G., & Marquardt, L. A. (Eds.). (1989). *Understanding chimpanzees.* Cambridge, MA: Harvard University Press.

Keith, J. (1990). Age in social and cultural context: Anthropological perspectives. In R. H. Binstock & L. K. George (Eds.), *Handbook of aging and the social sciences* (3rd ed., pp. 91–111). San Diego, CA: Academic Press.

Keith, J., Fry, C. L., Glascock, A. P., Ikels, C., Dickerson-Putman, J., Harpending, H. C, & Draper, P. (1994). *The aging experience: Diversity and commonality across cultures.* Thousand Oaks, CA : Sage Publications.

Kertzer, D. I. (1978). Theoretical developments in the study of age-group systems. *American Ethnologist, 5,* 368–374.

Kertzer, D. I. (1982). Generation and age in cross-cultural perspective. In M. W. Riley, R. P. Abeles, & M. S. Teitelbaum (Eds.), *Aging from birth to death: Sociotemporal perspectives* (pp. 27–50). Boulder, CO: Westview Press.

Kertzer, D. I. (1989). Age structuring in comparative and historical perspective. In D. I. Kertzer & K. W. Schaie (Eds.), *Age structuring in comparative perspective* (pp. 3–20). Hillsdale, NJ: Lawrence Erlbaum Associates.

Kertzer, D. I., & Keith, J. (Eds.) (1984). *Age and anthropological theory.* Ithaca, NY: Cornell University Press.

Kohli, M. (1986). Social organization and subjective construction of the life course. In A. B. Sorensen, F. E. Weinert, & L. R. Sherrod (Eds.), *Human development and subjective construction of the life course: Multidisciplinary perspectives.* (pp. 271–292). Hillsdale, NJ: Lawrence Erlbaum Associates.

Mayer, K. U., & Muller, W. (1986). The state and the structure of the life course. In A. B. Sorensen, F. E. Weinert, & L. R. Sherrod (Eds.), *Human development and subjective construction of the life course: Multidisciplinary perspectives* (pp. 217–246). Hillsdale, NJ: Lawrence Erlbaum Associates.

Mumford, L. (1956). For older people: Not segregation, but integration. *Architectural Record, 119,* 191–194.

Neugarten, B. L. (Ed.) (1982). *Age or need? Public policies for older people.* Beverly Hills, CA: Sage Publications.

Peterson, J. W. (1997). Age of wisdom: Elderly Black women in family and church. In J. Sokolovsky (Ed.), *The cultural context of aging: Worldwide perspectives* (2nd ed., pp. 276–292). Westport, CT: Bergin & Garvey.

Riley, M. W., Kahn, R. L., & Foner, A. (Eds.). (1994). *Age and structural lag: Society's failure to provide meaningful opportunities in work, family and leisure.* New York: John Wiley & Sons.

Settersten, R. A., Jr., & Hagestad, G. O. (1996a). What's the latest? Cultural age deadlines for family transitions. *Gerontologist, 36,* 178–188.

Settersten, R. A., Jr., & Hagestad, G. O. (1996b). What's the latest? 2. Cultural age deadlines for educational and work transitions. *Gerontologist, 36,* 602–613.

Simmons, L. W. (1945). *The role of the aged in primitive society.* New Haven, CT: Yale University Press.

Sokolovsky, J. (Ed.). (1997). *The cultural context of aging: Worldwide perspectives* (2nd ed.). Westport, CT: Bergin & Garvey.

Spencer, P. (1990). The riddled course: Theories of age and its transformations. In P. Spencer (Ed.), *Anthropology and the riddle of the sphinx: Paradoxes of change in the life course* (pp. 1–34). London: Routledge.

Stocking, G. W., Jr. (1995). *After Tylor: British social anthropology, 1888–1951.* Madison: University of Wisconsin Press.

Stocking, G. W., Jr. (1996). *Volksgeist as method and ethic: Essays on Boasian ethnography and the German anthropological tradition.* Madison: University of Wisconsin Press.

16

Constructionist Perspectives on Aging

Jaber F. Gubrium
James A. Holstein

S ocial constructionism includes a number of well-established perspectives, among them phenomenology, symbolic interactionism,
and ethnomethodology (Holstein & Gubrium, 1994). They are not
conceived as causal explanations of the social world but instead focus attention on problems of meaning in everyday life. As analytic perspectives, not
theories, they provide broadly sensitizing orientations to the socially constructed features of experience, including aging. Empirically, this results in
analytic descriptions of how the social categories and forms of age enter into
everyday life, how they are managed, and how they are socially organized. If
"theory" must be the necessary term of reference for the perspectives, it
would direct research toward the broad question of *how*, not why, ordinary
persons themselves "theorize" their worlds (Gubrium & Wallace, 1990). This
chapter discusses the question and exemplifies related empirical work in
aging from these constructionist viewpoints.

ANALYTIC ASSUMPTIONS AND KEY CONCEPTS

To start, let us consider the shared analytic assumptions and highlight the
key concepts of the perspectives. Because the perspectives draw ideas from
varied philosophical traditions, there are differences in emphasis, which we
will identify in the discussion.

Subjective Orientation

First, the perspectives share a *subjective* orientation to social reality. The view that the world of experience is constructed and given reality turns them away from considerations of the relation between social objects, implicating subjectivity. As Peter Berger and Thomas Luckmann (1966) describe the social construction of reality, before the world of experience is theorized, we must figure how that world is engaged and its order assembled by its participants. For Berger and Luckmann, this is a question of commonsense knowledge, meaning how those concerned, not researchers themselves, interpret social reality. The commonplace and ordinary are stressed, not formal hypotheses or theory-testing. The leading concerns are, what is the world of experience like from the subject's point of view, how does that world come to be viewed as objectively real, and what method of procedure can we use to examine it?

Berger and Luckmann (1966) draw much of their inspiration from Alfred Schutz's (1970) social phenomenology, which bridges sociology with philosophical phenomenology. Phenomenologists argue that the relation between perception and its objects is not passive but that human consciousness actively constitutes the objects of experience. Schutz was especially interested in the way ordinary members of society construct the world of everyday life. Stressing the constitutive nature of social action, Schutz (1964) turns our attention to the social construction of the life world, that is, the objective world that every person takes for granted. From this perspective, subjectivity is paramount, as the observer deals with how the objects of the world of experience are made meaningful. The emphasis is on *how* those concerned with objects of experience, including selves as objects, apprehend and act on them as "things" set apart from themselves.

To make the constitutive nature of social action visible requires that we temporarily turn our attention from the objective world and turn to the issue of how its objects or things have come to have a sense of being real and distinct. Phenomenologists refer to the temporary change in attention as *bracketing*, a key concept. Bracketing entails setting aside one's taken-for-granted orientation to a real world of things and their relationships. All ontological judgments about the nature and essence of things are suspended. The observer can then focus on the ways in which participants of the life world themselves interpretively produce the recognizable forms they treat as real. Ethnomethodologists similarly speak of a policy of *indifference* to the realities of everyday life (Garfinkel, 1967). The researcher suspends all commitments to an a priori or privileged version of social reality, focusing instead on how its members accomplish, manage, and reproduce a sense of the real. Constructionist symbolic interactionists routinely orient to social interaction and social situations with a good dose of "operating skepticism," as

Herbert Blumer (1969) suggested in his essays on method in sociology and psychology. The procedural imperative is clear, as Everett Hughes (1984) inveighs in his discussion of institutional analysis: "The term institution, in short, suffers from an overdose of respectability, if not of hypocrisy; perhaps also from overmuch definition and classification" (p. 52). If these orientations to social reality are not identical, they nonetheless commonly point adherents in constructionist directions.

Although a subjective orientation is shared by constructionists and the *subject* is a key concept, there are differences in emphasis. Generally speaking, within social constructionisms, subjectivity does not refer to the individual subject. When social phenomenologists refer to the "intentionality" of consciousness, it does not indicate a state of mind so much as it connotes the ontologically reflexive character of action. To think or to speak is, at the same time, to discursively constitute the objects of thought and communication. Things, in other words, are always already embedded in the language used to refer to them. They are subjective in that sense. When symbolic interactionists engage their healthy social skepticism, it usually doesn't reduce to introspection, although a group of scholars has recently taken that direction (Ellis & Flaherty, 1992). Ethnomethodologists are explicit about the socially contextual quality of subjectivity and argue that the construction of reality is, from start to finish, a reflexive feature of talk and interaction (Mehan & Wood, 1975). This is not the outward expression of an "inner" mind but a practical, working outcome of something shared.

A World of Meanings

Second, the perspectives share the understanding that the world of experience is a world composed of *meanings,* not of things. To formulate theory in relation to things is to treat those things as principally constituted in a space that is essentially separate and distinct from our actions. In this context, for example, it would not be our theorization of a possible relation between aging and health that constitutes that relationship. Rather, theory would be taken as merely describing a possible relationship in a world separate from theory. What's more, in the same context, should such a relationship be tested or otherwise examined empirically, care would necessarily have to be taken that contamination between the testing apparatus and the things was minimized. The language of bias and validity warrant this sense of the separateness.

A constructed world of meanings stands in a different relationship with its conceptualization and research apparatus. Because meanings are potential things, things have no ontological status separate from how meanings work in experience. Work and retirement may be social things in scientific research literatures, but they enter into the world of experience only as things-meaningful-to-those-in-question. The hyphenation is significant and, if awkward, is nonetheless an accurate way of writing, because it signals the existential link between things and the subjective meanings that give them the status they have for those in question.

In this context, the search for scientific answers to questions of work life, say, in a community where work "doesn't come up," would be like fishing for ocean fish in a freshwater pond. Finding "data" about work in such a community would be highly suspect, suggesting that the search itself was producing the "data." Haim Hazan's (1980) ethnography of the constitution of time in a London senior center is instructive. The study highlights a world of time that is discrepant with personal experience. Although we normally think of personal experience as extending across one's lifetime, center culture collapsed this into a present-restricted time framework. Certain parts of the past were obliterated, such as one's work life, and members referred to them at their social peril. Hazan explains that this indicates the "arrest of change and the negation of the outside, changeable world." In the center's social world, work was not a "thing" of the past in the same sense as it might be in a world where it is some-thing-for-participants, where we would expect it to enter into people's references to themselves and affect, say, their self-esteem or sense of themselves at leisure.

Some constructionists orient to this world of meanings more naturalistically than others do (see Gubrium & Holstein, 1997). They aim to document the what's of such worlds, the meanings that participants have constructed for themselves in a particular time and place. Many, but not all, symbolic interactionists, for example, view the social worlds of the elderly as established in their everyday habitats. These are worlds of meaning that can be carefully entered for research purposes, studied, and the pattern of meaningful relationships documented. David Unruh's (1983) study of the "invisible" social worlds of the elderly is exemplary. Unruh describes the various, separate, and distinctly meaningful worlds in which the elderly engage, which works against a picture of uniformity. It is naturalistic because it is taken for granted that the meanings under consideration are embedded in their adherents' habitats.

At the other end of the spectrum are constructionists who stress the how's of meaning construction. Ethnomethodologists are notable in this regard, as they set aside a naturalistic orientation to worlds of meaning in order to document how those worlds are assembled and managed. They don't take for granted that meaning is established in human experience but rather ask how it is that everyday life is experienced as filled with particular meanings, how it is that members of social life experience their lives and worlds as meaningfully given and real. Social phenomenologists have similar concerns, but it is ethnomethodology that has taken the lead in developing methods of procedure for studying the construction process at work building up social reality (see Heritage, 1984; Silverman, 1997).

The common understanding is that conceptualization on the part of the researcher is less a matter of theorizing than it is an effort to formulate analytic or sensitizing vocabularies that make the social world visible on its own terms. The aim is to document the various social organizations of those terms, not to test variations in their relationships and functioning. Constructionists tend to avoid extensive theorizing, lest members' own categories or their indigenous theory-work be displaced by a priori conceptualizations. This leads to what might be described as a minimalist orientation to theorizing, which ranges from Glaser and Strauss's (1967) mimimalist formulation of grounded theory to radically self-reflexive ethnomethodological ruminations about mundane theorizing (Pollner, 1991).

Contextuality

Third, constructionists share the view that *context* organizes meaning. Meanings are not set in stone. They aren't just "out there," so to speak, things to be theorized and hypothesized about, tested or evaluated, and variously acted on. Nor, at the opposite extreme, are meanings a matter of "anything goes." They aren't whatever we desire them to be. Whereas some constructionists, especially those guided by postmodern skepticism, see meanings as free-floating significations, most constructionists are informed by the understanding that context patterns meaning in its own right, separate from meaning-making (see Rosenau, 1992).

Context is a form of ontological stability. When it is said that the meaning of something depends on its context, it implies that, whereas all things are meaningful, context fills things with particular meanings. When Hazan (1980) argues, for example, that, in the context of the London day center he studied, time stands still, making the elderly participants into "limbo people," he informs us that in that place a particular set of meanings is assigned to experience, constituting the things of experience on its own terms. Meaning in that context is relatively stable. New participants soon learn that, in the context of center activities, the time-framing of their lives will take a particular shape. As long as they are there, experience takes on certain meanings. Renée Rose Shield's (1988) study of daily life in an American nursing home treats context similarly. In Shield's case, meaning-making in the context of the nursing home is viewed as an uneasy set of lived tensions between being at home and being hospitalized. The context presents a continuous tug-of-war between home and hospital as cultural categories.

Here, too, there are differences in emphasis among constructionists. Some view context in global terms and stress patterning, which highlights stability. At that end of the spectrum, contexts of meaning can take on a thing-like status, references to them signifying real and solid conditions of meaning that shape, if not actually determine, people's lives. The term *culture* is sometimes used in this way. As a distinct and stable set of shared meanings, culture is said to make people what they are, formulating their identities and lives in its terms. Those whose lives are in question are depicted as agents with very little to say in the process, designating them as virtual "cultural dopes" (Garfinkel, 1967). At the other end of the spectrum are construction-ists who view context in more fluid terms, taking the stability of meaning as something accomplished, not settled. Clifford Geertz (1983) gives culture this emphasis, describing participants as continually "spinning the webs of significance" that give culture its varied meanings. Ethnomethodologists are especially keen on documenting culture-producing activities in the making. Their orientation is to what ethnomethodologists call the "reflexive" and "indexical," or *mutually constitutive,* facets of meaning and context, which centers attention at the very heart of the construction process.

EXEMPLARY RESEARCH

These assumptions and key concepts are empirically realized in different ways within the various constructionisms. All apply a variety of qualitative methods, but their analytic aims and vocabularies differ (Gubrium & San-kar, 1994). For example, although some share the method of participant observation, their analytic orientation to empirical materials can be quite distinct. One perspective may focus on naturalistically describing the social organization of a particular social setting, such as a retirement community; another may consider how retirement is put together and managed as a local image of setting activities. The following exemplary studies provide a flavor of the differences. We begin by presenting symbolic interactionist research on the management of identity in old age and move on to examples of gerontological research with phenomenological and ethnomethodological orientations. The rapidly developing perspective of narrative analysis, which borrows from various constructionisms, also will be exemplified. Pseud-onyms for persons and places are used in all of the studies.

Identity Management

One of the most extensive areas of research in aging is the social construc-tion of identity. From traditional studies of role definition (Marshall, 1986) to deconstructions of aging and identity (Gubrium, Holstein, & Buckholdt, 1994; Hazan, 1994; Katz, 1996), the leading questions here are, who is the aged person and how are answers to the question managed in everyday life? Symbolic interactionists are apt to focus on identity management within a particular context of meaning such as age, whereas ethnomethodologists emphasize how various defining contexts, including the category of age, are used to designate applicable identities in particular social situations.

Sarah Matthews's (1979) research on the management of self-identity among old women is an exemplary study from a symbolic interactionist perspective. Her point of departure is Erving Goffman's (1959) concept of stigma, from which she argues that the category of old is likewise devalued in contemporary society. The old women she interviewed are continuously subjected to the stereotypic associations of this stigma, which include images of infirmity, senility, and worthlessness. In making her point, Matthews quotes from a local newspaper article, which is deeply discrediting.

> Sunday concerts of the Sacramento Symphony are Little Old Lady matinees: Scores of L.O.L.'s in their cloth coats with fur collars, tottering in pairs to their seats. It's not that there aren't plenty of students and other people in the audience—just that the L.O.L.'s seem to be the most noticeable element. Fortunately, the concert on Sunday, January 14, did not reflect the rather stodgy tastes of L.O.L.'s. (p. 62)

As Mike Featherstone and Mike Hepworth (1990) later argue, old people are perennially subject to these "masks of aging," behind which they personally cope with questions of who they actually are and how to relate that to what they are perceived as being.

Matthews (1979) uses a grounded theory approach to uncover the strategies used by a sample of old women to sustain positive identities. Some of the strategies are rhetorical: the older woman assembles her identity to present herself to others in a positive light, contrasting who she is with what many in her social category discredit. One strategy used by the women is to "suppress evidence" of age. As one respondent notes, "I don't think they know my age. I don't ask them theirs. People don't think I'm as old as I am, so I don't go around blabbin' it" (p. 74). Another strategy is to argue for different definitions of age, separating the age category that masks of aging assign from what inner definitions convey. One woman put it this way, "In the old vintage, eighty was the little black bonnet affair and that sort of thing. I don't think we should think of age chronologically at all. It's your outlook more than anything else" (p. 75). The use of others' testaments to one's age are a third strategy, such as suggesting that "other reputable people do not think of me as old."

Some strategies are more situational: the older woman manages her whereabouts to avoid circumstances that can threaten her identity. Several of the women stated that they organize their daily activities so that they never find themselves in situations that make them appear old. One explained, for example, that she avoids going to K-Mart when school is out because she risks being demeaned by the young people, especially "the way they look at you." Others carefully planned ahead so that, should they find themselves in potentially discrediting circumstances, they wouldn't come off negatively. For example, one woman deliberately left her umbrella in her car even though there was going to be a downpour, because, as the woman explained to others, "I thought you'd laugh at me if I brought it in—old grandma with her raincoat and her boots."

Still other strategies are self-presentational, in which the old woman presents an identity to herself different from what the category of old usually designates. One of these strategies effectively degerontologizes "elderly" behavior. As one respondent explained, "I used to be able to watch television. Now I fall asleep in the middle of the darn show. . . . But my son-in-law, Bob, he's half my age, and he falls asleep" (p. 80). Another of these self-presentational strategies is to attach new meaning to old activities, such as to redefine former leisure activities such as playing bridge as parts of very busy days. Yet another of these strategies is to subjectively reorient oneself from being old and dependent to being useful. As one woman stated, speaking of her daughter, "I have to depend on her for transportation, but she depends on me an awful lot. I still feel useful because if anybody is sick, or she gets behind on her ironing or something like that, she comes and gets me to help her" (p. 89).

The context of identity management can extend beyond the strategic. Certain settings have particular subjective meanings attached to them that mediate identity construction in their own right. For example, respondents who identified themselves as "newcomers" to the settings in which they resided, which were reserved for seniors, differed in their self-designations from those who identified themselves as "residents." Matthews (1979) explains that the newcomers typically felt old on becoming residents, whereas the established residents' identities were organized around different meanings, suggesting that there is likely to be a cycle of identity attribution when one moves into a new setting.

> The resident has a reputation; the newcomer is not so lucky. She arrives on the scene already old. Her move to the setting was probably precipitated by a negatively evaluated status passage [such as recent retirement or physical infirmity]. . . . The most salient characteristic of newcomers, then, is their oldness and their imputed, and often accepted, devalued status as no longer independent, financially, emotionally, or physically. (pp. 97–98)

Social Worlds

One of the authors, Jay Gubrium (1975/1997), made an ethnographic study of the social organization of care in a nursing home he called "Murray Manor" that turned constructionism's subjective orientation in a different direction. Whereas Matthews's (1979) subject is a category of person seen from the viewpoint of a stigmatized configuration of roles, Gubrium's subjects are the various everyday perspectives located within a particular long-term care facility. Gubrium's fieldwork showed that the meanings assigned to living and dying at the Manor were not homogeneous but constructed from the perspectives of its major categories of participant. He used the phenomenological concept of "worlds" to show how the nursing home, although a single organization, organized different worlds of meaning for administrative staff ("top staff"), front-line workers ("floor staff"), and the residents.

A social world is a broader context than a role. The concept *world* signifies social wholeness and perceptional borders. We might say, for example, that a group's world is limited to family, suggesting that anything outside of this realm of experience is irrelevant to the group members. Such persons organize their activities around family life, think of their past in those terms, and plan for the future in the same way. As a context, a social world is an entire perspective on everyday life, one that not only constructs identities but also conveys images of others and reasonable courses of action. It is an important concept because it suggests that, as we attempt to understand people's lives, we might well consider that there are experiential borders to what they think, feel, and do, that not everyone in effect constructs matters such as living and dying in the same way.

Worlds are the operating frameworks that make what participants do immediately reasonable in their everyday lives. To be part of a little world, for example, is to assume that what one and others do in the context of that world makes sense. Members of a world don't have to offer excuses or otherwise account for what they think, feel, and do. As members, they interact with each other in quite understandable terms. When worlds collide, and they regularly do in such close quarters as formal organizations, it not only disrupts working assumptions but is a clash between different senses of everyday reasonableness. A group of friends who live in their own little world not only have constructed a border that reasonably organizes their sentiments and social relations, but the border, for better or worse, also shields them from the reasoning of other worlds. As long as borders are intact and worlds remain relatively separate from each other, their respective members conduct their lives and interact in terms of their own shared understandings.

This is how Gubrium (1975/1997) came to view daily life at Murray Manor. Patterns of talk and social interaction attendant to living and dying showed that a single facility organized different worlds of conduct for their respective participants, the separate worlds of top staff, floor staff, and residents. A single organization, in other words, contained distinct worlds of meaning and, perhaps of greater significance in an evaluatory context, separate ways of acting reasonably. In that regard, Murray Manor was far from simply being just *an* organization or *a* better or worse nursing home. It was different organizations in practice, each with its own working sense of what it meant to be effective.

The daily lives and work of administrators, floor staff, and residents offered remarkably different perspectives on the meaning of care and caregiving. As well-intentioned as the top staff were found to be, they worked in a separate world from floor staff. What top staff saw as good and efficient caregiving, floor staff could resentfully consider "just getting the job done." Regular references by the floor staff to "them," meaning the administrative staff, conveyed a sense of being outside important channels of decision making affecting their work. What a resident felt was time well spent chatting with a friendly nurse's aide could, from the aide's point of view, be time away from her duties. The aide, after all, was not only providing care but also doing a job. Comments such as "we" know what we want, meaning what residents desire as opposed to that staff considers is best for "them," signaled a shared reasonableness among equals, that outsiders couldn't, or perhaps wouldn't, understand.

The indigenous reasonableness of these separate worlds was not only secured by perspective but by what Gubrium (1975/1997) called "place." By and large, top staff conducted their daily affairs in their offices and in meetings. Those places helped to keep their world separate and distinct from other worlds, its knowledge and sense of what is reasonable intact and unchallenged. Floor staff, especially nurse's aides, spent most of their work lives on resident floors, caring for and mingling with the residents and each other. Rarely did they attend patient care conferences, nor did they otherwise much enter into top staff's world. The residents, too, carried on life in their own places: their own rooms, the dining areas, lounges, and other locations on their floors. The residents were further subdivided into informal friendship circles, cliques, and mutually supportive dyads, which formed their own little worlds and customary places of interaction. In contrast to top staff, floor staff and residents regularly came into contact with each other. As a result, their worlds were more likely to collide than top and floor staff's, causing the usual kinds of related incidents and complaints. As long as worlds operated in separate places, these troubles were at a minimum. But they usually didn't operate that way, which caused routine clashes about what was reasonable.

Not only did those who worked, lived, and died at Murray Manor construct different worlds, which variously operated in separate places, but the result was a setting housing distinct moral universes. Although Gubrium (1975/1997) doesn't develop this concept in his ethnography, it does have important implications for how we evaluate the quality of care and life. Existing approaches homogenize worlds and moral universes into uniform definitions of quality, largely centered on administrative and/or legal criteria (see Gubrium, 1993). Constructionist analysis shows, on the contrary, that such homogenization is empirically unfair and produces concise and enforceable policy based on social fiction.

Narratives of Aging

A variety of commentators has noted that experience is not just lived but is continually shaped by how it is conveyed (Gubrium & Holstein, 1998). Narrative analysis is a very popular way of approaching experience through the examination of personal stories and storytelling. A number of gerontological researchers has shown that the personal story and other forms of individual narrative construct and reconstruct lifelong experiences in relation to ongoing developments in people's daily living (Birren, Kenyon, Ruth, Schroots, & Svensson, 1996). From diverse quarters, we are now being empirically convinced that the personal past has not simply gone by but is continually lived out in new terms as its storytellers speak of life. The present and the future, too, are implicated, as narrative unpacks and designs experience in relation to time as a whole.

The subjective is clearly at hand here. For some, the inventive individual storyteller is the focus of attention, a subject who actively, creatively constructs experience in the telling. Introspective skills can be of central concern, the emphasis on the free play of narration at times excessive (see Ellis & Bochner, 1996). For others the view is of a narrator who is him-or herself subject to the larger forces of storytelling, such as historical events that shape both how stories are told and what is conveyed (see Bertaux, 1981). The difference in emphasis results in deeply personalized narratives on the one hand and detailed subjective accounts of historical events on the other. Context varies accordingly. Those constructionists who emphasis the introspective skills of the storyteller can produce highly idiosyncratic contexts for telling lives. In contrast, constructionists who link storytelling to social forces tend to formulate overly typified historical contexts for the experiences in question.

We have chosen Sharon Kaufman's (1986) book *The Ageless Self* to exemplify narrative analysis in gerontology. Although Kaufman does not especially draw from any one of the constructionist perspectives we have discussed, she is concerned with how people's lives, especially the aging experience, are subjectively assembled, and she explicitly addresses the issue of contextual emphasis. As Kaufman explains, "I wanted to look at the meaning of aging to elderly people themselves, as it emerges in their personal reflections on growing old" (p. 5). Kaufman finds that her respondents construct and fashion their own accounts of aging, separate from the varied contexts that embed them in history. As Kaufman emphasizes, "The old Americans I studied do not perceive meaning in aging itself; rather, they perceive meaning in being themselves in old age" (p. 6).

Kaufman (1986) asks two questions in analyzing her data: What thematizes the life stories of these older Americans and from what do they draw meaning to construct their accounts? Sixty people participated in the open-ended interviews, important elements of which were organized around the life story. Kaufman focuses on three of her respondents to highlight the construction process. Their narratives show how personally inventive people are in assembling their lives. Millie, who is 80 years old and had been living in a nursing home before Kaufman met her, constructed her story around affective ties. Kaufman explains that most of the conversations she had with Millie over the course of the 8 months she interviewed her, centered on her emotional relations—her likes and dislikes, who she is attracted to, cares for, or loves. Millie uses the word *attach* repeatedly in her narrative: "I grew very attached to him and he to me." "I am so attached to her." "We developed an attachment to one another" (p. 33). The term *love,* too, is part of her vocabulary, embellishing the affectivity theme.

Ben and Stella present different themes. Ben, who is 74 years old, presents a dichotomous self in his story. According to Ben, his life has been a battle between his sober and responsible side and his carefree, romantic side. The theme crops up repeatedly as he talks of his past, his present, and the years to come. At one point he speaks of looking into the mirror and seeing his father, who, he explains, was "a very serious," "no-nonsense guy." Ben explains that that's the kind of image he conveys to the world, even though, he points out, "I don't *feel* that way. I feel carefree and happy . . . and I could easily slide or slip into a romantic adventure" (p. 48). Other themes are his need for financial security and his religion. Stella was born in 1897 in the rural South. The central theme of her life story is her achievement orientation. According to Stella, "I don't look back at all. I only look forward to what I'm going to do next." Even her past is something she competes with, not something she longs for. A second theme relates to the first: her aesthetic sense and need for perfection. Stella links both themes with a need for relationships, which, she explains, prompts her to create new roles for herself.

Although there are various ways these lives are given meaning, they have two important things in common. One is that none of them is thematized in terms of old age. Age comes up in the accounts or is brought up by the interviewer, but it is linked with more central anchor points. Another important commonality, which works against the idea that subjectivity is significantly mediated by larger social forces, is the lack of any emphasis on major historical events in the narratives. The two world wars and the Depression were key events in the lives of all 60 study participants, yet they draw very selectively from these events in assembling their narratives. It is evident that these lives narratively unfold in the meaning-making context of *active* storytellers, whose constructive skills communicate experience in varied and sundry ways, far removed from what a "late life" story might typically be.

Using Age to Construct Context

If Kaufman (1986) shows how the elderly select from contexts other than old age to thematize their stories, author Jim Holstein's (1990) ethnomethodological study of involuntary mental commitment hearings illustrates how age is applied to create locally useful contexts for interpreting conduct. Holstein's subjects are the judges, attorneys, consultants, witnesses, and candidate patients who use various features of the patient's life, including age, to give meaning to his or her conduct in relation to a commitment decision. An important question is how is age used in building a case for or against involuntary commitment.

Holstein (1990) reverses the typical research concern with age, not treating it as a background variable affecting the likelihood of involuntary commitment but rather as a condition that is selectively applied to construct a background or context for decision making. Emphasis is on the local management of age as an interpretive context. We are shown how standard background factors serve to assemble explanations, not to explain life events in their own right.

Holstein's (1990) empirical material is especially relevant for illustrating how an ethnomethodological perspective orients to theories of aging. He draws from the material to show how members of everyday social settings, such as an involuntary mental commitment hearings, themselves theorize old age. As Gubrium and Wallace (1990) have argued, gerontological theorizing is not exclusively gerontologists' stock-in-trade but is part and parcel of folk explanations of aging. Holstein illustrates how vernacular versions of disengagement and activity theories, for example, are used by judges in two different hearings as accounts or explanatory contexts for their decisions. As the following extracts from these hearings show, the theories in use are ways of constructing a context for action, rather than being the researcher's explanation for the causes or consequences of aging.

The following extract from proceedings at "Metropolitan Court," one of the commitment hearing settings studied, shows a version of disengagement theory being applied by a judge to construct a context warranting a decision against further hospitalization. Candidate patient Henry Brewer's hospitalization was initially ordered because his family believed he was, in their words, "depressed" and "responding badly" to his recent retirement. A psychiatrist had testified that Brewer was, in the psychiatrist's words, "withdrawn" and "suffered from acute depression." After being assured that medications would control these conditions, the judge nonetheless assimilates Brewer's behaviors to his own "theory" of aging, in effect normalizing Brewer's conduct by casting it as the inevitable withdrawal associated with aging. As a native disengagement theorist, the judge suggests that Brewer's increasing detachment from prior roles and activities is, in a sense, typical of persons entering the later years.

> I'm going to release Mr. Brewer if he'll agree to move back in with his daughter. It's pretty clear that he's slowing down a bit, but that's to be expected from a man his age. I think we just have to leave him to his own small pleasures and not worry so much about what he doesn't do anymore. As long as he's not causing anyone any trouble, and he's happy spending his time by himself, I don't see any reason for further hospitalization. We really can't expect him to keep up with the old pace if he doesn't feel up to it. (p. 124)

Compare this with the native gerontological theorizing implicit in an extract from similar material gathered at "Eastern Court." In this case, Dwight Berry's involuntary commitment is under consideration, and the extract illustrates a different explanatory context being constructed by the judge for his decision, one more reminiscent of activity theory.

> Mr. Berry hasn't been responding very well to his [mental] disability and I'm afraid he's not ready to leave [the psychiatric treatment center]. I think part of it is something we're all going to go through someday. Here's an older man who's not working, and now everyone wants to take care of him and he's been taking care of them all his life. He's having trouble figuring out what to do with himself. He might be okay in a retirement home, but I don't think he's ready for that yet. I like the idea of keeping him at Willowhaven [the psychiatric treatment center] because they've got all of those programs to try to get him involved. I'm hoping they can fit him into one of their vocational programs and get him on track, give him something to do that he can care about. Maybe then we can talk about a [retirement] home placement. (p. 124)

Here the judge views Berry's problems in terms of the typical difficulties of adjusting to the changing (and reduced) opportunities and demands of old age, in the judge's words, "something we're all going to go through someday." Berry has lost his well-defined roles due, in part, to his age, which, in the judge's opinion, can be addressed, by "[giving] him something to do that he can care about." The ending phrase, "that he can care about," suggests an activity that has a positive function. In contrast to the Brewer case, the judge here assembles an account justifying further remedial intervention rather than benign inattention.

At times, commitment hearing participants disagree about how to classify a candidate patient in terms of age, which focuses proceedings on the construction of age itself, not explanations of aging. Note how the local meaning of 51-year-old candidate patient Lois Kaplan's age emerges in her commitment hearing in "Northern Court." Kaplan's public defendant initially argued that

> a woman her age should do just fine in a board-and-care facility because she's gotten to the point where she's not likely to be too difficult to look after. She seems to have stabilized and at her age she's not likely to go looking for trouble. The best part about Crestview [the board-and-care facility] is she'll be able to live on her own but there'll be someone there to look after her. She's at a point in her life where that won't take much. (p. 125)

The judge is skeptical about the public defendant's claims and presents his own gloss on Kaplan's age.

> [To the public defendant] I'm not sure that I agree with you, Mr. Lyle. The problem with getting older is you sometimes need a little more attention. Little things seem like major problems. They seem to get out of hand a lot quicker. I know I have to do a lot more for my own mother now than just a couple of years ago. As far as I know, Crestview is a fine facility, but their policy is for residents to be able to pretty much do it on their own. I'm not convinced that Lois won't need more help than they can give her. (p. 125)

There was no disagreement here about Kaplan's place in the life course; everyone agreed she was "getting older." The disagreement, rather, centered on the implications this held for her manageability.

There were several further exchanges about Kaplan's age, specifically concerning how getting older related to how well Crestview could handle Kaplan's problems. The two perspectives were repeated and larded with related arguments. Eventually, the judge took a different tack:

> You know what's bothering me? I think it's the fact that we're talking about letting an older woman live alone, even if there is someone looking in on her. I can't help but worry that she's going to do something and nobody's going to notice until it's too late. It's so easy for someone like her—mental problems, getting a little older, not able to do everything she once did—to do something that might really be dangerous, something that could hurt her real bad. (p. 126)

In this extract, the judge transfers his concern from manageability to vulnerability, in the process reconstructing the meaning of Kaplan's age. In this context, "getting a little older" means that Kaplan is more susceptible to harm.

Over the course of these hearings, it became evident that age had no definitive meaning. Rather, it was used in a variety of ways to build contexts for the matters under consideration. In turn, these contexts supplied warrantable answers to questions of age, aging, and related issues of how to interpret the aging process. From the specification of "theories" of aging to transformations of age, interpretive practice sheds light on how context constructs meaning.

NEW DIRECTIONS

These varied perspectives continue to develop, adding to a growing fund of empirical knowledge. But there are new directions as well, which promise to further diversify and enrich the approach. Just as the postmodern debate, with its leading concern for theoretical reflexivity, has turned those engaged in theoretical work to ask how the social world itself informs what is theorized about it, constructionists have become increasingly self-conscious about the relation between analytic vocabularies, method, and the empirical world.

There has been extensive debate among constructionists over the meaning of the term *social construction* (Holstein & Miller 1993). Although the debate only marginally bears on gerontological topics, it nonetheless has tremendous implications for how such topics would develop both analytically and empirically. The debate largely centers on a question that has festered in the constructionist bailiwick from the start: If the social world is to be analytically opened to subjective formulation and the resulting empirical free play that implies, how are we to understand patterning in social life? Responses seem to fall along a continuum from advocating even more free play to advocating less, forming an uneasy alliance for doing qualitative research.

At the greater-free-play end of the continuum are constructionists who have distinct romanticist leanings. From the beginning they have focused on the way sentiments, feelings, and values mediate the social construction of experience (Douglas & Johnson, 1977). Empirical work has centered on the affective underpinnings of everyday life, emphasizing especially the need to develop methods of procedure that allow often hidden "emotional wellsprings" to be recognized and empirically documented. The earlier work in the area viewed the free play of feelings to be a integral, if not foundational, feature of experience and aimed to demonstrate the intensively irrational underlife of the reasonable surface of social order. Later romanticist constructionists have moved toward greater free play by incorporating postmodern sensibilities. The emphasis on greater free play here stems as much from a radically reflexive openness to the theoretical sources of the empirical world, as from a related, empirically foundational view of feelings. Methodological innovation is encouraged, relaxing the traditional boundary between theory and data (Ellis & Flaherty, 1992; Ellis & Bochner, 1996).

At the other end of the continuum are constructionists who have more rationalist leanings, even though ethnomethodologists especially eschew such analytic polarities. Early ethnomethodological work stressed the artful but methodical ways in which social order is constructed (Garfinkel, 1967). This was empirically realized in two ways. Some ethnomethodologists applied methods of participant observation to document the "ethnomethods" that members of social situations used to establish a sense of order in everyday life. Conversation analysts focused more on talk and interaction, examining their empirical material to show how the sequential machinery of talk served to systematically construct social reality in its own right. The most recent work in the area increasingly attends to the "external" institutional mediations of talk and interaction (Drew & Heritage, 1992). Some constructionists have formulated an analytic basis for reincorporating naturalistic and explanatory concerns into the rationalist equation (Gubrium & Holstein, 1997).

In between are other promising developments. The analysis of personal stories is a burgeoning area of interest. No longer are stories considered to more or less present the experiences they convey; it is increasingly recognized that the process of storytelling itself works to construct lives, which otherwise remain untold. The subjective here is also center stage, as researchers uncover the various ways that narrative works to construct experience. Still, the emphasis on narrative composition may now be excessive, overshadowing the local and practical conditioning of storytelling (Gubrium & Holstein, 1998). Other important developments that variously locate themselves along the continuum are feminist contributions (Harding 1987; Hekman, 1990), what has come to be called "queer theory" (Seidman, 1996), and African-American and ethnic perspectives (see, e.g., Collins, 1989). All aim to broaden significantly the working horizons of what it means to socially construct reality.

As constructionist perspectives continue to develop across this continuum, the heart of the orientation to everyday life has been and will continue to be focused on the question of how social categories and social forms develop and enter into experience. In a word, to construct is to *produce*, to work at the constitution of the world we live in, including aging as a set of categorical features of that world. The 21st century will move constructionism in various directions along the continuum we have described, but it will remain centered on the various processes by which the categories and structures of people's lives are assembled, managed, and sustained. Some constructionist analytics will increasingly offer modes of explanation focused on how the interplay between reality-constituting activities and variable conditions of possibility (Foucault, 1975) provide for the meaningful organization of everyday realities (see Gubrium & Holstein, 1997). As constructionist perspectives, they will stop short, however, of formulating causal models or predictive theories.

Newly emerging skeptical postmodernist insights (Rosenau 1992) might also move some constructionist perspectives in the direction of obviating broad theoretical formulations altogether as they continue to question the very possibility of both "theory" and "the empirical" itself. This presents constructionist researchers on aging with an extraordinarily broad horizon of choices regarding their analytic projects, methodological approaches, and end results.

REFERENCES

Berger, P. L., & Luckmann, T. (1966). *The social construction of reality.* Garden City, NY: Doubleday.

Bertaux, D. (Ed.). (1981. *Biography and society.* Newbury Park, CA: Sage.

Birren, J. E., Kenyon, G. M., Ruth, J-E, Schroots, J. J. F., & Svensson, T. (Eds.). (1996). *Aging and biography: Explorations in adult development.* New York: Springer Publishing Co.

Blumer. H. (1969). *Symbolic interactionism.* Englewood Cliffs, NJ: Prentice-Hall.

Collins, P. H. (1989). *Black feminist thought.* Boston: Unwin Hyman.

Douglas, J., & Johnson, J. (Eds.). (1977). *Existential sociology.* New York: Cambridge University Press.

Drew, P., & Heritage, J. (1992). *Talk at work.* Cambridge, U.K.: Cambridge University Press.

Ellis, C., & Bochner, A. (Eds.). (1996). *Composing ethnography.* Walnut Creek, CA: Altamira Press.

Ellis, C., & Flaherty, M. (Eds.). (1992). *Investigating subjectivity.* Newbury Park, CA: Sage.

Featherstone, M., & Hepworth, M. (1990). Images of ageing. In J. Bond & P. Coleman (Eds.), *Ageing in society* (pp. 250–275). London: Sage.

Foucault, M. (1975). *The birth of the clinic.* New York: Vintage.

Garfinkel, H. (1967). *Studies in ethnomethodology.* Englewood Cliffs, NJ: Prentice-Hall.

Geertz, C. (1983). *Local knowledge.* New York: Basic.

Glaser, B., & Strauss, A. (1967). *The discovery of grounded theory.* Chicago: Aldine.

Goffman, E. (1959). *The presentation of self in everyday life.* Garden City, NY: Doubleday.

Gubrium, J. F. (1993). *Speaking of life: Horizons of meaning for nursing home residents.* Hawthorne, NY: Aldine de Gruyter.

Gubrium, J. F. (1997). *Living and dying at Murray Manor.* Charlottesville: University Press of Virginia. (First published in 1975)

Gubrium, J. F., & Holstein, J. A. (1997). *The new language of qualitative method.* New York: Oxford University Press.

Gubrium, J. F., & Holstein, J. A. (1998). Narrative practice and the coherence of personal stories. *Sociological Quarterly, 39,* 163–187.

Gubrium, J. F., Holstein, J. A., & Buckholdt, D. (1994). *Constructing the life course.* Dix Hills, NY: General Hall.

Gubrium, J. F., & Sankar, A. (Eds.). (1994). *Qualitative methods in aging research.* Newbury Park, CA: Sage.

Gubrium, J. F., & Wallace, J. B.. (1990). Who theorizes age? *Ageing and Society, 10,* 131–149.

Harding, S. (Ed.). (1987). *Feminism and methodology.* Bloomington: Indiana University Press.

Hazan, H. (1980). *The limbo people.* London: Routledge.

Hazan, H. (1994). *Old age: Constructions and deconstructions.* Cambridge, U.K.: Cambridge University Press.

Hekman, S. J. (1990). *Gender and knowledge: Elements of postmodern feminism.* Boston: Northeastern University Press.

Heritage, J. (1984). *Garfinkel and ethnomethodology.* Cambridge, U.K.: Polity.

Holstein, J. A. (1990). The discourse of age in involuntary commitment proceedings. *Journal of Aging Studies, 4,* 111–130.

Holstein, J. A., & .Gubrium, J. F. (1994). Phenomenology, ethnomethodology, and interpretive practice. In N. K. Denzin & Y. S. Lincoln (Eds.), *Handbook of qualitative research* (pp. 262–272). Newbury Park, CA: Sage.

Holstein, J., & Miller, G. (Ed.). (1993). *Reconsidering social constructionism.* Hawthorne, NY: Aldine de Gruyter.

Hughes, E. C. (1984). *The sociological eye.* New Brunswick, NJ: Transaction Books.

Katz, S. (1996). *Disciplining old age: The formation of gerontological knowledge.* Charlottesville: University Press of Virginia.

Kaufman, S. (1986). *The ageless self.* Madison: University of Wisconsin Press.

Marshall, V. W. (Ed.). (1986). *Later life: A social psyhology of aging.* Newbury Park, CA: Sage.

Matthews, S. (1979). *The social world of old women: Management of self identity.* Newbury Park, CA: Sage.

Mehan, H., & Wood, H. (1975). *The reality of ethnomethodology.* New York: Wiley.

Pollner, M. (1991). Left of ethnomethodology: The rise and fall of radical reflexivity. *American Sociological Review, 56,* 370–380.

Rosenau, P. M. (1992). *Postmodernism and the social sciences.* Princeton, NJ: Princeton University Press.

Schutz, A. (1964). *Studies in social theory.* The Hague: Martinus Nijhoff.

Schutz, A. (1970). *On phenomenology and social relations.* Chicago: University of Chicago Press.

Seidman, S. (Ed.). (1996). *Queer theory/sociology.* Cambridge, MA: Blackwell.

Shield, R. R. (1988). *Uneasy Endings: Daily life in an American nursing home.* Ithaca, NY: Cornell University Press.

Silverman, D. (Ed.). (1997). *Qualitative research: Theory, method and practice.* London: Sage.

Unruh, D. (1983). *Invisible lives: Social worlds of the aged.* Newbury Park, CA: Sage.

17

Paths of the Life Course: A Typology

Dale Dannefer
Peter Uhlenberg

S ocial scientists who study the life course face the challenge of dealing with a subject matter of which everyone already has extensive "knowledge." Every individual possesses personal knowledge of her own life experiences, as well as knowledge about the lives of those in the social convoy with whom she travels through life (Kahn & Antonucci, 1980). And innumerable popular accounts by journalists and other critics inform us about the distinctive life course trajectories of the baby boom generation or generation X. The society at large, as well as much of the scientific community, holds widely shared beliefs about the distinctiveness of various life stages, which are often assumed to represent reliable "truths" of human nature: children are helpless and innocent; adolescents tend to engage in risky (indeed, deviant and criminal) behavior; young adults should settle down in families and careers; middle-aged persons face crises regarding the direction of their lives; the oldest members of a society are feeble and approaching death. Anyone conversant in the sociology of aging will immediately recognize such statements as cohort-centric and ethnocentric clichés that cannot withstand scrutiny as transcultural or transhistorical universals, despite their popular status as "factual depictions" of age differences.

A challenge to cohort-centric thinking occurred with the discovery in the late 1950s and early 1960s of dramatic differences in patterning between cross-sectional age comparisons and longitudinal patterns. These findings were an early empirical indication that the life course trajectories of most human characteristics were neither as obvious nor as inevitable as had often been assumed. Generalizations about age differences drawn from cross-sectional age patterns became suspect as representing nothing but the piling up of remarkably different cohorts at a single point in time. Actual human trajectories were seen to lack the predictability and rigidity that characterized the temporally precise and sequenced stages assumed by the standard paradigm of developmental biology (after which the organismic theories of developmental psychology and sociological functionalism were patterned [Buckley, 1967; Dannefer, 1984; Morss, 1990]).

The conceptual, methodological and analytical consequences following from the discovery that life course patterns could not be safely inferred from cross-sectional data is well known. The cohort concept was introduced into social science discourse by Ryder (1965), and cohort location was established as a central variable in both psychological and sociological analyses (e.g., Baltes & Schaie, 1968; Elder, 1974; Riley & Foner, 1968; Schaie, 1965). Cohort flow was identified as a ubiquitous social process that gave a new dynamism to the understanding of the constitution of societal age structure (Riley, Johnson, & Foner, 1972) as well as to the forces impinging on individuals as they moved through the life course (cf. Cain, 1964; Clausen 1972).

Explication of the cohort concept helped to stimulate an explosion of historical (Achenbaum, 1979; Fisher, 1977; Hareven, 1977; Modell, Furstenberg, & Strong, 1978), social-psychological (Bengtson, 1973; Elder, 1974), demographic (Glick, 1977; Hogan, 1981; Uhlenberg, 1977), and sociological research that demonstrated the fruitfulness of cohort analysis. Such work made it clear that cohorts differ in their age trajectories on a wide array of characteristics, from health, intelligence, and attitudes to income, lifestyle, and relationships. In response to these findings an analytical paradigm was forged in which age-specific *cohort* characteristics are treated as dependent variables, and the birth date of the cohort becomes, at least for purposes of analysis, the master independent variable.

In the decades since, research and theorizing about the life course has proliferated, stimulated by practical concerns (e.g., population "graying" in postindustrial societies), availability of new data (including large, high-quality longitudinal data sets), and methodological advances. As a consequence, methodologically sophisticated analyses focused on highly specific (albeit timely and interesting) questions have outpaced efforts at systematic theorizing (Bengtson, Burgess, & Parrott, 1997; Lynott & Lynott, 1996). Especially noteworthy has been the absence of a genuinely sociological approach to what is, at the level of surface description, manifestly and undeniably an individual phenomenon—the aging and life course patterning of human individuals.

This chapter offers a general sociological perspective on the study of the life course. It consists of two major components. The first sets forth the required founding premises—first principles—of a sociology of the life course and identifies problems in life course analysis that derive from the neglect of these first principles. The second component offers a typology based on the *explananda* and *explanans* of life course theory, with special reference to the explanatory potentials of life course theory.

FOUNDING PREMISES OF LIFE COURSE THEORY AND PROBLEMS DERIVING FROM THEIR NEGLECT

The first principles concern social interaction and social structure but not in isolation from the developing human organism. Indeed, the importance of interaction and social structure derive entirely from the unique physiological and developmental characteristics of humans, compared with other biological systems and especially with other higher mammals.

First Principles: Organism, Interaction, and Structure

Space does not permit a full treatment of the unique features of *yomo sapiens*. Treatments of these specific and well established—albeit neglected—features of human development are available elsewhere (Dannefer, in press; Gould, 1977b; Montagu, 1989; Morss, 1996). In brief, the constitutional potentials for flexibility and environmental responsiveness of human beings are not merely options to be occasionally exercised; they reflect broader constitutional requirements of external structuring and direction. In short, human organisms require human society to become human beings. *The form their humanity takes and the forms their aging and life course structures take depend on the nature of the society in which they participate.*

It is because of this uniquely potent and unavoidably necessary dependence of human development on social relations that social interaction, with all its complexity and dynamism, is a central principle of life course analysis. Social interaction involves processes whereby the human *organism* is transformed both physically and mentally into a human *being,* and the capability for human action is generated and maintained. Social interaction is often seen as most crucial in the early years of the life course, and arguably it is. However, interaction remains decisively important throughout the later life course (when it is often taken for granted and its effects unrecognized), as attested by the dramatic and sometimes bizarre effects of social isolation on individuals (whether occasioned by scientific experimentation or solitary confinement in prison).

The third term—social structure—entails the explication of social *forces* as regular, systematic influences on individuals of all ages at any given point in time. Social structure operates on individual lives in the immediacy of the present at every age. Of course, one need only compare patterns of aging in different historical periods or across cultures to recognize the profound significance of social structure. But the effects of interaction and structure also can be witnessed, even at the level of individual case studies, as when comparing the different aging trajectories experienced by two similarly disabled older persons after one enters a nursing home and the other continues living in a caring family unit.

In the life course area as a whole these two principles are often unrecognized, even though they describe the features of human dynamics that render cohort analysis so necessary, because they provide order to the diversity in human life course trajectories. But this ironic situation is exceeded by the further irony that the very focus on cohort analysis itself, important as it remains, has contributed to several persistent yet diverse intellectual problems in theorizing about the life course.

The power and utility of baseline intercohort comparisons generated considerable intellectual excitement and spawned a general approach to formulating empirical questions and research designs. The clarity and power of this straightforward approach made it a central analytical strategy. Although this strategy was highly fruitful, it had, as a by-product, the effect of directing inquiry within a sharply delimited field of problems. Within this field, debates raged and studies were conducted to disentangle cohort versus "true age" effects. Now that the cohort problem was recognized and more or less dealt with, efforts were made to resolve issues about particular life transitions or about continuity versus change in this or that aspect of the life course, as though such issues were general, all-or-nothing matters about which generalizations could safely be sought. Often, the required analytical tactic of comparing cohorts rather than age groups was not only seen as signaling the importance of context in shaping life course patterning but as analytically coterminous with the importance of context. Given this orientation, the central roles of social structure and interactional processes in producing life course phenomena tended to be overlooked.

These proclivities contributed to at least three significant intellectual problems in theorizing about the life course: (1) a tendency to equate the significance of social forces with social change, (2) a neglect of intracohort variability, (3) an unwarranted affirmation of choice as an unproblematized determinant of the life course.

The Life Course since Cohort Analysis: Four Conceptual Problems

Equating the Importance of Social Forces in Shaping the Life Course with Social Change

The initial rush of conceptual ferment that linked the newly discovered concept of cohorts to the proper analysis of the life course consistently emphasized *social change.* Clearly, social change does lead cohorts to age differently from one another. Indeed, observed differences in characteristics as diverse as marital status (Uhlenberg, 1977), health (Achenbaum, 1979), intelligence (Schaie & Willis, 1986), longevity (Preston, Keyfitz, & Schoen, 1972), and wealth (Pampel, 1981) could be clearly linked to changing social conditions. From the outset, therefore, linkage between social change and individual change was established as a dominant theme of the life course literature.

By the mid-1970s it had become conventional to recognize that cohort analysis was required for reliable and authoritative information about patterns of aging. By comparing across cohorts one could observe how social change and the resultant differences in social structure affected the aging process. Life course studies of aging since that time routinely have given the cohort variable a privileged conceptual status. This can be seen in the frequent pairing of social and individual change (as in countless references to "the changing person in the changing world") by both life course sociologists and psychologists, which implies the salience of social change in understanding individual aging (see, e.g., Elder, 1996; Hareven, 1977; Hogan, 1981.) This inclination to connect individual and social change shows no sign of abating, as it remains an emphasis of recent and exemplary treatments of the life course perspective (Elder, 1998; Elder & O'Rand, 1995; George, 1993). Within the life span framework the idea of cohort grading is given an explicit structural category equivalent to age grading (e.g., Baltes, 1987).

This emphasis invited the implicit assumption that the social mattered only in the case of social change. Absent was the acknowledgment that even if no social change occurred, human aging is still socially constituted through fundamental processes of social interaction and allocation, processes governed by "important institutions of informal and formal social control [that] vary across the life span (Sampson & Laub, 1993, p. 17). Recognizing this general problem of the association of change and the importance of the social, Sampson and Laub also note that "stability itself is quite compatible with a sociological perspective on the life course" (p. 12) (cf. Dannefer, 1984).

In contrast to this recognition of the universal involvement of social processes in the constitution of life course outcomes, researchers often treated each cohort as having a pattern derived from historical circumstance; thus, if there were no large-scale changes in circumstances, these cohort-specific patterns would be essentially identical. Such a condition of stability is improbable in any case, so there has been scant need to tease out this implication. Under stable conditions, then, one could worry less about historical and social effects and perhaps could more justifiably treat age as the master independent variable without worrying unduly about the specific factors that produced the age-related outcomes. And in any case, analyzing cohorts separately was proof of one's attention to social and historical influences and absolved one of further need for detailed sociological analysis. This logic is closely tied to the second problematic feature of life course analysis, the neglect of intracohort variability.

The Neglect of Intracohort Variability

Despite the dominance of the intercohort focus, which tended to typify entire cohorts and compare them in terms of their differences, some attention to internal differentiation of cohorts was evident in early life course work. Gribbin, Schaie and Parham (1980) had noted the differentiating effects of social status and lifestyle in their tracking of cognitive functioning over time. And an important finding from Elder's (1974) detailed longitudinal studies derived from his analysis of the differential effects of the Great Depression, based on social class and on the extent of experienced deprivation. Such analyses provided a powerful picture of systematic differences within, as well as between, cohorts).

Nevertheless, the heterogeneity within cohorts and the forces accounting for it received little sustained attention until fairly recently. In hindsight, this seems the more remarkable given the popular gerontological emphasis on diversity of the aged (Hickey, 1980; Maddox & Douglass, 1974; Neugarten, 1968; Riley, 1980). Subsequently, several studies and commentaries noted the systematic neglect of the issue of within-age heterogeneity as a topic of study and theoretical analysis (Bornstein & Smircana, 1982; Nelson & Dannefer, 1992; cf. Dannefer, 1988a), even as evidence of systematic increases in variability over the life course began to be more clearly documented (Crystal & Waehrer, 1996; Dannefer & Sell, 1988; O'Rand, 1996).

In fact, the theoretical predispositions of the field ensured such neglect. A logical by-product of the linkage of cohorts and social change discussed above was the focus on intercohort comparison, and this focus inevitably meant a neglect of questions concerning the range of variability within cohorts. However, as evidence of systematic changes in intracohort variability mounted, it became clear that life course theory must address these questions. If intracohort variability on key characteristics increases in similar fashion in successive cohorts, then it is a distortion to characterize cohorts in terms of averages or as undifferentiated aggregates (Dannefer, 1987).

As noted above, the analytical tactic of comparing cohorts not only indicated the importance of context but sometimes was treated as virtually coterminous with context. Thus, the relevance of the neglect of intracohort variability to the first principles is this: intercohort comparisons are based on the aggregation of intracohort outcomes. Yet the variation within cohorts is, to a significant degree, systematically organized by processes of social interaction and the allocational dynamics of social structure. Thus, the operation of these principles can be more directly and precisely observed in intracohort analysis, and the focus on cohort differences permits them to be altogether obfuscated.

In sum, the innovation of cohort analysis was seen as a corrective to naive assumptions of a biologically determined trajectory of "natural human aging." Yet at the same time, cohort analysis has allowed us to continue to view aging as a natural process within each cohort (so that each cohort had a characteristic age pattern), a tendency that has its roots in the organismic model that has always been powerful in studies of age and development (Lerner, 1986; Morss, 1990), and as a consequence to permit age alone to stand as the explanation rather than get behind age—that is, to ask what is it about age that produces a given age-related correlation. Thus, the underlying structure of an organismic model of natural aging has proved tenacious, surviving the claims of cohort analysts in only slightly modified form.

The Expanding Putative Role of Choice

The emphasis on individual choice making represents a final conceptual problem deriving from a neglect of first principles. In the study of action, choice is a problem to be analyzed, not an accomplishment to be asserted (Dannefer, in press). Given the problematic epistemological and ontological status of "choice" in the wider social science literature (compared with concepts such as "hidden curriculum," "alienation," "social control," etc.), its remarkably unproblematic appearance in life course theory cannot be defended. What is almost always measured in such discussions is behavior, and it is simply *presumed* that behavior is based on choice. In such a usage of choice, the degree of constraints an individual feels and the differential levels of constraints that confront individuals differently located in social structure (say, Ted Turner and Jane Fonda vs. a similarly middle-aged White couple who both work as nursing aides) is not analyzed. Even more, the degree to which perceptions and preferences are shaped by media-certified experts or by advertising is not analyzed.

Without a systematic analysis of the life circumstances and subjective experiences that lie behind the observed behavior, an appealing and culturally familiar image of a volitional and more or less autonomous individual obscures the analytical problem of the constraints within which choices are made, and the constitutive role of social interaction and social structure in constructing "choice" in the first place.

TYPES OF PHENOMENA AND TYPES OF EXPLANATION: THE EXPLANANS AND EXPLANANDA OF LIFE-COURSE THEORY

To develop a general perspective of work on the life course that encompasses the foregoing points, we present taxonomies of (a) the types of phenomena to be explained and (b) the types of explanation offered for these phenomena within the life course literature. This entails specifying precisely the focus of analysis in life course scholarship (i.e., what is to be explained—the *explanans,* in proper epistemological parlance) and also to specify as clearly as possible the types of explanation (the *explananda*). Focusing on the question of what is to be explained and how it is to be explained leads us to some categories that are reminiscent of but not identical with the usual micro-macro division.

We propose that the life course as an area encompasses phenomena representing at least three levels or foci of analysis: (1) the individual level (the structure of discrete human lives extended from birth to death and the characteristics of those lives), (2) the level of social aggregation (the *collective patterning* of individual life course structures in a population), and (3) the cultural or symbolic level—the *societal representation* of the life course in the socially shared stock of knowledge, including the nature of its socially recognized demarcations by life events and roles and the attendant meanings and norms. Each of these levels contains important phenomena that require careful description and analysis. At the individual level, for example, there are the identification of key transition points and the shape of trajectories on significant characteristics. At the collective level there is the aggregation of these individual-level characteristics in a population; at the sociocultural level are the social structuring of age-graded roles and the definition and evaluation of specific ages and life stages in the context of a given social system (e.g., adolescence, old age).

Then, for each of these types of outcomes the theoretical task is that of *explanation*: Why does the phenomenon assume the particular form that it does? Explanations offered for each of these classes of phenomena can be placed in two broad categories, which we term *personological and sociological.* We use the term *personological* to refer to any kind of individual characteristic. This includes characteristics that are assumed to be part of "human nature," or hardwired into the organism, and it includes individual choice making. But it also includes something that is often thought of as contextual: biographical characteristics that stem from earlier experience and earlier contextual factors, such as having grown up in a particular social class. That factor—social class of origin—*was* context while the person in question was growing up, but it is not context in the present. Its effects on outcomes in middle or later adulthood are conceived as being carried forward through time within the person. So personological factors include contextual factors that were internalized earlier, in ways that have an enduring significance for life course outcomes. The term *sociological,* by contrast, refers to social-structural and interactional forces that shape life course processes.

Both of these categories—sociological and personological—are quite broad and could readily be broken down into subtypes, although that task necessarily lies beyond the scope of this chapter. This logical bifurcation can be

Focus of Explanation

Life Course Outcome	Personological	Sociological
Individual	A	B
Population	C	D
Symbolic Construct	E	F

FIGURE 17.1 Framework for classifying life course studies by outcome of interest and type of explanation.

seen in citation patterns in the literature. For example, authoritative and recent reviews of the field by Elder (1998) and George (1993), exemplars of a personological approach, do not cite Martin Kohli, John Meyer, or Aage Sorensen, whom we regard as having made important contributions but from a social-structural perspective. And scholars working within a sociological framework often do not cite those whose work is primarily personological (see, e.g., Kohli & Meyer, 1986; Sorensen, 1986).

Cross-classifying our three categories of life course outcomes with the two types of explanations yields a 3 x 2 matrix, presented in Figure 17.1. Although classification for the sake of classification is a scholastic task of little intrinsic interest, we believe this framework is useful to clarify the explanatory objectives of studies of the life course whose theoretical models are often implicit.

Before embarking on this presentation of the various cells, several qualifiers and disclaimers are in order. First, because the life course has emerged as an area within the discipline of sociology, we focus primarily (though not exclusively) on the work of sociologists. Second, we borrow freely from the best work in the life course area to illustrate the kinds of argument that belong in each cell, which means locating researchers' names within the cells. But we recognize that this is a classification scheme of theories (explanations and outcomes), not of theorists and researchers. Often the work of individual scholars overlaps cell boundaries. In particular, those who have provided encompassing sociological frameworks, such as Riley's "aging and society" paradigm, could readily fit into multiple cells. We select the cell where the contribution is, in our view, clearest. This brings us to a third point: a very few exemplary empirical studies have seriously attempted to combine the personological and sociological. Examples are Kohn and associates' extensive analyses of work and personality (Kohn & Schooler, 1983; Kohn & Slomczynski, 1993), and the recent work on crime and the life course by Laub and Sampson and on stress by Pearlin (1989). Such studies could argue for a third column of explanation that combines personological and sociological in a single analysis. To date, however, rigorous efforts in this direction are few in number, and we are content just to mention them. Fourth, just as the typology can potentially be extended, it can also be refined. Both the personological and sociological categories encompass numerous subtypes (personological studies differentially emphasize genetic vs. early-experience effects; sociological studies differentially emphasize interaction and structure). Space limitations preclude a further refinement in the context of the present discussion.

Cell A: Personological Explanations for Individual Outcomes

Much of Glen Elder's voluminous work appears to belong in upper left-hand cell: individual-level outcomes explained in personological terms. Some readers may question this appraisal. Although the individual is the clearly the unit of analysis in most of Elder's work no one can doubt that his explanations utilize context extensively. As noted above, however, it is important to consider how context is being utilized. In Elder's work, it is primarily as part of the prior experience of individuals, experiences that are carried forward through time within the personality or in some cases the physiology of the individual. For example, whether or not one was deprived during the Depression was certainly a contextual factor, but its "effects" found in the 1980s are assumed to be carried forward in time largely through the effects of that early experience upon the person, whether through learning coping skills, personality change, or something else. There is no explicit conceptualization of present social structure as having an effect on individual outcomes.

As another example, consider John Clausen's (1993) analysis of "planful competence." Using the classic Berkeley and Oakland human development data, which trace cohorts born in the 1920s from early childhood or adolescence until 1990, Clausen argues that "planful competence"—a personality characteristic formed by adolescence—is a key predictor of life course success.

Cell B: Sociological Explanations for Individual Outcomes

Let us turn attention to Cell B, which contains explanations of individual-level outcomes in terms of proximal or immediate aspects of social context. This includes studies that utilize ethnographic methods to explain the immediate dynamics of interaction and their relevance to individual characteristics, including the diagnosis and labeling of individuals and their management by social systems. Applications of labeling theory and of interactional analyses more generally fall into this cell (e.g., Gubrium, Holstein, & Buckholdt, 1994; Kuypers & Bengtson, 1984).

Included here also are studies that attempt to explain what may be broadly called career outcomes in organizational terms—whether the organization is the workplace, the school, or the mental hospital; these also belong here, as do studies that focus on the effects on individuals of tournaments (Rosenbaum, 1978) and other organizational mobility processes (e.g., Kanter, 1977; Sorensen, 1986). The power of self-fulfilling prophecies to create cycles of cumulative advantage for some individuals and disadvantage for others (Dannefer, 1987; 1988a; O'Rand, 1996) has been observed in virtually all organizational settings—work, the military, higher education, and prisons, as well as schools, where it was first described and theorized (Buckley, 1967; Lemert, 1975). In each case, both the cumulative process itself and events that may break the cycle and redirect an individual's life course have implications for one's organizational career and potentially for psychological and physiological aging. Interestingly, this prospect has recently been considered from a personological perspective by Elder, who envisions this process in more volitional terms, describing it as a "knifing off" of the past from one's life history (Elder, 1998, p. 966). It may be useful to consider the conditions under which such a knifing off is possible, in order to link it explicitly to the social context in which it would occur.

Psychologists and biologists as well as sociologists have also utilized a sociological model of individual life course outcomes. Some clear examples are provided by experiments that have demonstrated how immediately affected individuals are by environmental changes. Baltes and Willis (1981) showed how the "normal" declining age trajectory of cognitive test performance can be altered by practice; in ingenious but very different types of studies, numerous scholars have demonstrated the effects of change in environment and experience on "normal aging" trajectories of human physiology (e.g., Langer, 1989; Stone et al., 1994).

The personological-sociological dichotomy encompasses the classic selection-versus-socialization debate. This becomes especially clear in those few studies that attempt to analyze comparatively the effects of the early life course on later outcomes (selection) with more proximal or contemporaneous effects (socialization). An exemplar of such research, often cited in the life course tradition although not conducted from within an explicit age or life course framework, is the work of Melvin Kohn and associates (Kohn, 1993; Kohn & Schooler, 1993). Their research looks at personality in relation to a highly refined conceptualization of *present* context, specifically the characteristics of people's jobs, which are hypothesized to shape thought and activity patterns in everyday life in adulthood. Kohn's explanatory effort is focused on an explicit characterization of the social structures people encounter in adulthood, especially the role requirements of jobs. These roles are seen as offering their incumbents differential opportunities for mental stimulation and growth and thus are hypothesized to have immediate but cumulative effects on subsequent intellectual functioning.

A second important example of such comparative work, which affords a direct test of theory, is the recent analysis of life course trajectories of criminal activity conducted by Sampson and Laub (1993). In a carefully designed study that attempts to assess both personological and sociological explanations simultaneously, these analysts examine the explanatory contributions of work and social support as proximal features of adulthood in the construction of life course trajectories of criminal activity, together with the effects of early experience and the presumed effects of personality.

Cell C: Personological Explanations for Population Outcomes

The collective character of the explanans in Role 2 may lead to an expectation of sociological modes of explanation. Nevertheless, population analysts often invoke personological explanations for collective cohort outcomes. Two recent population-level studies dealing with the transition to adulthood can serve as examples. Interestingly, both begin with structural explanations for behavior in the past but shift to personological explanations for behavior as we approach the present. In both cases, the structural forces that constrained behaviors in the past are not hard to detect; but when we get closer to the present, the social-structural mechanisms shaping human behavior disappear. Consequently, the tendency is to argue that these larger forces no longer operate, leaving individuals free to act on personal preference, or choice.

The first is John Modell's (1989) important book, *Into One's Own*. This study traces changes in patterns of movement into adulthood across cohorts in the period 1920–1975. In explaining cohort variations in such areas as schooling, premarital sex, marriage, and parenthood, he recognizes the powerful influences of factors like "the market demand for labor" and "needs of the family economy." But, he argues, because of increasing affluence, the social structure is losing its determinative force: "Young people . . . have increasingly taken control of the construction of the youthful life course" (p. 326) and "Young individuals . . . choose the timing of their own life course events and hence come increasingly to value the expression of personal choice in this as in other aspects of their lives" (p. 330).

The second example is Ronald Rindfuss's (1991) presidential address to the Population Association, which focuesd on changes in recent years in how young adults manage the timing and sequencing of their work, school, and family roles. He argued that recent changes "move toward allowing individuals more choice. . . . [y]oung adults will be pursuing their own preferences, with fewer constraints across and within roles" (p. 509).

The irony of this claim, as has been noted before (Dannefer, 1984), is that this presumed increase in personal freedom and choice has historically been associated with greater conformity in behavior. For example, in the United States, throughout the 20th century and especially after World War II, the degree of conformity among cohort members in transition to adulthood and in other life transitions has increased substantially. This can be seen in the reduction in the number of years it takes for each cohort to complete the transition. The interpretation typically offered for this finding has been, as in the examples above, an increase in prosperity in young adulthood, which increased the degree of choice and control young people had over their lives. So we have here the paradox that an increase in choice leads to an increase in conformity. What is required for this seeming paradox to make sense is to take as a premise that there is a strong set of impulses in human nature to differentiate from family of origin and marry soon after the period called adolescence. This is an example of the continued implicit reliance on the organismic model in sociological research.

Cell D: Sociological Explanations for Population Outcomes

The second row concerns life course patterns studied at the population level. The use of sociological explanations for life course patterns of cohorts in later life is illustrated by studies of labor force exit (Henretta, 1992) and economic status (Crystal & Waehrer, 1996). These studies acknowledge the influence of earlier life course experiences in determining later outcomes. Rather than being content with this as an explanation, however, both go on to indicate the significance of social factors encountered by cohorts as they move through later life structures created by the state (e.g., Social Security) and the workplace (e.g., pension programs). These structures are seen not only as factors having an impact on the aggregate experience of cohorts in later life but also as forces that produce heterogeneity and inequality within cohorts (Dannefer, 1988b; O'Rand, 1996).

We begin the discussion of population analysis with a sociological explanation, the right-hand cell of Row 2. Henretta (1992) tracks the pattern of labor force exit in later life for cohorts of men born in the first two decades of the 20th century. He notes how the expansion of Social Security and private pensions to encompass a growing proportion of men in each successive cohort, as well as increasing standardization of employers' rules over time, produced a steadily declining age of labor force exit. He then examines changes in intracohort diversity in patterns of exit. Increasing variability is found for men who retire early (before the median age) but increasing concentration of age for men who retire later. This interesting finding leads to a discussion of how the structural factors influencing retirement may change with age. The higher levels of Social Security and private pension income may account for the increasing uniformity of behavior for those who meet the age requirements for entitlement to those benefits. Among early retirees, however, several other structural factors may play a significant role. Examples of such factors include labor force composition, corporate use of early retirement incentives, and government requirements for disability benefits.

Crystal and Waehrer (1996) argue that income distributions characteristic of cohorts in later life are shaped "not only by the numerous vicissitudes of individual life events and choices, but also by policy choices implicitly in the design and regulation of retirement income systems" (p. S301).

Using longitudinal data for several cohorts moving from middle age into later life, they show average income declines and increasing inequality within each cohort. Individuals within a cohort differentially encounter such later life course events as retirement, loss of spouse, illness, disability, and inheritance. The effects of these transitions on economic status, however, are mediated by larger structural forces related to the income system. Without attention to the stratification of the occupational structure and to policies regulating public and private pensions, health care and taxes, one cannot understand cohort patterns of income distribution in later life.

Both of these studies suggest structural explanations for observed cohort patterns, but neither is able to examine in detail how particular social structures produce particular outcomes. Focusing on this limitation, Elder and O'Rand (1995) criticize cohort studies that "typically speculate about historical forces and fail to extend analysis to their actual investigation. At most we end with a plausible story that does not advance scientific understanding."

This observation can be accepted as a challenge to develop and test more fully structural explanations for observed cohort patterns of aging. Nothing is gained, however, if this critique is taken to justify a retreat to personological factors only. Clear understanding of life course trajectories is not enhanced by ignoring how the extrusion of individuals through regulative and often age-graded structures shapes collective patterns of aging.

Cells E and F: The Life Course as a Symbolic Construct

The third row concerns the life course as a social construction, as an institution. The phenomenon in question here is different from the first two. In both of the first two, the *explanans* consists of actual individual people, whether treated as individuals or aggregated. This third category of phenomena is really *symbolic or cultural* in nature—it refers to the life course as a *collective social concept*, as a set of publicly shared meanings and expectations for the course of human lives.

Accounts of the features of the life course as a symbolic construct are often cast in sociological terms, as indicated in Cell F. Notwithstanding certain organismic and logical constraints on role sequences (e.g., puberty precedes parenting), the dramatic historical and cross-cultural diversity in the timing, sequencing, content, and orderliness of roles and activities dictates the importance of a sociological approach here.

This approach is well illustrated by the work of Riley and associates, which has included a focus on the meaning of age and the processes by which it changes. Especially relevant are their discussions of age norms and expectations deriving from societal age grading (e.g., Riley, Johnson & Foner, 1972; Riley, Kahn & Foner, 1994; cf. Riley, Foner, & Riley, chapter 18 in this volume). Their treatment provides a framework for analyzing age as a formal and informal criterion to encourage or impede entrance into and exit from roles, thereby regulating access to resources and opportunities.

Studies of specific organizations or subcultures that have documented the operation of age norms in local settings are also important contributions to this cell. For example, Burton (1990, 1996) has documented a quite distinct set of life course and age-related expectations in poor minority communities. Organizations have their own cultural systems, of which age grading is often a part; Lawrence (1984, 1996) has demonstrated the presence of age consciousness and normative expectations about age-appropriateness for certain career levels and the like within a single corporation. The notion of a social system comprising age norms and age-stratified roles is made concrete in such studies. Sociological accounts of age norms envision both their content and their existence as closely tied to social-structural conditions.

From this perspective, age norms are explained in terms of the confluence of demographic change with social policies that have bureaucratized and increasingly institutionalized the life course in a matrix of formal and informal social regulation (cf. Kohli, 1988; Meyer, 1986). Over the past century these societal developments produced a steady increase in the use of age as a formal role criterion for education, work, and retirement, creating the "three boxes of life" (Riley, Kahn, & Foner 1994; cf. Riley, Foner, & Riley, chapter 18 in this volume), an unprecedented degree of life course transition and role conformity, especially for men (e.g., Modell, Furstenberg, & Strong, 1978; Glick, 1977; Hogan, 1981). Such a high degree of age-graded societal regulation (which tended to homogenize the major roles and transitions of tens of millions of people) produced a widely shared view of the life course and hence of age norms (Chudacoff, 1989). Historians have traced the forces underlying these changes back to earlier changes in the meaning and status of age, deriving from demographic changes in the age structure and technological change that shifted health expertise from the aged themselves to medicine (Achenbaum, 1979), and to still other technical and social changes that reshaped the age grading of work and school, creating new levels of age segregation and age awareness (Chudacoff, 1989). From this vantage point, then, the very concepts of age and life course are themselves historically contingent as culturally relevant and plausible constructs.

Although perhaps more commonly and plausibly cast in sociological terms, personological accounts of the source of the life course as a symbolic construct are also available, and examples are located in Cell E. One example of such an account is provided by the work of Riley and associates (Riley, 1978; Riley, Foner, & Riley, chapter 18 in this volume). Her concept of cohort norm formation is an attempt to provide an action complement to the strong structural emphasis of the basic aging and society framework by explicating the role of individual behavior in creating population patterns.

Most personological accounts derive, at least implicitly, from the same kind of argument used by the historical demography in the second row. This cell contains work that views the culturally shared *meaning* of age—both age in general and being a particular age—as deriving from factors in the individual person. This is, of course, precisely the notion that is explicitly applied to old age in disengagement theory, where an age norm of disengagement is said to be a realization of natural human tendencies. Despite its own age and its general disrepute, disengagement theory (Cumming & Henry, 1961) continues to resurface, as gerontological commentators regularly note. And in a context of a graying population, expanding health care potentials, and sharply rising health care costs, such theorizing is not irrelevant to economic arguments about aging. One recent reincarnation of disengagement can be found in Daniel Callahan's (1987) proposals that we think of a "full life" and an "expectable life course" of 70–odd years that comprises a criterion of access to care. Such approaches provide a personologically based, organismic justification of contemporary age norms and of the biases they justify. This general point is relevant to current public debates on issues like withholding needed medical treatment from the very old and physician-assisted suicide. If the life course is seen as having an organismically determined endpoint within a certain age range, it is another argument for such practices and another form of social pressure to be visited upon the aged individual in question.

SUMMARY

In the mid-1970s, Glen Elder (1975) correctly referred to the life course as an "emerging field of inquiry" (p. 186). By the mid-1990s the life course had become the dominant perspective from which social scientists approached the study of aging, as reflected by the renaming of the Sociology of Aging section of the American Sociological Association (ASA) the "Section on Aging and the Life Course in 1997. In the intervening decades, many researchers have contributed to the study of the life course through the collection of new data and through advancements in methodology. Nevertheless, the development and mobilization of social theory directed toward understanding the social forces that shape the life course is still in an early stage. From the perspective of social theory, the result is theoretical inadequacies in the formulation of life course issues, even though the term *life course* has a distinctly sociological heritage.

These theoretical inadequacies were the focus of the first section of this chapter. Discourse in the life course area has failed to acknowledge or utilize the basic insights concerning the unique role that social interaction and social structure play in the constitution of individual lives and in the symbolic understanding of the life course. This tendency is evident even in the ASA's section names, noted above. Notably absent from both section titles is *age* (which identifies a structural dimension of social organization as opposed to the individual level)—an absence that invites a continuation of the tendency to obscure social-structural aspects of the life course and to amplify the focus on individual aspects.

An adequate theory of the life course cannot ignore the unique features of the human organism (e.g., exterogestation, neoteny, and exceptional cognitive capacities). These features of human physical anthropology mean that human development and aging require social interaction processes, and therefore the *explanation* of human development also requires an understanding of the integral and irreducible role of social interaction. Social interaction processes are almost always institutionlized to some degree in group practices, which thereby organize and structure social interaction, giving *social structure* an important and irreducible role in organizing life course patterns. Accordingly, we have proposed that attention to social interaction and social structure stand as first principles of life course analysis. Without them, human organisms do not become human beings, and there is no life course. But it is not only social interaction in infancy and childhood nor social structures experienced in the earlier phases of the life course that matter. Throughout life, social interaction and social structure continue to operate as constitutive forces.

Given these principles, a theory of the life course cannot be based on the organismic model appropriate to other species, with its assumption of a "natural" aging trajectory. Common intellectual practices in the study of aging and the life course, such as the tendency to associate the importance of the social with change or the tendency to treat cohorts as undifferentiated aggregations, invite a reliance on unwarranted organismic assumptions.

The second section of the chapter offers a general classification scheme, based on types of phenomena *(explanans)* and types of explanations *(explananda)*—what is to be explained and how it is to be explained—in the life course literature. This classification scheme invites further refinement, but it provides a framework that enables explication of theoretical assumptions that have often been nascent and unrecognized in discussions of the life course. Each of the three types of phenomena or outcomes stands as a legitimate and important focus for life course analysis. An adequate theory cannot, however, avoid the problem of explicating causal assumptions and of clarifying whether one's explanation is personological or sociological. The complexity of dealing with the rich, dynamic, and extensive structure of lives over time, which always involves dimensions of social experience, has sometimes been confused with the separate explanatory role of the constitutive and age-graded social structure of the present. Too often, the explanatory force of present circumstances is neglected, leaving us with the popular but naive perspective of individuals aging outside a social world. One need not contend that the social has the primary explanatory contribution to make to every imaginable life course outcome in order to appreciate the value of clarity with respect to the kinds of explanation that are being assumed and the kinds that are being excluded by the causal assumptions and/or data available to the life course researcher.

REFERENCES

Achenbaum, W. A. (1979). *Old age in the new land: The American experience since 1790.* Baltimore: Johns Hopkins.

Baltes, P. B. (1987). Theoretical propositions of life-span developmental psychology: On the dynamics between growth and decline. *Developmental Psychology, 23,* 611–626.

Baltes, P. B., & Schaie, K. W. (1968). Longitudinal and cross sectional sequences in the study of age and generation effects. *Human Development, 11,* 145–171.

Baltes, P. B., & Willis, S. L. (1982). Enhancement (plasticity) of intellectual functioning in old age: Penn State's adult development and enrichment project (ADEPT). In F. I. M. Craik & S. E. Trehyb (Eds.), *Aging & Cognitive Process* (Pp. 353–89). New York: Plenum.

Bengtson, V. L. (1973). *The social psychology of aging.* Indianapolis: Bobbs-Merrill.

Bengtson, V. L., Burgess, E. O., & Parrott, T. M. (1997). Theory, explanation, and the third generation of theoretical development in social gerontology. *Journal of Gerontology: Social Sciences, 52B,* S72–S88.

Bornstein, R., & Smiricana, M. T. (1982). The status of empirical support for the hypothesis of increased variability in aging populations. *Gerontologist, 22,* 250–260.

Buckley, W. (1967). *Social and modern systems theory.* Englewood Cliffs, NJ: Prentice-Hall.

Burton, L. (1990). Teenage childbearing as an alternative life-course strategy in multigeneration black families. *Human Nature, 1,* 123–143.

Burton, L. (1996). Age norms, the timing of family role transitions, and the intergenerational caregiving among aging African American women. *Gerontologist, 36,* 199–208.

Cain, L. D. (1964). Life course and social structure. In R. E. L. Faris (Ed.), *Handbook of modern sociology* (pp. 272–309). Chicago: Rand, McNally.

Callahan, D. (1987). *Setting limits: Medical goals in an aging society.* New York: Simon & Schuster.

Chudacoff, H. (1989). *How old are you? Age consciousness in American culture.* Princeton, NJ: Princeton University Press.

Clausen, J. A. (1972). The life course of individuals. In M. W. Riley, M. E. Johnson, & A. Foner (Eds.), *Aging and society: Vol. 3. A sociology of age stratification.* New York: Russell Sage.

Clausen, J. A. (1993). *American lives: Looking back at the children of the Great Depression.* New York: Free Press.

Crystal, S., & & Waehrer, K. (1996). Later-life economic inequality in longitudinal perspective. *Journal of Gerontology: Social Sciences, 51B,* S307–S318.

Cumming, E., & Henry, W. F. (1961). *Growing old.* New York: Basic Books.

Dannefer, D. (1984). Adult development and social theory: A paradigmatic reappraisal. *American Sociological Review, 49,* 100–116.

Dannefer, D. (1987). Accentuation, the Matthew effect, and the life course: Aging as intracohort differentiation. *Sociological Forum, 2,* 211–236.

Dannefer, D. (1988a). Differential gerontology and the stratified life course: Conceptual and methodological issues. *Annual Review of Gerontology and Geriatrics, 8,* 3–36.

Dannefer, D. (1988b). What's in a name? An account of the neglect of variability in the study of aging. In J. E. Birren & V. L. Bengtson (Eds.), *Emergent theories of aging.* New York: Springer Publishing Co.

Dannefer, D. (ion press). Neoteny, naturalization and other constituents of human development. In C. Ryff & V. W. Marshall (Eds.), *Self and society in aging processes.*

Dannefer, D., & Sell, R. R. (1988). Age structure, the life course and "aged heterogeneity": Prospects for research and theory. *Contemporary Gerontology.*

Elder, G. H., Jr. (1974). *Children of the Great Depression: Social change in life experience.* Chicago: University of Chicago Press.

Elder, G. H., Jr. (1975). Age differentiation and the life course. *Annual Review of Sociology, 1,* 165–190.

Elder, G. H., Jr. (1996). Human lives in changing societies: Life course and developmental insights. In R. B. Cairns, G. H. Elder, Jr., & E. J. Costello (Eds.), *Developmental sciences* (pp. 31–62). New York: Cambridge University Press.

Elder, G. H., Jr. (1998). The life course and human development. In R. M. Lerner (Ed.), *Handbook of child psychology: Vol. 1. Theoretical models of human development.* New York: Wiley.

Elder, G. H., Jr., & Liker, J. (1982). Hard times in women's lives: Historical differences across 40 years. *American Journal of Sociology, 58,* 241–269.

Elder, G. H., Jr., & O'Rand, A. M. (1995). Adult lives in a changing society. In K. S. Cook, G. A. Fine, & J. S. House (Ed.), *Sociological perspectives on social psychology* (pp. 452–475). Boston: Allyn & Bacon.

Fisher, D. H. (1977). *Growing old in America.* New York: Oxford University Press.

George, L. (1993). Sociological perspective on life transitions. *Annual Review of Sociology, 19,* 353–373.

Glick, P. C. (1977). Updating the life cycle of the family. *Journal of Marriage and the Family, 39,* 5–13.

Gould, S. J. (1977a). Human babies as embryos. In S. J. Gould, *Ever since Darwin: Reflections on natural history.* New York: Norton.

Gould, S. J. (1977b). *Ontogeny and phylogeny.* Cambridge, MA: Belknap Harvard.

Gribbin, K., Schale, K. W., & Parham, I. A. (1980). Complexity of life style and maintenance of intellectual abilities. *Journal of Social Issues, 36,* 47–61.

Gubrium, J., Holstein, J., & Burkholdt, D. R. (1994). *Constructing the life course.* Dix Hills, NY: General Hall.

Hareven, T. K. (1977). *Transitions: The family and the life course in historical perspective.* New York: Academic Press.

Henretta, J. (1992). Uniformity and diversity: Life course institutionalization and late life exit. *Sociological Quarterly, 33,* 265–279.

Hickey, T. (1980). *Health and aging.* Monterey, CA: Brooks/Cole.

Hogan, D. (1981). *Transitions and social change: The early lives of American men.* New York: Academic Press.

Kahn, R., & Antonucci, T. (1980). Convoys over the life course: Attachments, roles, and social support. In P. B. Baltes & O. G. Brim (Eds.), *Life-span development and behavior* (Vol. 3, pp. 254–287). New York: Academic Press.

Kanter, R. M. (1977). *Man and work of the corporation.* New York: Basic Books.

Kohli, M. (1988). Social organization and subjective construction of the life course. In A. B. Sorensen, F. E. Weiner, & L. R. Sherrod (Eds.), *Human development and the life cycle* (pp. 271–292). Hillsdale, NJ: Erlbaum.

Kohli, M., & Meyer, J. W. (1986). Social structure and the construction of life stages. *Human Development, 29,* 145–180.

Kohn, M., & Schooler, C. (1983). *Work and personality: An inquiry into the impact of social stratification.* Norwood, NJ: Ablex.

Kohn, M. L., & Slomczynski, K. M. (1993). Social structure and self-direction: A comparative analysis of the United States and Poland. Cambridge, MA: Blackwell.

Kuypers, J., & Bengtson, V. L. (1984). Perspectives on the older family. In W. H. Quinn & C. A. Houghston (Eds.), *Independent aging: Family and social systems perspectives.* Rockville, MD: Aspen Systems.

Langer, E. (1989). *Mindfulness.* Reading, MA: Addison-Wesley.

Lawrence, B. (1984). Age grading: The implicit organizational timetable. *Journal of Occupational Behavior, 5,* 23–35.

Lawrence, B. S. (1996). Age norms: Why is it so hard to know one when you see one? *Gerontologist, 36,* 209–220.

Lemert, E. (1975). Primary and secondary deviation. In S. H. Traub & C. B. Little, *Theories of deviance* (pp. 167–179). Itasca, IL: F. E. Peacock.

Lerner, R. M. (1986). *Concepts and theories of human development* (2nd ed.). Reading, MA: Addison-Wesley.

Lynott, R. J., & Lynott, P. P. (1996). Tracing the course of theoretical development in the sociology of aging. *Gerontologist, 36,* 749–760.

Maddox, G., & Douglass, E. R. (1974). Aging and individual differences: A longitudinal analysis of social, psychological and physiological indicators. *Journal of Gerontology, 29,* 555–563.

Meyer, J. (1986). The self and the life course: Institutionalization and its effects. In A. B. Sorensen, F. B. Weinert, & L. R. Sherrod (Eds.), *Human development and the life course: Multidisciplinary perspectives* (pp. 199–206). Hillsdale, NJ: Lawrence Erlbaum.

Modell, J. (1989). *Into one's own: From youth to adulthood in the United States, 1920–1975.* Berkeley: University of California Press.

Modell, J., Furstenberg, F. F., Jr., & Strong, D. (1978). The timing of marriage in the transition to adulthood: Continuity and change, 1860–1975. *American Journal of Sociology, 84,* 8120–8150.

Montagu, A. (1989). *Growing young* (2nd ed.). Granby, MA: Bergin & Garvey.

Morss, J. (1990). *The biologising of childhood.* Hillsdale, NJ: lawrence Erlbaum.

Morss, J. (1996). *Critical developments.* London: Routledge.

Nelson, E. A., & Dannefer, D. (1992). Aged heterogeneity: Fact or fiction? The fate of diversity in gerontological research. *Gerontologist, 32,* 17–23.

Neugarten, B. L. (1968). *Middle age and aging.* Chicago: University of Chicago Press.

O'Rand, A. (1996). The precious and the precocious: The cumulation of disadvantage and advantage over the life course. *Gerontologist, 36,* 230–238.

Pampel, F. C. (1981). *Social change and the aged: Recent trends in the United States.* Lexington, MA: Lexington Books.

Pearlin, L. (1989). The sociological study of stress. *Journal of Health and Social Behavior, 30,* 241–256.

Preston, S., Keyfitz, N., & Schoen, R. (1972). *Causes of death: Life tables for national populations.* New York: Seminar Press.

Riley, M. W. (1978). Aging, social change and the power of ideas. *Daedaelus, 107,* 39–52.

Riley, M. W. (1980, September). *Social stratification and aging.* Paper presented at the Wilson Day proceedings, University of Rochester, Rochester, NY.

Riley, M. W., & Foner, A. (1968). *Aging and society: Vol. 1. An inventory of research findings.* New York: Russell Sage.

Riley, M. W., Kahn, R., & Foner, A. (1994). *Age and structural lag: Society's failure to provide meaningful opportunities in work, family, and leisure.* New York: Wiley-Interscience.

Riley, M. W., Johnson, M. E., & Foner, A. (1972). *Aging and society: Vol. 3. A sociology of age stratification.* New York: Russell Sage.

Rindfuss, R. R. (1991). The young adult years: Diversity, structural change, and fertility. *Demography, 28,* 493–512.

Rosenbaum, J. (1978). The structure of opportunity in school. *Social Forces, 57,* 236–256.

Rosenbaum, J. (1984). *Career mobility in a corporate hierarchy.* New York: Academic Press.

Ryder, N. B. (1965). The cohort as a concept in the study of social change. *American Sociological Review, 30,* 843–861.

Sampson, R. J., & Laub, J. H. (1993). *Crime in the making: Pathways and turning points through life.* Cambridge, MA: Harvard University Press.

Schaie, K. W. (1965). A general model for the study of developmental change. *Psychological Bulletin, 64,* 92–107.

Schaie, K. W., & Willis, S. (1986). *Adult development and aging.* Boston: Little, Brown.

Sorensen, A. B. (1986). Social structure and the mechanisms of life-course processes. In A. B. Sorensen, F. Weinert, & L. Sherrod (Eds.), *Human development: Multidisciplinary perspectives.* Hillsdale, NJ: Lawrence Erlbaum.

Stone, A. A., Neale, J. M., Cox, D. S., Napoli, A., Valdimarsdottir, H., & Kennedy-Moore, E. (1994). Daily events are associated with a secretory immune response to an oral antigen in men. *Health Psychology, 13,* 440–446.

Uhlenberg, P. (1978). Changing configurations of the life course. In T. K. Hareven (Ed.), *Transitions: The family and the life course in historical perspective.* New York: Academic Press.

18

The Aging and Society Paradigm

Matilda White Riley
Anne Foner
John W. Riley, Jr.

T
he aging and society (A&S) paradigm is a conceptual framework, or approach, for designing and interpreting studies of age and illuminating the place of age in both lives (as people age) and the surrounding social structures. Its central theme is that, against the backdrop of history, changes in people's lives influence and are influenced by changes in social structures and institutions. These reciprocal changes are linked to the meanings of age, which vary over time.

In this chapter we review the past and continuing experiences of our generation in developing and using this conceptual approach to age, hoping that it may be useful as prologue to some of the future work of oncoming generations—at any age and from any scientific discipline.[1]

MEANINGS OF AGE

This seems an exquisite moment for communicating ideas from generation to generation because, in the great swings of social change, society is now at a turning point; and the meaning attached to age, in popular usage and in scientific theory, has shifted in the past century and may well be utterly transformed in the next. This chapter will trace the early development of A&S in freeing the meaning of age from its almost complete dependence on biological determinants, and suggest a likely future approach in discovering new meaning in a society undergoing fundamental change.

Back in the 1960s, when A&S had its inception, social change had been pointing in one direction. The Roosevelt era and the New Deal had been building a strong central government. There was widespread confidence that government could provide safety nets for people as they aged. Today, in contrast, social change is taking a new turn. Much of the welfare state's central power is now diffusing to the individual states, to commercial organizations, or directly to "the people." Of particular interest, alterations in the economy, the polity, the judiciary, and communications are coinciding with unprecedented extensions of longevity and increasing numbers of older people. Many baffling issues currently involve age: issues about retirement, Social Security, health care, dying, social inequalities, education, intergenerational relations, individual responsibilities, and rights to privacy and decision making.[2] A new era may well be in the making.

These broad empirical changes in the place of age in society are reflected in the meanings attached to age and in the concepts used in A&S to describe these meanings. In the earlier era the meaning of age was being redefined, and aging became recognized as not entirely fixed or immutable. The theoretical emphasis was shifting from older people as "disengaged," a passive burden on society, to older people as active contributors *to* society. Now, as an oncoming generation enters a new era, the meanings of age will predictably change again, and the relevant scientific theories must keep pace. For the future, a key question is, what will the new meanings be?

We cannot predict the future. But we can extend into the future our thinking about age and its meanings as, in this chapter, we review the experience of A&S with the past (cf. Riley, 1994). The chapter will conclude by suggesting, for future development, several concepts for examining how, in the societal transformation, new meanings of age might be illuminated.

BACKGROUND OF THE PARADIGM

Our work on the A&S paradigm has developed gradually. We have been tracing historical shifts, seeking dynamic concepts that simplify the complex reality, and translating the changing meanings of age into workable theories to describe and explain the linkages between aging and social structures. These linkages have begun to revolutionize the potential at every age for health, effective functioning, and quality of life.

The A&S Trilogy

Our early studies culminated in publication of three volumes entitled *Aging and Society* (Vol. 1: Riley, Foner, et al. 1968—a codification of findings; Vol.

2: Riley, Riley, & Johnson, 1969—implications for practice and policy; Vol. 3: Riley, Johnson, & Foner, 1972—our first attempt at a general theory). We think of that early trilogy as exemplifying the way a scientific theory can develop through continuing interplay with research and practice, as each of the three works informs the others.

Development of the A&S paradigm had begun when the Ford and Russell Sage Foundations offered to support our then-ongoing Rutgers research on intergenerational relations—*provided* that we'd pause to summarize the existing social science findings on the middle and later years. "A simple task," they said, "easily accomplished by one or two graduate students in a couple of years." Well, 5 years later, 7 of us, with 50 consultants, finally accomplished that first volume! We had uncovered and reanalyzed some 3,000 studies. To our surprise, however, three quarters of these had to be discarded because the reported "findings" were not supported by appropriate research procedures. (Sampling was often severely biased, and analysis was faulty—as, in the absurd extreme, comparing young medical students and nurses with their elderly patients to "measure" the process of aging.)

It was that experience with research and its misinterpretation that demonstrated that many accepted "theories" of universal and inevitable aging decline were fallacious, that age barriers were blocking opportunities for older people, and that misleading "ageist" stereotypes were acting as self-fulfilling prophecies (cf. Butler, 1989).

Classical Roots

Our developing A&S paradigm, as first set out in Volume 3, was generated from the viable empirical findings in Volume 1 (after correcting for errors). A&S also attempted to integrate two long strands of thought from sociology: on age and social *structure* associated with such scholars as Sorokin, Mannheim, Parsons, Eisenstadt, and Cain; and on *aging* as a process, illuminated by Thomas and Znaniecki, Lazarsfeld, Clausen, Neugarten, Ryder, and Elder (Riley, Foner, & Waring, 1988). But, to examine the systemic relationship between these strands, a more general theory of age was needed (cf. the intertwining of "action" and structure by Alexander [1988] and Sztompka [1994]).

Distinctive Features

In its efforts to meet this need for a more general theory, the distinguishing emphasis of A&S is on *both* people and structures and the systemic relationship between them (cf. Foner, 1986). The paradigm (which corrected many of those early fallacies) includes the life course, but it avoids the widespread reduction of structure to mere "context" of people's lives—as if structural change had no meaning or guiding principles of its own (Riley, 1997b). Thus, we concluded that understanding the age-related changes in both people and structures requires a broad approach that, in relating abstract ideas to interpretation of empirical facts, transcends narrow boundaries.

As we have learned, and as possible guideposts for graduate students today, use of the paradigm—as appropriate for particular research objectives—should be as follows:

- *Multilevel.* People can be viewed either as individuals or as populations; just as structures can be viewed singly (as in a case study of a family) or as aggregates (as in comparing families with work organizations).
- *Age-inclusive.* Old age relates to all ages; aging takes place from conception to death, and changes at one age affect all ages.
- *Dynamic.* While people are growing older, society is changing around them.
- *Inclusive of subjective attitudes and feelings,* as well as overt actions, in the lives and structures involved.
- *Multidisciplinary,* following the model of James Birren's lifetime contributions. As sociologists, we had recognized in the early Volume 1 that social aspects of aging cannot be understood without reference to biology or psychology, nor can structures be understood without reference to history, anthropology, and all the social sciences.
- *Collaborative.* To cover this broad ground, our work has been aided by a wide array of colleagues here and abroad, including social, behavioral, biological, medical, and mathematical scholars at Rutgers, Russell Sage Foundation, the Social Science Research Council, and the National Institute on Aging (Riley & Abeles, 1990).[3]

PHASES OF DEVELOPMENT

In this chapter we describe four cumulative phases of paradigmatic development which aim to provide a basis for present and future theory. Each phase is designed to capture, simplify, and interpret the changing place of age and its meanings. Phase 1 defines the focus on lives and structures, formulated as age stratification. Phase 2 introduces the two dynamisms of changing lives and changing structures. Phase 3 specifies concepts connecting lives with structures through the interplay between the dynamisms. And Phase 4 anticipates possible future transformations in the place and meaning of age in lives and structures.

We illustrate those four phases of A&S development by describing some concepts and principles, as their meanings not only inform the scientific study of aging but also reflect and contribute to practice and policy. Each concept builds on its predecessors, and each has been undergoing continual clarification and specification. Still further evolution of emerging concepts remains for the oncoming generations of researchers.

LIVES AND STRUCTURES (PHASE 1)

Phase 1 began in the 1960s with the notion that, in every society, age organizes *both* people's lives and social structures into rough divisions (strata) from the youngest to the oldest. We labeled this seemingly simple notion age stratification (as the subtitle of our Volume 3). As a concept, AGE STRATIFICATION raised new and intriguing questions of how age strata of people and age-oriented structures arise and become interrelated.[4]

Lives

In dealing with such questions, Volume 3 theorized about several features of people's lives. First, aging is a process of growing *older* from birth to death. This definition aimed to correct the anomaly in the English language that *age* as a noun refers to any age, but *aging* as a verb has been used narrowly to mean growing *old*.

Second, aging is closely related to social structures. In growing older, people move through social roles in childhood and in middle and later life; they are exposed to diverse social and cultural conditions; and they participate in groups of people whose background and experience may differ from theirs.

Moreover, lifelong aging is a biopsychosocial process. At every age people's lives are influenced by interrelated biological, psychological, and social factors. Even newborns are not merely bundles of biological impulses: social learning occurs from the very beginning. The complex biopsychosocial makeup of individuals in the earliest years changes over the life course but can have long-term consequences, as, for example, fetal health can affect vulnerability to illness in old age (Fogel, 1993).

A&S efforts to understand the complex and often subtle connections among factors influencing the aging process have stimulated wide-ranging theoretical developments. As one example, Dannefer (1984) has explored the general phenomenon of heterogeneity—the prevalence at every age of wide differences among individual lives. Citing the work of Robert Merton, Dannefer shows how, through the aging process itself, individual lives become increasingly heterogeneous. He invokes the principle of accumulation (cf. Riley, 1976): the longer people live, the greater are their chances of having acquired irreversible characteristics (such as higher levels of education or of incurable diseases). Many advantages or disadvantages associated with gender, race, or class typically become intensified as people grow older.

A methodological implication of heterogeneity is that modal age differences among old, middle-aged, and young people can be defined by statistical averages; but for full theoretical understanding of age in people's lives, more fine-grained statistical or qualitative analyses are essential.

Structures

The early Volume 3 also explained how age operates in social structures: It serves as a criterion, or set of expectations or norms (cf. Hagestad & Neugarten, 1985), for entering and leaving particular structures, for performing roles in those structures, and for access to the associated resources (such as money, prestige, or power). Thus, structures provide opportunities or constraints at particular ages in people's lives.[5]

Among the familiar examples are schools in which age marks the divisions among grades (as strata). In the larger society, age marks the "three boxes" of education for the young, work and family for the middle aged, and retirement (or leisure) for the old. Age criteria are used in framing such critical issues as whether heroic medical treatments should be available to the very old or how public monies should be allocated between older people and children.

The power of age criteria in structures is illustrated by an unusual study of ex-nuns (San Giovanni, 1978) who had entered a convent as teenagers. As they grew older, they had no experience at the conventional ages with structures involving such roles as consumer, worker, friend, or lover. Years later, when they left the convent as adult women to return to the lay world, they had to resume life where they had left off—at age 17!

Heuristic Value of Age Stratification

Continuing development of the concept since the 1970s shows both strengths and weaknesses of age stratification. It is indispensable for understanding cross-sectional age differences and cross-sectional structural arrangements at given periods of time. And it laid the groundwork for later A&S concepts that specify interrelationships among coexisting people and structures (Phases 3 and 4).

Useful as the concept is, however, the term *age stratification* can conjure up images that are overly static. Strata (or layers) of people at a *single* point in time is a misleading image of the obviously dynamic process of growing up and growing older *over* time. Nor do social structures stay put. Examples of structures that change are not hard to find. Thus, inequalities of power, influence, or money have sometimes favored one age stratum, sometimes another. For example, Zuckerman and Merton (1972) counterpose "gerontocracy" in undeveloped societies, where old people are the chieftains, with "juvenocracy" in modern scientific establishments, where the newly educated hold sway; and in the United States there has been a shift from old to young in the age strata with highest levels of poverty (Foner, 1994). This recognition of *changeability* in age stratification demanded A&S attention to the dynamic processes underlying the changes.

TWO DYNAMISMS (PHASE 2)

To offset the unintentionally static overtones of age stratification, we introduced a dynamic emphasis (Phase 2) by defining TWO DYNAMISMS—changing lives and changing structures—as interdependent but distinct sets of processes. Here the apparently static strata of people who differ in age and the structures that are differentially appropriate for particular ages could be seen as *cross-section slices* through these two dynamisms. Today, of course, students of age recognize that age differences at given times cannot be used directly for understanding the aging process over time. Essential as cross-sections are for many purposes, their meanings can be comprehended only by examining the underlying dynamisms more closely.

Changing Lives

The dynamism of changing lives refers to the successive cohorts of people who are born, grow older, die, and are replaced by oncoming cohorts. Understanding of this dynamism began with recognition of COHORT DIFFERENCES: *Because society changes, members of different cohorts (i.e., born at different times) age in different ways.* Over their lives, from birth to death, people move through structures that are continually altered with the course of history; thus, the lives of those who are growing old today *cannot* be the same as the lives of those who grew old in the past or of those who will grow old in the future.

This concept is not easy to grasp, but its use has been gradually demonstrating its power. Large cohort differences have been found in people's standard of living, educational level and technical skills, diet and exercise, exposure to acute versus chronic diseases, attitudes toward other people, and views of the world. Cohort differences are manifest even at young ages: newborns now weigh more than their predecessors, and children now experiment with drugs or become sexually active much earlier. Such changed characteristics of cohort members now young are bound to have consequences for their later lives—their occupational trajectories, gender relationships, health and functioning.

Despite the many differences among cohorts, all cohorts share alike in one of the rare universal principles in social science, the *universality of aging and cohort succession* (Riley, 1973). As long as the society endures, people in every cohort invariably grow up, become fertile, grow old, die, and are replaced by oncoming cohorts. This universality in lives, when later seen as interdependent with structural change (Phase 3), led A&S to reaffirm the Heraclitean basis of the social system—not as "social order," as sometimes assumed, but as *inevitable change.*

Apart from this similarity among cohorts, the very existence of cohort differences demonstrates that social and structural changes are at work in people's lives—evolution of the human genome is too glacial to account for short-term changes from cohort to cohort (Riley & Abeles, 1990). However, cohort differences in lives provide only crude clues to the nature of their interrelationships with structures.

Changing Structures

Less well understood than the dynamism of changing lives through cohort differences is the dynamism of changing structures, in which age criteria are altered. Our thinking was influenced by many examples, such as changes in the expected ages for entering or retiring from work, or in the age-related expectations for continuing education. Age criteria are often altered directly, as changes are made by government in age of eligibility for Social Security or by companies in age of eligibility for pensions. Alternatively, age criteria are altered indirectly as part of other social changes. As a well-known example, structural changes associated with industrialization produced age barriers that have restricted participation of older people (as well as children) in the economy and of middle-aged people in education or leisure pursuits—the three boxes again. Here structural changes operate at particular ages to curtail (or in other instances to enlarge) opportunities, not only for income and power but also for affection, respect from others, self-esteem, and life experiences.

Once we had specified these two dynamisms, a wide avenue was opened for theoretical development. A&S could now examine *how* the dynamisms operate together through the intricate layers of the social system and how they influence each other to produce the central theme of the paradigm.

INTERPLAY (PHASE 3)

Phase 3 brings the dynamisms together by exploring the interplay between them. It begins to specify the nature and implications of two connecting concepts: the INTERDEPENDENCE and the inevitable ASYNCHRONY between the dynamisms.

Interdependence

How is it, we asked ourselves, that structural changes and changes in the patterns of people's lives continually influence each other? Why is it that neither can be understood without the other?

Several historical examples energized our understanding of these reciprocal influences. Among them was Smelser's (1968) account of changes in work, family, and lives of parents and children during the Industrial Revolution in England. First, a new technology that routinized tasks of spinning and weaving allowed the entire family to work together as a unit, either in the factory or in the home (structural innovation). Then, parents responded to this change through new behavior patterns in which, even though the children's work lasted from sunup to sundown, parents could provide discipline and even some recreation (changes in lives) and could hold their families together (structural change). Later, however, with still further technological developments, these family patterns broke down: spinners were required to hire more assistants than they had children, and home weavers were forced to send their children into the factories (structural change). Then, as fathers lost direct control and protection of their offspring (change in lives), the state interceded by providing schools for children during several hours of the parents' working day (structural change). Thus, the splitting apart of parents and children not only transformed structures of work and family but also created entirely new educational structures. Structural change had further impact on lives. And so on. (This example also illustrates how new meanings of childhood and adolescence emerged as new stages of life, anticipating our later work in Phase 4.)

In a more recent example, Henretta (1994) has analyzed the historical shift from lifetime employment toward contingent (temporary and part-time) employment, which has produced differences in career trajectories (lives) between today's cohort of older workers and the cohorts who will be old in the future; and these cohort differences, in turn, raise questions of possible future structural changes in both firms and families.

Such empirical examples have not only helped us to understand the conceptual interdependence between the dynamisms of changes in lives and in structures (cf. Schooler, Caplan, & Oates, 1997) but also serve to underscore the principle that neither lives nor structures can ever be stationary (cf. Foner & Kertzer, 1978).

Asynchrony

But this never-ending interplay between structures and lives does not run smoothly. Although the two dynamisms are interdependent, differences in *timing*, or ASYNCHRONY, are inherent in the interplay. The biological lifetime of people has a definite (though variable) rhythm from birth to death. But the timing of structural processes has no comparable rhythm or periodicity. While people are growing older, structures are going through entirely different historical sets of ups and downs in science, the economy, cultural values, or political leadership, to say nothing of cataclysmic events like wars or famines. Thus, lives and structures rarely, if ever, fit together. *Imbalances* arise between what people of given ages need and expect in their lives and what structures have to offer. These imbalances exert strains on both the people and the social institutions involved, creating pressures for further change.

Imbalances

As we pursued the implications of the lives/structures equation, it became clear that imbalances can occur in either direction. Where technology is highly developed, lives often lag behind structures: many people simply cannot keep up with sophisticated advances as in aeronautics or communication. (For example, some older people, because of fear of computers, do not benefit from direct access from home to shopping or banking; and some young people are not motivated to master the scientific knowledge needed in new jobs.) But in modern societies more generally (Kohli & Rein, 1991), the predominant imbalance has been a lag of structures behind lives; in particular, society has failed to provide opportunities in education, family, or work for the growing numbers of competent older people.

This structural lag (Riley, Kahn, & Foner, 1994) occurred because, during the 20th century, *lives* have undergone revolutionary changes. For the first time in history, *most* people live to be old. Not too long ago the statistical norm for dying was age 50; now we learn that people who survive to 85 may well live to 100 or even longer (Vaupel & Jeune, 1994). Moreover, today's older people (despite the minority who are seriously disabled) are on average healthier and more capable than their predecessors (Manton, Corder, & Stallard, 1997), as advances in technology, medicine, and public health have enhanced the biopsychosocial processes of aging over people's lives. Yet until recently, the complementary changes in social, cultural, and economic *structures* have been lagging behind. Older people's needs for involvement and esteem have been frustrated. Younger people too are affected. Middle-aged adults have been overburdened with responsibilities, and increasing numbers hold jobs without health care coverage. Children have few "real-world" opportunities, and for those whose mothers work outside the home few adequate care facilities are available. Thus, stubborn remnants of those three boxes, with their age constraints and "ageist" biases, still persist.

Social Homeostasis

However, such imbalances, or lags, cannot persist for long. When they become severe, they themselves become an inherent force for change. They tend to energize the interplay between lives and structures in the direction of the dynamism that is lagging. Here we speak in A&S of SOCIAL HOMEOSTASIS, as built-in pressures—*not* toward a stable equilibrium, but toward *new* changes that might improve the mesh between lives and structures.

One instance of homeostatic pressures focuses on the imbalances between cohorts of people too large or too small for the available age-appropriate roles. This had long ago been conceptualized as "disordered cohort flow" by our co-worker, Joan Waring (1975), who showed in detail how structures can be adjusted to make room for differing numbers and kinds of people. Sometimes the balance is redressed simply by changing the *numbers* of available roles, as by building new schools for increases in the school-age population or nursing homes for excessive numbers of elderly patients or by converting unneeded buildings for new uses. Alternatively, age criteria are modified. For example, with the baby boom, the age of entry to educational institutions was first raised; subsequently, with the dwindling of applications for college, age restrictions on entry of older adults were often removed. Also, changes in age of eligibility for retirement benefits can stimulate increases or decreases in the supply of older workers. In the interplay, of course, such structural alterations in turn disrupt the lives of the people involved.

As these and other forms of homeostatic pressure operate to reduce today's structural lag, they presage untold future changes, which will demand further conceptualization and refinement in the A&S paradigm or its functional equivalent. Thus, we bequeath a large theory-building agenda to the oncoming generation of students of age.

IMPENDING CHANGES (PHASE 4)

Phase 4 anticipates some of the possible future transformations in age and its meaning. Considering ways in which such transformations might emerge from the interplay between the dynamisms, we discuss two concepts, already emerging, that may lend themselves to further development: Age Integration and Cohort Norm Formation.

Age Integration

In our search for clearer understanding of possible responses to the structural lag, we postulated AGE INTEGRATION as an extreme type of structure, in opposition to the extreme age-differentiated type of the well-known three boxes. These types were originally defined as "ideal," in Max Weber's classic sense that they do not exist in reality. But there are signs that age integration is increasingly becoming real. For years the A&S paradigm had been predicting it. For years, however, it was regarded as visionary—until now, when many elements of age integration are already upon us (Riley & Riley, 1993, 1994).

Thus, the *age barriers* dividing education, work and family, and retirement are becoming more flexible. Role opportunities and responsibilities in all structures are more and more open to people of every age. More individuals can intersperse over their entire lives periods of education or work with periods of leisure or time with family. There are more arrangements for taking time off from jobs to retool for changes in employment. Increasingly, whether they realize it or not, people no longer need to hurry through life.

Particularly challenging is the fact that, as age barriers are removed, age integration *brings people of different ages together.* Thus, as education becomes lifelong, old and young are students together. More firms are integrating the workforce through "unretirement," or rehiring retired employees as consultants. In many families four generations are alive at the same time; and as people approach the end of life, home health care with wide access to others often replaces the age segregation of nursing homes (cf. Uhlenberg, 1997).

A possible shift toward an age-integrated society demands attention from A&S (Riley, 1997a) and from the next generation of theory builders. What might such a society be like? And what conceptual developments would be called for?

A&S is beginning to explore what potential *benefits* there might be. Older people's involvement in the wider society might enhance their health and functioning. It might also relieve the middle-aged of excessive burdens of work and family. Both old and young might benefit by socializing each other, as older people teach the young, and young people, even babies, evoke responses from the old. Each might gain new knowledge by sharing experiences with the other. They might come to understand each other's differences. And they might even recognize their common humanity—every old person was once young, and every young person will be old—a common humanness that transcends their many age-related differences. In such a society, members of older generations could be energized by the fresh ideas of the young, and members of younger generations could adapt the experience of their elders.

At the same time, theoretical attention must be given to the *disadvantages* entailed by age integration if it eventuates. People's differing experiences might lead to misunderstandings, tensions, even intergenerational conflict. Some older people might prefer the familiarity of age-differentiated structures and the hope of a financially secure retirement. Working part-time or starting over in new careers might often require accepting periods of reduced income or loss of benefits—an untenable requirement for many lower income workers. Even for those better off, giving precedence to family and leisure over work might involve sacrificing some of the traditional emphases on "success," materialism, consumerism, and economic security.

Thus, a shift toward age integration would challenge not only the place of age in the familiar rigid structures but also the age-related norms institutionalized in those structures and incorporated into people's lives. To the extent that formerly age-segregated people are now coming into increased contact with one another, the groundwork is laid in A&S for exploring *how* alterations in norms—in the very meanings of age—can occur. And this, it seems to us, is a clear mandate for the next generation.

Cohort Norm Formation

Whatever form of age integration may eventuate in the 21st century, the oncoming generation of researchers will confront a drastically altered society. In it the place and the meaning of age in structures and lives will predictably be changed. We focus here on another concept that is potentially useful, though still embryonic, for understanding mechanisms of change: COHORT NORM FORMATION. Here we think of a continuing process, in which behaviors and attitudes that develop within a cohort in response to social change become crystallized as new norms or ideologies—new meanings—that then pervade and influence all age strata and social structures. This concept requires much future development, although it has been foreshadowed in previous attempts to specify the interplay between lives and structures (as in the changing meanings of "childhood" during the Industrial Revolution).

An Early Example

Among the earlier examples of cohort norm formation we began with an analysis of changing meanings of *gender* that seems relevant also for *age*. Data on the century-long changes in the work lives of women provide clues to the interplay with changes in structures. Looking back over 100 years, we could begin to trace the interplay as larger and larger proportions of women in each successive cohort spent their adult *lives* in the labor force. Next, it became clear that *structures* also were changing, as more and more employers opened work roles for women. Gradually, too, the *norms* built into work and family structures also changed: first, it became acceptable for women to work; then it was often *expected* that women *should* work. As the interplay continues into the future, these alterations in both work and family *struc-*

tures will, in turn, bring still further changes into every aspect of women's *lives*. The meaning of women's roles, as well as the complementary roles of men, has been revolutionized (Riley, 1992).

Elements of Norm Formation

The conceptual elements of cohort norm formation, as gleaned from such historical accounts, may be described as a dialectical process (Riley 1978): (a) in response to social change, many individuals in a cohort begin to change their lives by developing new age-typical patterns and regularities of behavior and thought; (b) these patterns are then defined as age-appropriate norms, expectations, and rules, which become institutionalized as changed criteria in social structures; (c) in turn these structural changes redirect age-related behavior and thought into further changes in lives, which then affect structures, and so on and on.

Such elements are already visible in *today's* response to structural lag: each cohort is exerting a collective force as it moves through society, pressing for adjustments not only in the form of social roles but also in the underlying meanings and expectations. It is not surprising that many people no longer passively accept the age constraints that have confronted them as they grow older. Rather, they think and act in new ways that challenge the outdated social institutions that have marginalized both the old and the young in our society. Their new ways may gradually crystallize to become innovations in social structure. People themselves are creating original and rewarding opportunities that reduce the problems of structural lag. And it is not only the healthiest and most vigorous older people but also the disabled and the institutionalized who increasingly demand meaningful roles. Younger people too are encouraging change. Harried middle-aged people cry out for some share in the countless hours of free time that often hang heavy on older people in retirement. Children also are eager to be involved in useful activities.

Sources of Norm Formation

Of course, the dialectical process of changing norms does not always start with people whose individual actions in shaping their own fate coalesce to transform the social structures. Sometimes the process is initiated by leaders in government or industry. In other instances the impetus for change emanates from organized collective action on behalf of particular age groups, as the 1930s Townsend movement among older people influenced the enactment of Social Security legislation in the United States (Foner, 1974, 1994). Whatever its source, the process of norm formation involves a continuing interplay between structures and lives, which often ramifies through all age strata and several generations (cf. Mayer, 1988).

Future Meanings

But how, if the present trend toward age integration is sustained, can the concept of cohort norm formation be sharpened and specified? In a future age-integrated society, will younger people become accustomed to sharing paid jobs and material rewards with the elderly while older people share some of their leisure with the young? Will such changed behaviors generate new structures to provide support for old and young, rich and poor, to lead more flexible lives? Will structural changes, in turn, affect norms at the basic level of values—perhaps dissipating some of today's materialism, cynicism, and self-absorption? In the quest for answers in this era of change, a special challenge to future researchers is to intensify efforts to look *beneath the surface* of changing lives and structures, to search for possible fundamental changes in ideologies and values that could define entirely new meanings of age.

A PARTING WORD

For the next generation, the A&S paradigm has formulated several interrelated concepts for tracing the shape and meaning of age during the past century and into the next. This web of concepts has helped to identify what is important in describing and understanding age, as age affects individuals and also is embedded in and influences social structures. Our hope is that the oncoming cohorts of researchers in many disciplines will modify the concepts to reflect future changes, and will find them stimulating in the search for new interpretations, broad agendas, and innovative methods for the study of age in the 21st century.

NOTES

1. This chapter is a component of the Program on Age and Structural Change (PASC) at the National Institute on Aging.

2. Our discussion draws heavily on theory and research centered in the United States, although the underlying principles have broader applicability.

3. The current NIA emphasis is on the often neglected structural components, through the Program on Age and Structural Change (PASC).

4. Age stratification has since become fundamental in many theories of age; and although it has been enlarged and modified as the "A&S paradigm," it is often treated as a social science "perspective."

5. *Structures* refers broadly here to societal institutions, such as the family, the economy, and educational, political, and religious organizations; their component roles; their rules and resources; their built-in culture and values; and the social environment.

REFERENCES

Alexander, J. C. (1988). The new theoretical movement. In N. J. Smelser (Ed.), *Handbook of sociology* (pp. 77–101). Newbury Park, CA: Sage.

Butler, R. N. (1989). Dispelling ageism: The cross-cutting intervention. *Annals of the American Academy of Political and Social Science. "The Quality of Aging: Strategies for Interventions," 503,* 138–147.

Danncfer, D. (1984). Aging as intracohort differentiation: Acculturation, the Matthew effect and the life course, *Sociological Forum, 2,* 211–236.

Fogel, R. W. (1993). Economic growth, population theory, and physiology. *American Economic Review, 84,* 369–395.

Foner, A. (1974). Age stratification and age conflict in political life. *American Sociological Review, 39,* 187–196.

Foner, A. (1986). *The study of aging and old age.* Englewood Cliffs, NJ: Prentice-Hall.

Foner, A. (1994). Endnote: The reach of an idea. In M. W. Riley, R. L. Kahn, & A. Foner (Eds.), *Age and structural lag: Society's failure to provide meaningful opportunities in work, family, and leisure* (pp. 263–280). New York: Wiley.

Foner, A., & Kertzer, D. I. (1978). Transitions over the life course: Lessons from age-set societies. *American Journal of Sociology, 83,* 1081–1104.

Hagestad, G., & Neugarten, B. L. (1985). Age and the life course. In R. H. Binstock & E. Shanas (Eds.), *Handbook of aging and the social sciences.* New York: Van Nostrand Reinhold.

Henretta, J. C. (1994). Social structure and age-based careers. In M. W. Riley, R. L. Kahn, & A. Foner (Eds), *Age and structural lag* (pp. 57–79). New York: Wiley.

Kohli, M., & Rein, M. (1991). The changing balance of work and retirement. In M. Kohli, M. Rein, A. M. Guillemard, & H. van Gunsteren (Eds.), *Time for retirement* (pp. 1–35). New York: Cambridge University Press.

Manton, K. G., Corder, L., & Stallard, E. (1997). Chronic disability trends in elderly United States populations: 1982–1994. *Proceedings of the National Academy of Sciences, 94,* 2593–2598.

Mayer, K. U. (1988). German survivors of World War II: Impact on the life course of the collective experience of birth cohorts. In M. W. Riley, B. J. Huber, & B. B. Hess (Eds.), *Social structures and human lives* (pp. 229–246). Newbury Park, CA: Sage.

Riley, M. W. (1973). Aging and cohort succession: Interpretations and misinterpretations. *Public Opinion Quarterly, 37*(1), 35–49.

Riley, M. W. (1976). Age strata in social systems. In R. H. Binstock & E. Shanas (Eds.), *Handbook of aging and the social sciences* (pp. 179–217). New York: Van Nostrand Reinhold.

Riley, M. W. (1978). Aging, social change, and the power of ideas. *Daedalus, 107,* 39–52.

Riley, M. W. (1992, April). *Longevity and opportunity: The future for women.* Paper presented at the Radcliffe Conference on Women over 50, Cambridge, MA.

Riley, M. W. (1994). Aging and society: Past, present, and future (Kent Award Lecture). *Gerontologist, 34,* 436–446.

Riley, M. W. (1997a). *Age integration: Challenge to a new institute.* Raleigh: University of North Carolina, Institute on Aging.

Riley, M. W. (1997b). Rational choice and the sociology of age: Heuristic models. *The American Sociologist, special issue, 28*(2), 54–60.

Riley, M. W., & Abeles, R. P. (1990). *The behavioral and social research program at the National Institute on Aging: History of a decade.* Bethesda, MD: National Institute on Aging.

Riley, M. W., & Foner, A., in association with M. E. Moore, B. Hess, & B. Roth. (1968). *Aging and society, Vol. 1. An inventory of research findings.* New York: Russell Sage Foundation.

Riley, M. W., Foner, A., & Waring, J. (1988). Sociology of age. In N. J. Smelser (Ed.), *Handbook of sociology* (pp. 243–290). Newbury Park, CA: Sage.

Riley, M. W., Johnson, M., & Foner, A. (1972). *Aging and society, Vol. 3. A sociology of age stratification.* New York: Russell Sage Foundation.

Riley, M. W., Kahn, R. L., & Foner, A. (1994). *Age and structural lag: Society's failure to provide meaningful opportunities in work, family, and leisure.* New York: Wiley.

Riley, M. W., & Riley, J. W., Jr. (1993). Connections: Kin and cohort. In V. L. Bengtson & W. A. Achenbaum (Eds.), *The changing contract across generations* (pp. 169–189). New York: Aldine de Gruyter.

Riley, M. W., & Riley, J. W., Jr. (1994). Age integration and the lives of older people. *Gerontologist, 34,* 110–115.

Riley, M. W., Riley, J. W., Jr., & Johnson, M. (1969). *Aging and society, Vol. 2. Aging and the professions.* New York: Russell Sage Foundation.

San Giovanni, L. (1978). *Ex-nuns.* Norwood, NJ: Ablex.

Schooler, C., Caplan, L., & Oates, G. (1997). Aging and work: An overview. In K. W. Schaie & C. Schooler (Eds.), *Impact of work on older individuals* (pp. 1–19). Hillsdale, NJ: Erlbaum.

Smelser, N. J. (1968). Sociological history: The Industrial Revolution and the British working class family. In N. J. Smelser (Ed.), *Essays in Sociological Explanation* (pp. 76–91). Englewood Cliffs, NJ: Prentice-Hall.

Sztompka, P. (1994). Society as social becoming: Beyond individualism and collectivism. In P. Sztompka (Ed.), *Agency and structure: Reorienting social theory* (pp. 251–282). Langbourne, PA.: Gordon and Breach.

Uhlenberg, P. (1997). Replacing the nursing home. *Public Interest, 128,* 73–84.

Vaupel, J. W., & Jeune, B. (1994). The emergence and proliferation of centenarians. *Population Studies of Aging No. 12.* Odense, Denmark: Odense University.

Waring, J. M. (1975). Social replenishment and social change: The problem of disordered cohort flow. *American Behavioral Scientist, 19,* 237–256.

Zuckerman, H., & Merton, R. K. (1972). Age, aging, and age structure in science. In M. W. Riley, M. Jonson, & A. Foner, *Aging and society* (Vol. 3, pp. 292–356). New York: Russell Sage Foundation.

19

The Political Economy Perspective in Aging

Jill Quadagno
Jennifer Reid

T he political economy perspective is less a formal theory of aging than a framework for examining the larger social context of old age problems (Bengtson, Burgess, & Parrott, 1997). The term *political economy* sometimes simply refers to the interplay of public and private, state and market; at other times it implies a particular theoretical or methodological approach to analyzing society.

The political economy of aging framework recognizes old age as socially constructed, a product of struggles that result in the unequal distribution of societal resources. The central objective of the political economy of aging is to analyze the structural conditions that create inequality in old age and to emphasize the relevance of these struggles for understanding how the aged are defined and treated (Estes, Linkins, & Binney, 1996). As Estes (1991) explains, "The political economy of aging offers a theoretical and empirical perspective on the socioeconomic determinants of the experience of aging and old age and on the policy interventions that emerge in the context of capitalist society" (p. 19). Thus, the challenge for social gerontology is not simply to understand how people interpret their private troubles but rather to consider also how these private troubles become public issues, thereby generating a societal response (Estes, Gerard, Zones, & Swan, 1984). It is this emphasis on elucidating the underlying political and economic processes that create inequality in old age on the basis of class, gender, and race that distinguishes the political economy perspective from other macro-social theories of aging.

ORIGINS OF THE POLITICAL ECONOMY PERSPECTIVE

Contributions of Classical Social Theory

The basic conceptual elements of contemporary theories of inequality and social stratification are found in their original form in the theories of Karl Marx (1818–1883) and Max Weber (1864–1920). Both rejected the biopsychological approach of attributing inequality to "human nature" and instead viewed inequality as the product of economic and political forces.

For Marx the key determinant of human behavior and human consciousness was the relationship of humans to nature, by which he meant the material conditions of life. According to Marx, a given level of economic production creates a distinctive set of social relations. The crucial factor in the creation of classes is the ownership of the means of production. Marx's view of the class structure is based on the simple dichotomy between owner and nonowner, or capitalist and worker. All other factors (such as income, occupation, education, and political power) are derivative and secondary. In Marxian theory, economic classes based on the ownership of the means of production are synonymous with social classes because beliefs and values correspond to economic behavior (Giddens, 1971).

Marx's monocausal view of class stratification was subsequently modified by Max Weber (1946), who acknowledged the importance of economic forces in the formation of social strata but also regarded sociocultural variables as relevant to the distribution of material and symbolic benefits. Religious beliefs, canons of taste, the definition of work, and political forces could exert powerful controls over economic forces. Thus, Weber contended that a simple economic determinism was inconsistent with the historical record and that the analysis of inequality required that a distinction be made between class (market factors, income, wealth, property), status (cultural evaluations, and lifestyle), and party (access to the state, the ability to create and enforce the law).

Although Marx and Weber perceived the fundamental sources of social inequality differently, they agreed that systems of social stratification produced differences between human groups. That insight created a paradigm for sociological theory in the first four or five decades of the 20th century. Initially, research on stratification focused on the cultural and social determinants of inequality while ignoring the structural and economic sources. This emphasis was reflected in research on status attainment (Sewell & Hauser, 1995) and later in age stratification theory (Riley, Johnson & Foner, 1972).

Contributions of Contemporary Social Theory

Legacy of Status Attainment Research

Status attainment research in the social sciences originated in the postwar optimism generated by prosperity and economic growth (Bell, 1973). The underlying image of society in this literature was that affluent, postwar America was being classless, as more and more people were becoming incorporated into an expanding middle layer. The growth of industry, the spread of egalitarian norms, mass education, urbanization, bureaucratization, and professionalization—these trends suggested that economic and political inequality was declining, and social mobility between classes was increasing. The income scale was becoming compressed at both ends of the hierarchy: there were fewer rich and fewer poor (Knottnerus, 1987). The problem for research was to examine how ascriptive characteristics (like one's family of birth, one's gender or race) compared to achieved characteristics like education in determining an one's social and economic status. Because the United States had a fluid class structure, according to this view, all Americans had virtually unlimited opportunities for upward mobility. The research agenda was to determine the factors that influenced social mobility (Blau & Duncan, 1967).

Implicit in status attainment research and its underlying theory was a life course perspective because social mobility occurred across generations. Nearly all of these studies defined social mobility in terms of the transmission of occupational status among men within families. The focus was on the degree to which an individual's social standing was associated with the characteristics of his family of origin (Sewell & Hauser, 1975).

A more recent version of status attainment theory, promulgated by Dannefer (1991) and O'Rand (1996), is the theory of *cumulative disadvantage*, which applies a life course approach to the analysis of stratification among the aged. The central premise of the theory is that inequality is the product of institutional arrangements as well as aggregated individual actions over time. Although social mobility occurs at all points in the class structure, people who begin life in a position of social advantage generally are better positioned to acquire additional resources than those who begin life at the bottom of the stratification system. The major contribution of the theory of cumulative disadvantage is that it has provided a framework for analyzing inequality as a cumulative process that is produced over the life course. Although it recognizes that inequality is the result of differential opportunity structures, it fails to conceptualize why disadvantage is not randomly distributed but rather exhibits identifiable patterns.

Legacy of Age Stratification Theory

Age stratification theory (Riley et al., 1972) borrows concepts from class stratification and applies them to age. Deriving more from Weber than from

Marx, the implicit view of class stratification is that it is associated with societies with growing economies, which require specialized expertise that creates a ranking within the occupational system. The dimensions of social class include economic variables like income and wealth, prestige variables that refer to a subjective ranking, and power, such as political participation and the distribution of justice (Weber, 1946). When a full system of stratification is in place, social positions are ranked and rewarded differentially, acquired by individuals (and thus their families), and transmitted over generations.

The idea that age may be used as a criteria for organizing social relations was first elaborated by social theorists like Sorokin (1941), Parsons (1942) and Eisenstadt (1956), who attempted to understand "why and when age is used by society as a means for sorting people into positions and as a device for allocating goods and services" (Featherman, 1983, p. 9). Age stratification theory represents an effort to integrate these ideas into a formal statement (Riley, 1971). The underlying proposition of age stratification theory is that all societies group people into social categories on the basis of age, a practice that not only provides social identities but also determines the distribution of resources (Riley, 1971; Riley et al., 1972).

Despite the fact that the theory of age stratification contains an implicit focus on both individual life course rhythms and large-scale structural change, it came under attack in the 1970s by a new generation of sociologists, many of whom were influenced by Marxist theory. These critics contended that it relied on an inherently static concept of social structure, that it neglected political processes inherent in the creation of inequality, and that it ignored institutionalized patterns of inequality. Age stratification theory was criticized for defining social structure as relationships among positions and for ignoring the power relationships that determine how statuses and roles were allocated (Marshall, 1996). It also neglected the fact that age, although a pivotal source of social identity, often had less impact on an individual's life chances than other dimensions of stratification and that, within age cohorts, race, gender, and social class create wide variations between individuals (Dowd, 1987; Hogan & Astone, 1986).

From these criticisms of age stratification theory the political economy perspective emerged. The objective of this perspective is to explain age-related patterned inequality through a historical analysis of characteristics of societal organization that create differential opportunities over the life course and across generations. Because the state (or government) is the principal site of political organization, much of the research in the political economy tradition has focused on how the state ameliorates or augments inequality.

THE WELFARE STATE AS A SYSTEM OF STRATIFICATION

A core assumption of the political economy approach is that public policies for income, health, long-term care, and social services are an outcome of the social struggles and dominant power relations of the era, which are not merely components of private sector relationships but also are adjudicated within the state. To a large extent the state organizes class, gender, and race relations through the welfare state, which consists of social programs and tax policies that determine the distribution of societal resources (Estes, 1979; Quadagno, 1988). As Esping-Anderson (1990) explains, welfare states are "key institutions in the structuring of class and the social order. The organizational features of the welfare state help determine the articulation of social solidarity, divisions of class, and status differentiation" (p. 55). Although the welfare state may seek to lessen social inequality, it is in itself a system of stratification that contributes to the ranking of individuals in a social hierarchy (Smelser, 1988). By providing differential access to power and resources, the welfare state enables some individuals to protect and enhance their status while reducing the power and resources of others. Thus, welfare programs may reinforce gender, age, and racial stratification and thus reproduce inequality over the life course.

As the primary site of the civil functions of the state, the welfare state has become the central research focus of the political economy perspective. A large share of government expenditures in all Western, capitalist democracies is directed toward the aged. In consequence, much of the literature has been concerned with the organization of public pension systems and the distribution of public pension income. However, recent studies involve a broader array of programs targeted at reducing insecurity at various phases of the life course.

PRINCIPLES OF DISTRIBUTION

Welfare states are institutions designed to harmonize the production of wealth with its distribution. The welfare state is articulated by its power to tax, its power to distribute resources, and its power to regulate. Although much of the literature on the welfare state has focused on its distributional component, current policy directions cannot be understood as independent of the taxation and regulatory functions. Together, these functions consist of rules and policies that redistribute resources, by setting levels and forms of taxation and by establishing eligibility criteria and benefit formulas.

Cross-national comparisons have been based on two distinguishing characteristics of welfare states: the forms of provision and the bases of entitlement. Welfare programs can be classified into three types: social assistance, social insurance, and fiscal welfare. Each has its own set of rules regarding who pays for the benefit, who is eligible to receive it, and how much beneficiaries receive. Moreover, each type of program reflects a particular set of values and attitudes toward the needy.

Social Assistance

Social assistance benefits derive from the 16th century British system of poor relief, which was based on the principle of "less eligibility," meaning that the treatment of the poor was intended to be less desirable than the treatment of the lowest wage earners (Myles, 1989). They were incorporated into the principles governing "outdoor relief" in the American colonies. The basis of entitlement is need, determined through the administration of a means test. Means tests are often considered demeaning and humiliating by applicants for benefits, because individuals' private lives, income, assets, and behaviors are subject to scrutiny and judgment. In some cases, people who are poor enough to meet the eligibility criteria are still denied benefits because they are viewed as thriftless or immoral. Therefore, social assistance recipients are not viewed as entitled to their benefits; rather they are recipients of charity. Because means-tested benefits are quite low and accompanied by social stigma, they compel all but the most desperate to participate in the labor market (Marmor, Mashaw, & Harvey, 1990).

Reliance on social assistance implies an adherence to a residual welfare state strategy, which recognizes that social risk is unevenly distributed across the social strata. Aid is targeted to that strata—the disabled, single mothers, the poor—an approach that divides society into a self-reliant majority and a dependent core of welfare state clientele (Esping-Anderson, 1997).

Social Insurance

Social insurance recognizes that social risks are unevenly distributed over the life course, and its objective is to provide security against loss of income from such risks as unemployment, widowhood, or retirement. The central image of social insurance is an earned entitlement (Marmor et al., 1990). One factor that distinguishes social insurance from social assistance is the notion that people contribute to a common pool. Making contributions gives them an earned right to benefits, a distinct contrast to social assistance programs in which benefits are considered charity for the poor and not entitlements. A second distinguishing characteristic is the view that people share these life course risks. Pooling the risks means that the costs for one family or individual are shared across an entire population. In social insurance programs, criteria other than need determine who receives benefits. Often that criterion is age.

Fiscal Welfare

There is a third form of social provision that often goes unrecognized. Fiscal welfare consists of special income tax provisions that provide preferential tax treatment (i.e., tax breaks) for certain expenses (Shalev, 1996). These provisions in income tax laws decrease tax revenues from individuals and corporations to the federal government. The distinguishing feature of fiscal welfare is its linkage of benefits solely to the labor market. Because benefits are provided through the private sector but subsidized by the tax system, they are part of the "hidden welfare state."

In the United States fiscal welfare programs are called tax expenditures. Among the items that qualify as tax expenditures are employee contributions to employer-provided pensions, personal savings for retirement, employer-provided health insurance, and home mortgage interest. These programs represent an indirect approach to achieving public objectives such as encouraging savings for retirement, expanding health coverage insurance, and encouraging home ownership.

Tax expenditures are inherently unequal in their impact because they allow individuals receiving the same income to pay taxes at different rates (Street, 1996). For example, workers who contribute to an employer-provided pension fund pay less in taxes than do workers who do not. Similarly, individuals who receive health insurance though their employer pay lower taxes than those who have no health insurance. Home owners can deduct the interest they pay on their mortgage, whereas renters with similar incomes pay more in taxes. Tax expenditures also promote inequality because they disproportionately benefit the middle and upper middle class, whereas the working class and the poor receive little or no benefit from them because they are more likely to rent and less likely to have jobs with benefits.

Welfare states vary in the extent to which they rely on social assistance, social insurance, or fiscal welfare, as well as in how the bases of entitlement to benefits are organized. The structure of the welfare state has implications for class, gender, and racial equality.

PROCESSES OF STRATIFICATION

The central premise of the first generation of welfare state theorists was that the history of Western capitalist democracies was inextricably linked to the development of citizenship, defined as the rights and entitlements that attach to individuals by virtue of their membership in a national community rather than to their property, status, or market capacity. In evolutionary terms, civil and political rights were followed by social rights, defined as the right of protection from economic insecurity. Social rights reduce class inequality by providing power to workers in their conflicts with employers over wages and working conditions (Korpi, 1989). The locus of activity is the market, and the protagonists are capitalists and workers.

The second generation of theories of the welfare state originated in a feminist critique of class-based theorists for ignoring the gendered dimensions of the welfare state. Feminist theorists have emphasized that welfare states were created on a series of premises about the family, the economy, and the life course. The core premise was that the main recipient of social benefits was a male manufacturing worker who was the sole provider of family income and family entitlement and a female homemaker who would cease work with marriage and childbirth and thus be available to care for family members over the life course—first children, then aging parents. The ideal life course was one of continuous employment from leaving school to retirement, and programs most rewarded those who adhered to this model. Feminist theorists view the family as the locus of conflict and the protagonists as men and women.

There is a third generation of welfare state theory, less developed than the previous two, that emphasizes how the welfare state may promote racial stratification by mirroring the inequality embedded in other societal institutions. From this perspective, the objective of the welfare state is the promotion of equal opportunity, the locus of conflict is racially segregated institutions, and the protagonists are the White society and minorities.

Class Stratification

Class-based theorists view the welfare state as the result of political struggles between workers and capitalists, with the quality of social benefits serving as a measure of success (Stephens, 1979). Programs that "decommodify" workers provide an alternative to low wage work through unemployment or retirement benefits. Empirical tests of class-based theories typically involve comparisons across nations in levels of expenditures on public pensions. They generally confirm that nations with labor-dominated, social democratic parties have more generous social welfare programs than those without and that the presence of left-wing parties expands the public economy and leads to more redistributive policies of taxation and expenditure (Hicks & Swank, 1984; Myles, 1989).

The observation of regularities in patterns of social provision led to efforts to develop a typology of welfare state regimes. The concept of regimes provides a schema for classifying nations according to their dominant forms of social provision, basis of entitlement, and stratification outcomes. "Liberal" regimes are characterized by minimal intervention in the market. As Esping-Anderson (1990) explains, "Liberalism's ideal of stratification is the competitive individualism that the market supposedly cultivates" (p. 64). Liberal welfare states follow the Elizabethan poor relief tradition, relying heavily on means-tested social assistance. Need is the basic principle of eligibility, and benefits are designed to maintain existing patterns of stratification. The U.S. welfare state, for example, is classified as a liberal regime.

In "conservative" regimes, by contrast, benefits are based on participation in the labor market. The welfare state maintains traditional status relations by providing distinct programs for different class and status groups. In 19th century Germany, for example, Bismarck's pension plan constructed a myriad of social insurance schemes, each with its peculiar rules, finances, and benefit structure. Workers' pension plans were distinct from those of miners, and those of civil servants were distinct from those of white collar employees.

Finally, in "social democratic" regimes benefits are bestowed on the basis of citizenship. They promote status equality by endowing all citizens with similar rights, regardless of social class or occupation. The prototypical social democratic welfare state is Sweden, which provides benefits as a right of citizenship. The high quality of the benefits eliminates class and status cleavages and solidifies support for the welfare state (Esping-Anderson, 1990).

Gender Stratification

Feminist theories have stressed how the welfare state, through its public policies, political ideologies, and organizational principles, reproduces the gendered division of labor and male domination. Feminist analyses note that although social insurance is proclaimed superior to social assistance because it is based on the concept of an earned right, these benefits universally disadvantage women relative to men because they are based on labor market participation. For example, in Sweden, as the social insurance program has matured, the degree of inequality in benefits between men and women has increased (Sainsbury, 1996). Similarly, in the United States, women who receive Social Security through their own work histories receive lower benefits than male workers do; benefits are calculated to reward high earners with stable work histories—those who have never taken time out for family caregiving and who have rarely been unemployed (Harrington Meyer, 1990). Many older women have never worked outside the home for wages; most of those who did moved in and out of the labor force to care for children and aging parents (O'Rand & Henretta, 1982). As a result of their caregiving responsibilities, relatively few older women have contributed to Social Security long enough to qualify for maximum benefits.

Initially, feminist theorists agreed with class-based theorists that social assistance was an inferior form of social provision that primarily constructed women in terms of their relation to the household (Fraser, 1989). As O'Connor (1996) stresses, "The important distinction being emphasized here is that between rights and needs as the basis for access to benefits and services" (p. 60). Women whose lives did not mirror the traditional household arrangement of male breadwinner and female dependent were disadvantaged by the eligibility criteria. More recent feminist research has shown that although benefits based on the principle of need are often stigmatizing and minimal, they may also enhance the status of women if they are accompanied by an ideology that recognizes the right to a basic minimum income (Sainsbury, 1996).

Feminist theorists also criticize class-based models for emphasizing labor market status, need, and citizenship as the bases of entitlement while ignoring women's entitlements as wives, mothers, and informal caregivers to elderly or infirm parents. In her comparative research, for example, Sainsbury (1996) adds to the main bases of entitlement the principle of "care." Although benefits based on the principle of care may reinforce the traditional household of male breadwinner/female homemaker, they may also be more generous than those based on labor force participation. In the case of Social Security benefits, for example, the average monthly widow's benefit is substantially more generous than the average woman worker's benefit (Harrington Meyer, 1996).

An examination of benefits based on the principle of care also suggests that classed-based typologies of welfare state regimes often wrongly group countries by their stratifying effects. For example, Sweden and the Netherlands are typically classified as social democratic welfare states; however, along several gender-relevant dimensions, they represent polar opposites. In the Netherlands, benefits tend to be organized around the breadwinner model, whereas in Sweden they are based on individual entitlement independent of marital status (Sainsbury, 1996).

Feminist theories of the welfare state have added a gender dimension to class-based arguments about inequality. They have illuminated how gender inequality in old age is a consequence of political decisions about eligibility rules that create institutionalized mechanisms that penalize women for limited life choices and restricted labor market opportunities. Depending on the particular welfare state regime, women may be disadvantaged in their later years through welfare programs whose eligibility requirements are based on a male model of labor market participation.

Racial Stratification

Class-based models of welfare state provision emphasize the amelioration of life course risks but largely ignore the problem of the intergenerational transmission of risk that is ascriptively determined on the basis of race or ethnic origin (Esping-Anderson, 1997). Yet the risk of being a victim of racial discrimination, which is produced in the family and then compounded in the market, is not diminished by social programs that target life course risks but fail to redistribute life chances. In this case, the problem to be solved is the systematic reproduction of inequality that produces inherited disadvantages.

Analyses of the effect of social provision on racial equality have largely been ignored in theoretical debates about the welfare state. Yet in the United

States, statistics clearly indicate a wide disparity in income and wealth in old age on the basis of race, which represents the indicators of a process of systematic reproduction of intergenerational risk over the life course. In 1990, for example, median income among people over 65 was $14,839 for white males compared to $7,450 for African American males; for females the figures were $8,462 and $5,617, respectively (U.S. Bureau of the Census, 1993). Income inequality in old age reflects the consequences of racial discrimination in employment opportunities over the life course, which leads in turn to lower Social Security benefits and less access to private pension income.

An even greater racial disparity exists in the distribution of wealth. The home is the single most important asset of most Americans. African Americans are disadvantaged, compared to Whites, in home ownership and home value. In 1994 only 43.4% of African Americans owned their own homes, compared to 64% of Whites (*Statistical Abstract of the United States,* 1996). The Health and Retirement Survey (a nationally representative study of employment, income, assets, and health and retirement plans of individuals who were aged 51 to 61 in 1992) shows that the value of home equity was $36,658 for Blacks and $78,708 for Whites (Angel & Angel, 1996).

A theory based on the recognition that risk can be transmitted intergenerationally acknowledges that measures of the distribution of wealth tap not only present resources but also material assets that have historical origins. As Oliver and Shapiro (1995) note, "Wealth signifies the command over financial resources that a family has accumulated over its lifetime along with those resources that have been inherited across generations" (p. 2). Intergenerational risks are the product of political decisions compounded by market forces. Racial inequality in housing wealth, for example, is one of the legacies of federal housing policy and of racial discrimination by private lenders (Quadagno, 1994). Although the Fair Housing Act of 1968 made racial discrimination in the sale of housing illegal, a 1991 study by the Federal Reserve found that discrimination in the nation's banking system remains common practice. Nationwide, commercial banks rejected Black applicants for home mortgages twice as often as White applicants. Moreover, in some cities the rejection rate was three times higher: the poorest White applicant was three times more likely to be get a loan approved than an African American in the highest income bracket. The Federal Reserve study concluded that mortgage refusal rates have little, if any, relationship to neighborhood or income (Myers & Chung, 1996; Oliver & Shapiro, 1995).

Federal housing policy and continuing racial discrimination in lending practices have had a lasting impact on the asset accumulation of African Americans. Not only do fewer Blacks own their own homes, but also— because of housing segregation—most African American families that purchased homes were relegated to central cities. Unlike their White counterparts, instead of benefiting from the housing boom of the 1980s, when real estate prices rose dramatically, their investments often have declined in value (Oliver & Shapiro, 1995).

Because older African Americans have less wealth, they have less income security for their old age. Not only is there no fail-safe system if an emergency depletes their resources, there are also fewer resources for the next generation to inherit. Although members of the baby boom generation stand to inherit approximately $7 trillion from their parent's estates, this legacy will not be passed on to Black children (Oliver & Shapiro, 1995). Thus, the statistics cited above reflect underlying processes of cumulative disadvantage over the life course that are the product of institutional racism. The political economy perspective, combined with the life course perspective, provides a more comprehensive explanation of racial inequality, suitable for tracing sources of inequality in the racial distribution of wealth.

CONCLUSION

The political economy perspective on aging highlights how socioeconomic institutions affect individuals over the life course and how they continue to influence their social and economic well-being in old age. The political economy approach has shifted the focus of gerontological research from the individual's ability to adapt to aging to an examination of broader social processes that determine how resources are distributed (Bengtson, Parrott, and Burgess, 1997). It emphasizes that the analysis of social policy must not only consider political, social, and economic consequences of policy provisions but also the underlying processes that create structural barriers to equality.

The recent focus of the political economy of aging has centered on distributional issues of welfare state provision. Comparative research has demonstrated how governmental welfare policies can reinforce class, gender, and racial inequality at several points in the life course, resulting in unequal experiences in old age.

First, welfare provisions may *reproduce existing class divisions* and class stratification. This has been the outcome in welfare policies like those in the United States, which reproduce the existing social order by providing social assistance benefits to one group at the bottom of the class structure, social insurance for wage earners to protect against predictable life course risks, and fiscal welfare for those most securely located in the labor market, whose benefits are primarily provided by the market economy.

Second, the political economy of aging perspective examines how the welfare state reproduces *gender inequality* over the life course and reinforces traditional values about gender roles. Whereas men are the primary clients of *contributory* social insurance programs, women are the primary clients of *means-tested* social assistance programs. In old age, women may be disadvantaged by the welfare state because of the eligibility requirements of social insurance programs and private pensions, which are based on a male model of labor force participation that fails to account for women's roles as family caregivers.

Finally, the welfare state may reproduce existing patterns of *racial stratification* by failing to redistribute life chances within generations. In the United States, for example, racial discrimination in housing and lending has created unequal access to income and wealth in old age. Thus, racial inequality in old age is not only the result of historical patterns of racial discrimination but also of the institutionalization of those patterns in welfare state provision.

The political economy perspective in aging has developed recently as a useful framework for examining the social context of institutionalized sources of inequality over the life course. It not only helps to explain the experience of old age but also to determine why there are patterned inequalities in the experience of old age and how public policy (the "state" in its welfare provisions) may ameliorate or exacerbate such inequalities.

REFERENCES

Angel, R., & Angel, J. (1996). The extent of private and public health insurance coverage among adult Hispanics. *Gerontologist, 36,* 332–340.

Bell, D. (1973). *The coming of post-industrial society.* New York: Basic Books.

Bengtson, V., Parrott, T., and Burgess, E. (1997). Theory, explanation, and a third generation of theoretical developments in social gerontology. *Journal of Gerontology: Social Sciences, 52B,* S72–88.

Blau, P., & Duncan, O. (1967). *The American occupational structure.* New York: Wiley.

Dannefer, D. (1991). The race is to the swift: Images of collective aging. In G. Kenyon, J. Birren, and J. Schroots (Eds.), *metaphors of Aging in Science and the Humanities* (pp. 155–172). New York: Springer Publishing Co.

Dowd, J. (1987). The reification of age: Age stratification theory and the passing of the autonomous subject. *Journal of Aging Studies, 1,* 317–335.

Eisenstadt, S. (1956). *From Generation to Generation.* Glencoe, IL: Free Press.

Esping-Anderson, G. (1990). *The three worlds of welfare capitalism.* Cambridge, U.K.: Polity Press.

Esping-Anderson, G. (1997). *The new political economy of welfare states.* Unpublished manuscript.

Estes, C. (1979). *The aging enterprise.* San Francisco: Jossey-Bass.

Estes, C. (1991). The new political economy of aging: Introduction and critique. In M. Minkler & C. Estes (Eds.), *Critical perspectives on aging* (pp. 19–36). Amityville, NY: Baywood.

Estes, C. (1996). The political economy of aging. In R. Binstock & L. George (Eds.),

Handbook of aging and the social sciences (pp. 346–359). San Diego, CA: Academic Press.

Estes, C., Gerard, L., Sprague Zones, J., & Swan, J. (1984). *Political economy, health and aging.* Boston: Little Brown.

Estes, C., Linkins, K., & Binney, E. (1996). The political economy of aging. In R. Binstock & L. George (Eds.), *Handbook of aging and the social sciences* (pp. 346–360). San Diego, CA: Academic Press.

Featherman, D. (1983). Life-span perspectives in social science research. In P. Baltes & O. Brim (Eds.), *Life span development and behavior* (pp. 1–57). New York: Academic Press.

Fraser, N. (1989). *Unruly practices: Power, discourse and gender in contemporary social theory.* Minneapolis: University of Minnesota Press.

Giddens, A. (1971). *Capitalism and modern social theory.* Cambridge, U.K.: Cambridge University Press.

Harrington Meyer, M. (1990). Family status and poverty among older women: The gendered distribution of retirement income in the United States. *Social Problems, 37,* 551–563.

Harrington Meyer, M. (1996). *American Sociological Review, 61,* 651–669.

Hicks, A., & Swank, D. (1984). On the political economy of welfare expansion: A comparative analysis of eighteen advanced capitalist democracies, 1960–1971. *Comparative Political Studies, 17,* 81–119.

Hogan, D. P., & Astone, N. M. (1986). The transition to adulthood. *Annual Review of Sociology, 12,* 109–130.

Knottnerus, J. D. (1987). Status attainment research and its image of society. *American Sociological Review, 52,* 113–121.

Korpi, W. (1989). Power, politics and state autonomy in the development of social citizenship: Social rights during sickness in eighteen OECD Countries since 1930. *American Sociological Review, 54,* 309–328.

Marmor, T., Mashaw, J. L., & Harvey, P. (1990). *America's misunderstood welfare state.* New York: Basic Books.

Marshall, V. (1996). The state of theory of aging and the social sciences. In R. Binstock and L. George (Eds.), *Handbook of Aging and the Social Sciences* (pp. 12–30). San Diego: Academic Press.

Myers, S., & Chung, C. (1996). Racial differences in home ownership and home equity among preretirement-aged households. *Gerontologist, 36,* 350–360.

Myles, J. (1989). *Old age in the welfare state.* Lawrence: University Press of Kansas.

Myles, J. (1996). When markets fail: Social welfare in Canada and the United States. In G. Esping-Anderson (Ed.), *Welfare states in transition* (pp. 116–140). Thousand Oaks, CA: Sage.

O'Connor, J. S. (1996). Trend report: From women in the welfare state to gendering welfare state regimes. *Current Sociology, 44,* 48–77.

Oliver, M., & Shapiro, T. (1995). *Black wealth/White wealth: A new perspective on racial inequality.* New York: Routledge.

O'Rand, A. (1996). The cumulative stratification of the life course. In R. Binstock & L. George (Eds.), *Handbook of aging and the social sciences* (pp. 188–205). San Diego, CA: Academic Press.

O'Rand, A., & Henretta, J. (1982). Delayed career entry, industrial pension structure and early retirement in a cohort of unmarried women. *American Sociological Review, 47,* 365–373.

Parsons, T. (1942). Age and sex in the social structure of the United States. *American Sociological Review, 7,* 604–616.

Quadagno, J. (1988). *The transformation of old age security: Class and politics in the American welfare state.* Chicago: University of Chicago Press.

Quadagno, J. (1994). *The color of welfare: How racism undermined the war on poverty.* New York: Oxford University Press.

Riley, M. W. (1971). Social gerontology and the age stratification of society. *American Sociological Review, 52,* 1–14.

Riley, M. W., Johnson, M., & Foner, A. (1972). *Aging and society: Vol. 3. A sociology of age stratification.* New York: Russell Sage Foundation.

Sainsbury, D. (1996). *Gender, equality, and welfare states.* Cambridge, U.K.: Cambridge University Press.

Sewell, W., & Hauser, R. (1975). *Education, occupation and earnings: Achievements in the early career.* New York: Academic Press.

Shalev, M. (1996). *The privatization of social policy?* London: Macmillan.

Smelser, N. (1988). Social structure. In N. Smelser (Ed.), *Handbook of sociology* (pp. 103–130). Newbury Park, CA: Sage.

Sorokin, P. (1941). *Social and cultural dynamics.* New York: American Books.

Stephens, J. (1979). *The transition from capitalism to socialism.* London: Macmillan.

Street, D. (1996). *The Politics of Pensions.* Unpublished doctoral dissertation, Department of Sociology, Florida State University, Tallahassee, FL.

U.S. Bureau of the Census. (1993). *Statistical abstract of the United States.* Washington, D.C.: Government Printing Office.

Weber, M. (1946). Class, status and party. In H. Gerth & C. W. Mills (Trans. & Eds.), *From Max Weber,* New York: Oxford University Press.

SECTION V

Applications and Potentials for Theories of Aging

20

Public Policy and Theories of Aging: Constructing and Reconstructing Old Age

Alan Walker

T he purpose of this chapter is to examine the relationships between theories of aging and public policy. The relationship between old age and public policy is a close one—every welfare state began its active life in the form of income provision for older people (Guillemard, 1993). Yet in the fields of sociology and social gerontology, analysis of the aging and public policy interface remains relatively underdeveloped (Phillipson & Walker, 1986). Today the future of public welfare with regard to older people is being questioned in all industrial societies (Organization for Economic Cooperation and Development, 1988; World Bank, 1994); thus, it is more important than ever to understand the relationship between old age and public policy. In particular, social scientists must begin to evaluate the extent to which public policy derives from a consistent set of ideas or theories about old age and the aging process. This would contribute substantially to understanding policy formulation and impact, and it might also lay the foundations for better policies.

There has been an exponential growth since World War II in public provision with regard to older people as well as in the number of professional and allied groups with responsibility for providing old age services, a growth that is now itself under threat in some countries. This is uncontentious, as is the parallel spread of higher education and training in gerontology. More controversial perhaps is the statement that old age is itself partly a product of public policy. This contention is the central theme of this chapter. In the 20th century older people have been often the unwitting victims of policy. Old age has been constructed and reconstructed by social and economic policies and, for their part, older people have been expected to adjust to the reification of age into convenient social categories for the purposes of resource distribution and rationing; to the institutions of the welfare state set up to "manage" aging; and to the changing prescriptions of policymakers and bureau professionals (Estes, 1982; Phillipson, 1982; Townsend, 1981; Walker, 1980). This social construction of old age, through public policy, is derived from theoretical perspectives even if these are not explicit or conscious in the policy process.

In advancing this thesis concerning the relationship between public policy and old age it is important to distinguish three distinct phases in the postwar evolution of old age as a focus for public policy in industrial societies. First, from the 1940s to the early 1970s old age was regarded chiefly as a social problem. This was also a period that saw the rise of retirement as the key determinant of old age. Second was a transition phase from the early 1970s to the late 1980s when aging came to be defined by policymakers as an economic problem. This period also saw the blurring of the boundaries between economic activity and retirement. Third, there is the present phase, the central theme of which has yet to emerge but which seems to offer both pessimistic and optimistic scenarios. There is continuing panic among policymakers concerning the economic "burden" of aging, but this is accompanied by the growth of more flexible links between age and economic activity in later life and the advent of political movements of older people. This periodization has obvious parallels with the evolution of capitalist economies in the last half-century; from the entrenchment of large-scale modern ("Fordist") modes of production through the fiscal crisis and subsequent welfare restructuring to the advent of postmodernity.

Throughout these three phases old age has been constructed and reconstructed and continues to be so, though, as I shall argue, it cannot be assumed that this process of reconstruction has been a uniformly progressive one. Indeed, in the current phase there are early signs of new perspectives emerging, in which, for example, older people are challenging the received wisdom of welfare state services about their needs (Barnes & Walker, 1996); but at the same time, some of those services are under direct threat of closure or the indirect threat of privatization. Thus, just as groups of older people in different countries are beginning to assert their rights with regard to public services, some of those services are facing an uncertain future.

The thesis that public policy is an important determinant of the contemporary meaning of aging and age categories in different societies raises many questions, some of which are beyond the scope of this chapter. Does it mean, for example, that policymakers "theorize" age? Clearly not, if "theorise" means abstract reflections detached from concrete reality. Few policy makers will have the time, or inclination, to indulge in the obscure and often irrelevant writing that has frequently been labeled as theory. However, if we regard policy makers as active agents in the construction of social reality— agents with greater power and other resources than many citizens—then they may "theorise" in at least two ways.

On the one hand, policymakers bring to the subjects of their concern, older people, a set of beliefs and ideas about the particular group and its relationship with other groups—a theory of old age if you like. It may be incoherent, partial, or empirically untested, but in the process of policy-making it may be applied nonetheless. In other words, when policymakers propose practical solutions to social problems those solutions are based on an implicit set of beliefs about the nature of the social problem and its causation.

On the other hand, recognizing the three domains of social theory— methodology, substantive concerns, and critique (Layder, 1994; Scott, 1995)— we can see that some policymakers will make regular, if not necessarily consistent, excursions into the realm of theory. For example, they will be confronted constantly with new data on social phenomena and will question the nature of "evidence" and its appropriateness. Some will be driven by a critical theory aimed at transforming social reality and improving the human condition (though the values or ideologies involved in such a critique may be distinctly one-sided). Thus, policymakers may theorize in both implicit and explicit ways. They are contributors to the transmission of theoretical ideas, including those on aging, but this does not take a coherent or reflexive form. In other words, there is no evidence that gerontological theories have been consistently employed in the development of public policy with regard to aging.

This raises another question: do all policymakers theorize in the same way? Like the first question, this one should be subjected to rigorous empirical testing. My hypothesis is that they do not. For example, there will be distinct differences between those at the top of a public authority or agency and those "street-level bureaucrats" with day-to-day responsibility for practical implementation of policies (Lipsky, 1980). (Here I am purposely not separating practitioners from policymakers because, in the process of implementation, policy is usually produced and reproduced by the decisions taken by practitioners.) We know that many practicing gerontologists and others working with older people have employed specific theories, such as activity and life course theories, to inform their practice.

A further question is whether or not the policies of different countries reflect different theoretical perspectives. Here we can say with some certainty that they do. For example, the welfare regimes of the Western world differ substantially in their approach to general problems, such as poverty, as well as to specific ones, such as the health and social care needs of older people. In other words, the practical variations between these different national regimes reflect differences in the ideas, beliefs, and theories underlying them.

The main reference point for this chapter is Europe or, more specifically, the 15 member states of the European Union (EU). Maddox (1992) has said that "the European Communities provide a contemporary naturally occurring laboratory for the comparative study of social policy formation and implementation. This is particularly the case regarding social policies for aging populations" (p. 355). This chapter will use some results from recent EU research to illustrate differences and similarities between different countries in policy outcomes for older people (Walker, 1993; Walker, Guillemard, & Alber, 1993; Walker & Maltby, 1997). Yet at the same time, it is possible to argue empirically that there is a distinct European model of welfare provision that differs significantly from those of the United States and East Asia. The analysis focuses almost exclusively at the macro level. This is not intended to sidestep the crucial macro-micro distinctions nor the challenge to reconcile them, and it is not meant to exclude the potential for individual action by older people or practitioners. Individuals are never only the creatures of policyor policy makers; they are active agents in the reproduction of social reality (Walker, 1991). The macro focus is adopted because it is there that we can perceive most clearly the interaction between public policy and aging and the construction of age that results.

THEORIES OF AGING AND PUBLIC POLICY

The primary focus of both public policy and social policy analyses of aging is the welfare state. Consequently, a misconception has become entrenched that social policies are synonymous with state activity. Of course, this is no more the case than the contention that the state encompasses all social activity (Townsend, 1975; Walker, 1981). Social policies may stem from all social institutions and groups, public and private, and are distinguished by their functions rather than their perpetrators. The false equation of social policy with public policy has resulted, in Titmuss"s (1958, p. 40) words, in "a stereotype of social welfare which represents only the more visible parts of the real world of welfare." Nowhere is this a more important insight than with regard to older people: public pensions and, by association, those who claim them, have been portrayed recently as a burden on the economy, whereas private or occupational pensions and pensioners are seen in a wholly positive light (Walker, 1990). Yet both forms of transfers are welfare payments, and both are charges on national income. Therefore, it is important to bear in mind this distinction between public policy and social policy in the ensuing analysis.

It is also important to address a second common misconception regarding social policy: that it is possible to make a simple distinction between economic policies and social policies. It is not such a straightforward matter—the economic aims of government policies cannot be disassociated from their social effects. Economic policy and management embody assumptions about social policy and social relations, including welfare assumptions, and are therefore partly also social policies (Walker, 1981). Again, this is especially pertinent in the field of social gerontology because, as I will show, macroeconomic management and industrial policy, far outside the realms of what are perceived as being social policies, have had a devastating impact on the welfare of older people.

The false division between economic policy and social policy in public administration and practice and also in intellectual thought has led to the construction of two further misleading stereotypes: that social policies are only for the poor (what Miller & Rein [1975] called "poor persons'" economic policies) and that they are necessarily beneficial to those who receive them.

Such stereotypes derive from a set of theoretical perspectives on the welfare state and social policy, all of which stem from the liberal-pluralist tradition. In sociology this means *functionalism;* in political science, *democratic pluralism*; in economics, *neoclassical theory*. These are complementary theories that all stem from the liberal-pluralist tradition.

From structural functionalism has come the notion that social policy with regard to aging has emerged in response to the imperatives of technological and industrial change and the increased capacity to meet new needs as a result of the wealth generated by economic growth. Industrialization and urbanization create new social problems—disruption of traditional social support, health and housing needs—that require a policy response if order and consensus are to be maintained. A very similar version of the development of the welfare state can be found in traditional Marxist accounts; where the "logic of capitalism" substitutes for the "logic of industrialization."

From democratic pluralism has come the persuasive idea that social policy derives from successful political struggles—demands made on ruling elites by the people who have been empowered by universal suffrage and mass democracy. With regard to aging it is hypothesized that the demographic expansion in the numbers of older people has created a new interest group; this, with the support of others (including politicians hungry for votes), exerts political pressure; over time, policies emerge from the policy-making process in response to these demands.

From neoclassical economic theories has come the notion that the retirement of older people is a natural and inevitable result of the desirable course of industrial and technological change and the changing division of labor that accompanies it. The existence of low pay among older workers, their exclusion from training opportunities, and the tyranny of age-related retirement are all put down to individual characteristics. It is no wonder that Townsend (1981, 1986) has labeled this family of theories "*acquiescent* functionalism," in which the social experience of aging is a "natural consequence of physical decrescence and mental inflexibility or of the failures of individual adjustment to aging and retirement" (1986, p. 18).

The main problem with this theoretical orientation is that it cannot explain adequately the diversity of national responses to aging. If policies on aging are required or demanded, *when* and *how* they are fulfilled are not explained in these theories. Why is it, for example, that within the EU there are four distinct welfare state models with regard to older people: the Bismarckian employment-related system, the Beveridge residual model, the Scandinavian citizenship approach, and the southern family-oriented model (Leibfried, 1992). This diversity exists despite similar levels of economic development and parity in the level of development of formal democratic institutions. Among the northern EU countries, poverty rates among older people vary by as much as a ratio of 4:1 (Walker et al., 1993). It has been argued that there is little evidence of effective age-interest politics, in Europe at least (Walker, 1986, 1996a; Walker & Naegele, 1998). Moreover, as Myles (1983) has pointed out, "Since many who hold to [the liberal democratic] position view the United States as the most democratic of nations, the relative underdevelopment of welfare policies in that country constitutes a difficult negative case" (p. 468).

The pervasiveness and influence of this liberal-pluralist tradition should not be underestimated, particularly with regard to public policy. The meaning of aging projected by it—inevitable decline and disengagement from productive activity, inability to adjust to technological change, and an economic burden—still holds sway over policymakers, both public and private in all industrial societies. Also, in the scientific community of gerontologists it is important for us to be self-critical about the roles of both biomedical and social scientists, as researchers and advisers to policymakers, in helping to perpetuate a false positivistic separation between scientific fact gathering and policy-making and, in doing so, helping to sustain negative images of older people (Bytheway, 1995; McEwan, 1990; Townsend, 1986). All methodological approaches entail implicit theories about the groups being studied or ideas about the causes of the social problem in question. In other words, science is not value-free, and an important part of the task of the social scientist is to make those values explicit.

It was in response to the inadequacies of the liberal-pluralist accounts of the relationship between aging and social policy that a new theoretical perspective began to emerge in the late 1970s in both North America and Europe. Variously called the political economy, social construction of age, or structured dependency thesis, it focuses on the political, economic, and social processes that determine not just the nature of the aging experience but the very definition of old age itself (Minkler & Estes, 1991; Phillipson, 1992; Townsend, 1991; Walker, 1991). Any society's social policies on aging are located in the context of the economy (national and international), the state, the labor market, and the class, sex, race, and age divisions in that society. It is within this framework of institutions and rules that the meaning of aging is manufactured. The process of social construction entails major economic and industrial reorganization, for example, in response to technological change as well as in the common everyday management of the economy and the administration and development of social institutions that more subtly shape the position of older people.

Thus, the political economy perspective shifts the locus of analysis from the individual's adjustment to the aging process and the reactive policies that manage it toward the more generalized institutionalized policies of the state and industry that maintain or change social and economic structures. This is not to deny the importance of micro-sociological inputs to this scientific paradigm. For example, symbolic interactionist perspectives teach us that age may be socially constructed within interpersonal relationships— doctor and patient, social care worker and client, caring daughter and disabled mother. However, some groups in society have the power to impose their particular constructions of reality on others, for example, through the agencies of the state. Thus, as Estes (1991) has argued, experts, policymakers and the media have a disproportionate influence on the dominant definition of what aging consists of. She goes on to argue:

> Those who control definitions of aging in effect control access to old age benefits such as medical care, as well as the personal and public costs of care and the structure of health care delivery. Currently, public money and professional effort are disproportionately expended on institutional (hospital and nursing home) medical services for the elderly. Both reflect a definition of health care that is the product of the professional dominance of medicine and a guarantee of a profitable medical care industry. (p. 25)

The political economy perspective has been criticised for excluding the role of agency—the possibility of individual action. But this results from a misunderstanding. The political economy thesis suggests that the experience of aging is determined to a large extent by socioeconomic structures and policies. However, within this context, the outcome for particular individuals will depend on their precise location with regard to class, race, gender, and age structures and their own interpretation of their experiences of the aging process. In other words, the social meaning of old age is structurally determined, but there may be many different personal interpretations of this meaning by individual older people and their families. There is considerable scope for men and women to make their own life histories and therefore to determine their experience of aging. Older people too continue to interact with their environment in a reflexive way, to create their own social reality (Mouzelis, 1995).

Having established the theoretical paradigm I am operating within, the next stage is to apply it to the analysis of how aging is interpreted, or defined, in policy terms.

CONSTRUCTING AND RECONSTRUCTING THE MEANING OF OLD AGE

It is possible to distinguish three distinct phases in the postwar evolution of social policy with regard to older people. My analysis is based on the European experience, primarily the northern EU states, but it may be applicable to North America as well. During each of the periods discussed below, the meaning of old age was reconstructed, and although no theoretical perspective was made explicit by policymakers, the liberal-pluralist tradition was clearly dominant. Also, it is possible to discern in the approaches taken by public policy general ideas and beliefs about the place of older people in society.

Old Age as a Social Problem: 1940s–Early 1970s

In the years following World War II, aging became identified as a social problem. National pension systems were put in place and/or consolidated during this period, and social expenditure rose rapidly in what proved to be the heyday of the welfare state. Of course, the origins of social policy in the field of pensions predates this period by more than 50 years: Bismarck's system of worker insurance in Germany in 1889 and the first old age pensions in the United Kingdom in 1908 and in France in 1910. However, universal coverage was achieved in this period, and there is no mistaking the proliferation of social policy measures. In the period 1960–1975 the increase in pension expenditure in the OECD countries accounted for one quarter of the rise in the share of public expenditure in total expenditures. In France it was more than one third; in Germany, less than one fifth; and in the United Kingdom, less than one seventh (OECD, 1988). This reinforces the conclusion of Pampel, Williamson, and Stryker (1990) that there are "multiple paths to higher pension spending" (p. 547). Incidentally, in the period 1960–1975, pension spending in Canada contributed only 9% to the growth in size of the public sector.

The main goals of public policy in this period were to provide for income security in old age and, in doing so, to ensure the efficient transition of older workers from employment to retirement. The early postwar period was one of full employment; indeed, in the early 1950s in the United Kingdom the National Advisory Committee on the Employment of Older Men and Women was formed to encourage older people to remain in the labor market (Phillipson, 1982). While full employment lasted, there was some resistance to the assumptions of neoclassical economics and scientific management theories concerning declining productivity in older age (Taylor, 1947). Thus, the main focus of public policy was on those who had left the labor market. This focus was determined largely by economic management and policy because this group was, in effect, defined as "externalities" by the macroeconomic policy system. Public pensions were regarded as an appropriate way of socializing the costs of retirement as well as assisting industry to rejuvenate the workforce (Graebner, 1980). This was an important element of the post-war settlement between Keynesian economics and Beveridge (1942)-style (i.e., liberal) social policy: economic growth would generate sufficient resources for universal pension provision.

The establishment of public pension systems and, more important, their accompanying retirement conditions encouraged the rapid spread of fixed-age retirement. Thus, in policy terms aging came to be uniquely associated with retirement ages. In other words, old age was objictified as retirement age (Graebner, 1980; Townsend, 1981; Walker, 1980). What are the consequences of the institutionalization of age-related retirement? There are five key points.

In the first place, the economic dependency of older people has been enlarged substantially. One hundred years ago in the United Kindgom some two thirds of the male population aged 65 and over were economically active (in employment or seeking it); today it is only 7%. Older people were not helpless pawns in this social definition of old age. Individually and collectively, workers called for retirement and public pensions. But the creation of a fixed age barrier in European pension systems has led to widespread economic dependency.

Second, age-barrier retirement has been the main wellspring of age discrimination in employment, social security, and wider social relations (Bytheway, 1995; McEwan, 1990). It has not been the sole cause of age discrimination, but it has encouraged the view that, past a certain age, an individual's social worth is diminished.

Third, as a corollary to retirement, it has been accepted that the income needs of older people are lower than those of the "economically active." Typically, public pensions are set at rates considerably below average earnings, and even when occupational pensions are included and idealized projections made, some leading EU countries still have quite low replacement ratios: 69% in Germany and 64% in the United Kingdom, for example (Walker et al., 1993).

Fourth, age-barrier retirement and the foregoing factors have encouraged the view that older people are not just a social problem but an economic burden as well. Thus, in the early postwar phase there were occasional warnings, (e.g., from the UN in 1954) about the "burden" of population aging (Walker, 1990). This approach to aging is best exemplified in the old age dependency ratio, which crudely expresses a ratio between those over pension age and younger adults and thereby objectifies the assumption that economic dependency must be associated with aging. Such calculations are used frequently in European policy discourse in this field, despite their many flaws.

Fifth, with regard to health and social services policy and practice, it was the first phase that saw the major expansion of services and their professionalization. As policymakers had come to regard older people as largely dependent and passive objects, it is not surprising that the professional and institutional structures of the health and social services also reflected this view—for example, forms of education and training that encouraged professionals to regard themselves as experts operating autonomously. Thus, the expansion of health and social services in this period was a two-sided coin: it enhanced the welfare of older people, but it was delivered in ways that reinforced their dependency and powerlessness.

Old Age as the Solution to One Economic Problem and the Cause of Another: Mid 1970s–Late 1980s

A transitional phase stretched from the origins of the fiscal crises in the mid 1970s to the late 1980s. During this relatively short time the social meaning of aging was reconstructed along two dimensions.

First there was a massive fall in economic activity in later life throughout the EU and indeed all industrial countries with the exceptions of Sweden and Japan (Kohli, Rein, Guillemard, & van Gunsteren, 1991). The decline in activity is most marked among those aged 65 and over and those aged 60–64, but it is also clear in the age group 55–59. In most EU countries, working after the age of 65 has been eradicated. The position of older women is harder to disentangle from the cohort effect of rising rates of participation among younger women, but it does appear that a similar decline has taken place (Walker et al., 1993).

The main factors explaining this decline in Europe are demand-related, particularly the collapse of employment in the mid-1970s and early 1980s. My own research, on early retirement following redundancy in the Sheffield steel industry, shows two distinct paths being followed. On the one hand there were those who, faced with redundancy, chose early retirement as a preferable option to unemployment; on the other hand were those who were effectively coerced into it by a hostile labor market. Thus, early retirement was, for the first group, a welcome relief from the labor market and, for the second group, a refuge. The key explanatory factors in this social division were age (proximity to pension age) and income level (Westergaard, Noble, & Walker, 1989).

A key feature of the demand side of causation in the rise of early retirement was public policy. During this period there was a proliferation of employment and pension measures designed to encourage early retirement. Examples include the Job Release Scheme in the United Kingdom and pre-retirement benefits in Denmark and Germany (Walker et al., 1993).

During this transitional phase the growth of early retirement has reconstructed old age from a simple age-related status with a single lower entry point into a much broader category that stretches from age 50 to death. This has necessitated the widespread functional separation of the third (50–74) and fourth (75+) ages, the young-old and old-old, a distinction that first appeared in France in the 1960s. It has also meant, as Guillemard (1993) has shown, that public pension systems are no longer the key regulators of retirement. The traditional pattern of labor force exit at pension age has become a minority one—for example, in Germany (the former FDR) only 36% of entrants into the public pension system in 1989 came directly from employment.

Another important consequence of the unchecked growth of early retirement from the labor force is that it has reinforced the devaluation of older people in the labor market. The downward redefinition of aging has had consequences for the ways that employers perceive older workers and, in turn, the chances they offer them for reemployment. Indeed, there is a growing body of evidence in different EU countries to show that third-agers are frequently discriminated against with regard to job recruitment, promotions, and training (Drury, 1993, 1997; Walker, 1997). This is despite the fact that age is not a good proxy for the ability to work and learn; therefore, discrimination is not only unjust but wasteful of economic capacity and potential.

The only EU-wide survey evidence on this topic comes from 1992 (Walker, 1993). We asked the general public in each country whether or not older workers are discriminated against with regard to job recruitment and other aspects of employment. A remarkably high proportion—four out of five for the EU as a whole—said that such discrimination *does* exist with regard to recruitment. Moreover, there was hardly any difference based on the age of respondents; all age groups believe that discrimination against older workers takes place (Walker, 1993).

During this second phase the social meaning of aging was transformed from its long association with pension ages to labor market criteria such as employability. Public policy, particularly in the employment sphere, was one of the main engines driving this change. But while encouraging early retirement was seen as a solution to unemployment (though the policy does not seem to have been very effective), aging also came to be seen as an economic problem in its own right. From the late 1970s onward there has been mounting concern on the part of national governments about the economic consequences of population aging. Forward projections of dependency ratios have been used to paint a pessimistic picture of the socioeconomic implications of aging. Sometimes these border on the alarmist, as the following quotations show.

> Under existing regulations the evolution of public pension schemes is likely to put a heavy and increasing burden on the working population in coming decades. Such a financial strain may put inter-generational solidarity-a concept on which all public retirement provisions are based—at risk. (OECD, 1988)

> If no action is taken to deal with the incipient crisis of population aging, then it seems certain that western societies will experience major social and economic dislocation, and they may experience this relatively soon. (Johnson, Conrad, & Thomson, 1989)

The question as to why international agencies and European governments should adopt an avowedly pessimistic stance toward the societal implications of population aging takes us beyond the scope of this chapter. What it illustrates it that neoclassical assumptions about the burden of aging held sway in national and international policy arenas (Walker, 1990). In other words, the theory of old age that dominated public policy in this period was an extremely pessimistic economic one.

WHICH WAY FOR OLD AGE? BURDEN OR PRODUCTIVE CITIZENS?

The transition from the second to the third phase of aging-policy development was marked by the termination, in the late 1980s, of some of the main mechanisms for early retirement. One of the first EU countries to act was France, in 1986, when early retirement contracts were abolished. Soon after, similar actions were taken in Belgium, Germany, and the United Kingdom. However, the early retirement trend has developed its own momentum; it has become institutionalised in the labor market for the reasons outlined above. Although the transition has happened, European societies are only just on the threshold of this third phase, and therefore the future of aging and public policy is a matter of speculation. The future appears to offer two separate scenarios.

The first possibility is that aging will be regarded as a growing burden to society. In other words, aging would be constituted, in policy terms, as an economic burden, and national governments would attempt to reduce its economic cost in the form of pensions and health and social services. There is no doubt that in several leading EU countries the cost of pensions and long-term care is a major political issue. Some of them have already taken action to limit costs, and others are contemplating such action. In the pensions field the most favored policy is an increase in retirement age. For example, over the next decade, Germany and the United Kingdom are planning increases in their retirement ages, and Italy and the United Kingdom are discussing similar changes.

This public burden scenario for aging would reinforce the continuous thread in postwar policy discourse that associates aging with inevitable decline, decrescence, and unproductiveness. According to this account, the future of old age would be a bleak one, particularly for those heavily reliant on the welfare state. But in addition, the future of aging societies would be equally bleak because the undermining of intergenerational solidarity by the policies that flow from the public burden orientation, such as the privatization of pensions and health and social care, would have ramifications far beyond welfare policies. The alternative path leads to productive aging. Looking toward this future there are three interlinked sets of developments that suggest that age may be reconstructed, or perhaps deconstructed, in a new postmodern form.

First of all, in the labor market there are clear signs of change in the perceptions of aging on the part of employers. There are a growing number of private companies in France, Germany, and the United Kingdom (and in Sweden too) that are adopting employment practices different from those followed by the majority. Examples include the introduction of more flexible employment and retirement policies, special recruitment campaigns targeted at older workers, and perhaps most important, new holistic approaches to employment and lifelong training, in which aging is a key factor built into considerations of job planning and design. Although these policies have been adopted by only a minority of employers so far, there are sufficient indications to suggest the start of a trend. Moreover, some EU governments have been attempting to encourage flexibility in the form of partial retirement, though with little success so far.

Second, in the health and social services there are signs in some EU countries of a swing away from the traditional paternalism of service providers toward more active conceptions of old age. Over the past decade there has been a wide range of service innovations in the EU countries, despite funding shortages. Although traditional forms of service provision remain dominant, and pluralistic service innovation has been haphazard, there are sufficient indications of change to suggest that practitioners are beginning to face up to the challenges of involving older users of services in key decisions about the provision of their care. Some are developing new strategies designed to empower older people to some extent, and professional attitudes and values are beginning to encourage cooperation and partnership with older service users. In short, there is a gradual revolution underway in the approach to aging taken by some social service agencies. If this change is successful on a large scale, it may transform the meaning of aging in this sphere from its association with passivity and dependency to one concerned with activity and interdependence. This sort of development would represent a profound shift in the social status of older people.

Third, older Europeans themselves are beginning to seize the initiative and may not be prepared to wait for the pronouncements of experts on how the aging process should be interpreted. A growing number are actively demonstrating the potential for a new meaning to be applied to aging. Thus, in recent years new political groupings composed of older people have been formed, or existing ones have gained in strength (e.g., the creation of pensioners" political parties). In Germany a gray party was formed in 1989 to champion senior citizens" interests. Belgium saw the founding of a pensioners" party in 1990; Italy has one, and so does Portugal. There is a radical grass-roots movement of older people in Denmark; an organization called Aging Differently in the Netherlands (designed to campaign for alternative perceptions of old age); and in the United Kingdom, a National Pensioners' Convention. The growth of self-advocacy movements among older people has been echoed in some countries by the creation of local or national advisory councils composed of older people. These developments are finding support among the general public: more than four out of five EU citizens think that older people should stand up more actively for their rights (Walker, 1993). There is some indication in evidence such as this that the public thinks that aging should not be a simple matter of adjustment and peaceful retirement.

Together, these three sets of developments suggest that in the next century the meaning of old age may be reconstructed into a more productive form, where productivity includes not only economic activity in the form of paid employment but also a wide range of formal, quasi-formal, and informal activities that are productive in social, political, and economic terms. To the extent that such activities are economically productive they would also assist in quelling the fears of politicians concerning the costs of aging societies. On the negative side, however, it is likely that the deconstruction of the later life course, *in the absence of supportive social policies,* would leave older people very vulnerable, without rights to social protection and with access only to minimum social assistance–level benefits and services.

CONCLUSION

The purpose of this chapter has been to examine the relationship between theories of aging and public policy. Although recognizing that social theories are rarely explicit in public policies, it has been possible, at a macro level, to identify broad interpretations (or theories) of aging. Changes in these perspectives have been responsible for determining the nature of old age over the past 50 years, and today public policy will play a major role in determining the future of old age. The social construction of aging through public policy occurred first in the form of age-related retirement, which institutionalized the meaning of aging in terms of chronological age and which was concerned primarily with the exclusion of older workers from the labor market. Subsequently, it was regarded in terms of labor market criteria, such as employability, which moved the operational age barriers downward. At the same time, the focus of policy shifted from regarding aging as a social problem toward seeing it as an economic one. (Furthermore, public policy has not only played a major role in constructing the meaning of aging, it has also helped to determine the quality of the aging experience, through, for example, the provision of income maintenance and social support.) However, this review of the construction of old age in public policy has not revealed any consistent application of gerontological theory.

In looking forward to the next century, the legacy of the past is very influential. In particular the tendency in public policy to regard societal aging as an economic burden, rather than a social and economic triumph, is a strongly enduring one. It may well prove to be the dominant policy perspective in some EU countries, particularly the United Kingdom, in which neoliberal ideology has recently been a powerful force. Yet it is also possible to make out an alternative, more positive scenario in which the meaning of aging in both policy and practice would be created in a more flexible form than hitherto—as a process rather than a fixed chronological point, in which crude ageist stereotypes concerning the abilities of older people would diminish in importance and in which public policy would promote social inclusion or integration rather than exclusion. In this reconstructed form, aging would be less a matter of chronological age and more one of functional capacity, or to coin a phrase from Neugarten (1982), a case of need rather than age. If this positive future scenario is to be realized, the theoretical foundations on which public policies are based must become explicit, and social theories must begin to challenge economic ones for equal status in the policy arena.

REFERENCES

Barnes, M., & Walker, A. (1996). Consumerism versus empowerment: A principled approach to the involvement of older service users. *Policy and Politics, 24,* 375–393.

Beveridge, W. (1942). *Social insurance and allied services.* London: HMSO.

Bytheway, B. (1995). *Ageism.* Buckingham, UK: OU Press.

Drury, F. (Ed.). (1993). *Age discrimination against older workers in the European community.* London: Eurolink Age.

Drury, E. (1997). *Public policy options to assist older workers.* Brussels: Eurolink Age.

Estes, C. L. (1982). Austerity and aging in the US. *International Journal of Health Services, 12,* 573–584.

Estes, C. L. (1991). The new political economy of aging: Introduction and critique. In M. Minkler & C. Estes (Eds.), *Critical perspectives on aging* (pp. 3–18). New York: Baywood.

Graebner, W. (1980). *A history of retirement.* New Haven, CT: Yale University Press.

Guillemard, A.-M. (1993). Older workers and the labour market. In A. Walker, J. Alber, & A.-M. Guillemard (Eds.), *Older people in Europe: Social and economic policies* (pp. 35–51). Commission of the European Communities.

Johnson, P., Conrad, C., & Thomson, D. (Eds.). (1989). *Workers verses pensioners: Intergenerational justice in an ageing world.* Manchester: Manchester University Press.

Kohli, M., Rein, M., Guillemard, A.-M., & Van Gunsteren, H. (Eds.). (1991). *Time for retirement: Comparative studies of early exit from the labour force.* Cambridge, UK: Cambridge University Press.

Layder, D. (1994). *Understanding social theory.* London: Sage.

Leibfried, S. (1992). Towards a European welfare state? In Z. Ferge & J. Kolberg (Eds.), *Social policy in a changing Europe* (pp. 227–259). Vienna: Campus/Westview.

Lipsky, M. (1980). *Street-level bureaucracy: Dilemmas of the individual in public services.* New York: Russell Sage Foundation.

Maddox, G. (1992). Long-term care policies in comparative perspective. *Ageing and Society, 12,* 355–368.

McEwan, E. (Ed.). (1990). *Age: The unrecognised discrmination.* London: ACE Books.

Miller, S. M., & Rein, M. (1975, May/June). Can income redistribution work? *Social Policy,* 3–18.

Minkler, M., & Estes, C. (Eds.). (1991). *Critical perspectives on aging.* New York: Baywood.

Mouzelis, N. (1995). *Sociological theory: What went wrong?* London: Routledge.

Myles, J. (1983). Conflict, crisis, and the future of old age security. *Milbank Memorial Fund Quarterly, 61,* 462–472.

Neugarten, B. (Ed.). (1982). *Age or need?* London: Sage.

Organization for Economic Cooperation and Development. (1988). *Reforming public pensions.* Paris: Author.

Pampel, F., Williamson, J., & Stryker, R. (1990). Class context and pension response to demographic structure in advanced industrial democracies. *Social Problems,* *37,* 535–550.

Phillipson, C. (1982). *Capitalism and the construction of old age.* London: Macmillan.

Phillipson, C. (1992). Challenging the "spectre of old age": Community care for older people in the 1990s. In N. Manning & R. Page (Eds.), *Social Policy Review,* *4,* 111–133.

Phillipson, C., & Walker. A. (Eds.). (1986). *Ageing and social policy.* Aldershot, UK: Gower.

Scott, J. (1995). *Sociological theory.* Aldershot, UK: Edward Elgar.

Taylor, F. W. (1947). *Scientific management.* New York: Harper.

Titmuss, R. M. (1958). The social division of welfare. In R. M. Titmuss (Ed.), *Essays on the welfare state* (pp. 34–55) London: Allen & Unwin.

Townsend, P. (1975). *Sociology and social policy.* Harmondsworth, UK: Penguin Books.

Townsend, P. (1981). The structured dependency of the elderly: The creation of social policy in the twentieth century. *Ageing and Society, 1*(1), 5–28.

Townsend, P. (1986). Ageism and social policy. In C. Phillipson & A. Walker (Eds.), *Ageing and social policy: A critical assessment* (pp. 15–44). Aldershot, UK: Gower.

Townsend, P. (1991). Underclass and overclass: The widening gulf between social classes in Britain in the 1980s. In G. Payne & M. Gross (Eds.), *Sociology in action* (pp. 20–42). London: Macmillan.

Walker, A. (1980). The social creation of poverty and dependency in old age. *Journal of Social Policy, 9*(1), 49–75.

Walker, A. (1981). Social policy, social administration and the social construction of welfare. *Sociology, 5*(2), 225–250.

Walker, A. (1986). The politics of ageing in Britain. In C. Phillipson, M. Bernard, & P. Strang (Eds.), *Dependency and interdependency in old age* (pp. 30–45). London: Croom Helm.

Walker, A. (1990). The economic ʻburden' of ageing and the prospect of intergenerational conflict. *Ageing and Society, 10*(4), 377–396.

Walker, A. (1991). The relationship between the family and the state in the care of older people. *Canadian Journal on Aging, 10*(2), 94–112.

Walker, A. (1993). *Age and attitudes: Main results from a Eurobarometer survey.* Brussels: Commission of the European Communities.

Walker, A. (1996a). From acquiescence to dissent: A political sociology of ageing in the UK. In V. Minichiello, (Eds.), *The sociology of ageing* (pp. 31–45). Melbourne: ISA.

Walker, A. (Ed.). (1996b). *The new generational contract.* London: UCL Press.

Walker, A. (1997). *Combating age barriers in employment.* Luxembourg: Office of Official Publications of the European Communities.

Walker, A., Guillemard, A.-M., & Alber, J. (1993). *Older people in Europe: Social and economic policies.* Brussels: Commission of the European Communities.

Walker, A., & Maltby, T. (1997). *Ageing Europe.* Buckingham, UK: OU Press.

Walker, A., & Naegele, G. (Eds.). (1998). *The politics of old age in Europe.* Buckingham, UK: Open University Press.

Walker, A., & Taylor, P. (1993). Ageism vs productive ageing: The challenge of age discrimination in the labour market. In S. Bass, F. Caro, & Y. Chen (Eds.), *Achieving a productive ageing society* (pp. 61–80). Westport, CT: Greenwood.

Westergaard, J., Noble, I., & Walker, A. (1989). *After redundancy.* Oxford, UK: Polity Press.

World Bank. (1994). *Averting the old age crisis: Policies to protect the old and promote growth.* Oxford, UK: Oxford University Press.

21

Applying Theories of Aging to Gerontological Practice Through Teaching and Research

Peter G. Coleman
Dorothy Jerrome

The focus of this chapter is the link between gerontological theory and practice. There are several contexts for the application of gerontological theory, such as the health and social care of older adults; the creation of health and social policy at national, local, and institutional levels; and the training of practitioners. This discussion draws on our own experience as academic gerontologists, involved for two decades in the education and training of student practitioners and in collaborative research with professionals. Between us we have taught medical students, student nurses, and clinical psychologists, as well as trainee and qualified social workers, counselors, and occupational and physiotherapists. We have conducted collaborative research involving social work staff, occupational and physiotherapists, residential care staff, and medical practitioners, among others. The following discussion summarizes our experience of applying gerontological theory in training for practice and in research on practice.

Over the years we have become aware that there are topics of central concern to practitioners and that gerontological theory makes more or less of a contribution to professional intervention in the lives of older people. Practical issues we address in this chapter include the assessment of need, rehabilitation, and the long-term care of both the physically and mentally frail. We examine the interface between these areas of intervention and top-ics within social gerontology, such as the social construction of health and illness, management of identity in aging, attachment and separation over the life course, and structured dependency. Our aim is to identify the theoretical ideas that underpin our teaching and research to see how explicitly they inform our work and how closely they fit the practice orientation of stu-dents and research subjects.

Gerontologists' constructions of old age make various assumptions about the nature of social reality, about social causation, and about the importance of time. We might attend to internal realities and systems of meaning or to external, objective reality; we might emphasize individual choice and re-sponsibility in accounting for change; we might take the individual as our starting point rather than elements of social structure and examine the ex-periences of the individual rather than the cohort; and we might adopt a synchronic (snapshot) view of time rather than a diachronic (historical, or dynamic) view that encompasses the individual life course or the cohort in its historical setting.

Theoretical perspectives like these, which are offered to student practitio-ners, do not always correspond to the worldview of these students. The integration of theory and practice in teaching takes place against a back-ground of professional ideologies and intellectual preferences. Some theories are more easily translated into practice than others, for some groups of students and practitioners and in some topic areas. A contrast exists between social and health care workers, reflecting the systems of explanation and intervention that underlie their particular professional cultures. We can see a contrast specifically between the responses of medical students and stu-dent social workers to our particular kind of gerontological theory, which lies within the life course perspective and adopts a hermeneutic approach. Medical students are less comfortable with an approach that is interpretive and deals with individuals rather than statistical averages. Social work stu-dents, temperamentally and philosophically inclined to focus on individual cases, find our approach more familiar and meaningful. But in social work education there are other difficulties. From our point of view there are the-oretical problems in working with distinctions crucial to social policy and social casework—large versus small, public versus private, social forces versus individual strategies—that pose particular challenges in teaching.

From the practitioners' point of view, the crucial question is to what extent particular theoretical frameworks can take account of different pro-fessional concerns, in terms of what is important in health and social wel-fare, why social and health deficits become translated into need, how need can be forestalled or optimum conditions created for its alleviation, and what can be done to promote the quality of life in old age by practical means.

THINKING ABOUT IDENTITY

A thread running through our work has been an interest both in identity and in relationships in later life. The concept of the self is a vigorous area of research activity within gerontology, in which it is possible to discern at least two distinct theoretical perspectives or schools.

The dominant contemporary perspective is one that emphasizes active management of the self (Ruth & Coleman, 1996). In this tradition pride of place is given to the concept of self-esteem. From the 1960s onward, self-esteem has been seen as the linchpin of quality of life and well-being in old age, and research interest now focuses on the processes that maintain self-esteem.

We cannot assume that normal aging of itself gives people the experience and skills to cope with the sudden onset of disability and frailty in late life or with the loss in rapid succession of most long-term friendships (Atchley, 1991; Carstensen, 1993). Early research in the United States on institutional care identified the extreme strategies older people sometimes resorted to in order to maintain links with their past selves and dissociate themselves from unacceptable aspects of their present environment. A tolerant understanding of self-assertive behaviors is required of practitioners (Tobin, 1991). However, more recent studies of very old people living in the community present a gentler picture of the psychology of advanced old age in which accommodation and emotional disengagement play a larger role (C. L. Johnson & Barer, 1996).

Theories of the aging self have to account for the resilience of self-esteem in later life. Earlier models of the processes involved in self-maintenance emphasized social comparison and feedback from others, as well as temporal comparison of the self (Rosenberg, 1979). Older people have been shown to use the same methods, but research within the stress and coping paradigm indicates that the old-old are more likely to find ways of avoiding problems and accepting difficulties that they cannot avoid (Aldwin, Sutton, Chiara, & Spiro, 1996). Brandtstädter and Greve (1994) have provided a useful synthesis of the literature on self-management in late life. They argue that what we see operating across adulthood are three functionally interdependent processes: "immunizing" processes, which mitigate the impact of self-discrepant evidence by denial and by shifting focus to other types of evidence; "assimilative" processes, that is, those instrumental and compensatory activities aimed at preventing or alleviating losses in areas of life central to self-esteem and identity; and "accommodative" processes, involving readjustment of personal goals and aspirations, which as a result dampen or neutralize negative self-evaluations. Their model posits a shift from assimilative to accommodative coping styles in later life and suggests that depression can be a result of resistance to or failure to make this transition. Heckhausen and

Schulz (1995) have presented a similar argument from the perspective of control theory: that the increasing constraints with aging on the exercise of primary control are compensated for by a heightened investment in secondary control strategies (e.g., disengagement, positive reappraisal).

Control theory is one of the major theories to have influenced general psychology whose origins lie directly in gerontological research (Langer, 1989). It has obvious implications for practice. Professional carers tend to "prefer" elderly people who give up self-control and become easier to "manage" (Baltes, Wahl, & Reichert, 1991). Encouraging self-control and individual participation can often be more costly in staff time. Longitudinal study of the interaction between control and well-being in the course of aging are likely to provide important guidelines for practice (Lachman, 1991). Individual variation in optimum level of control at different ages is likely to emerge as an important factor.

The other popular perspective emphasizes identity as a quality of the self that gives it unity and purpose (McAdams, 1995). A major influence on this tradition is Erikson's model of psychosocial life tasks (see Erikson, Erikson, & Kivnick, 1986), in which the formation and development of identity in adolescence and early adulthood takes center place. Erikson's concepts have been a source of inspiration to many practitioners. Archer (1982), for example, provides a telling account of how she came to find added meaning in work with mentally infirm older people on British psychogeriatric wards through a consideration of Erikson's stages of development. It allowed her to recognize each person's individual history, in terms of both achievements and continuing problems. More recently, Helen Kivnick (1991) has developed a method for assessing what she describes as "life strengths" in elderly clients in long-term care. These strengths are based on updated versions of Erikson's eight concepts: hope and faith; willfulness, independence, and control; purposefulness, pleasure, and imagination; competence and hard work; values and sense of self; love and friendship; care and productivity; and wisdom and perspective (Erikson et al., 1986). As she points out, when care staff consider a resident's or client's functional needs in isolation from these strengths and values, they depersonalize that individual and exaggerate the relative importance of his or her disabilities.

Kivnick's (1991) approach to biographical assessment reflects the emphasis in Erikson's later thinking (Erikson et al., 1986) on the continuing relevance of previous life tasks. Although each task does have its focal period, these tasks continue to return in various forms throughout life. The need to work at early "themes" in late life is a function of current life demands, not only of previous success or failure with similar issues. Aging is viewed as ongoing reinvolvement in life, building on past strengths, interests, and achievements, as well as correcting past faults. This view provides a helpful context for defining rehabilitation and long-term care goals, and we will cite an example of a research application later in this chapter.

A major recent impetus to theory on identity development in adulthood has been provided by the American personologist Dan McAdams's (McAdams, 1993) life story model. He argues that identity is too big an issue in the human life cycle to be confined to a discrete stage at the end of adolescence and the beginning of adulthood. The adolescent or young adult may be preoccupied with certain facets of identity, especially the consolidation of an ideological setting to ground the emerging sense of self. But it is not enough to know what one believes in, whose side one is on. It is also important to consider what one has achieved and is presently achieving and the legacy one is likely to leave behind. Thus, for McAdams, Erikson's later task of generativity is part of lifelong identity formation that comes to completion in the final stage of integrity, in which the person accepts the story that has been created in his or her life.

The stories we tell of ourselves are ways in which we organize our principal motives and intentions. McAdams (1993) emphasizes agency and communion as the two superordinate dimensions of human motivation. The former, considered typically masculine, denotes themes of separation from and mastery of the world around; the latter, considered typically feminine, denotes themes of union and intimacy. Such a dualism is common to many psychological theories, and it is interesting that some authors point to the benefits of achieving greater integration between agency and communion in the later years—males becoming more nurturant and females more agentic (Gutmann, 1997; Henry, 1988). Both gender divergence and change of emphasis during later life are reflected in analyses of the projects of life that people describe during guided autobiography groups (Ruth, Birren, & Polkinghorne, 1996). In our own research and teaching about aging, therefore, we have been concerned to balance discussion of issues of empowerment, control, and achievement with those of love, friendship, and relationship. Although the former receive much emphasis because of the fear of loss of control that may accompany aging, we should not minimize the importance of maintenance of attachment relationships.

DEALINGS WITH INTIMACY

Much of our teaching draws on a range of related concepts—intimacy, social contact, sociability, connectedness, attachment, friendship, confidant relationships, social networks, loneliness—loosely described as issues of attachment and separation over the life course. The aim has been, broadly, to promote understanding of the nature of close relationships in later life; their role in the aging process; the influence of health on relationships, and vice versa; the objective characteristics of relationships; and their subjective meanings. The literature of social gerontology offers insights into the pattern of relationships and changes over time. The scope and intensity of relationships are variously constructed as adequate or inadequate, in which case the older adult is seen as being in a state of deprivation, characterized by loneliness, depression, and ill-health. The individual may be construed as an actor whose relationships are a product of personal strategy or as a victim of circumstances. The absence of relationships, whether or not it is experienced as loneliness and deprivation or an acceptable state of being, is explained in a variety of ways. It can be construed as denial of access to arenas of sociability or as a product of personal choice. The research literature also indicates implicit and explicit assumptions about the relative importance of different categories of close relationship—friends, relatives, and different classes of kin. Selectivity theory suggests an increasing emphasis on old social contacts that maximize the possibilities of positive emotion (Carstensen, 1993).

Of growing importance to this area of research is the application of attachment theory. This theory applies not only to accounts of child development but also to developmental and clinical perspectives on adult life, to the genesis of adult psychopathology, and to romantic and marital relationships (Crittenden, 1995; Hazan & Shaver, 1990). The British psychiatrist John Bowlby (1969, 1973, 1980) was the first to identify the significance of childhood attachment behavior in explaining the persisting distress experienced by infants when they are separated from their primary caregivers for long periods of time. Mary Ainsworth (Ainsworth, Bell, & Stayton, 1971) developed the so-called Strange Situation to study styles of attachment in young children. However, attachment may be one of the few concepts from child psychology that have the potential for linking different stages of the life span.

At present we can only speculate whether the striking variation that we see among older people in their response to loss—the ease or unease with which they are able to let people and things come and go from their lives—is a reflection of early attachment styles. But evidence is beginning to emerge that invites us to consider attitudes to friendship after bereavement and the impact of "giving up" a spouse with dementia (Stevens, 1995) in terms of early attachments. In the light of such evidence it seems worth investigating the value of this approach to late-life relationships, and we will refer later to research we have been involved in that examines the application of attachment theory to dementia care.

This is not the place for a review of the literature of intimacy but rather for an exploration of our own intellectual development and resolution of the theory-practice divide in this domain. We approach the teaching of relationships in old age from a life course and social constructionist perspective, drawing on attachment theory, selectivity theory, and anthropological ideas about the cultural construction of intimacy.

An underlying assumption we make, influenced by the work of John Bowlby, is that attachment relationships are crucial for the attainment of the self-concept. This is also supported by research from other traditions. Markus and Herzog (1991) refer to self-schemas as "packages of self-knowledge that derive from past experience" (p. 113). They remain vital in late life in providing protection in situations of stress (e.g., "I may have a heart problem, but I am very good as a grandfather"). Attachment is therefore a fundamental need, as is the need to be oneself. Attachment is a quality of relationships (though it becomes a feature of individual capacity) that makes us meaningful to each other over a lifetime. These basic premises inform the view that an absence of close relationships is problematic. They lead to questions about coping in the face of loss and social withdrawal. Attachment theory also prompts our concern for a life course approach to relationships. Long-term attachments have a special quality, and the early experience of intimacy can to some extent compensate for its current absence (Murphy, 1982; Bowlby, 1986). Current reactions to loss, equally, have their roots in earlier losses and indeed in initial attachment relationships, which produced the working model of self and other that is the basis for subsequent social experience (Stevens, 1995).

Moving on from the precepts of developmental psychology to those of social psychology and social anthropology, we regard older people as actors in a social arena, as authors of their own personal narratives, as sentient beings whose decisions reflect a lifetime of cumulative experience. Lives are lived in conjunction with others—parents, partners, children, siblings, and friends–who influence each other's perceptions of reality. Together, they construct social reality through conversation and other forms of communication (Vesperi, 1985). These fellow travelers, who move through time together, follow paths that sometimes run in parallel, sometimes diverge, and at other times intersect. Individual journeys are shaped by culture and personal preference. Plath (1982) talks metaphorically of shoals of fish swimming together down the biographical current. The patterns reflect prevailing social values concerning personal rights and responsibilities toward other people and ideas about personal space and freedom as the basis for individual identity and maturity (Jerrome, 1994). We view the individualistic values prevalent in mainstream British culture as a source of lifelong tension, played out in gender relations, in same-sex friendships, and in relationships across the generations between parents and children.

THE NEEDS OF STUDENT PRACTITIONERS

Medical students and student social workers vary in their experience of old age and their openness to issues of aging. This partly reflects their ages (in

Britain, medical students are typically in their early 20s; student social workers, more mature). Both groups are inspired by humanistic values, principally the importance of social justice and service. The social work ethic in the service of old age is expressed in a desire to help alleviate suffering. At a personal level the students need both to help and to avoid despair. The despair that comes from confronting pain, loss, and mortality in old age discourages many students from work in this area. But in training they either have to confront their own feelings of anguish or resist by withdrawing emotionally from lectures on the aging process.

For the practitioner, additional problems arise from the difficult circumstances of current social work practice. This takes place in a legislative framework that lays emphasis on the assessment of need. The assessment process drives the social work enterprise. Ironically, it has to some extent become an end in itself, reducing the opportunity for meaningful intervention. The professional task is now identified as the assessment of need in terms of strictly defined eligibility criteria and recommendation of appropriate services, to be provided by some other agency. Direct intervention in the lives of older clients, resulting in an improved quality of life and in emotional satisfaction for the practitioner, is less likely to happen.

In terms of social work training, the questions have not changed: What are the attachment needs of older adults and how can we satisfy them? How can we use informal social networks to improve the quality of life in old age? Insights from social gerontology are applied critically to the assessment of need in specific groups: spouse carers in partnerships where companionship has been corroded by one-sided caring, unattached people at risk of loneliness, residents in long-stay facilities where staff members have problems with intimacy, and dementia sufferers whose attachment needs are exacerbated by insecurity and fear (Leaper, 1997).

In the specialty of geriatric medicine students are exposed to a multidisciplinary approach that clashes with other models. They vary in their concern for personal suffering and their capacity to become involved in it. All are seeking the "right" tools for clinical intervention; they want to practice in a way that is emotionally rewarding and that leads to tolerable and ethical outcomes in terms of their basic value orientations (health and life). For most, this means relegating the psychosocial aspects of health and medicine to the sidelines; they are frustrated by the inclusion of social scientific discussion alongside clinical teaching. Just as the content of the sessions challenges these students, so does our preferred style of teaching, which is interactive and sometimes experiential. Accustomed to a more didactic, information-based approach that requires only that they take notes, they have difficulty in identifying with old people and sharing their reflections in the group.

The objective of social gerontology teaching is to acquaint students with the importance of a psychosocial framework and, within that, to examine the link between identity, relationships, and health. Implications for action are drawn out in respect of diagnosis and treatment (the equivalent of social work assessment and intervention). Insights from social gerontology are critically applied to notions of satisfactory outcomes from medical treatment— in the form of an acceptable life or a good death.

TEACHING ABOUT RELATIONSHIPS AND HEALTH

The session on relationships in our 3-week geriatric medicine program focuses on the psychological and social benefits of close relationships and the protective qualities of intimacy. Patterns of attachment and separation over the life course are followed by an account of the types of social contact typically experienced by older people—the size and scope of social networks in different settings—and variations in quality. The particular contributions of family, friends, and neighbors are detailed, with a focus on partnerships and parent-child relationships. Attention is given to the incidence of loneliness, its causes, and possibilities for therapeutic intervention. Reference is made to ongoing research on the link between social relationships and mortality in elderly people, which confirms that freely chosen, meaningful relationships are life-enhancing (Sabin, 1993). The challenge of accounting for this outcome is posed, because the mechanisms are still unclear and several social, psychological, and medical explanations have been proposed. A final topic, introduced in response to a need for relevance to clinical practice, is the issue of distance versus emotional involvement in the doctor-patient relationship.

Medical students have some difficulty with psychosocial discourse, summed up by a student as "just words!" Words are less meaningful than figures, and students are disturbed by the absence of recognizable proof. Subjective experience, even when reframed in an academic discourse, is anecdotal. There is no way of knowing the general significance of personal statements or how to translate them into clinically relevant propositions. The challenge for us as teachers has been to acknowledge and respond to the need for relevance by drawing out the clinical implications of gerontological theory.

Our theoretical propositions, derived from the writings of Bowlby and others, that "it is not right for human beings to stay alone" and that "it is not human nature to be emotionally self-sufficient" (Bowlby, 1986), lead to other propositions about loss, need, and the optimum conditions for an acceptable quality of life. They produce questions about adjustment to the loss of significant relationships and about coping in their absence.

The theoretical constructions of psychologists such as Sabin and Bowlby lead to practical propositions to promote good health. One such proposition might involve educating people about the need to cultivate certain relationships as they age. Another arena for educational work might be the training of professionals in how to take account of relationship needs while making clinically accurate decisions.

Selectivity theory (Carstensen, 1993) provides a useful model for practitioners considering the relative importance of different relationships to older people. The theory suggests that they concentrate on those that offer them most capacity for understanding, intimacy, and expression of emotions. The instrumental significance of relationships, on the other hand, diminishes. In accord with the observations of social anthropologists such as C. L. Johnson and Barer (1996), Carstensen (1993) argues that the very old reduce their need for contact to close family and old friends, allowing fewer and fewer persons the power to influence them. The emotional quality of relationships does not diminish, but the social network they comprise declines in size. The commonly observed lack of relationships among institutionalized residents reflects this reduced need to interact with new acquaintances, together with avoidance of the risks attached to communicating with unpredictable strangers.

The critical skill of the physician practicing with elderly people involves judgment of when to use medical procedures and when to suspend medical intervention. Clinical judgments might lead to a withdrawal resulting in death. But from the patient's point of view a good death is a positive outcome. Clinical decisions based on a medical model that ignores the psychosocial context of health might have the opposite effect: a clinical judgment, although defensible in strictly medical terms, might keep the patient alive but eventually result in a bad death from the patient's point of view (Gilmore & Gilmore, 1988).

In a revised version of our course for medical students, the social gerontologist (Jerrome) is joined by a geriatrician. The focus is on real cases, where the influence of relationships and the outcomes of different clinical decisions is clearly seen. The students are still involved in discussion and personal reflection, but the didactic input is limited to themes arising from the case material. They include concepts of illness, the importance of home and possessions in preservation of self, the psychological impact of loss, and the salience of relationships in advanced old age, drawing on the Bangor Longitudinal Study of Ageing (Wenger, 1997). The case studies allow the point to be made that in the outcome-led culture of health and social care, health measures in needs assessment are crudely instrumental and ignore the affective dimension. Reference is made finally to chronic illness as a social experience and the capacity of patients to incorporate illness into their personal narratives with the help of those around them (Kleinman, 1988).

The most important learning experience for the students is possibly hearing the geriatrician say that going along with the patient's wish to go home to her frail husband, knowing that early death is likely to be the outcome, represents a sound clinical decision. It is a judgment that recognizes the importance of meeting emotional needs at the expense of physical health, and that a good death, only 3 weeks after discharge, is an acceptable outcome. Case presentations clearly have an emotional impact on students. Nevertheless, their youth and lack of experience stand in the way of true appreciation of the professional and moral dilemmas involved in work with elderly patients. The geriatrician takes a personal risk in talking to students about clinical error in a cultural system built on medical expertise and authority. An additional challenge to conventional values lies in advocating a good death in a system where the subject of death is generally inadmissible.

For some of the students, perhaps most, the challenges of caring for elderly people as presented here are beyond their emotional capacity, for the time being. Steeped in the scientific discourse of modern medicine, they find individual and subjective interpretations of experience hard to accommodate. The session on cultural contexts of illness combines several intellectual traditions remote from their own.

Social anthropology, narrative psychology, and a life history approach inform our understanding of relationships in old age. Our preferred research methodologies—the qualitative case study, the intensive appraisal of subjective experience—are translated in teaching so that the usual emphasis on body and symptoms is tempered by consideration of self, emotions, and the meaning of health and illness. For some students it seems to work. We might expect to see them back one day as qualified physicians, as fascinated as we now are by the topic of aging, challenged by the multiple pathologies of older patients, and offering the kind of service, inspired by humanistic values, that we ourselves would find acceptable.

COLLABORATIVE RESEARCH

The following examples of collaborative research with practitioners, drawing on theory, that we wish to describe relate both to issues of identity management and to enhancement of relationships. The first example draws on research in the area of assessment of need, the second on improving quality of residential care.

A biographical approach to assessment of need was first taken seriously in the United Kingdom as a result of Malcolm Johnson's seminal paper (M. L. Johnson, 1976). He drew attention to the importance of elderly people's life experiences in defining their own needs, which were so often ignored by professional assessors who took a crudely functional view of needs. The principles were applied to subsequent projects evaluating social services provision in the United Kingdom, most notably in a project in Gloucester that was commissioned by the local health service (Gearing & Coleman, 1996).

In the Gloucester project, care coordinators were located in three primary health care teams. Their role included assessment, planning a care package, operating the package, and both monitoring and reviewing its effects. Their role differed from other contemporary approaches to case management because of the particular attention given to biographical assessment. Its value was demonstrated in various ways, for example, in the insight it provided into family relationships, in the understanding of people labeled as difficult, and in uncovering particular talents and aspirations that might suggest future activities. Although such an approach is initially more time-consuming, it has to be contrasted against the time and resources wasted in community care through hasty, superficial assessments and the inappropriate use of resources.

In Southampton we have recently applied similar principles in attempts to improve assessment of need for geriatric rehabilitation (Pomeroy, Conroy, & Coleman, 1997). The ultimate aim of rehabilitation is to secure social well-being or life satisfaction for rehabilitees and those close to them. Although it is generally acknowledged that in rehabilitation interventions all levels of the disease process, from pathology to handicap, must be considered, there is a tendency to emphasize reductions in disability. But these may not result automatically in reduction in handicap, which is more difficult to determine. The *International Classification of Impairments, Disabilities and Handicaps* defines handicap as "the disadvantage for a given individual, resulting from ill health that limits or prevents the fulfilment of a role that is normal (depending on age, sex, and social and cultural factors) for that individual" (World Health Organization, 1980). The focus is on the perceptions of the individual concerned and those of their social group about what is a normal role.

In our study we incorporated into the assessment procedure the Life Strengths Interview (LSI) (Kivnick, 1991) because it does not emphasize the disability but approaches people from their social context and was specifically developed for use with elderly people. We mentioned earlier Helen Kivnick's development of this instrument from Erikson's life cycle developmental theory. Although the LSI was designed for work in long-term settings, it appears to offer a framework for formulating rehabilitation goals in which considers the elderly person's view of his or her lifestyle is considered.

Our study (Pomeroy et al., 1997) demonstrated that the rehabilitation goals generated by the LSI process extended beyond the discharge plans the rehabilitees set with the professional teams. Among the types of goals identified were keeping contact by regular visits to more distant family members, attending church and clubs, providing a caring role to others through continuing to offer a listening ear, and even just getting out in the back garden. Often rehabilitation goals were stereotyped, and the LSI intervention allowed more individual goals to come to the fore. For example, whereas steps to the front door are usually seen as essential by therapists, the importance of back steps, which enable people to continue involvement with their garden, may be neglected. Yet for a particular individual such involvement could reinforce a more important part of his or her identity.

Our second example draws on the need of managers of residential care facilities to find ways of improving quality of care, particularly for residents suffering from dementia. Although there is currently much emphasis on finding ways of auditing quality of care, elderly mentally infirm people tend to be excluded from consideration because of the difficulty in obtaining their opinion. Those methods that have been recently developed for assessing quality of care for people with dementia, such as "dementia care mapping," which is based on a well articulated psychosocial theory (Kitwood, 1997), have attracted much attention.

Our own approach to improving training and care of people with dementia has also been based on consideration of developmental and gerontological theory. As mentioned earlier, one of the most promising areas of work in life span developmental theory is the application of attachment theory to adult development. Although not included in Bengtson, Burgess, and Parrott's (1997) review, it is likely that the coming years will see increasing application within gerontology (see, e.g., McAdams, Diamond, de St. Aubin, & Mansfield, 1997). Dementia care is one field where definite progress has been made.

For Bere Miesen (1992), a clinical psychogerontologist in the Netherlands, attachment theory has been the key that has unlocked much of the behavior of demented people that is typically found puzzling and disturbing. Emphasizing that we must see situations through the eyes of the person who experiences them, Miesen has suggested that the experience of becoming demented is like entering Ainsworth's Strange Situation. Behaviors such as crying, clinging, and calling out represent attachment behaviors in elderly people with dementia. The constant request and searching for parents, which becomes more common as the illness progresses, can be seen partly as a reflection of the greater clarity of the more distant past but even more so as an attachment behavior par excellence—a search for security and comfort in an increasingly uncertain world. Miesen has even gone so far as to suggest that if we knew enough in detail about people's attachment history, we would be able to predict the course their dementia might take as they progressively lose contact with successive stages of their life.

Through his training programs in the Netherlands, Miesen (1992) has had a significant impact on practice. Care staff are encouraged to see what it means to feel unsafe and insecure and so to appreciate what demented persons are looking for. Miesen shows how important it is for caregivers to understand their own previous experience of attachment. The goals of training are thus both psychoeducational and psychotherapeutic. Participants become familiar with both the demented person's emotional needs and their own characteristic responses, which are modified in the course of the training.

In Southampton we have developed a similar training course and are also evaluating its outcome. The Attachment Awareness and Dementia Care Course, as we call it, focuses on both skills and feelings and combines intellectual rigor with attention to personal and group dynamics. We have learned, however, that adhering closely to a theoretical framework produces particular challenges. In reviewing our course and its challenges we realized that our emphasis on attachment, combined with an experiential learning mode, involved the playing out of attachment relationships in the classroom. The expression of emotional difficulty around attachment affected both students and trainers alike. A high level of skill is required in working at both levels—creating shifts in knowledge and attitudes and changing feelings. The firmness of the foundation—knowledge of the subject and understanding of the subject matter, clear organization of material, good preparation and presentation, and communication skills-in combination with sensitive supervision of the trainers themselves has kept the project going. Above all, a commitment to the intellectual principle of attachment has underpinned the training and driven us to succeed.

CONCLUSION

Our contribution has emphasized both teaching and research. We would like to think that students who are well taught become effective practitioners. The intellectual coherence of our teaching provides students with a particular view of old age and its strengths and vulnerabilities that they take with them whether or not they choose to practice with older adults. Our ultimate goal is to convey a sense of common, if not shared, experience of intimacy and identity that brings together both personal and professional understandings.

If theory is explained well to practitioners, they themselves are often able to see research and practice applications. This was the case with our study of life strengths. The practitioners who had been interested in our discussion of the theoretical potential of life strengths assessment suggested its application to establishing rehabilitation goals. A two-way process of communication is involved, in which theories are introduced to practitioners and practical concerns to theorists.

REFERENCES

Aldwin, C. M., Sutton, K. J., Chiara, G., & Spiro, A. (1996). Age differences in stress, coping and appraisal: findings from the Normative Aging Study. *Journal of Gerontology: Psychological Sciences, 51B,* P179–P188.

Ainsworth, M. D. S., Bell, S. M., & Stayton, D. J. (1971). Individual differences in strange situation behaviour of one-year olds. In H. R. Schaffer (Ed.), *The origins of human social relations.* London: Academic Press.

Archer, J. L. (1982, Summer). Discovering a philosophy for working with the elderly mentally infirm. *Social Work Service, 43–49.*

Atchley, R. C. (1991). The influence of aging or frailty on perceptions and expressions of the self: theoretical and methodological issues. In J. E. Birren, J. E. Lubben, J. C. Rowe, & D. E. Deutchman (Eds.) *The concept and measurement of quality of life in the frail elderly* (pp. 207–225). New York: Academic Press.

Baltes, M. M., Wahl, H. W., & Reichert, M. (1991). Successful aging in long-term care institutions. *Annual Review of Gerontology and Geriatrics, 11,* 311–337.

Bengtson, V. L., Burgess, E. O., & Parrott, T. M. (1997). Theory, explanation and a third generation of theoretical development in social gerontology. *Journal of Gerontology: Social Sciences, 52B,* S72–S88.

Bowlby, J. (1969). *Attachment and loss: Vol. 1. Attachment.* London: The Hogarth Press.

Bowlby, J. (1973). *Attachment and loss: Vol. 2. Anxiety and anger.* London: The Hogarth Press.

Bowlby, J. (1980). *Attachment and loss: Vol. 3. Sadness and depression.* London: The Hogarth Press.

Bowlby, J. (1986). *Attachment, life-span and old-age.* Deventer, The Netherlands: Van Loghum Slaterus.

Brandstadter, J., & Greve, W. (1994). The aging self: stabilizing and protective processes. *Developmental Review, 14,* 52–80.

Carstensen, L. L. (1993). Motivation for social contact across the life span. In J. E. Jacobs (Ed.), *Developmental perspectives on motivation* (pp. 209–254). Lincoln: Nebraska University Press.

Crittenden, F. (1995). Attachment and psychopathology. In S. Goldberg, R. Muir, & J. Kerr (Eds.), *Attachment theory. Social, developmental and clinical perspectives* (pp. 367–406). Hillsdale, NJ: Analytic Press.

Erikson, E., Erikson, J., & Kivnick, H. (1986). *Vital involvement in old age. The experience of old age in our time.* New York: Norton.

Gearing, B., & Coleman, P. G. (1996). Biographical assessment in community care. In J. E. Birren, G. M. Kenyon, J.-E. Ruth, J. J. F. Schroots, & T. Svensson (Eds.), *Biography and aging: Explorations in adult development* (pp. 265–282). New York: Springer Publishing Co.

Gilmore, A., & Gilmore, S. (Eds.). (1988). *A safer death: Multidisciplinary aspects of terminal care.* New York: Plenum Press.

Gutmann, D. (1997). *The human elder in nature, culture and society.* New York: Westview Press.

Hazan, C., & Shaver, P. (1990). Love and work: An attachment-theoretical perspective. *Journal of Personality and Social Psychology, 59,* 270–280.

Heckhausen, J., & Schultz, R. (1995). A life-span theory of control. *Psychological Review, 102,* 284–304.

Henry, J. P. (1988). The archetypes of power and intimacy. In J. E. Birren, & V. E. Bengtson (Eds.), *Emergent theories of aging* (pp. 269–298). New York: Springer Publishing Co.

Jerrome, D. (1994). Family estrangement: Parents and children who "lose touch." *Journal of Family Therapy, 16,* 241–258.

Johnson, C. L., & Barer, B. M. (1996). *Life beyond 85 years: The aura of survivorship.* New York: Springer Publishing Co.

Johnson, M. L. (1976). That was your life: a biographical approach to later life. In J. M. A. Munnichs & W. J. A. Van Den Heuvel (Eds.), *Dependency and interdependency in old age* (pp. 147–161). The Hague: Martinus Nijhoff.

Kitwood, T. (1997). *Dementia reconsidered: The person comes first.* Milton Keynes, UK: Open University Press.

Kivnick, H. (1991). *Living with care, caring for life: The inventory of life strengths.* Minneapolis: University of Minnesota.

Kleinman, A (1988). *The illness narratives.* New York: Basic Books.

Lachman, M. E. (1991). Perceived control over memory aging: Developmental and intervention perspectives. *Journal of Social Issues, 47,* 159–175.

Langer, E. J. (1989). Minding matters: The consequences of mindlessness-mindfulness. *Advances in Experimental Social Psychology, 22,* 137–173.

Leaper, R. (1997). *Training and qualification for work with older people: An inventory with commentary.* London: Age Concern England.

Markus, H. R., & Herzog, R. A. (1991). The role of the self-concept in aging. *Annual Review of Gerontology and Geriatrics, 11,* 110–143.

McAdams, D. P. (1993). *Stories we live by: Personal myths and the making of the self.* New York: Morrow.

McAdams, D. P. (1995). What do we know when we know a person? *Journal of Personality, 63,* 365–396.

McAdams, D., Diamond, A., de St. Aubin, E., & Mansfield, E. (1997). Stories of commitment: The psychosocial construction of generative lives. *Journal of Personality and Social Psychology, 72,* 678–694.

Miesen B. M. L. (1992). Attachment theory and dementia. In G. M. M. Jones, & B. M. L. Miesen (Eds.), *Caregiving in dementia* (pp. 38–56). London: Routledge.

Murphy, E. (1982). Social origins of depression in old age. *British Journal of Psychiatry, 141,* 135–142.

Plath, D (1982). Resistance at forty-eight: old-age brinkmanship and Japanese life course pathways. In T. Hareven, & K. Adams (Eds.), *Ageing and life-course transitions.* (pp. 109–125). London: Tavistock.

Pomeroy, V. M., Conroy, M. C., & Coleman, P. G. (1997). Setting handicap goals with elderly people: A pilot study of the Life Strengths Interview. *Clinical Rehabilitation, 11,* 156–161.

Rosenberg, M. (1979). *Conceiving the self.* New York: Basic Books.

Ruth, J.-E., Birren, J. E., & Polkinghorne, D. E. (1996). The projects of life reflected in autobiographies of old age. *Ageing and Society, 16,* 677–699.

Ruth, J.-E., & Coleman, P. G. (1996). Personality and aging: Coping and management of the self in later life. In J. E. Birren & K. W. Schaie (Eds.), *Handbook of the psychology of aging* (4th ed., pp. 308–322). San Diego, CA: Academic Press.

Sabin, E. P. (1993). Social relationships and mortality among the elderly. *Journal of Applied Gerontology, 12,* 44–60.

Stevens, N. (1995, August). *Older women coping with loneliness: attachment style and friendship formation in later life.* Paper presented at 3rd European Congress of Gerontology, Amsterdam.

Tobin, S. S. (1991). *Personhood in advanced old age. Implications for practice.* New York: Springer Publishing Co.

Vesperi, M. (1985). *City of green benches.* Ithaca, NY: Cornell University Press.

Wenger, G. C. (1997). Reflections: Success and disappointment—octogenarians' current and retrospective perceptions. *Journal of Health Care in Later Life, 2,* 213–226.

World Health Organization. (1980). *International classification of impairments, disabilities and handicaps.* Geneva: Author.

22

A Good Old Age: Paradox or Possibility

Margaret Gatz
Steven H. Zarit

T he idea of having a good old age holds great appeal for individuals contemplating their own futures as well as the futures of their loved ones. Although it has been suggested that a good old age could be defined as "health and wealth," gerontologists typically have brought a more measured view and terminology to this definitional task. One term, "successful aging," has an especially long heritage (see Pfeiffer, 1974). Recently revived by the Research Network on Successful Aging of the John D. and Catherine T. MacArthur Foundation (Rowe & Kahn, 1987), the concept describes the segment of older adults who exhibit high functioning across a variety of domains. The more recent formulations place considerable emphasis on maintenance of cognitive functioning as well as physical, social, and economic status (e.g., Baltes & Smith, 1997).

Beyond objective indicators, such as lists of illnesses, financial assets, or size of social network, subjective perceptions are another critical component in most definitions (see George & Bearon, 1980). Subjective perceptions include sense of well-being, life satisfaction, and morale, as well as subjective evaluations of other dimensions, for example, self-rated health or judgments about loneliness. Once incorporating this subjective aspect, the idea of a good old age becomes a psychological variable.

Psychological well-being itself has a different standing from other variables in gerontological literature; to wit, sense of well-being, whether construed as positive affect or as an inference about oneself based on the result of some social comparison procedure, is often treated analytically as an outcome variable, a proxy for good old age. The other variables, such as physical health, functional level, finances, and social support, are treated as predictors, that is, influences on well-being (cf., Ryff & Essex, 1991).

The most elusive question, however, remains: How do we assure that we will have a good old age, by any definition? We turn to mental health theorists to elaborate our definition of life satisfaction and well-being and then to psychological research to suggest how to prepare ourselves now for a good old age in the future.

WHAT IS MENTAL HEALTH IN OLD AGE?

In a chapter by Birren and Renner (1980) we find an overview of Birren's convictions about mental health. In that chapter it is suggested that the concept of mental health encompasses absence of mental illness, absence of deficits in behavior, ability or capacity to deal effectively with the issues of life (issues such as dependency or bereavement), and contentment with one's life as lived. The authors argue further that any conceptualization of mental health in old age must include the biological status of the person, relevant characteristics of the environment, and the beliefs and cognitions that the person holds about himself or herself and about the environment. These beliefs and cognitions include an image of one's ideal, and with maturity, there is increased congruence between one's ideal and actual selves.

Conceptions of mental health in older adults can be found in the psychoanalytic tradition and in life course perspectives on human development. Whereas most psychodynamic theorists focused on development only during the beginning of life, both Jung and Erikson tackled the life cycle and discussed the inner life of the aging person.

Jung is perhaps the psychoanalytic theorist who had the most to say about old age (Kastenbaum, 1978). Jung's (1933) notion was that the second half of life is characterized by the emergence of the parts of oneself that have previously been hidden. Jung saw this process as different for men and for women. For men, softer, more tender, nurturant, or feminine qualities of personality could be allowed to appear. For women, more masculine aspects would be expected to surface, such as sense of agency. Mental health entails recognizing and integrating these emergent qualities. Jung also described a process of turning inward and making psychological accommodation to physical decline and other losses characteristic of the end of life (Neugarten, 1977).

The theme of different life pathways for men and for women has been elaborated by Gutmann (1977). His viewpoint is that, from middle age to old age, men move from active mastery to accommodative mastery—in other words, from an emphasis on changing external circumstances to an emphasis on changing one's inner self. Women, in contrast, move from accommodative to active mastery. Thus, both sexes are making a "contrasexual transition" toward androgyny (Gutmann, 1997).

Erikson (Erikson, 1963; Erikson, Erikson, & Kivnick, 1986) proposed eight stages of the life cycle that embody the sequence of fundamental conflicts faced by human beings. Although the resolution of each of the stages can influence old age, the seventh and eighth stages capture the special issues of the second half of life. The seventh stage concerns establishing a sense of generativity—in other words, working out one's relationship to the next generation. The eighth stage concerns the development of ego integrity, or the appreciation that one's life has had meaning, in the overall context of recognizing that one's life does not permit reliving. Mental health is harmonious resolution of these issues.

Processes of turning inward have been given fresh attention by Tornstam (1989), who proffers the concept of "gerotranscendence," comprising cosmic transcendence and ego transcendence (e.g., decrease in self-centeredness and decrease in interest in material things and superficial social interactions). Butler (1963) has elaborated the processes of life review that would occur in working one's way toward ego integrity, and Birren's interests in guided autobiography and in wisdom reflect similar issues (Birren, 1985; Birren & Deutschman, 1991).

The preponderance of mental health theories have, in reality, been theories of mental illness. In reaction to defining mental health in terms of absence of mental illness, Jahoda (1958) was asked to write a monograph summarizing criteria for positive mental health. Her monograph was one of the first sallies of the community mental health movement and the founding of community psychology, developments that changed the emphasis of intervention from treatment to prevention. Jahoda suggested six criteria: (1) sense of identity, including self-acceptance, self-esteem, and self-reliance; (2) investment in living and in realizing one's potential; (3) unifying outlook and sense of meaning and purpose to life; (4) autonomy, including self-determination with respect to demands from society; (5) accurate perception of reality and sensitivity to situations of others; and (6) mastery of the environment, manifested in interpersonal relationships, engagement in work and play, and ability to solve problems. Although Jahoda did not present these concepts as a theory of mental health in old age, they nicely serve this purpose, as was pointed out by Birren and Renner (1980) and later Ryff and Essex (1991) and M. M. Baltes and Lang (1997).

Gerontologists have tended to emphasize the positive mental health position, favoring life satisfaction as an indicator of well-being. Neugarten's view of life satisfaction, as reflected in the Life Satisfaction Index (Neugarten, Havighurst, & Tobin, 1961), incorporates notions similar to ego integrity, specifically, optimism, deriving pleasure from the activities that make up one's daily life, holding a positive view of oneself, accepting responsibility for one's life, and congruence between goals that were desired and that have been achieved.

Since the development of the Life Satisfaction Index, scales measuring life satisfaction, happiness, morale, and depression (as an indicator of absence of well-being) have been the most frequent way of operationalizing positive mental health. Ryff has been unusual in recent literature in seeking to identify dimensions of well-being (Ryff & Essex, 1991). Six are proposed: self-acceptance, positive relations with others, autonomy, environmental mastery, purpose in life, and personal growth. Notably, there is considerable overlap between these dimensions and Jahoda's (1958) theory of positive mental health.

The structure of affective experience in older adults has been explored by Lawton and colleagues (Lawton, Kleban, & Dean, 1993; Lawton, Kleban, Rajogopal, & Dean, 1992). These authors have found support for the existence of positive and negative affect dimensions. For older adults the quality of positive affect is a quieter experience, characterized less by excitement and arousal than in younger adults. They also found confirmation for greater propensity by older adults to arrange their lives to encounter fewer emotional highs and lows.

Thus, there seem to be substantial areas of convergence among different scholars concerning the qualities that comprise mental health or psychological well-being in older adults. Other scholars have addressed the mechanisms by which mental health is achieved in old age. One of the most important achievements entails putting one's own life in context in order to realize contentment, congruence, self-acceptance, sense of purpose, and emotional regulation. Whitbourne (1985) has proposed the concept of "the individual's own construction of the life course." The utility of Whitbourne's position is that it invites applying what we know about social cognition to the task of constructing a view of one's own life course.

Schulz and Heckhausen (1996) suggest a developmental theory of control in which they propose that old age is characterized by a decreased availability and use of primary control and an increase in secondary control. Whereas primary control is largely behavioral, secondary control involves cognition—for example, assigning values to alternative goals, estimating likelihood of goal attainment, and engaging in strategic social comparison in order to protect oneself. Brandtstädter and Renner (1990) developed scales to measure assimilative coping (actively and tenaciously solving problems) and accommodative coping (adjusting one's goals to take situational constraints into account). Cross-sectional data showed that use of assimilative strategies went down with age, and use of accommodative strategies went up. Accommodative coping was more highly correlated with optimism than was assimilative coping.

Optimism has been characterized by Seligman (1991) as a belief that one's actions matter and that change is possible. In this usage, optimism is an attributional style that (a) sees the causes of positive events as permanent but the causes of negative events as temporary, (b) generalizes from positive events but not from negative events, and (c) takes responsibility for bringing about positive events but not for bringing about negative events. In contrast, pessimists see negative events as due to permanent and global causes.

Social comparison processes have been shown by Heidrich and Ryff (1993) to be pertinent to maintenance of psychological well-being in old age. Downward comparison to those doing worse than oneself tends to be protective, for example, with respect to declines in physical health, whereas upward comparison to those doing slightly better seems to be motivational with respect to other areas of function, such as social activity. Temporal comparison, that is, comparing one's present to one's past self, may entail the most difficult conciliations (Suls, Marco, & Tobin, 1991). Various diseases and physical impairments increase with age; there are losses in intellectual areas such as psychomotor speed, and there are social losses such as death of parents, loss of work role and colleagues through retirement, and bereavement of spouse. Herzog and Markus (Chapter 13 in this volume) offer the idea of past, current, and possible selves. A good old age may involve not becoming preoccupied with feared possible selves while maintaining positive future selves that one can strive toward. It may also involve drawing on one's successes from past selves and not dwelling on disappointments or possible selves that were not realized.

Although there are areas that continue to improve, aging is characterized by the need to accommodate to physical limitations and other losses. An important model of these accommodative strategies is "selective optimization with compensation" (P. B. Baltes & Baltes, 1990). Selection entails concentrating on domains of functioning that are of highest priority. Priorities are established by taking environmental demands into account and also by emphasizing the individual's areas of greatest expertise. Optimization refers to methods of amplifying resources, such as opportunities for practice. Compensation means substituting available competencies and techniques, including use of environmental aids, when prior competencies are lost or reduced. Through selective optimization with compensation, then, it is possible to maintain ability to adapt to biological and environmental demands. Indeed, P. B. Baltes (1997) proposes selective optimization with compensation as a metatheory of adaptive human development.

In summary, keys to mental health in old age seem to include maintaining mastery in dealing with the issues of life, achieving congruence between

TABLE 22.1 Theoretical Perspective on Mental Health in Old Age

Maintaining mastery in dealing with the issues of life
Achieving congruence between one's aspirations and achievements
Deriving pleasure from life's activities
Sustaining an optimistic outlook

one's aspirations and one's achievements, deriving pleasure from life's activities, and sustaining an optimistic outlook (see Table 22.1). These attributes reflect the converging viewpoints of diverse theorists, in combination with the empirical support offered by these writers. Thus, they can be said to constitute an evolving theoretical perspective on mental health in older adults.

MENTAL HEALTH PROBLEMS IN LATER LIFE: A LIFE SPAN PERSPECTIVE

Old age is not without mental health problems. An important step in understanding mental health problems in later life is to take a life span perspective. The mental health problems of older adults represent either an extension of disorders they had when they were young or new occurrences in lives that heretofore were normal. In the latter case, those who might be described as having led a "previously normal life" are of greater interest to theories of aging. This distinction between late onset and recurrent is fundamental for clarifying the relation between mental health and the aging process. A schizophrenic who first experienced symptoms at age 20 and who has grown old while making marginal adjustments to work and social relationships will inform us more about the course and consequences of schizophrenia than about the aging process. Rather, it is the person who previously had a good adjustment in life but who develops major mental health problems for the first time in old age who can illuminate the role of aging in mental health and mental disorder.

There are several conditions in later life that affect people who led previously normal lives. In examining the possible role of aging in mental disorders, we review briefly the characteristics of four of these conditions: late-onset depression, dementia, delirium, and late-life paraphrenia.

Depression in Late Life: Late Onset and Recurrent

Depression is in many ways the most important disorder of later life. Depressive symptoms are widespread in the older population, and moreover, depression responds well to a variety of treatments (e.g., Blazer, 1994). Depression, of course, can have its onset throughout the life span. In fact, the median age of first onset has been reported to be an ungeriatric 25 (Burke, Burke, Regier, & Rae, 1990).

We want to approach the question of depression in later life in two ways: first, by reviewing studies that explicitly contrast late onset with recurrent depression and, second, by examining patterns of symptoms found among older people. Turning to the issue of first onset of depression in late life, there have been surprisingly few studies that focus on how these cases might differ from people with recurrent depression. Most of the available research points to more severe symptoms, on average, in late-onset cases, including more frequent psychotic or delusional symptoms (Meyers & Greenberg, 1986) and more hypochondriacal symptoms (Brown, Sweeney, Loutsch, Kocsis, & Frances, 1984). There is also less evidence of a family history in late-onset cases (Alexopoulos, Young, Abrams, Meyers, & Shamoian, 1989). Some studies, however, have found no differences in symptoms between early- and late-onset cases (e.g., Blazer, Bachar, & Hughes, 1987).

Lewinsohn and his colleagues (Lewinsohn, Fenn, Stanton, & Franklin, 1986; Lewinsohn, Hoberman, & Rosenbaum, 1988; Lewinsohn, Rohde, Fisher, & Seeley, 1991) have conducted an interesting series of studies that evaluate how age and age of onset affect depressive symptoms. Contrary to expectations, a later age of onset was not associated with longer duration of depressive episodes. Depression, but not aging, was associated with a variety of psychosocial variables, including greater life stress, lower social support, reduced social interaction and social skill, engaging in fewer pleasant activities, and holding more depressive beliefs. In sum, neither aging nor age of onset had a major role.

One important difference between the studies reporting more severe symptoms in late-onset cases and those that did not is the composition of their samples. Studies finding differences generally used psychiatric inpatient populations, whereas those reporting no differences recruited community-based samples. Two alternative conclusions can be drawn: more severe late-onset cases do differ from comparable early-onset cases or only more severe cases among the elderly compared to the young are likely to receive inpatient treatment.

There is much more information about differences in depressive symptoms of the older population as a whole compared with younger age groups. In reviewing that literature, two major findings emerge. First, it has been widely documented that rates of cases that meet operational criteria for major depression (or similar diagnostic categories) are lower among older people than among other age groups (e.g., Koenig & Blazer, 1992; Regier et al., 1988). At the same time, a relatively large proportion of the older population (20% to 25%) experience significant depressive symptoms. Rates of symptoms endorsed on depressive checklists, such as the Center for Epidemiological Studies Depression Scale (CES-D; Radloff, 1977), are highest in young adulthood and after age 75 (Blazer, Burchett, Service, & George, 1991; Lewinsohn et al., 1991). Furthermore, this elevation is not accounted for by higher rates of somatic symptoms such as fatigue or trouble sleeping.

One reason for this paradox of high symptoms yet low rates of diagnosis is that the criteria for classifying major depression that have been developed on a younger population may be too restrictive for the typical patterns of symptoms found in later life. Gallo, Anthony, and Muthén (1994), for example, report that older people endorse fewer items involving dysphoric or depressed mood than would be predicted from their other depressive symptoms. This difference in expression of depression may account for lower rates of diagnosis of major depression. Studies that have used Gurland's classification scheme for "pervasive depression," which was developed specifically for disorders in later life, find higher rates of cases (e.g., Gurland et al., 1983; Kay et al., 1985; Livingston, Hawkins, Graham, Blizard, & Mann, 1990). In one Australian investigation, which used both DSM criteria and the Gurland classification scheme, 10% of a sample aged 70 to 89 was found to have a major depression, whereas 16% were rated as having pervasive depression (Kay et al., 1985).

Taking a different perspective, Newmann, Engel, and Jensen (1991) suggest that the symptoms seen in many elderly people constitute a pattern that is distinct from major depression. They use the term "depletion syndrome" to describe this form of depression, which involves a loss of interest in activities and other aspects of life but without excessive dysphoric mood. Blazer (1994) proposes the term "minor depression" to describe older people with significant symptoms who do not meet diagnostic criteria for major depression. From this perspective, older people frequently suffer from occasional symptoms of depression but are less likely to experience a major, debilitating episode.

Does depression have a different etiology in later life? Here the evidence is scant, but two findings have emerged that contribute to an understanding of etiology. First, it is increasingly recognized that depressive symptoms in late life—especially late-onset depressive symptoms—are associated with brain abnormalities such as enlargement of the ventricles and changes in white matter (Alexopoulos, 1994; Alexopoulos et al., 1989; Leuchter, 1994). These markers may be early indicators of vascular dementia. Depression also can be an early symptom in Alzheimer's disease, appearing even before detectable cognitive changes. Second, prevalence of depression is high among a particular segment of the older population, those with medical illnesses. Estimates of major depression among hospital inpatients vary from 6% to 44%, with an average of about 12% (Koenig & Blazer, 1992). Less severe depressive symptoms have been found in 18% to 26% of hospital inpatients. Similarly high rates of symptoms are common among outpatient samples with medical problems (e.g., Horowitz, Reinhardt, McInerney, & Balistreri, 1994) and people in nursing homes (Parmalee, Katz, & Lawton, 1992). Clearly, then, biological factors play an important role in the etiology of late life depression.

One other ingredient to consider is the people who have been omitted from these studies. One such group is people who experienced major depressive episodes in earlier life but do not have recurrences in old age. These individuals might reveal a great deal about processes of successful adaptation in adulthood and old age. A second group is people whose lives were foreshortened as a result of depression, either because of suicide or poor health behaviors (e.g., smoking, alcohol consumption). The reduced life expectancy associated with depression has sometimes been posited as part of the reason that rates of depression are lower in old age.

Although there are many contradictory findings about late-life depression, one compelling conclusion emerges: rates of disabling depression (major depression) are surprisingly low. Even allowing for problems in classification criteria and for selective attrition in the population, older people are not more likely to have a major depression than are younger age groups; indeed, they may be less so. This finding is all the more striking in light of the age-related changes in neurotransmitters and other biological factors that would suggest a greater predisposition toward depression in later life (e.g., Alexopoulos et al., 1989; Morgan, 1992).

Our understanding of late-life depression and, in particular, cases with first onset in old age is still limited in some critical respects. Nonetheless, the available information points to the finding that biological changes play a major role in disrupting the previously normal life, causing depression in old age. That is not to say that psychosocial factors are not important. They may be critical in at least some cases of late-onset depression But stressful life events have generally not been found to have as strong a relation to depression in later life as at younger ages (George, 1994).

There are two important caveats to this conclusion. First, the socioeconomic position of older people is dramatically better in the United States and Western Europe than at any time in human history. Older people no longer routinely suffer the economic uncertainties that were common in the past, nor do they need to be dependent on children for housing and sustenance. They are also better educated and healthier than previous cohorts. Relatively low rates of depression in later life may reflect the fact that people are able to maintain a preferred lifestyle in old age and that the major threat to them is illness, not loss of economic or social status.

The second caveat is that one type of stressful event, family caregiving, is associated with higher rates of depressive symptoms and diagnosis of major depression (Aneshensel, Pearlin, Mullan, Zarit, & Whitlatch, 1995; Gallagher, Rose, Rivera, Lovett, & Thompson, 1989; Schulz, O'Brien, Bookwala, & Fleissner, 1995). Depression and other psychiatric symptoms have a high prevalence, particularly among caregivers of dementia patients. What differentiates caregiving from most other stressors in late life is its chronicity. Family members usually provide assistance for several years. The demanding routine, in combination with limited opportunities to get occasional relief or assistance with caregiving tasks, results in a depletion of resources and increased emotional distress (Aneshensel et al., 1995). In this way caring for a dementia patient may be the psychosocial equivalent of a major biological event, leading to depression in the previously normal person by overwhelming available resources and coping strategies. Indeed, caregivers may be experiencing stress-related immunological and cardiovascular changes (Kiecolt-Glaser, Dura, Speicher, Trask, & Glaser, 1991; Wright, Clipp, & George, 1993). Psychosocial and biological changes, then, may influence the mental health of caregivers.

Past Experience and the Risk of Alzheimer's Disease

We turn next to a brief examination of dementia, in particular, Alzheimer's disease (AD), perhaps the best example of a disorder that affects the previously normal person. Apart from Down's syndrome, diseases earlier in one's life are not notably related to increased risk of AD in later life.

An interesting picture is emerging regarding the etiology of AD. Epidemiological investigations have identified several protective factors that reduce somewhat the risk of developing AD. These factors include higher education (Liu et al., 1995; Stern et al., 1994), use of anti-inflammatory medications (Breitner, 1996), estrogen replacement therapy (ERT) in postmenopausal women (Henderson, Paganini-Hill, Emanuel, Dunn, & Buckwalter, 1994), vitamin E (Sano et al., 1997), and nicotine (Brenner et al., 1993). The common element with all these factors, except perhaps the use of anti-inflammatories, is that they bear a general relationship to better cognitive functioning. Higher education is likely a proxy for premorbid intelligence. Nicotine enhances neurotransmitter functioning and improves attentional processes; vitamin E is an antioxidant and thus may slow normal brain aging. ERT also may enhance neurotransmitter functioning and may be more commonly used by women with higher education.

As a result, the reduced risk of AD found in cross-sectional epidemiological studies may actually be due to delay in the onset of significant symptoms. As with late-onset depression, it takes a catastrophic biological event to affect the previously normal person, and those with greater intellectual reserves may actually be able to delay or ward off this occurrence.

Consequences of Multiple Threats: Delirium

Delirium is an often overlooked though common problem in late life, especially in hospitals. The etiology of delirium is diverse. Common risk factors include medications, fractures, general anesthesia, metabolic disorders, electrolyte imbalances, sensory deprivation, dementia, and movement to a new location. A general finding, however, has been that the more risk factors involved, the greater the likelihood of an episode (Lipowski, 1990). In other words, the more ways that brain function is compromised, the greater the likelihood of a generalized failure. As with depression and AD, massive events that undermine the reserve capacities of the previously normal person lead to a catastrophic change.

Fragile Resources and Decompensation: Late Onset Paranoia

We turn to one last example of a late-onset disorder, paraphrenia. Though relatively rare, late-life paraphrenia presents an interesting variation on the pattern we have been describing. There are, in fact, two relatively distinct etiologies of late-life paraphrenia. In the first type the major cause appears to be sensory loss, particularly bilateral hearing loss suffered in mid-life. The second pattern is found typically among older women who present with a long history of poor social relationships, although they have often had a good work history. They are typically estranged from any family. If they married, the marriage usually did not last long. Problems often begin after retirement, when they lose the structure and the few social contacts they had previously had. Such women, then, did not have what we have characterized as a previously normal life but rather had long-standing interpersonal problems that perhaps warranted a diagnosis of a personality disorder. Changes associated with aging, however, put them at increased risk.

One other factor may play a role in these cases. Neuroradiological investigations have found evidence of infarcts in critical regions of the brain in many cases of late-onset paraphrenia (Cummings, 1985). Etiology, then, may be an interaction of risk factors. People with sensory loss or those who have poor interpersonal adjustment may be at greater risk, and small strokes in critical regions of the brain may facilitate the appearance of symptoms. As with the other disorders we observed, there is evidence that biological factors overwhelm the person's available reserves, which are more restricted to begin with in this population.

In summary, the idea of the previously normal life constitutes a pivotal component in formulating a model for mental health problems of later life. Four important distinctions are contained in this idea: First, it is *not* a normal part of aging to experience major depression, paranoia, or dementia. Second, mental disorders that occur for the first time in old age often have a strong biological component and do not represent a continuation of previous problems. Third, individuals who are first afflicted with mental disorder in old age almost certainly have a reservoir of past successes in coping with difficulties that can be harnessed in managing this new problem. Fourth, the idea of the previously normal life reflects the more general view that psychopathology must be considered developmentally. Whether a mental disorder occurs for the first time in old age or represents the recurrence of a previous episode, the problem is embedded in a context of life events and personal and social resources and deficiencies that have their own developmental trajectories.

IMPLICATIONS FOR TREATMENT

Beliefs about treatment of the elderly with mental health problems have historically been characterized by a pessimism derived from focusing on actual or perceived age-related declines. Older people may be reluctant to seek help for fear of running out of money or because of the stigma that many people of all ages associate with mental health care. By contrast, the implication of the concept of the previously normal life is that there will be many positive points of leverage for interventions. A point of leverage is a resource that can be drawn upon to make a change in the immediate situation. The previously normal person will have many points of leverage, namely, personal, social, and economic resources that have accumulated over the years. By focusing on points of leverage, treatment can support areas of functioning that are still normal, enhance recovery and rehabilitation, and optimize remaining abilities in the face of chronic or progressive disorder.

The resources that the previously normal person can draw upon are usually greater than those available to people who have had severe, chronic problems throughout their adult years, such as schizophrenia or personality disorders. Such individuals typically have limited adaptive abilities and an already depleted social network. Similarly, a young person just starting out in life will often have little practical experience at coping with complex and challenging situations. In contrast to older clients who have led a rich and varied life, young adults in therapy sometimes seem empty, needing to learn so much and often without the skills to do so. Many therapists prefer the blank screen that young clients present, assuming that they have greater flexibility and possibility for change, but that unlimited potential is partly illusory. Younger adults do not necessarily have the skills yet to make use of the opportunities that are available to them. In contrast, older clients have a record of coping and adaptation that, although not always successful, contains strengths that can be drawn upon in coping with adversity in later life.

When working with older clients, therapists can uncover and activate adaptive abilities, even in the face of seemingly overwhelming problems. A depressed person, for example, may claim that there is nothing she can do about her current situation, but a review of past experiences may uncover incidents in which she coped effectively with similarly challenging situations. Another strength is the previously normal person's ability to form relationships. Therapists can use the relationship they develop with older clients to provide support and encourage new behavior.

An important point of leverage has to do with the accumulated benefits the previously normal person has with family and friends. Those whose lives have been characterized by positive and reciprocal exchanges with the important people in their lives can more readily draw upon help and support when they need it. That is not to say that relationships have been conflict-free but rather that the amount of goodwill outweighs lingering grievances.

The effect of accumulated benefits can be illustrated in caregiving situations. When caregivers and care recipients have had a good relationship in the past, help is more forthcoming, and caregivers experience less emotional burden, even in the face of significant changes in behavior and personality, as in cases of dementia (Williamson & Schulz, 1990). An important aspect of the past relationship is a sense of reciprocity, that caregivers received help in the past and that the care recipient would help them if their situations were reversed. Caregivers with a greater sense of reciprocity experience less strain in this role than do those with lower feelings of reciprocity (Goodman, Zarit, & Steiner, 1997).

The opposite side of building on strengths is not to delve into problems or deficits unnecessarily. Kahn (1975) proposed that mental health interventions with older people be guided by the principle of minimum intervention, that is, doing the least possible needed to address current problems. Kahn believed that doing too much could upset an older person's precarious hold on independence and lead to the development of unnecessary dependencies. Minimum intervention is often embodied in geriatric medicine, which stresses not making unneeded changes and doing less, not more—for example, reducing the number of medications that a patient is taking. In a similar way, mental health interventions should address problems in the most direct way. Therapists do not need to explore areas that are not of immediate concern to the client or do not bear on the client's problems. Caregiving families, for example, may have long-standing conflicts or problems with each other, but it is often unnecessary to get into old tensions or grievances in order for everyone to contribute more help and support to the primary caregiver. The philosophy of minimum intervention can also allay concerns about running out of resources. Solving the practical need created by present circumstances makes a big difference in the situation and also addresses the problem that the family sought help with in the first place.

One of the most critical decisions in treatment is whether to support autonomy or dependence. This decision is often seen as a choice between two extremes, either doing nothing to help the person or taking away all independence, such as occurs in typical institutional settings. On this point, selective optimization with compensation suggests the importance of some letting go in the service of maintaining autonomy in other domains. Compromise is sometimes necessary on the details of autonomy, but the larger goal of optimizing control over one's life can be preserved. Although people can sometimes choose to be dependent, clinicians should not push them into dependencies nor take away more independence than necessary.

A severe test of optimizing independence is treatment of dementia patients. With dementia there is a growing lack of judgment and reasonableness, so people cannot make decisions in their own best interests or even assure their own safety. But even though autonomy cannot be preserved in usual ways, it can still be supported by the use of creative approaches. Dementia-specific units in nursing homes and assisted living facilities provide autonomy in a paradoxical manner by securing the exits. As a result, residents are free to roam within the facility and do not have to be restrained. Group homes for dementia in Sweden take autonomy a further step (Malmberg & Zarit, 1993). Residents sign a lease for their own apartment, which includes a bathroom and small cooking area. They furnish the apartment with their own belongings. They are given a key to their apartment and can lock the door if they want to. Not saddled with roommates and given control over their personal environments, residents of group homes are surprisingly calm, especially compared to those in typical dementia facilities. These group homes also illustrate identification of points of leverage at the cultural level.

In situations where there is limited possibility of changing the person, it may be feasible to change the physical or social environment. Interventions may be made with families, as has been noted above, or with medical or social services. Changes in the structure of the setting in which the person resides can also be important. Changes can be relatively minimal, such as providing frail older people with alarm systems to call for help if they need it, or may involve more substantial architectural modifications to accommodate people with mobility or sensory problems. Finally, there can be change at the community level in how services are organized or delivered or in how the community responds to problems associated with aging.

IMPLICATIONS FOR PREVENTION

What are the keys to preventing mental health problems in old age? Our examination of theory and research about successful aging suggests some practical and promising strategies. Unlike easy aphorisms or magical elixirs, these strategies are not always intuitive, and they require long term changes in behavior and habits (see Table 22.2).

TABLE 22.2   Preventive Strategies Reflecting a Life Span View of Mental
Health Problems in Later Life

Practice sound health habits to assure a healthy body and a healthy brain.
Develop good habits of thought, including an optimistic cognitive style and an
attitude of interest in things.
Maintain a social circle of choice.
Develop sound economic habits.

---

1. Straighten out your health habits to assure a healthy body and a healthy brain. Health habits are behaviors pertaining to physical exercise, diet, environmental hazards, and so forth. Among younger adults considerable attention has been paid to perceptions of personal risk and strategies to improve compliance with a variety of health-related behaviors (U.S. Department of Health and Human Services, 1991; Weinstein, 1988; Weinstein & Klein, 1996). The same notions should apply to habits that are most relevant to good mental health in old age.

Although we do not know how to prevent the more catastrophic problems of life, such as AD, evidence is accumulating about ways to delay its onset and that of other disorders. Protective factors such as such as higher education, ERT, and vitamin E bear a general relationship to cognitive reserve. Given the apparent relevance of cognitive reserve to both dementia and delirium and the strong association between depression and physical health, health habits have implications for mental health that have not heretofore been sufficiently emphasized.

2. Before old age, develop good habits of thought. One key habit of thought is optimism. Health psychologists have written about the importance of optimism in response to severe physical illness, that is, refusing to expect the worst to happen and trying to find meaning from adverse life circumstances (Scheier & Carver, 1992). Optimism is also a preventive factor with respect to depression (Seligman, 1996).

Another habit of thought is being an "interested person."[1] Preretirees are often advised to start a hobby that they can continue after retiring, and productive activity has been held by many older adults and their advocates to be the key to sustaining physical and psychological well-being in old age (e.g., Svanborg, 1985). We submit that the cognitions are more important than the activity per se, namely, the attitude of being intellectually curious or interested in things.

Habits of thought are relevant to cognitive as well as physical and emotional health. Dealing with environmental complexity, seizing opportunities for self-direction, and experiencing self-efficacy all lead to more effective cognitive functioning throughout old age (Schooler, 1990).

3. Maintain a social circle of choice. This advice should not be confused with maximizing social activity, a point that becomes clear if one extends the logic of selective optimization with compensation to social relationships in old age (see Carstensen, 1993). As people age, they become more selective about their social companions, tending more and more toward people to whom they already feel close. Being more selective may help to conserve both physical and emotional energy, particularly through limiting the risk of negative feelings. Tornstam (1989) has argued that forcing social interaction can actually impede the important processes of gerotranscendence. He has shown not only that loneliness decreases decade by decade but also that interaction with other people is progressively less relevant as a remedy for loneliness. That is not to say that older people cannot form new relationships, but the key to successful aging may lie in the nature of the relationships we form earlier in life.

4. Develop good economic habits. Gregg and Cutler (1992) have proposed the idea of a human wealth span. Choices in earlier decades, called the accumulation stage, can have important positive effects in later decades, called the expenditure stage. Good economic habits include: saving money, achieving some degree of financial literacy (i.e., understanding compound interest, risk and return), and conducting regular reviews of one's financial situation. The goal is to prevent financial dependency in old age.

For the past three decades, social policies in the United States as well as in other Western countries, have supported the economic well-being of older people to an unprecedented extent. With growing economic pressures of an aging society, the future may not be as secure, and older people may be asked to accept lower benefits and pay a greater share of current health care and other costs. Good economic habits may become all the more important in this uncertain future.

CONCLUSION

We have posed and tried to answer the question of how to have a good old age. We argued that this question is fundamentally psychological, both because well-being is a psychological construct and because the development of good habits is built on psychological principles. We proposed the concept of the previously normal life for understanding psychopathology and the potential for treatment and prevention in later life. Although first onset of mental health problems in later life is more likely to be indicative of a biological source, older patients may have greater psychological, social, and economic resources that can be of assistance in confronting the problem. Similarly, the key to preparing for a good old age is the cultivation of strengths and resources—in particular, the kind of cognitive habits that characterize the mentally healthy older adult. Widely advocated approaches such as diet and exercise play a role, but equally important are the development of good habits of thought that lead people to be interested in things about them, engaged with other people, more able to cope with adversity, and more adherent to health-related behaviors and good economic practices. Mental health problems are not an inevitable accompaniment to aging but occur when events overwhelm an individual's capability to compensate and adapt. A life span perspective on the basic processes by which people acquire the skills and resources of living can lead to new approaches to conceptualizing disorder and intervention. Theory-building thus has practical implications for treating late-life disorders and for improving people's chances of experiencing a good old age.

NOTE

1. This idea should be credited to Joseph Kahn (personal communication, December 23, 1989). In the summer of 1989, Kahn and a retired U.S. Air Force officer took a 100–mile bicycle trip together. One topic of conversation while they rode was the ingredients of a successful retirement. The term "interested person" evolved during those discussions.

REFERENCES

Alexopoulos, G. S. (1994). Biological correlates of late-life depression. In L. S. Schneider, C. F. Reynolds, B. D. Lebowitz, & A. J. Friedhoff (Eds.), *Diagnosis and treatment of depression in late life* (pp. 99–116). Washington, DC: American Psychiatric Press.

Alexopoulos, G. S., Young, R. C., Abrams, R. C., Meyers, B., & Shamoian, C. A. (1989). Chronicity and relapse in geriatric depression. *Biological Psychiatry, 26,* 551–564.

Aneshensel, C. S., Pearlin, L. I., Mullan, J. T., Zarit, S. H., & Whitlatch, C. J. (1995). *Profiles in caregiving: The unexpected career.* New York: Academic Press.

Baltes, M. M., & Lang, F. R. (1997). Everyday functioning and successful aging: The impact of resources. *Psychology and Aging, 12,* 433–443.

Baltes, P. B. (1997). On the incomplete architecture of human ontogeny: Selection, optimization, and compensation as foundation of developmental theory. *American Psychologist, 52,* 366–380.

Baltes, P. B., & Baltes, M. M. (1990). Psychological perspectives on successful aging: The model of selective optimization with compensation. In P. B. Baltes & M. M. Baltes (Eds.), *Successful aging: Perspectives from the behavioral sciences* (pp. 1–34). New York: Cambridge University Press.

Baltes, P. B., & Smith, J. (1997). A systemic-wholistic view of psychological functioning in very old age: Introduction to a collection of articles from the Berlin Aging Study. *Psychology and Aging, 12,* 395–409.

Birren, J. E. (1985). Age, competence, creativity, and wisdom. In R. N. Butler & H. P. Gleason (Eds.), *Productive aging* (pp. 29–36). New York: Springer Publishing Co.

Birren, J. E., & Deutchman, D. E. (1991). *Guiding autobiography groups for older adults.* Baltimore: Johns Hopkins University Press.

Birren, J. E., & Renner, J. (1980). Concepts and issues of mental health and aging. In J. E. Birren & R. B. Sloane (Eds.), *Handbook of mental health and aging* (pp. 3–33). Englewood Cliffs, NJ: Prentice-Hall.

Blazer, D. (1994). Epidemiology of late-life depression. In L. S. Schneider, C. F. Reynolds, B. D. Lebowitz, & A. J. Friedhoff (Eds.), *Diagnosis and treatment of depression in late life* (pp. 9–20). Washington, DC: American Psychiatric Press.

Blazer, D., Bachar, J. R., & Hughes, D. C. (1987). Major depression with melancholia: A comparison of middle-aged and elderly adults. *Journal of the American Geriatrics Society, 35,* 927–932.

Blazer, D., Burchett, B., Service, C., & George, L. K. (1991). The association of age and depression among the elderly: An epidemiologic exploration. *Journal of Gerontology: Medical Sciences, 46,* M210–M215.

Brandtstädter, J., & Renner, G. (1990). Tenacious goal pursuit and flexible goal adjustment: Explication and age-related analysis of assimilative and accommodative strategies of coping. *Psychology and Aging, 5,* 58–67.

Breitner, J. (1996). Inflammatory processes and antiinflammatory drugs in Alzheimer's disease: A current appraisal. *Neurobiology of Aging, 17,* 789–94.

Brenner, D. E., Kukull, W. A., van Belle, G., Bowen, J. D., McCormick, W. C., Teri, L., & Larson, E. B. (1993). Relationship between cigarette smoking and Alzheimer's disease in a population-based case-control study. *Neurology, 43,* 293–300.

Brown, R., Sweeney, J., Loutsch, E., Kocsis, J., & Frances, A. (1984). Involutional melancholia revisited. *American Journal of Psychiatry, 141,* 24–28.

Burke, K. C., Burke, J. D., Regier, D. A., & Rae, D. S. (1990). Age at onset of selected mental disorders in five community populations. *Archives of General Psychiatry, 47,* 511–518.

Butler, R. N. (1963). The life review: An interpretation of reminiscence in the aged. *Psychiatry, 26,* 65–76.

Carstensen, L. L. (1993). Motivation for social contact across the life span: A theory of socioemotional selectivity. In J. Jacobs (Ed.), *Nebraska Symposium on Motivation: 1992: Developmental perspectives on motivation* (Vol. 40, pp. 209–254). Lincoln: University of Nebraska Press.

Cummings, J. L. (1985). Organic delusions: Phenomenology, anatomical correlations, and review. *British Journal of Psychiatry, 146,* 184–197.

Erikson, E. H. (1963). *Childhood and society* (2nd ed.). New York: Norton.

Erikson, E. H., Erikson, J. M., & Kivnick, H. (1986). *Vital involvement in old age: The experience of old age in our time.* New York: Norton.

Gallagher, D., Rose, J., Rivera, P., Lovett, S., & Thompson, L. W. (1989). Prevalence of depression in family caregivers. *Gerontologist, 29,* 449–456.

Gallo, J. J., Anthony, J. C., & Muthén, B. O. (1994). Age differences in the symptoms of depression: A latent trait analysis. *Journal of Gerontology: Psychological Sciences, 49,* P251–P264.

George, L. K. (1994). Social factors and depression in late life. In L. S. Schneider, C.

F. Reynolds, B. D. Lebowitz, & A. J. Friedhoff (Eds.), *Diagnosis and treatment of depression in late life* (pp. 131–154). Washington, DC: American Psychiatric Press.

George, L. K., & Bearon, L. B. (1980). *Quality of life in older persons: Meaning and measurement.* New York: Human Sciences Press.

Goodman, C. R., Zarit, S. H., & Steiner, V. L. (1997). Personal orientation as a predictor of caregiver strain. *Aging and Mental Health, 1,* 149–157.

Gregg, D. W., & Cutler, N. E. (1992). *The human wealth span: A life span view of financial well-being.* Philadelphia: Boettner Institute of Financial Gerontology.

Gurland, B. J., Copeland, J., Kuriansky, J., Kelleher, M. J., Sharpe, L., & Dean, L. (1983). *The mind and mood of aging.* New York: Haworth.

Gutmann, D. (1997). *The human elder in nature, culture, and society.* Boulder, CO: Westview Press.

Heidrich, S. M., & Ryff, C. D. (1993). The role of social comparison processes in the psychological adaptation of elderly adults. *Journal of Gerontology: Psychological Sciences, 48,* P127–P136.

Henderson, V. W., Paganini-Hill, A., Emanuel C. K., Dunn, M. E., & Buckwalter, J. G. (1994). Estrogen replacement therapy in older women. Comparisons between Alzheimer's disease cases and nondemented control subjects. *Neurology, 51,* 896–900.

Horowitz, A., Reinhardt, J. P., McInerney, R., & Balistreri, E. (1994, November). *Psychosocial adaptation to age-related vision loss over time.* Paper presented at the Annual Scientific Meeting of the Gerontological Society of America, Atlanta.

Jahoda, M. (1958). *Current concepts of positive mental health.* New York: Basic Books.

Jung, C. G. (1933). *Modern man in search of a soul.* New York: Harcourt, Brace & World.

Kahn, R. L. (1975). The mental health system and the future aged. *Gerontologist, 15*(1, pt. 2), 24–31.

Kastenbaum, R. (1978). Personality theory, therapeutic approaches, and the elderly client. In M. Storandt, I. C. Siegler, & M. F. Elias (Eds.), *The clinical psychology of aging* (pp. 199–224). New York: Plenum.

Kay, D. W. K., Henderson, A. S., Scott, R., Wilson, J., Rickwood, D., & Grayson, D. A. (1985). Dementia and depression among the elderly living in the Hobart community: The effect of the diagnostic criteria on the prevalence rates. *Psychological Medicine, 15,* 771–788.

Kiecolt-Glaser, J. K., Dura, J. R., Speicher, C. E., Trask, O. J., & Glaser, R. (1991). Spousal caregivers of dementia victims: Longitudinal changes in immunity and health. *Psychosomatic Medicine, 53,* 345–362.

Koenig, H. G., & Blazer, D. G. (1992). Mood disorders and suicide. In J. E. Birren, R. B. Sloane, G. D. Cohen, N. R. Hooyman, B. D. Lebowitz, M. Wykle, & D. E. Deutchman (Eds.), *Handbook of mental health and aging* (2nd ed., pp. 380–400). New York: Academic Press.

Lawton, M. P., Kleban, M. H., & Dean, J. (1993). Affect and age: Cross-sectional comparisons of structure and prevalence. *Psychology and Aging, 8,* 165–175.

Lawton, M. P., Kleban, M. H., Rajogopal, D., & Dean, J. (1992). Dimensions of affective experience in three age groups. *Psychology and Aging, 7,* 171–184.

Leuchter, A. F. (1994). Brain structural and functional correlates of late-life depression. In L. S. Schneider, C. F. Reynolds, B. D. Lebowitz, & A. J. Friedhoff (Eds.), *Diagnosis and treatment of depression in late life* (pp. 117–130). Washington, DC: American Psychiatric Press.

Lewinsohn, P. M., Fenn, D. S., Stanton, A. K., & Franklin, J. (1986). Relation of age at onset to duration of episode in unipolar depression. *Psychology and Aging, 1,* 63–68.

Lewinsohn, P. M., Hoberman, H. M., & Rosenbaum, M. (1988). A prospective study of risk factors for unipolar depression. *Journal of Abnormal Psychology, 97,* 251–264.

Lewinsohn P. M., Rohde, P., Fischer, S. A., & Seeley, J. R. (1991). Age and depression: Unique and shared effects. *Psychology and Aging, 6,* 247–260.

Lipowski, Z. J. (1990). *Delirium: Acute confusional states.* New York: Oxford University Press.

Liu, H., Lin, K., Teng, E., Wang, S., Fuh, J., Guo, N., Chou, P., Hu, H., & Chiang, B. (1995). Prevalence and subtypes of dementia in Taiwan: A community survey of 5297 individuals. *Journal of the American Geriatrics Society, 43,* 144–149.

Livingston, G., Hawkins, A., Graham, N., Blizard, B., & Mann, A. (1990). The Gospel Oak Study: Prevalence rates of dementia, depression and activity limitation among elderly residents in inner London. *Psychological Medicine, 20,* 137–146.

Malmberg, B., & Zarit, S. H. (1993). Group homes for dementia patients: An innovative model in Sweden. *Gerontologist, 31,* 682–686.

Meyers, B. S., & Greenberg, R. (1986). Late-life delusional depression. *Journal of Affective Disorders, 11,* 133–137.

Morgan, D. G. (1992). Neurochemical changes with aging: Predisposition towards age-related mental disorders. In J. E. Birren, R. B. Sloane, & G. D. Cohen (Eds.), *Handbook of mental health and aging* (2nd ed., pp. 175–200). San Diego, CA: Academic Press.

Neugarten, B. L. (1977). Personality and aging. In J. E. Birren & K. W. Schaie (Eds.), *Handbook of the psychology of aging* (pp. 626–649). New York: Van Nostrand Reinhold.

Neugarten, B. L., Havighurst, R. J., & Tobin, S. S. (1961). the measurement of life satisfaction. *Journal of Gerontology, 16,* 134–143.

Newmann, J. P., Engel, R. J., & Jensen, J. E. (1991). Changes in depressive-symptom experiences among older women. *Psychology and Aging, 6,* 212–222.

Parmalee, P. A., Katz, I. R., & Lawton, M. P. (1992). Incidence of depression in long-term care settings. *Journal of Gerontology: Medical Sciences, 47,* M189–M196.

Pfeiffer, E. (Ed.). (1974). *Successful aging: A conference report.* Durham, NC: Duke University Center for the Study of Aging and Human Development.

Radloff, L. S. (1977). The CES-D Scale: A self-report depression scale for research in the general population. *Applied Psychological Measurement, 1,* 385–401.

Regier, D. A., Boyd, J. H., Burke, J. D., Jr., Rae, D. S., Myers, J. K., Kraemer, M., Robins, L. N., George, L. K., Karno, M., & Locke, B. Z. (1988). One-month prevalence of mental disorders in the United States. *Archives of General Psychiatry, 45,* 977–986.

Rowe, J. W., & Kahn, R. L. (1987). Human aging: Usual and successful. *Science, 237,* 143–149.

Ryff, C. D., & Essex, M. J. (1991). Psychological well-being in adulthood and old age:

Descriptive markers and explanatory processes. *Annual Review of Gerontology and Geriatrics, 11,* 144–171.

Sano, M., Ernesto, C., Thomas, R. G., Klauber, M. R., Schafer, K., Grundman, M., Woodbury, P., Growdon, J., Cotman, C. W., Pfeiffer, E., Schneider, L. S., & Thal, L. J. (1997). A controlled trial of selegiline, alpha-tocopheral, or both as treatment for Alzheimer's disease. *New England Journal of Medicine, 336,* 1216–1222.

Schooler, C. (1990). Psychosocial factors and effective cognitive functioning in adulthood. In J. E. Birren & K. W. Schaie (Eds.), *Handbook of the psychology of aging* (3rd ed., pp. 347–358). San Diego, CA: Academic Press.

Schulz, R., & Heckhausen, J. (1996). A life span model of successful aging. *American Psychologist, 51,* 702–714.

Schulz, R., O'Brien, A. T., Bookwala, J., Fleissner, K. (1995). Psychiatric and physical morbidity effects of dementia caregiving: Prevalence, correlates, and causes. *Gerontologist, 35,* 771–791.

Scheier, M. F. & Carver, C. S. (1992). Effects of optimism on psychological and physical well-being: Theoretical overview and empirical update. *Cognitive Therapy and Research, 16,* 201–228.

Seligman, M. E. P. (1991). *Learned optimism.* New York: A. A. Knopf.

Seligman, M. E. P. (1996, August). *Predicting and preventing depression.* Master Lecture Series, annual convention of the American Psychological Association. Toronto.

Stern, Y., Gurland, B., Tatemichi, T., Tang, M., Wilder, D., & Mayeux, R. (1994). Influence of education and occupation on the incidence of Alzheimer's disease. *Journal of the American Medical Association, 271,* 1004–1010.

Suls, J., Marco, C. A., & Tobin, S. (1991). The role of temporal comparison, social comparison, and direct appraisal in the elderly's self-evaluations of health. *Journal of Applied Social Psychology, 21,* 1125–1144.

Svanborg, A. (1985). Biomedical and environmental influences on aging. In R. N Butler & H. P. Gleason (Eds.), *Productive aging* (pp. 15–27). New York: Springer Publishing Co.

Tornstam, L. (1989). Gero-transcendence: A reformulation of disengagement theory. *Aging, 1,* 55–63.

U.S. Department of Health and Human Services. (1991). *Healthy People 2000* (DHHS Publication No. PHS 91–50212). Washington, DC: U.S. Government Printing Office.

Weinstein, N. D. (1988). The precaution adoption process. *Health Psychology, 7,* 355–386.

Weinstein, N. D., & Klein, W. M. (1996). Unrealistic optimism: Present and future. *Journal of Social and Clinical Psychology, 15,* 1–8.

Whitbourne, S. K. (1985). The psychological construction of the lifespan. In J. E. Birren & K. W. Schaie (Eds.), *Handbook of the psychology of aging* (2nd ed., pp. 594–618). New York: Van Nostrand Reinhold.

Williamson, G. M., & Schulz, R. (1990). Relationship orientation, quality of prior relationship and distress among caregivers of Alzheimer's patients. *Psychology and Aging, 5,* 502–509.

Wright, L., Clipp, E., & George, L. K. (1993). Health consequences of caregiver stress. *Medicine, exercise, nutrition, and health, 2,* 181–195.

23

On the Dynamics of
Development and Aging

Johannes J. F. Schroots
F. Eugene Yates

D evelopment and aging are both dynamic processes. Traditionally, development and aging are thought of as two successive processes of change, with the transition point or apex at maturity. These traditional conceptions can be reduced to the implications of the well-known Gompertz or mortality curve for population data. This exponential function can be characterized by two or three distinct phases, depending on the theoretical orientation. The first of these is a rapid decrease in mortality rate during infancy and childhood (i.e., birth to about age 10). This is followed by a period roughly between 10 and 30 years of age, during which there is a slowly increasing mortality rate. The third phase consists of a period of logarithmic increase in death rate—the so-called Gompertzian period—which extends from about age 30 to age 90 in a variety of different human populations (Strehler, 1977).

Dependent on the theoretical emphasis on or neglect of the second phase (10–30 years), the apex or transition point of development and aging is located around maturity or adulthood. From this perspective, development is compared with incremental processes of change (e.g., biological growth) and aging with decremental processes or senescence. The classic metaphor for these processes is that of the hill (Schroots, 1991). For a few decades, however, the notion has been growing that psychological processes of change do not necessarily parallel biological changes along the life span. The psychological attribute of wisdom, for instance, represents a progressive aspect of change in middle and late adulthood and challenges the traditional decline view of aging (Sternberg, 1990). A major cross-disciplinary question, then, concerns the diachronic and synchronic relations of development and aging. For instance, are development and aging just different stages of a unitary life trajectory, or are they two sides of the same coin?

In this chapter, theory formation will be discussed at the level of both biophysics and behavior. From a biophysical perspective the discussion will focus on the dynamics of senescence as a subset of aging phenomena. The informational, genetic aspects will not be emphasized. At the behavioral level the dynamics of both development and aging will be discussed. This dynamic approach considers the organization of behavior over the course of life (Schroots, 1988). To provide theoretical integration, dynamic systems theory (DST) will be introduced as the metatheoretical, content-free framework for the study of the content-specific field of development and aging. It should be noted, however, that the following description of DST is necessarily an oversimplification (for a comprehensive overview, see Yates, 1987).

DYNAMIC SYSTEMS THEORY

The human individual can be conceived of as a living system, hierarchically organized from many subsystems, such as cells, cell tissues, organs, and so on, according to levels of complexity. As a system the individual can be conceived as part of an even more complex ecological system—for example, the social and physical environment (Miller, 1978). From a thermodynamic or energy point of view, a living system of any sort is open. That is to say, a current of energy passes through the hierarchically organized (sub)systems in a chain of reactions. Essentially, living systems in their environments are ruled by the Second Law of Thermodynamics, which states that there is an increase of entropy, or disorder, with age, resulting in the system's death.

Living systems are continuously fluctuating. Strong fluctuations in individuals, as might be the case with increased age, do not fit well with the classical model of near-equilibrium thermodynamics, developed during the 19th century. To solve the problem of fit for fluctuating, open systems in nonequilibrium conditions, Prigogine (1979) and his associates developed the theory of dissipative structures, also called chaos theory or DST. This theory postulates that a single fluctuation or combination of fluctuations may become so powerful, as a result of positive feedback, that a critical level is passed and the preexisting form or structure is shattered. At this moment it is inherently impossible to determine in advance which direction change will take: whether the system will disintegrate into chaos or leap to a new, more differentiated order, that is, a dissipative structure. However, the more complex the structure is, the more energy the system must dissipate or disperse to sustain its complexity. In other words, living systems, which behave in complex (nonlinear) ways, are stabilized far from equilibrium by way of self-organizing, autocatalytic structures that serve as pathways for the dissipation of unusable energy and material. Because living systems are dissipative structures in this sense, entropy (disorder) production and organization (order) are positively correlated (Weber et al., 1989). Summarizing, it may be stated that internal or external fluctuations of nonequilibrium systems can pass a critical point—the transformation point—and create order out of disorder through a process of self-organization.

BIOPHYSICAL PERSPECTIVE

In gerontology, particularly in the biological and medical sciences, the term *aging* regularly induces conceptual and semantic confusion. Literally speaking, aging (or "to age") denotes change of any kind in living or inanimate systems that is associated with the passage of external, geophysical time (i.e., calendar or clock time). The changes may be good, bad, or indifferent from the point of view of a human observer, but the term *aging* is neutral. In this part the term *senescence* will be used to describe damage, harm, loss, or failure associated with aging in a human individual (Yates & Benton, 1995a). From the reference frame of any living system, time can be conceptualized as an emergent, intrinsic property of energy transformations. Such times are scaled by the systems from which they emerge. The half-life of a metabolite is an example. Although it may be referenced to some device (calendar or clock), calibrated in units of external, geophysical time, the half-life itself arises out of biophysical processes in the living system. Aging can be expressed with reference to the external, calendar time, but the biophysical process of senescence is a function of the emergent, intrinsic time. Therefore, calendar or chronological age (geophysical time reference) is not necessarily identical to biological age (intrinsic time reference) (Schroots, 1996a). In the biophysical part of this chapter the term *senescence* will be used to distinguish the unidirectional, pernicious manifestations of the passage of biophysical time from the effects of general aging consequent to the passage of geophysical time (i.e. "to age").

Dynamics of Development and Senescence

Development and senescence possess broadly similar features. Both processes of change are thermodynamic, requiring potential gradients, and in tapping these they construct and dissipate Gibbs free energy (the form of energy that can be used for work or syntheses). The informational, genetic aspects of these processes will not be emphasized. Rather, it should be noted that development is an execution-driven, regular process, just like senescence. It is not program-driven. Each stage or step after execution leads to new structures with new functions, and these provide new dynamical constraints and new information, through feedback to the genome, for the next round of construction involving a new pattern of gene expression.

Although broadly similar, there are also differences in dynamics. A newborn organism, for example, is less stable than it will be at maturity. The dynamics of development are neither gradual nor smooth, whereas those of senescence proceed in a slow, uniform manner. For the human being the achievement of maturity and maximal stability occurs at approximately 30 years of age, at which time the capacity of many physiological processes is at its peak. After age 30 there is a monotonic decline and loss of "reserve" even when the data are corrected to eliminate disease. We have used a linear approximation of this decline, following Bortz and Bortz (1996). Death from "old age" occurs when the physiological losses beginning at maturity have progressed to the point that the stability crosses the minimum threshold required for system autonomy. In dynamic terms the life span trajectory of the self-organizing system begins with growth, development, and differentiation, all of which are internally negentropic processes that initially mask the ongoing entropic process of senescence. After maturity is reached, the entropic processes become dominant or manifest, leading to a destruction of order in the organism (Yates & Benton, 1995b) .

In Figure 23.1 the ordinate shows the energetics (metabolism) of the self-organizing system during growth and maturity. Negentropic (anabolic) processes exceed the entropic (katabolic) costs of repair and maintenance during the stage of growth. After maturity is reached, no further net gain in differentiation occurs and the metabolic process becomes entropic in the net. Figure 23.1 shows that the process of aging is considered to run concurrent with growth, development, and differentiation in a self-organizing system; but until the growing phase is completed, senescing is masked and not easily detected. In the following, the senescing phase will be discussed in more detail.

Rate of Senescence

In reviewing the data on energetics and body composition we examined the senescence rate for exercise-related variables, because these integrate many physiological systems. Bortz and Bortz (1996) have suggested that the global senescence rate for the healthiest people is a linear loss of 0.50% per year of capacities at age 30. Using the same approach, we have divided the data of healthy subjects into three groups: (1) sedentary, (2) physically active, and (3) master athletes. Most of the data are from cross-sectional studies. In most of the few longitudinal studies the levels of physical activity or training fell off over time, so deconditioning effects could not be clearly separated from senescence effects. Unfortunately, cross-sectional studies often present

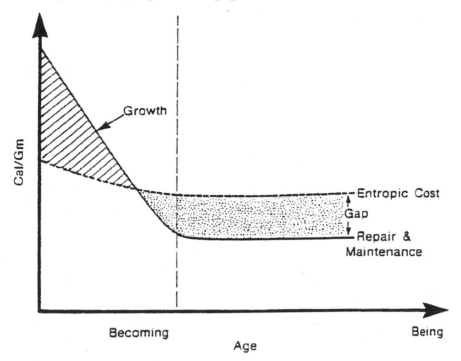

FIGURE 23.1   Energetics of a self-organizing system during growth, development, and maturity. From Yates & Benton (1995b). Reprinted with permission.

only two points: a value for a "young" group (e.g., average age 30 years) and another for a group of higher average age—the "old." The data on the old group are subject to the classical "survivor" bias. In such cases, to estimate the rate of change we took the difference between the two averages, then divided it by the number of years separating the ages of the two groups and expressed the yearly change as a percentage or fraction of the initial value for the young group. The result is a forced, normalized, 2-point line, whose slope is the rate estimate. The actual character of the slope, whether constant, monotonically changing, or more complicated is unknown. However, some studies did provide intermediate points (e.g., Suominen, Heikkinen, Parkatti, Forsberg, & Kiiskinen, 1980), so we could apply various linear and nonlinear least-squares models to fit. Linear models proved to be most effective. Therefore, we adopted the model of Equation 1 for all (Yates, 1996):

$$y_x = s\,(x - x_0) + 1 \qquad\qquad (1)$$

where

   $x_0 = 30$ years (the marker for end of development and beginning of maturity)

y_x is the fraction of capacity at age 30 that is left at age x
x is chronological age rounded to the nearest year ($30 < x < 70$)
s is the constant, relative senescence rate, as fractional change per year.

Note that the senescence rate s will be positive for measures that increase with senescence, such as reaction times, but still represent a loss of capacity. It will be negative for direct losses. Also, this simple model addresses only the *relative, fractional* change rate, normalized to an initial value of 1.0 at age 30. The *absolute initial value* at age 30 can be quite different for sedentary subjects, for moderately active people, and for master athletes—a fact concealed by the above model. There are cases in which master athletes in their late 60s or older had residual capacities equal to those with which a young, sedentary group started at about age 30 (Heath, Hagberg, Ehrani, & Holloszy, 1981; Suominen et al., 1980).

Variance

It is to be expected that different physiological processes will have different s values even in the same subject. The dispersion around the global, average s would be an indicator of the degree of *uniformity* of senescing across tissues and organs and their network connections. Our modeling further suggests that the larger the standard deviation of the sample of s values for an individual, the greater is the risk of dying. A late death from "old age" eventuates if the dispersion of the s values is small, so senescing is uniformly expressed. That is so-called *system death* (Yates & Benton, 1995a). In contrast, a catecholamine-driven, lethal cardiac arrhythmia occurring in a master athlete during a competition would be an example of an outlier value for the s of one organ while all others remain optimal. This situation results in an earlier *component death.*

Lean Body Mass

For healthy subjects, the study by Fukagawa, Bandini, and Young (1990) with two groups, average ages 21 and 75, gave a loss rate of lean body mass of –0.26%/year (normalized to the initial, young value). Similar studies by others have indicated loss rates varying from –0.10%/year to –0.22%/year. These results suggest that there is a loss of lean body mass (mostly muscle—the well-known sarcopenia of senescence [Holloszy, 1995]) in healthy people, which, taking into account measurement errors and other sources, we set at a maximum value of –0.5% per year.

Exercise Performance as Biomarker

Following the lead from Bortz and Bortz (1996), we examined men's marathon times, as well as data on maximal oxygen consumption, for strong indicators of cardiopulmonary, aerobic fitness at different ages.

Marathon Times

The large data set used was provided by Professor Rodney A. Pearson (personal communication); he assembled it from the National Running Data Center. The 100th percentile (best) performers at age 30 finished in 124:53 (min:sec). The best performers at age 60, in the same races, finished in 153:14. The *increase* in time expressed as a percent slowing, was 0.77%/year—presumably reflecting a *decrease* in aerobic capacity.

Maximum Oxygen Consumption Rate

Studies by Babcock, Paterson, Cunningham, and Dickins (1994), Proctor, Sinning, Bredle, and Joyner (1996), Rogers, Hagberg, Martin, Ehsani, and Holloszy (1990), and Schwartz et al. (1991) in healthy subjects showed loss rates for VO_{2max} ranging from −0.88 to −1.16%/year over the age range of about 24–82 years. However, in master athletes, Davies (1979), Rogers et al.(1990), Heath et al. (1981), and Pollack, Foster, Knapp, Rod, and Schmidt (1987) discovered a much smaller loss rate: only −0.13 to −0.50%/year (ages 22–69 years). Kasch, Boyer, van Camp, Verity, and Wallace (1990) found a rate of about −0.56%/year in the trained and untrained. These data suggest that exercise training slows the rate of senescence.

However, the results of Suominen et al. (1980) give exactly the opposite impression. In a cross-sectional design they studied 22 men aged 33–68 (11 smokers) and compared them to 22 men aged 34–70 (only 2 smoked, occasionally) who had sustained a vigorous exercise program for all of their adult lives. At all ages the exercise-related functions (e.g., VO_{2max}) were higher in the trained group, including anaerobic power. Blood pressures and lipids were lower. The groups did not differ in lean body mass, grip strength, or vital capacity, or any of the psychophysiological measures. The *rate of loss* of aerobic capacity was greater in the exercise group even though the remaining values of those aged 70 were as high as the initial values of the young sedentary group at age 30! The faster loss in the trained group compared to sedentary men (−1.0% vs. −0.5%/year, respectively) was not the result of deconditioning, because in this unusual case the intensity of the exercise programs had not diminished over time. The authors concluded that exercise-related variables are not biomarkers of senescence and that vigorous exercise does not slow senescence itself. We have another interpretation. When sedentary people undertake an exercise program, they can rapidly increase their maximum oxygen consumption by 10%–20% at any age. Therefore, their apparent maximum while they are relatively inactive is not a true physiological ceiling. In contrast, superior athletes reach the true maximum, and their values can only decrease under the influence of senescence, revealing its actual rate (regression to the mean). We conclude that VO_{2max} is a clear biomarker of aging—but only in master athletes.

Although body cell mass (mainly muscle) in well people decreases at a rate of only about −0.5%/year from ages 30 to 69, soon after 70 it accelerates to −1.0%/year (Aniansson, Hedberg, Henning, & Grimby, 1986; Tanzikoff & Norris, 1972; Grimby, 1995). Whatever advantage intense athletic training may bestow in the years from the 20s through the 70s, after 80 that advantage will vanish, if for no other reason than a failure to continue to meet the requirement of sustaining master-level performance. We do not know how to describe senescence rates for humans in their advanced years past 70. There may be "flat spots" in age-specific mortality curves, in which the probability of dying in the next interval is constant for a while (Carey, Liedo, Orozco, & Vaupel, 1992; Curtsinger, Fukui, Townsend, & Vaupel, 1992), but senescence rates might also follow the cascade or terminal drop model (Birren & Schroots, 1996). In the final analysis, the ultimate death rate is always one per individual.

BEHAVIORAL PERSPECTIVE

As noted before, psychological processes of change do not necessarily parallel biological changes along the life span. From this perspective the question might be raised to what extent the dynamics of age-related psychological processes of change are different from the dynamics of biological development and senescence. In 1960, James E. Birren presented a general theory of aging as a counterpart of development. The use of the metaphor *counterpart* is meant to express the idea that there are latent structures of behavior (emotions, cognitions, and motivations) carried forward from earlier experience that interact with present situations. Aging is viewed as a transformation of the biological and behavioral development of the organism expressed in a "counterpart manner" in variable ecological contexts.

Dynamics of Development and Aging

Counterpart theory describes primarily the diachronic relationship between development and aging and does not address explicitly the issue of their synchronic relations. To fill the gap, Birren and Schroots (1984) developed a simple diagram of human ontogenesis, in which development and aging—defined as negentropic and entropic processes, respectively—are conceptualized as two parallel but related processes of change or as two sides of a unitary life trajectory. At the start of ontogenesis (conception) the developmental process is most visible or manifest while at the same time the signs of aging are still obscure or latent—and vice versa at the end of ontogenesis. At the biophysical system level, Figure 23.1 might be interpreted as the illustration of this diagram for developmental (negentropic, anabolic) and aging (entropic, katabolic) processes of change. Thus, from an ontogenetic perspective, aging is the diachronic and synchronic counterpart of development both before and after the transition point. Expressed in dynamic terms, this point represents the moment at which entropic (disorderly) processes become dominant or manifest, leading to a destruction of order, that is, a higher probability of dying (mortality) or lower life expectancy.

It should be noted (1) that transition points vary across the life span from system level to system level, from individual to individual, and from system to system even in the same subject; (2) dynamic systems theory emphasizes that not all transitions or transformations lead to a destruction of order in the individual—under far-from-equilibrium conditions certain systems may run down (lower order) and other systems simultaneously evolve and grow more coherent at a higher level of organization (higher order); (3) the phenomenon that under certain conditions order can arise from disorder, applies primarily to low-energetic behavioral systems and to a lesser degree to high-energetic biophysical systems. For example, during the constructive phase of biophysical development the possibilities for varied behavior increase, paradoxically. When the destructive phase of senescence starts, however, these behavioral possibilities will decrease, stabilize, or even increase further, depending on the *strength of the connection* between specific behavioral functions and their biophysical substrate. Fluid abilities, for example, which show strong connections, will reach their apex or transition point early in life, whereas crystallized abilities may develop until late life. From the above perspective, the unitary life trajectory of series of transformations, as presented in Figure 23.2, provides a suitable illustration of the dynamics of development and aging at the behavioral system level.

Figure 23.2 shows, first, that in the absence of strong fluctuations the individual maintains a dynamic equilibrium and moves through time in a straight line until emerging fluctuations direct the life trajectory distinctly toward a higher or lower order behavioral structure. Second, the two life trajectories illustrate differential mortality, as well as the correlation between chronological age and mortality in the sense that more and more of the later transformations (bifurcations, branching points) that uniquely define an individual's trajectory lead to mortality (Nesselroade, 1988). Third, Figure 23.2 shows the transformations expressed in terms of mortality, probability of dying, or life expectancy; however, they can be translated equally well in terms of morbidity, disease, disorder, and disability or dysfunction or in terms of quality of life, well-being, life satisfaction, and healthy life expectancy. For example, traumatic life events and a healthy lifestyle may result in lower and higher order behavior, respectively (i.e., higher and lower probabilities of dying or lower and higher quality of life). Briefly summarized, the biobehavioral life trajectory of an individual can be described as *a nonlinear series of transformations into higher and/or lower order behavior, showing a*

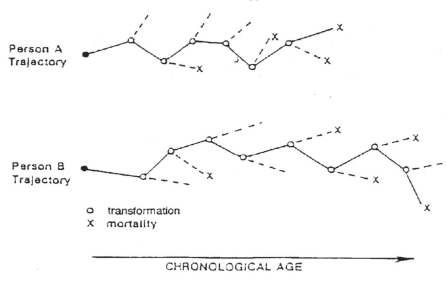

FIGURE 23.2   Individual life trajectories. Adapted from Nesselroade (1988).

progressive trend toward more disorderly than orderly behavior over the life span (Schroots, 1995).

Formalization in Ontogenetic Psychology

The dynamic approach in behavioral science is reflected in ontogenetic psychology, which studies the organization of behavior over the course of an individual's life (Schroots, 1988). Increasingly, ontogenetic research is dependent on longitudinal and time-series data to gain insights into the dynamics of behavior. In this respect, life trajectory data can be conceived as a series of data points over time. These data points are not independent but coupled according to the principle of *iteration;* that is, a process of change takes its output as its new input, produces new output, which it takes as input, and so on. In brief, life trajectories can be conceived as the product of a series of iterations or conditionally coupled events over the course of life. All ontogenetic (life span, developmental, or aging) theories basically agree on an elementary iterative form. It is so elementary that it appears almost trivial; it states that the next ontogenetic state of the system (i.e., the level of combined developmental and aging phenomena) is a function of the previous ontogenetic state (iteration principle).

There are a number of mathematical equations that specify ontogenetic phenomena. The most familiar differential equation, known as the *logistic growth equation,* was developed by the Belgian mathematician Pierre Francois Verhulst in 1847 to model population growth à la Malthus given limited resources. (The term *logistic* (from the French *logis,* "lodging") refers to logistics, a branch of military science having to do with procuring, maintaining, and transporting materiel, personnel, and facilities). More than a century later, May (1976) reduced the Verhulst equation to the more practical "difference form" (Equation 2), which shows a rich spectrum of solutions, ranging from the simple dynamic equilibrium state to chaos:

$$L_t + 1 = L_t(1 + r - a \cdot L_t) \tag{2}$$

where

L_t is the ontogenetic state or level of ontogenetic change at time *t*
r is the growth (developmental) rate
a is the aging rate (including senescence)

Equation 2 describes how a later ontogenetic level, at time *t* + 1, is caused by an earlier ontogenetic level, at time *t*, and by two additional parameters, r and a, which stand for growth (developmental) rate or positive resources and for aging rate or negative resources, respectively. Thus designated, aging includes senescence as a subset of aging phenomena. Because *t* is undefined, the equation describes how any later level of ontogenetic change depends on an earlier one. If applied iteratively, starting with *t* and proceeding to *t* + 1, *t* + 2, *t* + 3, and so on, the equation generates a sequence of ontogenetic levels that follow one another and form a curve, or life-trajectory.

Paraphrasing Van Geert's (1994) *Dynamic Systems of Development,* which has been liberally used in the foregoing, we might add that the trajectory of ontogenetic change is not only the result of a positive term (the growth rate, or "grower") but also of a negative term (the aging rate or "ager"). In the case of biological populations the positive term is birth; the negative term is death. If ontogenetic change applies to biophysical phenomena, the positive term could be anabolism, the negative term katabolism; and in the case of behavioral or psychological phenomena, the positive and negative terms could be higher and lower order behavior, respectively, or gains and losses, learning and forgetting, and so on.

A major property of the logistic equation is its *nonlinearity,* which becomes expressed in different types of curves, depending on the values of the parameters r and a, respectively. Another property of the equation is its *bifurcation* or branching behavior; that is a sudden shift in the nature of the outcome of the equation as some quantitative threshold for the parameter values is crossed. Figure 23.2, for example, shows the different bifurcation, branching, or transformation patterns of two different life trajectories. Briefly summarized, the logistic equation with two parameters, r and a—development (growth) and aging (senescence), respectively—lies at the root of the dynamic systems model of ontogenetic change in reference to biophysical, behavioral, and psychological phenomena.

Variability

From the foregoing it may be concluded that, essentially, dynamic systems modeling amounts to logistic curve fitting, in which efforts are made to estimate the parameter values of **r** and **a** that lead to the best fit between theoretical and empirical (longitudinal or time-series) data. At the behavioral and psychological systems level, this type of empirical data has been produced in the Stanford Terman Study, the Duke Longitudinal Study, and the Baltimore Longitudinal Study on Aging, even though not all data lend themselves directly to dynamic modeling (Schroots, 1993). The monumental Seattle Longitudinal Study (SLS), however, may provide a rich source for the requisite longitudinal estimates. For example, on the basis of SLS data, Schaie (1996) was able to formulate an unambiguous answer to the question of whether intelligence changes uniformly through adulthood or there are different life course ability patterns: "Neither at the level of analysis of the tests actually given nor at the level of the inferred latent ability constructs do we find uniform patterns of developmental change across the entire ability spectrum" (p. 350). With regard to the more limited data on the latent construct estimates (obtained only in the fifth and sixth SLS study cycles), Schaie summarizes the findings as follows:

> . . . it appears that peak ages of performance are still shifting and that we now see these peaks occurring in the 50s for Inductive Reasoning and Spatial Orientation and in the 60s for Verbal Ability and Verbal Memory. By contrast, Perceptual Speed peaks in the 20s and Numeric Ability in the late 30s. Even by the late 80s, declines for Verbal Ability and Inductive Reasoning are modest, but they are severe in very old age for Perceptual Speed and Numeric Ability, with Spatial Orientation and Verbal Memory in between.
>
> Again I must caution that these are average patterns of age-change profiles. Individual profiles depend to a large extent on individual patterns of use and disuse and on the presence or absence of neuropathology. Indeed, virtually every possible permutation of individual profiles has been observed in our study. (p. 351)

Note that Schaie's longitudinal study addresses *interindividual change* patterns over extended periods of time. Long-term, average patterns of change, however, take no account of short-term *intraindividual variability*, that is, systematic patterns of fluctuations that are defined over relatively short intervals of time (e.g., day to day, week to week) (Nesselroade, 1991). Consequently, short-term fluctuations of the individual system, which refer to the system's dynamic equilibrium, are not interpreted in classical, longitudinal studies, even though they could contribute to a better understanding of the dynamics of individual life trajectories.

In the not so distant past, many attempts have been made to quantify the amount of variability, regularity, fluctuations or *entropy* of dynamic systems. (Entropy is a concept that addresses system randomness and regularity or predictability, with greater entropy associated with more randomness and less system order [lower order], and vice versa [higher order]). There are many different entropy formulations, but the two statistics of potential interest in psychometrics require impractical time series of at least 200–1,000 data values (Pincus, 1991) or are awkward to compute (Weisberg, 1992). Recently, however, Nesselroade and colleagues (Eizenman, Nesselroade, Featherman, & Rowe, 1997) introduced successfully a classical statistic—the well known standard deviation-to quantify the amount of intraindividual variability in Perceived Control over weekly measurements during a period of 7 months. Thus defined, the concept of short-term intraindividual variability is not only closely related—if not similar—to entropy-based measures of spread but also a promising indicator of the individual's dynamic equilibrium in the sense that the amount of variability is indicative of changes of state in the system. Eizenman and colleagues (1997) collected strong evidence for this *entropy measure* as predictor of mortality by relating amount of variability in Perceived Control with mortality status 5.5 years later:

> The mortality status of the individuals 5.5 years after the intraindividual variability data were collected was used as a dichotomous outcome variable in a logistic regression. First, the means of LOC and COM (= Perceived Control) for each individual were used to predict the probability of that individual having a certain mortality status 5.5 years later. . . . [T]he mean scores showed very little ability to differentiate between those individuals who were still alive and those who had died. Next, the variability scores were added to the equation to see if they added predictive power over and above that given by the means. . . . [I]ndividuals' standard deviations on LOC and COM across the 25 occasions of measurement added considerably to the predictive power, yielding a pseudo R^2 of .33. Those individuals who were less variable on perceived control measures over the testing interval had a significantly higher probability of still being alive some years later. This rather striking evidence argues both for the usefulness of variability as a predictor variable and for its general value as an object of scientific study. (p. 498)

As noted before, it would be worthwhile replacing mortality as outcome variable with (concurrent) health expectancy indicators (Mathers, Robine, & Wilkins, 1994) to test the power of short-term intraindividual variability, as both predictor and entropy construct. (*Health expectancy* is a generic term for life expectancy in any discrete state of health, including both positive and negative states). In conclusion we can say that short-term intraindividual variability data, in combination with long-term interindividual change data, offer the best prospects for the dynamic systems modeling of ontogenetic change in reference to biophysical, behavioral, and psychological phenomena.

Finally, after many years of theory formation, developments in methodology have reached the point that theoretical conceptions of the dynamics of development and aging can be tested empirically (Schroots, 1996b). After all, the proof of the pudding is in the eating.

SUMMARY

In this chapter the dynamics of development and aging is discussed at different levels of theorizing, varying from the level of metaphor and model to the level of theory and metatheory.

Dynamic systems theory is presented as the metatheoretical framework for the study of development and aging from both biophysical and behavioral perspectives. Living systems are continuously fluctuating and achieve a dynamic stability. Dynamic systems theory hypothesizes that internal or external fluctuations of nonequilibrium systems can pass a critical point—the transformation point—and create order out of disorder through a process of self-organization.

From a *biophysical* perspective, the discussion is focused on the dynamics of senescence as a subset of aging phenomena consisting of a constellation of deleterious processes in each person. One striking manifestation is failure of repair and maintenance. For each individual there is a global, average rate of loss of competence (here designated as s). The greater the variance for s within an individual, the greater the probability of his or her dying in the next interval.

By definition, senescence starts at maturity and proceeds ineluctably toward death at a uniform, global rate in healthy people between the ages of 30 and 70 years. The common global rate, s = −0.5% to −0.75% per year, possibly can be slowed by exercise, antioxidants, or caloric restriction (within limits), but the data are inconclusive for humans. Conversely, many behaviors or experiences can accelerate s (alcoholism; smoking; high intakes of fat, sugar, and possibly salt in some; chronic stress; physical inactivity; chronic lack of sleep).

At advanced ages (> 70 years) normal senescence spontaneously accelerates (i.e., s exceeds −1%/year for awhile) but then may decelerate to nearly zero, so death results from a random fluctuation.

From a *behavioral* perspective, the dynamics of both development and aging are discussed. Development and aging, defined as primarily negentropic and entropic processes, respectively, are conceptualized as two parallel but related processes of ontogenetic change or as two sides of a unitary life trajectory.

The ontogenetic (biobehavioral) life trajectory of an individual system can be described as a nonlinear series of transformations into higher and/or lower order behavior, showing a progressive trend toward more disorderly than orderly behavior over the life span.

The logistic equation with two parameters **r** and **a** (including **s**)—development (growth) and aging (including senescence)—lies at the root of the dynamic systems model of ontogenetic change in reference to biophysical, behavioral, and psychological phenomena.

Developments in methodology have reached the point that theoretical conceptions of the dynamics of development and aging can be tested empirically. Short-term intraindividual variability data, in combination with long-term interindividual change data, offer the best prospects for the dynamic systems modeling of development and aging.

REFERENCES

Aniansson, A., Hedberg, M., Henning, G.-B., & Grimby, G. (1986). Muscle morphology, enzymatic activity, and muscle strength in elderly men: A follow-up study. *Muscle and Nerve, 9,* 585–591.

Babcock, M. A., Paterson, D. H., Cunningham, D. A., & Dickins, J. R. (1994). Exercise on-transient gas exchange kinetics are slowed as a function of age. *Medical Science, Sports and Exercise, 26,* 440–446.

Birren, J. E. (1960). Behavioral theories of aging. In N. W. Shock (Ed.), *Aging: Some social and biological aspects* (pp. 305–332). Washington, DC: American Association for the Advancement of Science.

Birren, J. E. & Schroots, J. J. F. (1984). Steps to an ontogenetic psychology. *Academic Psychology Bulletin, 6,* 177–190.

Birren, J. E. & Schroots, J. J. F. (1996). History, concepts, and theory in the psychology of aging. In J. E. Birren & K. W. Schaie (Eds.), *Handbook of the psychology of aging* (4th ed., pp. 3–23). San Diego, CA: Academic Press.

Bortz, W. M. IV, & Bortz, W. M. II. (1996). How fast do we age? Exercise performance as a biomarker. *Journal of Gerontology Medical Science, 51A,* M223–M225.

Carey, J. R., Liedo, P., Orozco, D., & Vaupel, J. W. (1992). Slowing of mortality rates at older ages in large medfly cohorts. *Science, 258,* 457–461.

Curtsinger, J. W., Fukui, H. H., Townsend, D. R., & Vaupel, J. W. (1992). Demography of geneotypes: Failure of the limited life-span paradigm in *Drosophila melanogaster. Science, 258,* 461–463.

Davies, C. T. M. (1979). Thermoregulation during exercise in relation to sex and age. *Journal of Applied Physiology, 42,* 71–79.

Eizenman, D. R., Nesselroade, J. R., Featherman, D. L., & Rowe, J. W. (1997). Intraindividual variability in perceived control in an older sample: The MacArthur Successful Aging Studies. *Psychology and Aging, 12,* 489–502.

Fukagawa, N. K., Bandini, L. B., & Young, J. B. (1990). Effect of age on body composition and resting metabolic rate. *American Journal of Physiology: Endocrinology and Metabolism, 22,* E233–E238.

Grimby, G. (1995). Muscle performance and structure in the elderly as studied cross-sectionally and longitudinally. *Journal of Gerontology, Series A, 50A,* 17–22.

Heath, G., Hagberg, J., Ehrani, A. A., & Holloszy, J. O. (1981). Physical comparison of young and old endurance athletes. *Journal of Applied Physiology, 51,* 634–640.

Holloszy, J. O. (Ed.) (1995). Workshop on sarcopenia: Muscle atrophy in old age [Special issue]. *Journal of Gerontology Series A, 50A.*

Kasch, F. W., Boyer, J. L., van Camp, S. P., Verity, L. S., & Wallace, S. P. (1990). The effect of physical activity and inactivity on aerobic power in older men (a longitudinal study). *Journal of Physicians' Sports Medicine, 18,* 73–83.

Mathers, C. D., Robine, J. M., & Wilkins, R. (1994). Health expectancy indicators: Recommendations for terminology. In C. D. Mathers, J. McCallum, & J. M. Robine (Eds.), *Advances in health expectancies* (pp. 34–41). Canberra: Australian Institute of Health and Welfare: AGPS.

May, R. M. (1976). Simple mathematical models with very complicated dynamics. *Nature, 261,* 459–467.

Miller, J. G. (1978). *Living systems.* New York: McGraw-Hill.

Nesselroade, J. R. (1988). Sampling and generalizability: Adult development and aging research issues examined within the general methodological framework of selection. In K. W. Schaie, R. T. Campbell, W. Meredith, & S. C. Rawlings (Eds.), *Methodological issues in aging research* (pp. 13–42). New York: Springer Publishing Co.

Nesselroade, J. R. (1991). The warp and the woof of the developmental fabric. In R. M. Downs, L. S. Liben, & D. S. Palermo (Eds.), *Visions of aesthetics, the enviromnent and development: The legacy of Joachim F. Wohlwill* (pp. 213–240). Hillsdale, NJ: Lawrence Erlbaum Associates.

Pincus, S. M. (1991). Approximate entropy as a measure of system complexity. *Proceedings of the National Academy of Sciences, USA, 88,* 2297–2301.

Pollack, M. L., Foster, C., Knapp, D., Rod, J. L., & Schmidt, D. H. (1987). Effect of age and training on aerobic capacity and body composition of master athletes. *Journal of Applied Physiology, 62,* 725–731.

Prigogine, I. (1979). *From being to becoming.* San Francisco: W.H. Freeman.

Proctor, D. N., Sinning, W. E., Bredle, J. L., & Joyner, M. J. (1996). Cardiovascular and peak VO_2 responses to supine exercise: Effects of age and training status. *Medical Science, Sports and Exercise, 28,* 892–899.

Rogers, M. A., Hagberg, J. M., Martin, III, W. H., Ehsani, A. A., & Holloszy, J. O. (1990). Decline in $VO_{2\,max}$ with aging in master athletes and sedentary men. *Journal of Applied Physiology, 68,* 2195–2199.

Schaie, K. W. (1996). *Intellectual development in adulthood: The Seattle Longitudinal Study.* New York: Cambridge University Press.

Schroots, J. J. F. (1988). On growing, formative change and aging. In J. E. Birren & V. L. Bengtson (Eds.), *Emergent theories of aging* (pp. 299–329). New York: Springer Publishing Co.

Schroots, J. J. F. (1991). Methaphors of aging and complexity. In G. M. Kenyon, J. E. Birren, & J. J. F. Schroots (Eds.), *Methaphors of aging in science and the humanities* (pp. 219–243). New York: Springer Publishing Co.

Schroots, J. J. F. (Ed.). (1993). *Aging, health and competence: The next generation of longitudinal research.* Amsterdam: Elsevier Science Publishers.

Schroots, J. J. F. (1995). Gerodynamics: Toward a branching theory of aging. *Canadian Journal on Aging, 14,* 74–81.

Schroots, J. J. F. (1996a). Time: Concepts and perceptions. In J. E. Birren (Ed.), *Encyclopedia of gerontology* (Vol. 2, pp. 583–590). San Diego: Academic Press.

Schroots, J. J. F. (1996b). Theoretical developments in the psychology of aging. *The Gerontologist, 36,* 742–748.

Schwartz, R. S., Shuman, W. S., Larson, V., Cain, K. C., Fellingham, G. W., Beard, J. C., Kahn, S. E., Stratton, J. R., Cerqueria, M. D., & Abrass, I. B. (1991). The effect of intensive endurance exercise training on body fat distribution in young and older men. *Metabolism, 40,* 545–551.

Sternberg, R. J. (1990). *Metaphors of mind; Conceptions of the nature of intelligence.* Cambridge, U.K.: Cambridge University Press.

Strehler, B. L. (1977). *Time, cells and aging.* New York: Academic Press.

Suominen, H., Heikkinen, E., Parkatti, T., Forsberg, S., & Kiiskinen, A. (1980). Effects of lifelong physical training on functional aging in men. *Scandinavian Journal of the Society of Medicine, 14*(Suppl.), 225–240.

Tanzikoff, S. P., & Norris, A. H. (1972). Effect of muscle mass decrease on age-related BMR changes. *Journal of Applied Physiology, 43,* 1001–1006.

Van Geert, P. (1994). *Dynamic systems of development; Change between complexity and chaos.* New York: Harvester Wheatsheaf.

Weber, B. H., Depew, D. J., Dyke, C., Salthe, S. N., Schneider, E. D., Ulanowicz, R. E., & Wicken, J. S. (1989). Evolution in thermodynamic perspective: An ecological approach. *Biology and Philosophy, 4,* 373–405.

Weisberg, H.F. (1992). *Central tendency and variability* (Sage University Paper Series on Quantitative Applications in the Social Sciences, 07–083). Newbury Park, CA: Sage.

Yates, F. E. (Ed.). (1987). *Self-organizing systems: The emergence of order.* New York: Plenum Press.

Yates, F. E. (1996). Theories of aging: Biological. In J. E. Birren (Ed.), *Encyclopedia of gerontology* (Vol. 2, pp. 545–555). San Diego, CA: Academic Press.

Yates, F. E., & Benton, L. A. (1995a). Loss of integration and resiliency with age: A dissipative destruction. In E. J. Masoro (Ed.), *Handbook of physiology; Section 11. Aging* (pp. 591–610). New York: Oxford University Press.

Yates, F. E., & Benton, L. A. (1995b). Rejoinder to Rosen's comments on Biological senescence: Loss of integration and resilience. *Canadian Journal on Aging, 14,* 125–130.

24

Analyzing Social Theories of Aging

Victor W. Marshall

ithin the past few years, several scholars have undertaken to analyze social theories of aging. This exercise has led them to develop classifications of such theories, but these classifications do
not agree. It may be time to examine this process—to analyze the analyses—
and that is the intention of this chapter.

What is theory? In a recent paper, Bengtson, Burgess and Parrott (1997)
define theory as "the construction of explicit explanations in accounting for
empirical findings" (p. S72). To this I would add, "Theory in the social
sciences is discourse" (Marshall, 1996, p. 13). Theoretical disputes are not
just about the fit between abstract statements and statements about data. In
fact, theoretical disputes are rarely resolved by data, but more often the
disputes concern the characterization of the theoretical statements. Thus, as
Alexander (1988) puts it theoretical discourse involves arguments about "logical coherence, expansiveness of scope, interpretive insight, value relevance,
rhetorical force, beauty, and texture of argument" (p. 80). This makes talking
about and analyzing theory much more interesting than if theoretical debates dealt only with abstract ideas.

In this chapter, I argue that understanding theory is important and that

An earlier version of this chapter was presented as a Distinguished Teacher lecture at the Association for Gerontology and Higher Education meetings, Winston-Salem, North Carolina, February
1998. The lecture and this chapter are dedicated to the late Donald Spence, friend and mentor,
who engendered in me a love of sociological theory.

classification of theories is a more useful guide to understanding them if the classification supports stories about theories, theorizing, and theorists.

THE ROLE OF THEORY

The majority of researchers in the field are, on the whole, quite unconcerned with theory. Bengtson and colleagues (Bengtson et al., 1997) go so far as to say that "much recent research in gerontology appears to have disinherited theory. In their quest to examine aspects of individual and social aging, researchers have been quick to provide facts but slow to integrate them within a larger explanatory framework, connecting findings to established explanations of social phenomena" (p. S72). They reviewed a number of major journals publishing sociological work in aging and found that only 27% made explicit reference to sociological or more specific social gerontological theories—even though these authors also correctly point out that there is always at least an explicit theory in any analysis that links two or more variables in an explanatory model. The problem is that, unless such models are explicitly linked to broader theories, the publication of research results cannot have a cumulative impact on knowledge.

Most fundamentally, theory is useful in making generalizations about particular cases of anything we want to understand. If we can locate a given event—for example, the way a younger person treats an older person with respect or without respect—within a theoretical context, we can begin to understand two things: why that event occurs and what the consequences of that event are. And our goal as social scientists is understanding.

The French mathematician Jules Henri Poincarré (who lived from 1854 to 1912) noted that "science is built of facts the way a house is built of bricks; but an accumulation of facts is no more science than a pile of bricks is a house" (quoted in Marshall, 1996). I agree with this view. I have had students go out and gather data for their theses and then try to reproduce every ounce of their hard-gained data in those theses. But that is not our goal. Our goal is understanding of the world, not reproduction of the world, as a model might do (Bengtson, Rice, & Johnson, Chapter 1; Marshall, 1996) And that involves making abstractions, generalizing.

Bengtson and his colleagues have summarized some of the purposes or benefits of theory. First, theory serves the integration of knowledge. "A good theory summarizes the many discrete findings from many empirical studies and incorporates them into a brief statement that summarizes linkages among concepts and empirical results" (Bengtson, Parrott, & Burgess, 1996, p. 769). Second, "a useful theory provides not only description of the ways empirically-observed phenomena are related (this is what 'models' reflect), but also *how* and especially *why* they are related, in a logically sound account incorporating antecedents and consequences of empirical results" (p. 769). Third, theory can lead to predictions; and fourth, it can lead to interventions. These authors note that scholars in the interpretive and critical traditions are concerned not with prediction and intervention but with understanding and description of processes. Theories in this sense pursue meaning.

Many sociologists have the misguided idea that we should commence our research with absolutely no presuppositions at all, with our minds as empty as a tabula rasa (blank slate). Some scholars who like to use qualitative methods want to just go out there, find out what is going on, describe it, and perhaps make some generalizations about it, bringing their understanding to a level of abstraction that we could call theory. But it is surely foolish to undertake research on a topic without trying to find out what is already known about it. It is also a bit disrespectful of our predecessors in research, who put a lot of time and effort into researching something and thinking it through. Theoretical formulations are the most convenient way to summarize what is known about a phenomenon. If you doubt this, consider any topic, such as aging and family relations. There must be literally thousands of research publications in such an area. You cannot "know" this literature by remembering each specific study. You formulate a knowledge of it by identifying generalizations, and in doing so you are either constructing or using theory.

WAYS TO UNDERSTAND THEORY

In the remainder of the chapter, I review some different, although related, ways to understand, or to foster an understanding, of theory. I focus on approaches that have been used in the literature of the past few years, in which there has been somewhat of a resurgence of interest in social theories of aging.

Theoretical Contrast and Conflict

One common way to approach the understanding of social theory is to develop a typology that classifies theoretical approaches into different groups. This approach is quite commonly found in social gerontology textbooks, and of course it begins with making some kind of theoretical distinction. But it also occurs as a device used by those who are constructing theory. For example, when Cumming and Henry (1961) wanted to establish the disengagement theory of aging, they postulated that it was an alternative to a widely shared theory arguing that continuing high levels of activity were desirable for successful aging. Although it was years before the alternative theory was formalized (Lemon, Bengtson & Peterson, 1972; later, Longino &

Kart, 1982), Cumming and Henry in a sense created activity theory as a foil against which to advocate their own approach.

When Joseph Tindale and I (Marshall & Tindale, 1978) wanted to advocate what is now called a political economy approach in gerontological theory, we presented a paper called "Notes for a Radical Gerontology." Our intention was to contrast our own position with "the mainstream perspectives in social gerontology for their normative, or sociology of order assumptions; and . . . present the outlines of a radical scholarship as a desired alternative" (p. 163). In contrast to the social-psychological and individualistic stance that dominated the field at that time, we argued for a political economy approach drawing on Marxist origins but one that linked the macro and the micro. We invoked C. Wright Mills's (1959) often cited injunction that sociologists should attempt to link personal troubles and public issues, biography and history. In another early paper, "No Exit: A Symbolic Interactionist Perspective on Aging" (Marshall, 1978–1979), I took Irving Rosow's (1974) functionalist and normative work on socialization for old age as the foil for a symbolic interactionist, interpretive approach. It was easy to do and useful, because Rosow's functionalism was so pure and also good theory of its type and such a strong contrast, in it assumptions about human agency, to the symbolic interactionist perspective.

The Typology as an Approach to Understanding Theory

Subsequently, I brought together the two dimensions of contrast in these two papers into a cross-classification of normative versus interpretive theories, on the one hand, and macro versus micro theories on the other hand, with intermediate categories in both cases (Marshall, 1980). A revised version forms the organizing principle for my recent "State of Theory" chapter (Marshall, 1996). This typology appears as Table 24.1.

Across the top, I distinguish normative from interpretive theoretical perspectives; the vertical axis contrasts macro and micro levels of analysis. These dimensions refer to broad aspects of theoretical perspective and not to theories themselves, which are more specific and generally seek to explain the relationships among variables. Perspectives, in contrast, direct one's attention to certain phenomena and incorporate quite abstract assumptions about the way the social world works. Examples of assumptions about basic properties of human nature might be that humans are motivated to reduce complexity, to give meaning to life experience, or to reduce psychosexual tension. Examples about social relationships might be that they are characterized by consensus or by conflict, that they are inherently exploitative or not. Theories, which are of greater specificity than perspectives, are entered into the cells formed by this cross-tabular arrangement. This distinction is somewhat arbitrary, and in fact, some of the cell entries, such as age stratification, are

TABLE 24.1   Social Science Theories in the Field of Aging

Level of Analysis	Normative	Bridging	Interpretive
Macro	Structuralism, modernization, and aging theory	Interest group theory, Institutional theory	Political economy
Linking	Disengagement and activity theory, "birth and fortune thesis, age stratification perspective	Life course perspective, feminist theories	Critical theory, symbolic interactionism and phenomenology, cultural anthropology
Micro	Role theory, developmental theory, conventional economic and rational choice theory	Exchange theory	Self and identity theories (continuity theory, career/status passage, dramaturgical)

Source: Marshall, V. W. (1996), The state of theory in aging and the social sciences. Pp. 12–30 in R. H. Binstock and Linda K. George (Eds.), *Handbook of Aging and the Social Sciences,* Fourth Edition. San Diego: Academic Press. Reprinted with permission.

really perspectives, not theories. However, these are more specific than the general perspectives of normative and interpretive.

Intermediate categories are entered in both dimensions of this typology. There is nothing special about using the term *bridging* to describe theoretical approaches that are intermediate between normative and interpretive and the term *linking* for the intermediate level in the other dimension. Two different words are used to avoid confusion when talking about the typology. The two could well be interchanged, or some other word chosen, such as *meso,* might have been used instead of *linking.* But *linking* is a good term because all the theories or perspectives described as linking go beyond the view that there is a middle level of analysis to argue that social processes operating at one level (the micro or the macro) are somehow linked to those at the other level. Theories differ in the ways they postulate these linkages to occur.

Normative approaches give priority to the society over the individual, in the sense that they give little credit to the individual for human agency—for the capacity to act or choose as opposed to reacting or simply having things happen to them. Note that rational choice theory falls into this category even though it has the term "choice" in it. This is because choice is seen as highly constrained by rational choice theorists—to one form of rationality in which people are assumed to always choose that which maximizes their own utility. They evaluate the costs and benefits of various lines of activity and will inevitably choose the line that has the highest value of the equation, "utility = rewards minus costs." How much choice is that? Similarly, in conventional role theory, which is incorporated into not only Irving Rosow's (1974) conception of socialization for old age but also into Matilda Riley's earlier versions of the age stratification perspective (Riley, Johnson, & Foner, 1972) and Bernice Neugarten's writings on socialization and age norms (Neugarten, Moore, & Lowe, 1965), people follow norms; their behavior is highly determined by norms. For the most part (Rosow's argument is more complex) these authors accept Parsons's assumption that norms are well learned and internalized. There is not much choice here, as Giddens (1976) has noted in observing that "there is no action in Parsons' 'action frame of reference,'" only behaviour which is propelled by need-dispositions or role expectations" (p. 16).

In contrast, symbolic interactionists, phenomenologists, ethnomethodologists, and others of similar theoretical persuasion give much more credit to the individual for making choices and at least attempting to exercise his or her own will. It definitely does not follow, from the assumption that people are willful, that people's behavior is unconstrained. It is constrained, if for no other reason than that social behavior occurs with other people, who are willful in their own right. But different interpretive theorists will take different positions as to the degree of freedom or constraint and as to the extent to which agency, the capacity for and exercise of choice, is limited or curtailed.

There are both normative and interpretive approaches to macro-level theorizing. The theory of aging and modernization is rooted in functionalist or normative theoretical assumptions, as is the age-stratification perspective. But political economy perspectives at the macro level are classified as interpretive because the notion of collective action implies choice and the social production of social behavior, rather than a highly deterministic view.

Political economy perspectives at the macro level draw heavily on the Marxist theoretical tradition, and there are certainly structuralist Marxist theorists who give no or little place to human agency (Layder, 1994). But agency was accepted by Marx himself. Marx viewed social structure as the product of human action, especially economic action. As Derek Layder (1994) summarizes, "Marx emphasized that social arrangements are human products. History is not some impersonal process moved simply by great ideals or political objectives removed from the grasp of human activity" (p. 36). Rather, history is made by the actions of real people—otherwise why would he have advocated a revolution by the proletariat?

This emphasis on the importance of real people resonates very nicely with the view of the individual that is found in symbolic interactionism or phenomenological approaches. But the agency of people comes to be constrained because they participate in complex systems of social relationships that assume a reality of their own. People "make their own history, but they do not make it just as they please; they do not make it under circumstances chosen by themselves, but under circumstances directly encountered, given and transmitted from the past" (Marx & Engels, 1968, p. 96; see also Layder, 1994, on this point). This position is not different from that of the phenomenological sociologist, Alfred Schutz (1964), who maintained that

> . . . there are regions of social reality which are neither actually nor potentially accessible to direct experience. They transcend not only my present situation but also my life. There is the world of my predecessors, i.e., a world of Others of whom I may have knowledge and whose actions may influence my own life, but upon whom I cannot act in any manner. (p 23)

Moreover, political economy approaches draw also quite heavily on Weber, who is viewed by some as working directly in the Marxian tradition (Zeitlin, 1997) but whose views of social action inspired theorizing at the social-psychological level by people such as Parsons and Schutz. Symbolic interactionists see social interaction as occurring in a "negotiated order," in which people struggle with one another, use presentation of self, information control strategies, and other strategic devices to pursue their own ends, often in conflict with others. The people they see in interaction are called actors—by which is meant they act, or possess agency and make choices; but which also has a metaphorical connection to the theater. However, this theatrical or dramaturgical metaphor is not that of actors simply acting out the parts that are written in cultural scripts. Rather, it is a kind of "free theater" metaphor, in which actors are simultaneously writing their own scripts as they enact the parts they are writing. But free theater is not unconstrained agency. Actors are not free to do just whatever they want to. There are other actors on the stage, to whom they throw cues and who are themselves writing and enacting scripts that throw off their own cues. So the actors in a free theater are constrained by the conditions of their interaction. This is a view of human nature and social interaction that is highly congruent with the views of Marx when he talked about people creating a world through their actions but not a world that is solely of their own choosing.

A great deal of research in social gerontology has focused on macro issues and even more on micro or social psychological issues but I consider the linking of micro and macro to be the most exciting theoretical challenge before us at this time. The theoretical approaches that will best link the lives of individuals with social structure will likely draw on the interpretive sociologies rooted in Marx and post-Marxists, Weber, Mead, and Schutz. If these perspectives are incorporated into the life course perspective, to enhance the sense of agency that is sometimes missing from that perspective, we might find a way to theorize aging and later life that is faithful to the facts of social structure and of human agency. Such a move would put the field into the central square of the topology—linking micro and macro and bridging normative and interpretive perspectives.

This typological approach is, in a way, ahistorical, but it is always possible to make comparisons and contrasts in some historical framework, and the next approaches to be considered do that.

Telling Stories and Making Connections as an Approach to Understanding Theory

Another approach to understanding theory is to make connections between different theoretical approaches, through either individual linkages or other historical connections. Either way, these approaches put a more human face on theory by linking theoretical ideas and traditions to the individuals who developed or worked within them.

The Hendricks Story

Joe Hendricks (1992) has made a kind of story about the development of theory in social gerontology in his paper "Generations and the Generation of Theory in Social Gerontology." The abstract of this paper reads:

> "The process of theorizing, creating theoretical explanations, and disseminating theoretical perspectives is most frequently discussed in terms of disembodied ideas. A more insightful rendering of how theory is used in the sociology of aging literature would attend to the real individuals who promulgate the ideas." (p. 31)

He uses the sociological concept of generations for this purpose. One advantage of doing so is the emphasis that theoretical approaches a person might adopt early on—say, in the formative years as an undergraduate or graduate student—are likely to "stick." Younger generations may, through fresh contact with a set of problems, come up with different theoretical approaches. Thus, we no doubt find a younger average age of critical and feminist theorists in the field than of modernization theorists or other structural functionalists.

The early adoption of a theoretical perspective, Hendricks (1992) suggests, is linked to the problems newcomers have in finding a place and a career in the field:

> Training and professionalization entail, at least in part, a picking of the right explanatory framework. Research is undertaken, and findings announced in terms of an accepted genealogy of explanations that tie back to respected precedents. Successful entry into a community of scholars requires that one not be too obvious a heretic, and it is not uncommon for citations, at least in part, to be used to buttress that point. Mentors, abetted by reviewers, colleagues, funding

agencies, journal editors, and all the other sentries one encounters in the company of learned societies, help insure the launch pad is at least mainstream. (p. 34)

Such conditions might lead to a perpetuation, ad infinitum, of a theoretical tradition, were it not for two related things: the accumulation of anomalies and the succession of generations. In Thomas Kuhn's (1962) analysis of theoretical change through paradigmatic revolutions, the idea is that people working within one shared theoretical perspective tend to ignore any facts that do not fit theoretical expectations. For example, if findings do not meet expectations, they might be dismissed as relating to problems of sampling, measurement error, or missing data. Theories usually try to explain differences in a dependent variable in terms of some postulated independent variables that are theoretically related to the dependent variable. It is well established that it is more difficult to publish papers that show "no difference" (i.e., that fail to meet theoretical expectations) than to publish findings of differences. However, over time an accumulation of anomalies might be grouped together to lead investigators to think about the problem in a radically different way, and it is this that leads to a paradigmatic shift.

Both Kuhn and Hendricks reject an "internalist" view of paradigmatic change; that is, theoretical advances do not occur simply because of the conflict of ideas. People and the contingencies of their lives influence whether and how theoretical paradigms are established, become legitimized, and sometime become marginalized or overthrown. Moreover—and this is important for the argument Hendricks wants to make about the importance of generations in theory development—a new paradigm is more likely to attract adherents if it does *not* solve all the problems. There has to be work to do and careers to build through work in the context of the new theoretical paradigm. Who will do this work? Not those who are already committed strongly to existing paradigms, on record as adherents of the earlier paradigms, funded to do research in the older paradigms. Rather, younger, less established generations of scholars will do this work. Thus, a second advantage of the generational approach, as Hendricks (1992) puts it, is that "there are real people and very real careers lying behind paradigmatic assertions" (p. 34). That is to say, theorizing is a completely human activity, and this activity occurs within a framework of generations of scholars—real, interacting people who reinforce each other's ideas or band together to support one another in an alternative set of ideas.

What are the generations of theorizing that Hendricks identifies? They are three major generations, which I have illustrated in Table 24.2. Hendricks (1992) offered the thoughts in his paper as very preliminary and invited people to "refine, review, and debunk" (p. 36), so I have taken some liberties with his formulation. He sees a first generation as emerging in the 1960s

TABLE 24.2   Three Generations of Theory: Hendricks's Version

Generation/Focus	Subtypes	Foundations	People
Thesis (1960s–)	Disengagement	Functionalism	Cumming and Henry, Williams and Wirths
Individual	Activity	Symbolic interaction	Havighurst, Maddox, Palmore
	Subcultural	Symbolic interaction	Rose
	Continuity	Symbolic interaction	Atchley
Antithesis (1970s–	Age stratification	Functionalism	Riley, Foner
Structure	Modernization	Functionalism	Burgess, Cowgill
Synthesis (mid 1970s–	Political economy	Marxism, Weber's sociology of domination	Estes, Guillemard, Marshall, Myles, Walker
Individual-society linkage	Life course perspective	Mead	Bengtson, Elder, Marshall, Matthews, Ryff
Intentionality	Interpretive	Foucault, Mead, Schutz	Breytspraak, Gubrium, Hendricks, Marshall
Power and politics		Weber	Binstock, Estes

Developed by V. Marshall, based loosely on J. Hendricks (1992). Generations and the generation of theory in social gerontology. *International Journal of Aging and Human Development 35(1)*, 31–47.

from structural-functional and symbolic-interactionist roots and emphasizing the individual to the neglect of social structure. Here came the famous "debate" between activity and disengagement theory, which I will address later in this chapter. The core references, which can serve as generational markers, would be Cumming and Henry's (1961) *Growing Older: The Process of Disengagement*, Maddox's (1964) "Disengagement Theory: A Critical Evaluation", in which he argued a competing activity theory; and Havighurst, Neugarten, and Tobin's (1968) "Disengagement and Patterns of Aging" (first published in 1968 but widely disseminated prior to that date), which in a sense sought a middle ground. But it should be noted that the debate had been simmering, even boiling at times, in several conference papers since the first preliminary conference presentation of disengagement theory in 1958 (Achenbaum & Bengtson, 1994; for a review, see Orbach, 1974, chap. 3).

A second generation emerged in the 1970s, focusing on social structure through the age stratification perspective and the theory of aging and modernization. The core references here are Riley's (1971) "Social Gerontology and the Age Stratification of Society" and Cowgill and Holmes's (1972) *Aging and Modernization.*

A third generation, Hendricks (1992) argues, arose in the mid1970s, developing a political economy approach that emphasized social structure while trying to link social structure to the experiences of aging individuals and of the aged. Two key sources in this development were Carol Estes, with her 1979 book, *The Aging Enterprise*; and Anne-Marie Guillemard's edited collection, *Old Age and the Welfare State*, which appeared in 1983.

In Hendricks's view, the second generation emerged partly in reaction to the first, and the third partly in reaction to the second. You cannot really understand what a generation was doing without seeing it in the context of predecessor generations.

Bengtson's Story

Vern Bengtson and his colleagues (1997) have also used a generations approach to talk about social theories of aging, and Bengtson (1996) recommends this approach as a vehicle for the teaching of graduate-level courses in the sociology of aging. Whereas 10 years ago, Passuth and Bengtson (1988) differentiated 10 sociological theories of aging, they now distinguish 16 theoretical approaches in social gerontology, of which they place 4 in the first generation, 5 in the second, and 7 in the third. These are linked to one another and to some general theoretical perspectives in sociology in Figure 24.1.

The chronological markers for these generations do not coincide completely with those used by Hendricks (1992). They agree that the first generation was in the 1960s and the second started about 1970. But Hendricks sees the third generation as beginning in the mid1970s, whereas Bengtson (1996) suggests that it begins around 1985—quite a difference. The generational placement of these theories does not coincide exactly with that used by Hendricks either. Hendricks put modernization theory in the second generation; Bengtson puts it in the first generation. Hendricks puts continuity theory in the first generation, and Bengtson puts it in the second generation. Finally, Hendricks and Bengtson do not coincide exactly in the delineation of theories, although they do not contradict each other either. The classification of theories and theoretical perspectives is obviously somewhat arbitrary, and there is not just one correct answer to how to break up these theories. But engaging in the classification exercise is helpful to explore connections among theories and theorists and thereby to better understand each theoretical approach.

What the Bengtson chart does not make clear, however, is the dynamics of the relationships between different types of theory. He sees the relationship between generations as either resting on continuity or drawing on earlier sociological theory—or as the reaction of a new generation to prior theories. Well, what else might there be? The only other logical alternative seems to be the emergence, de novo, of a new, intellectually rootless theory as a pure product of the imagination. This practically all-inclusive set of criteria for

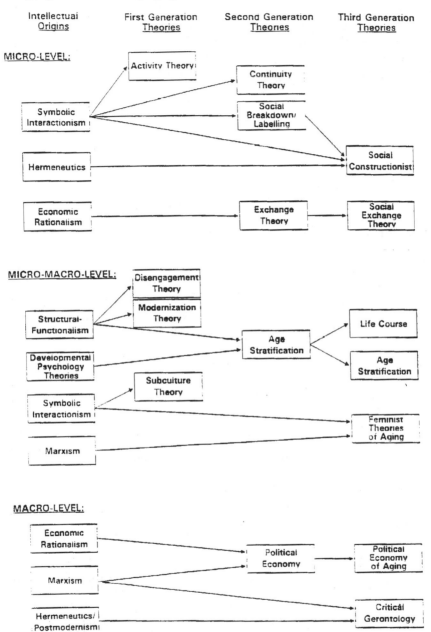

FIGURE 24.1   The generation of theories in social gerontology. From Bengtson, V. L., Burgess, E. O., and Parrott, T. M. (1997). Theory, explanation, and a third generation of theoretical development in social gerontology. *Journal of Gerontology: Social Sciences 52B* (2): S72–S88.

distinguishing generations fails, in fact, to provide a clear theoretical or conceptual criterion for distinguishing one generation from another.

I suggest that this criterion should rest on a notion of dynamic opposition, in which a new generation of scholars explicitly sets forth a new view in the context of a critique of an earlier view. As mentioned earlier, there is a dynamic between activity theory and disengagement theory, in that Cumming and Henry (1961) explicitly contrasted disengagement theory with what came to be formalized as activity theory. Another example of the dynamic is between modernization theory and the political economy of aging. The modernization theory of aging quite clearly grew out of functionalist sociology. An early statement of the theory, suggesting that modernization led to lower status of the older person within the family, can be found in a work by the great functionalist Emile Durkheim (1893/1964), *The Division of Labor in Society.* Long before Cowgill and Holmes (1972), Ernest Burgess (1960) related modernization to loss of status through its removal of roles from the aged that are functionally important for the survival of society. Asking, "What are the criteria by which Western cultures may be differentiated from those of other peoples?" he listed "industrialization and the growth of cities," "the rise of science and technology," "medical science and the prolongation of life," "the growth of democracy," and "the development of social gerontology" (p. 3). Many of these features of modernization (but not, presumably, the growth of democracy nor the development of social gerontology), Burgess held, have had an adverse impact on the social status of the aged, leading to a "role-less role" for the elderly (pp. 20–21). The term was cited by Cowgill and Holmes in their book, and the dimensions of modernization were incorporated into their theorizing. More generally, the theory of modernization and economic development that is foundational to the theory of modernization and aging is explicitly functionalist. But Cowgill and Holmes's careful laying out of the linked hypotheses that form the theory of aging and modernization made it a wonderful foil or reference point for other scholars—notably, Jill Quadagno (1982) in her book *Aging in Early Industrial Society* and James Dowd (1980) in his book *Stratification among the Aged*—to develop a strong critique of the theory while laying some of the important foundations for a political economy theory of aging.

Bengtson's graphical presentation (Bengtson et al., 1997) of the links between different theories across the generations is intended to show the continuities underlying changes in theory; it is a kind of developmental theory of aging theories but one that postulates the changes as relatively smooth rather than rooted in crisis or conflict. As such, the graphical presentation perhaps underplays the importance of contrast and conflict in theory development, which is somewhat better recognized in the text of the article itself, yet still not very explicit.

However, all theoretical changes are not necessarily revolutionary, involving the overthrowing of a paradigm. For example, Marshall, Matthews, and Rosenthal (1993) suggest a "rough historical or evolutionary classification of the development of aging and family research" (p. 41) by delineating four historical categories. The first we called the Burgess era, marked by Ernest Burgess's (1960) formulation in modernization theory terms of the role-less role of the older person in the family context. The second, the Shanas era was reactive to this, and her research provided an empirical challenge to Burgess in showing that older people in American society, as well as cross-culturally in two other modern societies, still had strong family ties and roles (Shanas et al., 1968). Her work laid a foundation for the third, the Bengtson era, which added important cultural and social psychological dimensions to the analysis of aging and the family and provided important conceptual and theoretical advances by viewing intergenerational relations in the context of family solidarity. Finally, we reviewed other recent developments in which gender, caregiving, elder abuse, and other substantive concerns came to be addressed coincident with continuing research in the solidarity framework. This classification is not quite generational but provides another example of historical story-telling about theoretical developments.

Lynott and Lynott's Story

Yet another story is told by Robert Lynott and Patricia Passuth Lynott (1996) in "Tracing the Course of Theoretical Development in the Sociology of Aging." They see a sequence of two transformations: a transformation from a pretheoretical period to a first serious attempt at theorizing, beginning with Cumming and Henry's 1961 book, and a transformation from that period to a metatheoretical stance toward theorizing, beginning in the late 1970s and early 1980s. In this second transformation, social gerontologists supposedly turned a critical eye toward theorizing itself, reflecting the influence of social constructionism, critical sociology, the political economy approach, and postmodernism. Thus, theory is seen as socially constructing age categories and structures that create or shape the aging process. This is, then, a story not about the content of theories but about the stance toward theory and theorizing. Their two transformations create three periods, and these do not coincide with the time periods outlined by Hendricks (1992). Bengtson, Parrott, and Burgess (1996), correctly in my view, challenge them on the reality of their second transformation:

> The second [transformation] involves what Kuhn (1962) has described as a process wherein two competing scientific worldviews challenge each other, re-sulting in a 'paradigm shift' for the field. Many who do research in gerontology would dispute that a transformation of this order has occurred. Certainly it is yet to be determined which worldview—the 'critical theory' perspective Lynott

and Lynott suggest, or the life-course and social stratification perspectives more often cited in current empirical studies—will succeed. (p. 771)

Bengtson, Parrott, and Burgess (1996) also question the Lynnotts for failing to consider the potential of the life course perspective to provide a new paradigm. This is a serious oversight, given the widespread adoption of this perspective (Marshall, 1995), and the value of their generational story is thereby lessened.

We have, then, three different generational stories about sociological theories of aging, developed by Hendricks, Bengtson and colleagues, and the Lynotts; these stories are not wholly consistent, yet each challenges us to think in new ways about theoretical continuity and change. Bengtson, Burgess, and Parrott (1997) emphasize an important point, that "understanding or discovery of phenomena is seldom achieved by the solo investigator, but rather is a social process within a community of investigators involving discussion and criticism between new and previous findings and explanations" (p. S84). Theories help to organize observations that are pooled by the community of scientists within theory groups, and it thereby helps these observations to be seen as either consistent with existing theory or anomalous. "These anomalies (and their emergent explanations) are the basis for 'paradigm shifts' and 'scientific revolutions' which can leapfrog the progress of knowledge forward (Kuhn, 1962)" (Bengtson et al., 1997, p. S84).

It warrants emphasis that theorizing is done by real people. There is a tendency, particularly among students, to think of theorists as a race apart—in a way as godlike creatures. But there are no gods, at least among theorists. As Hendricks (1992) puts it, "The way we think of theory in gerontology should not be divorced from the gerontologists who worked so hard and whose careers were devoted to formulating meaningful theoretical explanations" (p. 43). One prominent social gerontologist, a former president of the Gerontological Society of America and recipient of several awards for the quality of his research, confessed to me that he felt inadequately trained in theory. When I pointed out to an internationally recognized leader in the political economy perspective on aging that she did not adequately handle the ways in which age groups resembled classes, her reaction was not defensive, but instead she declared, "Yeah. I just can't seem to get it. I keep working on this problem but I haven't solved it." I think of these theorists as craftspeople, working away at theoretical problems. Theorists are not gods but humans. They are even capable of making mistakes and of changing their minds. A story is told (and I have no reason to doubt its veracity) of the famous social theorist Talcott Parsons. At a conference of the International Sociological Association, a young scholar presented a paper attacking Parsons for inconsistencies. It was the common criticism of the form "in a paper in 1951 you said that X is true, but in 1960 you wrote that not X, but

Y is true." Parsons happened to be in the audience, and he simply stated, "I changed my mind."

One of the giants of our field, Bernice Neugarten, has successively embraced and advocated a number of theoretical positions, beginning with developmental psychology in her early work and in some of her work on the Kansas City Studies of Aging. She then turned to a very deterministic, structural-functionalist perspective when she emphasized the power of normative determination in shaping age-appropriate behavior and later advocated an interpretive theoretical approach that emphasizes the capacity for choice and human agency. This takes me to another example of how to make theoretical developments clear, which is to tell the story of a theoretical development as a kind of case study. The example will be the Kansas City Studies of Aging, from which sprang the disengagement theory of aging and, in a sense, also the activity theory.

The Kansas City Studies of Aging

Because it was so important in the development of the field, a number of scholars have examined the debate between the activity and disengagement theorists in some detail. Collectively, these metatheoretical works provide an interesting way to learn about some of the important theoretical debates that continue to shape social gerontology.

The most thorough such examination is unpublished but has a wide circulation in its doctoral dissertation form. Harold Orbach's (1974) dissertation at the University of Minnesota examined the scientific controversies about the disengagement theory of aging and showed that this debate was largely an "intra-mural one within the various segments of the Kansas City Studies of Adult Life" (p. 80). He characterized most of the players as very much influenced by developmental psychology. The Kansas City studies were originally conceptualized using the assumptions of activity theory (although this theory had not been formalized); but the study director and field director, both of whom were new to the field of aging "and were not committed to the theoretical assumptions of the study interpreted early analyses of the interview data in its first stages as requiring a different approach" (p. 83). A stream of papers came out of that study, pitting two main subsets of the large research team against one another. Thus, the configuration of investigators and staff led to a split into two camps, each of which was analyzing the same data but with different theoretical assumptions. These groups rarely published together. Robert Havighurst and Bernice Neugarten, with Crotty and Tobin, advanced the activity theory in their publications. Cumming, Henry, and Dean advanced the disengagement theory, but in fact they soon withdrew from the debate to pursue other interests. Other subgroupings developed specific work on intrinsic disengagement (Neugarten did participate in this), personality approaches, lifestyles (Williams and Wirths, 1965), and the importance of age-status norms; and the connections among these groups were exceedingly complex (they were outlined by Harold Orbach [1974] in his doctoral dissertation). The two major groups and the other groups orbiting around them were connected—and equally they were divided—by disciplinary ties and faculty-student ties.

Orbach (1974) and others (Achenbaum & Bengtson, 1994) have noted that one of the major reasons the disengagement theory became such a strong focus of research was that it was put forth in a set of explicit, testable hypotheses; and according to Orbach, the disputants had no difficulty understanding the positions of the other groups. They just approached the same data from different perspectives and came up with different answers. Achenbaum and Bengtson (1994) have noted that the initial investigators of the Kansas City studies were remarkably gentle in expressing their criticisms of the disengagement theory in print while reaching vividly contrasting conclusions from their investigations.

As Achenbaum and Bengtson (1994) argue, the disengagement theory "was the first truly comprehensive, truly explicit, and truly multidisciplinary theory advanced by social and behavioral scientists in gerontology" (p. 762). Despite its failure to find empirical support or to secure long-lasting adherents, it influenced the field of social gerontology quite directly for over a decade, and its indirect effects continue to this day. One of its virtues—a virtue shared by the theory of aging and modernization, another theory that found little empirical support and few long-term adherents—was that it was formulated explicitly enough to stimulate construction of alternative theories, as with the subsequent formalization of the activity theory of aging (Lemon et al., 1969; Longino & Kart, 1982). Although Hochschild (1975) argued that the theory was "unfalsifiable" because it was not operationalized adequately, the theory did stimulate a plethora of operational tests and also theoretical elaborations—for example, bringing in personality constructs—and thereby moved the pursuit of knowledge along. A major contribution of this debate was that the testing and elaboration of the theory and the formalization of alternative approaches, led to a progressively greater appreciation of diversity among the aged, even though the Kansas City Studies were not themselves based on a broadly diverse population (Marshall, 1994; Neugarten, 1987).

The rich social dynamics of this debate are captured in Orbach's (1974) account of this case study in social theory of aging. The disengagement theory debate and the Kansas City studies from which it emanated should be studied and taught by theorists in the sociology of aging, because this case shows what happens when real people come together from different disciplines. It shows that theory development is socially accomplished. Study is warranted here as well because there are living connections to the Kansas

City studies, and mentor-student connections (Bengtson's [1967] dissertation with Havighurst and Neugarten forming one of those connections; [see also Achenbaum & Bengtson, 1994; Bengtson, 1969]).

Taken more broadly than the disengagement theory controversy itself but related to it, continuing analyses of the Kansas City data supported investigations by Neugarten and associates (Neugarten et al., 1964) that led Neugarten to the conclusion that personality and developmental psychology approaches could explain little of either the behavior or the phenomenological meanings, beliefs, and attitudes of the people being studied. She concluded (1970) that a growing developmental move toward "interiority" that could be described through psychodynamic methodologies "seems, however, to be relatively independent of adaptation or purposive behavior. Our studies suggest that interiority is age-related and adaptation is not" (p. 85). This led her to a research phase in which she drew on a much more sociological, less individualistic theoretical stance, emphasizing the importance of age structure and of socialization to ensure age-appropriate role performance (Neugarten, Moore, & Lowe, 1965). The Kansas City Studies are therefore as important for what they ignored—social structure—as for the highly individualistic social psychology on which they focused (Marshall, 1976, 1994). Although the intention in the study was to link the individual and society, a study of the social structure of Kansas City (Coleman & Neugarten, 1971) was not published until long after the core findings of the project had been published. But the Kansas City studies show the use of theoretical comparisons and contrasts in the development of social theory.

CONCLUSION

I have reviewed different approaches to understanding social theory in aging and, by implication, different approaches to teaching it. Contrast is as essential to theoretical understanding as comparison is essential to the scientific process. Making contrasts, such as between functionalist and social-constructionist theoretical approaches, highlights what is special about each pole in a contrast. But I continue to believe that the complexities of theorizing are better served by the cross-classification of contrasts, such as in the typology that I used to organize my review of the "state of theory" (Marshall, 1996). In developing this typology by the cross-classification of theory in terms of the normative-interpretive distinction on the one hand and the macro-micro distinction on the other, I direct the theoretical gaze to challenge some conceptions that are widely held. For example, it is not always the case that social constructionists theorize at the micro, or social psychological, level. As another example, macro-level theorists who focus on social structure do not always or inevitably deny human agency; they face the great challenge of showing how agency operates through complex social action processes.

The typological approach does not go far in making theory come alive, live and breathe. Here a generations approach is helpful, because it ties the development of theoretical ideas to real individuals and, more important, to social configurations of individuals. Theorizing is inherently and fundamentally a social process. Any conceptions that theory is disembodied, standing apart from the theorists who struggle to fashion, elaborate, test, and critique it, should be abandoned. Theory is a living process.

The generational stories that I have reviewed do not provide completely consistent views of the development of social theory in gerontology, but that is just fine. Some of the disparities between these views might be diminished through investigation, and all the authors are quite tentative in putting forward their generational frameworks. Further investigation of any one theoretical line might, for example, reveal an earlier development—a theorist or a significant publication—that would lead to shifts in the dates at which a generation began. For example, I suggest that more weight (and thus an early start date) in the theory of aging and modernization be given to Ernest Burgess's (1960) "Aging in Western Culture" than has been given in these generational accounts. But identifying precise dates for a generation is less important than understanding the theoretical ideas and their value. The generational stories help us to do that, providing a story line that makes theoretical comparisons more comprehensible and interesting. These stories, however told, can be read across the framework of the typology I have proposed. Thus, Hendricks's (1992) generational framework leads to a journey from the normative micro cell of the typology to the normative macro cell and thence to the cells depicting interpretive approaches that attempt to link micro and macro.

Finally, focusing on a specific case of theory development (or controversy) can be useful in fostering theoretical understanding. The case of the Kansas City studies and disengagement theory reveals how theoretical controversy is generated when people from different disciplines and status come together in the research enterprise. Similar analyses could trace the emergence and intellectual lineage of modernization theory, and the oppositional theorizing it stimulated. One could inquire systematically about the role of organizations such as the Social Science Research Council in shaping theoretical agendas in the early development of the field. In determining to promote gerontology it likely had little choice but to stress that gerontology ought to take a multidisciplinary approach. Could a council that brings together all the social sciences do otherwise? What of the impact of the National Institute on Aging in shaping theory? Here one might be interested in mapping linkages, including funding, conference participation, cross-citation, faculty-student ties, and formal acknowledgments in books and other publications, in the development and popularization of the age stratification perspective and subsequently the life course perspective.

Similarly, it would be informative to try to identify what theoretical developments emanated from the Midwest Council for Social Research on Aging, an influential group of sociologists, now formally defunct and hence truly an "invisible college" spread throughout the Midwest and engaged in graduate education.

All of the approaches described should be useful and will be most useful if brought together synergistically. Several observers have recently decried the low level of explicit attention to theory in the sociology of aging. But these same sources testify to a growing interest in theory. Doing theory well requires a broadly based and deeply historically textured sense of the field, and it involves processes of comparing and contrasting theoretical approaches. An explicit focus on theory will serve the field well, and the approaches I have described will assist in getting theory in focus.

REFERENCES

Achenbaum, W. A., & Bengtson, V. L. (1994). Re-engaging the disengagement theory of aging: On the history and assessment of theory development in gerontology. *Gerontologist, 34,* 756–763.

Alexander, J. C. (1988). The new theoretical movement. In N. J. Smelser (Ed.), *Handbook of sociology* (pp. 77–101). Newbury Park, CA: Sage.

Bengtson, V. L. (1967). A cross-national study of patterns of social interaction in aged males. Unpublished doctoral dissertation, University of Chicago.

Bengtson, V. L. (1969). Cultural and occupational differences in level of present role activity in retirement. In R. J. Havighurst, J. M. A. Munnichs, B. L. Neugarten, & H. Thomae (Eds.), *Adjustment to retirement: A cross-national study* (pp. 35–53). Assen, Netherlands: Van Gorkum.

Bengtson, V. L. (1996). Teaching concepts and theories in the sociology of aging. In V. Minichiello, N. Chappell, H. Kendig, & A. Walker (Eds.), *Sociology of aging: International perspectives* (pp. 112–123). Melbourne: International Sociological Association Research Committee on Aging.

Bengtson, V. L., Burgess, E. O., & Parrott, T. M. (1997). Theory, explanation, and a third generation of theoretical development in social gerontology. *Journal of Gerontology: Social Sciences, 52B,* S72–S88.

Bengtson, V. L., Parrott, T. M., & Burgess, E. O. (1996). Progress and pitfalls in gerontological theorizing. *Gerontologist, 36,* 768–772.

Burgess, E. W. (1960). Aging in Western culture. In E. W. Burgess (Ed.), Aging in Western societies (pp. 3–28). Chicago and London: University of Chicago Press.

Coleman, R. P., & Neugarten, B. L. (1971). *Social status in the city.* San Francisco: Jossey-Bass.

Cowgill, D. O., & Holmes, L. D. (Eds.) (1972). *Aging and modernization.* New York: Appleton-Century-Crofts.

Cumming, E., & Henry, W. E. (1961). *Growing older: The process of disengagement.* New York: Basic Books.

Dowd, J. (1980). *Stratification among the aged.* Monterey, CA: Brooks/Cole.

Durkheim, E. (1964). *The division of labor in society.* New York: The Free Press. (Originally published in France, 1893).

Estes, C. L. (1979). *The aging enterprise.* San Francisco: Jossey Bass.

Giddens, A. (1976). *New rules of sociological method: A positive critique of interpretative sociologies.* New York: Basic Books.

Guillemard, A.-M. (Ed.) (1983). Old age and the welfare state. Beverly Hills, CA: Sage.

Havighurst, R. J., Neugarten, B. L., & Tobin, S. S. (1968). Disengagement and patterns of aging. In B. L. Neugarten (Ed.), *Middle age and aging: A reader in social psychology* (pp. 161–172). Chicago: University of Chicago Press.

Hendricks, J. (1992). Generations and the generation of theory in social gerontology. *International Journal Of Aging And Human Development, 35(1),* 31–47.

Hochschild, A. (1975). Disengagement theory: A critique and a proposal. *American Sociological Review, 40,* 553–569.

Kuhn, T. S. (1962). *The structure of scientific revolutions.* New York: Norton.

Layder, D. (1994). *Understanding social theory.* London: Sage.

Lemon, B. W., Bengtson, V. L., & Peterson, J. A. (1972). An exploration of the activity theory of aging: Activity types and life satisfaction among in-movers to a retirement community. *Journal of Gerontology, 27,* 511–523.

Longino, C. F., & Kart, C. S. (1982). Explicating activity theory: A formal replication. *Journal of Gerontology, 37,* 713–722.

Lynott, R. J., & Lynott, P. P. (1996). Tracing the course of theoretical development in the sociology of aging. *Gerontologist, 36,* 749–760.

Maddox, G. L. (1964). Disengagement theory: A critical evaluation. *Gerontologist, 6,* 80–82.

Marshall, V. W. (1976, November). *Bernice Neugarten: Gerontologist in search of a theory.* Paper presented at the annual meeting of the Gerontological Society of America, New York.

Marshall, V. W. (1978–1979). No exit: A symbolic interactionist perspective on aging. *International Journal of Aging and Human Development, 9,* 345–358.

Marshall, V. W. (1980). *Last chapters: A sociology of aging and dying.* Monterey, CA: Brooks/Cole.

Marshall, V. W. (1994). Sociology, psychology, and the theoretical legacy of the Kansas City studies. *Gerontologist, 34,* 768–774.

Marshall, V. W. (1995). Social models of aging. *Canadian Journal on Aging, 14(1),* 12–34.

Marshall, V. W. (1996). The state of theory in aging and the social sciences. In R. H. Binstock & L. George (Eds.), *Handbook of Aging and the Social Sciences* (4th ed., pp. 12–30). San Diego, CA: Academic Press.

Marshall, V. W., Matthews, S. H., & Rosenthal, C. J. (1993). Elusiveness of family life: A challenge for the sociology of aging. *Annual Review of Gerontology and Geriatrics, 13,* 39–72.

Marshall, V. W., & Tindale, J. A. (1978). Notes for a radical gerontology. *International Journal of Aging and Human Development, 9,* 163–175.

Marx, K., & Engels, F. (1968). *Selected works.* London: Lawrence and Wishart.

Mills, C. W. (1959). *The sociological imagination.* New York: Oxford University Press.

Neugarten, B. L. (1970). Dynamics of transition of middle age to old age. *Journal of Geriatric Psychiatry, 4,* 71–87.

Neugarten, B. L. (1987). Kansas City Studies of Adult Life. In G. K. Maddox (Ed.), *The encyclopedia of aging* (pp. 372–373). New York: Springer Publishing Co.

Neugarten, B. L., and associates. (1964). *Personality in middle and late life: Empirical studies.* New York: Atherton.

Neugarten, B. L., Moore, J. W., & Lowe, J. C. (1965). Age norms, age constraints, and adult socialization. *American Journal of Sociology, 70,* 710–717.

Orbach, H. L. (1974). *The disengagement theory of aging, 1960–1970: A case study of a scientific controversy.* Unpublished doctoral dissertation, University of Michigan.

Passuth, P. M., & Bengtson, V. L. (1988). Sociological theories of aging: Current perspectives and future directions. In J. E. Birren and V. L. Bengtson (Eds.). *Emergent theories of aging* (pp. 333–355). New York: Springer Publishing Co.

Quadagno, J. (1982). *Aging in early industrial society: Work, family, and social policy in nineteenth-century England.* New York: Academic Press.

Riley, M. W. (1971). Social gerontology and the age stratification of society. *Gerontologist, 11,* 79–87.

Riley, M. W., Johnson, M., & Foner, A. (1972). *Aging and society: Vol. 3. A sociology of age stratification.* New York: Russell Sage Foundation.

Rosow, I. (1974). *Socialization to old age.* Berkeley, CA: University of California Press.

Schutz, A. (1964). The dimensions of the social world. In A. Schutz, *Collected papers II. Studies in social theory* (A. Brodersen, Ed.). The Hague: Martinus Nijhoff.

Shanas, E., Townsend, P., Wedderburn, D., Friis, H., Milhoj, P., & Stehouwer, J. (1968). *Old people in three industrial societies.* New York: Atherton Press.

Williams, R. H., & Wirths, C. G. (1965). *Lives through the years.* New York: Atherton Press.

Zeitlin, I. M. (1997). *Ideology and the development of sociological theory* (6th ed.). Upper Saddle River, NJ: Prentice-Hall.

Afterword

25

Theories of Aging: A Personal Perspective

James E. Birren

T he history of a subject or a field of scientific inquiry is broader than a history of its theories. The history of gerontology, like the history of any scholarly or scientific field, reflects the influence of events of war, depression, personalities, and discoveries along with the development of methods of research and ideas. In this concluding chapter in the *Handbook of Theories of Aging,* I want to emphasize ideas—although ideas and theories cannot be completely separated from their times and the persons who contributed them. Thus, you must permit me some latitude here, particularly as this is a personal view of development of theories of aging.

One benefit of being in a field of study for a long time is the historical and intellectual perspective it provides on trends in theories and concepts. The field of aging has vastly changed since 1947, when I presented a paper at the first meeting of the Gerontological Society of America. In my view, aging has emerged as one of the most complex subjects facing modern science.

Some time ago I said that gerontology, the study of aging, was data-rich and theory-poor. This has come about, I believe, because of the inherent complexity of the phenomena of aging. Today I would add that the field is also in need of integration, a by-product of the fact that so many different factors have come to be recognized as being involved in human aging. Integration and theory go hand in hand. It will not be possible to fit together in an integrated picture the many factors involved in aging without broad theory and concepts. Theory leads us to the questions we ask and the kinds of explanations we offer for observed phenomena.

One weakness of the field is the general use of the word *aging* to cover all aspects of change in adult organisms. Investigators often don't define what it is they have in mind when they use the term *aging*. Simply defined, aging consists of the forces that govern the length of life of organisms and how well they survive. More detailed reviews of various definitions of aging are available elsewhere (Birren & Renner, 1977).

Accompanying the emergence of the field has been a lack of specificity in what investigators have in mind when they study aging and attempt to explain some observed phenomena. By itself, the collection of large amounts of data showing relationships with chronological age does not help because chronological age is not a cause of anything. Chronological age is only an index, and unrelated sets of data show correlations with chronological age that have no intrinsic or causal relationship with each other. Thus, a goal of theory and research is to replace chronological age with variables that reflect the *causes* of change we initially identify as being closely related to chronological age.

It is perhaps not chance that Francis Galton, an English gentleman scientist in the early 19th century, developed what appears to be the first quantitative measure of the closeness of association of a relationship between two variables. He was interested in how closely various health and behavioral measurements were correlated with age. There being no existing means to measure such phenomena, he set about to develop one. The ease with which complex measures of relationships can be made today obscures the fact that the underlying issues lie in specifying the forces that shape the organism in a sequential way. These forces are presumably reducible to categories like energy, metabolism, and information, but in their intermediate concept form they are expressed in terms of genetics and social and environmental influences.

That there are many facets of aging to be explained was first identified by Quetelet (1835) in his book. However, only in the late 20th century has aging become a focus of scientific study. Although the subject matter has some roots in 19th-century thought and in the growth of scientific research it fostered, organized research on aging has primarily been a post–World War II development. The earliest excursions into theorizing about aging looked upon aging as a "lock and key" problem: it would take the understanding of just one key variable or phenomenon to unlock the puzzle.

The man who first used the term *gerontology*, Methchnikoff (1903), in the early part of 20th century, held a rather simple view: aging was the result of "gastrointestinal putrefaction." Methchnikoff's explanation looks naive in retrospect, although he was a talented and highly recognized biological scientist. He won a Nobel Prize for his research and served at a member of the Pasteur Institute in Paris. Likely he was influenced by the biomedical climate of the time, which was enthusiastically pursuing the control of infectious diseases and making great progress in their control.

Infectious diseases are invasions of a host by a foreign agent. Medicine waged successful warfare upon the invading agents, and in consequence much was added to life expectancy in the early part of the 20th century. When aging emerged as a phenomenon or set of phenomena to be explained, seeking for its "causes" involved the search for a single agent. Metchnikoff, for example, attributed the cause to parasitic plant life growing in the host's gastrointestinal tract. But by the mid 20th century it had become apparent that chronic diseases were replacing infectious diseases as the major causes of death, and these occurred later in life. Although chronic disease is still a target for prevention and cure, the host is part of the problem. It was obvious that one does not wage biological warfare on the human hosts of debilitating and terminal chronic diseases. In the middle of the 20th century there was a decided shift away from simplistic single-causal variable views of aging, and this coincided with the founding of the Gerontological Society of America in 1945. Something appeared to lurk behind the expression of the chronic diseases that were limiting late life. With recent advances in research on genetics it has been an easy shift in emphasis from the infectious disease model of invasion by a foreign agent to genetic determination of aging and its evolutionary basis.

Dominant today is an interactionist view of aging, specifying that the generic background of the organism is expressed in interaction with its environment. One of the early bits of evidence for an interaction concept of aging was the data of Clive McKay (1935) at Cornell showing that his underfed rats lived longer than control rats eating at liberty, which were heavier. For a long time this information remained on the fringe of gerontological science. Anton Carlson (1952, Personal Communication) at the University of Chicago later underfed rats and found that they not only lived longer than normally ad lib–fed rats but also that they expressed later the chronic diseases to which they seem predisposed. In other words, dietary intake was modulating the appearance of the chronic diseases to which the animals seemed predisposed by possible genetic background.

To the above thinking should be added the consequences of mankind's changes of the environment in ways that have potential effects on the manne in which we express our genetic potentials. These changes can be both beneficial or deleterious. To give just one example, we have achieved the virtual elimination of transient nutritional deficiencies in developed countries, but at the same time we are increasingly at risk for the carcinogenic influences of air pollution.

THE GRAY AREA BETWEEN THEORY AND THE PRACTICAL

While at the University of Chicago, 1950–1953, I worked with some colleagues on the Committee on Mathematical Biology and sat in on their research seminars. One day I read a paper by the chairman, Nicholas Rashevsky, reporting on an equation describing the spread of atheism in a population. It dawned on me that the equation was hardly a theory in itself. Subsequently, I have been less awed by the neatness of an equation purportedly expressing a causal theory.

I was exposed to several examples of the close proximity of theory and the practical while a staff member in the intramural program at the National Institutes of Health (NIH) from 1947 to 1965. One example was the resistance of the senior staff of the National Institute of Mental Health to the use of drugs in the treatment of mental disorders. Given their psychoanalytic orientation about the origin of mental disorders, the use of drugs was regarded as barbaric. It was in response to external pressures that resistance to projects using drugs for the control of mental states and behavior was lowered.

Other examples of theoretical bias came to my attention from the NIH files. Dyes added as color to foods were not thought to be possible carcinogens, but later studies demonstrated that they were. Also, studies finding that urban residents were more likely than rural residents to have high blood pressure were earlier thought to be implausible because of theoretical bias, but subsequently, controlled studies demonstrated that these findings were robust.

Within my personal experience there was strong opposition to reporting data that psychosocial loss experienced by older persons could be a factor in physical health status. At that time the dominant perspective was that the risk factors for late-life illness were biological in character. Indeed, a 1964 call for suggestions for the early Framingham studies of heart disease discarded psychosocial factors as being disposers to risk. Later evidence modified this opinion. I had another personal exposure to such matters when, as a matter of convenience, I was using hypertensive subjects in a pilot study. The internist in charge of the patients told me that the patients were taken off all medication when they entered the program and that their blood pressures returned to normal while they were in residence in the NIH clinical facility. I became puzzled about the situation and eventually came to the conclusion that the patients were reacting to their normal environmental conditions with elevated blood pressure and that the pharmacological treatment was dealing with the proximal cause rather than the remote cause. Interpretation of data and theories thus vary, depending on whether one is dealing with proximal or distal causes of outcomes. The choice of treatment may rest less on theory than on the pragmatics of treating outcomes.

In human aging there are long causal chains with sequences of biological, behavioral, and social environmental factors influencing length of life and well-being. Our theories tend to deal with segments of these long causal chains, and we must be aware of the congruency of the theories, measurements, and the questions being asked.

My generalization from this background of experiences is that we must avoid giving way to fads of interpretation while the bases for the ideas are examined and also that we should not cling too rigidly to concepts and interpretations that may be archaic. From an analytical perspective it is apparent that there are several levels of analysis of aging phenomena and that there has to be a congruency between the questions asked, the measurements made, and the theoretical interpretations. The evaluation of theory obviously takes time—but hopefully not time spent in obfuscation in defense of dated theory.

DUST BOWL EMPIRICISM

A considerable influence was exercised by the Josiah Macy Jr. Foundation in the late 1930s by conducting colloquia with scientists of different backgrounds. This gave organization to the book edited by E. V. Cowdry, (1939), *Problems of Ageing*. This multidisciplinary approach still characterizes many efforts in the field and provided the structure for the Gerontological Society of America's formation in 1945. Following this there was a growing wariness of broad theorizing about aging, perhaps as a rebound from some of the early enthusiasts who, in the absence of much data, speculated freely about rather simplistic models or theories of aging. This began a phase in gerontology that I call "dust bowl empiricism," a phase in which each investigator in each discipline reported data on some phenomenon that was correlated with chronological age. A problem of dust bowl empiricism is that the information thus produced was not notably additive. Mounds of data were collected, much of high quality, that were difficult to weave together. Moreover, the common denominator of chronological age as correlated with some observed phenomenon is only a first step. Explanations of aging require the tracing of the effects of causal variables, the dynamic forces that transform young organisms to old organisms.

The heritage of dust bowl empiricism, which still characterizes the study of aging to date, is the staggering amount of age-related data that are difficult or impossible to integrate. Perhaps there will emerge an integrating influence through more meta-analysis of studies in which the additivity of information is a primary value.

I confess that I was a participant in the dust bowl empirical phase of the study of aging. This was a phase in which any dependent variable of interest could be chosen for study because of the rationale for the importance of the independent variable—age—and not because of its dependence on some underlying process of aging.

In my studies at the Gerontology Center in Baltimore, 1947–1950, a wide range of physiological and behavioral measurements were studied in relation to chronological age. Nathan Shock, the director of the Gerontology Center, was a great stimulator of the direct empirical approach. His criteria of importance seemed to be the refinement of the measurements and the selection of subjects. Less important were underlying questions and their potential for generalizations about aging. Nathan was the product of 10 years of work in the Berkeley Growth Studies at the University of California, Berkeley. His energy encouraged further work and led to the Baltimore Longitudinal Studies. It is perhaps not surprising that the early reports of this work consisted of descriptions of measurements laid side by side with others but with little synthesis of interrelationships or the identification of underlying influences. This period of research in gerontology shows that highly sophisticated measurements described in relation to chronological age do not automatically lead to a broader understanding of aging and the stimulation of theory.

In subsequent years we have appreciated the direct descriptions of the life course of many functions such as cardiac output, renal clearance, lung capacity, muscle strength, visual dark adaptation, memory, learning, and social competence. Yet the interrelatedness of change in these functions with age appears to be the more general scientific issue, and this requires the development. Some knowledge of the commonality in the pathways of change can lead to the replacement of chronological age with dynamic variables and encourage deeper understanding.

Perhaps in the future of theory development in aging there should be an extension of the period of preoccupation with single function measurement in relation to age, in order to develop a broader encyclopedic catalog of important facts about aspects of aging. But the danger would seem to be an overload of facts and a deficiency of explanations.

An emphasis on integration and theory appears to be encouraged by the meta-analysis of sets of data. However, such efforts are not generally encouraged by graduate study, in which the value of a contribution is judged more on the basis of individual data gathering than on integration and interpretation of sets of data.

COMPLEXITY OF AGING

While at the University of Chicago, 1950–1953, I met Ralph Gerard, a physiologist, who posed the question about the level of organization at which aging appears. In an evolutionary sense the question is at what level of biological development aging emerged as a phenomenon. It seems quite likely that we share phenomena of aging with other primates and mammals. In addition to shared processes of aging, evolution also brings with it a hierarchy of complex systems (e.g., nervous, immune, vascular). A complex nervous system has evolved that is the primary regulatory organ of the human body, controlling such vital processes as metabolism, respiration, blood pressure, and temperature, as well as survival behaviors. Theory has not yet addressed this hierarchical question: Do we age primarily because of earlier evolved and shared phylogenetic functions, or do we age because of changes controlled by later evolved structures such as the nervous system or the cardiovascular system?

This line of thought gives rise to other questions about the level at which the more important forces controlling human aging appear. There is a temptation to take the "bottom-up" approach of physics and attach greater theoretical importance to molecular changes in cell particles and cells than to changes in the regulating mechanisms of the more complex systems of tissues and organs or to a nervous system that modifies its functioning on the basis or experience or learning. This leads to the question of whether a top-down or a bottom-up approach to both theory and the empirical study of aging will be more productive of understanding and control of the processes.

DEVELOPMENT AND AGING

Philip Handler, professor of biochemistry at Duke University, once said to me that in his generation of biochemistry he and his colleagues were discovering the building blocks of metabolism. He then said that the next generation of biochemistry was going to be dominated by matters of differentiation and aging. This thought sets in opposition two groups of forces, one leading to further development of an organism and the other to its degradation. Both forces are dependent on energy and metabolism.

Students of life span developmental psychology have given emphasis to the study of the life span as a whole unit. In practice this is difficult because of the long survival time of humans and also because it tends to study the products of the two forces and not separate the processes of differentiation, growth, and repair from those of degradation.

It would seem that throughout the organization of living systems, from cells to societies, there are developing and degrading forces. At the social level there is elimination of old jobs and creation of new ones, at the behavioral level there is the replacement of old learning with new learning, and biologically there is the replacement of old cells with new ones. Still further, at the subcellular level, there is the task of regulating demands for energy, as in the case of repair processes, and of increasing its supply. Changing gene expression in order to adapt to changing energy needs of cell processes would seem to represent a balance of expanding and contracting regulation, such as the activity of the mitochondrial genes (Wiesner, 1997).

This gives rise to the view that any abstract dynamic characterization of aging requires at least two terms in the rational equation. The two terms presumably have different limits of response, which is the basis of the potential collapse of the complex system of an aging organism.

The aspects of aging that are currently being studied range from apoptosis to wisdom, from accidents to work. From which of these levels will come our most useful models of aging of the organism is not clear. At present, encouragement is needed at all levels, with integration of information being a high priority.

A PERSPECTIVE ON CURRENT THEORIES OF AGING

In addition to what appears to be the inherent complexity of the subject of aging, there is also the influence of effects of disciplinary specialization contributing to the fragmentation of theory. Yates (1996), in his characterization of theories of aging, points out that there are many "aspect" theories. These are theories that attempt to explain particular facets of aging without attempting to deal with the whole range. He listed 23 aspect theories that have been proposed, ranging from "wear and tear" to gerontogenes and also pointed out that the list was not definitive. The contemporary picture of theories of aging is obviously a very fragmented one. If one adds to this the theories of life span development, which attempt to embrace both developments and senescence, then a further broadening of the scope is often made without any apparent means of integration.

In the developing organism the systems move toward more differentiation and from less to more capacity for self-repair. In aging, or senescence, the organism moves toward less repair capacity and greater likelihood of developing a fatal illness from which it cannot protect itself. A question for contemporary thought about theory is whether it is desirable to attempt to blend both processes into a single conceptual system. To resolve such issues it seems necessary to specify increasingly what independent variables (causes) are being considered in a theory, and what dependent variables or outcomes are being considered.

A PERSPECTIVE ON BIOLOGICAL, BEHAVIORAL, AND
SOCIAL THEORIES OF AGING

It is difficult to compare developments in theory in the biological, behavioral, and social areas. One obvious problem is the fact that the three areas of study explain different outcomes. Biologists are interested in predicting length of life or the viability of an organ system or cell line. Psychologists are interested in the changes in a wide range of behavioral capacities, such as perception, learning, and memory. Social scientists are concerned with other dependent variables, including social status, life satisfaction, and adjustment. To this group should be added a fourth category: the personal experience of aging, or the subjective interpretation of events. Manifestly little of all the information processed in the aging body is read out by conscious mind. How the personal experience of aging relates to organic and social change is itself an evolving field of study, which is beginning to present itself as subject to theoretical interpretations and related to our probabilities of survival.

The common denominator of these fields of study is that they use chronological age as a substitute index for their intrinsic independent variables. These include genetics, metabolic rates, disease, central nervous system integrity, practice, stress, social roles, and social structure. It is not surprising that, because the areas of study of aging use different dependent and independent variables, with only a sometimes shared use of chronological age, there is little overlap in theory. One also detects an element of extreme relativism in some approaches, particularly in the social and behavioral areas. This makes it still more difficult to integrate theory and findings across the sciences when as a point of departure they pose as autonomous.

Little progress seem to have been made in mathematical models of biological systems in relation to time since Landahl's (1959) treatment of the subject. Because he believed that time was inseparable from biological processes of aging, he thought it necessary to consider the role of time more explicitly.

> To a large extent the study of aging consists of the measurement of variables of interest at various ages and the subsequent search for relationships among these variables. Mathematics is an ideal tool for this latter undertaking, and the construction of simple mathematical models can be useful in the understanding of the observed events. Thus it may turn out that it is more useful to know the effect of age on a parameter of the model than the effect of age on the observed measurements, since a change of a single value of the former may explain several kinds of observed effects. (p. 81)

Another relevant point, made elegantly by Reichenbach and Mathers (1959), is that temporal order is reducible to causal order. Our descriptions of data are given in terms of temporal order. The more theoretical step consists of creating a causal order of changes. In the case of irreversible flow of events, destruction of the system (organism) can result. A significant point was made by Reichenbach and Mathers about the denial of time as a psychological defense against the recognition of irreversible biological processes.

Since temporality leads to destruction, it is often identified with the evil in the world. If time is an illusion, evil can also be denied and regarded as illusory. The mythics of ages have declared that time is an illusion both as an attribute of physical events and as an aspect of subjective experience and they have preached that this illusion must be overcome. (p. 79)

There is little doubt that aging invokes strong reactions of denial. The extent to which denial as such enters theorizing is unclear, but at the personal level denial may reduce the level of stress and influence the parameters that govern irreversible processes (e.g., accumulation of insoluble proteins such as amyloids) but not change the form of the relationships.

In the description of organisms' changes with time, there appear qualitative shifts in which there is discontinuity with previous states (e.g., fever and delirium or congestive heart failure). When subsystems reach boundary conditions, a qualitatively new state may be reached (e.g., terminal decline). The modeling of such shifts in behavioral and physiological states may gain from consideration of other areas of science in which concepts of entropy and negentropy are used. In this volume (Chapter 23), Schroots and Yates attempt to explore the dynamics of development and aging. Following this approach would encourage the description of transition points in dynamic systems of aging organisms (e.g., those contributing to terminal decline).

The characterization and modeling of the processes of aging is a task for both medicine and the life sciences. Medicine faces end products of aging dependent diseases, and the exponential rise of such diseases with age suggests link with changes in component biological processes that predispose to manifest disease (see Chapter 8 by Solomon in this volume).

Overlapping theoretical interests in human aging may arise as more comprehensive longitudinal studies permit the analysis of the four broad areas of interest. That is, newer studies are beginning to examine length of life, illnesses, behavioral capacities, social functioning, and subjective states in the same matrix of measurements. Furthermore, additional samples of subject cohorts can lead to detection of drift in the effects of supposed independent variables. It is perhaps surprising to think that our theories may be deeply influenced by the way we gather data in large longitudinal studies of aging populations. Those theories may also lead to new hypotheses about the upper limits of human functioning and capacities over the life span.

Noteworthy additions to our knowledge base about aging are the reports from longitudinal studies of identical twins reared together and reared apart (Pedersen, 1996). These studies not only provide quantitative data on the relative contributions of heredity and environment; they have measurements from a wide domain of sciences that may prod thinking about causal mechanisms and promote integrative theory of the underlying causes. Given the complexity of aging and its practical significance, perhaps some encouragement should be given to establishing a "think tank" that would offer serious scholars of the subject more than the hit-and-run interactions that are provided by annual meetings. The creation of a think tank for mature scholars, where they would spend ample time sharing and refining their theorizing in the presence of scholars from other fields, might help to integrate our growing knowledge of aspects of aging. An added feature would be the sharing of data on which theories are built. Particularly useful would be the mutual examination of data from large-scale sequential longitudinal studies.

SUMMARY

Fifty years in a scientific career such as mine provides a perspective on trends but doesn't necessarily lend itself to more accurate predictions of the future development of theories of aging. Nonetheless, it is tempting to put the past, present, and future into an organized picture.

The earliest speculations about aging appeared to regard it simplistically. It was as though understanding of the characteristics regarded as results of aging waited only on the identification of one pervading variable, analogous to an infectious agent. Slowly, it became obvious that the organism itself was an active participant in the development of the chronic diseases that limited the life span. Less often was aging cast as a disease or a product of disease.

The formation of scientific societies for exchanging information about aging after World War II was accompanied by a great growth in research about aging. The published literature grew exponentially, with many new journals and books appearing on topics where previously there had been none. The recent epoch has been a golden era for research on aging. Much of it has been descriptive empirical research reporting on an aspect of organisms related to chronological age. The field rapidly became data-rich and theory-poor as studies reported on particular features. Perhaps impressed by the naïveté of early thought, later researchers avoided theory in favor of well-designed aspect studies.

At present we face a field that has a mountain of information but little integration across disciplines and phenomena. Along with aspect research we now have many aspect theories. This seems to be in part a product of the inherent complexity of aging and also of the way intellectual life is departmentalized in modern universities. In intellectual self-defense against the complexity of aging, scientists appear to have limited their theorizing about aging to small areas of improved data. Data gathering and methods of analysis have improved dramatically. Longitudinal studies have separated different classes of influences, endogenous and exogenous. Longitudinal studies of identical twins have separated in a quantitative manner sources of genetic and environmental influences on a range of outcomes.

Once the main forces have been identified and placed in a theoretical framework, their expression and their quantitative importance may be expected to vary over time as mankind intentionally shifts the environment and increasing attention is given to the conditions that affect the well-being of individuals. Although the quantitative balance of explanatory power of variables may be expected to shift in the future, that should not detract from the validity of the need to encourage ecological theorizing about human aging in a way that reflects our evolution, ontogeny, and environments.

In the complex human organism there are questions about the survival of the organisms as well as the weakening and failure of component systems, such as the nervous, immune, cardiovascular, and musculoskeletal systems. This gives rise to the question of whether theories might best be built from the top down or the bottom up. The successes of the physical sciences in moving in their explanations from small particles to large systems has produced an aura of validity of the bottom-up approach. Whether this is as relevant for complex biological organisms must be examined, that is, for systems in which there are repair functions and in which a component failure can limit the functioning of the entire organism. In the human organism there is a continuing balance between expanding and repairing and degradation processes that can lead to organ failures and death of the organism. This seems to require theory to have at least two terms governing rates of change in a rational equation depicting the trajectories of individual lives.

The growth of research brings me to the perspective that aging is one of the most complex sets of phenomena facing science. It is also one of the most important influencing the quality of lives and the organization of society. What seems clear to me is that aging is a product of the interaction of many forces—genetic, environmental—and the accumulation of the products of chance events. Given this view, it seems desirable to adopt an ecological point of view of aging, and that theory should embrace many forces not commonly grouped together as a result of disciplinary specialization.

REFERENCES

Birren, J. E., & Renner, V. J. (1977). Research on the psychology of aging: Principles and experimentation. In J. E. Birren (Ed.), *Handbook of the psychology of aging* (pp. 3–38).
New York: Van Nostrand Reinhold.
Birren, J. E. (1996). History of gerontology. In J. E. Birren (Ed.), *Encyclopedia of gerontology* (pp. 655–665). San Diego, CA: Academic Press.
Birren, J. E. & Bengtson, V. L. (Eds.). (1986). *Emergent theories of aging.* New York: Springer Publishing Co.
Cowdry, E. V. (Ed.). (1939). *Problems of ageing.* Baltimore: Williams & Wilkins.

Landahl, H. D. (1959). Biological periodicities, mathematical biology, and aging. In J. E. Birren (Ed.), *Handbook of aging and the individual* (pp. 81–115). Chicago: University of Chicago Press.

MacKay, C. M., Crowell, M. F., & Maynard, L. A. (1935). The effect of retarded growth upon the length of life span and upon ultimate life span. *J. Nature, 10,* 63–79.

Marshall, V. W. (1996). Theories of aging: Social. In J. E. Birren (Ed.), *Encyclopedia of gerontology* (pp. 569–572). San Diego, CA: Academic Press.

Metchnikoff, E. (1903). *The nature of man.* New York: G. P. Putnam's Sons.

Pedersen, N. L. (1996). Gerontological behavior genetics. In J. E. Birren (Ed.), *Handbook of the psychology of aging* (pp. 59–77). San Diego, CA: Academic Press.

Quetelet, A. (1835). Sur l'homme et dévellopment de ses facultes. Paris: Bachilier, Imprimeur-Libraire, 2 vols.

Reichenbach, M., & Mathers, R. A. (1959). The place of time and aging in the natural sciences and scientific philosophy. In J. E. Birren (Ed.), *Handbook of aging and the individual* (pp. 43–80). Chicago: University of Chicago Press.

Schroots, J. J. F. (1997). Theories of aging: Psychological. In J. E. Birren (Ed.), *Encyclopedia of gerontology* (pp. 557–567). San Diego, CA: Academic Press.

Wiesner, R. J. (1997). Adaptation of mitochondrial gene expression to changing cellular energy demands. *News in Physiological Sciences, 12,* 178–184.

Yates, F. E. (1996). Theories of aging: Biological. In J. E. Birren (Ed.), *Encyclopedia of gerontology* (pp. 545–55). San Diego, CA: Academic Press.

Dedication to James E. Birren

This volume was conceptualized as a *Festschrift* in honor of James E. Birren's 80th birthday, commemorating his remarkable career as a scientist, scholar, teacher, and institution builder in the field of gerontology. It contains chapters by many of his students and colleagues as well as others for whom he served as a major role model.

James Emmett Birren was born on April 4, 1918 in Chicago, Illinois, the child of second-generation immigrants from Germany and Luxembourg. Although his early education was in Catholic schools, he found himself in conflict with some ideas suggested by the nuns, so he finished his secondary education in the Chicago public school system. His original career goal was to become an engineer, but since no one in his family had gone to college he had no clear plan to follow to reach this goal. Following his elder brother's lead, he decided to go to Wright Junior College in Chicago to continue his interest in technical subjects. But America was still in the depth of the Great Depression, and he decided that an engineering degree might not be very useful. Thus Jim transferred to Chicago Teachers College, where he took his first course in psychology. A summer volunteer position at Elgin State Hospital whetted Jim's interest in the field. The head of the psychology department, Dr. Phyllis Whittman, recommended that he go to the graduate program in psychology at Northwestern University, where he was admitted in the summer of 1941. He soon caught the attention of Robert H. Seashore, who became his mentor. In his first graduate class during that summer quarter he met his lifelong partner, Betty, who was also a first-year graduate student. They were married in December, 1942, and eventually three children were born to their union: Barbara, Jeff, and Bruce.

With America's entering World War II the, work of Jim and many of the other psychologists at Northwestern became war-related; he soon became involved in studies such as the affect of amphetamines in combating fatigue. Although he had been granted a deferment by the Draft Board because of the importance of this research, Jim volunteered for a commission as an ensign in the Hospital Corps of the U.S. Navy. He was assigned to the Naval Medical Research Institute in Bethesda, Maryland, where he had the opportunity to interact with major biomedical scientists who had been recruited to aid the naval war effort. He participated in a variety of projects ranging from the study of motion sickness to visual dark-adaptation, foreshadowing the wide-ranging interests in many aspects of behavior that would characterize his career.

Following the war Jim returned to Northwestern in 1946 with the aid of a pre-doctoral National Institutes of Health (NIH) fellowship and the G.I. Bill of Rights. It took him only one year to finish his Ph.D. requirements. He was recruited by Nathan W. Shock to work at the newly established Gerontology Unit of the Public Health Service (later to become the National Institutes of Health) in Baltimore, Maryland. There he focused his research on the mechanisms associated with the slowing of behavior with age. His reading of the work of Edward Thorndike and Irving Lorge convinced him that they had minimized the significance of behavioral slowing as an important factor in explaining decline in abilities with age. He shortly initiated a program of research that explored the basis for age-related slowing within the organism, focusing not only on the speed of input and output mechanisms, but also on slowness attributable to the mediating central nervous system itself. His work with Jack Botwinick and others showed that much of the variance in individual differences between older persons could be attributed to the central nervous system itself, and not only to changes in peripheral sensory factors and motor responses. This was a startling idea at the time.

Jim moved to the University of Chicago to continue his research while the NIH was building new facilities in Bethesda. The theories he was developing about mechanisms of aging were further reinforced in animal experiments he developed in collaboration with neurophysiologist Patrick D. Wall. Other work during this period showed that age changes in perceptual judgement could also not be fully accounted for by peripheral processes, but required consideration of central nervous system aging. Additional seminal influences during his work at Chicago included research with L. L. Thurstone and neurophysiologist Ralph Gerard, leading Jim to formulate two principles establishing the course for behavioral gerontology ever since: that multiple methods are required to study phenomena of aging, and that the research question being studied should determine the research methodologies to be used.

Jim's next major contribution involved his leadership of a multidisciplinary team at the National Institute of Mental Health (NIMH), which included Robert N. Butler. They developed a study of "normal aging" with comprehensive data collected from a group of healthy older men, using behavioral measures as well as assessments of cerebral circulation, psychiatric symptomology, social functioning, and subclinical disease. Their findings indicated that healthy aged subjects maintained high levels of general metabolic activity, and in addition demonstrated higher than expected global verbal information scores, despite slower reaction times. This suggested the principle that healthy older adults continue to acquire information just as younger adults do; they just process it more slowly. Subsequent work indicated that slowness is exacerbated by disease. The work of Jim and his colleagues at NIMH added up to a revolutionary conclusion: that the performance of healthy older adults is much more like that of younger adults than it is to unhealthy older adults.

Throughout this period Jim also contributed to the development of criteria for distinguishing between normal and pathological aging. He gathered the prominent researchers of the period to produce a definitive compendium of gerontological knowledge which he edited, the influential *Hand-*

book of Aging and the Individual, published by the University of Chicago Press. This was the first in a three-volume *Handbooks* series that has chronicled emerging research in gerontology for almost four decades now.

As part of his responsibilities at the NIH, Jim was involved in stimulating extramural research and research training in aging. While program officer for aging research, first at the NIMH and later at the National Institute of Child Health and Human Development (NICHD), he was the leader in recruiting developmental scientists into the field of aging and in laying the groundwork for the research and training programs that would eventually find a prominent and independent place when the National Institute on Aging (NIA) was established in 1974.

In 1965, Jim left the NIH to move west and take advantage of a major opportunity offered to him at the University of Southern California. USC had obtained a major pledge from Ross Cortese, founder of Leisure World, to start an Institute for the Study of Retirement and Aging. Jim became founding director of what was to become the Andrus Gerontology Center. He quickly developed a series of comprehensive programs that included basic research, applied research, graduate education, and community outreach programs at USC. He secured funding from NIH for a training grant to support predoctoral as well as postdoctoral trainees in multidisciplinary research training; this grant is currently in its 33rd year of continuous funding and has produced over 200 Ph.D.s in gerontology. Jim then obtained support from the American Association of Retired Persons to build a facility in honor of Ethel Percy Andrus, one of USC's first female Ph.D.s who, after retiring from a memorable career in education, founded the National Retired Teacher's Association in 1950 and AARP in 1953. More than 200,000 individuals and AARP chapters gave donations ranging from 25 cents to $50,000 to the building program. It became the Ethel Percy Andrus Gerontology Center when it was dedicated in 1972.

Two years later a large gift to USC from Leonard Davis, a former colleague of Dr. Andrus and the founder of Colonial Penn Insurance Company, led to the establishment of the nation's first School of Gerontology. With degree programs at the undergraduate, Masters, and Ph.D. levels, the Leonard Davis School of Gerontology has graduated over 400 students, many of whom have gone on to leadership positions in gerontology. In 1981 Jim also received funding for an Institute for the Advanced Study in Gerontology from the Andrew Norman Foundation. This provided support for international researchers in aging to be in residence at the Andrus Gerontology Center for a year, and the Institute produced a series of yearly volumes between 1983 and 1989 that helped define and advance the field. One of these was *Emergent Theories of Aging,* the precursor to this volume, published in 1988.

Before coming to USC, Jim had relatively few opportunities to teach and mentor students. It quickly became apparent that this was a role he relished, and, one at which he was incredibly successful. Throughout his years at USC (1965–1989), one of his major contributions was to advance the careers of students and young faculty who then went on to develop major contributions to gerontology. Many of these individuals are represented in this volume as authors: Vern Bengtson, Dale Dannefer, Walter Cunningham, Caleb Finch, Margaret Gatz, Gary Kenyon, Jan-Erik Ruth, Hans Schroots, Diana Woodruff-Pak, and Steve Zarit.

The years from 1965 to 1989 represented a remarkable period of achievement for Jim Birren. He built USC's Gerontology Center from its modest beginnings–one full-time administrative assistant and two second-story offices in an old house on the far corner of the USC campus–into a world-recognized center for gerontological research and training. He taught and mentored several cohorts of graduate students and young researchers, helping them establish their own leadership in gerontological research. At the same time he also continued his own amazing contributions to the research literature on aging: first in terms of the neurological basis of speed of behavior with age, then in the study of creativity and wisdom with age. He formalized a new field of research in the psychology of aging, the study of autobiography, and developed it as both a research technique and a means for teaching enrichment in seminars and classes for older adults. Throughout this period he continued to produce, as senior editor, the landmark *Handbooks of Aging* which are now in their fourth edition. These, as well as his *Handbook of Mental Health and Aging* (two editions) and the *Encyclopedia of Gerontology,* will remain as lasting testimony to his astonishingly wide intellectual interests as well as his amazing organizational abilities.

Becoming emeritus at USC at 71 years of age, Jim did not rest on his laurels, but started a third career with the "cross-town competition" at UCLA. There he was instrumental in developing the Borun Center for Gerontological Research. Once again, as at USC, Jim took on the inertia of an academic system that had difficulties thinking beyond traditional disciplinary boundaries and succeeded in guiding the new Center through its early growing pains and into nationally recognized status.

Throughout his long career, Jim not only has been an exemplary institution-builder but also has contributed vastly to the development of gerontological science. He helped develop the Gerontology Society (now the Gerontological Society of America) after 1946 and served as its President in 1963. He was one of the earliest members of the Division on maturity and old age (now Division 20, the Division of Adulthood and Aging) of the American Psychological Association and was its president in 1956–57.

Despite the astonishing breadth of his scientific, academic, and institution-building contributions, Jim has always seen himself as a research developmental psychologist. Of the many honors which he has received, perhaps nothing pleased him more than being the first gerontologist ever to receive the American Psychological Association's Distinguished Scientific Contributions Award. Jim's message on that occasion was that geropsychology must not remain an encapsulated special interest group, but must become an essential part of general psychology and the other developmental sciences, since differentiation and aging are among the most universal of human phenomena.

With this volume we recognize Jim Birren for his truly remarkable record of scholarly contributions and thank him for enriching our lives. In dedicating the volume to him we honor one of the true giants of gerontology. We know that he will continue to be a role model for successful aging and that we will learn more from him as he continues to inspire us in the years to come.

Vern L. Bengtson
K. Warner Schaie
Editors, August 1998

Postcript from VLB:

Jim Birren got me my first job, my first professional publication, and helped me get my first research grant–all within three years from the first time I met him. This is eloquent testimony to his legendary mentorship and to his ability to bring out the best in even the most inexperienced of his associates. He has remained one of the most important influences in my adult life ever since.

Jim hired me as an assistant professor at USC in 1967, even before my dissertation was completed at the University of Chicago. He encouraged my raw confidence by saying that I could be instrumental in helping him build a world-class multidisciplinary research and training program in gerontology; he inflated my self-confidence further by adding the then-magnificent sum of $500 per year to the offer I was considering from UC Berkeley. He and Betty welcomed us to their home, helped us find our first apartment, and got us our first USC season football tickets. Shortly thereafter Jim and I published our first paper together–a 1968 article on "New generational tensions in American society"–and then he guided me through the mystifying NIH grants submission process to achieve funding for a study titled "Intergenerational relationships and mental health." This study of three-generations has become the Longitudinal Study of Generations, now in its 27th year and now including the fourth generation as they move into adulthood. Jim and Betty provided my daughters Julie and Kristina with their first Paddington bear books in 1970 and 1973. They helped me find my way after the death of Denise, my first wife in 1977. They helped me celebrate my marriage to Hannah in 1983 after a courtship including "double-dates" with Jim and Betty to USC basketball games.

Above all, beyond Jim's accomplishments in developing gerontology as a science and his abilities as an academic mentor and institution-builder, I think he will be remembered by those who have worked with him for his ability to inspire confidence. He has brought out the best in those who worked with him—his staff, students, faculty, administrators, international scholars. He has the ability to make them more confident in their abilities than they would have been by themselves. Related to this is Jim's unfailing personal courtesy. He takes the time to make contact, to listen, to become interested. Throughout his career, wherever he has gone, Jim's courtesy and affirmation have created an atmosphere of support and productivity that made people feel good about themselves.

Postcript from KWS:

I first met Jim Birren in 1951, when as a college junior I attended my first gerontological meeting at the Second International Congress of Gerontology at St. Louis, Missouri. Jim was already well established then and in very much of a leadership role for the small contingent of psychologists interested in the aging process and the aged.

I don't think he remembers me from that meeting, but I got to know Jim well four years later when I showed him around the San Francisco Bay area during the 1955 meeting of the American Psychological Association. He amazed me with his encyclopedic knowledge of gerontology and knew that I would like nothing better than to have an opportunity to work with him. This opportunity arose many years later, in 1973, when I joined Jim at USC's Andrus Gerontology Center for eight productive years. During that period we began our continuing collaboration on the *Handbook of the Psychology of Aging* project which continues to date.

Jim continues to amaze me with his vitality and breadth of interest; and from being a role model for my professional career, he has now become a role model for my own successful aging.

REFERENCES

Birren, J. E. (1996). James Emmet Birren. In D. Thompson & J. D. Hogan (Eds.), *A history of developmental psychology in autobiography.* Chicago: Westview Press.

Birren, J. E. (In press). James E. Birren. In J. E. Birren & J.J.F. Schroots (Eds.), *The history of geropsychology.* Washington, D.C.: American Psychological Association.

Author and Name Index

Subject Index